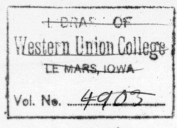

Post Office Department

THE POST-OFFICE DEPARTMENT stands on the site of the Department's former building, destroyed in 1836. It is in the Corinthian style and connoisseurs class it among the beautiful buildings of the city. It was completed in 1855 at a cost of about $2,000,000.

A COMPILATION

OF THE

MESSAGES AND PAPERS

OF THE

PRESIDENTS

1789 - 1902

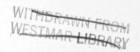

BY

JAMES D. RICHARDSON

A REPRESENTATIVE FROM THE STATE OF TENNESSEE

VOLUME III

PUBLISHED BY

BUREAU OF NATIONAL LITERATURE AND ART

1904

Copyright 1897,

BY

JAMES D. RICHARDSON

Prefatory Note

The second volume of this compilation, issued a few weeks since, was received with the same degree of favor as the first volume. It was a matter of surprise that only sixteen years of our history, or eight Congresses, could be comprised within the second volume, while the first covered twenty-eight years, or fourteen Congresses. There is greater surprise that this volume includes only the period covered by the four years of the second term of Andrew Jackson and the four years of Martin Van Buren's term—eight years in all, or four Congresses. However, it will be found almost, if not quite, as interesting as the preceding ones. In it will be found the conclusion of the controversy over the United States Bank, including President Jackson's reasons for the removal of the deposits from that bank; his Farewell Address, and other important papers, all of which are characteristic of the man. It was during the second Administration of President Jackson that the act changing the ratio between the gold and silver dollar was passed.

This volume contains President Van Buren's message recommending the independent treasury or subtreasury, and the discussion of that subject, which terminated in what has been termed "the divorce of the bank and state in the fiscal affairs of the Federal Government," and which President Van Buren considered a second Declaration of Independence. The controversy with Great Britain in relation to the northeastern boundary of the United States is also included in Van Buren's Administration, and will prove highly interesting.

The omission of indexes to Volumes I and II has been commented on. The answer to such comments is, it was deemed best to omit the index to each volume and publish a general and comprehensive index to the entire work in a separate volume. This index will be ready for distribution soon after the issuance of the last volume.

JAMES D. RICHARDSON.

NOVEMBER 26, 1896.

III

Andrew Jackson

March 4, 1833, to March 4, 1837

Andrew Jackson

SECOND INAUGURAL ADDRESS.

FELLOW-CITIZENS: The will of the American people, expressed through their unsolicited suffrages, calls me before you to pass through the solemnities preparatory to taking upon myself the duties of President of the United States for another term. For their approbation of my public conduct through a period which has not been without its difficulties, and for this renewed expression of their confidence in my good intentions, I am at a loss for terms adequate to the expression of my gratitude. It shall be displayed to the extent of my humble abilities in continued efforts so to administer the Government as to preserve their liberty and promote their happiness.

So many events have occurred within the last four years which have necessarily called forth—sometimes under circumstances the most delicate and painful—my views of the principles and policy which ought to be pursued by the General Government that I need on this occasion but allude to a few leading considerations connected with some of them.

The foreign policy adopted by our Government soon after the formation of our present Constitution, and very generally pursued by successive Administrations, has been crowned with almost complete success, and has elevated our character among the nations of the earth. To do justice to all and to submit to wrong from none has been during my Administration its governing maxim, and so happy have been its results that we are not only at peace with all the world, but have few causes of controversy, and those of minor importance, remaining unadjusted.

In the domestic policy of this Government there are two objects which especially deserve the attention of the people and their representatives, and which have been and will continue to be the subjects of my increasing solicitude. They are the preservation of the rights of the several States and the integrity of the Union.

These great objects are necessarily connected, and can only be attained by an enlightened exercise of the powers of each within its appropriate sphere in conformity with the public will constitutionally expressed. To this end it becomes the duty of all to yield a ready and patriotic submission to the laws constitutionally enacted, and thereby promote and strengthen a proper confidence in those institutions of the several States and of the United States which the people themselves have ordained for their own government.

My experience in public concerns and the observation of a life somewhat advanced confirm the opinions long since imbibed by me, that the destruction of our State governments or the annihilation of their control over the local concerns of the people would lead directly to revolution and anarchy, and finally to despotism and military domination. In proportion, therefore, as the General Government encroaches upon the rights of the States, in the same proportion does it impair its own power and detract from its ability to fulfill the purposes of its creation. Solemnly impressed with these considerations, my countrymen will ever find me ready to exercise my constitutional powers in arresting measures which may directly or indirectly encroach upon the rights of the States or tend to consolidate all political power in the General Government. But of equal, and, indeed, of incalculable, importance is the union of these States, and the sacred duty of all to contribute to its preservation by a liberal support of the General Government in the exercise of its just powers. You have been wisely admonished to "accustom yourselves to think and speak of the Union as of the palladium of your political safety and prosperity, watching for its preservation with jealous anxiety, discountenancing whatever may suggest even a suspicion that it can in any event be abandoned, and indignantly frowning upon the first dawning of any attempt to alienate any portion of our country from the rest or to enfeeble the sacred ties which now link together the various parts." Without union our independence and liberty would never have been achieved; without union they never can be maintained. Divided into twenty-four, or even a smaller number, of separate communities, we shall see our internal trade burdened with numberless restraints and exactions; communication between distant points and sections obstructed or cut off; our sons made soldiers to deluge with blood the fields they now till in peace; the mass of our people borne down and impoverished by taxes to support armies and navies, and military leaders at the head of their victorious legions becoming our lawgivers and judges. The loss of liberty, of all good government, of peace, plenty, and happiness, must inevitably follow a dissolution of the Union. In supporting it, therefore, we support all that is dear to the freeman and the philanthropist.

The time at which I stand before you is full of interest. The eyes of all nations are fixed on our Republic. The event of the existing crisis will be decisive in the opinion of mankind of the practicability of our federal system of government. Great is the stake placed in our hands; great is the responsibility which must rest upon the people of the United States. Let us realize the importance of the attitude in which we stand before the world. Let us exercise forbearance and firmness. Let us extricate our country from the dangers which surround it and learn wisdom from the lessons they inculcate.

Deeply impressed with the truth of these observations, and under the obligation of that solemn oath which I am about to take, I shall continue to exert all my faculties to maintain the just powers of the Constitution and to transmit unimpaired to posterity the blessings of our Federal Union. At the same time, it will be my aim to inculcate by my official acts the necessity of exercising by the General Government those powers only that are clearly delegated; to encourage simplicity and economy in the expenditures of the Government; to raise no more money from the people than may be requisite for these objects, and in a manner that will best promote the interests of all classes of the community and of all portions of the Union. Constantly bearing in mind that in entering into society "individuals must give up a share of liberty to preserve the rest," it will be my desire so to discharge my duties as to foster with our brethren in all parts of the country a spirit of liberal concession and compromise, and, by reconciling our fellow-citizens to those partial sacrifices which they must unavoidably make for the preservation of a greater good, to recommend our invaluable Government and Union to the confidence and affections of the American people.

Finally, it is my most fervent prayer to that Almighty Being before whom I now stand, and who has kept us in His hands from the infancy of our Republic to the present day, that He will so overrule all my intentions and actions and inspire the hearts of my fellow-citizens that we may be preserved from dangers of all kinds and continue forever a united and happy people.

MARCH 4, 1833.

REMOVAL OF THE PUBLIC DEPOSITS.

[Read to the Cabinet September 18, 1833.]

Having carefully and anxiously considered all the facts and arguments which have been submitted to him relative to a removal of the public deposits from the Bank of the United States, the President deems it his duty to communicate in this manner to his Cabinet the final conclusions of his own mind and the reasons on which they are founded, in order to put them in durable form and to prevent misconceptions.

The President's convictions of the dangerous tendencies of the Bank of the United States, since signally illustrated by its own acts, were so overpowering when he entered on the duties of Chief Magistrate that he felt it his duty, notwithstanding the objections of the friends by whom he was surrounded, to avail himself of the first occasion to call the attention of Congress and the people to the question of its recharter. The opinions expressed in his annual message of December, 1829, were reiterated in those of December, 1830 and 1831, and in that of 1830 he threw out for consideration some suggestions in relation to a substitute. At the session of 1831–32 an act was passed by a majority of both Houses of Congress rechartering the present bank, upon which the President felt it his duty to put his constitutional veto. In his message returning that act he repeated and enlarged upon the principles and views briefly asserted in his annual message, declaring the bank to be, in his opinion, both inexpedient and unconstitutional, and announcing to his countrymen very unequivocally his firm determination never to sanction by his approval the continuance of that institution or the establishment of any other upon similar principles.

There are strong reasons for believing that the motive of the bank in asking for a recharter at that session of Congress was to make it a leading question in the election of a President of the United States the ensuing November, and all steps deemed necessary were taken to procure from the people a reversal of the President's decision.

Although the charter was approaching its termination, and the bank was aware that it was the intention of the Government to use the public deposit as fast as it has accrued in the payment of the public debt, yet did it extend its loans from January, 1831, to May, 1832, from $42,402,304.24 to $70,428,070.72, being an increase of $28,025,766.48 in sixteen months. It is confidently believed that the leading object of this immense extension of its loans was to bring as large a portion of the people as possible under its power and influence, and it has been disclosed that some of the largest sums were granted on very unusual terms to the conductors of the public press. In some of these cases the motive was made manifest by the nominal or insufficient security taken for the loans, by the large amounts discounted, by the extraordinary time allowed for payment, and especially by the subsequent conduct of those receiving the accommodations.

Having taken these preliminary steps to obtain control over public opinion, the bank came into Congress and asked a new charter. The object avowed by many of the advocates of the bank was to *put the President to the test*, that the country might know his final determination relative to the bank prior to the ensuing election. Many documents and articles were printed and circulated at the expense of the bank to bring the people to a favorable decision upon its pretensions. Those whom the bank appears to have made its debtors for the special occasion were warned of the ruin which awaited them should the President be sustained, and attempts were made to alarm the whole people by painting the depression in the price of property and produce and the general loss, inconvenience, and distress which it was represented would immediately follow the reelection of the President in opposition to the bank.

Can it now be said that the question of a recharter of the bank was not decided at the election which ensued? Had the veto been equivocal, or had it not covered the whole ground; if it had merely taken exceptions to the details of the bill or to the time of its passage; if it had not met the whole ground of constitutionality and expediency, then there might have been some plausibility for the allegation that the question was not decided by the people. It was to compel the President to take his stand that the question was brought forward at that particular time. He met the challenge, willingly took the position into which his adversaries sought to force him, and frankly declared his unalterable opposition to the bank as being both unconstitutional and inexpedient. On that ground the case was argued to the people; and now that the people have sustained the President, notwithstanding the array of influence and power which was brought to bear upon him, it is too late, he confidently thinks, to say that the question has not been decided. Whatever may be the opinions of others, the President considers his reelection as a decision of the people against the bank. In the concluding paragraph of his veto message he said:

I have now done my duty to my country. If sustained by my fellow-citizens, I shall be grateful and happy; if not, I shall find in the motives which impel me ample grounds for contentment and peace.

He was sustained by a just people, and he desires to evince his gratitude by carrying into effect their decision so far as it depends upon him.

Of all the substitutes for the present bank which have been suggested, none seems to have united any considerable portion of the public in its favor. Most of them are liable to the same constitutional objections for which the present bank has been condemned, and perhaps to all there are strong objections on the score of expediency. In ridding the country of an irresponsible power which has attempted to control the Government, care must be taken not to unite the same power with the executive branch. To give a President the control over the currency and the power over individuals now possessed by the Bank of the United States, even with the material difference that he is responsible to the people, would be as objectionable and as dangerous as to leave it as it is. Neither one nor the other is necessary, and therefore ought not to be resorted to.

On the whole, the President considers it as conclusively settled that the charter of the Bank of the United States will not be renewed, and he has no reasonable ground to believe that any substitute will be established. Being bound to regulate his course by the laws as they exist, and not to anticipate the interference of the legislative power for the purpose of framing new systems, it is proper for him seasonably to consider the means by which the services rendered by the Bank of the United States are to be performed after its charter shall expire.

The existing laws declare that—

The deposits of the money of the United States in places in which the said bank and branches thereof may be established shall be made in said bank or branches thereof unless the Secretary of the Treasury shall at any time otherwise order and direct, in which case the Secretary of the Treasury shall immediately lay before Congress, if in session, and, if not, immediately after the commencement of the next session, the reasons of such order or direction.

The power of the Secretary of the Treasury over the deposits is *unqualified*. The provision that he shall report his reasons to Congress is no limitation. Had it not been inserted he would have been responsible to Congress had he made a removal for any other than good reasons, and his responsibility now ceases upon the rendition of sufficient ones to Congress. The only object of the provision is to make his reasons accessible to Congress and enable that body the more readily to judge of their soundness and purity, and thereupon to make such further provision by law as the legislative power may think proper in relation to the deposit of the public money. Those reasons may be very diversified. It was asserted by the Secretary of the Treasury, without contradiction, as early as 1817, that he had power ''to control the proceedings'' of the Bank of the United States at any moment ''by changing the deposits to the State banks'' should it pursue an illiberal course toward those institutions; that ''the Secretary of the Treasury will always be disposed to support the credit of the State banks, and will invariably direct transfers from the deposits of the public money in aid of their legitimate exertions to maintain their credit;'' and he asserted a right to employ the State banks when the Bank of the United States should refuse to receive on deposit the notes of such State banks as the public interest required should be received in payment of the public dues. In several instances he did transfer the public deposits to State banks in the immediate vicinity of branches, for reasons connected only with the safety of those banks, the public convenience, and the interests of the Treasury.

If it was lawful for Mr. Crawford, the Secretary of the Treasury at that time, to act on these principles, it will be difficult to discover any sound reason against the application of similar principles in still stronger cases. And it is a matter of surprise that a power which in the infancy of the bank was freely asserted as one of the ordinary and familiar duties of the Secretary of the Treasury should now be gravely questioned, and attempts made to excite and alarm the public mind as if some new and unheard-of power was about to be usurped by the executive branch of the Government.

It is but a little more than two and a half years to the termination of the charter of the present bank. It is considered as the decision of the country that it shall then cease to exist, and no man, the President believes, has reasonable ground for expectation that any other Bank of the United States will be created by Congress.

To the Treasury Department is intrusted the safe-keeping and faithful application of the public moneys. A plan of collection different from the present must therefore be introduced and put in complete operation before the dissolution of the present bank. When shall it be commenced? Shall no step be taken in this essential concern until the charter expires and the Treasury finds itself without an agent, its accounts in confusion, with no depository for its funds, and the whole business of the Government deranged, or shall it be delayed until six months, or a year, or two years before the expiration of the charter? It is obvious that any new system which may be substituted in the place of the Bank of the United States could not be suddenly carried into effect on the termination of its existence without serious inconvenience to the Government and the people. Its vast amount of notes are then to be redeemed and withdrawn from circulation and its immense debt collected. These operations must be gradual, otherwise much suffering and distress will be brought upon the community.

It ought to be not a work of months only, but of years, and the President thinks it can not, with due attention to the interests of the people, be longer postponed. It is safer to begin it too soon than to delay it too long.

It is for the wisdom of Congress to decide upon the best substitute to be adopted in the place of the Bank of the United States, and the President would have felt himself relieved from a heavy and painful responsibility if in the charter to the bank Congress had reserved to itself the power of directing at its pleasure the public money to be elsewhere deposited, and had not devolved that power exclusively on one of the Executive Departments. It is useless now to inquire why this high and important power was surrendered by those who are peculiarly and appropriately the guardians of the public money. Perhaps it was an oversight. But as the President presumes that the charter to the bank is to be considered as a contract on the part of the Government, it is not now in the power of Congress to disregard its stipulations; and by the terms of that contract the public money is to be deposited in the bank during the continuance of its charter unless the Secretary of the Treasury shall otherwise direct. Unless, therefore, the Secretary of the Treasury first acts, Congress have no power over the subject, for they can not add a new clause to the charter or strike one out of it without the consent of the bank, and consequently the public money must remain in that institution to the last hour of its existence unless the Secretary of the Treasury shall remove it at an earlier day. The responsibility is thus thrown upon the executive branch of the Government of deciding how long before the expiration of the charter the public interest will require the deposits to be placed elsewhere; and although according to the frame and principle of our Government this decision would seem more properly to belong to the legislative power, yet as the law has imposed it upon the executive department the duty ought to be faithfully and firmly met, and the decision made and executed upon the best lights that can be obtained and the best judgment that can be formed.

It would ill become the executive branch of the Government to shrink from any duty which the law imposes on it, to fix upon others the responsibility which justly belongs to itself. And while the President anxiously wishes to abstain from the exercise of doubtful powers and to avoid all interference with the rights and duties of others, he must yet with unshaken constancy discharge his own obligations, and can not allow himself to turn aside in order to avoid any responsibility which the high trust with which he has been honored requires him to encounter; and it being the duty of one of the Executive Departments to decide in the first instance, subject to the future action of the legislative power, whether the public deposits shall remain in the Bank of the United States until the end of its existence or be withdrawn some time before, the President has felt himself bound to examine the question carefully and deliberately in order to make up his judgment on the subject, and in his opinion the near approach of the termination of the charter and the public considerations heretofore mentioned are of themselves amply sufficient to justify the removal of the deposits, without reference to the conduct of the bank or their safety in its keeping.

But in the conduct of the bank may be found other reasons, very imperative in their character, and which require prompt action. Developments have been made from time to time of its faithlessness as a public agent, its misapplication of public funds, its interference in elections, its efforts by the machinery of committees to deprive the Government directors of a full knowledge of its concerns, and, above all, its flagrant misconduct as recently and unexpectedly disclosed in placing all the funds of the bank, including the money of the Government, at the disposition of the president of the bank as means of operating upon public opinion and procuring a new charter, without requiring him to render a voucher for their disbursement. A brief recapitulation of the facts which justify these charges, and which have come to the knowledge of the public and the President, will, he thinks, remove every reasonable doubt as to the course which it is now the duty of the President to pursue.

We have seen that in sixteen months ending in May, 1832, the bank had extended its loans more than $28,000,000, although it knew the Government intended to appropriate most of its large deposit during that year in payment of the public debt. It was in May, 1832, that its loans arrived at the maximum, and in the preceding March so sensible was the bank that it would not be able to pay over the public deposit when it would be required by the Government that it commenced a secret negotiation, without the approbation or knowledge of the Government, with the agents for about $2,700,000 of the 3 per cent stocks held in Holland, with a view of inducing them not to come forward for payment for one or more years after notice should be given by the Treasury Department. This arrangement would have enabled the bank to keep and use during that time the public money set apart for the payment of these stocks.

After this negotiation had commenced, the Secretary of the Treasury informed the bank that it was his intention to pay off one-half of the 3 percents on the 1st of the succeeding July, which amounted to about $6,500,000. The president of the bank, although the committee of investigation was then looking into its affairs at Philadelphia, came immediately to Washington, and upon representing that the bank was desirous of accommodating the importing merchants at New York (which it failed to do) and undertaking to pay the interest itself, procured the consent of the Secretary, after consultation with the President, to postpone the payment until the succeeding 1st of October.

Conscious that at the end of that quarter the bank would not be able to pay over the deposits, and that further indulgence was not to be expected of the Government, an agent was dispatched to England secretly to negotiate with the holders of the public debt in Europe and induce them by the offer of an equal or higher interest than that paid by the Government to hold back their claims for one year, during which the bank expected thus to retain the use of $5,000,000 of the public money, which the Government should set apart for the payment of that debt. The agent made an arrangement on terms, in part, which were in direct violation of the charter of the bank, and when some incidents connected with this secret negotiation accidentally came to the knowledge of the public and the Government, then, and not before, so much of it as was palpably in violation of the charter was disavowed. A modification of the rest was attempted with the view of getting the certificates without payment of the money, and thus absolving the Government from its liability to the holders. In this scheme the bank was partially successful, but to this day the certificates of a portion of these stocks have not been paid and the bank retains the use of the money.

This effort to thwart the Government in the payment of the public debt that it might retain the public money to be used for their private interests, palliated by pretenses notoriously unfounded and insincere, would have justified the instant withdrawal of the public deposits. The negotiation itself rendered doubtful the ability of the bank to meet the demands of the Treasury, and the misrepresentations by which it was attempted to be justified proved that no reliance could be placed upon its allegations.

If the question of a removal of the deposits presented itself to the Executive in the same attitude that it appeared before the House of Representatives at their last session, their resolution in relation to the safety of the deposits would be entitled to more weight, although the decision of the question of removal has been confided by law to another department of the Government. But the question now occurs attended by other circumstances and new disclosures of the most serious import. It is true that in the message of the President which produced this inquiry and resolution on the part of the House of Representatives it was his object to obtain the aid of that body in making a thorough examination into the conduct and condition of the bank and its branches in order to enable the executive department to decide whether the public money was longer safe in its hands.   The limited power of the Secretary of the Treasury over the subject disabled him from making the investigation as fully and satisfactorily as it could be done by a committee of the House of Representatives, and hence the President desired the assistance of Congress to obtain for the Treasury Department a full knowledge of all the facts which were necessary to guide his judgment.   But it was not his purpose, as the language of his message will show, to ask the representatives of the people to assume a responsibility which did not belong to them and relieve the executive branch of the Government from the duty which the law had imposed upon it.   It is due to the President that his object in that proceeding should be distinctly understood, and that he should acquit himself of all suspicion of seeking to escape from the performance of his own duties or of desiring to interpose another body between himself and the people in order to avoid a measure which he is called upon to meet.   But although as an act of justice to himself he disclaims any design of soliciting the opinion of the House of Representatives in relation to his own duties in order to shelter himself from responsibility under the sanction of their counsel, yet he is at all times ready to listen to the suggestions of the representatives of the people, whether given voluntarily or upon solicitation, and to consider them with the profound respect to which all will admit that they are justly entitled. Whatever may be the consequences, however, to himself, he must finally form his own judgment where the Constitution and the law make it his duty to decide, and must act accordingly; and he is bound to suppose that such a course on his part will never be regarded by that elevated body as a mark of disrespect to itself, but that they will, on the contrary, esteem it the strongest evidence he can give of his fixed resolution conscientiously to discharge his duty to them and the country.

A new state of things has, however, arisen since the close of the last session of Congress, and evidence has since been laid before the President which he is persuaded would have led the House of Representatives to a different conclusion if it had come to their knowledge. The fact that the bank controls, and in some cases substantially *owns*, and by its money *supports* some of the leading presses of the country is now more clearly established.   Editors to whom it loaned extravagant sums in 1831 and 1832, on unusual time and nominal security, have since turned out to be insolvent, and to others apparently in no better condition accommodations still more extravagant, on terms more unusual, and some without any security, have also been heedlessly granted.

The allegation which has so often circulated through these channels that the Treasury was bankrupt and the bank was sustaining it, when for many years there has not been less, on an average, than six millions of public money in that institution, might be passed over as a harmless misrepresentation; but when it is attempted by substantial acts to impair the credit of the Government and tarnish the honor of the country, such charges require more serious attention. With six millions of public money in its vaults, after having had the use of from five to twelve millions for nine years without interest, it became the purchaser of a bill drawn by our Government on that of France for about $900,000, being the first installment of the French indemnity. The purchase money was left in the use of the bank, being simply added to the Treasury deposit. The bank sold the bill in England, and the holder sent it to France for collection, and arrangements not having been made by the French Government for its payment, it was taken up by the agents of the bank in Paris with the funds of the bank in their hands. Under these circumstances it has through its organs openly assailed the credit of the Government, and has actually made and persists in a demand of 15 per cent, or $158,842.77, as damages, when no damage, or none beyond some trifling expense, has in fact been sustained, and when the bank had in its own possession on deposit several millions of the public money which it was then using for its own profit. Is a fiscal agent of the Government which thus seeks to enrich itself at the expense of the public worthy of further trust?

There are other important facts not in the contemplation of the House of Representatives or not known to the members at the time they voted for the resolution.

Although the charter and the rules of the bank both declare that "not less than seven directors" shall be necessary to the transaction of business, yet the most important business, even that of granting discounts to any extent, is intrusted to a committee of five members, who do not report to the board.

To cut off all means of communication with the Government in relation to its most important acts at the commencement of the present year, not one of the Government directors was placed on any one committee; and although since, by an unusual remodeling of those bodies, some of those directors have been placed on some of the committees, they are yet entirely excluded from the committee of exchange, through which the greatest and most objectionable loans have been made.

When the Government directors made an effort to bring back the business of the bank to the board in obedience to the charter and the existing regulations, the board not only overruled their attempt, but altered the rule so as to make it conform to the practice, in direct violation of one of the most important provisions of the charter which gave them existence.

It has long been known that the president of the bank, by his single will, originates and executes many of the most important measures connected with the management and credit of the bank, and that the committee as well as the board of directors are left in entire ignorance of many acts done and correspondence carried on in their names, and apparently under their authority. The fact has been recently disclosed that an unlimited discretion has been and is now vested in the president of the bank to expend its funds in payment for preparing and circulating articles and purchasing pamphlets and newspapers, calculated by their contents to operate on elections and secure a renewal of its charter. It appears from the official report of the public directors that on the 30th November, 1830, the president submitted to the board an article published in the American Quarterly Review containing favorable notices of the bank, and suggested the expediency of giving it a wider circulation at the expense of the bank; whereupon the board passed the following resolution, viz:

Resolved, That the president be authorized to take such measures in regard to the circulation of the contents of the said article, either in whole or in part, as he may deem most for the interest of the bank.

By an entry in the minutes of the bank dated March 11, 1831, it appears that the president had not only caused a large edition of that article to be issued, but had also, before the resolution of 30th November was adopted, procured to be printed and widely circulated numerous copies of the reports of General Smith and Mr. McDuffie in favor of the bank; and on that day he suggested the expediency of extending his power to the printing of other articles which might subserve the purposes of the institution, whereupon the following resolution was adopted, viz:

Resolved, That the president is hereby authorized to cause to be prepared and circulated such documents and papers as may communicate to the people information in regard to the nature and operations of the bank.

The expenditures purporting to have been made under authority of these resolutions during the years 1831 and 1832 were about $80,000. For a portion of these expenditures vouchers were rendered, from which it appears that they were incurred in the purchase of some hundred thousand copies of newspapers, reports and speeches made in Congress, reviews of the veto message and reviews of speeches against the bank, etc. For another large portion no vouchers whatever were rendered, but the various sums were paid on orders of the president of the bank, making reference to the resolution of the 11th of March, 1831.

On ascertaining these facts and perceiving that expenditures of a similar character were still continued, the Government directors a few weeks ago offered a resolution in the board calling for a specific account of these expenditures, showing the objects to which they had been applied and the persons to whom the money had been paid. This reasonable proposition was voted down.

They also offered a resolution rescinding the resolutions of November, 1830, and March, 1831. This also was rejected.

Not content with thus refusing to recall the obnoxious power or even to require such an account of the expenditure as would show whether the money of the bank had in fact been applied to the objects contemplated by these resolutions, as obnoxious as they were, the board renewed the power already conferred, and even enjoined renewed attention to its exercise by adopting the following in lieu of the propositions submitted by the Government directors, viz:

Resolved, That the board have confidence in the wisdom and integrity of the president and in the propriety of the resolutions of 30th November, 1830, and 11th March, 1831, and entertain a full conviction of the necessity of a renewed attention to the object of those resolutions, and that the president be authorized and requested to continue his exertions for the promotion of said object.

Taken in connection with the nature of the expenditures heretofore made, as recently disclosed, which the board not only tolerate, but approve, this resolution puts the funds of the bank at the disposition of the president for the purpose of employing the whole press of the country in the service of the bank, to hire writers and newspapers, and to pay out such sums as he pleases to what person and for what services he pleases without the responsibility of rendering any specific account. The bank is thus converted into a vast electioneering engine, with means to embroil the country in deadly feuds, and, under cover of expenditures in themselves improper, extend its corruption through all the ramifications of society.

Some of the items for which accounts have been rendered show the construction which has been given to the resolutions and the way in which the power it confers has been exerted. The money has not been expended merely in the publication and distribution of speeches, reports of committees, or articles written for the purpose of showing the constitutionality or usefulness of the bank, but publications have been prepared and extensively circulated containing the grossest invectives against the officers of the Government, and the money which belongs to the stockholders and to the public has been freely applied in efforts to degrade in public estimation those who were supposed to be instrumental in resisting the wishes of this grasping and dangerous institution. As the president of the bank has not been required to settle his accounts, no one but himself knows how much more than the sum already mentioned may have been squandered, and for which a credit may hereafter be claimed in his account under this most extraordinary resolution. With these facts before us can we be surprised at the torrent of abuse incessantly poured out against all who are supposed to stand in the way of the cupidity or ambition of the Bank of the United States? Can we be surprised at sudden and unexpected changes of opinion in favor of an institution which has millions to lavish and avows its determination not to spare its means when they are necessary to accomplish its purposes? The refusal to render an account of the manner in which a part of the money expended has been applied gives just cause for the suspicion that it has been used for purposes which it is not deemed prudent to expose to the eyes of an intelligent and virtuous people. Those who act justly do not shun the light, nor do they refuse explanations when the propriety of their conduct is brought into question.

With these facts before him in an official report from the Government directors, the President would feel that he was not only responsible for all the abuses and corruptions the bank has committed or may commit, but almost an accomplice in a conspiracy against that Government which he has sworn honestly to administer, if he did not take every step within his constitutional and legal power likely to be efficient in putting an end to these enormities. If it be possible within the scope of human affairs to find a reason for removing the Government deposits and leaving the bank to its own resource for the means of effecting its criminal designs, we have it here. Was it expected when the moneys of the United States were directed to be placed in that bank that they would be put under the control of one man empowered to spend millions without rendering a voucher or specifying the object? Can they be considered safe with the evidence before us that tens of thousands have been spent for highly improper, if not corrupt, purposes, and that the same motive may lead to the expenditure of hundreds of thousands, and even millions, more? And can we justify ourselves to the people by longer lending to it the money and power of the Government to be employed for such purposes?

It has been alleged by some as an objection to the removal of the deposits that the bank has the power, and in that event will have the disposition, to destroy the State banks employed by the Government, and bring distress upon the country. It has been the fortune of the President to encounter dangers which were represented as equally alarming, and he has seen them vanish before resolution and energy. Pictures equally appalling were paraded before him when this bank came to demand a new charter. But what was the result? Has the country been ruined, or even distressed? Was it ever more prosperous than since that act? The President verily believes the bank has not the power to produce the calamities its friends threaten. The funds of the Government will not be annihilated by being transferred. They will immediately be issued for the benefit of trade, and if the Bank of the United States curtails its loans the State banks, strengthened by the public deposits, will extend theirs. What comes in through one bank will go out through others, and the equilibrium will be preserved. Should the bank, for the mere purpose of producing distress, press its debtors more heavily than some of them can bear, the consequences will recoil upon itself, and in the attempts to embarrass the country it will only bring loss and ruin upon the holders of its own stock. But if the President believed the bank possessed all the power which has been attributed to it, his determination would only be rendered the more inflexible. If, indeed, this corporation now holds in its hands the happiness and prosperity of the American people, it is high time to take the alarm. If the despotism be already upon us and our only safety is in the mercy of the despot, recent developments in relation to his designs and the means he employs show how necessary it is to shake it off. The struggle can never come with less distress to the people or under more favorable auspices than at the present moment.

All doubt as to the willingness of the State banks to undertake the service of the Government to the same extent and on the same terms as it is now performed by the Bank of the United States is put to rest by the report of the agent recently employed to collect information, and from that willingness their own safety in the operation may be confidently inferred. Knowing their own resources better than they can be known by others, it is not to be supposed that they would be willing to place themselves in a situation which they can not occupy without danger of annihilation or embarrassment. The only consideration applies to the safety of the public funds if deposited in those institutions, and when it is seen that the directors of many of them are not only willing to pledge the character and capital of the corporations in giving success to this measure, but also their own property and reputation, we can not doubt that they at least believe the public deposits would be safe in their management. The President thinks that these facts and circumstances afford as strong a guaranty as can be had in human affairs for the safety of the public funds and the practicability of a new system of collection and disbursement through the agency of the State banks.

From all these considerations the President thinks that the State banks ought immediately to be employed in the collection and disbursement of the public revenue, and the funds now in the Bank of the United States drawn out with all convenient dispatch. The safety of the public moneys if deposited in the State banks must be secured beyond all reasonable doubts; but the extent and nature of the security, in addition to their capital, if any be deemed necessary, is a subject of detail to which the Treasury Department will undoubtedly give its anxious attention. The banks to be employed must remit the moneys of the Government without charge, as the Bank of the United States now does; must render all the services which that bank now performs; must keep the Government advised of their situation by periodical returns; in fine, in any arrangement with the State banks the Government must not in any respect be placed on a worse footing than it now is. The President is happy to perceive by the report of the agent that the banks which he has consulted have, in general, consented to perform the service on these terms, and that those in New York have further agreed to make payments in London without other charge than the mere cost of the bills of exchange.

It should also be enjoined upon any banks which may be employed that it will be expected of them to facilitate domestic exchanges for the benefit of internal commerce; to grant all reasonable facilities to the payers of the revenue; to exercise the utmost liberality toward the other State banks, and do nothing uselessly to embarrass the Bank of the United States.

As one of the most serious objections to the Bank of the United States is the power which it concentrates, care must be taken in finding other agents for the service of the Treasury not to raise up another power equally formidable. Although it would probably be impossible to produce such a result by any organization of the State banks which could be devised, yet it is desirable to avoid even the appearance. To this end it would be expedient to assume no more power over them and interfere no more in their affairs than might be absolutely necessary to the security of the public deposit and the faithful performance of their duties as agents of the Treasury. Any interference by them in the political contests of the country with a view to influence elections ought, in the opinion of the President, to be followed by an immediate discharge from the public service.

It is the desire of the President that the control of the banks and the currency shall, as far as possible, be entirely separated from the political power of the country as well as wrested from an institution which has already attempted to subject the Government to its will. In his opinion the action of the General Government on this subject ought not to extend beyond the grant in the Constitution, which only authorizes Congress "to coin money and regulate the value thereof;" all else belongs to the States and the people, and must be regulated by public opinion and the interests of trade.

In conclusion, the President must be permitted to remark that he looks upon the pending question as of higher consideration than the mere transfer of a sum of money from one bank to another. Its decision may affect the character of our Government for ages to come. Should the bank be suffered longer to use the public moneys in the accomplishment of its purposes, with the proofs of its faithlessness and corruption before our eyes, the patriotic among our citizens will despair of success in struggling against its power, and we shall be responsible for entailing it upon our country forever. Viewing it as a question of transcendent importance, both in the principles and consequences it involves, the President could not, in justice to the responsibility which he owes to the country, refrain from pressing upon the Secretary of the Treasury his view of the considerations which impel to immediate action. Upon him has been devolved by the Constitution and the suffrages of the American people the duty of superintending the operation of the Executive Departments of the Government and seeing that the laws are faithfully executed. In the performance of this high trust it is his undoubted right to express to those whom the laws and his own choice have made his associates in the administration of the Government his opinion of their

CARTOON ON ANDREW JACKSON'S SECOND TERM CAM-
PAIGN, SHOWING HOW HE PLEASED THE MASSES BY
OVERTHROWING THE NATIONAL BANK MONOPOLY.

CARTOON AGAINST THE NATIONAL BANK SYSTEM, WHICH
ANDREW JACKSON OVERTHREW.

duties under circumstances as they arise. It is this right which he now exercises. Far be it from him to expect or require that any member of the Cabinet should at his request, order, or dictation do any act which he believes unlawful or in his conscience condemns. From them and from his fellow-citizens in general he desires only that aid and support which their reason approves and their conscience sanctions.

In the remarks he has made on this all-important question he trusts the Secretary of the Treasury will see only the frank and respectful declarations of the opinions which the President has formed on a measure of great national interest deeply affecting the character and usefulness of his Administration, and not a spirit of dictation, which the President would be as careful to avoid as ready to resist. Happy will he be if the facts now disclosed produce uniformity of opinion and unity of action among the members of the Administration.

The President again repeats that he begs his Cabinet to consider the proposed measure as his own, in the support of which he shall require no one of them to make a sacrifice of opinion or principle. Its responsibility has been assumed after the most mature deliberation and reflection as necessary to preserve the morals of the people, the freedom of the press, and the purity of the elective franchise, without which all will unite in saying that the blood and treasure expended by our forefathers in the establishment of our happy system of government will have been vain and fruitless. Under these convictions he feels that a measure so important to the American people can not be commenced too soon, and he therefore names the 1st day of October next as a period proper for the change of the deposits, or sooner, provided the necessary arrangements with the State banks can be made.

ANDREW JACKSON.

FIFTH ANNUAL MESSAGE.

DECEMBER 3, 1833.

Fellow-Citizens of the Senate and House of Representatives:

On your assembling to perform the high trusts which the people of the United States have confided to you, of legislating for their common welfare, it gives me pleasure to congratulate you upon the happy condition of our beloved country. By the favor of Divine Providence health is again restored to us, peace reigns within our borders, abundance crowns the labors of our fields, commerce and domestic industry flourish and increase, and individual happiness rewards the private virtue and enterprise of our citizens.

Our condition abroad is no less honorable than it is prosperous at home. Seeking nothing that is not right and determined to submit to nothing that is wrong, but desiring honest friendships and liberal intercourse with all nations, the United States have gained throughout the world the confidence and respect which are due to a policy so just and so congenial to the character of the American people and to the spirit of their institutions.

In bringing to your notice the particular state of our foreign affairs, it affords me high gratification to inform you that they are in a condition which promises the continuance of friendship with all nations.

With Great Britain the interesting question of our northeastern boundary remains still undecided. A negotiation, however, upon that subject has been renewed since the close of the last Congress, and a proposition has been submitted to the British Government with the view of establishing, in conformity with the resolution of the Senate, the line designated by the treaty of 1783. Though no definitive answer has been received, it may be daily looked for, and I entertain a hope that the overture may ultimately lead to a satisfactory adjustment of this important matter.

I have the satisfaction to inform you that a negotiation which, by desire of the House of Representatives, was opened some years ago with the British Government, for the erection of light-houses on the Bahamas, has been successful. Those works, when completed, together with those which the United States have constructed on the western side of the Gulf of Florida, will contribute essentially to the safety of navigation in that sea. This joint participation in establishments interesting to humanity and beneficial to commerce is worthy of two enlightened nations, and indicates feelings which can not fail to have a happy influence upon their political relations. It is gratifying to the friends of both to perceive that the intercourse between the two people is becoming daily more extensive, and that sentiments of mutual good will have grown up befitting their common origin and justifying the hope that by wise counsels on each side not only unsettled questions may be satisfactorily terminated, but new causes of misunderstanding prevented.

Notwithstanding that I continue to receive the most amicable assurances from the Government of France, and that in all other respects the most friendly relations exist between the United States and that Government, it is to be regretted that the stipulations of the convention concluded on the 4th July, 1831, remain in some important parts unfulfilled.

By the second article of that convention it was stipulated that the sum payable to the United States should be paid at Paris, in six annual installments, into the hands of such person or persons as should be authorized by the Government of the United States to receive it, and by the same article the first installment was payable on the 2d day of February, 1833. By the act of Congress of the 13th July, 1832, it was made the duty of the Secretary of the Treasury to cause the several installments, with the interest thereon, to be received from the French Government and transferred to the United States in such manner as he may deem best; and by the same act of Congress the stipulations on the part of the United States in the convention were in all respects fulfilled. Not doubting that a treaty thus made and ratified by the two Governments, and faithfully executed by the United States, would be promptly complied with by the other party, and desiring to avoid the risk and expense of intermediate agencies, the Secretary of the Treasury deemed it advisable to receive and transfer the first installment by means of a draft upon the French minister of finance. A draft for this purpose was accordingly drawn in favor of the cashier of the Bank of the United States for the amount accruing to the United States out of the first installment, and the interest payable with it. This bill was not drawn at Washington until five days after the installment was payable at Paris, and was accompanied by a special authority from the President authorizing the cashier or his assigns to receive the amount. The mode thus adopted of receiving the installment was officially made known to the French Government by the American chargé d'affaires at Paris, pursuant to instructions from the Department of State. The bill, however, though not presented for payment until the 23d day of March, was not paid, and for the reason assigned by the French minister of finance that no appropriation had been made by the French Chambers. It is not known to me that up to that period any appropriation had been required of the Chambers, and although a communication was subsequently made to the Chambers by direction of the King, recommending that the necessary provision should be made for carrying the convention into effect, it was at an advanced period of the session, and the subject was finally postponed until the next meeting of the Chambers.

Notwithstanding it has been supposed by the French ministry that the financial stipulations of the treaty can not be carried into effect without an appropriation by the Chambers, it appears to me to be not only consistent with the character of France, but due to the character of both Governments, as well as to the rights of our citizens, to treat the convention, made and ratified in proper form, as pledging the good faith of the French Government for its execution, and as imposing upon each department an obligation to fulfill it; and I have received assurances through our chargé d'affaires at Paris and the French minister plenipotentiary at Washington, and more recently through the minister of the United States at Paris, that the delay has not proceeded from any indisposition on the part of the King and his ministers to fulfill the treaty, and that measures will be presented at the next meeting of the Chambers, and with a reasonable hope of success, to obtain the necessary appropriation.

It is necessary to state, however, that the documents, except certain lists of vessels captured, condemned, or burnt at sea, proper to facilitate the examination and liquidation of the reclamations comprised in the stipulations of the convention, and which by the sixth article France engaged to communicate to the United States by the intermediary of the legation, though repeatedly applied for by the American chargé d'affaires under instructions from this Government, have not yet been communicated; and this delay, it is apprehended, will necessarily prevent the completion of the duties assigned to the commissioners within the time at present prescribed by law.

The reasons for delaying to communicate these documents have not been explicitly stated, and this is the more to be regretted as it is not understood that the interposition of the Chambers is in any manner required for the delivery of those papers.

Under these circumstances, in a case so important to the interests of our citizens and to the character of our country, and under disappointments so unexpected, I deemed it my duty, however I might respect the general assurances to which I have adverted, no longer to delay the appointment of a minister plenipotentiary to Paris, but to dispatch him in season to communicate the result of his application to the French Government at an early period of your session. I accordingly appointed a distinguished citizen for this purpose, who proceeded on his mission in August last and was presented to the King early in the month of October. He is particularly instructed as to all matters connected with the present posture of affairs, and I indulge the hope that with the representations he is instructed to make, and from the disposition manifested by the King and his ministers in their recent assurances to our minister at Paris, the subject will be early considered, and satisfactorily disposed of at the next meeting of the Chambers.

As this subject involves important interests and has attracted a considerable share of the public attention, I have deemed it proper to make this explicit statement of its actual condition, and should I be disappointed in the hope now entertained the subject will be again brought to the notice of Congress in such manner as the occasion may require.

The friendly relations which have always been maintained between the United States and Russia have been further extended and strengthened by the treaty of navigation and commerce concluded on the 6th of December last, and sanctioned by the Senate before the close of its last session. The ratifications having been since exchanged, the liberal provisions of the treaty are now in full force, and under the encouragement which they have secured a flourishing and increasing commerce, yielding its benefits to the enterprise of both nations, affords to each the just recompense of wise measures, and adds new motives for that mutual friendship which the two countries have hitherto cherished toward each other.

It affords me peculiar satisfaction to state that the Government of Spain has at length yielded to the justice of the claims which have been so long urged in behalf of our citizens, and has expressed a willingness to provide an indemnification as soon as the proper amount can be agreed upon. Upon this latter point it is probable an understanding had taken place between the minister of the United States and the Spanish Government before the decease of the late King of Spain; and, unless that event may have delayed its completion, there is reason to hope that it may be in my power to announce to you early in your present session the conclusion of a convention upon terms not less favorable than those entered into for similar objects with other nations. That act of justice would well accord with the character of Spain, and is due to the United States from their ancient friend. It could not fail to strengthen the sentiments of amity and good will between the two nations which it is so much the wish of the United States to cherish and so truly the interest of both to maintain.

By the first section of an act of Congress passed on the 13th of July, 1832, the tonnage duty on Spanish ships arriving from the ports of Spain was limited to the duty payable on American vessels in the ports of Spain previous to the 20th of October, 1817, being 5 cents per ton. That act was intended to give effect on our side to an arrangement made with the Spanish Government by which discriminating duties of tonnage were to be abolished in the ports of the United States and Spain on the vessels of the two nations. Pursuant to that arrangement, which was carried into effect on the part of Spain on the 20th of May, 1832, by a royal order dated the 29th of April, 1832, American vessels in the ports of Spain have paid 5 cents per ton, which rate of duty is also paid in those ports by Spanish ships; but as American vessels pay no tonnage duty in the ports of the United States, the duty of 5 cents payable in our ports by Spanish vessels under the act above mentioned is really a discriminating duty, operating to the disadvantage of Spain. Though no complaint has yet been made on the part of Spain, we are not the less bound by the obligations of good faith to remove the discrimination, and I recommend that the act be amended accordingly. As the royal order above alluded to includes the ports of the Balearic and Canary islands as well as those of Spain, it would seem that the provisions of the act of Congress should be equally extensive, and that for the repayment of such duties as may have been improperly received an addition should be made to the sum appropriated at the last session of Congress for refunding discriminating duties.

As the arrangement referred to, however, did not embrace the islands of Cuba and Puerto Rico, discriminating duties to the prejudice of American shipping continue to be levied there. From the extent of the commerce carried on between the United States and those islands, particularly the former, this discrimination causes serious injury to one of those great national interests which it has been considered an essential part of our policy to cherish, and has given rise to complaints on the part of our merchants. Under instructions given to our minister at Madrid, earnest representations have been made by him to the Spanish Government upon this subject, and there is reason to expect, from the friendly disposition which is entertained toward this country, that a beneficial change will be produced. The disadvantage, however, to which our shipping is subjected by the operation of these discriminating duties requires that they be met by suitable countervailing duties during your present session, power being at the same time vested in the President to modify or discontinue them as the discriminating duties on American vessels or their cargoes may be modified or discontinued at those islands. Intimations have been given to the Spanish Government that the United States may be obliged to resort to such measures as are of necessary self-defense, and there is no reason to apprehend that it would be unfavorably received. The proposed proceeding if adopted would not be permitted, however, in any degree to induce a relaxation in the efforts of our minister to effect a repeal of this irregularity by friendly negotiation, and it might serve to give force to his representations by showing the dangers to which that valuable trade is exposed by the obstructions and burdens which a system of discriminating and countervailing duties necessarily produces.

The selection and preparation of the Florida archives for the purpose of being delivered over to the United States, in conformity with the royal order as mentioned in my last annual message, though in progress, has not yet been completed. This delay has been produced partly by causes which were unavoidable, particularly the prevalence of the cholera at Havana; but measures have been taken which it is believed will expedite the delivery of those important records.

Congress were informed at the opening of the last session that "owing, as was alleged, to embarrassments in the finances of Portugal, consequent upon the civil war in which that nation was engaged," payment had been made of only one installment of the amount which the Portuguese Government had stipulated to pay for indemnifying our citizens for property illegally captured in the blockade of Terceira. Since that time a postponement for two years, with interest, of the two remaining installments was requested by the Portuguese Government, and as a consideration it offered to stipulate that rice of the United States should be admitted into Portugal at the same duties as Brazilian rice. Being satisfied that no better arrangement could be made, my consent was given, and a royal order of the King of Portugal was accordingly issued on the 4th of February last for the reduction of the duty on rice of the United States. It would give me great pleasure if in speaking of that country, in whose prosperity the United States are so much interested, and with whom a long-subsisting, extensive, and mutually advantageous commercial intercourse has strengthened the relations of friendship, I could announce to you the restoration of its internal tranquillity.

Subsequently to the commencement of the last session of Congress the final installment payable by Denmark under the convention of the 28th day of March, 1830, was received. The commissioners for examining the claims have since terminated their labors, and their awards have been paid at the Treasury as they have been called for. The justice rendered to our citizens by that Government is thus completed, and a pledge is thereby afforded for the maintenance of that friendly intercourse becoming the relations that the two nations mutually bear to each other.

It is satisfactory to inform you that the Danish Government have recently issued an ordinance by which the commerce with the island of St. Croix is placed on a more liberal footing than heretofore. This change can not fail to prove beneficial to the trade between the United States and that colony, and the advantages likely to flow from it may lead to greater relaxations in the colonial systems of other nations.

The ratifications of the convention with the King of the Two Sicilies have been duly exchanged, and the commissioners appointed for examining the claims under it have entered upon the duties assigned to them by law. The friendship that the interests of the two nations require of them being now established, it may be hoped that each will enjoy the benefits which a liberal commerce should yield to both.

A treaty of amity and commerce between the United States and Belgium was concluded during the last winter and received the sanction of the Senate, but the exchange of the ratifications has been hitherto delayed, in consequence, in the first instance, of some delay in the reception of the treaty at Brussels, and, subsequently, of the absence of the Belgian minister of foreign affairs at the important conferences in which his Government is engaged at London. That treaty does but embody those enlarged principles of friendly policy which it is sincerely hoped will always regulate the conduct of the two nations having such strong motives to maintain amicable relations toward each other and so sincerely desirous to cherish them.

With all the other European powers with whom the United States have formed diplomatic relations and with the Sublime Porte the best understanding prevails. From all I continue to receive assurances of good will toward the United States—assurances which it gives me no less pleasure to reciprocate than to receive. With all, the engagements which have been entered into are fulfilled with good faith on both sides. Measures have also been taken to enlarge our friendly relations and extend our commercial intercourse with other States. The system we have pursued of aiming at no exclusive advantages, of dealing with all on terms of fair and equal reciprocity, and of adhering scrupulously to all our engagements is well calculated to give success to efforts intended to be mutually beneficial.

The wars of which the southern part of this continent was so long the theater, and which were carried on either by the mother country against the States which had formerly been her colonies or by the States against each other, having terminated, and their civil dissensions having so far subsided as with few exceptions no longer to disturb the public tranquillity, it is earnestly hoped those States will be able to employ themselves without interruption in perfecting their institutions, cultivating the arts of peace, and promoting by wise councils and able exertions the public and private prosperity which their patriotic struggles so well entitle them to enjoy.

With those States our relations have undergone but little change during the present year. No reunion having yet taken place between the States which composed the Republic of Colombia, our chargé d'affaires at Bogota has been accredited to the Government of New Grenada, and we have, therefore, no diplomatic relations with Venezuela and Equator, except as they may be included in those heretofore formed with the Colombian Republic.

It is understood that representatives from the three States were about to assemble at Bogota to confer on the subject of their mutual interests, particularly that of their union, and if the result should render it necessary, measures will be taken on our part to preserve with each that friendship and those liberal commercial connections which it has been the constant desire of the United States to cultivate with their sister Republics of this hemisphere. Until the important question of reunion shall be settled, however, the different matters which have been under discussion between the United States and the Republic of Colombia, or either of the States which composed it, are not likely to be brought to a satisfactory issue.

In consequence of the illness of the chargé d'affaires appointed to Central America at the last session of Congress, he was prevented from proceeding on his mission until the month of October. It is hoped, however, that he is by this time at his post, and that the official intercourse, unfortunately so long interrupted, has been thus renewed on the part of the two nations so amicably and advantageously connected by engagements founded on the most enlarged principles of commercial reciprocity.

It is gratifying to state that since my last annual message some of the most important claims of our fellow-citizens upon the Government of Brazil have been satisfactorily adjusted, and a reliance is placed on the friendly dispositions manifested by it that justice will also be done in others. No new causes of complaint have arisen, and the trade between the two countries flourishes under the encouragement secured to it by the liberal provisions of the treaty.

It is cause of regret that, owing, probably, to the civil dissensions which have occupied the attention of the Mexican Government, the time fixed by the treaty of limits with the United States for the meeting of the commissioners to define the boundaries between the two nations has been suffered to expire without the apppointment of any commissioners on the part of that Government. While the true boundary remains in doubt by either party it is difficult to give effect to those measures which are necessary to the protection and quiet of our numerous citizens residing near that frontier. The subject is one of great solicitude to the United States, and will not fail to receive my earnest attention.

The treaty concluded with Chili and approved by the Senate at its last session was also ratified by the Chilian Government, but with certain additional and explanatory articles of a nature to have required it to be again submitted to the Senate. The time limited for the exchange of the ratifications, however, having since expired, the action of both Governments on the treaty will again become necessary.

The negotiations commenced with the Argentine Republic relative to the outrages committed on our vessels engaged in the fisheries at the Falkland Islands by persons acting under the color of its authority, as well as the other matters in controversy between the two Governments, have been suspended by the departure of the chargé d'affaires of the United States from Buenos Ayres. It is understood, however, that a minister was subsequently appointed by that Government to renew the negotiation in the United States, but though daily expected he has not yet arrived in this country.

With Peru no treaty has yet been formed, and with Bolivia no diplomatic intercourse has yet been established. It will be my endeavor to encourage those sentiments of amity and that liberal commerce which belong to the relations in which all the independent States of this continent stand toward each other.

I deem it proper to recommend to your notice the revision of our consular system. This has become an important branch of the public service, inasmuch as it is intimately connected with the preservation of our national character abroad, with the interest of our citizens in foreign countries, with the regulation and care of our commerce, and with the protection of our seamen. At the close of the last session of Congress I communicated a report from the Secretary of State upon the subject, to which I now refer, as containing information which may be useful in any inquiries that Congress may see fit to institute with a view to a salutary reform of the system.

It gives me great pleasure to congratulate you upon the prosperous condition of the finances of the country, as will appear from the report which the Secretary of the Treasury will in due time lay before you. The receipts into the Treasury during the present year will amount to more than $32,000,000. The revenue derived from customs will, it is believed, be more than $28,000,000, and the public lands will yield about $3,000,000. The expenditures within the year for all objects, including $2,572,240.99 on account of the public debt, will not amount to $25,000,000, and a large balance will remain in the Treasury after satisfying all the appropriations chargeable on the revenue for the present year.

The measures taken by the Secretary of the Treasury will probably enable him to pay off in the course of the present year the residue of the exchanged 4½ per cent stock, redeemable on the 1st of January next. It has therefore been included in the estimated expenditures of this year, and forms a part of the sum above stated to have been paid on account of the public debt. The payment of this stock will reduce the whole debt of the United States, funded and unfunded, to the sum of $4,760,082.08, and as provision has already been made for the 4½ percents above mentioned, and charged in the expenses of the present year, the sum last stated is all that now remains of the national debt; and the revenue of the coming year, together with the balance now in the Treasury, will be sufficient to discharge it, after meeting the current expenses of the Government. Under the power given to the commissioners of the sinking fund, it will, I have no doubt, be purchased on favorable terms within the year.

From this view of the state of the finances and the public engagements yet to be fulfilled you will perceive that if Providence permits me to meet you at another session I shall have the high gratification of announcing to you that the national debt is extinguished. I can not refrain from expressing the pleasure I feel at the near approach of that desirable event. The short period of time within which the public debt will have been discharged is strong evidence of the abundant resources of the country and of the prudence and economy with which the Government has heretofore been administered. We have waged two wars since we became a nation, with one of the most powerful kingdoms in the world, both of them undertaken in defense of our dearest rights, both successfully prosecuted and honorably terminated; and many of those who partook in the first struggle as well as in the second will have lived to see the last item of the debt incurred in these necessary but expensive conflicts faithfully and honestly discharged. And we shall have the proud satisfaction of bequeathing to the public servants who follow us in the administration of the Government the rare blessing of a revenue sufficiently abundant, raised without injustice or oppression to our citizens, and unencumbered with any burdens but what they themselves shall think proper to impose upon it.

The flourishing state of the finances ought not, however, to encourage us to indulge in a lavish expenditure of the public treasure. The receipts of the present year do not furnish the test by which we are to estimate the income of the next. The changes made in our revenue system by the acts of Congress of 1832 and 1833, and more especially by the former, have swelled the receipts of the present year far beyond the amount to be expected in future years upon the reduced tariff of duties. The shortened credits on revenue bonds and the cash duties on woolens which were introduced by the act of 1832, and took effect on the 4th of March last, have brought large sums into the Treasury in 1833, which, according to the credits formerly given, would not have been payable until 1834, and would have formed a part of the income of that year. These causes would of themselves produce a great diminution of the receipts in the year 1834 as compared with the present one, and they will be still more diminished by the reduced rates of duties which take place on the 1st of January next on some of the most important and productive articles. Upon the best estimates that can be made the receipts of the next year, with the aid of the unappropriated amount now in the Treasury, will not be much more than sufficient to meet the expenses of the year and pay the small remnant of the national debt which yet remains unsatisfied. I can not, therefore, recommend to you any alteration in the present tariff of duties. The rate as now fixed by law on the various articles was adopted at the last session of Congress, as a matter of compromise, with unusual unanimity, and unless it is found to produce more than the necessities of the Government call for there would seem to be no reason at this time to justify a change.

But while I forbear to recommend any further reduction of the duties beyond that already provided for by the existing laws, I must earnestly and respectfully press upon Congress the importance of abstaining from all appropriations which are not absolutely required for the public interest and authorized by the powers clearly delegated to the United States. We are beginning a new era in our Government. The national debt, which has so long been a burden on the Treasury, will be finally discharged in the course of the ensuing year. No more money will afterwards be needed than what may be necessary to meet the ordinary expenses of the Government. Now, then, is the proper moment to fix our system of expenditure on firm and durable principles, and I can not too strongly urge the necessity of a rigid economy and an inflexible determination not to enlarge the income beyond the real necessities of the Government and not to increase the wants of the Government by unnecessary and profuse expenditures. If a contrary course should be pursued, it may happen that the revenue of 1834 will fall short of the demands upon it, and after reducing the tariff in order to lighten the burdens of the people, and providing for a still further reduction to take effect hereafter, it would be much to be deplored if at the end of another year we should find ourselves obliged to retrace our steps and impose additional taxes to meet unnecessary expenditures.

It is my duty on this occasion to call your attention to the destruction of the public building occupied by the Treasury Department, which happened since the last adjournment of Congress. A thorough inquiry into the causes of this loss was directed and made at the time, the result of which will be duly communicated to you. I take pleasure, however, in stating here that by the laudable exertions of the officers of the Department and many of the citizens of the District but few papers were lost, and none that will materially affect the public interest.

The public convenience requires that another building should be erected as soon as practicable, and in providing for it it will be advisable to enlarge in some manner the accommodations for the public officers of the several Departments, and to authorize the erection of suitable depositories for the safe-keeping of the public documents and records.

Since the last adjournment of Congress the Secretary of the Treasury has directed the money of the United States to be deposited in certain State banks designated by him, and he will immediately lay before you his reasons for this direction.   I concur with him entirely in the view he has taken of the subject, and some months before the removal I urged upon the Department the propriety of taking that step.   The near approach of the day on which the charter will expire, as well as the conduct of the bank, appeared to me to call for this measure upon the high considerations of public interest and public duty.   The extent of its misconduct, however, although known to be great, was not at that time fully developed by proof.   It was not until late in the month of August that I received from the Government directors an official report establishing beyond question that this great and powerful institution had been actively engaged in attempting to influence the elections of the public officers by means of its money, and that, in violation of the express provisions of its charter, it had by a formal resolution placed its funds at the disposition of its president to be employed in sustaining the political power of the bank.   A copy of this resolution is contained in the report of the Government directors before referred to, and however the object may be disguised by cautious language, no one can doubt that this money was in truth intended for electioneering purposes, and the particular uses to which it was proved to have been applied abundantly show that it was so understood.   Not only was the evidence complete as to the past application of the money and power of the bank to electioneering purposes, but that the resolution of the board of directors authorized the same course to be pursued in future.

It being thus established by unquestionable proof that the Bank of the United States was converted into a permanent electioneering engine, it appeared to me that the path of duty which the executive department of the Government ought to pursue was not doubtful.   As by the terms of the bank charter no officer but the Secretary of the Treasury could remove the deposits, it seemed to me that this authority ought to be at once exerted to deprive that great corporation of the support and countenance of the Government in such an use of its funds and such an exertion of its power.   In this point of the case the question is distinctly presented whether the people of the United States are to govern through representatives chosen by their unbiased suffrages or whether the money and power of a great corporation are to be secretly exerted to influence their judgment and control their decisions.   It must now be determined whether the bank is to have its candidates for all offices in the country, from the highest to the lowest, or whether candidates on both sides of political questions shall be brought forward as heretofore and supported by the usual means.

At this time the efforts of the bank to control public opinion, through the distresses of some and the fears of others, are equally apparent, and, if possible, more objectionable. By a curtailment of its accommodations more rapid than any emergency requires, and even while it retains specie to an almost unprecedented amount in its vaults, it is attempting to produce great embarrassment in one portion of the community, while through presses known to have been sustained by its money it attempts by unfounded alarms to create a panic in all.

These are the means by which it seems to expect that it can force a restoration of the deposits, and as a necessary consequence extort from Congress a renewal of its charter. I am happy to know that through the good sense of our people the effort to get up a panic has hitherto failed, and that through the increased accommodations which the State banks have been enabled to afford, no public distress has followed the exertions of the bank, and it can not be doubted that the exercise of its power and the expenditure of its money, as well as its efforts to spread groundless alarm, will be met and rebuked as they deserve. In my own sphere of duty I should feel myself called on by the facts disclosed to order a *scire facias* against the bank, with a view to put an end to the chartered rights it has so palpably violated, were it not that the charter itself will expire as soon as a decision would probably be obtained from the court of last resort.

I called the attention of Congress to this subject in my last annual message, and informed them that such measures as were within the reach of the Secretary of the Treasury had been taken to enable him to judge whether the public deposits in the Bank of the United States were entirely safe; but that as his single powers might be inadequate to the object, I recommended the subject to Congress as worthy of their serious investigation, declaring it as my opinion that an inquiry into the transactions of that institution, embracing the branches as well as the principal bank, was called for by the credit which was given throughout the country to many serious charges impeaching their character, and which, if true, might justly excite the apprehension that they were no longer a safe depository for the public money. The extent to which the examination thus recommended was gone into is spread upon your journals, and is too well known to require to be stated. Such as was made resulted in a report from a majority of the Committee of Ways and Means touching certain specified points only, concluding with a resolution that the Government deposits might safely be continued in the Bank of the United States. This resolution was adopted at the close of the session by the vote of a majority of the House of Representatives.

Although I may not always be able to concur in the views of the public interest or the duties of its agents which may be taken by the other departments of the Government or either of its branches, I am, notwithstanding, wholly incapable of receiving otherwise than with the most sincere respect all opinions or suggestions proceeding from such a source, and in respect to none am I more inclined to do so than to the House of Representatives. But it will be seen from the brief views at this time taken of the subject by myself, as well as the more ample ones presented by the Secretary of the Treasury, that the change in the deposits which has been ordered has been deemed to be called for by considerations which are not affected by the proceedings referred to, and which, if correctly viewed by that Department, rendered its act a matter of imperious duty.

Coming as you do, for the most part, immediately from the people and the States by election, and possessing the fullest opportunity to know their sentiments, the present Congress will be sincerely solicitous to carry into full and fair effect the will of their constituents in regard to this institution. It will be for those in whose behalf we all act to decide whether the executive department of the Government, in the steps which it has taken on this subject, has been found in the line of its duty.

The accompanying report of the Secretary of War, with the documents annexed to it, exhibits the operations of the War Department for the past year and the condition of the various subjects intrusted to its administration.

It will be seen from them that the Army maintains the character it has heretofore acquired for efficiency and military knowledge. Nothing has occurred since your last session to require its services beyond the ordinary routine of duties which upon the seaboard and the inland frontier devolve upon it in a time of peace. The system so wisely adopted and so long pursued of constructing fortifications at exposed points and of preparing and collecting the supplies necessary for the military defense of the country, and thus providently furnishing in peace the means of defense in war, has been continued with the usual results. I recommend to your consideration the various subjects suggested in the report of the Secretary of War. Their adoption would promote the public service and meliorate the condition of the Army.

Our relations with the various Indian tribes have been undisturbed since the termination of the difficulties growing out of the hostile aggressions of the Sac and Fox Indians. Several treaties have been formed for the relinquishment of territory to the United States and for the migration of the occupants of the region assigned for their residence west of the Mississippi. Should these treaties be ratified by the Senate, provision will have been made for the removal of almost all the tribes now remaining east of that river and for the termination of many difficult and embarrassing questions arising out of their anomalous political condition. It is to be hoped that those portions of two of the Southern tribes, which in that event will present the only remaining difficulties, will realize the necessity of emigration, and will speedily resort to it. My original convictions upon this subject have been confirmed by the course of events for several years, and experience is every day adding to their strength.

That those tribes can not exist surrounded by our settlements and in continual contact with our citizens is certain. They have neither the intelligence, the industry, the moral habits, nor the desire of improvement which are essential to any favorable change in their condition. Established in the midst of another and a superior race, and without appreciating the causes of their inferiority or seeking to control them, they must necessarily yield to the force of circumstances and ere long disappear. Such has been their fate heretofore, and if it is to be averted—and it is—it can only be done by a general removal beyond our boundary and by the reorganization of their political system upon principles adapted to the new relations in which they will be placed. The experiment which has been recently made has so far proved successful. The emigrants generally are represented to be prosperous and contented, the country suitable to their wants and habits, and the essential articles of subsistence easily procured. When the report of the commissioners now engaged in investigating the condition and prospects of these Indians and in devising a plan for their intercourse and government is received, I trust ample means of information will be in possession of the Government for adjusting all the unsettled questions connected with this interesting subject.

The operations of the Navy during the year and its present condition are fully exhibited in the annual report from the Navy Department.

Suggestions are made by the Secretary of various improvements, which deserve careful consideration, and most of which, if adopted, bid fair to promote the efficiency of this important branch of the public service. Among these are the new organization of the Navy Board, the revision of the pay to officers, and a change in the period of time or in the manner of making the annual appropriations, to which I beg leave to call your particular attention.

The views which are presented on almost every portion of our naval concerns, and especially on the amount of force and the number of officers, and the general course of policy appropriate in the present state of our country for securing the great and useful purposes of naval protection in peace and due preparation for the contingencies of war, meet with my entire approbation.

It will be perceived from the report referred to that the fiscal concerns of the establishment are in an excellent condition, and it is hoped that Congress may feel disposed to make promptly every suitable provision desired either for preserving or improving the system.

The general Post-Office Department has continued, upon the strength of its own resources, to facilitate the means of communication between the various portions of the Union with increased activity. The method, however, in which the accounts of the transportation of the mail have always been kept appears to have presented an imperfect view of its expenses. It has recently been discovered that from the earliest records of the Department the annual statements have been calculated to exhibit an amount considerably short of the actual expense incurred for that service. These illusory statements, together with the expense of carrying into effect the law of the last session of Congress establishing new mail routes, and a disposition on the part of the head of the Department to gratify the wishes of the public in the extension of mail facilities, have induced him to incur responsibilities for their improvement beyond what the current resources of the Department would sustain. As soon as he had discovered the imperfection of the method he caused an investigation to be made of its results and applied the proper remedy to correct the evil. It became necessary for him to withdraw some of the improvements which he had made to bring the expenses of the Department within its own resources. These expenses were incurred for the public good, and the public have enjoyed their benefit. They are now but partially suspended, and that where they may be discontinued with the least inconvenience to the country.

The progressive increase in the income from postages has equaled the highest expectations, and it affords demonstrative evidence of the growing importance and great utility of this Department. The details are exhibited in the accompanying report of the Postmaster-General.

The many distressing accidents which have of late occurred in that portion of our navigation carried on by the use of steam power deserve the immediate and unremitting attention of the constituted authorities of the country. The fact that the number of those fatal disasters is constantly increasing, notwithstanding the great improvements which are everywhere made in the machinery employed and in the rapid advances which have been made in that branch of science, shows very clearly that they are in a great degree the result of criminal negligence on the part of those by whom the vessels are navigated and to whose care and attention the lives and property of our citizens are so extensively intrusted.

That these evils may be greatly lessened, if not substantially removed, by means of precautionary and penal legislation seems to be highly probable. So far, therefore, as the subject can be regarded as within the constitutional purview of Congress I earnestly recommend it to your prompt and serious consideration.

I would also call your attention to the views I have heretofore expressed of the propriety of amending the Constitution in relation to the mode of electing the President and the Vice-President of the United States. Regarding it as all important to the future quiet and harmony of the people that every intermediate agency in the election of these officers should be removed and that their eligibility should be limited to one term of either four or six years, I can not too earnestly invite your consideration of the subject.

Trusting that your deliberations on all the topics of general interest to which I have adverted, and such others as your more extensive knowledge of the wants of our beloved country may suggest, may be crowned with success, I tender you in conclusion the cooperation which it may be in my power to afford them,

ANDREW JACKSON.

SPECIAL MESSAGES.

WASHINGTON, *December 5, 1833.*

To the Senate of the United States:

In compliance with the resolution of the Senate at its last session, requesting the President "to cause to be prepared and laid before the Senate at the commencement of its next session a plan for equalizing the pay of the officers in the Army and Navy according to their relative rank, and providing a stated salary or fixed compensation for their services in lieu of present allowances," I submit herewith a report from the Secretaries of the War and Navy Departments, to whom the subject was referred. It is believed the plan they have presented meets substantially the objects of the resolution.

ANDREW JACKSON.

WASHINGTON, *December 6, 1833.*

To the House of Representatives:

I transmit herewith to the House of Representatives a communication from the War Department, showing the circumstances under which the sum of $5,000, appropriated for subsistence of the Army, was transferred to the service of the medical and hospital department, and which, by the law authorizing the transfer, are required to be laid before Congress during the first week of their session.

ANDREW JACKSON.

WASHINGTON, *December 6, 1833.*

To the House of Representatives:

I transmit herewith, for the information of the House, the report of the survey made in pursuance of the fourth section of the act of Congress of the 4th July, 1832, authorizing the survey of canal routes in the Territory of Florida.

ANDREW JACKSON.

WASHINGTON, *December 11, 1833.*

To the House of Representatives:

I transmit herewith a report from the Secretary of the Treasury, exhibiting certain transfers of appropriations that have been made in that Department in pursuance of the power vested in the President by the first section of the act of Congress of the 3d March, 1809, entitled "An act further to amend the several acts for the establishment and regulation of the Treasury, War, and Navy Departments."

ANDREW JACKSON.

WASHINGTON, *December 12, 1833.*

To the Senate of the United States:

I have attentively considered the resolution of the Senate of the 11th instant, requesting the President of the United States to communicate to the Senate "a copy of the paper which has been published, and which purports to have been read by him to the heads of the Executive Departments, dated the 18th day of September last, relating to the removal of the deposits of the public money from the Bank of the United States and its offices."

The executive is a coordinate and independent branch of the Government equally with the Senate, and I have yet to learn under what constitutional authority that branch of the Legislature has a right to require of me an account of any communication, either verbally or in writing, made to the heads of Departments acting as a Cabinet council. As well might I be required to detail to the Senate the free and private conversations I have held with those officers on any subject relating to their duties and my own.

Feeling my responsibility to the American people, I am willing upon all occasions to explain to them the grounds of my conduct, and I am willing upon all proper occasions to give to either branch of the Legislature any information in my possession that can be useful in the execution of the appropriate duties confided to them.

Knowing the constitutional rights of the Senate, I shall be the last man under any circumstances to interfere with them. Knowing those of the Executive, I shall at all times endeavor to maintain them agreeably to the provisions of the Constitution and the solemn oath I have taken to support and defend it.

I am constrained, therefore, by a proper sense of my own self-respect and of the rights secured by the Constitution to the executive branch of the Government to decline a compliance with your request.

ANDREW JACKSON.

WASHINGTON, *December 23, 1833.*

To the House of Representatives:

The rules and regulations herewith submitted have been prepared by a board of officers in conformity with an act passed May 19, 1832.*

They are approved by me, and in pursuance of the provisions of said

---

* An act authorizing the revision and extension of the rules and regulations of the naval service.

act are now communicated to the House of Representatives for the purpose of obtaining to them the sanction of Congress.

ANDREW JACKSON.

WASHINGTON, *December 24, 1833.*

To the Senate:

I transmit herewith, for the consideration of the Senate as to the ratification thereof, the following Indian treaties that have been received since the adjournment of the last session of Congress, viz:

No. 1. Treaty with the Seminole Indians, made May 9, 1832.

No. 2. Treaty with the Cherokees west of the Mississippi, made 14th February, 1833.

No. 3. Treaty with the Creeks west of the Mississippi, made 14th February, 1833.

No. 4. Assignment to the Seminoles of a tract of land for their residence west of the Mississippi, made 28th March, 1833.

No. 5. Agreement with the Apalachicola band of Indians, made 18th June, 1833.

No. 6. Treaty with the united bands of Ottoes and Missourians, made 21st September, 1833.

No. 7. Treaty with the four confederated bands of Pawnees residing on the Platt and Loup Fork, made 9th October, 1833.

ANDREW JACKSON.

WASHINGTON, *January 6, 1834.*

To the Senate and House of Representatives:

I communicate to Congress an extract of a letter recently received from R. J. Leib, consul of the United States at Tangier, by which it appears that that officer has been induced to receive from the Emperor of Morocco a present of a lion and two horses, which he holds as belonging to the United States. There being no funds at the disposal of the Executive applicable to the objects stated by Mr. Leib, I submit the whole subject to the consideration of Congress for such direction as in their wisdom may seem proper.

I have directed instructions to be given to all our ministers and agents abroad requiring that in future, unless previously authorized by Congress, they will not under any circumstances accept presents of any description from any foreign state.

I deem it proper on this occasion to invite the attention of Congress to the presents which have heretofore been made to our public officers, and which have been deposited under the orders of the Government in the Department of State. These articles are altogether useless to the Government, and the care and preservation of them in the Department of State are attended with considerable inconvenience.

The provision of the Constitution which forbids any officer, without the consent of Congress, to accept any present from any foreign power may be considered as having been satisfied by the surrender of the articles to the Government, and they might now be disposed of by Congress to those for whom they were originally intended, or to their heirs, with obvious propriety in both cases, and in the latter would be received as grateful memorials of the surrender of the present.

As under the positive order now given similar presents can not hereafter be received, even for the purpose of being placed at the disposal of the Government, I recommend to Congress to authorize by law that the articles already in the Department of State shall be delivered to the persons to whom they were originally presented, if living, and to the heirs of such as may have died.

ANDREW JACKSON.

WASHINGTON, *January 7, 1834.*

To the House of Representatives:

In compliance with the resolution requesting the President of the United States to lay before the House "a copy of any contract which may have been made for the construction of a bridge across the Potomac opposite to the city of Washington, together with the authority under which such contract may have been made, the names of the contractors and their securities, if any, and the plan and estimate of the cost of such a bridge," I transmit herewith a report from the Secretary of the Treasury, to whom the resolution was referred, containing all the information upon the subject which he is now able to communicate.

ANDREW JACKSON.

WASHINGTON, *January 9, 1834.*

To the Senate of the United States:

I transmit to the Senate, for their constitutional action, a treaty concluded between the commissioners on the part of the United States and the united nation of Chippewas, Ottawas, and Potawatamies, at Chicago, on the 26th of September, 1833, to the cession of certain lands in the State of Illinois and Territory of Michigan.

I transmit also sundry documents relating thereto that I think proper should be laid before the Senate.

I understand the country ceded by this treaty is considered a valuable one and its acquisition important to that section of the Union. Under these circumstances, as the objection to a ratification applies to those stipulations in the third article which provide that $100,000 and $150,000 shall be granted in satisfaction of claims to reservations and for debts due from the Indians to individuals, I recommend that the treaty be ratified. with the condition that an agent be appointed to proceed to Chicago and investigate the justice of these claims. If they are all well founded and have been assented to by the Indians with a full knowledge of the circumstances, a proper investigation of them will do the claimants no injury, but will place the matter beyond suspicion. If, on the other hand, they are unjust and have not been fully understood by the Indians, the fraud will in that event vitiate them, and they ought not to be paid. To the United States, in a mere pecuniary point of view, it is of no importance to whom the money provided by this treaty is paid. They stipulate to pay a given amount, and that amount they must pay, but the consideration is yielded by the Indians, and they are entitled to its value. Whatever is granted in claims must be withheld from them, and if not so granted it becomes theirs. Considering the relations in which the Indians stand to the United States, it appears to me just to exercise their supervisory authority. It has been done in more than one instance, and as its object in this case is to ascertain whether any fraud exists, and if there does to correct it, I consider such a ratification within the proper scope of the treaty-making power. ANDREW JACKSON.

WASHINGTON, *January 22, 1834.*

To the Senate:

I transmit to the Senate a report* from the Secretary of State, containing the information requested by their resolution of the 9th instant, with the documents which accompany that report.

ANDREW JACKSON.

WASHINGTON, *January 25, 1834.*

To the House of Representatives of the United States:

I transmit herewith to the House of Representatives a letter from the Secretary of State, together with the accompanying papers, relating to a claim preferred to that Department, through the British legation at Washington, for indemnification for losses alleged to have been sustained by the owners of the ship *Francis and Eliza*, libeled at New Orleans in 1819, and condemned and sold by the sentence and decree of the district court of the United States for the district of Louisiana, but afterwards restored upon an appeal to the Supreme Court of the United States, that such legislative provision may be made by Congress in behalf of those interested as shall appear just and proper in the case.

ANDREW JACKSON.

FEBRUARY 4, 1834.

To the Senate and House of Representatives:

I deem it my duty to communicate to Congress the recent conduct of the Bank of the United States in refusing to deliver the books, papers, and funds in its possession relating to the execution of the act of Congress

*Relating to presents from foreign governments to officers of the United States.

of June 7, 1832, entitled "An act supplementary to the 'Act for the relief of certain surviving officers and soldiers of the Revolution.'" The correspondence reported by the Secretary of War, and herewith transmitted, will show the grounds assumed by the bank to justify its refusal to make the transfer directed by the War Department. It does not profess to claim the privilege of this agency as a right secured to it by contract, nor as a benefit conferred by the Government, but as a burden, from which it is willing to be relieved. It places its refusal upon the extraordinary ground that the corporation has a right to sit in judgment upon the legality of the acts of the constituted authorities in a matter in which the stockholders are admitted to have no interest, and it impedes and defeats, as far as its power will permit, the execution of a measure of the Administration, because the opinion of the corporation upon the construction of an act of Congress differs from that of the proper officers of the United States.

The claim of this corporation thus to usurp the functions of the judicial power and to prescribe to the executive department the manner in which it shall execute the trust confided to it by law is without example in the history of our country. If the acts of the public servants, who are responsible to the people for the manner in which they execute their duty, may thus be checked and controlled by an irresponsible money corporation, then indeed the whole frame of our Government is changed, and we have established a power in the Bank of the United States above what we derive from the people.

It will be seen from the accompanying statement (marked A) that according to the latest accounts received at the War Department the Bank of the United States and its branches have in their possession near half a million of the public money, received by them under the law of 1832, which they have not yet accounted for, and which they refuse to pay over to the proper agents for the use of those persons for whose benefit it was withdrawn from the Treasury. It is to be regretted that this attempt on the part of the bank to guide and direct the Executive upon the construction and execution of an act of Congress should have been put forward and insisted on in a case where the immediate sufferers from their conduct will be the surviving veterans of the Revolutionary war, for this evil falls exclusively upon the gallant defenders of their country and delays and embarrasses the payment of the debt which the gratitude of the nation has awarded to them, and which in many instances is necessary for their subsistence and comfort in their declining years.

The character of the claim set up by the bank and the interest of the parties to be immediately affected by it make it my duty to submit the whole subject to the consideration of Congress, and I leave it to their wisdom to adopt such measures as the honor of the Government and the just claims of the individuals injured by the proceedings may be deemed to require.

Having called for the opinion of the Attorney-General upon this occasion with a view to a thorough investigation of the question which has thus been presented for my consideration, I inclose a copy of the report of that officer and add my entire concurrence in the views he has taken.

ANDREW JACKSON.

WASHINGTON, *February 12, 1834.*

To the House of Representatives:

I transmit to the House of Representatives a report* from the Secretary of State, in relation to the subject of a resolution of the 8th of this month. ANDREW JACKSON.

WASHINGTON, *February 12, 1834.*

To the House of Representatives:

I transmit to the House of Representatives a report from the Secretary of State, containing the information requested† by the resolution of the 14th ultimo, with the documents which accompanied that report.

ANDREW JACKSON.

WASHINGTON, *February 22, 1834.*

To the Senate of the United States:

I transmit herewith to the Senate, for their advice concerning its ratification, an additional and explanatory convention to the treaty of peace, amity, commerce, and navigation between the United States and the Republic of Chile, which additional and explanatory convention was concluded at the city of Santiago by the plenipotentiaries of the United States and of Chile on the 1st of September, 1833. I also transmit a report from the Secretary of State on the subject. ANDREW JACKSON.

WASHINGTON, *March 8, 1834.*

To the House of Representatives:

I transmit herewith to the House a report from the Secretary of State, containing the instructions and other papers called for by the resolution of the House of the 14th ultimo, "relative to the trade between the United States and the islands of Cuba and Porto Rico," etc.

ANDREW JACKSON.

WASHINGTON, *March 11, 1834.*

To the Senate:

I renominate Henry D. Gilpin, Peter Wager, and John T. Sullivan, of Philadelphia, and Hugh McEldery, of Baltimore, to be directors in the Bank of the United States for the year 1834.

---

*Relating to the boundary line between Georgia and Florida.

†List of presents from foreign governments to officers of the United States, deposited in the State Department.

I disclaim all pretension of right on the part of the President officially to inquire into or call in question the reasons of the Senate for rejecting any nomination whatsoever. As the President is not responsible to them for the reasons which induce him to make a nomination, so they are not responsible to him for the reasons which induce them to reject it. In these respects each is independent of the other and both responsible to their respective constituents. Nevertheless, the attitude in which certain vital interests of the country are placed by the rejection of the gentlemen now renominated require of me frankly to communicate my views of the consequences which must necessarily follow this act of the Senate if it be not reconsidered.

The characters and standing of these gentlemen are well known to the community, and eminently qualify them for the offices to which I propose to appoint them. Their confirmation by the Senate at its last session to the same offices is proof that such was the opinion of them entertained by the Senate at that time, and unless something has occurred since to change it this act may now be referred to as evidence that their talents and pursuits justified their selection. The refusal, however, to confirm their nominations to the same offices shows that there is something in the conduct of these gentlemen during the last year which, in the opinion of the Senate, disqualifies them, and as no charge has been made against them as men or citizens, nothing which impeaches the fair private character they possessed when the Senate gave them their sanction at its last session, and as it, moreover, appears from the Journal of the Senate recently transmitted for my inspection that it was deemed unnecessary to inquire into their qualifications or character, it is to be inferred that the change in the opinion of the Senate has arisen from the official conduct of these gentlemen. The only circumstances in their official conduct which have been deemed of sufficient importance to attract public attention are the two reports made by them to the executive department of the Government, the one bearing date the 22d day of April and the other the 19th day of August last, both of which reports were communicated to the Senate by the Secretary of the Treasury with his reasons for removing the deposit.

The truth of the facts stated in these reports is not, I presume, questioned by anyone. The high character and standing of the citizens by whom they were made prevent any doubt upon the subject. Indeed, the statements have not been denied by the president of the bank and the other directors. On the contrary, they have insisted that they were authorized to use the money of the bank in the manner stated in the two reports, and have not denied that the charges there made against the corporation are substantially true.

It must be taken, therefore, as admitted that the statements of the public directors in the reports above mentioned are correct, and they disclose the most alarming abuses on the part of the corporation and the most strenuous exertions on their part to put an end to them. They prove that enormous sums were secretly lavished in a manner and for purposes that can not be justified, and that the whole of the immense capital of the bank has been virtually placed at the disposal of a single individual, to be used, if he thinks proper, to corrupt the press and to control the proceedings of the Government by exercising an undue influence over elections.

The reports are made in obedience to my official directions, and I herewith transmit copies of my letters calling for information of the proceedings of the bank. Were they bound to disregard the call? Was it their duty to remain silent while abuses of the most injurious and dangerous character were daily practiced? Were they bound to conceal from the constituted authorities a course of measures destructive to the best interests of the country and intended gradually and secretly to subvert the foundations of our Government and to transfer its powers from the hands of the people to a great moneyed corporation? Was it their duty to sit in silence at the board and witness all these abuses without an attempt to correct them, or, in case of failure there, not to appeal to higher authority? The eighth fundamental rule authorizes any one of the directors, whether elected or appointed, who may have been absent when an excess of debt was created, or who may have dissented from the act, to exonerate himself from personal responsibility by giving notice of the fact to the President of the United States, thus recognizing the propriety of communicating to that officer the proceedings of the board in such cases. But independently of any argument to be derived from the principle recognized in the rule referred to, I can not doubt for a moment that it is the right and the duty of every director at the board to attempt to correct all illegal proceedings, and, in case of failure, to disclose them, and that every one of them, whether elected by the stockholders or appointed by the Government, who had knowledge of the facts and concealed them, would be justly amenable to the severest censure.

But in the case of the public directors it was their peculiar and official duty to make the disclosures, and the call upon them for information could not have been disregarded without a flagrant breach of their trust. The directors appointed by the United States can not be regarded in the light of the ordinary directors of a bank appointed by the stockholders and charged with the care of their pecuniary interests in the corporation. They have higher and more important duties. They are public officers. They are placed at the board not merely to represent the stock held by the United States, but to observe the conduct of the corporation and to watch over the public interests. It was foreseen that this great moneyed monopoly might be so managed as to endanger the interests of the country, and it was therefore deemed necessary as a measure of precaution to place at the board watchful sentinels, who should observe its conduct and stand ready to report to the proper officers of the Government every act of the board which might affect injuriously the interests of the people.

The whole frame of the charter, as well as the manner of their appointment, proves this to be their true character. The United States are not represented at the board by these directors merely on account of the stock held by the Government. The right of the United States to appoint directors and the number appointed do not depend upon the amount of the stock, for if every share should be sold and the United States cease to be a stockholder altogether, yet under the charter the right to appoint five directors would still remain. In such a case what would be the character of the directors? They would represent no stock and be chosen by no stockholders. Yet they would have a right to sit at the board, to vote on all questions submitted to it, and to be made acquainted with all the proceedings of the corporation. They would not in such a case be ordinary directors chosen by the stockholders in proportion to their stock, but they would be public officers, appointed to guard the public interest, and their duties must conform to their office. They are not the duties of an ordinary director chosen by a stockholder, but they are the peculiar duties of a public officer who is bound on all occasions to protect to the utmost of his lawful means the public interests, and, where his own authority is not sufficient to prevent injury, to inform those to whom the law has confided the necessary power. Such, then, is the character and such are the duties of the directors appointed by the United States, whether the public be stockholders or not. They are officers of the United States, and not the mere representatives of a stockholder.

The mode of their appointment and their tenure of office confirm this position. They are appointed like other officers of the Government and by the same authority. They do not hold their offices irrevocably a year after their appointment; on the contrary, by the express terms of the law, they are liable to be removed from office at any time by the President when in his judgment the public interest shall require it. In every aspect, therefore, in which the subject can be considered it is evident that the five directors appointed by the United States are to be regarded as public officers who are placed there in order to observe the conduct of the corporation and to prevent abuses which might otherwise be committed.

Such being the character of the directors appointed on behalf of the United States, it is obviously their duty to resist, and in case of failure to report to the President or to the Secretary of the Treasury, any proceedings of the board by which the public interests may be injuriously affected. The President may order a *scire facias* against the bank for a violation of its charter, and the Secretary of the Treasury is empowered to direct the money of the United States to be deposited elsewhere when in his judgment the public interest requires it to be done. The directors of this bank, like all others, are accustomed to sit with closed doors, and do not report their proceedings to any department of the Government.

The monthly return which the charter requires to be made to the Treasury Department gives nothing more than a general statement of its pecuniary condition, and of that but an imperfect one; for although it shows the amount loaned at the bank and its different branches, it does not show the condition of its debtors nor the circumstances under which the loans were made. It does not show whether they were in truth accommodations granted in the regular and ordinary course of business upon fair banking principles or from other motives. Under the name of loans advances may be made to persons notoriously insolvent for the most corrupt and improper purposes, and a course of proceeding may be adopted in violation of its charter, while upon the face of its monthly statement everything would appear to be fair and correct.

How, then, is the executive branch of the Government to become acquainted with the official conduct of the public directors or the abuses practiced by the corporation for its private ends and in violation of its duty to the public? The power of displacing the public directors and that of issuing a *scire facias* and of removing the deposits were not intended to be idle and nugatory provisions without the means of enforcement. Yet they must be wholly inoperative and useless unless there be some means by which the official conduct of the public directors and the abuses of power on the part of the corporation may be brought to the knowledge of the executive department of the Government.

Will it be said that the power is given to the Secretary of the Treasury to examine himself, or by his authorized agent, into the conduct and condition of the bank? The answer is obvious. It could not have been expected or intended that he would make an examination unless information was first given to him which excited his suspicions; and if he did make such a general examination without previous information of misconduct, it is most probable that in the complex concerns and accounts of a bank it would result in nothing, whatever abuses might have been practiced.

It is, indeed, the duty of every director to give information of such misconduct on the part of the board. But the power to issue a *scire facias* and to remove the deposits presupposes that the directors elected by the stockholders might abuse their power, and it can not be presumed that Congress intended to rely on these same directors to give information of their own misconduct. The Government is not accustomed to rely on the offending party to disclose his offense. It was intended that the power to issue a *scire facias* and remove the deposits be real and effective. The necessary means of information were therefore provided in the charter, and five officers of the Government, appointed in the usual manner, responsible to the public and not to the stockholders, were placed as sentinels at the board, and are bound by the nature and character of their office to resist, and if unsuccessful to report to the proper authority, every infraction of the charter and every abuse of power, in order that due measures should be taken to punish or correct it; and in like manner it is their duty to give, when called upon, any explanation of their own official conduct touching the management of the institution.

It was perhaps scarcely necessary to present to the Senate these views of the power of the Executive and of the duties of the five directors appointed by the United States. But the bank is believed to be now striving to obtain for itself the government of the country, and is seeking by new and strained constructions to wrest from the hands of the constituted authorities the salutary control reserved by the charter; and as misrepresentation is one of its most usual weapons of attack, I have deemed it my duty to put before the Senate in a manner not to be misunderstood the principles on which I have acted.

Entertaining as I do a solemn conviction of the truth of these principles, I must adhere to them and act upon them with constancy and firmness. Aware as I now am of the dangerous machinations of the bank, it is more than ever my duty to be vigilant in guarding the rights of the people from the impending danger. And I should feel that I ought to forfeit the confidence with which my countrymen have honored me if I did not require regular and full reports of everything in the proceedings of the bank calculated to affect injuriously the public interests from the public directors; and if the directors should fail to give the information called for, it would be my imperious duty to exercise the power conferred on me by law of removing them from office and of appointing others who would discharge their duties with more fidelity to the public. I can never suffer anyone to hold office under me who would connive at corruption or who should fail to give the alarm when he saw the enemies of liberty endeavoring to sap the foundations of our free institutions and to subject the free people of the United States to the dominion of a great moneyed corporation.

Any directors of the bank, therefore, who might be appointed by the Government would be required to report to the Executive as fully as the late directors have done, and more frequently, because the danger is more imminent; and it would be my duty to require of them a full detail of every part of the proceedings of the corporation, or any of its officers, in order that I might be enabled to decide whether I should exercise the power of ordering a *scire facias*, which is reserved to the President by the charter, or adopt such other lawful measures as the interests of the country might require. It is too obvious to be doubted that the misconduct of the corporation would never have been brought to light by the aid of a public proceeding at the board of directors. The board when called on by the Government directors refused to institute an inquiry or require an account, and the mode adopted by the latter was the only one by which the object could be attained. It would be absurd to admit the right of the Government directors to give information and at the same time deny the means of obtaining it. It would be but another mode of enabling the bank to conceal its proceedings and practice with impunity its corruptions. In the mode of obtaining the information, therefore, and in their efforts to put an end to the abuses disclosed, as well as in reporting them, the conduct of the late directors was judicious and praiseworthy, and the honesty, firmness, and intelligence which they have displayed entitle them, in my opinion, to the gratitude of the country.

But if I do not mistake the principles on which the Senate have recently rejected them, the conduct which I deem worthy of praise they treat as a breach of duty, and in their judgment the measures which they took to obtain the informations and their efforts to put an end to the practices disclosed and the reports they have made to the Executive, although true in all their parts, are regarded as an offense and supposed to require some decisive mark of strong disapprobation.

If the views of the Senate be such as I have supposed, the difficulty of sending to the Senate any other names than those of the late directors will be at once apparent. I can not consent to place before the Senate the name of anyone who is not prepared with firmness and honesty to discharge the duties of a public director in the manner they were fulfilled by those whom the Senate have refused to confirm. If for performing a duty lawfully required of them by the Executive they are to be punished by the subsequent rejection of the Senate, it would not only be useless, but cruel, to place men of character and honor in that situation, if even such men could be found to accept it. If they failed to give the required information or to take proper measures to obtain it, they would be removed by the Executive. If they gave the information and took proper measures to obtain it, they would upon the next nomination be rejected by the Senate. It would be unjust in me to place any other citizens in the predicament in which this unlooked-for decision of the Senate has placed the estimable and honorable men who were directors during the last year.

If I am not in error in relation to the principles upon which these gentlemen have been rejected, the necessary consequence will be that the bank will hereafter be without Government directors, and the people of the United States must be deprived of their chief means of protection against its abuses, for whatever conflicting opinions may exist as to the right of the directors appointed in January, 1833, to hold over until new appointments shall be made, it is very obvious that whilst their rejection by the Senate remains in force they can not with propriety attempt to exercise such a power. In the present state of things, therefore, the corporation will be enabled effectually to accomplish the object it has been so long endeavoring to attain. Its exchange committees and its delegated powers to its president may hereafter be dispensed with without incurring the danger of exposing its proceedings to the public view. The sentinels which the law had placed at its board can no longer appear there.

Justice to myself and to the faithful officers by whom the public has been so well and so honorably served without compensation or reward during the last year has required of me this full and frank exposition of my motives for nominating them again after their rejection by the Senate.   I repeat that I do not question the right of the Senate to confirm or reject at their pleasure, and if there had been any reason to suppose that the rejection in this case had not been produced by the causes to which I have attributed it, or if my views of their duties and the present importance of their rigid performance were other than they are, I should have cheerfully acquiesced and attempted to find others who would accept the unenviable trust; but I can not consent to appoint directors of the bank to be the subservient instruments or silent spectators of its abuses and corruptions, nor can I ask honorable men to undertake the thankless duty with the certain prospect of being rebuked by the Senate for its faithful performance in pursuance of the lawful directions of the Executive.

I repeat that I do not claim a right to inquire into or officially to censure the acts of the Senate, but the situation in which the important interests of the American people vested in the Bank of the United States and affected by its arrangements must necessarily be left by the rejection of the gentlemen now renominated has made it my duty to give this explanation to the Senate and submit the matter to their reconsideration.   If it shall be determined by the Senate that all channels of information in relation to the corrupt proceedings of this dangerous corporation shall be cut off and the Government and country left exposed to its unrestrained machinations against the purity of the press and public liberty, I shall, after having made this effort to avert so great an evil, rest for the justification of my official course with respectful confidence on the judgment of the American people.

In conclusion it is proper I should inform the Senate that there is now no Government director appointed for the present year, Mr. Bayard, who was nominated, and confirmed by the Senate, having refused to accept that appointment.

ANDREW JACKSON.

WASHINGTON, *March 14, 1834.*

To the Senate and House of Representatives:

I transmit herewith a report from the Secretary of State, accompanied by a copy of a letter from the commissioners appointed to adjust the claims of our citizens under the late treaty with Naples, and suggest for the consideration of Congress the expediency of extending the term allowed for the performance of the duties assigned to them.

ANDREW JACKSON.

WASHINGTON, *March 20, 1834.*

To the Senate of the United States:

I transmit herewith to the Senate a report * from the Secretary of State, with the documents accompanying it, in pursuance of their resolution of the 7th instant, relative to the ship *Olive Branch.*

ANDREW JACKSON.

WASHINGTON, *March 22, 1834.*

To the House of Representatives of the United States:

I transmit to the House of Representatives a report † from the Secretary of State, upon the subject of a resolution of the 10th instant, which was referred to that officer.

ANDREW JACKSON.

WASHINGTON, *April 1, 1834.*

To the Senate and House of Representatives:

I transmit for the consideration of Congress a report from the Secretary of State, and recommend that legislative measures may be taken to prevent the counterfeiting of foreign coins and the exporting of counterfeit coins from the United States.

ANDREW JACKSON.

WASHINGTON, *April 2, 1834.*

To the Senate and House of Representatives:

I lay before Congress a communication from the governor of New York and a copy of a communication from the governor of New Jersey, addressed to me with a view of obtaining the consent of Congress to an agreement which has been entered into by the States of New York and New Jersey to settle the boundary line between those States. The agreement and authenticated copies of the acts of the legislatures of New York and New Jersey relating to it are also transmitted.

ANDREW JACKSON.

WASHINGTON, *April 8, 1834.*

To the Senate:

I transmit herewith a report from the Commissioner of the General Land Office, made in compliance with the resolution of the Senate of the 29th ultimo, calling for "the dates of the proclamations and the times

---

* Transmitting memorial of the heir at law of General Ira Allen, relative to the capture, detention, and condemnation of the ship *Olive Branch* and her cargo by the British Government; also copy of instructions given to the United States minister to Great Britain and of correspondence between him and the British Government on the subject.

† Transmitting correspondence and papers relating to the claim of Don Juan Madrazo, a Spanish subject, for losses occasioned by acts of the United States and Georgia.

of sale specified in each of the sales of the public lands in the district of country acquired from the Choctaw tribe of Indians by the treaty of Dancing Rabbit Creek and from the Creek tribe of Indians in Alabama; and also the causes, if any existed, of a shorter notice being given for the sale of these lands than is usual in the sale of the other public lands."

ANDREW JACKSON.

WASHINGTON, *April 17, 1834.*

To the Senate of the United States:

I transmit to the Senate, for their consideration and advice with regard to its ratification, a convention for the settlement of claims between the United States of America and Her Catholic Majesty, concluded at Madrid on the 17th of February, 1834.

ANDREW JACKSON.

WASHINGTON, *May 1, 1834.*

The SPEAKER OF THE HOUSE OF REPRESENTATIVES:

I submit for the sanction of Congress certain proposals for amending the present laws in relation to the naval service, prepared and reported by the board constituted under the act of May 19, 1832.

The papers on this subject are Nos. 1 to 5, inclusive.

These proposals are approved by me, and if adopted in the form of laws appear well suited "to the present and future exigencies of that important arm of national defense."

ANDREW JACKSON.

WASHINGTON, *May 12, 1834.*

To the Senate and House of Representatives of the United States:

I communicate to Congress copies of a treaty of navigation and commerce between the United States and His Majesty the Emperor of all the Russias, concluded at St. Petersburg on the 6th (18th) of December, 1832, and the ratifications of which were exchanged in this city on the 11th of May, 1833.

ANDREW JACKSON.

WASHINGTON, *May 13, 1834.*

To the Senate and House of Representatives of the United States:

I communicate to Congress copies of a convention between the United States and His Majesty the King of the Kingdom of the Two Sicilies, to terminate the reclamations of the former for the depredations inflicted upon American commerce by Murat during the years 1809, 1810, 1811, and 1812, concluded at Naples on the 14th of October, 1832, and the ratifications of which were exchanged at the same place on the 8th of June, 1833.

ANDREW JACKSON.

WASHINGTON, *May 15, 1834.*

To the Senate and House of Representatives:

I transmit herewith to Congress copies of a treaty of peace, amity, commerce, and navigation between the United States and the Republic of Chilé, concluded at Santiago de Chilé on the 1st of September, 1833, and the ratifications of which were exchanged in this city on the 29th of April last.

ANDREW JACKSON.

WASHINGTON, *May 19, 1834.*

To the House of Representatives of the United States:

I transmit a letter from the Marquis de Rochambeau to the minister of the United States in France, together with a translation of the same, referring to the petition of certain descendants of the Count de Rocham-beau, which was communicated to the House of Representatives with my message of the 22d of February, 1833. Extracts from the dispatches of Mr. Livingston to the Secretary of State respecting the same subject are also sent.

I likewise transmit, for the consideration of the House, a petition from the heirs of the Baron de Kalb, accompanied by a note from General Lafayette, praying remuneration for the services rendered by the Baron to the United States during the War of the Revolution.

ANDREW JACKSON.

MAY 21, 1834.

To the Senate of the United States:

I nominate Arthur St. Clair to be register of the land office for the district of lands subject to sale at Indianapolis, in the State of Indiana, in the place of William B. Slaughter, appointed during the recess of the Senate.

As Arthur St. Clair was heretofore appointed to this office and was removed during the recess, it is proper to state the reasons which induce me again to nominate him to the Senate.

During the last summer an agent was appointed by the Treasury Department to examine the land offices in Indiana, and upon his report to the Department of the proceedings in the register's and receiver's offices at Indianapolis I deemed it proper to remove both of those officers without delay. A subsequent examination by a different agent enabled the parties to offer explanations of the charges against them in the first report, and although I am satisfied that the duty of the first agent was honestly and faithfully performed by him, yet the circumstances on which his report is founded have since been so explained as to acquit both of the officers who were removed of any intentional misconduct. In the case of Mr. St. Clair, however, it appears from both of the reports that he had permitted the clerk in his office to be the agent of speculations in land scrip contrary to the instructions received by him from the Treasury Department, but I am convinced that he himself did not participate in the speculation nor share in the profits, and that he gave the permission under a mistaken construction of the order and erroneous views of his duty as an officer. His mistake in this respect seems to have arisen in a great measure from his reliance on the judgment of others in whom he might well have supposed he could confide, and who appear to have sanctioned the course he adopted without sufficiently examining the subject and the evils to which such a practice would necessarily lead. Under these circumstances I have believed it to be an act of justice to Mr. St. Clair to present his name again to the Senate, as he can be reinstated in the office from which he was removed without injury to the person who in the recess was selected to succeed him. And I should have adopted the same course in relation to the receiver but for the peculiar circumstances in which his successor has been placed, and which would render it an act of injustice to him not to submit his name to the Senate for confirmation.

The reports and papers in relation to these removals are herewith transmitted to the Senate, in order that they may act in the case with the whole evidence before them.

ANDREW JACKSON.

WASHINGTON, *May 21, 1834.*

To the House of Representatives:

I lay before the House of Representatives a copy of a "convention for the settlement of claims between the United States of America and Her Catholic Majesty," concluded on the 17th of February last.

This convention has been ratified by me, agreeably to the Constitution, and will be immediately transmitted to Madrid, where it will doubtless be ratified by Her Majesty.

It is deemed proper to communicate the convention thus early, that provision may be made for carrying the first article into effect as soon as the ratifications shall have been exchanged, in order that our citizens may with as little delay as possible obtain the stipulated compensation.

ANDREW JACKSON.

WASHINGTON, *May 28, 1834.*

To the Senate of the United States:

I transmit herewith to the Senate, for their advice and consent as to the ratification of the same, a treaty and a supplement thereto, concluded between John H. Eaton, a commissioner on the part of the United States, and a delegation from the Chickasaw tribe of Indians, together with the journal of proceedings.

ANDREW JACKSON.

WASHINGTON, *May 30, 1834.*

To the Senate of the United States:

It having been represented to me by persons whose statements and opinions were thought worthy of confidence that the trade of the United States might be extended and rendered more lucrative by commercial arrangements with the countries bordering on the Indian Ocean, and being informed that the success of any efforts which might be made to accomplish that object would materially depend upon the secrecy with which they should be conducted, I appointed Mr. Edmund Roberts a special agent of this Government for the purpose of visiting those seas and concluding such commercial conventions as might have the effect of securing additional advantages to our trade in that quarter. This agency has resulted in the conclusion of treaties with the King of Siam and the Sultan of Muscat, whereby the commerce of the United States with the countries subject to the dominion of those princes, which had been previously embarrassed by serious disadvantages and obstructions, is placed upon a footing with that of the most favored nation. These treaties, the former of which was signed at the city of Siayuthia (commonly called Bankok) on the 20th day of March, 1833, and the latter at the city of Muscat on the 21st day of September of the same year, are submitted to the Senate for their consideration and advice.

I transmit a copy of the instructions which were given to the special agent and a communication made by him to the Secretary of State, containing particular and important information respecting the countries with which these treaties have been concluded. The expenses of the agency have been defrayed out of the contingent fund for foreign intercourse.

ANDREW JACKSON.

WASHINGTON, *June 13, 1834.*

To the Senate:

I have this day received a resolution of the 12th instant, requesting me to communicate to the Senate a copy of the first official communication which was made to Andrew Stevenson of the intention of the President to nominate him as a minister plenipotentiary and envoy extraordinary to the United Kingdom of Great Britain and Ireland, and his answer thereto.

As a compliance with this resolution might be deemed an admission of the right of the Senate to call upon the President for confidential correspondence of this description, I consider it proper on this occasion to remark that I do not acknowledge such a right. But to avoid misrepresentation I herewith transmit a copy of the paper in question, which was the only communication made to Mr. Stevenson on the subject.

This communication merely intimated the intention of the President in a particular contingency to offer to Mr. Stevenson the place of minister to the Court of St. James, and as the negotiations to which it refers were commenced early in April, 1833, in this city instead of London, and have been since conducted here, no further communication was made to him. I have no knowledge that an answer was received from Mr. Stevenson; none is to be found in the Department of State and none has been received by me.

ANDREW JACKSON.

WASHINGTON, *June 18, 1834.*

To the Senate and House of Representatives of the United States:

I transmit to Congress an extract of a dispatch from Mr. Livingston, the minister of the United States at Paris, dated the 7th ultimo, and the copy of a communication made to him by Captain Ballard, commander of the frigate *United States*, by which it appears that in firing a national salute from that ship at Toulon, in honor of the birthday of the King of the French, two men were killed and four others wounded on board the French ship of war *Suffren*. Suitable explanations were immediately made to the French admiral; and the officers and crew of the American frigate, with that generosity which distinguishes their profession, promptly contributed, by a liberal subscription, toward providing for the families of the unfortunate sufferers. I am sure, however, that I should not do justice to the feelings of the American people on this occasion if I did not invite Congress to assume, on their part, this melancholy duty. I propose, therefore, that the same provision be made by law for these French seamen and their families as would be made for American seamen killed or wounded in battle. This proceeding will show the deep sensibility with which the disastrous accident is viewed by the United States, and their readiness to alleviate those consequences which can not be remedied.

ANDREW JACKSON.

WASHINGTON, *June 20, 1834.*

To the House of Representatives of the United States:

I transmit to the House of Representatives, for their consideration, a memorial from the granddaughters of the Count de Rochambeau, together with their letter to the minister of the United States in France, from whom these papers have been recently received.

Translations of these documents accompany them.

ANDREW JACKSON.

WASHINGTON, *June 21, 1834.*

To the Senate and House of Representatives of the United States:

The afflicting intelligence of the death of the illustrious Lafayette has been received by me this morning.

I have issued the general order inclosed* to cause appropriate honors to be paid by the Army and Navy to the memory of one so highly venerated and beloved by my countrymen, and whom Providence has been pleased to remove so unexpectedly from the agitating scenes of life.

ANDREW JACKSON.

JUNE 23, 1834.

To the Senate of the United States:

I transmit for the consideration and action of the Senate a treaty concluded with the Cherokees for the cession of their lands east of the Mississippi River.

It is known to the Senate that for some years great difficulties have been experienced in the relations of that tribe. Without further allusion to these than as they furnish strong inducements to a final settlement of all the questions involved in our intercourse with these Indians, it is obvious from the existing state of things that they can not continue in their present position with any hope of ultimate prosperity. I have been, therefore, desirous that a just and satisfactory arrangement should be made for their removal, and propositions to that effect upon a liberal scale have been repeatedly made to them. These have until now been rejected, and their rejection, I have been induced to believe, has been owing more to the ascendency acquired by individuals who are unwilling to go than to the deliberative opinion of a majority of the Cherokee people. Some years since a form of government was established among them, but since the extension of the laws of Georgia and Alabama over them this government can have no binding effect upon a great majority of them. Its obligation is also denied by many of them in consequence of the continuance of certain persons in power contrary to the principles of their fundamental articles of association. A delegation from the persons claiming to hold their authority under the former existing state of things is in this city, and have communicated with the War Department on the subject of their situation and removal. They deny the right of the persons who have negotiated this treaty to perform such an act, and have remonstrated against it. Copies of their communications are herewith transmitted.

The delegation who have signed the present treaty have produced an authority from William Hicks, designating himself as principal chief, and others, signing the same in an official capacity. It is understood from the report of Major Currie, the enrolling agent, that public notice was given to all persons desirous of emigrating to attend upon a particular day and place in order to appoint representatives to communicate with the Government and to arrange the terms of cession and removal. In conformity with this notice a meeting was held and the authority herein referred to was the result.

*See under Executive Orders, pp. 94-95.

In consequence of this application John H. Eaton was appointed to meet and confer with them and to report their views to the War Department. These are embodied in the treaty which is presented to your consideration.

Under these circumstances I submit the matter to the decision of the Senate. The practice of the Government has not been very strict on the subject of the authority of the persons negotiating treaties on the part of the Indians. Sometimes it has been done by persons representing the tribe and sometimes by the individuals composing it. I am not aware that a case similar in its features to the present has ever before required the action of the Government. But, independently of the considerations which so forcibly urge a settlement of this matter, no injustice can be done to the Indians by the ratification of this treaty. It is expressly provided that it will not be binding upon them till a majority has assented to its stipulations. When that assent is given no one can justly deny its obligation.

The Cherokees east of the Mississippi occupy a portion of the territories of four States, to wit, Georgia, North Carolina, Tennessee, and Alabama. The treaty provides that the communities inhabiting those divisions shall each be considered as acting for themselves independently of the others. We have frequently in our intercourse with the Indians treated with different portions of the same tribe as separate communities. Nor is there any injustice in this as long as they are separated into divisions without any very strong bond of union, and frequently with different interests and views. By requiring the assent of a majority to any act which will bind them we insure the preservation of a principle which wil' afford adequate security to their rights.

ANDREW JACKSON.

VETO MESSAGE.*

DECEMBER 4, 1833.

To the Senate of the United States:

At the close of the last session of Congress I received from that body a bill entitled "An act to appropriate for a limited time the proceeds of the sales of the public lands of the United States and for granting lands to certain States." The brief period then remaining before the rising of Congress and the extreme pressure of official duties unavoidable on such occasions did not leave me sufficient time for that full consideration of the subject which was due to its great importance. Subsequent consideration and reflection have, however, confirmed the objections to the bill which presented themselves to my mind upon its first perusal, and

* Pocket veto.

have satisfied me that it ought not to become a law. I felt myself, therefore, constrained to withhold from it my approval, and now return it to the Senate, in which it originated, with the reasons on which my dissent is founded.

I am fully sensible of the importance, as it respects both the harmony and union of the States, of making, as soon as circumstances will allow of it, a proper and final disposition of the whole subject of the public lands, and any measure for that object providing for the reimbursement to the United States of those expenses with which they are justly chargeable that may be consistent with my views of the Constitution, sound policy, and the rights of the respective States will readily receive my cooperation. This bill, however, is not of that character. The arrangement it contemplates is not permanent, but limited to five years only, and in its terms appears to anticipate alterations within that time, at the discretion of Congress; and it furnishes no adequate security against those continued agitations of the subject which it should be the principal object of any measure for the disposition of the public lands to avert.

Neither the merits of the bill under consideration nor the validity of the objections which I have felt it to be my duty to make to its passage can be correctly appreciated without a full understanding of the manner in which the public lands upon which it is intended to operate were acquired and the conditions upon which they are now held by the United States. I will therefore precede the statement of those objections by a brief but distinct exposition of these points.

The waste lands within the United States constituted one of the early obstacles to the organization of any government for the protection of their common interests. In October, 1777, while Congress were framing the Articles of Confederation, a proposition was made to amend them to the following effect, viz:

That the United States in Congress assembled shall have the sole and exclusive right and power to ascertain and fix the western boundary of such States as claim to the Mississippi or South Sea, and lay out the land beyond the boundary so ascertained into separate and independent States from time to time as the numbers and circumstances of the people thereof may require.

It was, however, rejected, Maryland only voting for it, and so difficult did the subject appear that the patriots of that body agreed to waive it in the Articles of Confederation and leave it for future settlement.

On the submission of the Articles to the several State legislatures for ratification the most formidable objection was found to be in this subject of the waste lands. Maryland, Rhode Island, and New Jersey instructed their delegates in Congress to move amendments to them providing that the waste or Crown lands should be considered the common property of the United States, but they were rejected. All the States except Maryland acceded to the Articles, notwithstanding some of them did so with the reservation that their claim to those lands as common property was not thereby abandoned.

On the sole ground that no declaration to that effect was contained in the Articles, Maryland withheld her assent, and in May, 1779, embodied her objections in the form of instructions to her delegates, which were entered upon the Journals of Congress. The following extracts are from that document, viz:

Is it possible that those States who are ambitiously grasping at territories to which in our judgment they have not the least shadow of exclusive right will use with greater moderation the increase of wealth and power derived from those territories when acquired than what they have displayed in their endeavors to acquire them? * * *

We are convinced policy and justice require that a country unsettled at the commencement of this war, claimed by the British Crown and ceded to it by the treaty of Paris, if wrested from the common enemy by the blood and treasure of the thirteen States, should be considered as a common property, subject to be parceled out by Congress into free, convenient, and independent governments, in such manner and at such times as the wisdom of that assembly shall hereafter direct. * * *

Virginia proceeded to open a land office for the sale of her Western lands, which produced such excitement as to induce Congress, in October, 1779, to interpose and earnestly recommend to "the said State and all States similarly circumstanced to forbear settling or issuing warrants for such unappropriated lands, or granting the same, during the continuance of the present war."

In March, 1780, the legislature of New York passed an act tendering a cession to the United States of the claims of that State to the Western territory, preceded by a preamble to the following effect, viz:

Whereas nothing under Divine Providence can more effectually contribute to the tranquillity and safety of the United States of America than a federal alliance on such liberal principles as will give satisfaction to its respective members; and whereas the Articles of Confederation and Perpetual Union recommended by the honorable Congress of the United States of America have not proved acceptable to all the States, it having been conceived that a portion of the waste and uncultivated territory within the limits or claims of certain States ought to be appropriated as a common fund for the expenses of the war, and the people of the State of New York being on all occasions disposed to manifest their regard for their sister States and their earnest desire to promote the general interest and security, and more especially to accelerate the federal alliance, by removing as far as it depends upon them the before-mentioned impediment to its final accomplishment. * * *

This act of New York, the instructions of Maryland, and a remonstrance of Virginia were referred to a committee of Congress, who reported a preamble and resolutions thereon, which were adopted on the 6th September, 1780; so much of which as is necessary to elucidate the subject is to the following effect, viz:

That it appears advisable to press upon those States which can remove the embarrassments respecting the Western country a liberal surrender of a portion of their territorial claims, since they can not be preserved entire without endangering the stability of the General Confederacy; to remind them how indispensably necessary it is to establish the Federal Union on a fixed and permanent basis and on principles acceptable to all its respective members; how essential to public credit and confidence, to the support of our Army, to the vigor of our counsels and success of our measures, to our tranquillity at home, our reputation abroad, to our very existence as a free, sovereign, and independent people; that they are fully persuaded the wisdom of the several legislatures will lead them to a full and impartial consideration of a subject so interesting to the United States, and so necessary to the happy establishment of the Federal Union; that they are confirmed in these expectations by a review of the before-mentioned act of the legislature of New York, submitted to their consideration. * * *

Resolved, That copies of the several papers referred to the committee be transmitted, with a copy of the report, to the legislatures of the several States, and that it be earnestly recommended to those States who have claims to the Western country to pass such laws and give their delegates in Congress such powers as may effectually remove the only obstacle to a final ratification of the Articles of Confederation, and that the legislature of Maryland be earnestly requested to authorize their delegates in Congress to subscribe the said Articles.

Following up this policy, Congress proceeded, on the 10th October, 1780, to pass a resolution pledging the United States to the several States as to the manner in which any lands that might be ceded by them should be disposed of, the material parts of which are as follows, viz:

Resolved, That the unappropriated lands which may be ceded or relinquished to the United States by any particular State pursuant to the recommendation of Congress of the 6th day of September last shall be disposed of for the common benefit of the United States and be settled and formed into distinct republican States, which shall become members of the Federal Union and have the same rights of sovereignty, freedom, and independence as the other States; * * * that the said lands shall be granted or settled at such times and under such regulations as shall hereafter be agreed on by the United States in Congress assembled, or nine or more of them.

In February, 1781, the legislature of Maryland passed an act authorizing their delegates in Congress to sign the Articles of Confederation. The following are extracts from the preamble and body of the act, viz:

Whereas it hath been said that the common enemy is encouraged by this State not acceding to the Confederation to hope that the union of the sister States may be dissolved, and therefore prosecutes the war in expectation of an event so disgraceful to America, and our friends and illustrious ally are impressed with an idea that the common cause would be promoted by our formally acceding to the Confederation. * * *

The act of which this is the preamble authorizes the delegates of that State to sign the Articles, and proceeds to declare ''that by acceding to the said Confederation this State doth not relinquish, nor intend to relinquish, any right or interest she hath with the other united or confederated States to the back country,'' etc.

On the 1st of March, 1781, the delegates of Maryland signed the Articles of Confederation, and the Federal Union under that compact was complete. The conflicting claims to the Western lands, however, were not disposed of, and continued to give great trouble to Congress. Repeated and urgent calls were made by Congress upon the States claiming them to make liberal cessions to the United States, and it was not until long after the present Constitution was formed that the grants were completed.

The deed of cession from New York was executed on the 1st of March, 1781, the day the Articles of Confederation were ratified, and it was accepted by Congress on the 29th October, 1782. One of the conditions of this cession thus tendered and accepted was that the lands ceded to the United States "*shall be and inure for the use and benefit of such of the United States as shall become members of the federal alliance of the said States, and for no other use or purpose whatsoever.*"

The Virginia deed of cession was executed and accepted on the 1st day of March, 1784. One of the conditions of this cession is as follows, viz:

That all the lands within the territory as ceded to the United States, and not reserved for or appropriated to any of the before-mentioned purposes or disposed of in bounties to the officers and soldiers of the American Army, *shall be considered as a common fund for the use and benefit of such of the United States as have become or shall become members of the confederation or federal alliance of the said States, Virginia inclusive, according to their usual respective proportions in the general charge and expenditure, and shall be faithfully and bona fide disposed of for that purpose, and for no other use or purpose whatsoever.*

Within the years 1785, 1786, and 1787 Massachusetts, Connecticut, and South Carolina ceded their claims upon similar conditions. The Federal Government went into operation under the existing Constitution on the 4th of March, 1789. The following is the only provision of that Constitution which has a direct bearing on the subject of the public lands, viz:

The Congress shall have power to dispose of and make all needful rules and regulations respecting the territory or other property belonging to the United States, and nothing in this Constitution shall be so construed as to prejudice any claims of the United States or of any particular State.

Thus the Constitution left all the compacts before made in full force, and the rights of all parties remained the same under the new Government as they were under the Confederation.

The deed of cession of North Carolina was executed in December, 1789, and accepted by an act of Congress approved April 2, 1790. The third condition of this cession was in the following words, viz:

That all the lands intended to be ceded by virtue of this act to the United States of America, and not appropriated as before mentioned, *shall be considered as a common fund for the use and benefit of the United States of America, North Carolina inclusive, according to their respective and usual proportions of the general charge and expenditure, and shall be faithfully disposed of for that purpose, and for no other use or purpose whatever.*

The cession of Georgia was completed on the 16th June, 1802, and in its leading condition is precisely like that of Virginia and North Carolina. This grant completed the title of the United States to all those lands generally called *public lands* lying within the original limits of the Confederacy. Those which have been acquired by the purchase of Louisiana and Florida, having been paid for out of the common treasure of the United States, are as much the property of the General Government, to be disposed of for the common benefit, as those ceded by the several States.

By the facts here collected from the early history of our Republic it appears that the subject of the public lands entered into the elements of its institutions. It was only upon the condition that those lands should be considered as common property, to be disposed of for the benefit of the United States, that some of the States agreed to come into a "perpetual union." The States claiming those lands acceded to those views and transferred their claims to the United States upon certain specific conditions, and on those conditions the grants were accepted. These solemn compacts, invited by Congress in a resolution declaring the purposes to which the proceeds of these lands should be applied, originating before the Constitution and forming the basis on which it was made, bound the United States to a particular course of policy in relation to them by ties as strong as can be invented to secure the faith of nations.

As early as May, 1785, Congress, in execution of these compacts, passed an ordinance providing for the sales of lands in the Western territory and directing the proceeds to be paid into the Treasury of the United States. With the same object other ordinances were adopted prior to the organization of the present Government.

In further execution of these compacts the Congress of the United States under the present Constitution, as early as the 4th of August, 1790, in "An act making provision for the debt of the United States," enacted as follows, viz:

That the proceeds of sales which shall be made of lands in the Western territory now belonging or that may hereafter belong to the United States shall be and are hereby appropriated toward sinking or discharging the debts for the payment whereof the United States now are or by virtue of this act may be holden, and shall be applied solely to that use until the said debt shall be fully satisfied.

To secure to the Government of the United States forever the power to execute these compacts in good faith the Congress of the Confederation, as early as July 13, 1787, in an ordinance for the government of the territory of the United States northwest of the river Ohio, prescribed to the people inhabiting the Western territory certain conditions which were declared to be "articles of compact between the original States and the people and States in the said territory," which should "forever remain unalterable, unless by common consent." In one of these articles it is declared that—

The legislatures of those districts, or new States, shall never interfere with the primary disposal of the soil by the United States in Congress assembled, nor with any regulations Congress may find necessary for securing the title in such soil to the *bona fide purchasers.*

This condition has been exacted from the people of all the new territories, and to put its obligation beyond dispute each new State carved out of the public domain has been required explicitly to recognize it as one of the conditions of admission into the Union. Some of them have declared through their conventions in separate acts that their people "forever disclaim all right and title to the waste and unappropriated lands lying within this State, and that the same shall be and remain at the sole and entire disposition of the United States."

With such care have the United States reserved to themselves, in all their acts down to this day, in legislating for the Territories and admitting States into the Union, the unshackled power to execute in good faith the compacts of cession made with the original States. From these facts and proceedings it plainly and certainly results—

1. That one of the fundamental principles on which the Confederation of the United States was originally based was that the waste lands of the West within their limits should be the common property of the United States.

2. That those lands were ceded to the United States by the States which claimed them, and the cessions were accepted on the express condition that they should be disposed of for the common benefit of the States, according to their respective proportions in the general charge and expenditure, and for no other purpose whatsoever.

3. That in execution of these solemn compacts the Congress of the United States did, under the Confederation, proceed to sell these lands and put the avails into the common Treasury, and under the new Constitution did repeatedly pledge them for the payment of the public debt of the United States, by which pledge each State was expected to profit in proportion to the general charge to be made upon it for that object.

These are the first principles of this whole subject, which I think can not be contested by anyone who examines the proceedings of the Revolutionary Congress, the cessions of the several States, and the acts of Congress under the new Constitution. Keeping them deeply impressed upon the mind, let us proceed to examine how far the objects of the cessions have been completed, and see whether those compacts are not still obligatory upon the United States.

The debt for which these lands were pledged by Congress may be considered as paid, and they are consequently released from that lien. But that pledge formed no part of the compacts with the States, or of the conditions upon which the cessions were made. It was a contract between new parties—between the United States and their creditors. Upon payment of the debt the compacts remain in full force, and the obligation of the United States to dispose of the lands for the common benefit is neither destroyed nor impaired. As they can not now be executed in that mode, the only legitimate question which can arise is, In what other way are these lands to be hereafter disposed of for the common benefit of the several States, *"according to their respective and usual proportion in the general charge and expenditure"?* The cessions of Virginia, North Carolina, and Georgia in express terms, and all the rest impliedly, not only provide thus specifically the proportion according to which each State shall profit by the proceeds of the land sales, but they proceed to declare that they shall be *"faithfully and bona fide disposed of for that purpose, and for no other use or purpose whatsoever."* This is the fundamental law of the land at this moment, growing out of compacts which are older than the Constitution, and formed the corner stone on which the Union itself was erected.

In the practice of the Government the proceeds of the public lands have not been set apart *as a separate fund* for the payment of the public debt, but have been and are now paid into the Treasury, where they constitute a part of the aggregate of revenue upon which the Government draws as well for its current expenditures as for payment of the public debt. In this manner they have heretofore and do now lessen the general charge upon the people of the several States in the exact proportions stipulated in the compacts.

These general charges have been composed not only of the public debt and the usual expenditures attending the civil and military administrations of the Government, but of the amounts paid to the States with which these compacts were formed, the amounts paid the Indians for their right of possession, the amounts paid for the purchase of Louisiana and Florida, and the amounts paid surveyors, registers, receivers, clerks, etc., employed in preparing for market and selling the Western domain.

From the origin of the land system down to the 30th September, 1832, the amount expended for all these purposes has been about $49,701,280, and the amount received from the sales, deducting payments on account of roads, etc., about $38,386,624. The revenue arising from the public lands, therefore, has not been sufficient to meet the general charges on the Treasury which have grown out of them by about $11,314,656. Yet in having been applied to lessen those charges the conditions of the compacts have been thus far fulfilled, and each State has profited according to its usual proportion in the general charge and expenditure. The annual proceeds of land sales have increased and the charges have diminished, so that at a reduced price those lands would now defray all current charges growing out of them and save the Treasury from further advances on their account. Their original intent and object, therefore, would be accomplished as fully as it has hitherto been by reducing the price and hereafter, as heretofore, bringing the proceeds into the Treasury. Indeed, as this is the only mode in which the objects of the original compact can be attained, it may be considered for all practical purposes that it is one of their requirements.

The bill before me begins with an entire subversion of every one of the compacts by which the United States became possessed of their

Western domain, and treats the subject as if they never had existence and as if the United States were the original and unconditional owners of all the public lands. The first section directs—

That from and after the 31st day of December, 1832, there shall be allowed and paid to each of the States of Ohio, Indiana, Illinois, Alabama, Missouri, Mississippi, and Louisiana, over and above what each of the said States is entitled to by the terms of the compacts entered into between them respectively upon their admission into the Union and the United States, the sum of 12½ per cent upon the net amount of the sales of the public lands which subsequent to the day aforesaid shall be made within the several limits of the said States, which said sum of 12½ per cent shall be applied to some object or objects of internal improvement or education within the said States under the direction of their several legislatures.

This 12½ per cent is to be taken out of the net proceeds of the land sales before any apportionment is made, and the same seven States which are first to receive this proportion are also to receive their due proportion of the residue according to the ratio of general distribution.

Now, waiving all considerations of equity or policy in regard to this provision, what more need be said to demonstrate its objectionable character than that it is in direct and undisguised violation of the pledge given by Congress to the States before a single cession was made, that it abrogates the condition upon which some of the States came into the Union, and that it sets at naught the terms of cession spread upon the face of every grant under which the title to that portion of the public land is held by the Federal Government?

In the apportionment of the remaining seven-eighths of the proceeds this bill, in a manner equally undisguised, violates the conditions upon which the United States acquired title to the ceded lands. Abandoning altogether the ratio of distribution according to the general charge and expenditure provided by the compacts, it adopts that of the Federal representative population. Virginia and other States which ceded their lands upon the express condition that they should receive a benefit from their sales in proportion to their part of the general charge are by the bill allowed only a portion of seven-eighths of their proceeds, and that not in the proportion of general charge and expenditure, but in the ratio of their Federal representative population.

The Constitution of the United States did not delegate to Congress the power to abrogate these compacts. On the contrary, by declaring that nothing in it "*shall be so construed as to prejudice any claims of the United States or of any particular State*," it virtually provides that these compacts and the rights they secure shall remain untouched by the legislative power, which shall only make all "*needful rules and regulations*" for carrying them into effect. All beyond this would seem to be an assumption of undelegated power.

These ancient compacts are invaluable monuments of an age of virtue, patriotism, and disinterestedness. They exhibit the price that great

States which had won liberty were willing to pay for that union without which they plainly saw it could not be preserved. It was not for territory or state power that our Revolutionary fathers took up arms; it was for individual liberty and the right of self-government. The expulsion from the continent of British armies and British power was to them a barren conquest if through the collisions of the redeemed States the individual rights for which they fought should become the prey of petty military tyrannies established at home. To avert such consequences and throw around liberty the shield of union, States whose relative strength at the time gave them a preponderating power magnanimously sacrificed domains which would have made them the rivals of empires, only stipulating that they should be disposed of for the common benefit of themselves and the other confederated States. This enlightened policy produced union and has secured liberty. It has made our waste lands to swarm with a busy people and added many powerful States to our Confederation. As well for the fruits which these noble works of our ancestors have produced as for the devotedness in which they originated, we should hesitate before we demolish them.

But there are other principles asserted in the bill which would have impelled me to withhold my signature had I not seen in it a violation of the compacts by which the United States acquired title to a large portion of the public lands. It reasserts the principle contained in the bill authorizing a subscription to the stock of the Maysville, Washington, Paris and Lexington Turnpike Road Company, from which I was compelled to withhold my consent for reasons contained in my message of the 27th May, 1830, to the House of Representatives.

The leading principle then asserted was that Congress possesses no constitutional power to appropriate any part of the moneys of the United States for objects of a local character within the States. That principle I can not be mistaken in supposing has received the unequivocal sanction of the American people, and all subsequent reflection has but satisfied me more thoroughly that the interests of our people and the purity of our Government, if not its existence, depend on its observance. The public lands are the common property of the United States, and the moneys arising from their sales are a part of the public revenue. This bill proposes to raise from and appropriate a portion of this public revenue to certain States, providing expressly that it shall "*be applied to objects of internal improvement or education within those States,*" and then proceeds to appropriate the balance to all the States, with the declaration that it shall be applied "*to such purposes as the legislatures of the said respective States shall deem proper.*" The former appropriation is expressly for internal improvements or education, without qualification as to the kind of improvements, and therefore in express violation of the principle maintained in my objections to the turnpike-road bill above referred to. The latter appropriation is more broad, and gives the money to be applied to any local purpose whatsoever. It will not be denied that under the provisions of the bill a portion of the money might have been applied to making the very road to which the bill of 1830 had reference, and must of course come within the scope of the same principle. If the money of the United States can not be applied to local purposes *through its own agents,* as little can it be permitted to be thus expended *through the agency of the State governments.*

It has been supposed that with all the reductions in our revenue which could be speedily effected by Congress without injury to the substantial interests of the country there might be for some years to come a surplus of moneys in the Treasury, and that there was in principle no objection to returning them to the people by whom they were paid. As the literal accomplishment of such an object is obviously impracticable, it was thought admissible, as the nearest approximation to it, to hand them over to the State governments, the more immediate representatives of the people, to be by them applied to the benefit of those to whom they properly belonged. The principle and the object were to return to the people an unavoidable surplus of revenue which might have been paid by them under a system which could not at once be abandoned, but even this resource, which at one time seemed to be almost the only alternative to save the General Government from grasping unlimited power over internal improvements, was suggested with doubts of its constitutionality.

But this bill assumes a new principle. Its object is not to return to the people an unavoidable surplus of revenue paid in by them, but to create a surplus for distribution among the States. It seizes the entire proceeds of one source of revenue and sets them apart as a surplus, making it necessary to raise the moneys for supporting the Government and meeting the general charges from other sources. It even throws the entire land system upon the customs for its support, and makes the public lands a perpetual charge upon the Treasury. It does not return to the people moneys accidentally or unavoidably paid by them to the Government, by which they are not wanted, but compels the people to pay moneys into the Treasury for the mere purpose of creating a surplus for distribution to their State governments. If this principle be once admitted, it is not difficult to perceive to what consequences it may lead. Already this bill, by throwing the land system on the revenues from imports for support, virtually distributes among the States a part of those revenues. The proportion may be increased from time to time, without any departure from the principle now asserted, until the State governments shall derive all the funds necessary for their support from the Treasury of the United States, or, if a sufficient supply should be obtained by some States and not by others, the deficient States might complain; and to put an end to all further difficulty Congress, without assuming any new principle, need go but one step further and put the

salaries of all the State governors, judges, and other officers, with a sufficient sum for other expenses, in their general appropriation bill.

It appears to me that a more direct road to consolidation can not be
devised. Money is power, and in that Government which pays all the
public officers of the States will all political power be substantially concentrated. The State governments, if governments they might be called,
would lose all their independence and dignity; the economy which now
distinguishes them would be converted into a profusion, limited only by
the extent of the supply. Being the dependents of the General Government, and looking to its Treasury as the source of all their emoluments,
the State officers, under whatever names they might pass and by whatever forms their duties might be prescribed, would in effect be the mere
stipendiaries and instruments of the central power.

I am quite sure that the intelligent people of our several States will
be satisfied on a little reflection that it is neither wise nor safe to release
the members of their local legislatures from the responsibility of levying the taxes necessary to support their State governments and vest it
in Congress, over most of whose members they have no control. They
will not think it expedient that Congress shall be the taxgatherer and
paymaster of all their State governments, thus amalgamating all their
officers into one mass of common interest and common feeling. It is too
obvious that such a course would subvert our well-balanced system of
government, and ultimately deprive us of all the blessings now derived
from our happy Union.

However willing I might be that any unavoidable surplus in the
Treasury should be returned to the people through their State governments, I can not assent to the principle that a surplus may be created
for the purpose of distribution. Viewing this bill as in effect assuming
the right not only to create a surplus for that purpose, but to divide the
contents of the Treasury among the States without limitation, from whatever source they may be derived, and asserting the power to raise and
appropriate money for the support of every State government and institution, as well as for making every local improvement, however trivial,
I can not give it my assent.

It is difficult to perceive what advantages would accrue to the old States
or the new from the system of distribution which this bill proposes if
it were otherwise unobjectionable. It requires no argument to prove
that if $3,000,000 a year, or any other sum, shall be taken out of the
Treasury by this bill for distribution it must be replaced by the same
sum collected from the people through some other means. The old
States will receive annually a sum of money from the Treasury, but they
will pay in a larger sum, together with the expenses of collection and
distribution. It is only their proportion of *seven-eighths* of the proceeds
of land sales which they are *to receive*, but they must *pay* their due proportion of the *whole*. Disguise it as we may, the bill proposes to them a

dead loss in the ratio of *eight* to *seven*, in addition to expenses and other incidental losses. This assertion is not the less true because it may not at first be palpable. Their receipts will be in large sums, but their payments in small ones. The *governments* of the States will receive *seven* dollars, for which the *people* of the States will pay *eight*. The large sums received will be palpable to the senses; the small sums paid it requires thought to identify. But a little consideration will satisfy the people that the effect is the same as if *seven hundred dollars* were given them from the public Treasury, for which they were at the same time required to pay in taxes, direct or indirect, *eight hundred*.

I deceive myself greatly if the new States would find their interests promoted by such a system as this bill proposes. Their true policy consists in the rapid settling and improvement of the waste lands within their limits. As a means of hastening those events, they have long been looking to a reduction in the price of public lands upon the final payment of the national debt. The effect of the proposed system would be to prevent that reduction. It is true the bill reserves to Congress the power to reduce the price, but the effect of its details as now arranged would probably be forever to prevent its exercise.

With the just men who inhabit the new States it is a sufficient reason to reject this system that it is in violation of the fundamental laws of the Republic and its Constitution. But if it were a mere question of interest or expediency they would still reject it. They would not sell their bright prospect of increasing wealth and growing power at such a price. They would not place a sum of money to be paid into their treasuries in competition with the settlement of their waste lands and the increase of their population. They would not consider a small or a large annual sum to be paid to their governments and immediately expended as an equivalent for that enduring wealth which is composed of flocks and herds and cultivated farms. No temptation will allure them from that object of abiding interest, the settlement of their waste lands, and the increase of a hardy race of free citizens, their glory in peace and their defense in war.

On the whole, I adhere to the opinion, expressed by me in my annual message of 1832, that it is our true policy that the public lands shall cease as soon as practicable to be a source of revenue, except for the payment of those general charges which grow out of the acquisition of the lands, their survey and sale. Although these expenses have not been met by the proceeds of sales heretofore, it is quite certain they will be hereafter, even after a considerable reduction in the price. By meeting in the Treasury so much of the general charge as arises from that source they will hereafter, as they have been heretofore, be disposed of for the common benefit of the United States, according to the compacts of cession. I do not doubt that it is the real interest of each and all the States in the Union, and particularly of the new States, that the price of these lands shall be reduced and graduated, and that after they have been offered for a certain number of years the refuse remaining unsold shall be abandoned to the States and the machinery of our land system entirely withdrawn. It can not be supposed the compacts intended that the United States should retain forever a title to lands within the States which are of no value, and no doubt is entertained that the general interest would be best promoted by surrendering such lands to the States.

This plan for disposing of the public lands impairs no principle, violates no compact, and deranges no system. Already has the price of those lands been reduced from $2 per acre to $1.25, and upon the will of Congress it depends whether there shall be a further reduction. While the burdens of the East are diminishing by the reduction of the duties upon imports, it seems but equal justice that the chief burden of the West should be lightened in an equal degree at least. It would be just to the old States and the new, conciliate every interest, disarm the subject of all its dangers, and add another guaranty to the perpetuity of our happy Union.

Sensible, however, of the difficulties which surround this important subject, I can only add to my regrets at finding myself again compelled to disagree with the legislative power the sincere declaration that any plan which shall promise a final and satisfactory disposition of the question and be compatible with the Constitution and public faith shall have my hearty concurrence.   ANDREW JACKSON.

[NOTE.—For reasons for the pocket veto of "An act to improve the navigation of the Wabash River," see Sixth Annual Message, dated December 1, 1834, pp. 118–123.]

PROTEST.*

APRIL 15, 1834.

To the Senate of the United States:

It appears by the published Journal of the Senate that on the 26th of December last a resolution was offered by a member of the Senate, which after a protracted debate was on the 28th day of March last modified by the mover and passed by the votes of twenty-six Senators out of forty-six who were present and voted, in the following words, viz:

Resolved, That the President, in the late Executive proceedings in relation to the public revenue, has assumed upon himself authority and power not conferred by the Constitution and laws, but in derogation of both.

Having had the honor, through the voluntary suffrages of the American people, to fill the office of President of the United States during the

*The Senate ordered that it be not entered on the Journal.

period which may be presumed to have been referred to in this resolution, it is sufficiently evident that the censure it inflicts was intended for myself. Without notice, unheard and untried, I thus find myself charged on the records of the Senate, and in a form hitherto unknown in our history, with the high crime of violating the laws and Constitution of my country.

It can seldom be necessary for any department of the Government, when assailed in conversation or debate or by the strictures of the press or of popular assemblies, to step out of its ordinary path for the purpose of vindicating its conduct or of pointing out any irregularity or injustice in the manner of the attack; but when the Chief Executive Magistrate is, by one of the most important branches of the Government in its official capacity, in a public manner, and by its recorded sentence, but without precedent, competent authority, or just cause, declared guilty of a breach of the laws and Constitution, it is due to his station, to public opinion, and to a proper self-respect that the officer thus denounced should promptly expose the wrong which has been done.

In the present case, moreover, there is even a stronger necessity for such a vindication. By an express provision of the Constitution, before the President of the United States can enter on the execution of his office he is required to take an oath or affirmation in the following words:

I do solemnly swear (or affirm) that I will faithfully execute the office of President of the United States and will to the best of my ability preserve, protect, and defend the Constitution of the United States.

The duty of defending so far as in him lies the integrity of the Constitution would indeed have resulted from the very nature of his office, but by thus expressing it in the official oath or affirmation, which in this respect differs from that of any other functionary, the founders of our Republic have attested their sense of its importance and have given to it a peculiar solemnity and force. Bound to the performance of this duty by the oath I have taken, by the strongest obligations of gratitude to the American people, and by the ties which unite my every earthly interest with the welfare and glory of my country, and perfectly convinced that the discussion and passage of the above-mentioned resolution were not only unauthorized by the Constitution, but in many respects repugnant to its provisions and subversive of the rights secured by it to other coordinate departments, I deem it an imperative duty to maintain the supremacy of that sacred instrument and the immunities of the department intrusted to my care by all means consistent with my own lawful powers, with the rights of others, and with the genius of our civil institutions. To this end I have caused this my *solemn protest* against the aforesaid proceedings to be placed on the files of the executive department and to be transmitted to the Senate.

It is alike due to the subject, the Senate, and the people that the views which I have taken of the proceedings referred to, and which compel me to regard them in the light that has been mentioned, should be exhibited at length, and with the freedom and firmness which are required by an occasion so unprecedented and peculiar.

Under the Constitution of the United States the powers and functions of the various departments of the Federal Government and their responsibilities for violation or neglect of duty are clearly defined or result by necessary inference. The legislative power is, subject to the qualified negative of the President, vested in the Congress of the United States, composed of the Senate and House of Representatives; the executive power is vested exclusively in the President, except that in the conclusion of treaties and in certain appointments to office he is to act with the advice and consent of the Senate; the judicial power is vested exclusively in the Supreme and other courts of the United States, except in cases of impeachment, for which purpose the accusatory power is vested in the House of Representatives and that of hearing and determining in the Senate. But although for the special purposes which have been mentioned there is an occasional intermixture of the powers of the different departments, yet with these exceptions each of the three great departments is independent of the others in its sphere of action, and when it deviates from that sphere is not responsible to the others further than it is expressly made so in the Constitution. In every other respect each of them is the coequal of the other two, and all are the servants of the American people, without power or right to control or censure each other in the service of their common superior, save only in the manner and to the degree which that superior has prescribed.

The responsibilities of the President are numerous and weighty. He is liable to impeachment for high crimes and misdemeanors, and on due conviction to removal from office and perpetual disqualification; and notwithstanding such conviction, he may also be indicted and punished according to law. He is also liable to the private action of any party who may have been injured by his illegal mandates or instructions in the same manner and to the same extent as the humblest functionary. In addition to the responsibilities which may thus be enforced by impeachment, criminal prosecution, or suit at law, he is also accountable at the bar of public opinion for every act of his Administration. Subject only to the restraints of truth and justice, the free people of the United States have the undoubted right, as individuals or collectively, orally or in writing, at such times and in such language and form as they may think proper, to discuss his official conduct and to express and promulgate their opinions concerning it. Indirectly also his conduct may come under review in either branch of the Legislature, or in the Senate when acting in its executive capacity, and so far as the executive or legislative proceedings of these bodies may require it, it may be exercised by them. These are believed to be the proper and only modes in which the

President of the United States is to be held accountable for his official conduct.

Tested by these principles, the resolution of the Senate is wholly unauthorized by the Constitution, and in derogation of its entire spirit. It assumes that a single branch of the legislative department may for the purposes of a public censure, and without any view to legislation or impeachment, take up, consider, and decide upon the official acts of the Executive. But in no part of the Constitution is the President subjected to any such responsibility, and in no part of that instrument is any such power conferred on either branch of the Legislature.

The justice of these conclusions will be illustrated and confirmed by a brief analysis of the powers of the Senate and a comparison of their recent proceedings with those powers.

The high functions assigned by the Constitution to the Senate are in their nature either legislative, executive, or judicial. It is only in the exercise of its judicial powers, when sitting as a court for the trial of impeachments, that the Senate is expressly authorized and necessarily required to consider and decide upon the conduct of the President or any other public officer. Indirectly, however, as has already been suggested, it may frequently be called on to perform that office. Cases may occur in the course of its legislative or executive proceedings in which it may be indispensable to the proper exercise of its powers that it should inquire into and decide upon the conduct of the President or other public officers, and in every such case its constitutional right to do so is cheerfully conceded. But to authorize the Senate to enter on such a task in its legislative or executive capacity the inquiry must actually grow out of and tend to some legislative or executive action, and the decision, when expressed, must take the form of some appropriate legislative or executive act.

The resolution in question was introduced, discussed, and passed not as a joint but as a separate resolution. It asserts no legislative power, proposes no legislative action, and neither possesses the form nor any of the attributes of a legislative measure. It does not appear to have been entertained or passed with any view or expectation of its issuing in a law or joint resolution, or in the repeal of any law or joint resolution, or in any other legislative action.

Whilst wanting both the form and substance of a legislative measure, it is equally manifest that the resolution was not justified by any of the executive powers conferred on the Senate. These powers relate exclusively to the consideration of treaties and nominations to office, and they are exercised in secret session and with closed doors. This resolution does not apply to any treaty or nomination, and was passed in a public session.

Nor does this proceeding in any way belong to that class of incidental resolutions which relate to the officers of the Senate, to their Chamber and other appurtenances, or to subjects of order and other matters of the like nature, in all which either House may lawfully proceed without any cooperation with the other or with the President.

On the contrary, the whole phraseology and sense of the resolution seem to be judicial. Its essence, true character, and only practical effect are to be found in the conduct which it charges upon the President and in the judgment which it pronounces on that conduct. The resolution, therefore, though discussed and adopted by the Senate in its legislative capacity, is in its office and in all its characteristics essentially judicial.

That the Senate possesses a high judicial power and that instances may occur in which the President of the United States will be amenable to it is undeniable; but under the provisions of the Constitution it would seem to be equally plain that neither the President nor any other officer can be rightfully subjected to the operation of the judicial power of the Senate except in the cases and under the forms prescribed by the Constitution.

The Constitution declares that "the President, Vice-President, and all civil officers of the United States shall be removed from office on impeachment for and conviction of treason, bribery, or other high crimes and misdemeanors;" that the House of Representatives "shall have the sole power of impeachment;" that the Senate "shall have the sole power to try all impeachments;" that "when sitting for that purpose they shall be on oath or affirmation;" that "when the President of the United States is tried the Chief Justice shall preside;" that "no person shall be convicted without the concurrence of two-thirds of the members present," and that "judgment shall not extend further than to removal from office and disqualification to hold and enjoy any office of honor, trust, or profit under the United States."

The resolution above quoted charges, in substance, that in certain proceedings relating to the public revenue the President has usurped authority and power not conferred upon him by the Constitution and laws, and that in doing so he violated both. Any such act constitutes a high crime—one of the highest, indeed, which the President can commit—a crime which justly exposes him to impeachment by the House of Representatives, and, upon due conviction, to removal from office and to the complete and immutable disfranchisement prescribed by the Constitution. The resolution, then, was in substance an impeachment of the President, and in its passage amounts to a declaration by a majority of the Senate that he is guilty of an impeachable offense. As such it is spread upon the journals of the Senate, published to the nation and to the world, made part of our enduring archives, and incorporated in the history of the age. The punishment of removal from office and future disqualification does not, it is true, follow this decision, nor would it have followed the like decision if the regular forms of proceeding had been pursued, because the requisite number did not concur in the result. But the moral influence of a solemn declaration by a majority of the Senate that the accused is guilty of the offense charged upon him has been as effectually secured as if the like declaration had been made upon an impeachment expressed in the same terms. Indeed, a greater practical effect has been gained, because the votes given for the resolution, though not sufficient to authorize a judgment of guilty on an impeachment, were numerous enough to carry that resolution.

That the resolution does not expressly allege that the assumption of power and authority which it condemns was intentional and corrupt is no answer to the preceding view of its character and effect. The act thus condemned necessarily implies volition and design in the individual to whom it is imputed, and, being unlawful in its character, the legal conclusion is that it was prompted by improper motives and committed with an unlawful intent. The charge is not of a mistake in the exercise of supposed powers, but of the assumption of powers not conferred by the Constitution and laws, but in derogation of both, and nothing is suggested to excuse or palliate the turpitude of the act. In the absence of any such excuse or palliation there is only room for one inference, and that is that the intent was unlawful and corrupt. Besides, the resolution not only contains no mitigating suggestions, but, on the contrary, it holds up the act complained of as justly obnoxious to censure and reprobation, and thus as distinctly stamps it with impurity of motive as if the strongest epithets had been used.

The President of the United States, therefore, has been by a majority of his constitutional triers accused and found guilty of an impeachable offense, but in no part of this proceeding have the directions of the Constitution been observed.

The impeachment, instead of being preferred and prosecuted by the House of Representatives, originated in the Senate, and was prosecuted without the aid or concurrence of the other House. The oath or affirmation prescribed by the Constitution was not taken by the Senators, the Chief Justice did not preside, no notice of the charge was given to the accused, and no opportunity afforded him to respond to the accusation, to meet his accusers face to face, to cross-examine the witnesses, to procure counteracting testimony, or to be heard in his defense. The safeguards and formalities which the Constitution has connected with the power of impeachment were doubtless supposed by the framers of that instrument to be essential to the protection of the public servant, to the attainment of justice, and to the order, impartiality, and dignity of the procedure. These safeguards and formalities were not only practically disregarded in the commencement and conduct of these proceedings, but in their result I find myself convicted by less than two-thirds of the members present of an impeachable offense.

In vain may it be alleged in defense of this proceeding that the form of the resolution is not that of an impeachment or of a judgment thereupon, that the punishment prescribed in the Constitution does not follow its adoption, or that in this case no impeachment is to be expected from the House of Representatives. It is because it did not assume the form of an impeachment that it is the more palpably repugnant to the Constitution, for it is through that form only that the President is judicially responsible to the Senate; and though neither removal from office nor future disqualification ensues, yet it is not to be presumed that the framers of the Constitution considered either or both of those results as constituting the whole of the punishment they prescribed. The judgment of *guilty* by the highest tribunal in the Union, the stigma it would inflict on the offender, his family, and fame, and the perpetual record on the Journal, handing down to future generations the story of his disgrace, were doubtless regarded by them as the bitterest portions, if not the very essence, of that punishment. So far, therefore, as some of its most material parts are concerned, the passage, recording, and promulgation of the resolution are an attempt to bring them on the President in a manner unauthorized by the Constitution. To shield him and other officers who are liable to impeachment from consequences so momentous, except when really merited by official delinquencies, the Constitution has most carefully guarded the whole process of impeachment. A majority of the House of Representatives must think the officer guilty before he can be charged. Two-thirds of the Senate must pronounce him guilty or he is deemed to be innocent. Forty-six Senators appear by the Journal to have been present when the vote on the resolution was taken. If after all the solemnities of an impeachment thirty of those Senators had voted that the President was guilty, yet would he have been acquitted; but by the mode of proceeding adopted in the present case a lasting record of conviction has been entered up by the votes of twenty-six Senators without an impeachment or trial, whilst the Constitution expressly declares that to the entry of such a judgment an accusation by the House of Representatives, a trial by the Senate, and a concurrence of two-thirds in the vote of guilty shall be indispensable prerequisites.

Whether or not an impeachment was to be expected from the House of Representatives was a point on which the Senate had no constitutional right to speculate, and in respect to which, even had it possessed the spirit of prophecy, its anticipations would have furnished no just ground for this procedure. Admitting that there was reason to believe that a violation of the Constitution and laws had been actually committed by the President, still it was the duty of the Senate, as his sole constitutional judges, to wait for an impeachment until the other House should think proper to prefer it. The members of the Senate could have no right to infer that no impeachment was intended. On the contrary, every legal and rational presumption on their part ought to have been that if there was good reason to believe him guilty of an impeachable offense the House of Representatives would perform its constitutional duty by arraigning the offender before the justice of his country. The contrary presumption would involve an implication derogatory to the integrity and honor of the representatives of the people. But suppose the suspicion thus implied were actually entertained and for good cause, how can it justify the assumption by the Senate of powers not conferred by the Constitution?

It is only necessary to look at the condition in which the Senate and the President have been placed by this proceeding to perceive its utter incompatibility with the provisions and the spirit of the Constitution and with the plainest dictates of humanity and justice.

If the House of Representatives shall be of opinion that there is just ground for the censure pronounced upon the President, then will it be the solemn duty of that House to prefer the proper accusation and to cause him to be brought to trial by the constitutional tribunal. But in what condition would he find that tribunal? A majority of its members have already considered the case, and have not only formed but expressed a deliberate judgment upon its merits. It is the policy of our benign systems of jurisprudence to secure in all criminal proceedings, and even in the most trivial litigations, a fair, unprejudiced, and impartial trial, and surely it can not be less important that such a trial should be secured to the highest officer of the Government.

The Constitution makes the House of Representatives the exclusive judges, in the first instance, of the question whether the President has committed an impeachable offense. A majority of the Senate, whose interference with this preliminary question has for the best of all reasons been studiously excluded, anticipate the action of the House of Representatives, assume not only the function which belongs exclusively to that body, but convert themselves into accusers, witnesses, counsel, and judges, and prejudge the whole case, thus presenting the appalling spectacle in a free State of judges going through a labored preparation for an impartial hearing and decision by a previous *ex parte* investigation and sentence against the supposed offender.

There is no more settled axiom in that Government whence we derived the model of this part of our Constitution than that "the lords can not impeach any to themselves, nor join in the accusation, *because they are judges.*" Independently of the general reasons on which this rule is founded, its propriety and importance are greatly increased by the nature of the impeaching power. The power of arraigning the high officers of government before a tribunal whose sentence may expel them from their seats and brand them as infamous is eminently a popular remedy—a remedy designed to be employed for the protection of private right and public liberty against the abuses of injustice and the encroachments of arbitrary power. But the framers of the Constitution were also undoubtedly aware that this formidable instrument had been and might be abused, and that from its very nature an impeachment for high crimes and misdemeanors, whatever might be its result, would in most cases be accompanied by so much of dishonor and reproach, solicitude and suffering, as to make the power of preferring it one of the highest solemnity and importance. It was due to both these considerations that the impeaching power should be lodged in the hands of those who from the mode of their election and the tenure of their offices would most accurately express the popular will and at the same time be most directly and speedily amenable to the people. The theory of these wise and benignant intentions is in the present case effectually defeated by the proceedings of the Senate. The members of that body represent not the people, but the States; and though they are undoubtedly responsible to the States, yet from their extended term of service the effect of that responsibility during the whole period of that term must very much depend upon their own impressions of its obligatory force. When a body thus constituted expresses beforehand its opinion in a particular case, and thus indirectly invites a prosecution, it not only assumes a power intended for wise reasons to be confined to others, but it shields the latter from that exclusive and personal responsibility under which it was intended to be exercised, and reverses the whole scheme of this part of the Constitution.

Such would be some of the objections to this procedure, even if it were admitted that there is just ground for imputing to the President the offenses charged in the resolution. But if, on the other hand, the House of Representatives shall be of opinion that there is no reason for charging them upon him, and shall therefore deem it improper to prefer an impeachment, then will the violation of privilege as it respects that House, of justice as it regards the President, and of the Constitution as it relates to both be only the more conspicuous and impressive.

The constitutional mode of procedure on an impeachment has not only been wholly disregarded, but some of the first principles of natural right and enlightened jurisprudence have been violated in the very form of the resolution. It carefully abstains from averring in *which* of "the late proceedings in relation to the public revenue the President has assumed upon himself authority and power not conferred by the Constitution and laws." It carefully abstains from specifying *what laws* or *what parts* of the Constitution have been violated. Why was not the certainty of the offense—"the nature and cause of the accusation"—set out in the manner required in the Constitution before even the humblest individual, for the smallest crime, can be exposed to condemnation? Such a specification was due to the accused that he might direct his defense to the real points of attack, to the people that they might clearly understand in what particulars their institutions had been violated, and to the truth and certainty of our public annals. As the record now stands, whilst the resolution plainly charges upon the President at least one act of usurpation in "the late Executive proceedings in relation to the public revenue," and is so framed that those Senators who believed that one such act, and only one, had been committed could assent to it, its language is yet broad enough to include several such acts, and so it may have been regarded by some of those who voted for it. But though the accusation is thus comprehensive in the censures it implies, there is no such certainty of time, place, or circumstance as to exhibit the particular conclusion of fact or law which induced any one Senator to vote for it; and it may well have happened that whilst one Senator believed that some particular act embraced in the resolution was an arbitrary and unconstitutional assumption of power, others of the majority may have deemed that very act both constitutional and expedient, or, if not expedient, yet still within the pale of the Constitution; and thus a majority of the Senators may have been enabled to concur in a vague and undefined accusation that the President, in the course of ''the late Executive proceedings in relation to the public revenue,'' had violated the Constitution and laws, whilst if a separate vote had been taken in respect to each particular act included within the general terms the accusers of the President might on any such vote have been found in the minority.

Still further to exemplify this feature of the proceeding, it is important to be remarked that the resolution as originally offered to the Senate specified with adequate precision certain acts of the President which it denounced as a violation of the Constitution and laws, and that it was not until the very close of the debate, and when perhaps it was apprehended that a majority might not sustain the specific accusation contained in it, that the resolution was so modified as to assume its present form. A more striking illustration of the soundness and necessity of the rules which forbid vague and indefinite generalities and require a reasonable certainty in all judicial allegations, and a more glaring instance of the violation of those rules, has seldom been exhibited.

In this view of the resolution it must certainly be regarded not as a vindication of any particular provision of the law or the Constitution, but simply as an official rebuke or condemnatory sentence, too general and indefinite to be easily repelled, but yet sufficiently precise to bring into discredit the conduct and motives of the Executive. But whatever it may have been intended to accomplish, it is obvious that the vague, general, and abstract form of the resolution is in perfect keeping with those other departures from first principles and settled improvements in jurisprudence so properly the boast of free countries in modern times. And it is not too much to say of the whole of these proceedings that if they shall be approved and sustained by an intelligent people, then will that great contest with arbitrary power which had established in statutes, in bills of rights, in sacred charters, and in constitutions of government the right of every citizen to a notice before trial, to a hearing before conviction, and to an impartial tribunal for deciding on the charge have been waged in vain.

If the resolution had been left in its original form it is not to be presumed that it could ever have received the assent of a majority of the Senate, for the acts therein specified as violations of the Constitution and laws were clearly within the limits of the Executive authority. They are the "dismissing the late Secretary of the Treasury because he would not, contrary to his sense of his own duty, remove the money of the United States in deposit with the Bank of the United States and its branches in conformity with the President's opinion, and appointing his successor to effect such removal, which has been done." But as no other specification has been substituted, and as these were the "Executive proceedings in relation to the public revenue" principally referred to in the course of the discussion, they will doubtless be generally regarded as the acts intended to be denounced as "an assumption of authority and power not conferred by the Constitution or laws, but in derogation of both." It is therefore due to the occasion that a condensed summary of the views of the Executive in respect to them should be here exhibited.

By the Constitution "the executive power is vested in a President of the United States." Among the duties imposed upon him, and which he is sworn to perform, is that of "taking care that the laws be faithfully executed." Being thus made responsible for the entire action of the executive department, it was but reasonable that the power of appointing, overseeing, and controlling those who execute the laws—a power in its nature executive—should remain in his hands. It is therefore not only his right, but the Constitution makes it his duty, to "nominate and, by and with the advice and consent of the Senate, appoint" all "officers of the United States whose appointments are not in the Constitution otherwise provided for," with a proviso that the appointment of inferior officers may be vested in the President alone, in the courts of justice, or in the heads of Departments.

The executive power vested in the Senate is neither that of "nominating" nor "appointing." It is merely a check upon the Executive power of appointment. If individuals are proposed for appointment by the President by them deemed incompetent or unworthy, they may withhold their consent and the appointment can not be made. They check the action of the Executive, but can not in relation to those very subjects act themselves nor direct him. Selections are still made by the President, and the negative given to the Senate, without diminishing his responsibility, furnishes an additional guaranty to the country that the subordinate executive as well as the judicial offices shall be filled with worthy and competent men.

The whole executive power being vested in the President, who is responsible for its exercise, it is a necessary consequence that he should have a right to employ agents of his own choice to aid him in the performance of his duties, and to discharge them when he is no longer willing to be responsible for their acts.   In strict accordance with this principle, the power of removal, which, like that of appointment, is an original executive power, is left unchecked by the Constitution in relation to all executive officers, for whose conduct the President is responsible, while it is taken from him in relation to judicial officers, for whose acts he is not responsible.   In the Government from which many of the fundamental principles of our system are derived the head of the executive department originally had power to appoint and remove at will all officers, executive and judicial.   It was to take the judges out of this general power of removal, and thus make them independent of the Executive, that the tenure of their offices was changed to good behavior.   Nor is it conceivable why they are placed in our Constitution upon a tenure different from that of all other officers appointed by the Executive unless it be for the same purpose.

But if there were any just ground for doubt on the face of the Constitution whether all executive officers are removable at the will of the President, it is obviated by the cotemporaneous construction of the instrument and the uniform practice under it.

The power of removal was a topic of solemn debate in the Congress of 1789 while organizing the administrative departments of the Government, and it was finally decided that the President derived from the Constitution the power of removal so far as it regards that department for whose acts he is responsible.   Although the debate covered the whole ground, embracing the Treasury as well as all the other Executive Departments, it arose on a motion to strike out of the bill to establish a Department of Foreign Affairs, since called the Department of State, a clause declaring the Secretary "to be removable from office by the President of the United States."   After that motion had been decided in the negative it was perceived that these words did not convey the sense of the House of Representatives in relation to the true source of the power of removal.   With the avowed object of preventing any future inference that this power was exercised by the President in virtue of a grant from Congress, when in fact that body considered it as derived from the Constitution, the words which had been the subject of debate were struck out, and in lieu thereof a clause was inserted in a provision concerning the chief clerk of the Department, which declared that "whenever the said principal officer shall be removed from office by the President of the United States, or in any other case of vacancy," the chief clerk should during such vacancy have charge of the papers of the office. This change having been made for the express purpose of declaring the sense of Congress that the President derived the power of removal from the Constitution, the act as it passed has always been considered as a full expression of the sense of the Legislature on this important part of the American Constitution.

Here, then, we have the concurrent authority of President Washington, of the Senate, and the House of Representatives, numbers of whom had taken an active part in the convention which framed the Constitution and in the State conventions which adopted it, that the President derived an unqualified power of removal from that instrument itself, which is "beyond the reach of legislative authority." Upon this principle the Government has now been steadily administered for about forty-five years, during which there have been numerous removals made by the President or by his direction, embracing every grade of executive officers from the heads of Departments to the messengers of bureaus.

The Treasury Department in the discussions of 1789 was considered on the same footing as the other Executive Departments, and in the act establishing it were incorporated the precise words indicative of the sense of Congress that the President derives his power to remove the Secretary from the Constitution, which appear in the act establishing the Department of Foreign Affairs. An Assistant Secretary of the Treasury was created, and it was provided that he should take charge of the books and papers of the Department "whenever the Secretary shall be removed from office by the President of the United States." The Secretary of the Treasury being appointed by the President, and being considered as constitutionally removable by him, it appears never to have occurred to anyone in the Congress of 1789, or since until very recently, that he was other than an executive officer, the mere instrument of the Chief Magistrate in the execution of the laws, subject, like all other heads of Departments, to his supervision and control. No such idea as an officer of the Congress can be found in the Constitution or appears to have suggested itself to those who organized the Government. There are officers of each House the appointment of which is authorized by the Constitution, but all officers referred to in that instrument as coming within the appointing power of the President, whether established thereby or created by law, are "officers of the United States." No joint power of appointment is given to the two Houses of Congress, nor is there any accountability to them as one body; but as soon as any office is created by law, of whatever name or character, the appointment of the person or persons to fill it devolves by the Constitution upon the President, with the advice and consent of the Senate, unless it be an inferior office, and the appointment be vested by the law itself "in the President alone, in the courts of law, or in the heads of Departments."

But at the time of the organization of the Treasury Department an incident occurred which distinctly evinces the unanimous concurrence of the First Congress in the principle that the Treasury Department is wholly executive in its character and responsibilities. A motion was made to strike out the provision of the bill making it the duty of the Secretary "to digest and report plans for the improvement and management of the revenue and for the support of public credit," on the ground that it would give the executive department of the Government too much influence and power in Congress. The motion was not opposed on the ground that the Secretary was the officer of Congress and responsible to that body, which would have been conclusive if admitted, but on other ground, which conceded his executive character throughout. The whole discussion evinces an unanimous concurrence in the principle that the Secretary of the Treasury is wholly an executive officer, and the struggle of the minority was to restrict his power as such. From that time down to the present the Secretary of the Treasury, the Treasurer, Register, Comptrollers, Auditors, and clerks who fill the offices of that Department have in the practice of the Government been considered and treated as on the same footing with corresponding grades of officers in all the other Executive Departments.

The custody of the public property, under such regulations as may be prescribed by legislative authority, has always been considered an appropriate function of the executive department in this and all other Governments. In accordance with this principle, every species of property belonging to the United States (excepting that which is in the use of the several coordinate departments of the Government as means to aid them in performing their appropriate functions) is in charge of officers appointed by the President, whether it be lands, or buildings, or merchandise, or provisions, or clothing, or arms and munitions of war. The superintendents and keepers of the whole are appointed by the President, responsible to him, and removable at his will.

Public money is but a species of public property. It can not be raised by taxation or customs, nor brought into the Treasury in any other way except by law; but whenever or howsoever obtained, its custody always has been and always must be, unless the Constitution be changed, intrusted to the executive department. No officer can be created by Congress for the purpose of taking charge of it whose appointment would not by the Constitution at once devolve on the President and who would not be responsible to him for the faithful performance of his duties. The legislative power may undoubtedly bind him and the President by any laws they may think proper to enact; they may prescribe in what place particular portions of the public property shall be kept and for what reason it shall be removed, as they may direct that supplies for the Army or Navy shall be kept in particular stores, and it will be the duty of the President to see that the law is faithfully executed; yet will the custody remain in the executive department of the Government. Were the Congress to assume, with or without a legislative act, the power of appointing officers, independently of the President, to take the charge and custody of the public property contained in the military and naval arsenals, magazines, and storehouses, it is believed that such an act would be regarded by all as a palpable usurpation of executive power, subversive of the form as well as the fundamental principles of our Government. But where is the difference in principle whether the public property be in the form of arms, munitions of war, and supplies or in gold and silver or bank notes? None can be perceived; none is believed to exist. Congress can not, therefore, take out of the hands of the executive department the custody of the public property or money without an assumption of executive power and a subversion of the first principles of the Constitution.

The Congress of the United States have never passed an act imperatively directing that the public moneys shall be kept in any particular place or places. From the origin of the Government to the year 1816 the statute book was wholly silent on the subject. In 1789 a Treasurer was created, subordinate to the Secretary of the Treasury, and through him to the President. He was required to give bond safely to keep and faithfully to disburse the public moneys, without any direction as to the manner or places in which they should be kept. By reference to the practice of the Government it is found that from its first organization the Secretary of the Treasury, acting under the supervision of the President, designated the places in which the public moneys should be kept, and especially directed all transfers from place to place. This practice was continued, with the silent acquiescence of Congress, from 1789 down to 1816, and although many banks were selected and discharged, and although a portion of the moneys were first placed in the State banks, and then in the former Bank of the United States, and upon the dissolution of that were again transferred to the State banks, no legislation was thought necessary by Congress, and all the operations were originated and perfected by Executive authority. The Secretary of the Treasury, responsible to the President, and with his approbation, made contracts and arrangements in relation to the whole subject-matter, which was thus entirely committed to the direction of the President under his responsibilities to the American people and to those who were authorized to impeach and punish him for any breach of this important trust.

The act of 1816 establishing the Bank of the United States directed the deposits of public money to be made in that bank and its branches in places in which the said bank and branches thereof may be established, "unless the Secretary of the Treasury should otherwise order and direct," in which event he was required to give his reasons to Congress. This was but a continuation of his preexisting power as the head of an Executive Department to direct where the deposits should be made, with the superadded obligation of giving his reasons to Congress for making them elsewhere than in the Bank of the United States and its branches. It is not to be considered that this provision in any degree altered the relation between the Secretary of the Treasury and the President as the responsible head of the executive department, or released the latter from his constitutional obligation to "take care that the laws be faithfully executed." On the contrary, it increased his responsibilities by adding another to the long list of laws which it was his duty to carry into effect.

It would be an extraordinary result if because the person charged by law with a public duty is one of his Secretaries it were less the duty of the President to see that law faithfully executed than other laws enjoining duties upon subordinate officers or private citizens.   If there be any difference, it would seem that the obligation is the stronger in relation to the former, because the neglect is in his presence and the remedy at hand.

It can not be doubted that it was the legal duty of the Secretary of the Treasury to order and direct the deposits of the public money to be made elsewhere than in the Bank of the United States *whenever sufficient reasons existed for making the change.*   If in such a case he neglected or refused to act, he would neglect or refuse to execute the law.   What would be the sworn duty of the President?   Could he say that the Constitution did not bind him to see the law faithfully executed because it was one of his Secretaries and not himself upon whom the service was specially imposed?   Might he not be asked whether there was any such limitation to his obligations prescribed in the Constitution?   Whether he is not equally bound to take care that the laws be faithfully executed, whether they impose duties on the highest officer of State or the lowest subordinate in any of the Departments?   Might he not be told that it was for the sole purpose of causing all executive officers, from the highest to the lowest, faithfully to perform the services required of them by law that the people of the United States have made him their Chief Magistrate and the Constitution has clothed him with the entire executive power of this Government?   The principles implied in these questions appear too plain to need elucidation.

But here also we have a cotemporaneous construction of the act which shows that it was not understood as in any way changing the relations between the President and Secretary of the Treasury, or as placing the latter out of Executive control even in relation to the deposits of the public money.   Nor on that point are we left to any equivocal testimony. The documents of the Treasury Department show that the Secretary of the Treasury did apply to the President and obtained his approbation and sanction to the original transfer of the public deposits to the present Bank of the United States, and did carry the measure into effect in obedience to his decision.   They also show that transfers of the public deposits from the branches of the Bank of the United States to State banks at Chillicothe, Cincinnati, and Louisville, in 1819, were made with the approbation of the President and by his authority.   They show that upon all important questions appertaining to his Department, whether they related to the public deposits or other matters, it was the constant practice of the Secretary of the Treasury to obtain for his acts the approval and sanction of the President.   These acts and the principles on which they were founded were known to all the departments of the Government, to Congress and the country, and until very recently appear never to have been called in question.

Thus was it settled by the Constitution, the laws, and the whole practice of the Government that the entire executive power is vested in the President of the United States; that as incident to that power the right of appointing and removing those officers who are to aid him in the execution of the laws, with such restrictions only as the Constitution prescribes, is vested in the President; that the Secretary of the Treasury is one of those officers; that the custody of the public property and money is an Executive function which, in relation to the money, has always been exercised through the Secretary of the Treasury and his subordinates; that in the performance of these duties he is subject to the supervision and control of the President, and in all important measures having relation to them consults the Chief Magistrate and obtains his approval and sanction; that the law establishing the bank did not, as it could not, change the relation between the President and the Secretary—did not release the former from his obligation to see the law faithfully executed nor the latter from the President's supervision and control; that afterwards and before the Secretary did in fact consult and obtain the sanction of the President to transfers and removals of the public deposits, and that all departments of the Government, and the nation itself, approved or acquiesced in these acts and principles as in strict conformity with our Constitution and laws.

During the last year the approaching termination, according to the provisions of its charter and the solemn decision of the American people, of the Bank of the United States made it expedient, and its exposed abuses and corruptions made it, in my opinion, the duty of the Secretary of the Treasury, to place the moneys of the United States in other depositories. The Secretary did not concur in that opinion, and declined giving the necessary order and direction. So glaring were the abuses and corruptions of the bank, so evident its fixed purpose to persevere in them, and so palpable its design by its money and power to control the Government and change its character, that I deemed it the imperative duty of the Executive authority, by the exertion of every power confided to it by the Constitution and laws, to check its career and lessen its ability to do mischief, even in the painful alternative of dismissing the head of one of the Departments. At the time the removal was made other causes sufficient to justify it existed, but if they had not the Secretary would have been dismissed for this cause only.

His place I supplied by one whose opinions were well known to me, and whose frank expression of them in another situation and generous sacrifices of interest and feeling when unexpectedly called to the station he now occupies ought forever to have shielded his motives from suspicion and his character from reproach. In accordance with the views long before expressed by him he proceeded, with my sanction, to make arrangements for depositing the moneys of the United States in other safe institutions.

The resolution of the Senate as originally framed and as passed, if it refers to these acts, presupposes a right in that body to interfere with this exercise of Executive power. If the principle be once admitted, it is not difficult to perceive where it may end. If by a mere denunciation like this resolution the President should ever be induced to act in a matter of official duty contrary to the honest convictions of his own mind in compliance with the wishes of the Senate, the constitutional independence of the executive department would be as effectually destroyed and its power as effectually transferred to the Senate as if that end had been accomplished by an amendment of the Constitution. But if the Senate have a right to interfere with the Executive powers, they have also the right to make that interference effective, and if the assertion of the power implied in the resolution be silently acquiesced in we may reasonably apprehend that it will be followed at some future day by an attempt at actual enforcement. The Senate may refuse, except on the condition that he will surrender his opinions to theirs and obey their will, to perform their own constitutional functions, to pass the necessary laws, to sanction appropriations proposed by the House of Representatives, and to confirm proper nominations made by the President. It has already been maintained (and it is not conceivable that the resolution of the Senate can be based on any other principle) that the Secretary of the Treasury is the officer of Congress and independent of the President; that the President has no right to control him, and consequently none to remove him. With the same propriety and on similar grounds may the Secretary of State, the Secretaries of War and the Navy, and the Postmaster-General each in succession be declared independent of the President, the subordinates of Congress, and removable only with the concurrence of the Senate. Followed to its consequences, this principle will be found effectually to destroy one coordinate department of the Government, to concentrate in the hands of the Senate the whole executive power, and to leave the President as powerless as he would be useless—the shadow of authority after the substance had departed.

The time and the occasion which have called forth the resolution of the Senate seem to impose upon me an additional obligation not to pass it over in silence. Nearly forty-five years had the President exercised, without a question as to his rightful authority, those powers for the recent assumption of which he is now denounced. The vicissitudes of peace and war had attended our Government; violent parties, watchful to take advantage of any seeming usurpation on the part of the Executive, had distracted our councils; frequent removals, or forced resignations in every sense tantamount to removals, had been made of the Secretary and other officers of the Treasury, and yet in no one instance is it known that any man, whether patriot or partisan, had raised his voice against it as a violation of the Constitution. The expediency and justice of such changes in reference to public officers of all grades have frequently been the topic of discussion, but the constitutional right of the President to appoint, control, and remove the head of the Treasury as well as all other Departments seems to have been universally conceded. And what is the occasion upon which other principles have been first officially asserted? The Bank of the United States, a great moneyed monopoly, had attempted to obtain a renewal of its charter by controlling the elections of the people and the action of the Government. The use of its corporate funds and power in that attempt was fully disclosed, and it was made known to the President that the corporation was putting in train the same course of measures, with the view of making another vigorous effort, through an interference in the elections of the people, to control public opinion and force the Government to yield to its demands. This, with its corruption of the press, its violation of its charter, its exclusion of the Government directors from its proceedings, its neglect of duty and arrogant pretensions, made it, in the opinion of the President, incompatible with the public interest and the safety of our institutions that it should be longer employed as the fiscal agent of the Treasury. A Secretary of the Treasury appointed in the recess of the Senate, who had not been confirmed by that body, and whom the President might or might not at his pleasure nominate to them, refused to do what his superior in the executive department considered the most imperative of his duties, and became in fact, however innocent his motives, the protector of the bank. And on this occasion it is discovered for the first time that those who framed the Constitution misunderstood it; that the First Congress and all its successors have been under a delusion; that the practice of near forty-five years is but a continued usurpation; that the Secretary of the Treasury is not responsible to the President, and that to remove him is a violation of the Constitution and laws for which the President deserves to stand forever dishonored on the journals of the Senate.

There are also some other circumstances connected with the discussion and passage of the resolution to which I feel it to be not only my right, but my duty, to refer. It appears by the Journal of the Senate that among the twenty-six Senators who voted for the resolution on its final passage, and who had supported it in debate in its original form, were one of the Senators from the State of Maine, the two Senators from New Jersey, and one of the Senators from Ohio. It also appears by the same Journal and by the files of the Senate that the legislatures of these States had severally expressed their opinions in respect to the Executive proceedings drawn in question before the Senate.

The two branches of the legislature of the State of Maine on the 25th of January, 1834, passed a preamble and series of resolutions in the following words:

Whereas at an early period after the election of Andrew Jackson to the Presidency, in accordance with the sentiments which he had uniformly expressed, the attention of Congress was called to the constitutionality and expediency of the renewal of the charter of the United States Bank; and

Whereas the bank has transcended its chartered limits in the management of its business transactions, and has abandoned the object of its creation by engaging in political controversies, by wielding its power and influence to embarrass the Administration of the General Government, and by bringing insolvency and distress upon the commercial community; and

Whereas the public security from such an institution consists less in its present pecuniary capacity to discharge its liabilities than in the fidelity with which the trusts reposed in it have been executed; and

Whereas the abuse and misapplication of the powers conferred have destroyed the confidence of the public in the officers of the bank and demonstrated that such powers endanger the stability of republican institutions: Therefore,

Resolved, That in the removal of the public deposits from the Bank of the United States, as well as in the manner of their removal, we recognize in the Administration an adherence to constitutional rights and the performance of a public duty.

Resolved, That this legislature entertain the same opinion as heretofore expressed by preceding legislatures of this State, that the Bank of the United States ought not to be rechartered.

Resolved, That the Senators of this State in the Congress of the United States be instructed and the Representatives be requested to oppose the restoration of the deposits and the renewal of the charter of the United States Bank.

On the 11th of January, 1834, the house of assembly and council composing the legislature of the State of New Jersey passed a preamble and a series of resolutions in the following words:

Whereas the present crisis in our public affairs calls for a decided expression of the voice of the people of this State; and

Whereas we consider it the undoubted right of the legislatures of the several States to instruct those who represent their interests in the councils of the nation in all matters which intimately concern the public weal and may affect the happiness or well-being of the people: Therefore,

1. *Be it resolved by the council and general assembly of this State,* That while we acknowledge with feelings of devout gratitude our obligations to the Great Ruler of Nations for His mercies to us as a people that we have been preserved alike from foreign war, from the evils of internal commotions, and the machinations of designing and ambitious men who would prostrate the fair fabric of our Union, that we ought nevertheless to humble ourselves in His presence and implore His aid for the perpetuation of our republican institutions and for a continuance of that unexampled prosperity which our country has hitherto enjoyed.

2. *Resolved,* That we have undiminished confidence in the integrity and firmness of the venerable patriot who now holds the distinguished post of Chief Magistrate of this nation, and whose purity of purpose and elevated motives have so often received the unqualified approbation of a large majority of his fellow-citizens.

3. *Resolved,* That we view with agitation and alarm the existence of a great moneyed incorporation which threatens to embarrass the operations of the Government and by means of its unbounded influence upon the currency of the country to scatter distress and ruin throughout the community, and that we therefore solemnly believe the present Bank of the United States ought not to be rechartered.

4. *Resolved,* That our Senators in Congress be instructed and our members of the House of Representatives be requested to sustain, by their votes and influence, the course adopted by the Secretary of the Treasury, Mr. Taney, in relation to the Bank of the United States and the deposits of the Government moneys, believing as

we do the course of the Secretary to have been constitutional, and that the public good required its adoption.

5. *Resolved,* That the governor be requested to forward a copy of the above resolutions to each of our Senators and Representatives from this State to the Congress of the United States.

On the 21st day of February last the legislature of the same State reiterated the opinions and instructions before given by joint resolutions in the following words:

Resolved by the council and general assembly of the State of New Jersey, That they do adhere to the resolutions passed by them on the 11th day of January last, relative to the President of the United States, the Bank of the United States, and the course of Mr. Taney in removing the Government deposits.

Resolved, That the legislature of New Jersey have not seen any reason to depart from such resolutions since the passage thereof, and it is their wish that they should receive from our Senators and Representatives of this State in the Congress of the United States that attention and obedience which are due to the opinion of a sovereign State openly expressed in its legislative capacity.

On the 2d of January, 1834, the senate and house of representatives composing the legislature of Ohio passed a preamble and resolutions in the following words:

Whereas there is reason to believe that the Bank of the United States will attempt to obtain a renewal of its charter at the present session of Congress; and

Whereas it is abundantly evident that said bank has exercised powers derogatory to the spirit of our free institutions and dangerous to the liberties of these United States; and

Whereas there is just reason to doubt the constitutional power of Congress to grant acts of incorporation for banking purposes out of the District of Columbia; and

Whereas we believe the proper disposal of the public lands to be of the utmost importance to the people of these United States, and that honor and good faith require their equitable distribution: Therefore,

Resolved by the general assembly of the State of Ohio, That we consider the removal of the public deposits from the Bank of the United States as required by the best interests of our country, and that a proper sense of public duty imperiously demanded that that institution should be no longer used as a depository of the public funds.

Resolved also, That we view with decided disapprobation the renewed attempts in Congress to secure the passage of the bill providing for the disposal of the public domain upon the principles proposed by Mr. Clay, inasmuch as we believe that such a law would be unequal in its operations and unjust in its results.

Resolved also, That we heartily approve of the principles set forth in the late veto message upon that subject; and

Resolved, That our Senators in Congress be instructed and our Representatives requested to use their influence to prevent the rechartering of the Bank of the United States, to sustain the Administration in its removal of the public deposits, and to oppose the passage of a land bill containing the principles adopted in the act upon that subject passed at the last session of Congress.

Resolved, That the governor be requested to transmit copies of the foregoing preamble and resolutions to each of our Senators and Representatives.

It is thus seen that four Senators have declared by their votes that the President, in the late Executive proceedings in relation to the revenue, had been guilty of the impeachable offense of "assuming upon himself authority and power not conferred by the Constitution and laws, but in derogation of both," whilst the legislatures of their respective States had deliberately approved those very proceedings as consistent with the Constitution and demanded by the public good. If these four votes had been given in accordance with the sentiments of the legislatures, as above expressed, there would have been but twenty-two votes out of forty-six for censuring the President, and the unprecedented record of his conviction could not have been placed upon the Journal of the Senate.

In thus referring to the resolutions and instructions of the State legislatures I disclaim and repudiate all authority or design to interfere with the responsibility due from members of the Senate to their own consciences, their constituents, and their country. The facts now stated belong to the history of these proceedings, and are important to the just development of the principles and interests involved in them as well as to the proper vindication of the executive department, and with that view, and that view only, are they here made the topic of remark.

The dangerous tendency of the doctrine which denies to the President the power of supervising, directing, and controlling the Secretary of the Treasury in like manner with the other executive officers would soon be manifest in practice were the doctrine to be established. The President is the direct representative of the American people, but the Secretaries are not. If the Secretary of the Treasury be independent of the President in the execution of the laws, then is there no direct responsibility to the people in that important branch of this Government to which is committed the care of the national finances. And it is in the power of the Bank of the United States, or any other corporation, body of men, or individuals, if a Secretary shall be found to accord with them in opinion or can be induced in practice to promote their views, to control through him the whole action of the Government (so far as it is exercised by his Department) in defiance of the Chief Magistrate elected by the people and responsible to them.

But the evil tendency of the particular doctrine adverted to, though sufficiently serious, would be as nothing in comparison with the pernicious consequences which would inevitably flow from the approbation and allowance by the people and the practice by the Senate of the unconstitutional power of arraigning and censuring the official conduct of the Executive in the manner recently pursued. Such proceedings are eminently calculated to unsettle the foundations of the Government, to disturb the harmonious action of its different departments, and to break down the checks and balances by which the wisdom of its framers sought to insure its stability and usefulness.

The honest differences of opinion which occasionally exist between the Senate and the President in regard to matters in which both are obliged to participate are sufficiently embarrassing; but if the course recently adopted by the Senate shall hereafter be frequently pursued, it is not only obvious that the harmony of the relations between the President and the Senate will be destroyed, but that other and graver effects will ultimately ensue. If the censures of the Senate be submitted to by the President, the confidence of the people in his ability and virtue and the character and usefulness of his Administration will soon be at an end, and the real power of the Government will fall into the hands of a body holding their offices for long terms, not elected by the people and not to them directly responsible. If, on the other hand, the illegal censures of the Senate should be resisted by the President, collisions and angry controversies might ensue, discreditable in their progress and in the end compelling the people to adopt the conclusion either that their Chief Magistrate was unworthy of their respect or that the Senate was chargeable with calumny and injustice. Either of these results would impair public confidence in the perfection of the system and lead to serious alterations of its framework or to the practical abandonment of some of its provisions.

The influence of such proceedings on the other departments of the Government, and more especially on the States, could not fail to be extensively pernicious. When the judges in the last resort of official misconduct themselves overleap the bounds of their authority as prescribed by the Constitution, what general disregard of its provisions might not their example be expected to produce? And who does not perceive that such contempt of the Federal Constitution by one of its most important departments would hold out the strongest temptations to resistance on the part of the State sovereignties whenever they shall suppose their just rights to have been invaded? Thus all the independent departments of the Government, and the States which compose our confederated Union, instead of attending to their appropriate duties and leaving those who may offend to be reclaimed or punished in the manner pointed out in the Constitution, would fall to mutual crimination and recrimination and give to the people confusion and anarchy instead of order and law, until at length some form of aristocratic power would be established on the ruins of the Constitution or the States be broken into separate communities.

Far be it from me to charge or to insinuate that the present Senate of the United States intend in the most distant way to encourage such a result. It is not of their motives or designs, but only of the tendency of their acts, that it is my duty to speak. It is, if possible, to make Senators themselves sensible of the danger which lurks under the precedent set in their resolution, and at any rate to perform my duty as the responsible head of one of the coequal departments of the Government, that I have been compelled to point out the consequences to which the discussion and passage of the resolution may lead if the tendency of the measure be not checked in its inception. It is due to the high trust with which I have been charged, to those who may be called to succeed me in it, to the representatives of the people whose constitutional prerogative has been unlawfully assumed, to the people and to the States, and to the Constitution they have established that I should not permit its provisions to be broken down by such an attack on the executive department without at least some effort "to preserve, protect, and defend" them. With this view, and for the reasons which have been stated, I do hereby *solemnly protest* against the aforementioned proceedings of the Senate as unauthorized by the Constitution, contrary to its spirit and to several of its express provisions, subversive of that distribution of the powers of government which it has ordained and established, destructive of the checks and safeguards by which those powers were intended on the one hand to be controlled and on the other to be protected, and calculated by their immediate and collateral effects, by their character and tendency, to concentrate in the hands of a body not directly amenable to the people a degree of influence and power dangerous to their liberties and fatal to the Constitution of their choice.

The resolution of the Senate contains an imputation upon my private as well as upon my public character, and as it must stand forever on their journals, I can not close this substitute for that defense which I have not been allowed to present in the ordinary form without remarking that I have lived in vain if it be necessary to enter into a formal vindication of my character and purposes from such an imputation. In vain do I bear upon my person enduring memorials of that contest in which American liberty was purchased; in vain have I since periled property, fame, and life in defense of the rights and privileges so dearly bought; in vain am I now, without a personal aspiration or the hope of individual advantage, encountering responsibilities and dangers from which by mere inactivity in relation to a single point I might have been exempt, if any serious doubts can be entertained as to the purity of my purposes and motives. If I had been ambitious, I should have sought an alliance with that powerful institution which even now aspires to no divided empire. If I had been venal, I should have sold myself to its designs. Had I preferred personal comfort and official ease to the performance of my arduous duty, I should have ceased to molest it. In the history of conquerors and usurpers, never in the fire of youth nor in the vigor of manhood could I find an attraction to lure me from the path of duty, and now I shall scarcely find an inducement to commence their career of ambition when gray hairs and a decaying frame, instead of inviting to toil and battle, call me to the contemplation of other worlds, where conquerors cease to be honored and usurpers expiate their crimes. The only ambition I can feel is to acquit myself to Him to whom I must soon render an account of my stewardship, to serve my fellow-men, and live respected and honored in the history of my country. No; the ambition which leads me on is an anxious desire and a fixed determination to return to the people unimpaired the sacred trust they have confided to my charge; to heal the wounds of the Constitution and preserve it from further violation; to persuade my countrymen, so far as I may, that it is not in a splendid government supported by powerful monopolies and aristocratical establishments that they will find happiness or their liberties protection, but in a plain system, void of pomp, protecting all and granting favors to none, dispensing its blessings, like the dews of Heaven, unseen and unfelt save in the freshness and beauty they contribute to produce. It is such a government that the genius of our people requires; such an one only under which our States may remain for ages to come united, prosperous, and free. If the Almighty Being who has hitherto sustained and protected me will but vouchsafe to make my feeble powers instrumental to such a result, I shall anticipate with pleasure the place to be assigned me in the history of my country, and die contented with the belief that I have contributed in some small degree to increase the value and prolong the duration of American liberty.

To the end that the resolution of the Senate may not be hereafter drawn into precedent with the authority of silent acquiescence on the part of the executive department, and to the end also that my motives and views in the Executive proceedings denounced in that resolution may be known to my fellow-citizens, to the world, and to all posterity, I respectfully request that this message and protest may be entered at length on the journals of the Senate.   ANDREW JACKSON.

APRIL 21, 1834.

To the Senate of the United States:

Having reason to believe that certain passages contained in my message and protest transmitted to the Senate on the 17th [15th] instant may be misunderstood, I think it proper to state that it was not my intention to deny in the said message the power and right of the legislative department to provide by law for the custody, safe-keeping, and disposition of the public money and property of the United States.

Although I am well satisfied that such a construction is not warranted by anything contained in that message, yet aware from experience that detached passages of an argumentative document, when disconnected from their context and considered without reference to previous limitations and the particular positions they were intended to refute or to establish, may be made to bear a construction varying altogether from the sentiments really entertained and intended to be expressed, and deeply solicitous that my views on this point should not, either now or hereafter, be misapprehended, I have deemed it due to the gravity of the subject, to the great interests it involves, and to the Senate as well as to myself to embrace the earliest opportunity to make this communication.

I admit without reserve, as I have before done, the constitutional power of the Legislature to prescribe by law the place or places in which the public money or other property is to be deposited, and to make such regulations concerning its custody, removal, or disposition as they may think proper to enact. Nor do I claim for the Executive any right to the possession or disposition of the public property or treasure or any authority to interfere with the same, except when such possession, disposition, or authority is given to him by law. Nor do I claim the right in any manner to supervise or interfere with the person intrusted with such property or treasure, unless he be an officer whose appointment, under the Constitution and laws, is devolved upon the President alone or in conjunction with the Senate, and for whose conduct he is constitutionally responsible.

As the message and protest referred to may appear on the Journal of the Senate and remain among the recorded documents of the nation, I am unwilling that opinions should be imputed to me, even through misconstruction, which are not entertained, and more particularly am I solicitous that I may not be supposed to claim for myself or my successors any power or authority not clearly granted by the Constitution and laws to the President. I have therefore respectfully to request that this communication may be considered a part of that message and that it may be entered therewith on the journals of the Senate.

ANDREW JACKSON.

EXECUTIVE ORDERS.

HEADQUARTERS OF THE ARMY,
ADJUTANT-GENERAL'S OFFICE,
Washington, June 21, 1834.

ORDER 46.

The Major-General Commanding the Army has received through the War Department the following General Order from the President of the United States:

GENERAL ORDER.

WASHINGTON, *June 21, 1834.*

Information having been received of the death of General Lafayette, the President considers it due to his own feelings as well as to the character and services of that lamented man to announce the event to the Army and Navy.

Lafayette was a citizen of France, but he was the distinguished friend

of the United States. In early life he embarked in that contest which
secured freedom and independence to our country. His services and sacrifices constitute a part of our Revolutionary history, and his memory
will be second only to that of Washington in the hearts of the American
people. In his own country and in ours he was the zealous and uniform
friend and advocate of rational liberty. Consistent in his principles and
conduct, he never during a long life committed an act which exposed him
to just accusation or which will expose his memory to reproach. Living
at a period of great excitement and of moral and political revolutions,
engaged in many of the important events which fixed the attention of
the world, and invited to guide the destinies of France at two of the most
momentous eras of her history, his political integrity and personal disinterestedness have not been called in question. Happy in such a life, he
has been happy in his death. He has been taken from the theater of
action with faculties unimpaired, with a reputation unquestioned, and
an object of veneration wherever civilization and the rights of man
have extended; and mourning, as we may and must, his departure, let
us rejoice that this associate of Washington has gone, as we humbly
hope, to rejoin his illustrious commander in the fullness of days and of
honor.

He came in his youth to defend our country. He came in the maturity
of his age to witness her growth in all the elements of prosperity, and
while witnessing these he received those testimonials of national gratitude which proved how strong was his hold upon the affections of the
American people.

One melancholy duty remains to be performed. The last major-general of the Revolutionary army has died. Himself a young and humble
participator in the struggles of that period, the President feels called on
as well by personal as public considerations to direct that appropriate
honors be paid to the memory of this distinguished patriot and soldier.
He therefore orders that the same honors be rendered upon this occasion
at the different military and naval stations as were observed upon the
decease of Washington, the Father of his Country, and his contemporary
in arms.

In ordering this homage to be paid to the memory of one so eminent
in the field, so wise in council, so endeared in private life, and so well and
favorably known to both hemispheres the President feels assured that he
is anticipating the sentiments not of the Army and Navy only, but of the
whole American people.

ANDREW JACKSON.

In obedience to the commands of the President, the following funeral
honors will be paid at the several stations of the Army:

At daybreak twenty-four guns will be fired in quick succession, and
one gun at the interval of every half hour thereafter till sunset.

The flags of the several stations will during the day be at half-mast. The officers of the Army will wear crape on the left arm for the period of six months.

This order will be carried into effect under the direction of the commanding officer of each post and station the day after its reception.

By command of Major-General Macomb, commanding in chief:

R. JONES, *Adjutant-General.*

GREEN HILL, *October 12, 1834.*

Hon. LEVI WOODBURY,
    Secretary of the Treasury.

MY DEAR SIR: I inclose you two letters from two of our most respectable citizens. They are good men and true. The letters relate to matters under your immediate charge, and when I come on to Washington will see about them.

Marshall was our candidate for the legislature, and has no doubt lost his election through the influence of the United States officers at that post, who are all of them opposed to us, and if we lose *Brown* this winter from the Senate it will be owing mainly and chiefly to this. The county of Carterett sends three members to the legislature, and is Jackson to the *hub;* but Major Kirby, who commands at Fort Macon, has used his influence in conjunction with D. Borden, who finds the troops with provisions, in favor of the opposition, and have beaten our men by small majorities. The troops, it seems, were paid off in Virginia money, which is below *par* in our State, and this just on the eve of the election, and hence you may see the turn that was given to the matter. Dr. Hunt, who wishes to be appointed surgeon at Occracock, is a fine man, and I should like for him to have it; but of these matters more when I see you.

You see our new bank has gone into operation. Suppose you open a correspondence [with] them about the matter we have been talking about. It is *all important* that this matter should be attended to.

With sentiments of great respect, I am, dear sir, yours, etc.,

J. SPEIGHT.

[Indorsement.]

Let a strict inquiry be had into the conduct of the officers complained of, and particularly why the paymaster has paid the troops in depreciated paper when he could as easily paid them in specie. It is his duty in all cases so to do, as all the revenue is specie and all public dues are payable in specie.

A. J.

SIXTH ANNUAL MESSAGE.

DECEMBER 1, 1834.

Fellow-Citizens of the Senate and House of Representatives:

In performing my duty at the opening of your present session it gives me pleasure to congratulate you again upon the prosperous condition of our beloved country. Divine Providence has favored us with general health, with rich rewards in the fields of agriculture and in every branch of labor, and with peace to cultivate and extend the various resources which employ the virtue and enterprise of our citizens. Let us trust that in surveying a scene so flattering to our free institutions our joint deliberations to preserve them may be crowned with success.

Our foreign relations continue, with but few exceptions, to maintain the favorable aspect which they bore in my last annual message, and promise to extend those advantages which the principles that regulate our intercourse with other nations are so well calculated to secure.

The question of the northeastern boundary is still pending with Great Britain, and the proposition made in accordance with the resolution of the Senate for the establishment of a line according to the treaty of 1783 has not been accepted by that Government. Believing that every disposition is felt on both sides to adjust this perplexing question to the satisfaction of all the parties interested in it, the hope is yet indulged that it may be effected on the basis of that proposition.

With the Governments of Austria, Russia, Prussia, Holland, Sweden, and Denmark the best understanding exists. Commerce with all is fostered and protected by reciprocal good will under the sanction of liberal conventional or legal provisions.

In the midst of her internal difficulties the Queen of Spain has ratified the convention for the payment of the claims of our citizens arising since 1819. It is in the course of execution on her part, and a copy of it is now laid before you for such legislation as may be found necessary to enable those interested to derive the benefits of it.

Yielding to the force of circumstances and to the wise counsels of time and experience, that power has finally resolved no longer to occupy the unnatural position in which she stood to the new Governments established in this hemisphere. I have the great satisfaction of stating to you that in preparing the way for the restoration of harmony between those who have sprung from the same ancestors, who are allied by common interests, profess the same religion, and speak the same language the United States have been actively instrumental. Our efforts to effect this good work will be persevered in while they are deemed useful to the parties and our entire disinterestedness continues to be felt and understood. The act of Congress to countervail the discriminating duties to the prejudice of our navigation levied in Cuba and Puerto Rico has been transmitted to the minister of the United States at Madrid, to be communicated to the Government of the Queen.   No intelligence of its receipt has yet reached the Department of State.   If the present condition of the country permits the Government to make a careful and enlarged examination of the true interests of these important portions of its dominions, no doubt is entertained that their future intercourse with the United States will be placed upon a more just and liberal basis.

The Florida archives have not yet been selected and delivered.   Recent orders have been sent to the agent of the United States at Havana to return with all that he can obtain, so that they may be in Washington before the session of the Supreme Court, to be used in the legal questions there pending to which the Government is a party.

Internal tranquillity is happily restored to Portugal.   The distracted state of the country rendered unavoidable the postponement of a final payment of the just claims of our citizens.   Our diplomatic relations will be soon resumed, and the long-subsisting friendship with that power affords the strongest guaranty that the balance due will receive prompt attention.

The first installment due under the convention of indemnity with the King of the Two Sicilies has been duly received, and an offer has been made to extinguish the whole by a prompt payment—an offer I did not consider myself authorized to accept, as the indemnification provided is the exclusive property of individual citizens of the United States.   The original adjustment of our claims and the anxiety displayed to fulfill at once the stipulations made for the payment of them are highly honorable to the Government of the Two Sicilies.   When it is recollected that they were the result of the injustice of an intrusive power temporarily dominant in its territory, a repugnance to acknowledge and to pay which would have been neither unnatural nor unexpected, the circumstances can not fail to exalt its character for justice and good faith in the eyes of all nations.

The treaty of amity and commerce between the United States and Belgium, brought to your notice in my last annual message as sanctioned by the Senate, but the ratifications of which had not been exchanged owing to a delay in its reception at Brussels and a subsequent absence of the Belgian minister of foreign affairs, has been, after mature deliberation, finally disavowed by that Government as inconsistent with the powers and instructions given to their minister who negotiated it.   This disavowal was entirely unexpected, as the liberal principles embodied in the convention, and which form the groundwork of the objections to it, were perfectly satisfactory to the Belgian representative, and were supposed to be not only within the powers granted, but expressly conformable to the instructions given to him.   An offer, not yet accepted, has been made by Belgium to renew negotiations for a treaty less liberal in its provisions on questions of general maritime law,

Our newly established relations with the Sublime Porte promise to be useful to our commerce and satisfactory in every respect to this Government. Our intercourse with the Barbary Powers continues without important change, except that the present political state of Algiers has induced me to terminate the residence there of a salaried consul and to substitute an ordinary consulate, to remain so long as the place continues in the possession of France. Our first treaty with one of these powers, the Emperor of Morocco, was formed in 1786, and was limited to fifty years. That period has almost expired. I shall take measures to renew it with the greater satisfaction as its stipulations are just and liberal and have been, with mutual fidelity and reciprocal advantage, scrupulously fulfilled.

Intestine dissensions have too frequently occurred to mar the prosperity, interrupt the commerce, and distract the governments of most of the nations of this hemisphere which have separated themselves from Spain. When a firm and permanent understanding with the parent country shall have produced a formal acknowledgment of their independence, and the idea of danger from that quarter can be no longer entertained, the friends of freedom expect that those countries, so favored by nature, will be distinguished for their love of justice and their devotion to those peaceful arts the assiduous cultivation of which confers honor upon nations and gives value to human life. In the meantime I confidently hope that the apprehensions entertained that some of the people of these luxuriant regions may be tempted, in a moment of unworthy distrust of their own capacity for the enjoyment of liberty, to commit the too common error of purchasing present repose by bestowing on some favorite leaders the fatal gift of irresponsible power will not be realized. With all these Governments and with that of Brazil no unexpected changes in our relations have occurred during the present year. Frequent causes of just complaint have arisen upon the part of the citizens of the United States, sometimes from the irregular action of the constituted subordinate authorities of the maritime regions and sometimes from the leaders or partisans of those in arms against the established Governments. In all cases representations have been or will be made, and as soon as their political affairs are in a settled position it is expected that our friendly remonstrances will be followed by adequate redress.

The Government of Mexico made known in December last the appointment of commissioners and a surveyor on its part to run, in conjunction with ours, the boundary line between its territories and the United States, and excused the delay for the reasons anticipated—the prevalence of civil war. The commissioners and surveyors not having met within the time stipulated by the treaty, a new arrangement became necessary, and our chargé d'affaires was instructed in January last to negotiate in Mexico an article additional to the preexisting treaty. This instruction was acknowledged, and no difficulty was apprehended in the accomplishment of that object. By information just received that additional article to the treaty will be obtained and transmitted to this country as soon as it can receive the ratification of the Mexican Congress.

The reunion of the three States of New Grenada, Venezuela, and Equador, forming the Republic of Colombia, seems every day to become more improbable. The commissioners of the two first are understood to be now negotiating a just division of the obligations contracted by them when united under one government. The civil war in Equador, it is believed, has prevented even the appointment of a commissioner on its part.

I propose at an early day to submit, in the proper form, the appointment of a diplomatic agent to Venezuela, the importance of the commerce of that country to the United States and the large claims of our citizens upon the Government arising before and since the division of Colombia rendering it, in my judgment, improper longer to delay this step.

Our representatives to Central America, Peru, and Brazil are either at or on their way to their respective posts.

From the Argentine Republic, from which a minister was expected to this Government, nothing further has been heard. Occasion has been taken on the departure of a new consul to Buenos Ayres to remind that Government that its long-delayed minister, whose appointment had been made known to us, had not arrived.

It becomes my unpleasant duty to inform you that this pacific and highly gratifying picture of our foreign relations does not include those with France at this time. It is not possible that any Government and people could be more sincerely desirous of conciliating a just and friendly intercourse with another nation than are those of the United States with their ancient ally and friend. This disposition is founded as well on the most grateful and honorable recollections associated with our struggle for independence as upon a well-grounded conviction that it is consonant with the true policy of both. The people of the United States could not, therefore, see without the deepest regret even a temporary interruption of the friendly relations between the two countries—a regret which would, I am sure, be greatly aggravated if there should turn out to be any reasonable ground for attributing such a result to any act of omission or commission on our part. I derive, therefore, the highest satisfaction from being able to assure you that the whole course of this Government has been characterized by a spirit so conciliatory and forbearing as to make it impossible that our justice and moderation should be questioned, whatever may be the consequences of a longer perseverance on the part of the French Government in her omission to satisfy the conceded claims of our citizens.

The history of the accumulated and unprovoked aggressions upon our commerce committed by authority of the existing Governments of France between the years 1800 and 1817 has been rendered too painfully familiar to Americans to make its repetition either necessary or desirable. It will be sufficient here to remark that there has for many years been scarcely a single administration of the French Government by whom the justice and legality of the claims of our citizens to indemnity were not to a very considerable extent admitted, and yet near a quarter of a century has been wasted in ineffectual negotiations to secure it.

Deeply sensible of the injurious effects resulting from this state of things upon the interests and character of both nations, I regarded it as among my first duties to cause one more effort to be made to satisfy France that a just and liberal settlement of our claims was as well due to her own honor as to their incontestable validity. The negotiation for this purpose was commenced with the late Government of France, and was prosecuted with such success as to leave no reasonable ground to doubt that a settlement of a character quite as liberal as that which was subsequently made would have been effected had not the revolution by which the negotiation was cut off taken place. The discussions were resumed with the present Government, and the result showed that we were not wrong in supposing that an event by which the two Governments were made to approach each other so much nearer in their political principles, and by which the motives for the most liberal and friendly intercourse were so greatly multiplied, could exercise no other than a salutary influence upon the negotiation. After the most deliberate and thorough examination of the whole subject a treaty between the two Governments was concluded and signed at Paris on the 4th of July, 1831, by which it was stipulated that "the French Government, in order to liberate itself from all the reclamations preferred against it by citizens of the United States for unlawful seizures, captures, sequestrations, confiscations, or destruction of their vessels, cargoes, or other property, engages to pay a sum of 25,000,000 francs to the United States, who shall distribute it among those entitled in the manner and according to the rules it shall determine;" and it was also stipulated on the part of the French Government that this 25,000,000 francs should "be paid at Paris, in six annual installments of 4,166,666 francs and 66 centimes each, into the hands of such person or persons as shall be authorized by the Government of the United States to receive it," the first installment to be paid "at the expiration of one year next following the exchange of the ratifications of this convention and the others at successive intervals of a year, one after another, till the whole shall be paid. To the amount of each of the said installments shall be added interest at 4 per cent thereupon, as upon the other installments then remaining unpaid, the said interest to be computed from the day of the exchange of the present convention."

It was also stipulated on the part of the United States, for the purpose of being completely liberated from all the reclamations presented by

France on behalf of its citizens, that the sum of 1,500,000 francs should be paid to the Government of France in six annual installments, to be deducted out of the annual sums which France had agreed to pay, interest thereupon being in like manner computed from the day of the exchange of the ratifications. In addition to this stipulation, important advantages were secured to France by the following article, viz:

The wines of France, from and after the exchange of the ratifications of the present convention, shall be admitted to consumption in the States of the Union at duties which shall not exceed the following rates by the gallon (such as it is used at present for wines in the United States), to wit: 6 cents for red wines in casks; 10 cents for white wines in casks, and 22 cents for wines of all sorts in bottles. The proportions existing between the duties on French wines thus reduced and the general rates of the tariff which went into operation the 1st January, 1829, shall be maintained in case the Government of the United States should think proper to diminish those general rates in a new tariff.

In consideration of this stipulation, which shall be binding on the United States for ten years, the French Government abandons the reclamations which it had formed in relation to the eighth article of the treaty of cession of Louisiana. It engages, moreover, to establish on the *long-staple* cottons of the United States which after the exchange of the ratifications of the present convention shall be brought directly thence to France by the vessels of the United States or by French vessels the same duties as on *short-staple* cottons.

This treaty was duly ratified in the manner prescribed by the constitutions of both countries, and the ratification was exchanged at the city of Washington on the 2d of February, 1832. On account of its commercial stipulations it was in five days thereafter laid before the Congress of the United States, which proceeded to enact such laws favorable to the commerce of France as were necessary to carry it into full execution, and France has from that period to the present been in the unrestricted enjoyment of the valuable privileges that were thus secured to her. The faith of the French nation having been thus solemnly pledged through its constitutional organ for the liquidation and ultimate payment of the long-deferred claims of our citizens, as also for the adjustment of other points of great and reciprocal benefits to both countries, and the United States having, with a fidelity and promptitude by which their conduct will, I trust, be always characterized, done everything that was necessary to carry the treaty into full and fair effect on their part, counted with the most perfect confidence on equal fidelity and promptitude on the part of the French Government. In this reasonable expectation we have been, I regret to inform you, wholly disappointed. No legislative provision has been made by France for the execution of the treaty, either as it respects the indemnity to be paid or the commercial benefits to be secured to the United States, and the relations between the United States and that power in consequence thereof are placed in a situation threatening to interrupt the good understanding which has so long and so happily existed between the two nations.

Not only has the French Government been thus wanting in the performance of the stipulations it has so solemnly entered into with the United States, but its omissions have been marked by circumstances which would seem to leave us without satisfactory evidences that such performance will certainly take place at a future period. Advice of the exchange of ratifications reached Paris prior to the 8th April, 1832. The French Chambers were then sitting, and continued in session until the 21st of that month, and although one installment of the indemnity was payable on the 2d of February, 1833, one year after the exchange of ratifications, no application was made to the Chambers for the required appropriation, and in consequence of no appropriation having then been made the draft of the United States Government for that installment was dishonored by the minister of finance, and the United States thereby involved in much controversy. The next session of the Chambers commenced on the 19th November, 1832, and continued until the 25th April, 1833. Notwithstanding the omission to pay the first installment had been made the subject of earnest remonstrance on our part, the treaty with the United States and a bill making the necessary appropriations to execute it were not laid before the Chamber of Deputies until the 6th of April, nearly five months after its meeting, and only nineteen days before the close of the session. The bill was read and referred to a committee, but there was no further action upon it. The next session of the Chambers commenced on the 26th of April, 1833, and continued until the 26th of June following. A new bill was introduced on the 11th of June, but nothing important was done in relation to it during the session. In the month of April, 1834, nearly three years after the signature of the treaty, the final action of the French Chambers upon the bill to carry the treaty into effect was obtained, and resulted in a refusal of the necessary appropriations. The avowed grounds upon which the bill was rejected are to be found in the published debates of that body, and no observations of mine can be necessary to satisfy Congress of their utter insufficiency. Although the gross amount of the claims of our citizens is probably greater than will be ultimately allowed by the commissioners, sufficient is, nevertheless, shown to render it absolutely certain that the indemnity falls far short of the actual amount of our just claims, independently of the question of damages and interest for the detention. That the settlement involved a sacrifice in this respect was well known at the time—a sacrifice which was cheerfully acquiesced in by the different branches of the Federal Government, whose action upon the treaty was required from a sincere desire to avoid further collision upon this old and disturbing subject and in the confident expectation that the general relations between the two countries would be improved thereby.

The refusal to vote the appropriation, the news of which was received from our minister in Paris about the 15th day of May last, might have been considered the final determination of the French Government not to execute the stipulations of the treaty, and would have justified an immediate communication of the facts to Congress, with a recommendation of such ultimate measures as the interest and honor of the United States might seem to require. But with the news of the refusal of the Chambers to make the appropriation were conveyed the regrets of the King and a declaration that a national vessel should be forthwith sent out with instructions to the French minister to give the most ample explanations of the past and the strongest assurances for the future. After a long passage the promised dispatch vessel arrived. The pledges given by the French minister upon receipt of his instructions were that as soon after the election of the new members as the charter would permit the legislative Chambers of France should be called together and the proposition for an appropriation laid before them; that all the constitutional powers of the King and his cabinet should be exerted to accomplish the object, and that the result should be made known early enough to be communicated to Congress at the commencement of the present session. Relying upon these pledges, and not doubting that the acknowledged justice of our claims, the promised exertions of the King and his cabinet, and, above all, that sacred regard for the national faith and honor for which the French character has been so distinguished would secure an early execution of the treaty in all its parts, I did not deem it necessary to call the attention of Congress to the subject at the last session.

I regret to say that the pledges made through the minister of France have not been redeemed. The new Chambers met on the 31st July last, and although the subject of fulfilling treaties was alluded to in the speech from the throne, no attempt was made by the King or his cabinet to procure an appropriation to carry it into execution. The reasons given for this omission, although they might be considered sufficient in an ordinary case, are not consistent with the expectations founded upon the assurances given here, for there is no constitutional obstacle to entering into legislative business at the first meeting of the Chambers. This point, however, might have been overlooked had not the Chambers, instead of being called to meet at so early a day that the result of their deliberations might be communicated to me before the meeting of Congress, been prorogued to the 29th of the present month—a period so late that their decision can scarcely be made known to the present Congress prior to its dissolution. To avoid this delay our minister in Paris, in virtue of the assurance given by the French minister in the United States, strongly urged the convocation of the Chambers at an earlier day, but without success. It is proper to remark, however, that this refusal has been accompanied with the most positive assurances on the part of the executive government of France of their intention to press the appropriation at the ensuing session of the Chambers.

The executive branch of this Government has, as matters stand, exhausted all the authority upon the subject with which it is invested and which it had any reason to believe could be beneficially employed.

The idea of acquiescing in the refusal to execute the treaty will not, I am confident, be for a moment entertained by any branch of this Government, and further negotiation upon the subject is equally out of the question.

If it shall be the pleasure of Congress to await the further action of the French Chambers, no further consideration of the subject will at this session probably be required at your hands. But if from the original delay in asking for an appropriation, from the refusal of the Chambers to grant it when asked, from the omission to bring the subject before the Chambers at their last session, from the fact that, including that session, there have been five different occasions when the appropriation might have been made, and from the delay in convoking the Chambers until some weeks after the meeting of Congress, when it was well known that a communication of the whole subject to Congress at the last session was prevented by assurances that it should be disposed of before its present meeting, you should feel yourselves constrained to doubt whether it be the intention of the French Government, in all its branches, to carry the treaty into effect, and think that such measures as the occasion may be deemed to call for should be now adopted, the important question arises what those measures shall be.

Our institutions are essentially pacific. Peace and friendly intercourse with all nations are as much the desire of our Government as they are the interest of our people. But these objects are not to be permanently secured by surrendering the rights of our citizens or permitting solemn treaties for their indemnity, in cases of flagrant wrong, to be abrogated or set aside.

It is undoubtedly in the power of Congress seriously to affect the agricultural and manufacturing interests of France by the passage of laws relating to her trade with the United States. Her products, manufactures, and tonnage may be subjected to heavy duties in our ports, or all commercial intercourse with her may be suspended. But there are powerful and to my mind conclusive objections to this mode of proceeding. We can not embarrass or cut off the trade of France without at the same time in some degree embarrassing or cutting off our own trade. The injury of such a warfare must fall, though unequally, upon our own citizens, and could not but impair the means of the Government and weaken that united sentiment in support of the rights and honor of the nation which must now pervade every bosom. Nor is it impossible that such a course of legislation would introduce once more into our national councils those disturbing questions in relation to the tariff of duties which have been so recently put to rest. Besides, by every measure adopted by the Government of the United States with the view of injuring France the clear perception of right which will induce our own people and the rulers and people of all other nations, even of France herself, to pronounce our quarrel just will be obscured and the support rendered to us in a final resort to more decisive measures will be more limited and equivocal.   There is but one point in the controversy, and upon that the whole civilized world must pronounce France to be in the wrong.   We insist that she shall pay us a sum of money which she has acknowledged to be due, and of the justice of this demand there can be but one opinion among mankind.   True policy would seem to dictate that the question at issue should be kept thus disencumbered and that not the slightest pretense should be given to France to persist in her refusal to make payment by any act on our part affecting the interests of her people.   The question should be left, as it is now, in such an attitude that when France fulfills her treaty stipulations all controversy will be at an end.

It is my conviction that the United States ought to insist on a prompt execution of the treaty, and in case it be refused or longer delayed take redress into their own hands.   After the delay on the part of France of a quarter of a century in acknowledging these claims by treaty, it is not to be tolerated that another quarter of a century is to be wasted in negotiating about the payment.   The laws of nations provide a remedy for such occasions.   It is a well-settled principle of the international code that where one nation owes another a liquidated debt which it refuses or neglects to pay the aggrieved party may seize on the property belonging to the other, its citizens or subjects, sufficient to pay the debt without giving just cause of war.   This remedy has been repeatedly resorted to, and recently by France herself toward Portugal, under circumstances less unquestionable.

The time at which resort should be had to this or any other mode of redress is a point to be decided by Congress.   If an appropriation shall not be made by the French Chambers at their next session, it may justly be concluded that the Government of France has finally determined to disregard its own solemn undertaking and refuse to pay an acknowledged debt.   In that event every day's delay on our part will be a stain upon our national honor, as well as a denial of justice to our injured citizens. Prompt measures, when the refusal of France shall be complete, will not only be most honorable and just, but will have the best effect upon our national character.

Since France, in violation of the pledges given through her minister here, has delayed her final action so long that her decision will not probably be known in time to be communicated to this Congress, I recommend that a law be passed authorizing reprisals upon French property in case provision shall not be made for the payment of the debt at the approaching session of the French Chambers.   Such a measure ought not to be considered by France as a menace.   Her pride and power are too well known to expect anything from her fears and preclude the necessity of a declaration that nothing partaking of the character of intimidation is intended by us. She ought to look upon it as the evidence only of an inflexible determination on the part of the United States to insist on their rights. That Government, by doing only what it has itself acknowledged to be just, will be able to spare the United States the necessity of taking redress into their own hands and save the property of French citizens from that seizure and sequestration which American citizens so long endured without retaliation or redress. If she should continue to refuse that act of acknowledged justice and, in violation of the law of nations, make reprisals on our part the occasion of hostilities against the United States, she would but add violence to injustice, and could not fail to expose herself to the just censure of civilized nations and to the retributive judgments of Heaven.

Collision with France is the more to be regretted on account of the position she occupies in Europe in relation to liberal institutions, but in maintaining our national rights and honor all governments are alike to us. If by a collision with France in a case where she is clearly in the wrong the march of liberal principles shall be impeded, the responsibility for that result as well as every other will rest on her own head.

Having submitted these considerations, it belongs to Congress to decide whether after what has taken place it will still await the further action of the French Chambers or now adopt such provisional measures as it may deem necessary and best adapted to protect the rights and maintain the honor of the country. Whatever that decision may be, it will be faithfully enforced by the Executive as far as he is authorized so to do.

According to the estimate of the Treasury Department, the revenue accruing from all sources during the present year will amount to $20,624,717, which, with the balance remaining in the Treasury on the 1st of January last of $11,702,905, produces an aggregate of $32,327,623. The total expenditure during the year for all objects, including the public debt, is estimated at $25,591,390, which will leave a balance in the Treasury on the 1st of January, 1835, of $6,736,232. In this balance, however, will be included about $1,150,000 of what was heretofore reported by the Department as not effective.

Of former appropriations it is estimated that there will remain unexpended at the close of the year $8,002,925, and that of this sum there will not be required more than $5,141,964 to accomplish the objects of all the current appropriations. Thus it appears that after satisfying all those appropriations and after discharging the last item of our public debt, which will be done on the 1st of January next, there will remain unexpended in the Treasury an effective balance of about $440,000. That such should be the aspect of our finances is highly flattering to the industry and enterprise of our population and auspicious of the wealth and prosperity which await the future cultivation of their growing resources. It is not deemed prudent, however, to recommend any change for the present in our impost rates, the effect of the gradual reduction now in progress in many of them not being sufficiently tested to guide us in determining the precise amount of revenue which they will produce.

Free from public debt, at peace with all the world, and with no complicated interests to consult in our intercourse with foreign powers, the present may be hailed as the epoch in our history the most favorable for the settlement of those principles in our domestic policy which shall be best calculated to give stability to our Republic and secure the blessings of freedom to our citizens.

Among these principles, from our past experience, it can not be doubted that simplicity in the character of the Federal Government and a rigid economy in its administration should be regarded as fundamental and sacred. All must be sensible that the existence of the public debt, by rendering taxation necessary for its extinguishment, has increased the difficulties which are inseparable from every exercise of the taxing power, and that it was in this respect a remote agent in producing those disturbing questions which grew out of the discussions relating to the tariff. If such has been the tendency of a debt incurred in the acquisition and maintenance of our national rights and liberties, the obligations of which all portions of the Union cheerfully acknowledged, it must be obvious that whatever is calculated to increase the burdens of Government without necessity must be fatal to all our hopes of preserving its true character. While we are felicitating ourselves, therefore, upon the extinguishment of the national debt and the prosperous state of our finances, let us not be tempted to depart from those sound maxims of public policy which enjoin a just adaptation of the revenue to the expenditures that are consistent with a rigid economy and an entire abstinence from all topics of legislation that are not clearly within the constitutional powers of the Government and suggested by the wants of the country. Properly regarded under such a policy, every diminution of the public burdens arising from taxation gives to individual enterprise increased power and furnishes to all the members of our happy Confederacy new motives for patriotic affection and support. But above all, its most important effect will be found in its influence upon the character of the Government by confining its action to those objects which will be sure to secure to it the attachment and support of our fellow-citizens.

Circumstances make it my duty to call the attention of Congress to the Bank of the United States. Created for the convenience of the Government, that institution has become the scourge of the people. Its interference to postpone the payment of a portion of the national debt that it might retain the public money appropriated for that purpose to strengthen it in a political contest, the extraordinary extension and contraction of its accommodations to the community, its corrupt and partisan loans, its exclusion of the public directors from a knowledge of its most important proceedings, the unlimited authority conferred on the president to expend its funds in hiring writers and procuring the execution of printing, and the use made of that authority, the retention of the pension money and books after the selection of new agents, the groundless claim to heavy damages in consequence of the protest of the bill drawn on the French Government, have through various channels been laid before Congress. Immediately after the close of the last session the bank, through its president, announced its ability and readiness to abandon the system of unparalleled curtailment and the interruption of domestic exchanges which it had practiced upon from the 1st of August, 1833, to the 30th of June, 1834, and to extend its accommodations to the community. The grounds assumed in this annunciation amounted to an acknowledgment that the curtailment, in the extent to which it had been carried, was not necessary to the safety of the bank, and had been persisted in merely to induce Congress to grant the prayer of the bank in its memorial relative to the removal of the deposits and to give it a new charter. They were substantially a confession that all the real distresses which individuals and the country had endured for the preceding six or eight months had been needlessly produced by it, with the view of affecting through the sufferings of the people the legislative action of Congress. It is a subject of congratulation that Congress and the country had the virtue and firmness to bear the infliction, that the energies of our people soon found relief from this wanton tyranny in vast importations of the precious metals from almost every part of the world, and that at the close of this tremendous effort to control our Government the bank found itself powerless and no longer able to loan out its surplus means. The community had learned to manage its affairs without its assistance, and trade had already found new auxiliaries, so that on the 1st of October last the extraordinary spectacle was presented of a national bank more than one-half of whose capital was either lying unproductive in its vaults or in the hands of foreign bankers.

To the needless distresses brought on the country during the last session of Congress has since been added the open seizure of the dividends on the public stock to the amount of $170,041, under pretense of paying damages, cost, and interest upon the protested French bill. This sum constituted a portion of the estimated revenues for the year 1834, upon which the appropriations made by Congress were based. It would as soon have been expected that our collectors would seize on the customs or the receivers of our land offices on the moneys arising from the sale of public lands under pretenses of claims against the United States as that the bank would have retained the dividends. Indeed, if the principle be established that anyone who chooses to set up a claim against the United States may without authority of law seize on the public property or money wherever he can find it to pay such claim, there will remain no assurance that our revenue will reach the Treasury or that it will be applied after the appropriation to the purposes designated in the law. The paymasters of our Army and the pursers of our Navy may under like pretenses apply to their own use moneys appropriated to set in motion the public force, and in time of war leave the country without defense. This measure resorted to by the bank is disorganizing and revolutionary, and if generally resorted to by private citizens in like cases would fill the land with anarchy and violence.

It is a constitutional provision "that no money shall be drawn from the Treasury but in consequence of appropriations made by law." The palpable object of this provision is to prevent the expenditure of the public money for any purpose whatsoever which shall not have been first approved by the representatives of the people and the States in Congress assembled. It vests the power of declaring for what purposes the public money shall be expended in the legislative department of the Government, to the exclusion of the executive and judicial, and it is not within the constitutional authority of either of those departments to pay it away without law or to sanction its payment. According to this plain constitutional provision, the claim of the bank can never be paid without an appropriation by act of Congress. But the bank has never asked for an appropriation. It attempts to defeat the provision of the Constitution and obtain payment without an act of Congress. Instead of awaiting an appropriation passed by both Houses and approved by the President, it makes an appropriation for itself and invites an appeal to the judiciary to sanction it. That the money had not technically been paid into the Treasury does not affect the principle intended to be established by the Constitution. The Executive and the judiciary have as little right to appropriate and expend the public money without authority of law before it is placed to the credit of the Treasury as to take it from the Treasury. In the annual report of the Secretary of the Treasury, and in his correspondence with the president of the bank, and the opinions of the Attorney-General accompanying it, you will find a further examination of the claims of the bank and the course it has pursued.

It seems due to the safety of the public funds remaining in that bank and to the honor of the American people that measures be taken to separate the Government entirely from an institution so mischievous to the public prosperity and so regardless of the Constitution and laws. By transferring the public deposits, by appointing other pension agents as far as it had the power, by ordering the discontinuance of the receipt of bank checks in the payment of the public dues after the 1st day of January, the Executive has exerted all its lawful authority to sever the connection between the Government and this faithless corporation.

The high-handed career of this institution imposes upon the constitutional functionaries of this Government duties of the gravest and most imperative character—duties which they can not avoid and from which I trust there will be no inclination on the part of any of them to shrink. My own sense of them is most clear, as is also my readiness to discharge those which may rightfully fall on me. To continue any business relations with the Bank of the United States that may be avoided without a violation of the national faith after that institution has set at open defiance the conceded right of the Government to examine its affairs, after it has done all in its power to deride the public authority in other respects and to bring it into disrepute at home and abroad, after it has attempted to defeat the clearly expressed will of the people by turning against them the immense power intrusted to its hands and by involving a country otherwise peaceful, flourishing, and happy, in dissension, embarrassment, and distress, would make the nation itself a party to the degradation so sedulously prepared for its public agents and do much to destroy the confidence of mankind in popular governments and to bring into contempt their authority and efficiency. In guarding against an evil of such magnitude considerations of temporary convenience should be thrown out of the question, and we should be influenced by such motives only as look to the honor and preservation of the republican system. Deeply and solemnly impressed with the justice of these views, I feel it to be my duty to recommend to you that a law be passed authorizing the sale of the public stock; that the provision of the charter requiring the receipt of notes of the bank in payment of public dues shall, in accordance with the power reserved to Congress in the fourteenth section of the charter, be suspended until the bank pays to the Treasury the dividends withheld, and that all laws connecting the Government or its officers with the bank, directly or indirectly, be repealed, and that the institution be left hereafter to its own resources and means.

Events have satisfied my mind, and I think the minds of the American people, that the mischiefs and dangers which flow from a national bank far overbalance all its advantages. The bold effort the present bank has made to control the Government, the distresses it has wantonly produced, the violence of which it has been the occasion in one of our cities famed for its observance of law and order, are but premonitions of the fate which awaits the American people should they be deluded into a perpetuation of this institution or the establishment of another like it. It is fervently hoped that thus admonished those who have heretofore favored the establishment of a substitute for the present bank will be induced to abandon it, as it is evidently better to incur any inconvenience that may be reasonably expected than to concentrate the whole moneyed power of the Republic in any form whatsoever or under any restrictions.

Happily it is already illustrated that the agency of such an institution is not necessary to the fiscal operations of the Government. The State banks are found fully adequate to the performance of all services which were required of the Bank of the United States, quite as promptly and with the same cheapness. They have maintained themselves and discharged all these duties while the Bank of the United States was still powerful and in the field as an open enemy, and it is not possible to conceive that they will find greater difficulties in their operations when that enemy shall cease to exist.

The attention of Congress is earnestly invited to the regulation of the deposits in the State banks by law. Although the power now exercised by the executive department in this behalf is only such as was uniformly exerted through every Administration from the origin of the Government up to the establishment of the present bank, yet it is one which is susceptible of regulation by law, and therefore ought so to be regulated. The power of Congress to direct in what places the Treasurer shall keep the moneys in the Treasury and to impose restrictions upon the Executive authority in relation to their custody and removal is unlimited, and its exercise will rather be courted than discouraged by those public officers and agents on whom rests the responsibility for their safety. It is desirable that as little power as possible should be left to the President or the Secretary of the Treasury over those institutions, which, being thus freed from Executive influence, and without a common head to direct their operations, would have neither the temptation nor the ability to interfere in the political conflicts of the country. Not deriving their charters from the national authorities, they would never have those inducements to meddle in general elections which have led the Bank of the United States to agitate and convulse the country for upward of two years.

The progress of our gold coinage is creditable to the officers of the Mint, and promises in a short period to furnish the country with a sound and portable currency, which will much diminish the inconvenience to travelers of the want of a general paper currency should the State banks be incapable of furnishing it. Those institutions have already shown themselves competent to purchase and furnish domestic exchange for the convenience of trade at reasonable rates, and not a doubt is entertained that in a short period all the wants of the country in bank accommodations and exchange will be supplied as promptly and as cheaply as they have heretofore been by the Bank of the United States. If the several States shall be induced gradually to reform their banking systems and prohibit the issue of all small notes, we shall in a few years have a currency as sound and as little liable to fluctuations as any other commercial country.

The report of the Secretary of War, together with the accompanying documents from the several bureaus of that Department, will exhibit the situation of the various objects committed to its administration.

No event has occurred since your last session rendering necessary any movements of the Army, with the exception of the expedition of the regiment of dragoons into the territory of the wandering and predatory tribes inhabiting the western frontier and living adjacent to the Mexican boundary. These tribes have been heretofore known to us principally by their attacks upon our own citizens and upon other Indians entitled to the protection of the United States. It became necessary for the peace of the frontiers to check these habitual inroads, and I am happy to inform you that the object has been effected without the commission of any act of hostility. Colonel Dodge and the troops under his command have acted with equal firmness and humanity, and an arrangement has been made with those Indians which it is hoped will assure their permanent pacific relations with the United States and the other tribes of Indians upon that border. It is to be regretted that the prevalence of sickness in that quarter has deprived the country of a number of valuable lives, and particularly that General Leavenworth, an officer well known, and esteemed for his gallant services in the late war and for his subsequent good conduct, has fallen a victim to his zeal and exertions in the discharge of his duty.

The Army is in a high state of discipline. Its moral condition, so far as that is known here, is good, and the various branches of the public service are carefully attended to. It is amply sufficient under its present organization for providing the necessary garrisons for the seaboard and for the defense of the internal frontier, and also for preserving the elements of military knowledge and for keeping pace with those improvements which modern experience is continually making. And these objects appear to me to embrace all the legitimate purposes for which a permanent military force should be maintained in our country. The lessons of history teach us its danger and the tendency which exists to an increase. This can be best met and averted by a just caution on the part of the public itself, and of those who represent them in Congress.

From the duties which devolve on the Engineer Department and upon the topographical engineers, a different organization seems to be demanded by the public interest, and I recommend the subject to your consideration.

No important change has during this season taken place in the condition of the Indians. Arrangements are in progress for the removal of the Creeks, and will soon be for the removal of the Seminoles. I regret that the Cherokees east of the Mississippi have not yet determined as a community to remove. How long the personal causes which have heretofore retarded that ultimately inevitable measure will continue to operate I am unable to conjecture. It is certain, however, that delay will bring with it accumulated evils which will render their condition more and more unpleasant. The experience of every year adds to the conviction that emigration, and that alone, can preserve from destruction the remnant of the tribes yet living amongst us. The facility with which the necessaries of life are procured and the treaty stipulations providing aid for the emigrant Indians in their agricultural pursuits and in the important concern of education, and their removal from those causes which have heretofore depressed all and destroyed many of the tribes, can not fail to stimulate their exertions and to reward their industry.

The two laws passed at the last session of Congress on the subject of Indian affairs have been carried into effect, and detailed instructions for their administration have been given. It will be seen by the estimates for the present session that a great reduction will take place in the expenditures of the Department in consequence of these laws, and there is reason to believe that their operation will be salutary and that the colonization of the Indians on the western frontier, together with a judicious system of administration, will still further reduce the expenses of this branch of the public service and at the same time promote its usefulness and efficiency.

Circumstances have been recently developed showing the existence of extensive frauds under the various laws granting pensions and gratuities for Revolutionary services. It is impossible to estimate the amount which may have been thus fraudulently obtained from the National Treasury. I am satisfied, however, it has been such as to justify a reexamination of the system and the adoption of the necessary checks in its administration. All will agree that the services and sufferings of the remnant of our Revolutionary band should be fully compensated; but while this is done, every proper precaution should be taken to prevent the admission of fabricated and fraudulent claims. In the present mode of proceeding the attestations and certificates of the judicial officers of the various States form a considerable portion of the checks which are interposed against the commission of frauds. These, however, have been and may be fabricated, and in such a way as to elude detection at the examining offices. And independently of this practical difficulty, it is ascertained that these documents are often loosely granted; sometimes even blank certificates have been issued; sometimes prepared papers have been signed without inquiry, and in one instance, at least, the seal of the court has been within reach of a person most interested in its improper application. It is obvious that under such circumstances no severity of administration can check the abuse of the law. And information has from time to time been communicated to the Pension Office questioning or denying the right of persons placed upon the pension list to the bounty of the country. Such cautions are always attended to and examined, but a far more general investigation is called for, and I therefore recommend, in conformity with the suggestion of the Secretary of War, that an actual inspection should be made in each State into the circumstances and claims of every person now drawing a pension. The honest veteran has nothing to fear from such a scrutiny, while the fraudulent claimant will be detected and the public Treasury relieved to an amount, I have reason to believe, far greater than has heretofore been suspected. The details of such a plan could be so regulated as to interpose the necessary checks without any burdensome operation upon the pensioners. The object should be twofold:

1. To look into the original justice of the claims, so far as this can be done under a proper system of regulations, by an examination of the

claimants themselves and by inquiring in the vicinity of their residence into their history and into the opinion entertained of their Revolutionary services.

2. To ascertain in all cases whether the original claimant is living, and this by actual personal inspection.

This measure will, if adopted, be productive, I think, of the desired results, and I therefore recommend it to your consideration, with the further suggestion that all payments should be suspended till the necessary reports are received.

It will be seen by a tabular statement annexed to the documents transmitted to Congress that the appropriations for objects connected with the War Department, made at the last session, for the service of the year 1834, excluding the permanent appropriation for the payment of military gratuities under the act of June 7, 1832, the appropriation of $200,000 for arming and equipping the militia, and the appropriation of $10,000 for the civilization of the Indians, which are not annually renewed, amounted to the sum of $9,003,261, and that the estimates of appropriations necessary for the same branches of service for the year 1835 amount to the sum of $5,778,964, making a difference in the appropriations of the current year over the estimates of the appropriations for the next of $3,224,297.

The principal causes which have operated at this time to produce this great difference are shown in the reports and documents and in the detailed estimates. Some of these causes are accidental and temporary, while others are permanent, and, aided by a just course of administration, may continue to operate beneficially upon the public expenditures.

A just economy, expending where the public service requires and withholding where it does not, is among the indispensable duties of the Government.

I refer you to the accompanying report of the Secretary of the Navy and to the documents with it for a full view of the operations of that important branch of our service during the present year. It will be seen that the wisdom and liberality with which Congress has provided for the gradual increase of our navy material have been seconded by a corresponding zeal and fidelity on the part of those to whom has been confided the execution of the laws on the subject, and that but a short period would be now required to put in commission a force large enough for any exigency into which the country may be thrown.

When we reflect upon our position in relation to other nations, it must be apparent that in the event of conflicts with them we must look chiefly to our Navy for the protection of our national rights. The wide seas which separate us from other Governments must of necessity be the theater on which an enemy will aim to assail us, and unless we are prepared to meet him on this element we can not be said to possess the power requisite to repel or prevent aggressions. We can not, therefore, watch with too much attention this arm of our defense, or cherish with too much care the means by which it can possess the necessary efficiency and extension. To this end our policy has been heretofore wisely directed to the constant employment of a force sufficient to guard our commerce, and to the rapid accumulation of the materials which are necessary to repair our vessels and construct with ease such new ones as may be required in a state of war.

In accordance with this policy, I recommend to your consideration the erection of the additional dry dock described by the Secretary of the Navy, and also the construction of the steam batteries to which he has referred, for the purpose of testing their efficacy as auxiliaries to the system of defense now in use.

The report of the Postmaster-General herewith submitted exhibits the condition and prospects of that Department. From that document it appears that there was a deficit in the funds of the Department at the commencement of the present year beyond its available means of $315,599.98, which on the 1st July last had been reduced to $268,092.74. It appears also that the revenues for the coming year will exceed the expenditures about $270,000, which, with the excess of revenue which will result from the operations of the current half year, may be expected, independently of any increase in the gross amount of postages, to supply the entire deficit before the end of 1835. But as this calculation is based on the gross amount of postages which had accrued within the period embraced by the times of striking the balances, it is obvious that without a progressive increase in the amount of postages the existing retrenchments must be persevered in through the year 1836 that the Department may accumulate a surplus fund sufficient to place it in a condition of perfect ease.

It will be observed that the revenues of the Post-Office Department, though they have increased, and their amount is above that of any former year, have yet fallen short of the estimates more than $100,000. This is attributed in a great degree to the increase of free letters growing out of the extension and abuse of the franking privilege. There has been a gradual increase in the number of executive offices to which it has been granted, and by an act passed in March, 1833, it was extended to members of Congress throughout the whole year. It is believed that a revision of the laws relative to the franking privilege, with some enactments to enforce more rigidly the restrictions under which it is granted, would operate beneficially to the country, by enabling the Department at an earlier period to restore the mail facilities that have been withdrawn, and to extend them more widely, as the growing settlements of the country may require.

To a measure so important to the Government and so just to our constituents, who ask no exclusive privileges for themselves and are not willing to concede them to others, I earnestly recommend the serious attention of Congress.

The importance of the Post-Office Department and the magnitude to which it has grown, both in its revenues and in its operations, seem to demand its reorganization by law. The whole of its receipts and disbursements have hitherto been left entirely to Executive control and individual discretion. The principle is as sound in relation to this as to any other Department of the Government, that as little discretion should be confided to the executive officer who controls it as is compatible with its efficiency. It is therefore earnestly recommended that it be organized with an auditor and treasurer of its own, appointed by the President and Senate, who shall be branches of the Treasury Department.

Your attention is again respectfully invited to the defect which exists in the judicial system of the United States. Nothing can be more desirable than the uniform operation of the Federal judiciary throughout the several States, all of which, standing on the same footing as members of the Union, have equal rights to the advantages and benefits resulting from its laws. This object is not attained by the judicial acts now in force, because they leave one-fourth of the States without circuit courts.

It is undoubtedly the duty of Congress to place all the States on the same footing in this respect, either by the creation of an additional number of associate judges or by an enlargement of the circuits assigned to those already appointed so as to include the new States. Whatever may be the difficulty in a proper organization of the judicial system so as to secure its efficiency and uniformity in all parts of the Union and at the same time to avoid such an increase of judges as would encumber the supreme appellate tribunal, it should not be allowed to weigh against the great injustice which the present operation of the system produces.

I trust that I may be also pardoned for renewing the recommendation I have so often submitted to your attention in regard to the mode of electing the President and Vice-President of the United States. All the reflection I have been able to bestow upon the subject increases my conviction that the best interests of the country will be promoted by the adoption of some plan which will secure in all contingencies that important right of sovereignty to the direct control of the people. Could this be attained, and the terms of those officers be limited to a single period of either four or six years, I think our liberties would possess an additional safeguard.

At your last session I called the attention of Congress to the destruction of the public building occupied by the Treasury Department. As the public interest requires that another building should be erected with as little delay as possible, it is hoped that the means will be seasonably provided and that they will be ample enough to authorize such an enlargement and improvement in the plan of the building as will more effectually accommodate the public officers and secure the public documents deposited in it from the casualties of fire.

I have not been able to satisfy myself that the bill entitled ''An act to improve the navigation of the Wabash River,'' which was sent to me at the close of your last session, ought to pass, and I have therefore withheld from it my approval and now return it to the Senate, the body in which it originated.

There can be no question connected with the administration of public affairs more important or more difficult to be satisfactorily dealt with than that which relates to the rightful authority and proper action of the Federal Government upon the subject of internal improvements. To inherent embarrassments have been added others resulting from the course of our legislation concerning it.

I have heretofore communicated freely with Congress upon this subject, and in adverting to it again I can not refrain from expressing my increased conviction of its extreme importance as well in regard to its bearing upon the maintenance of the Constitution and the prudent management of the public revenue as on account of its disturbing effect upon the harmony of the Union.

We are in no danger from violations of the Constitution by which encroachments are made upon the personal rights of the citizen. The sentence of condemnation long since pronounced by the American people upon acts of that character will, I doubt not, continue to prove as salutary in its effects as it is irreversible in its nature. But against the dangers of unconstitutional acts which, instead of menacing the vengeance of offended authority, proffer local advantages and bring in their train the patronage of the Government, we are, I fear, not so safe. To suppose that because our Government has been instituted for the benefit of the people it must therefore have the power to do whatever may seem to conduce to the public good is an error into which even honest minds are too apt to fall. In yielding themselves to this fallacy they overlook the great considerations in which the Federal Constitution was founded. They forget that in consequence of the conceded diversities in the interest and condition of the different States it was foreseen at the period of its adoption that although a particular measure of the Government might be beneficial and proper in one State it might be the reverse in another; that it was for this reason the States would not consent to make a grant to the Federal Government of the general and usual powers of government, but of such only as were specifically enumerated, and the probable effects of which they could, as they thought, safely anticipate; and they forget also the paramount obligation upon all to abide by the compact then so solemnly and, as it was hoped, so firmly established. In addition to the dangers to the Constitution springing from the sources I have stated, there has been one which was perhaps greater than all. I allude to the materials which this subject has afforded for sinister appeals to selfish feelings, and the opinion heretofore so extensively entertained of its adaptation to the purposes of personal ambition. With such stimulants it is not surprising that the acts and pretensions of the Federal Government in this behalf should sometimes have been carried to an alarming extent. The questions which have arisen upon this subject have related—

First. To the power of making internal improvements within the limits of a State, with the right of territorial jurisdiction, sufficient at least for their preservation and use.

Second. To the right of appropriating money in aid of such works when carried on by a State or by a company in virtue of State authority, surrendering the claim of jurisdiction; and

Third. To the propriety of appropriation for improvements of a particular class, viz, for light-houses, beacons, buoys, public piers, and for the removal of sand bars, sawyers, and other temporary and partial impediments in our navigable rivers and harbors.

The claims of power for the General Government upon each of these points certainly present matter of the deepest interest. The first is, however, of much the greatest importance, inasmuch as, in addition to the dangers of unequal and improvident expenditures of public moneys common to all, there is superadded to that the conflicting jurisdictions of the respective governments. Federal jurisdiction, at least to the extent I have stated, has been justly regarded by its advocates as necessarily appurtenant to the power in question, if that exists by the Constitution. That the most injurious conflicts would unavoidably arise between the respective jurisdictions of the State and Federal Governments in the absence of a constitutional provision marking out their respective boundaries can not be doubted. The local advantages to be obtained would induce the States to overlook in the beginning the dangers and difficulties to which they might ultimately be exposed. The powers exercised by the Federal Government would soon be regarded with jealousy by the State authorities, and originating as they must from implication or assumption, it would be impossible to affix to them certain and safe limits. Opportunities and temptations to the assumption of power incompatible with State sovereignty would be increased and those barriers which resist the tendency of our system toward consolidation greatly weakened. The officers and agents of the General Government might not always have the discretion to abstain from intermeddling with State concerns, and if they did they would not always escape the suspicion of having done so. Collisions and consequent irritations would spring up; that harmony which should ever exist between the General Government and each member of the Confederacy would be frequently interrupted; a spirit of contention would be engendered and the dangers of disunion greatly multiplied.

Yet we all know that notwithstanding these grave objections this dangerous doctrine was at one time apparently proceeding to its final establishment with fearful rapidity. The desire to embark the Federal

Government in works of internal improvement prevailed in the highest degree during the first session of the first Congress that I had the honor to meet in my present situation. When the bill authorizing a subscription on the part of the United States for stock in the Maysville and Lexington Turnpike Company passed the two Houses, there had been reported by the Committees of Internal Improvements bills containing appropriations for such objects, inclusive of those for the Cumberland road and for harbors and light-houses, to the amount of $106,000,000. In this amount was included authority to the Secretary of the Treasury to subscribe for the stock of different companies to a great extent, and the residue was principally for the direct construction of roads by this Government. In addition to these projects, which had been presented to the two Houses under the sanction and recommendation of their respective Committees on Internal Improvements, there were then still pending before the committees, and in memorials to Congress presented but not referred, different projects for works of a similar character, the expense of which can not be estimated with certainty, but must have exceeded $100,000,000.

Regarding the bill authorizing a subscription to the stock of the Maysville and Lexington Turnpike Company as the entering wedge of a system which, however weak at first, might soon become strong enough to rive the bands of the Union asunder, and believing that if its passage was acquiesced in by the Executive and the people there would no longer be any limitation upon the authority of the General Government in respect to the appropriation of money for such objects, I deemed it an imperative duty to withhold from it the Executive approval. Although from the obviously local character of that work I might well have contented myself with a refusal to approve the bill upon that ground, yet sensible of the vital importance of the subject, and anxious that my views and opinions in regard to the whole matter should be fully understood by Congress and by my constituents, I felt it my duty to go further. I therefore embraced that early occasion to apprise Congress that in my opinion the Constitution did not confer upon it the power to authorize the construction of ordinary roads and canals within the limits of a State and to say, respectfully, that no bill admitting such a power could receive my official sanction. I did so in the confident expectation that the speedy settlement of the public mind upon the whole subject would be greatly facilitated by the difference between the two Houses and myself, and that the harmonious action of the several departments of the Federal Government in regard to it would be ultimately secured.

So far, at least, as it regards this branch of the subject, my best hopes have been realized. Nearly four years have elapsed, and several sessions of Congress have intervened, and no attempt within my recollection has been made to induce Congress to exercise this power. The applications for the construction of roads and canals which were formerly multiplied upon your files are no longer presented, and we have good reason to infer that the current of public sentiment has become so decided against the pretension as effectually to discourage its reassertion. So thinking, I derive the greatest satisfaction from the conviction that thus much at least has been secured upon this important and embarrassing subject.

From attempts to appropriate the national funds to objects which are confessedly of a local character we can not, I trust, have anything further to apprehend. My views in regard to the expediency of making appropriations for works which are claimed to be of a national character and prosecuted under State authority—assuming that Congress have the right to do so—were stated in my annual message to Congress in 1830, and also in that containing my objections to the Maysville road bill.

So thoroughly convinced am I that no such appropriations ought to be made by Congress until a suitable constitutional provision is made upon the subject, and so essential do I regard the point to the highest interests of our country, that I could not consider myself as discharging my duty to my constituents in giving the Executive sanction to any bill containing such an appropriation. If the people of the United States desire that the public Treasury shall be resorted to for the means to prosecute such works, they will concur in an amendment of the Constitution prescribing a rule by which the national character of the works is to be tested, and by which the greatest practicable equality of benefits may be secured to each member of the Confederacy. The effects of such a regulation would be most salutary in preventing unprofitable expenditures, in securing our legislation from the pernicious consequences of a scramble for the favors of Government, and in repressing the spirit of discontent which must inevitably arise from an unequal distribution of treasures which belong alike to all.

There is another class of appropriations for what may be called, without impropriety, internal improvements, which have always been regarded as standing upon different grounds from those to which I have referred. I allude to such as have for their object the improvement of our harbors, the removal of partial and temporary obstructions in our navigable rivers, for the facility and security of our foreign commerce. The grounds upon which I distinguished appropriations of this character from others have already been stated to Congress. I will now only add that at the first session of Congress under the new Constitution it was provided by law that all expenses which should accrue from and after the 15th day of August, 1789, in the necessary support and maintenance and repairs of all light-houses, beacons, buoys, and public piers erected, placed, or sunk before the passage of the act within any bay, inlet, harbor, or port of the United States, for rendering the navigation thereof easy and safe, should be defrayed out of the Treasury of the United States, and, further, that it should be the duty of the Secretary of the Treasury to provide by contracts, with the approbation of the President, for rebuilding when necessary and keeping in good repair the light-houses, beacons, buoys, and public piers in the several States, and for furnishing them with supplies. Appropriations for similar objects have been continued from that time to the present without interruption or dispute. As a natural consequence of the increase and extension of our foreign commerce, ports of entry and delivery have been multiplied and established, not only upon our seaboard, but in the interior of the country upon our lakes and navigable rivers. The convenience and safety of this commerce have led to the gradual extension of these expenditures; to the erection of light-houses, the placing, planting, and sinking of buoys, beacons, and piers, and to the removal of partial and temporary obstructions in our navigable rivers and in the harbors upon our Great Lakes as well as on the seaboard. Although I have expressed to Congress my apprehension that these expenditures have sometimes been extravagant and disproportionate to the advantages to be derived from them, I have not felt it to be my duty to refuse my assent to bills containing them, and have contented myself to follow in this respect in the footsteps of all my predecessors. Sensible, however, from experience and observation of the great abuses to which the unrestricted exercise of this authority by Congress was exposed, I have prescribed a limitation for the government of my own conduct by which expenditures of this character are confined to places below the ports of entry or delivery established by law. I am very sensible that this restriction is not as satisfactory as could be desired, and that much embarrassment may be caused to the executive department in its execution by appropriations for remote and not well-understood objects. But as neither my own reflections nor the lights which I may properly derive from other sources have supplied me with a better, I shall continue to apply my best exertions to a faithful application of the rule upon which it is founded. I sincerely regret that I could not give my assent to the bill entitled "An act to improve the navigation of the Wabash River;" but I could not have done so without receding from the ground which I have, upon the fullest consideration, taken upon this subject, and of which Congress has been heretofore apprised, and without throwing the subject again open to abuses which no good citizen entertaining my opinions could desire.

I rely upon the intelligence and candor of my fellow-citizens, in whose liberal indulgence I have already so largely participated, for a correct appreciation of my motives in interposing as I have done on this and other occasions checks to a course of legislation which, without in the slightest degree calling in question the motives of others, I consider as sanctioning improper and unconstitutional expenditures of public treasure.

I am not hostile to internal improvements, and wish to see them extended to every part of the country. But I am fully persuaded, if they are not commenced in a proper manner, confined to proper objects, and conducted under an authority generally conceded to be rightful, that a successful prosecution of them can not be reasonably expected. The attempt will meet with resistance where it might otherwise receive support, and instead of strengthening the bonds of our Confederacy it will only multiply and aggravate the causes of disunion.

ANDREW JACKSON.

SPECIAL MESSAGES.

WASHINGTON, *December 4, 1834.*

To the Senate and House of Representatives:

I transmit to Congress a communication addressed to me by M. George Washington Lafayette, accompanying a copy of the Declaration of Independence engraved on copper, which his illustrious father bequeathed to Congress to be placed in their library as a last tribute of respect, patriotic love, and affection for his adopted country.

I have a mournful satisfaction in transmitting this precious bequest of that great and good man who through a long life, under many vicissitudes and in both hemispheres, sustained the principles of civil liberty asserted in that memorable Declaration, and who from his youth to the last moment of his life cherished for our beloved country the most generous attachment.

ANDREW JACKSON.

The bequest accompanies the message to the House of Representatives.

A. J.

PARIS, *June 15, 1834.*

SIR: A great misfortune has given me more than one solemn and important duty to fulfill, and the ardent desire of accomplishing with fidelity my father's last will emboldens me to claim the patronage of the President of the United States and his benevolent intervention when I am obliged respectfully and mournfully to address the Senate and Representatives of a whole nation.

Our forever beloved parent possessed a copper plate on which was inscribed the first engraved copy of the American Declaration of Independence, and his last intention in departing this world was that the precious plate should be presented to the Congress of the United States, to be deposited in their library as a last tribute of respect, patriotic love, and affection for his adopted country.

Will it be permitted to me, a faithful disciple of that American school whose principles are so admirably exposed in that immortal Declaration, to hope that you, sir, would do me the honor to communicate this letter to both Houses of Congress at the same time that in the name of his afflicted family you would present to them my venerated father's gift?

In craving such an important favor, sir, the son of General Lafayette, the adopted grandson of Washington, knows and shall never forget that he would become unworthy of it if he was ever to cease to be a French and American patriot.

With the utmost respect, I am, sir, your devoted and obedient servant,

GEORGE W. LAFAYETTE.

WASHINGTON, *December 10, 1834.*

To the Senate and House of Representatives of the United States:

The joint resolutions of Congress unanimously expressing their sensibility on the intelligence of the death of General Lafayette were communicated, in compliance with their will, to George Washington Lafayette and the other members of the family of that illustrious man. By their request I now present the heartfelt acknowledgments of the surviving descendants of our beloved friend for that highly valued proof of the sympathy of the United States.

ANDREW JACKSON.

WASHINGTON, *June 27, 1834.*

GEORGE WASHINGTON LAFAYETTE AND THE OTHER MEMBERS OF THE FAMILY OF THE LATE GENERAL LAFAYETTE:

In compliance with the will of Congress, I transmit to you the joint resolutions of the two Houses unanimously expressing the sensibility with which they received the intelligence of the death of "General Lafayette, the friend of the United States, the friend of Washington, and the friend of liberty;" and I also assure you of the condolence of this whole nation in the irreparable bereavement which by that event you have sustained.

In complying with the request of Congress I can not omit the occasion of offering you my own condolence in the great loss you have sustained, and of expressing my admiration of the eminent virtues of the distinguished patriot whom it has pleased Providence to remove to his high reward.

I also pray you to be persuaded that your individual welfare and prosperity will always be with me objects of that solicitude which the illustrious services of the great friend and benefactor of my country are calculated to awaken.

ANDREW JACKSON,
President of the United States.

RESOLUTION manifesting the sensibility of the two Houses of Congress and of the nation on the occasion of the decease of General Lafayette.

Resolved by the Senate and House of Representatives of the United States of America in Congress assembled, That the two Houses of Congress have received with the profoundest sensibility intelligence of the death of General Lafayette, the friend of the United States, the friend of Washington, and the friend of liberty.

And be it further resolved, That the sacrifices and efforts of this illustrious person in the cause of our country during her struggle for independence, and the affectionate interest which he has at all times manifested for the success of her political institutions, claim from the Government and people of the United States an expression of condolence for his loss, veneration for his virtues, and gratitude for his services.

And be it further resolved, That the President of the United States be requested to address, together with a copy of the above resolutions, a letter to George Washington Lafayette and the other members of his family, assuring them of the condolence of this whole nation in their irreparable bereavement.

And be it further resolved, That the members of the two Houses of Congress will wear a badge of mourning for thirty days, and that it be recommended to the people of the United States to wear a similar badge for the same period.

And be it further resolved, That the halls of the Houses be dressed in mourning for the residue of the session.

And be it further resolved, That John Quincy Adams be requested to deliver an oration on the life and character of General Lafayette before the two Houses of Congress at the next session.

JNO. BELL,
Speaker of the House of Representatives.

M. VAN BUREN,
Vice-President of the United States and President of the Senate.

Approved, June 26, 1834.

ANDREW JACKSON.

LA GRANGE, *October 21, 1834.*

SIR: The resolution of Congress communicated to me by your honored favor of the 27th of June, that glorious testimony of American national affection for my beloved and venerated father, has been received by his family with the deepest sense of the most respectful and, give me leave to say, filial gratitude.

And now, sir, that we experience the benefits of such a high and soothing sympathy, we find ourselves called to the honor of addressing to the people and Congress of the United States our heartfelt and dutiful thanks.

Sir, you were the friend of my father, and the kind letter which accompanied the precious message seems to be for us a sufficient authorization to our claiming once more your honorable assistance for the accomplishment of a duty dear to our hearts. We most fervently wish that the homage of our everlasting devotion to a nation whose tears have deigned to mingle with ours should be offered to both Houses of Congress. Transmitted by you, sir, that homage shall be rendered acceptable, and we earnestly pray you, sir, to present it in our name. Our gratitude shall be forever adequate to the obligation.

The resolution which so powerfully honors my father's memory shall be deposited as a most sacred family property in that room of mourning where once his son and grandsons used to receive with avidity from him lessons of patriotism and active love of liberty. There the daily contemplation of it will more and more impress their minds with that encouraging conviction that the affection and esteem of a free nation is the most desirable reward that can be obtained on earth.

With the utmost respect, sir, I have the honor to be, your devoted and obedient servant,

GEORGE W. LAFAYETTE.

WASHINGTON, *December 12, 1834.*

To the House of Representatives:

In compliance with the resolution of the House of Representatives of the 10th instant, calling for any information which the President may possess respecting the burning of the building occupied by the Treasury Department in the year 1833, I transmit herewith the papers containing the inquiry into the cause of that disaster, which was directed and made soon after its occurrence.

Accompanying this inquiry I also transmit a particular report from

Mr. McLane, who was then Secretary of the Treasury, stating all the facts relating to the subject which were within the knowledge of the officers of the Department and such losses of records and papers as were ascertained to have been sustained.

ANDREW JACKSON.

To the Senate:

I transmit herewith, for the consideration of the Senate, papers showing the terms on which the united tribes of the Chippewas, Ottawas, and Potawatamies are willing to accede to the amendments contained in the resolution of the Senate of the 22d of May last, ratifying conditionally the treaty which had been concluded with them on the 26th day of September, 1833.

ANDREW JACKSON.

DECEMBER 15, 1834.

WASHINGTON, *December 27, 1834.*

To the Senate of the United States:

I transmit to the Senate a report from the Secretary of State, together with the papers relative to the execution of the treaty of the 4th of July, 1831, between the United States and France, requested by their resolution of the —— instant.

ANDREW JACKSON.

WASHINGTON, *December 27, 1834.*

To the House of Representatives of the United States:

I transmit to the House a report from the Secretary of State, together with the papers relating to the refusal of the French Government' to make provision for the execution of the treaty between the United States and France concluded on the 4th July, 1831, requested by their resolution of the 24th instant.

ANDREW JACKSON.

DEPARTMENT OF STATE,
Washington, December 27, 1834.

The PRESIDENT OF THE UNITED STATES:

The Secretary of State, to whom has been referred the resolution of the House of Representatives of the 24th instant, requesting the President of the United States "to communicate to the House, if not in his opinion incompatible with the public interest, any communications or correspondence which may have taken place between our minister at Paris and the French Government, or between the minister from France to this Government and the Secretary of State, on the subject of the refusal of the French Government to make provision for the execution of the treaty concluded between the United States and France on the 4th July, 1831," has the honor of reporting to the President copies of the papers desired by that resolution.

It will be perceived that no authority was given to either of the chargés d'affaires who succeeded Mr. Rives to enter into any correspondence with the French Government in regard to the merits of the convention, or in relation to its execution, except to urge the prompt delivery of the papers stipulated for in the sixth article and to apprise that Government of the arrangement made for receiving payment of the first installment.

All which is respectfully submitted.   JOHN FORSYTH.

WASHINGTON, *January 5, 1835.*

To the House of Representatives:

: In answer to the resolution of the House of Representatives passed on the 24th ultimo, I transmit a report* from the Secretary of State upon the subject.   ANDREW JACKSON.

WASHINGTON, *January 6, 1835.*

To the House of Representatives of the United States:

In answer to a resolution of the House of Representatives passed on the 27th ultimo, I transmit a report made to me by the Secretary of State on the subject; and I have to acquaint the House that the negotiation for the settlement of the northeastern boundary being now in progress, it would, in my opinion, be incompatible with the public interest to lay before the House any communications which have been had between the two Governments since the period alluded to in the resolution.

ANDREW JACKSON.

WASHINGTON, *January 13, 1835.*

To the House of Representatives:

In compliance with the resolution of the House of the 8th instant, requesting "copies of every circular or letter of instruction emanating from the Treasury or War Departments since the 30th day of June last, and addressed to either the receiving or the disbursing officers stationed in States wherein land offices are established or public works are constructing under the authority of Congress," I transmit herewith reports from the Secretaries of the Treasury and War Departments, containing the information sought for.   ANDREW JACKSON.

WASHINGTON, *January 13, 1835.*

To the Senate of the United States:

I have received the resolution of the Senate of the 9th instant, requesting me to communicate "a copy of any report made by any director or directors of the Bank of the United States appointed by the Government, purporting to give information to the Executive of certain notes and bills of exchange discounted at the Bank of the United States for account and benefit of George Poindexter, a member of the Senate; also the name or names of such director or directors."

*Relating to claims of American citizens upon the Mexican Government.

In my replies to the resolutions of the Senate of the 11th December, 1833, and of 12th of June, 1834, the former passed in their legislative and the latter in their executive capacity, I had occasion to state the objections to requests of this nature, and to vindicate in this respect the constitutional rights of the executive department. The views then expressed remain unchanged, and as I think them peculiarly applicable to the present occasion I should feel myself required to decline any reply to the resolution before me were there not reason to apprehend that persons now in nomination before the Senate might possibly by such a course be exposed to improper and injurious imputations.

The resolution of the Senate, standing alone, would seem to be adopted with the view of obtaining information in regard to the transactions which may have been had between a particular member of the Senate and the Bank of the United States. It can, however, scarcely be supposed that such was its object, inasmuch as the Senate have it in their power to obtain any information they may desire on this subject from their own committee, who have been freely allowed, as appears by their published report, to make examinations of the books and proceedings of the bank, peremptorily denied to the Government directors, and not even allowed to the committee of the House of Representatives. It must therefore be presumed that the resolution has reference to some other matter, and on referring to the Executive Journal of the Senate I find therein such proceedings as in my judgment fully to authorize the apprehension stated.

Under these circumstances, and for the purpose of preventing misapprehension and injustice, I think it proper to communicate herewith a copy of the only report made to me by any director or directors of the Bank of the United States appointed by the Government, since the report of the 19th of August, 1833, which is already in the possession of the Senate. It will be perceived that the paper herewith transmitted contains no information whatever as to the discounting of notes or bills of exchange for the account and benefit of the member of the Senate named in their resolution, nor have I at any time received from the Government directors any report purporting to give any such information.

ANDREW JACKSON.

WASHINGTON, January 29, 1835.

To the House of Representatives of the United States :

I transmit to the House of Representatives a report* from the Secretary of State, upon the subject of a resolution of the 22d instant, which was referred to that officer, together with the papers referred to in the said report.

ANDREW JACKSON.

* Relating to Commerce with Cuba and Puerto Rico.

WASHINGTON, *January 30, 1835.*

To the House of Representatives of the United States:

With reference to the claim of the granddaughters of the Marshal de Rochambeau, and in addition to the papers formerly communicated relating to the same subject, I now transmit to the House of Representatives, for their consideration, a memorial to the Congress of the United States from the Countess d'Ambrugeac and the Marquise de la Gorée, together with the letter which accompanied it. Translations of these documents are also sent.

ANDREW JACKSON.

WASHINGTON, *February 6, 1835.*

To the House of Representatives:

I submit to Congress a report from the Secretary of War, containing the evidence of certain claims to reservations under the fourteenth article of the treaty of 1830 with the Choctaws, which the locating agent has reserved from sale in conformity with instructions from the President, who did not consider himself authorized to direct their location.

Should Congress consider the claims just, it will be proper to pass a law authorizing their location, or satisfying them in some other way.

ANDREW JACKSON.

WASHINGTON, *February 6, 1835.*

To the House of Representatives of the United States:

I transmit to the House of Representatives a report of the Secretary of State, accompanied with extracts from certain dispatches received from the minister of the United States at Paris, which are communicated in compliance with a resolution of the House of the 31st ultimo. Being of opinion that the residue of the dispatches of that minister can not at present be laid before the House consistently with the public interest, I decline transmitting them. In doing so, however, I deem proper to state that whenever any communication shall be received exhibiting any change in the condition of the business referred to in the resolution information will be promptly transmitted to Congress.

ANDREW JACKSON.

DEPARTMENT OF STATE,
Washington, February 5, 1835.

The PRESIDENT OF THE UNITED STATES:

The Secretary of State, to whom has been referred the resolution of the House of Representatives of the 31st ultimo, requesting the President "to communicate to that House, if not incompatible with the public interest, any correspondence with the Government of France and any dispatches received from the minister of the United States at Paris, not hitherto communicated to the House, in relation to the failure of the French Government to carry into effect any stipulation of the treaty of the 4th day of July, 1831," has the honor to report to the President that as far as is known to the Department no correspondence has taken place with the Government of France since that communicated to the House on the 27th December last. The Secretary is not aware that the dispatches received from the minister of the United States at Paris present any material fact which does not appear in the correspondence already transmitted. He nevertheless incloses so much of those dispatches written subsequently to the commencement of the present session of the French Chambers as may serve to shew the state of the business to which they relate since that time, and also that portion of an early dispatch which contains the substance of the assurances made to him by His Majesty the King of the French at a formal audience granted to him for the purpose of presenting his credentials, and he submits for the President's consideration whether the residue can consistently with the public interest be now laid before the House.

JOHN FORSYTH.

Mr. Livingston to the Secretary of State of the United States.

[Extracts.]

PARIS, *October 4, 1833.*

SIR: On Monday I presented my letter of credence to the King, on which occasion I made the address to him a copy of which is inclosed.

*   *   *   *   *   *   *

His answer was long and earnest. I can not pretend to give you the words of it, but in substance it was a warm expression of his good feeling toward the United States for the hospitality he had received there, etc. * * * "As to the convention," he said, "assure your Government that unavoidable circumstances alone prevented its immediate execution, but it will be faithfully performed. Assure your Government of this," he repeated, "the necessary laws will be passed at the next meeting of the Chambers. I tell you this not only as King, but as an individual whose promise will be fulfilled."

Mr. Livingston to the Secretary of State.

[Extracts.]

PARIS, *November 22, 1834.*

*   *   *   *   *   *   *

I do not hope for any decision on our affairs before the middle of January. One motive for delay is an expectation that the message of the President may arrive before the discussion, and that it may contain something to show a strong national feeling on the subject. *This is not mere conjecture; I know the fact.* And I repeat now from a full knowledge of the case what I have more than once stated in my former dispatches as my firm persuasion, that the moderate tone taken by our Government when the rejection was first known was attributed by some to indifference or to a conviction on the part of the President that he would not be supported in any strong measure by the people, and by others to a consciousness that the convention had given us more than we were entitled to ask.

*   *   *   *   *   *   *

I saw last night an influential member of the Chamber, who told me that, * * * and that the King had spoken of our affairs and appeared extremely anxious to secure the passage of the law. I mention this as one of the many circumstances which, independent of official assurances, convince me that the King is sincere, and now I have no doubt of the sincerity of his cabinet. From all this you may imagine the anxiety I shall feel for the arrival of the President's message. On its tone will depend very much, not only the payment of our claims, but our national reputation for energy. I have no doubt it will be such as to attain both of these important objects.

Mr. Livingston to Mr. Forsyth.

[Extract.]

PARIS, *December 6, 1834.*

*   *   *   *   *   *   *

The Chambers were convened on the 1st instant under very exciting circumstances, the ministers individually and the papers supposed to speak their language having previously announced a design to enter into a full explanation of their conduct, to answer all interrogations, and place their continuance in office on the question of approval by the Chambers of their measures.

This, as you will see by the papers, they have frankly and explicitly done, and after a warm debate of two days, which has just closed, they have gained a decided victory. This gives them confidence, permanence, and, I hope, influence enough to carry the treaty. I shall now urge the presentation of the law at as early a day as possible, and although I do not yet feel very certain of success, my hopes of it are naturally much increased by the vote of this evening. The conversations I have had with the King and with all the ministers convince me that now they are perfectly in earnest and united on the question, and that it will be urged with zeal and ability.

Many of the deputies, too, with whom I have entered into explanations on the subject, seem now convinced that the interest as well as the honor of the nation requires the fulfillment of their engagements. This gives me hopes that the endeavors I shall continue to make without ceasing until the question is decided may be successful.

The intimation I have conceived myself authorized to make of the serious consequences that may be expected from another rejection of the law, and of the firm determination of our Government to admit of no reduction or change in the treaty, I think has had an effect. On the whole, I repeat that without being at all confident I now entertain better hopes than I have for some time past done.

Mr. Livingston to the Secretary of State.

[Extracts.]

PARIS, *December 22, 1834.*

Hon. JOHN FORSYTH,
    Secretary of State, etc.

SIR: Our diplomatic relations with this Government are on the most extraordinary footing. With the executive branch I have little to discuss, for they agree with me in every material point on the subject of the treaty. With the legislature, where the great difficulty arises, I can have no official communication. Yet, deeply impressed with the importance to my fellow-citizens of securing the indemnity to which they are entitled, and to the country of enforcing the execution of engagements solemnly made to it, as well as of preventing a rupture, which must infallibly follow the final refusal to execute the convention, I have felt it a duty to use every proper endeavor to avoid this evil. This has been and continues to be a subject of much embarrassment.

*   *   *   *   *   *   *

My last dispatch (6th December) was written immediately after the vote of the Chamber of Deputies had, as it was thought, secured a majority to the administration, and it naturally excited hopes which that supposition was calculated to inspire. I soon found, however, both from the tone of the administration press and from the language of the King and all the ministers with whom I conferred on the subject, that they were not willing to put their popularity to the test on our question.

It will not be made one on the determination of which the ministers are willing to risk their portfolios. The very next day after the debate the ministerial gazette (Les Débats) declared that, satisfied with the approbation the Chamber had given to their system, it was at perfect liberty to exercise its discretion as to particular measures which do not form *an essential part of that system;* and the communications I subsequently had with the King and the ministers confirmed me in the opinion that the law for executing our convention was to be considered as one of those free questions. I combated this opinion, and asked whether the faithful observance of treaties was not *an essential part of their* system, and, if so, whether it did not come within their rule. Without answering this argument, I was told of the endeavors they were making to secure the passage of the law by preparing the statement* mentioned in my former dispatch. This, it is said, is nearly finished, and from what I know of its tenor it will produce all the effect that truth and justice can be expected to have on prejudice and party spirit.

The decision not to make it a cabinet question will not be without its favorable operation; * * * some of the leaders of the opposition, who may not be willing to take the responsibility of a rupture between the two nations by breaking the treaty, when they are convinced that instead of forcing the ministers to resign they will themselves only incur the odium of having caused the national breach. In this view of the subject I shall be much aided if by the tenor of the President's message it is seen that we shall resent the breach of faith they contemplate.

It is on all hands conceded that it would be imprudent to press the decision before the next month, when the exposition will be printed and laid before the Chambers.

　* 　　　 * 　　　 * 　　　 * 　　　 * 　　　 * 　　　 *

On the whole, I am far from being sanguine of success in the endeavors which I shall not cease to make for the accomplishment of this important object of my mission, and I expect with some solicitude the instructions for my conduct in the probable case of a rejection of the law.

　　　I have the honor to be, etc.,　　　　　　　　　EDW. LIVINGSTON.

　　　　　　　　　　　　　　WASHINGTON, *February 10, 1835.*

To the Senate of the United States:

I have received the resolution of the Senate of the 2d instant, requesting me to communicate copies of the charges, if any, which may have been made to me against the official conduct of Gideon Fitz, late surveyor-general south of the State of Tennessee, which caused his removal from office.

The resolution is preceded by a preamble which alleges as reasons for this request that the causes which may have produced the removal of the officer referred to may contain information necessary to the action of the Senate on the nomination of his successor and to the investigation now in progress respecting the frauds in the sales of the public lands.

This is another of those calls for information made upon me by the Senate which have, in my judgment, either related to the subjects exclusively belonging to the executive department or otherwise encroached on the constitutional powers of the Executive. Without conceding the right of the Senate to make either of these requests, I have yet, for the various reasons heretofore assigned in my several replies, deemed it expedient

---

*A memoir to be laid before the commission which may be appointed to examine the law, intended to contain all the arguments and facts by which it is to be supported.

to comply with several of them. It is now, however, my solemn conviction that I ought no longer, from any motive nor in any degree, to yield to these unconstitutional demands. Their continued repetition imposes on me, as the representative and trustee of the American people, the painful but imperious duty of resisting to the utmost any further encroachment on the rights of the Executive. This course is especially due to the present resolution. The President in cases of this nature possesses the exclusive power of removal from office, and, under the sanctions of his official oath and of his liability to impeachment, he is bound to exercise it whenever the public welfare shall require. If, on the other hand, from corrupt motives he abuses this power, he is exposed to the same responsibilities. On no principle known to our institutions can he be required to account for the manner in which he discharges this portion of his public duties, save only in the mode and under the forms prescribed by the Constitution. The suggestion that the charges a copy of which is requested by the Senate "may contain information necessary to their action" on a nomination now before them can not vary the principle. There is no necessary connection between the two subjects, and even if there were the Senate have no right to call for that portion of these matters which appertains to the separate and independent action of the Executive. The intimation that these charges may also be necessary "to the investigation now in progress respecting frauds in the sales of public lands" is still more insufficient to authorize the present call. Those investigations were instituted and have thus far been conducted by the Senate in their legislative capacity, and with the view, it is presumed, to some legislative action. If the President has in his possession any information on the subject of such frauds, it is his duty to communicate it to Congress, and it may undoubtedly be called for by either House sitting in its legislative capacity, though even from such a call all matters properly belonging to the exclusive duties of the President must of necessity be exempted.

The resolution now before me purports to have been passed in executive session, and I am bound to presume that if the information requested therein should be communicated it would be applied in secret session to "the investigation of frauds in the sales of the public lands." But, if so applied, the distinction between the executive and legislative functions of the Senate would not only be destroyed, but the citizen whose conduct is impeached would lose one of his valuable securities, that which is afforded by a public investigation in the presence of his accusers and of the witnesses against him. Besides, a compliance with the present resolution would in all probability subject the conduct and motives of the President in the case of Mr. Fitz to the review of the Senate when not sitting as judges on an impeachment, and even if this consequence should not occur in the present case the compliance of the Executive might hereafter be quoted as a precedent for similar and repeated applications.

Such a result, if acquiesced in, would ultimately subject the independent constitutional action of the Executive in a matter of great national concernment to the domination and control of the Senate; if not acquiesced in, it would lead to collisions between coordinate branches of the Government, well calculated to expose the parties to indignity and reproach and to inflict on the public interest serious and lasting mischief.

I therefore decline a compliance with so much of the resolution of the Senate as requests "copies of the charges, if any," in relation to Mr. Fitz, and in doing so must be distinctly understood as neither affirming nor denying that any such charges were made; but as the Senate may lawfully call upon the President for information properly appertaining to nominations submitted to them, I have the honor, in this respect, to reply that I have none to give them in the case of the person nominated as successor to Mr. Fitz, except that I believe him, from sources entitled to the highest credit, to be well qualified in abilities and character to discharge the duties of the office in question.

ANDREW JACKSON.

WASHINGTON, *February 14, 1835.*
To the Senate of the United States:

I beg leave to call the attention of Congress to the accompanying communication from the Secretary of War, from which it appears that the "act for the relief of Benedict Alford and Robert Brush," although signed and duly certified by the proper officers as having passed the two Houses of Congress at their last session, had not in fact obtained the sanction of that body when it was presented to the President for his approval.

Under these circumstances it is thought that the subject is worthy of the consideration of Congress.

ANDREW JACKSON.

WASHINGTON, *February 16, 1835.*
To the House of Representatives of the United States:

I transmit to the House of Representatives, for their consideration, a petition to the Congress of the United States from Adelaide de Grasse de Grochamps, one of the surviving daughters of the Count de Grasse, together with the letter which accompanied it. Translations of these papers are also sent.

ANDREW JACKSON.

WASHINGTON, *February 18, 1835.*
To the House of Representatives:

Since my message a few days ago relating to Choctaw reservations other documents on the same subject have been received from the locating agent, which are mentioned in the accompanying report of the Secretary of War, and which I also transmit herewith for the information and consideration of Congress.

ANDREW JACKSON.

WASHINGTON, *February 21, 1835.*

To the Senate of the United States:

I transmit herewith, for the advice and consent of the Senate as to the ratification of the same, four treaties for Potawatamie reservations, concluded by General Marshall in December last.

ANDREW JACKSON.

WASHINGTON, *February 25, 1835.*

To the Senate and House of Representatives of the United States:

I transmit to Congress a report from the Secretary of State, with copies of all the letters received from Mr. Livingston since the message to the House of Representatives of the 6th instant, of the instructions given to that minister, and of all the late correspondence with the French Government in Paris or in Washington, except a note of Mr. Sérurier, which, for the reasons stated in the report, is not now communicated.

It will be seen that I have deemed it my duty to instruct Mr. Livingston to quit France with his legation and return to the United States if an appropriation for the fulfillment of the convention shall be refused by the Chambers.

The subject being now in all its present aspects before Congress, whose right it is to decide what measures are to be pursued in that event, I deem it unnecessary to make further recommendation, being confident that on their part everything will be done to maintain the rights and honor of the country which the occasion requires.

ANDREW JACKSON.

DEPARTMENT OF STATE,
Washington, February 25, 1835.

The PRESIDENT OF THE UNITED STATES:

The Secretary of State has the honor to submit to the President copies of all the letters received from Mr. Livingston since the message to the House of Representatives of the 6th instant, of the instructions given to that minister, and of all the late correspondence with the French Government in Paris or in Washington, except the last note of M. Sérurier, which it has been considered necessary to submit to the Government of France before it is made public or answered, that it may be ascertained whether some exceptionable expressions are to be taken as the result of a settled purpose in that Government or as the mere ebullition of the minister's indiscretion.

JOHN FORSYTH.

Mr. Livingston to Mr. Forsyth.

No. 70.

LEGATION OF THE UNITED STATES,
Paris, January 11, 1835.

Hon. JOHN FORSYTH.

SIR: Believing that it would be important for me to receive the dispatches you might think it necessary to send with the President's message, I ventured on incurring the expense of a courier to bring it to me as soon as it should arrive at Havre. Mr. Beasley accordingly, on the arrival of the *Sully*, dispatched a messenger with my letters received by that vessel, and a New York newspaper containing the message, but without any communication from the Department, so that your No. 43 is still the last which I have to acknowledge. The courier arrived at 2 o'clock on the morning of the 8th. Other copies were the same morning received by the estafette, and the contents, being soon known, caused the greatest sensation, which as yet is, I think, unfavorable—the few members of the opposition who would have voted for the execution of the treaty now declaring that they can not do it under the threat of reprisals, and the great body of that party making use of the effect it has on national pride to gain proselytes from the ministerial side of the Chamber, in which I have no doubt they have in a great degree for the time succeeded.

The ministers are aware of this, and will not, I think, immediately urge the consideration of the law, as I have no doubt they were prepared to do when the message arrived. Should Congress propose commercial restrictions or determine to wait to the end of the session before they act, this will be considered as a vote against reprisals, and then the law will be proposed and I think carried. But I ought not to conceal from you that the excitement is at present very great; that their pride is deeply wounded by what they call an attempt to coerce them by threats to the payment of a sum which they persist, in opposition to the plainest proof, in declaring not to be due. This feeling is fostered by the language of our opposition papers, particularly by the Intelligencer and New York Courier, extracts from which have been sent on by Americans, declaring them to be the sentiments of a majority of the people. These, as you will see, are translated and republished here, with such comments as they might have been expected and undoubtedly were intended to produce, and if hostilities should take place between the two countries those persons may flatter themselves with having the credit of a great share in producing them. The only letter I have received from home is from one of my family. This, to my great satisfaction, informs me that the President will be supported by all parties, and I am told that this is the language of some of the opposition papers; but as they are not sent to the legation I can not tell in what degree this support can be depended upon. Whether the energetic language of the message will be made the pretext with some or be the cause with others among the deputies for rejecting the law can not, of course, be yet conjectured with any great degree of probability, but I think it will have a good effect. It has certainly raised us in the estimation of other powers, if I may judge from the demeanor of their representatives here, and my own opinion is that as soon as the first excitement subsides it will operate favorably on the counsels of France. Already some of the journals begin to change their tone, and I am much mistaken if the opposition here, finding that we are in earnest, will incur the responsibility of a rupture between the two nations, which they see must take place if the treaty be rejected. The funds experienced a considerable fall as soon as the message was known, and insurance rose. In short, it has made them feel the commercial as well as political importance of our country.

The Comte de Rigny had requested me to communicate the message to him as soon as it should be received. This I promised to do, and accordingly on the morning of the 8th, to avoid any mistake as to the mode of making the communication, I carried the paper to him myself, telling him that I had received a gazette containing a paper said to be the message of the President, which I delivered to him in compliance with my promise; but I requested him to observe that it was not an authentic paper, nor was it delivered in pursuance of instructions, nor in my official character. I thought it, for obvious reasons, necessary to be very explicit on this point, and he properly understood me, as he had not yet read the message. Little more passed at the interview, and I thought of it, but not immediately, to seek another. I shall probably, however, see him to-night, and shall then appoint some time for a further conference, of which I will by this same packet give you the result.

Mr. Middleton has just arrived from Madrid with the inscriptions for the Spanish indemnity and a draft for the first payment of interest. His instructions are, he says, to leave them with me, but as I have heard nothing from the Department I shall advise the depositing them with Rothschild to wait the directions of the President.

The importance of obtaining the earliest intelligence at this crisis of our affairs with France has induced me to direct that my letters should be sent by the estafette from Havre, and that if any important advice should be received at such an hour in the day as would give a courier an advance of some hours over the estafette, that a special messenger should be dispatched with it.

I have the honor to be, very respectfully, sir, your most obedient servant,

EDW. LIVINGSTON.

Mr. Livingston to Mr. Forsyth.

No. 71.

LEGATION OF THE UNITED STATES,
Paris, January 14, 1835.

Hon. JOHN FORSYTH.

SIR: The intended conference with the minister for foreign affairs of which I spoke to you in my last (No. 70) took place yesterday morning. I began it by expressing my regret that a communication from the President to Congress had been so much misrepresented in that part which related to France as to be construed into a measure of hostilities. It was, I said, part of a consultation between different members of our Government as to the proper course to be pursued if the legislative body of France should persevere in refusing to provide the means of complying with a treaty formally made; that the President, as was his duty, stated the facts truly and in moderate language, without any irritating comment; that in further pursuance of his official duty he declared the different modes of redress which the law of nations permitted in order to avoid hostilities, expressing, as he ought to do, his reasons for preferring one of them; that in all this there was nothing addressed to the French nation; and I likened it to a proceeding well known in the French law (a family council in which the concerns and interests are discussed), but of which in our case the debates were necessarily public; that a further elucidation of the nature of this document might be drawn from the circumstance that no instructions had been given to communicate it to the French Government, and that if a gazette containing it had been delivered it was at the request of his excellency, and expressly declared to be a private communication, not an official one. I further stated that I made this communication without instructions, merely to counteract misapprehensions and from an earnest desire to rectify errors which might have serious consequences. I added that it was very unfortunate that an earlier call of the Chambers had not been made in consequence of Mr. Sérurier's promise, the noncompliance with which was of a nature to cause serious disquietude with the Government of the United States. I found immediately that this was the part of the message that had most seriously affected the King, for Comte de Rigny immediately took up the argument, endeavoring to show that the Government had acted in good faith, relying principally on the danger of a second rejection had the Chambers been called at an early day expressly for this object. I replied by repeating that the declaration made by Mr. Sérurier was a positive and formal one, and that it had produced a forbearance on the part of the President to lay the state of the case before Congress. In this conference, which was a long one, we both regretted that any misunderstanding should interrupt the good intelligence of two nations having so many reasons to preserve it and so few of conflicting interests. He told me (what I knew before) that the exposition was prepared, and that the law would have been presented the day after that on which the message was received. He showed me the document, read part of it to me, and expressed regret that the language of the message prevented it being sent in. I said that I hoped the excitement would soon subside and give place to better feelings, in which I thought he joined with much sincerity. It is perhaps necessary to add that an allusion was made by me to the change of ministry in November and the reinstatement of the present ministers, which I told him I had considered as a most favorable occurrence, and that I had so expressed myself in my communications to you, but that this circumstance was unknown at Washington when the message was delivered; and I added that the hopes of success held out in the communication to which I referred and the assurances it contained that the ministers would zealously urge the adoption of the law might probably have imparted the same hopes to the President and have induced some change in the measure he had recommended, but that the formation of the Dupin ministry, if known, must have had a very bad effect on the President's mind, as many of that ministry were known to be hostile to the treaty.

When I took leave the minister requested me to reflect on the propriety of presenting a note of our conversation, which he said should be formal or otherwise, as I should desire. I told him I would do so, and inform him on the next morning by 11 o'clock. We parted, as I thought, on friendly terms, and in the evening, meeting him at the Austrian ambassador's, I told him that on reflection I had determined to wait the arrival of the packet of the 16th before I gave the note, to which he made no objection. After all this you may judge of my surprise when last night about 10 o'clock I received the letter copy of which is inclosed, and which necessarily closes my mission. In my reply I shall take care to throw the responsibility of breaking up the diplomatic intercourse between the countries where it ought to rest, and will not fail to expose the misstatements which you will observe are contained in the minister's note, both as respects my Government and myself; but the late hour at which I received the Comte de Rigny's note and the almost immediate departure of the packet may prevent my sending you a copy of my communication to him, which I shall use the utmost diligence in preparing.

The law, it is said, will be presented to-day, and I have very little doubt that it will pass. The ministerial phalanx, reenforced by those of the opposition (and they are not a few) who will not take the responsibility of involving the country in the difficulties which they now see must ensue, will be sufficient to carry the vote. The recall of Sérurier and the notice to me are measures which are resorted to to save the pride of the Government and the nation.

I have the honor to be, very respectfully, sir, your most obedient servant,

EDW. LIVINGSTON.

From Count de Rigny to Mr. Livingston.

[Translation.]

DEPARTMENT OF FOREIGN AFFAIRS,
Paris, January 13, 1835.

Hon. EDWARD LIVINGSTON, etc.

SIR: You have well comprehended the nature of the impressions produced upon the King's Government by the message which His Excellency President Jackson addressed on the 1st of December to the Congress of the United States. Nothing certainly could have prepared us for it. Even though the complaints expressed in it had been as just as they are in reality unjust, we should still have had a right to be astonished on receiving the first communication of them in such a form.

In the explanations which I am now about to make I can not enter upon the consideration of any facts other than those occurring subsequently to the vote by which the last Chamber of Deputies refused the appropriation necessary for the payment stipulated in the treaty of July 4. However this vote may have been regarded by the Government of the United States, it is evident that by accepting (*accueillant*) the promise of the King's Government to bring on a second deliberation before the new legislature it had in fact postponed all discussion and all recrimination on the subject of this first refusal until another decision should have either repealed or confirmed it. This postponement therefore sets aside for the time all difficulties arising either justly or unjustly from the rejection of the treaty or from the delay by which it had been preceded; and although the message begins by enumerating them, I think proper, in order to confine myself to the matter in question, only to reply to the imputations made on account of subsequent occurrences.

The reproaches which President Jackson considers himself authorized to address to France may be summed up in a few words. The King's Government promised to present the treaty of July 4 again to the Chambers as soon as they could be assembled. They were assembled on the 31st of July, and the treaty has not yet been presented to them. Such is exactly the whole substance of the President's argumentation, and nothing can be easier than to refute it.

I may first observe that the assembling of the Chambers on the 31st of July, in obedience to a legal prescription that they should be called together within a stated period after a dissolution of the Chamber of Deputies, was nothing more than a piece of formality, and if President Jackson had attended to the internal mechanism of our administrative system he would have been convinced that the session of 1835 could not have really commenced at that session of 1834. Everyone knew beforehand that after a fortnight spent in the forms of installation it would be adjourned.

The President of the United States considers that the bill relative to the American claims should have been presented to the Chamber within that fortnight. I can not understand the propriety of this reproach. The bill was explicitly announced in the speech from the throne on the very day on which the Chambers met. This was all that was required to make known the opinion and design of the Government, and to prevent that species of moral proscription to which absolute silence would have given authority. With regard to the mere act of presentation so long before discussion could possibly take place, this proceeding would have been so unusual and extraordinary that it might have increased the unfavorable prepossessions of the public, already too numerous, without producing any real advantage in return. Above all, the result which the President had in view, of being able to announce the new vote of the Chamber of Deputies in his message, would not have been attained.

President Jackson expresses his regrets that your solicitations (*instances*) had not determined the King's Government to call the Chambers together at an earlier day. How soon soever they may have been called, the simplest calculation will serve to shew that the discussions in our Chambers could not have been known in the United States at the opening of Congress, and the President's regret is therefore unfounded.

Moreover, the same obstacles and the same administrative reasons which rendered a real session impossible during the months of July or August were almost equally opposed to its taking place before the last weeks of the year. The head of a government like that of the United States should be able to comprehend more clearly than anyone else those moral impossibilities which arise from the fixed character of the principles of a constitutional régime, and to see that in such a system the administration is subject to constant and regular forms, from which no special interest, however important, can authorize a deviation.

It is, then, evident that far from meriting the reproach of failing to comply with its engagements, far from having deferred, either voluntarily or from negligence, the accomplishment of its promises, the King's Government, ever occupied in the design of fulfilling them, was only arrested for a moment by insurmountable obstacles. This appears from the explanations now given, and I must add that the greater part of them have already been presented by M. Sérurier to the Government of the United States, which by its silence seemed to acknowledge their full value.

It is worthy of remark that on the 1st of December, the day on which President Jackson signed the message to Congress, and remarked with severity that nearly a month was to elapse before the assembling of the Chambers, they were in reality assembled in virtue of a royal ordinance calling them together at a period earlier than that first proposed. Their assemblage was not indeed immediately followed by the presentment of the bill relative to the American claims, but you, sir, know better than any other person the causes of this new delay. You yourself requested us not to endanger the success of this important affair by mingling its discussion with debates of a different nature, as their mere coincidence might have the effect of bringing other influences into play than those by which it should naturally be governed. By this request, sir, you clearly shewed that you had with your judicious spirit correctly appreciated the situation of things and the means of advancing the cause which you were called to defend. And permit me to add that the course which you have thought proper to adopt on this point is the best justification of that which we ourselves have for some months been pursuing in obedience to the necessities inherent in our political organization, and in order to insure as far as lies in our power the success of the new attempt which we were preparing to make in the Chamber.

However this may be, the King's Government, freed from the internal difficulties the force of which you have yourself so formally admitted, was preparing to present the bill for giving sanction to the treaty of July 4, when the strange message of December 1 came and obliged it again to deliberate on the course which it should pursue.

The King's Government, though deeply wounded by imputations to which I will not give a name, having demonstrated their purely gratuitous character, still does not wish to retreat absolutely from a determination already taken in a spirit of good faith and justice. How great soever may be the difficulties caused by the provocation which President Jackson has given, and by the irritation which it has produced in the public mind, it will ask the Chambers for an appropriation of twenty-five millions in order to meet the engagements of July 4; but at the same time His Majesty has considered it due to his own dignity no longer to leave his minister exposed to hear language so offensive to France. M. Sérurier will receive orders to return to France.

Such, sir, are the determinations of which I am charged immediately to inform you, in order that you may make them known to the Government of the United States and that you may yourself take those measures which may seem to you to be the natural consequences of this communication. The passports which you may desire are therefore at your disposition.

Accept, sir, the assurance of my high consideration.

DE RIGNY.

Mr. Livingston to Mr. Forsyth.

No. 72.

LEGATION OF THE UNITED STATES,
Paris, January 15, 1835.

SIR: Having determined to send Mr. Brown, one of the gentlemen attached to the legation, to Havre with my dispatches, I have just time to add to them the copy of the note which I have sent to the Comte de Rigny. The course indicated by it was adopted after the best reflections I could give to the subject, and I hope will meet the approbation of the President. My first impressions were that I ought to follow my inclinations, demand my passports, and leave the Kingdom. This would at once have freed me from a situation extremely painful and embarrassing; but a closer attention convinced me that by so doing I should give to the French Government the advantage they expect to derive from the equivocal terms of their note, which, as occasions might serve, they might represent as a suggestion only, leaving upon me the responsibility of breaking up the diplomatic intercourse between the two countries if I demanded my passports; or, if I did not, and they found the course convenient, they might call it an order to depart which I had not complied with. Baron Rothschild also called on me yesterday, saying that he had conversed with the Comte de Rigny, who assured him that the note was not intended as a notice to depart, and that he would be glad to see me on the subject. I answered that I could have no verbal explanations on the subject, to which he replied that he had suggested the writing a note on the subject, but that the minister had declined any written communication. Rothschild added that he had made an appointment with the Comte de Rigny for 6 o'clock, and would see me again at night, and he called to say that there had been a misunderstanding as to the time of appointment, and that he had not seen Mr. de Rigny, but would see him this morning. But in the meantime I determined on sending my note, not only for the reasons contained in it, which appeared to me conclusive, but because I found that the course was the correct one in diplomacy, and that to ask for a passport merely because the Government near which the minister was accredited had suggested it would be considered as committing the dignity of his own; that the universal practice in such cases was to wait the order to depart, and not by a voluntary demand of passports exonerate the foreign Government from the odium and responsibility of so violent a measure. My note will force them to take their ground. If the answer is that they intended only a suggestion which I may follow or not, as I choose, I will remain, but keep aloof until I receive your directions. If, on the other hand, I am told to depart, I will retire to Holland or England, and there wait the President's orders. In either case the derangement will be extremely expensive and my situation very disagreeable. The law was not presented yesterday, but will be to-day, and I have been informed that it is to be introduced by an exposé throwing all the blame of the present state of things on Mr. Sérurier and me for not truly representing the opinions of our respective Governments. They may treat their own minister as they please, but they shall not, without exposure, presume to judge of my conduct and make me the scapegoat for their sins. The truth is, they are sadly embarrassed. If the law should be rejected, I should not be surprised if they anticipated our reprisals by the seizure of our vessels in port or the attack of our ships in the Mediterranean with a superior force. I shall without delay inform Commodore Patterson of the state of things, that he may be on his guard, having already sent him a copy of the message.

I have the honor to be, sir, your obedient servant,

EDW. LIVINGSTON.

Mr. Livingston to the Count de Rigny.

LEGATION OF THE UNITED STATES OF AMERICA,
Paris, January 14, 1835.

His Excellency COUNT DE RIGNY, etc.:

The undersigned, envoy extraordinary and minister plenipotentiary of the United States of America, received late last night the note of His Excellency the Count de Rigny, minister secretary of state for foreign affairs, dated the 13th instant.

The undersigned sees with great surprise as well as regret that a communication made by one branch of the Government of the United States to another, not addressed to that of His Majesty the King of the French, nor even communicated to it, is alleged as the motive for a measure which not only increases actual subjects of irritation, but which necessarily cuts off all the usual means of restoring harmony to two nations who have the same interests, commercial and political, to unite them, and none but factitious subjects for collision.

The grave matter in the body of his excellency's note demands and will receive a full answer. It is to the concluding part that his attention is now requested. The undersigned, after being informed that it is the intention of His Majesty's Government to recall Mr. Sérurier, is told ''that this information is given to the undersigned in order that he may communicate it to his Government and in order that he may himself take those measures which may appear to him the natural result of that communication, and that in consequence thereof the passports which he might require are at his disposition.'' This phrase may be considered as an intimation of the course which, in the opinion of His Majesty's Government, the undersigned ought to pursue as the natural result of Mr. Sérurier's recall, or it may be construed, as it seems to have been by the public, into a direction by His Majesty's Government to the minister of the United States to cease his functions and leave the country.

It is necessary in a matter involving such grave consequences that there should be no misunderstanding, the two categories demanding a line of conduct entirely different the one from the other.

In the first, he can take no directions or follow no suggestions but those given by his own Government, which he has been sent here to represent. The recall of the minister of France on the grounds alleged could not have been anticipated. Of course no instructions have been given to the undersigned on the subject, and he will not take upon himself the responsibility which he would incur by a voluntary demand of his passports, although made on the suggestion of His Majesty's Government. If this be the sense of the passage in question, the duty of the undersigned can not be mistaken. He will transmit the note of His Excellency the Comte de Rigny to his Government and wait its instructions. Widely different will be his conduct if he is informed that the conclusion of the Comte de Rigny's note is intended as a direction that he should quit the French territory. This he will without delay comply with on being so informed and on receiving the passports necessary for his protection until he shall leave the Kingdom.

Leaving the responsibility of this measure where it ought to rest, the undersigned has the honor to renew to His Excellency the Comte de Rigny the assurance, etc.

EDW'D LIVINGSTON.

Mr. Livingston to Mr. Forsyth.

No. 73.

LEGATION OF THE UNITED STATES,
Paris, January 16, 1835.

Hon. J. FORSYTH, etc.

SIR: The wind being unfavorable, I hope that this letter may arrive in time for the packet.

By the inclosed semiofficial paper you will see that a law has been presented for effecting the payment of 25,000,000 francs capital to the United States, for which the budgets of the six years next succeeding this are affected, and with a condition annexed that our Government shall have done nothing to affect the interests of France. It would seem from this that they mean to pay nothing but the capital, and that only in six years from this time; but as the law refers to the treaty for execution of which it provides, I presume the intention of the ministry can not be to make any change in it, and that the phraseology is in conformity to their usual forms.

At any rate, I shall, notwithstanding the situation in which I am placed in relation to this Government, endeavor to obtain some explanation on this point.

The packet of the 16th arrived, but to my great regret brought me no dispatches, and having received none subsequent to your No. 43, and that not giving me any indication of the conduct that would be expected from me in the event of such measures as might have been expected on the arrival of the President's message, I have been left altogether to the guidance of my own sense of duty under circumstances of much difficulty. I have endeavored to shape my course through them in such a way as to maintain the dignity of my Government and preserve peace, and, if possible, restore the good understanding that existed between the two countries. From the view of the motives of the President's message contained in the answer of the Globe to the article in the Intelligencer I am happy in believing that the representations I have made to the Comte de Rigny, as detailed in my No. 71, are those entertained by the Government, and that I have not, in this at least, gone further than it would have directed me to do had I been favored with your instructions.

I have no answer yet to my note to the Comte de Rigny, a copy of which was sent by my last dispatch, nor can I form any new conjecture as to the event.

The inclosed paper contains a notice that I had been received by the King. This is unfounded, and shall be contradicted. I shall not in the present state of things make my appearance at court, and only in cases where it is indispensable have any communication with the minister.

I have the honor to be, with great respect, your obedient, humble servant,

EDW. LIVINGSTON.

Mr. Forsyth to Mr. Livingston.

DEPARTMENT OF STATE,
Washington, February 13, 1835.

EDWARD LIVINGSTON, Esq.

SIR: To relieve the anxiety expressed in your late communication to the Department of State as to the course to be pursued in the event of the rejection by the Chamber of Deputies of the law to appropriate funds to carry into effect the treaty of 4th July, 1831, I am directed by the President to inform you that if Congress shall adjourn without prescribing some definite course of action, as soon as it is known here that the law of appropriation has been again rejected by the French Chamber a frigate will be immediately dispatched to Havre to bring you back to the United States, with such instructions as the state of the question may then render necessary and proper.

I am, sir, etc.,

JOHN FORSYTH.

Mr. Forsyth to Mr. Livingston.

No. 49.

DEPARTMENT OF STATE,
Washington, February 24, 1835.

EDWARD LIVINGSTON, Esq.,
Envoy Extraordinary and Minister Plenipotentiary.

SIR: Your dispatches to No. 73 have been received at the Department—No. 73 by yesterday's mail. Nos. 70, 71, 72 were delayed until this morning by the mismanagement of the young man to whose care they were committed by the captain of the packet *Sully* in New York.

In the very unexpected and unpleasant position in which you have been placed I am directed by the President to say to you that he approves of your conduct as well becoming the representative of a Government ever slow to manifest resentment and eager only to fulfill the obligations of justice and good faith, but at the same time to inform you that he should have felt no surprise and certainly would have expressed no displeasure had you yielded to the impulse of national pride and at once have quitted France, with the whole legation, on the receipt of the Count de Rigny's note of the 13th of January. M. Sérurier, having received his orders, has terminated his ministerial career by the transmission of a note, a copy of which and of all the correspondence had with him is herewith inclosed. M. Pageot has been presented to me as charged with the affairs of France on the recall of the minister.

The note of the Count de Rigny having no doubt, according to your intention, received from you an appropriate reply, it is only necessary for me now to say that the Count is entirely mistaken in supposing that any explanations have been given here by M. Sérurier of the causes that have led to the disregard or postponement of the engagements entered into by France after the rejection of the appropriation by the last Chamber of Deputies, and of which he was the organ. No written communication whatever has been made on the subject, and none verbally made of sufficient importance to be recorded, a silence with regard to which could have been justly the foundation of any inference that the President was satisfied that the course of the French administration was either reconcilable to the assurances given him or necessary to secure a majority of the Chamber of Deputies.

The last note of M. Sérurier will be the subject of separate instructions, which will be immediately prepared and forwarded to you.

In the present position of our relations with France the President directs that if the appropriation to execute the treaty shall be or shall have been rejected by the French legislature, you forthwith quit the territory of France, with all the legation, and return to the United States by the ship of war which shall be in readiness at Havre to bring you back to your own country. If the appropriation be made, you may retire to England or Holland, leaving Mr. Barton in charge of affairs. Notify the Department of the place selected as your temporary residence and await further instructions.

I am, sir, your obedient servant,

JOHN FORSYTH.

Mr. Sérurier to Mr. Forsyth.

[Translation.]

WASHINGTON, *February 23, 1835.*

Hon. JOHN FORSYTH,
   Secretary of State of the United States.

SIR: I have just received orders from my Government which make it necessary for me to demand of you an immediate audience. I therefore request you to name the hour at which it will suit you to receive me at the Department of State.

I have the honor to be, with great consideration, sir, your obedient, humble servant,

SÉRURIER.

Mr. Forsyth to Mr. Sérurier.

DEPARTMENT OF STATE,
   Washington, February 23, 1835.

M. SÉRURIER,
   Envoy Extraordinary, etc., of the King of the French:

Official information having been received by the President of the recall of Mr. Sérurier by his Government, and the papers of the morning having announced the arrival of a French sloop of war at New York for the supposed object of carrying him from the United States, the undersigned, Secretary of State of the United States, tenders to Mr. Sérurier all possible facilities in the power of this Government to afford to enable him to comply speedily with the orders he may have received or may receive.

The undersigned avails himself of the occasion to renew to Mr. Sérurier the assurance of his very great consideration.

JOHN FORSYTH.

Mr. Forsyth to Mr. Sérurier.

DEPARTMENT OF STATE,
Washington, February 23, 1835.

The undersigned, Secretary of State of the United States, informs M. Sérurier, in reply to his note of this instant, demanding the indication of an hour for an immediate audience, that he is ready to receive in writing any communication the minister of France desires to have made to the Government of the United States.

The undersigned has the honor to offer M. Sérurier the assurances of his very great consideration.

JOHN FORSYTH.

Mr. Sérurier to Mr. Forsyth.

[Translation.]

WASHINGTON, *February 23, 1835.*

Hon. JOHN FORSYTH,
    Secretary of State.

SIR: My object in asking you this morning to name the hour at which it would suit you to receive me was in order that I might, in consequence of my recall as minister of His Majesty near the United States, present and accredit M. Pageot, the first secretary of this legation, as chargé d'affaires of the King. This presentation, which, according to usage, I calculated on making in person, I have the honor, in compliance with the desire expressed to me by you, to make in the form which you appear to prefer.

I thank you, sir, for the facilities which you have been kind enough to afford me in the note preceding that now answered, also of this morning's date, and which crossed the letter in which I demanded an interview.

I have the honor to renew to you, sir, the assurance of my high consideration.

SÉRURIER.

WASHINGTON, *February 28, 1835.*

To the Senate of the United States:

I transmit to the Senate of the United States a report* of the Secretary of State, to whom was referred the resolutions of that body passed on the 2d and 17th days of the present month, together with such portion of the correspondence and instructions requested by the said resolutions as could be transcribed within the time that has elapsed since they were received and as can be communicated without prejudice to the public interest

ANDREW JACKSON.

* Relating to the treaty of indemnity with Spain of February 17, 1834.

VETO MESSAGE.

WASHINGTON, *March 3, 1835.*

To the Senate:

I respectfully return to the Senate, where it originated, the "act to authorize the Secretary of the Treasury to compromise the claims allowed by the commissioners under the treaty with the King of the Two Sicilies, concluded October 14, 1832," without my signature.

The act is, in my judgment, inconsistent with the division of powers in the Constitution of the United States, as it is obviously founded on the assumption that an act of Congress can give power to the Executive or to the head of one of the Departments to negotiate with a foreign government. The debt due by the King of the Two Sicilies will, after the commissioners have made their decision, become the private vested property of the citizens of the United States to whom it may be awarded. Neither the Executive nor the Legislature can properly interfere with it without their consent. With their consent the Executive has competent authority to negotiate about it for them with a foreign government—an authority Congress can not constitutionally abridge or increase.

ANDREW JACKSON.

PROCLAMATION.

[From Statutes at Large (Little, Brown & Co.), Vol. XI, p. 781.]

BY THE PRESIDENT OF THE UNITED STATES OF AMERICA.

A PROCLAMATION.

Whereas by an act of Congress of the United States of the 24th of May, 1828, entitled "An act in addition to an act entitled 'An act concerning discriminating duties of tonnage and impost' and to equalize the duties on Prussian vessels and their cargoes," it is provided that, upon satisfactory evidence being given to the President of the United States by the government of any foreign nation that no discriminating duties of tonnage or impost are imposed or levied in the ports of the said nation upon vessels wholly belonging to citizens of the United States or upon the produce, manufactures, or merchandise imported in the same from the United States or from any foreign country, the President is hereby authorized to issue his proclamation declaring that the foreign discriminating duties of tonnage and impost within the United States are and shall be suspended and discontinued so far as respects the vessels of the said foreign nation and the produce, manufactures, or merchandise imported into the United States in the same from the said foreign nation or from any other foreign country, the said suspension to take effect from the time of such notification being given to the President of the United States and to continue so long as the reciprocal exemption of vessels belonging to citizens of the United States and their cargoes, as aforesaid, shall be continued, and no longer; and

Whereas satisfactory evidence has lately been received by me from His Royal Highness the Grand Duke of Mechlenberg Schwerin, through an official communication of Leon Herckenrath, his consul at Charleston, in the United States, under date of the 13th April, 1835, that no discriminating duties of tonnage or impost are imposed or levied in the ports of the Grand Duchy of Mechlenberg Schwerin upon vessels wholly belonging to citizens of the United States or upon the produce, manufactures, or merchandise imported in the same from the United States or from any foreign country:

Now, therefore, I, Andrew Jackson, President of the United States of America, do hereby declare and proclaim that the foreign discriminating duties of tonnage and impost within the United States are and shall be suspended and discontinued so far as respects the vessels of the Grand Duchy of Mechlenberg Schwerin and the produce, manufactures, or merchandise imported into the United States in the same from the said Grand Duchy or from any other foreign country, the said suspension to take effect from the 13th day of April, 1835, above mentioned, and to continue so long as the reciprocal exemption of vessels belonging to citizens of the United States and their cargoes, as aforesaid, shall be continued, and no longer.

Given under my hand at the city of Washington, the 28th day of [SEAL.] April, A. D. 1835, and of the Independence of the United States the fifty-ninth.

ANDREW JACKSON.

By the President:
JOHN FORSYTH,
Secretary of State.

SEVENTH ANNUAL MESSAGE.

WASHINGTON, *December 7, 1835.*

Fellow-Citizens of the Senate and House of Representatives:

In the discharge of my official duty the task again devolves upon me of communicating with a new Congress. The reflection that the representation of the Union has been recently renewed, and that the constitutional term of its service will expire with my own, heightens the solicitude with which I shall attempt to lay before it the state of our national concerns and the devout hope which I cherish that its labors to improve them may be crowned with success.

You are assembled at a period of profound interest to the American patriot. The unexampled growth and prosperity of our country having given us a rank in the scale of nations which removes all apprehension of danger to our integrity and independence from external foes, the career of freedom is before us, with an earnest from the past that if true to ourselves there can be no formidable obstacle in the future to its peaceful and uninterrupted pursuit. Yet, in proportion to the disappearance of those apprehensions which attended our weakness, as once contrasted with the power of some of the States of the Old World, should we now be solicitous as to those which belong to the conviction that it is to our own conduct we must look for the preservation of those causes on which depend the excellence and the duration of our happy system of government.

In the example of other systems founded on the will of the people we trace to internal dissension the influences which have so often blasted the hopes of the friends of freedom. The social elements, which were strong and successful when united against external danger, failed in the more difficult task of properly adjusting their own internal organization, and thus gave way the great principle of self-government. Let us trust that this admonition will never be forgotten by the Government or the people of the United States, and that the testimony which our experience thus far holds out to the great human family of the practicability and the blessings of free government will be confirmed in all time to come.

We have but to look at the state of our agriculture, manufactures, and commerce and the unexampled increase of our population to feel the magnitude of the trust committed to us. Never in any former period of our history have we had greater reason than we now have to be thankful to Divine Providence for the blessings of health and general prosperity. Every branch of labor we see crowned with the most abundant rewards. In every element of national resources and wealth and of individual comfort we witness the most rapid and solid improvements. With no interruptions to this pleasing prospect at home which will not yield to the spirit of harmony and good will that so strikingly pervades the mass of the people in every quarter, amidst all the diversity of interest and pursuits to which they are attached, and with no cause of solicitude in regard to our external affairs which will not, it is hoped, disappear before the principles of simple justice and the forbearance that mark our intercourse with foreign powers, we have every reason to feel proud of our beloved country.

The general state of our foreign relations has not materially changed since my last annual message.

In the settlement of the question of the northeastern boundary little progress has been made. Great Britain has declined acceding to the proposition of the United States, presented in accordance with the resolution of the Senate, unless certain preliminary conditions were admitted, which I deemed incompatible with a satisfactory and rightful adjustment of the controversy. Waiting for some distinct proposal from the Government of Great Britain, which has been invited, I can only repeat the expression of my confidence that, with the strong mutual disposition which I believe exists to make a just arrangement, this perplexing question can be settled with a due regard to the well-founded pretensions and pacific policy of all the parties to it. Events are frequently occurring on the northeastern frontier of a character to impress upon all the necessity of a speedy and definitive termination of the dispute. This consideration, added to the desire common to both to relieve the liberal and friendly relations so happily existing between the two countries from all embarrassment, will no doubt have its just influence upon both.

Our diplomatic intercourse with Portugal has been renewed, and it is expected that the claims of our citizens, partially paid, will be fully satisfied as soon as the condition of the Queen's Government will permit the proper attention to the subject of them. That Government has, I am happy to inform you, manifested a determination to act upon the liberal principles which have marked our commercial policy. The happiest effects upon the future trade between the United States and Portugal are anticipated from it, and the time is not thought to be remote when a system of perfect reciprocity will be established.

The installments due under the convention with the King of the Two Sicilies have been paid with that scrupulous fidelity by which his whole conduct has been characterized, and the hope is indulged that the adjustment of the vexed question of our claims will be followed by a more extended and mutually beneficial intercourse between the two countries.

The internal contest still continues in Spain. Distinguished as this struggle has unhappily been by incidents of the most sanguinary character, the obligations of the late treaty of indemnification with us have been, nevertheless, faithfully executed by the Spanish Government.

No provision having been made at the last session of Congress for the ascertainment of the claims to be paid and the apportionment of the funds under the convention made with Spain, I invite your early attention to the subject. The public evidences of the debt have, according to the terms of the convention and in the forms prescribed by it, been placed in the possession of the United States, and the interest as it fell due has been regularly paid upon them. Our commercial intercourse with Cuba stands as regulated by the act of Congress. No recent information has been received as to the disposition of the Government of Madrid on this subject, and the lamented death of our recently appointed minister on his way to Spain, with the pressure of their affairs at home, renders it scarcely probable that any change is to be looked for during the coming year. Further portions of the Florida archives have been sent to the United States, although the death of one of the commissioners at a critical moment embarrassed the progress of the delivery of them. The higher officers of the local government have recently shewn an anxious desire, in compliance with the orders from the parent Government, to facilitate the selection and delivery of all we have a right to claim.

Negotiations have been opened at Madrid for the establishment of a lasting peace between Spain and such of the Spanish American Governments of this hemisphere as have availed themselves of the intimation given to all of them of the disposition of Spain to treat upon the basis of their entire independence. It is to be regretted that simultaneous appointments by all of ministers to negotiate with Spain had not been made. The negotiation itself would have been simplified, and this long-standing dispute, spreading over a large portion of the world, would have been brought to a more speedy conclusion.

Our political and commercial relations with Austria, Prussia, Sweden, and Denmark stand on the usual favorable bases. One of the articles of our treaty with Russia in relation to the trade on the northwest coast of America having expired, instructions have been given to our minister at St. Petersburg to negotiate a renewal of it. The long and unbroken amity between the two Governments gives every reason for supposing the article will be renewed, if stronger motives do not exist to prevent it than with our view of the subject can be anticipated here.

I ask your attention to the message of my predecessor at the opening of the second session of the Nineteenth Congress, relative to our commercial intercourse with Holland, and to the documents connected with that subject, communicated to the House of Representatives on the 10th of January, 1825, and 18th of January, 1827. Coinciding in the opinion of my predecessor that Holland is not, under the regulations of her present system, entitled to have her vessels and their cargoes received into the United States on the footing of American vessels and cargoes as regards duties of tonnage and impost, a respect for his reference of it to the Legislature has alone prevented me from acting on the subject. I should still have waited without comment for the action of Congress, but recently a claim has been made by Belgian subjects to admission into our ports for their ships and cargoes on the same footing as American, with the allegation we could not dispute that our vessels received in their ports the identical treatment shewn to them in the ports of Holland, upon whose vessels no discrimination is made in the ports of the United States. Giving the same privileges the Belgians expected the same benefits—benefits that were, in fact, enjoyed when Belgium and Holland were united under one Government. Satisfied with the justice of their pretension to be placed on the same footing with Holland, I could not, nevertheless, without disregard to the principle of our laws, admit their claim to be treated as Americans, and at the same time a respect for Congress, to whom the subject had long since been referred, has prevented me from producing a just equality by taking from the vessels of Holland privileges conditionally granted by acts of Congress, although the condition upon which the grant was made has, in my judgment, failed since 1822. I recommend, therefore, a review of the act of 1824, and such a modification of it as will produce an equality on such terms as Congress shall think best comports with our settled policy and the obligations of justice to two friendly powers.

With the Sublime Porte and all the Governments on the coast of Barbary our relations continue to be friendly. The proper steps have been taken to renew our treaty with Morocco.

The Argentine Republic has again promised to send within the current year a minister to the United States.

A convention with Mexico for extending the time for the appointment of commissioners to run the boundary line has been concluded and will be submitted to the Senate. Recent events in that country have awakened the liveliest solicitude in the United States. Aware of the strong temptations existing and powerful inducements held out to the citizens of the United States to mingle in the dissensions of our immediate neighbors, instructions have been given to the district attorneys of the United States where indications warranted it to prosecute without respect to persons all who might attempt to violate the obligations of our neutrality, while at the same time it has been thought necessary to apprise the Government of Mexico that we should require the integrity of our territory to be scrupulously respected by both parties.

From our diplomatic agents in Brazil, Chile, Peru, Central America, Venezuela, and New Granada constant assurances are received of the continued good understanding with the Governments to which they are severally accredited. With those Governments upon which our citizens have valid and accumulating claims, scarcely an advance toward a settlement of them is made, owing mainly to their distracted state or to the pressure of imperative domestic questions. Our patience has been and will probably be still further severely tried, but our fellow-citizens whose interests are involved may confide in the determination of the Government to obtain for them eventually ample retribution.

Unfortunately, many of the nations of this hemisphere are still self-tormented by domestic dissensions. Revolution succeeds revolution; injuries are committed upon foreigners engaged in lawful pursuits; much time elapses before a government sufficiently stable is erected to justify expectation of redress; ministers are sent and received, and before the discussions of past injuries are fairly begun fresh troubles arise; but too frequently new injuries are added to the old, to be discussed together with the existing government after it has proved its ability to sustain the assaults made upon it, or with its successor if overthrown.   If this unhappy condition of things continues much longer, other nations will be under the painful necessity of deciding whether justice to their suffering citizens does not require a prompt redress of injuries by their own power, without waiting for the establishment of a government competent and enduring enough to discuss and to make satisfaction for them.

Since the last session of Congress the validity of our claims upon France, as liquidated by the treaty of 1831, has been acknowledged by both branches of her legislature, and the money has been appropriated for their discharge; but the payment is, I regret to inform you, still withheld.

A brief recapitulation of the most important incidents in this protracted controversy will shew how utterly untenable are the grounds upon which this course is attempted to be justified.

On entering upon the duties of my station I found the United States an unsuccessful applicant to the justice of France for the satisfaction of claims the validity of which was never questionable, and has now been most solemnly admitted by France herself.   The antiquity of these claims, their high justice, and the aggravating circumstances out of which they arose are too familiar to the American people to require description.   It is sufficient to say that for a period of ten years and upward our commerce was, with but little interruption, the subject of constant aggressions on the part of France—aggressions the ordinary features of which were condemnations of vessels and cargoes under arbitrary decrees, adopted in contravention as well of the laws of nations as of treaty stipulations, burnings on the high seas, and seizures and confiscations under special imperial rescripts in the ports of other nations occupied by the armies or under the control of France.   Such it is now conceded is the character of the wrongs we suffered—wrongs in many cases so flagrant that even their authors never denied our right to reparation.   Of the extent of these injuries some conception may be formed from the fact that after the burning of a large amount at sea and the necessary deterioration in other cases by long detention the American property so seized and sacrificed at forced sales, excluding what was adjudged to privateers before or without condemnation, brought into the French treasury upward of 24,000,000 francs, besides large customhouse duties.

The subject had already been an affair of twenty years' uninterrupted negotiation, except for a short time when France was overwhelmed by the military power of united Europe.   During this period, whilst other nations were extorting from her payment of their claims at the point of the bayonet, the United States intermitted their demand for justice out of respect to the oppressed condition of a gallant people to whom they felt under obligations for fraternal assistance in their own days of suffering and of peril.   The bad effects of these protracted and unavailing discussions, as well upon our relations with France as upon our national character, were obvious, and the line of duty was to my mind equally so. This was either to insist upon the adjustment of our claims within a reasonable period or to abandon them altogether. I could not doubt that by this course the interests and honor of both countries would be best consulted. Instructions were therefore given in this spirit to the minister who was sent out once more to demand reparation. Upon the meeting of Congress in December, 1829, I felt it my duty to speak of these claims and the delays of France in terms calculated to call the serious attention of both countries to the subject. The then French ministry took exception to the message on the ground of its containing a menace, under which it was not agreeable to the French Government to negotiate. The American minister of his own accord refuted the construction which was attempted to be put upon the message and at the same time called to the recollection of the French ministry that the President's message was a communication addressed, not to foreign governments, but to the Congress of the United States, in which it was enjoined upon him by the Constitution to lay before that body information of the state of the Union, comprehending its foreign as well as its domestic relations, and that if in the discharge of this duty he felt it incumbent upon him to summon the attention of Congress in due time to what might be the possible consequences of existing difficulties with any foreign government, he might fairly be supposed to do so under a sense of what was due from him in a frank communication with another branch of his own Government, and not from any intention of holding a menace over a foreign power. The views taken by him received my approbation, the French Government was satisfied, and the negotiation was continued. It terminated in the treaty of July 4, 1831, recognizing the justice of our claims in part and promising payment to the amount of 25,000,000 francs in six annual installments.

The ratifications of this treaty were exchanged at Washington on the 2d of February, 1832, and in five days thereafter it was laid before Congress, who immediately passed the acts necessary on our part to secure to France the commercial advantages conceded to her in the compact. The treaty had previously been solemnly ratified by the King of the French in terms which are certainly not mere matters of form, and of which the translation is as follows:

We, approving the above convention in all and each of the dispositions which are contained in it, do declare, by ourselves as well as by our heirs and successors, that it is accepted, approved, ratified, and confirmed, and by these presents, signed by our hand, we do accept, approve, ratify, and confirm it; promising, on the faith and word of a king, to observe it and to cause it to be observed inviolably, without ever contravening it or suffering it to be contravened, directly or indirectly, for any cause or under any pretense whatsoever.

Official information of the exchange of ratifications in the United States reached Paris whilst the Chambers were in session. The extraordinary and to us injurious delays of the French Government in their action upon the subject of its fulfillment have been heretofore stated to Congress, and I have no disposition to enlarge upon them here. It is sufficient to observe that the then pending session was allowed to expire without even an effort to obtain the necessary appropriations; that the two succeeding ones were also suffered to pass away without anything like a serious attempt to obtain a decision upon the subject, and that it was not until the fourth session, almost three years after the conclusion of the treaty and more than two years after the exchange of ratifications, that the bill for the execution of the treaty was pressed to a vote and rejected.

In the meantime the Government of the United States, having full confidence that a treaty entered into and so solemnly ratified by the French King would be executed in good faith, and not doubting that provision would be made for the payment of the first installment which was to become due on the 2d day of February, 1833, negotiated a draft for the amount through the Bank of the United States. When this draft was presented by the holder with the credentials required by the treaty to authorize him to receive the money, the Government of France allowed it to be protested. In addition to the injury in the nonpayment of the money by France, conformably to her engagement, the United States were exposed to a heavy claim on the part of the bank under pretense of damages, in satisfaction of which that institution seized upon and still retains an equal amount of the public money. Congress was in session when the decision of the Chambers reached Washington, and an immediate communication of this apparently final decision of France not to fulfill the stipulations of the treaty was the course naturally to be expected from the President. The deep tone of dissatisfaction which pervaded the public mind and the correspondent excitement produced in Congress by only a general knowledge of the result rendered it more than probable that a resort to immediate measures of redress would be the consequence of calling the attention of that body to the subject. Sincerely desirous of preserving the pacific relations which had so long existed between the two countries, I was anxious to avoid this course if I could be satisfied that by doing so neither the interests nor the honor of my country would be compromitted. Without the fullest assurances upon that point, I could not hope to acquit myself of the responsibility to be incurred in suffering Congress to adjourn without laying the subject before them. Those received by me were believed to be of that character.

That the feelings produced in the United States by the news of the rejection of the appropriation would be such as I have described them to have been was foreseen by the French Government, and prompt measures were taken by it to prevent the consequences. The King in person expressed through our minister at Paris his profound regret at the decision of the Chambers, and promised to send forthwith a national ship with dispatches to his minister here authorizing him to give such assurances as would satisfy the Government and people of the United States that the treaty would yet be faithfully executed by France. The national ship arrived, and the minister received his instructions. Claiming to act under the authority derived from them, he gave to this Government in the name of his the most solemn assurances that as soon after the new elections as the charter would permit the French Chambers would be convened and the attempt to procure the necessary appropriations renewed; that all the constitutional powers of the King and his ministers should be put in requisition to accomplish the object, and he was understood, and so expressly informed by this Government at the time, to engage that the question should be pressed to a decision at a period sufficiently early to permit information of the result to be communicated to Congress at the commencement of their next session. Relying upon these assurances, I incurred the responsibility, great as I regarded it to be, of suffering Congress to separate without communicating with them upon the subject.

The expectations justly founded upon the promises thus solemnly made to this Government by that of France were not realized. The French Chambers met on the 31st of July, 1834, soon after the election, and although our minister in Paris urged the French ministry to bring the subject before them, they declined doing so. He next insisted that the Chambers, if prorogued without acting on the subject, should be reassembled at a period so early that their action on the treaty might be known in Washington prior to the meeting of Congress. This reasonable request was not only declined, but the Chambers were prorogued to the 29th of December, a day so late that their decision, however urgently pressed, could not in all probability be obtained in time to reach Washington before the necessary adjournment of Congress by the Constitution. The reasons given by the ministry for refusing to convoke the Chambers at an earlier period were afterwards shewn not to be insuperable by their actual convocation on the 1st of December under a special call for domestic purposes, which fact, however, did not become known to this Government until after the commencement of the last session of Congress.

Thus disappointed in our just expectations, it became my imperative duty to consult with Congress in regard to the expediency of a resort to retaliatory measures in case the stipulations of the treaty should not be speedily complied with, and to recommend such as in my judgment the occasion called for. To this end an unreserved communication of the case in all its aspects became indispensable. To have shrunk in making it from saying all that was necessary to its correct understanding, and that the truth would justify, for fear of giving offense to others, would have been unworthy of us. To have gone, on the other hand, a single step further for the purpose of wounding the pride of a Government and people with whom we had so many motives for cultivating relations of amity and reciprocal advantage would have been unwise and improper. Admonished by the past of the difficulty of making even the simplest statement of our wrongs without disturbing the sensibilities of those who had by their position become responsible for their redress, and earnestly desirous of preventing further obstacles from that source, I went out of my way to preclude a construction of the message by which the recommendation that was made to Congress might be regarded as a menace to France in not only disavowing such a design, but in declaring that her pride and her power were too well known to expect anything from her fears. The message did not reach Paris until more than a month after the Chambers had been in session, and such was the insensibility of the ministry to our rightful claims and just expectations that our minister had been informed that the matter when introduced would not be pressed as a cabinet measure.

Although the message was not officially communicated to the French Government, and notwithstanding the declaration to the contrary which it contained, the French ministry decided to consider the conditional recommendation of reprisals a menace and an insult which the honor of the nation made it incumbent on them to resent. The measures resorted to by them to evince their sense of the supposed indignity were the immediate recall of their minister at Washington, the offer of passports to the American minister at Paris, and a public notice to the legislative Chambers that all diplomatic intercourse with the United States had been suspended. Having in this manner vindicated the dignity of France, they next proceeded to illustrate her justice. To this end a bill was immediately introduced into the Chamber of Deputies proposing to make the appropriations necessary to carry into effect the treaty. As this bill subsequently passed into a law, the provisions of which now constitute the main subject of difficulty between the two nations, it becomes my duty, in order to place the subject before you in a clear light, to trace the history of its passage and to refer with some particularity to the proceedings and discussions in regard to it.

The minister of finance in his opening speech alluded to the measures which had been adopted to resent the supposed indignity, and recommended the execution of the treaty as a measure required by the honor and justice of France. He as the organ of the ministry declared the message, so long as it had not received the sanction of Congress, a mere expression of the personal opinion of the President, for which neither the Government nor people of the United States were responsible, and that an engagement had been entered into for the fulfillment of which the honor of France was pledged. Entertaining these views, the single condition which the French ministry proposed to annex to the payment of the money was that it should not be made until it was ascertained that the Government of the United States had done nothing to injure the interests of France, or, in other words, that no steps had been authorized by Congress of a hostile character toward France.

What the disposition or action of Congress might be was then unknown to the French cabinet; but on the 14th of January the Senate resolved that it was at that time inexpedient to adopt any legislative measures in regard to the state of affairs between the United States and France, and no action on the subject had occurred in the House of Representatives. These facts were known in Paris prior to the 28th of March, 1835, when the committee to whom the bill of indemnification had been referred reported it to the Chamber of Deputies. That committee substantially reechoed the sentiments of the ministry, declared that Congress had set aside the proposition of the President, and recommended the passage of the bill without any other restriction than that originally proposed. Thus was it known to the French ministry and Chambers that if the position assumed by them, and which had been so frequently and solemnly announced as the only one compatible with the honor of France, was maintained and the bill passed as originally proposed, the money would be paid and there would be an end of this unfortunate controversy.

But this cheering prospect was soon destroyed by an amendment introduced into the bill at the moment of its passage, providing that the money should not be paid until the French Government had received satisfactory explanations of the President's message of the 2d December, 1834, and, what is still more extraordinary, the president of the council of ministers adopted this amendment and consented to its incorporation in the bill. In regard to a supposed insult which had been formally resented by the recall of their minister and the offer of passports to ours, they now for the first time proposed to ask explanations. Sentiments and propositions which they had declared could not justly be imputed to the Government or people of the United States are set up as obstacles to the performance of an act of conceded justice to that Government and people. They had declared that the honor of France required the fulfillment of the engagement into which the King had entered, unless Congress adopted the recommendations of the message. They ascertained that Congress did not adopt them, and yet that fulfillment is refused unless they first obtain from the President explanations of an opinion characterized by themselves as personal and inoperative.

The conception that it was my intention to menace or insult the Government of France is as unfounded as the attempt to extort from the fears of that nation what her sense of justice may deny would be vain and ridiculous. But the Constitution of the United States imposes on the President the duty of laying before Congress the condition of the country in its foreign and domestic relations, and of recommending such measures as may in his opinion be required by its interests. From the performance of this duty he can not be deterred by the fear of wounding the sensibilities of the people or government of whom it may become necessary to speak; and the American people are incapable of submitting to an interference by any government on earth, however powerful, with the free performance of the domestic duties which the Constitution has imposed on their public functionaries. The discussions which intervene between the several departments of our Government belong to ourselves, and for anything said in them our public servants are only responsible to their own constituents and to each other. If in the course of their consultations facts are erroneously stated or unjust deductions are made, they require no other inducement to correct them, however informed of their error, than their love of justice and what is due to their own character; but they can never submit to be interrogated upon the subject as a matter of right by a foreign power. When our discussions terminate in acts, our responsibility to foreign powers commences, not as individuals, but as a nation. The principle which calls in question the President for the language of his message would equally justify a foreign power in demanding explanation of the language used in the report of a committee or by a member in debate.

This is not the first time that the Government of France has taken exception to the messages of American Presidents. President Washington and the first President Adams in the performance of their duties to the American people fell under the animadversions of the French Directory. The objection taken by the ministry of Charles X, and removed by the explanations made by our minister upon the spot, has already been adverted to. When it was understood that the ministry of the present King took exception to my message of last year, putting a construction upon it which was disavowed on its face, our late minister at Paris, in answer to the note which first announced a dissatisfaction with the language used in the message, made a communication to the French Government under date of the 29th of January, 1835,* calculated to remove all impressions which an unreasonable susceptibility had created. He repeated and called the attention of the French Government to the disavowal contained in the message itself of any intention to intimidate by menace; he truly declared that it contained and was intended to contain no charge of ill faith against the King of the French, and properly distinguished between the right to complain in unexceptionable terms of the omission to execute an agreement and an accusation of bad motives in withholding such execution, and demonstrated that the necessary use of that right ought not to be considered as an offensive imputation. Although this communication was made without instructions and entirely on the minister's own responsibility, yet it was afterwards made the act of this Government by my full approbation, and that approbation was officially made known on the 25th of April, 1835, to the French Government. It, however, failed to have any effect. The law, after this friendly

* For communication, see pp. 202-208.

explanation, passed with the obnoxious amendment, supported by the King's ministers, and was finally approved by the King.

The people of the United States are justly attached to a pacific system in their intercourse with foreign nations. It is proper, therefore, that they should know whether their Government has adhered to it. In the present instance it has been carried to the utmost extent that was consistent with a becoming self-respect. The note of the 29th of January, to which I have before alluded, was not the only one which our minister took upon himself the responsibility of presenting on the same subject and in the same spirit. Finding that it was intended to make the payment of a just debt dependent on the performance of a condition which he knew could never be complied with, he thought it a duty to make another attempt to convince the French Government that whilst self-respect and regard to the dignity of other nations would always prevent us from using any language that ought to give offense, yet we could never admit a right in any foreign government to ask explanations of or to interfere in any manner in the communications which one branch of our public councils made with another; that in the present case no such language had been used, and that this had in a former note been fully and voluntarily stated, before it was contemplated to make the explanation a condition; and that there might be no misapprehension he stated the terms used in that note, and he officially informed them that it had been approved by the President, and that therefore every explanation which could reasonably be asked or honorably given had been already made; that the contemplated measure had been anticipated by a voluntary and friendly declaration, and was therefore not only useless, but might be deemed offensive, and certainly would not be complied with if annexed as a condition.

When this latter communication, to which I especially invite the attention of Congress, was laid before me, I entertained the hope that the means it was obviously intended to afford of an honorable and speedy adjustment of the difficulties between the two nations would have been accepted, and I therefore did not hesitate to give it my sanction and full approbation. This was due to the minister who had made himself responsible for the act, and it was published to the people of the United States and is now laid before their representatives to shew how far their Executive has gone in its endeavors to restore a good understanding between the two countries. It would have been at any time communicated to the Government of France had it been officially requested.

The French Government having received all the explanation which honor and principle permitted, and which could in reason be asked, it was hoped it would no longer hesitate to pay the installments now due. The agent authorized to receive the money was instructed to inform the French minister of his readiness to do so. In reply to this notice he was told that the money could not then be paid, because the formalities required by the act of the Chambers had not been arranged.

Not having received any official information of the intentions of the French Government, and anxious to bring, as far as practicable, this unpleasant affair to a close before the meeting of Congress, that you might have the whole subject before you, I caused our chargé d'affaires at Paris to be instructed to ask for the final determination of the French Government, and in the event of their refusal to pay the installments now due, without further explanations to return to the United States.

The result of this last application has not yet reached us, but is daily expected. That it may be favorable is my sincere wish. France having now, through all the branches of her Government, acknowledged the validity of our claims and the obligation of the treaty of 1831, and there really existing no adequate cause for further delay, will at length, it may be hoped, adopt the course which the interests of both nations, not less than the principles of justice, so imperiously require. The treaty being once executed on her part, little will remain to disturb the friendly relations of the two countries—nothing, indeed, which will not yield to the suggestions of a pacific and enlightened policy and to the influence of that mutual good will and of those generous recollections which we may confidently expect will then be revived in all their ancient force. In any event, however, the principle involved in the new aspect which has been given to the controversy is so vitally important to the independent administration of the Government that it can neither be surrendered nor compromitted without national degradation. I hope it is unnecessary for me to say that such a sacrifice will not be made through any agency of mine. The honor of my country shall never be stained by an apology from me for the statement of truth and the performance of duty; nor can I give any explanation of my official acts except such as is due to integrity and justice and consistent with the principles on which our institutions have been framed. This determination will, I am confident, be approved by my constituents. I have, indeed, studied their character to but little purpose if the sum of 25,000,000 francs will have the weight of a feather in the estimation of what appertains to their national independence, and if, unhappily, a different impression should at any time obtain in any quarter, they will, I am sure, rally round the Government of their choice with alacrity and unanimity, and silence forever the degrading imputation.

Having thus frankly presented to you the circumstances which since the last session of Congress have occurred in this interesting and important matter, with the views of the Executive in regard to them, it is at this time only necessary to add that whenever the advices now daily expected from our chargé d'affaires shall have been received they will be made the subject of a special communication.

The condition of the public finances was never more flattering than at the present period.

Since my last annual communication all the remains of the public debt have been redeemed, or money has been placed in deposit for this purpose whenever the creditors choose to receive it. All the other pecuniary engagements of the Government have been honorably and promptly fulfilled, and there will be a balance in the Treasury at the close of the present year of about $19,000,000. It is believed that after meeting all outstanding and unexpended appropriations there will remain near eleven millions to be applied to any new objects which Congress may designate or to the more rapid execution of the works already in progress. In aid of these objects, and to satisfy the current expenditures of the ensuing year, it is estimated that there will be received from various sources twenty millions more in 1836.

Should Congress make new appropriations in conformity with the estimates which will be submitted from the proper Departments, amounting to about twenty-four millions, still the available surplus at the close of the next year, after deducting all unexpended appropriations, will probably not be less than six millions. This sum can, in my judgment, be now usefully applied to proposed improvements in our navy-yards, and to new national works which are not enumerated in the present estimates or to the more rapid completion of those already begun. Either would be constitutional and useful, and would render unnecessary any attempt in our present peculiar condition to divide the surplus revenue or to reduce it any faster than will be effected by the existing laws. In any event, as the annual report from the Secretary of the Treasury will enter into details, shewing the probability of some decrease in the revenue during the next seven years and a very considerable deduction in 1842, it is not recommended that Congress should undertake to modify the present tariff so as to disturb the principles on which the compromise act was passed. Taxation on some of the articles of general consumption which are not in competition with our own productions may be no doubt so diminished as to lessen to some extent the source of this revenue, and the same object can also be assisted by more liberal provisions for the subjects of public defense, which in the present state of our prosperity and wealth may be expected to engage your attention. If, however, after satisfying all the demands which can arise from these sources the unexpended balance in the Treasury should still continue to increase, it would be better to bear with the evil until the great changes contemplated in our tariff laws have occurred and shall enable us to revise the system with that care and circumspection which are due to so delicate and important a subject.

It is certainly our duty to diminish as far as we can the burdens of taxation and to regard all the restrictions which are imposed on the trade and navigation of our citizens as evils which we shall mitigate whenever we are not prevented by the adverse legislation and policy of foreign nations or those primary duties which the defense and independence of our country enjoin upon us. That we have accomplished much toward the relief of our citizens by the changes which have accompanied the payment of the public debt and the adoption of the present revenue laws is manifest from the fact that compared with 1833 there is a diminution of near twenty-five millions in the last two years, and that our expenditures, independently of those for the public debt, have been reduced near nine millions during the same period. Let us trust that by the continued observance of economy and by harmonizing the great interests of agriculture, manufactures, and commerce much more may be accomplished to diminish the burdens of government and to increase still further the enterprise and the patriotic affection of all classes of our citizens and all the members of our happy Confederacy. As the data which the Secretary of the Treasury will lay before you in regard to our financial resources are full and extended, and will afford a safe guide in your future calculations, I think it unnecessary to offer any further observations on that subject here.

Among the evidences of the increasing prosperity of the country, not the least gratifying is that afforded by the receipts from the sales of the public lands, which amount in the present year to the unexpected sum of $11,000,000. This circumstance attests the rapidity with which agriculture, the first and most important occupation of man, advances and contributes to the wealth and power of our extended territory. Being still of the opinion that it is our best policy, as far as we can consistently with the obligations under which those lands were ceded to the United States, to promote their speedy settlement, I beg leave to call the attention of the present Congress to the suggestions I have offered respecting it in my former messages.

The extraordinary receipts from the sales of the public lands invite you to consider what improvements the land system, and particularly the condition of the General Land Office, may require. At the time this institution was organized, near a quarter of a century ago, it would probably have been thought extravagant to anticipate for this period such an addition to its business as has been produced by the vast increase of those sales during the past and present years. It may also be observed that since the year 1812 the land offices and surveying districts have been greatly multiplied, and that numerous legislative enactments from year to year since that time have imposed a great amount of new and additional duties upon that office, while the want of a timely application of force commensurate with the care and labor required has caused the increasing embarrassment of accumulated arrears in the different branches of the establishment.

These impediments to the expedition of much duty in the General Land Office induce me to submit to your judgment whether some modification of the laws relating to its organization, or an organization of a new character, be not called for at the present juncture, to enable the office to accomplish all the ends of its institution with a greater degree of facility and promptitude than experience has proved to be practicable under existing regulations. The variety of the concerns and the magnitude and complexity of the details occupying and dividing the attention of the Commissioner appear to render it difficult, if not impracticable, for that officer by any possible assiduity to bestow on all the multifarious subjects upon which he is called to act the ready and careful attention due to their respective importance, unless the Legislature shall assist him by a law providing, or enabling him to provide, for a more regular and economical distribution of labor, with the incident responsibility among those employed under his direction. The mere manual operation of affixing his signature to the vast number of documents issuing from his office subtracts so largely from the time and attention claimed by the weighty and complicated subjects daily accumulating in that branch of the public service as to indicate the strong necessity of revising the organic law of the establishment. It will be easy for Congress hereafter to proportion the expenditure on account of this branch of the service to its real wants by abolishing from time to time the offices which can be dispensed with.

The extinction of the public debt having taken place, there is no longer any use for the offices of Commissioners of Loans and of the Sinking Fund. I recommend, therefore, that they be abolished, and that proper measures be taken for the transfer to the Treasury Department of any funds, books, and papers connected with the operations of those offices, and that the proper power be given to that Department for closing finally any portion of their business which may remain to be settled.

It is also incumbent on Congress in guarding the pecuniary interests of the country to discontinue by such a law as was passed in 1812 the receipt of the bills of the Bank of the United States in payment of the public revenue, and to provide for the designation of an agent whose duty it shall be to take charge of the books and stock of the United States in that institution, and to close all connection with it after the 3d of March, 1836, when its charter expires. In making provision in regard to the disposition of this stock it will be essential to define clearly and strictly the duties and powers of the officer charged with that branch of the public service.

It will be seen from the correspondence which the Secretary of the Treasury will lay before you that notwithstanding the large amount of the stock which the United States hold in that institution no information has yet been communicated which will enable the Government to anticipate when it can receive any dividends or derive any benefit from it.

Connected with the condition of the finances and the flourishing state of the country in all its branches of industry, it is pleasing to witness the advantages which have been already derived from the recent laws regulating the value of the gold coinage. These advantages will be more apparent in the course of the next year, when the branch mints authorized to be established in North Carolina, Georgia, and Louisiana shall have gone into operation. Aided, as it is hoped they will be, by further reforms in the banking systems of the States and by judicious regulations on the part of Congress in relation to the custody of the public moneys, it may be confidently anticipated that the use of gold and silver as a circulating medium will become general in the ordinary transactions connected with the labor of the country. The great desideratum in modern times is an efficient check upon the power of banks, preventing that excessive issue of paper whence arise those fluctuations in the standard of value which render uncertain the rewards of labor. It was supposed by those who established the Bank of the United States that from the credit given to it by the custody of the public moneys and other privileges and the precautions taken to guard against the evils which the country had suffered in the bankruptcy of many of the State institutions of that period we should derive from that institution all the security and benefits of a sound currency and every good end that was attainable under that provision of the Constitution which authorizes Congress alone to coin money and regulate the value thereof. But it is scarcely necessary now to say that these anticipations have not been realized.

After the extensive embarrassment and distress recently produced by the Bank of the United States, from which the country is now recovering, aggravated as they were by pretensions to power which defied the public authority, and which if acquiesced in by the people would have changed the whole character of our Government, every candid and intelligent individual must admit that for the attainment of the great advantages of a sound currency we must look to a course of legislation radically different from that which created such an institution.

In considering the means of obtaining so important an end we must set aside all calculations of temporary convenience, and be influenced by those only which are in harmony with the true character and the permanent interests of the Republic. We must recur to first principles and see what it is that has prevented the legislation of Congress and the States on the subject of currency from satisfying the public expectation and realizing results corresponding to those which have attended the action of our system when truly consistent with the great principle of equality upon which it rests, and with that spirit of forbearance and mutual concession and generous patriotism which was originally, and must ever continue to be, the vital element of our Union.

On this subject I am sure that I can not be mistaken in ascribing our want of success to the undue countenance which has been afforded to the spirit of monopoly. All the serious dangers which our system has yet encountered may be traced to the resort to implied powers and the use of corporations clothed with privileges, the effect of which is to advance the interests of the few at the expense of the many. We have felt but one class of these dangers exhibited in the contest waged by the Bank of the United States against the Government for the last four years. Happily they have been obviated for the present by the indignant resistance of the people, but we should recollect that the principle whence they sprung is an ever-active one, which will not fail to renew its efforts in the same and in other forms so long as there is a hope of success, founded either on the inattention of the people or the treachery of their representatives to the subtle progress of its influence. The bank is, in fact, but one of the fruits of a system at war with the genius of all our institutions—a system founded upon a political creed the fundamental principle of which is a distrust of the popular will as a safe regulator of political power, and whose great ultimate object and inevitable result, should it prevail, is the consolidation of all power in our system in one central government. Lavish public disbursements and corporations with exclusive privileges would be its substitutes for the original and as yet sound checks and balances of the Constitution—the means by whose silent and secret operation a control would be exercised by the few over the political conduct of the many by first acquiring that control over the labor and earnings of the great body of the people. Wherever this spirit has effected an alliance with political power, tyranny and despotism have been the fruit. If it is ever used for the ends of government, it has to be incessantly watched, or it corrupts the sources of the public virtue and agitates the country with questions unfavorable to the harmonious and steady pursuit of its true interests.

We are now to see whether, in the present favorable condition of the country, we can not take an effectual stand against this spirit of monopoly, and practically prove in respect to the currency as well as other important interests that there is no necessity for so extensive a resort to it as that which has been heretofore practiced. The experience of another year has confirmed the utter fallacy of the idea that the Bank of the United States was necessary as a fiscal agent of the Government. Without its aid as such, indeed, in despite of all the embarrassment it was in its power to create, the revenue has been paid with punctuality by our citizens, the business of exchange, both foreign and domestic, has been conducted with convenience, and the circulating medium has been greatly improved. By the use of the State banks, which do not derive their charters from the General Government and are not controlled by its authority, it is ascertained that the moneys of the United States can be collected and disbursed without loss or inconvenience, and that all the wants of the community in relation to exchange and currency are supplied as well as they have ever been before. If under circumstances the most unfavorable to the steadiness of the money market it has been found that the considerations on which the Bank of the United States rested its claims to the public favor were imaginary and groundless, it can not be doubted that the experience of the future will be more decisive against them.

It has been seen that without the agency of a great moneyed monopoly the revenue can be collected and conveniently and safely applied to all the purposes of the public expenditure. It is also ascertained that instead of being necessarily made to promote the evils of an unchecked paper system, the management of the revenue can be made auxiliary to the reform which the legislatures of several of the States have already commenced in regard to the suppression of small bills, and which has only to be fostered by proper regulations on the part of Congress to secure a practical return to the extent required for the security of the currency to the constitutional medium. Severed from the Government as political engines, and not susceptible of dangerous extension and combination, the State banks will not be tempted, nor will they have the power, which we have seen exercised, to divert the public funds from the legitimate purposes of the Government. The collection and custody of the revenue, being, on the contrary, a source of credit to them, will increase the security which the States provide for a faithful execution of their trusts by multiplying the scrutinies to which their operations and accounts will be subjected. Thus disposed, as well from interest as the obligations of their charters, it can not be doubted that such conditions as Congress may see fit to adopt respecting the deposits in these institutions, with a view to the gradual disuse, of the small bills will be cheerfully complied with, and that we shall soon gain in place of the Bank of the United States a practical reform in the whole paper system of the country. If by this policy we can ultimately witness the suppression of all bank bills below $20, it is apparent that gold and silver will take their place and become the principal circulating medium in the common business of the farmers and mechanics of the country. The attainment of such a result will form an era in the history of our country which will be dwelt upon with delight by every true friend of its liberty and independence. It will lighten the great tax which our paper system has so long collected from the earnings of labor, and do more to revive and perpetuate those habits of economy and simplicity which are so congenial to the character of republicans than all the legislation which has yet been attempted.

To this subject I feel that I can not too earnestly invite the special attention of Congress, without the exercise of whose authority the opportunity to accomplish so much public good must pass unimproved. Deeply impressed with its vital importance, the Executive has taken all the steps within his constitutional power to guard the public revenue and defeat the expectation which the Bank of the United States indulged of renewing and perpetuating its monopoly on the ground of its necessity as a fiscal agent and as affording a sounder currency than could be obtained without such an institution. In the performance of this duty much responsibility was incurred which would have been gladly avoided if the stake which the public had in the question could have been otherwise preserved. Although clothed with the legal authority and supported by precedent, I was aware that there was in the act of the removal of the deposits a liability to excite that sensitiveness to Executive power which it is the characteristic and the duty of freemen to indulge; but I relied on this feeling also, directed by patriotism and intelligence, to vindicate the conduct which in the end would appear to have been called for by the best interests of my country. The apprehensions natural to this feeling that there may have been a desire, through the instrumentality of that measure, to extend the Executive influence, or that it may have been prompted by motives not sufficiently free from ambition, were not overlooked. Under the operation of our institutions the public servant who is called on to take a step of high responsibility should feel in the freedom which gives rise to such apprehensions his highest security. When unfounded the attention which they arouse and the discussions they excite deprive those who indulge them of the power to do harm; when just they but hasten the certainty with which the great body of our citizens never fail to repel an attempt to procure their sanction to any exercise of power inconsistent with the jealous maintenance of their rights. Under such convictions, and entertaining no doubt that my constitutional obligations demanded the steps which were taken in reference to the removal of the deposits, it was impossible for me to be deterred from the path of duty by a fear that my motives could be misjudged or that political prejudices could defeat the just consideration of the merits of my conduct. The result has shewn how safe is this reliance upon the patriotic temper and enlightened discernment of the people. That measure has now been before them and has stood the test of all the severe analysis which its general importance, the interests it affected, and the apprehensions it excited were calculated to produce, and it now remains for Congress to consider what legislation has become necessary in consequence.

I need only add to what I have on former occasions said on this subject generally that in the regulations which Congress may prescribe respecting the custody of the public moneys it is desirable that as little discretion as may be deemed consistent with their safe-keeping should be given to the executive agents. No one can be more deeply impressed than I am with the soundness of the doctrine which restrains and limits, by specific provisions, executive discretion, as far as it can be done consistently with the preservation of its constitutional character. In respect to the control over the public money this doctrine is peculiarly applicable, and is in harmony with the great principle which I felt I was sustaining in the controversy with the Bank of the United States, which has resulted in severing to some extent a dangerous connection between a moneyed and political power. The duty of the Legislature to define, by clear and positive enactments, the nature and extent of the action which it belongs to the Executive to superintend springs out of a policy analogous to that which enjoins upon all the branches of the Federal

Government an abstinence from the exercise of powers not clearly granted.

In such a Government, possessing only limited and specific powers, the spirit of its general administration can not be wise or just when it opposes the reference of all doubtful points to the great source of authority, the States and the people, whose number and diversified relations, securing them against the influences and excitements which may mislead their agents, make them the safest depository of power. In its application to the Executive, with reference to the legislative branch of the Government, the same rule of action should make the President ever anxious to avoid the exercise of any discretionary authority which can be regulated by Congress. The biases which may operate upon him will not be so likely to extend to the representatives of the people in that body.

In my former messages to Congress I have repeatedly urged the propriety of lessening the discretionary authority lodged in the various Departments, but it has produced no effect as yet, except the discontinuance of extra allowances in the Army and Navy and the substitution of fixed salaries in the latter. It is believed that the same principles could be advantageously applied in all cases, and would promote the efficiency and economy of the public service, at the same time that greater satisfaction and more equal justice would be secured to the public officers generally.

The accompanying report of the Secretary of War will put you in possession of the operations of the Department confided to his care in all its diversified relations during the past year.

I am gratified in being able to inform you that no occurrence has required any movement of the military force, except such as is common to a state of peace. The services of the Army have been limited to their usual duties at the various garrisons upon the Atlantic and inland frontier, with the exceptions stated by the Secretary of War. Our small military establishment appears to be adequate to the purposes for which it is maintained, and it forms a nucleus around which any additional force may be collected should the public exigencies unfortunately require any increase of our military means.

The various acts of Congress which have been recently passed in relation to the Army have improved its condition, and have rendered its organization more useful and efficient. It is at all times in a state for prompt and vigorous action, and it contains within itself the power of extension to any useful limit, while at the same time it preserves that knowledge, both theoretical and practical, which education and experience alone can give, and which, if not acquired and preserved in time of peace, must be sought under great disadvantages in time of war.

The duties of the Engineer Corps press heavily upon that branch of the service, and the public interest requires an addition to its strength. The nature of the works in which the officers are engaged renders necessary professional knowledge and experience, and there is no economy in committing to them more duties than they can perform or in assigning these to other persons temporarily employed, and too often of necessity without all the qualifications which such service demands. I recommend this subject to your attention, and also the proposition submitted at the last session of Congress and now renewed, for a reorganization of the Topographical Corps. This reorganization can be effected without any addition to the present expenditure and with much advantage to the public service. The branch of duties which devolves upon these officers is at all times interesting to the community, and the information furnished by them is useful in peace and war.

Much loss and inconvenience have been experienced in consequence of the failure of the bill containing the ordinary appropriations for fortifications which passed one branch of the National Legislature at the last session, but was lost in the other. This failure was the more regretted not only because it necessarily interrupted and delayed the progress of a system of national defense, projected immediately after the last war and since steadily pursued, but also because it contained a contingent appropriation, inserted in accordance with the views of the Executive, in aid of this important object and other branches of the national defense, some portions of which might have been most usefully applied during the past season. I invite your early attention to that part of the report of the Secretary of War which relates to this subject, and recommend an appropriation sufficiently liberal to accelerate the armament of the fortifications agreeably to the proposition submitted by him, and to place our whole Atlantic seaboard in a complete state of defense. A just regard to the permanent interests of the country evidently requires this measure, but there are also other reasons which at the present juncture give it peculiar force and make it my duty to call to the subject your special consideration.

The present system of military education has been in operation sufficiently long to test its usefulness, and it has given to the Army a valuable body of officers. It is not alone in the improvement, discipline, and operation of the troops that these officers are employed. They are also extensively engaged in the administrative and fiscal concerns of the various matters confided to the War Department; in the execution of the staff duties usually appertaining to military organization; in the removal of the Indians and in the disbursement of the various expenditures growing out of our Indian relations; in the formation of roads and in the improvement of harbors and rivers; in the construction of fortifications, in the fabrication of much of the *matériel* required for the public defense, and in the preservation, distribution, and accountability of the whole, and in other miscellaneous duties not admitting of classification.

These diversified functions embrace very heavy expenditures of public money, and require fidelity, science, and business habits in their execution, and a system which shall secure these qualifications is demanded by the public interest. That this object has been in a great measure obtained by the Military Academy is shewn by the state of the service and by the prompt accountability which has generally followed the necessary advances. Like all other political systems, the present mode of military education no doubt has its imperfections, both of principle and practice; but I trust these can be improved by rigid inspections and by legislative scrutiny without destroying the institution itself.

Occurrences to which we as well as all other nations are liable, both in our internal and external relations, point to the necessity of an efficient organization of the militia. I am again induced by the importance of the subject to bring it to your attention. To suppress domestic violence and to repel foreign invasion, should these calamities overtake us, we must rely in the first instance upon the great body of the community whose will has instituted and whose power must support the Government. A large standing military force is not consonant to the spirit of our institutions nor to the feelings of our countrymen, and the lessons of former days and those also of our own times shew the danger as well as the enormous expense of these permanent and extensive military organizations. That just medium which avoids an inadequate preparation on one hand and the danger and expense of a large force on the other is what our constituents have a right to expect from their Government. This object can be attained only by the maintenance of a small military force and by such an organization of the physical strength of the country as may bring this power into operation whenever its services are required. A classification of the population offers the most obvious means of effecting this organization. Such a division may be made as will be just to all by transferring each at a proper period of life from one class to another and by calling first for the services of that class, whether for instruction or action, which from age is qualified for the duty and may be called to perform it with least injury to themselves or to the public. Should the danger ever become so imminent as to require additional force, the other classes in succession would be ready for the call. And if in addition to this organization voluntary associations were encouraged and inducements held out for their formation, our militia would be in a state of efficient service. Now, when we are at peace, is the proper time to digest and establish a practicable system. The object is certainly worth the experiment and worth the expense. No one appreciating the blessings of a republican government can object to his share of the burden which such a plan may impose. Indeed, a moderate portion of the national funds could scarcely be better applied than in carrying into effect and continuing such an arrangement, and in giving the necessary elementary instruction. We are happily at peace with all the world. A sincere desire to continue so and a fixed determination to give no just cause of offense to other nations furnish, unfortunately, no certain grounds of expectation that this relation will be uninterrupted. With this determination to give no offense is associated a resolution, equally decided, tamely to submit to none. The armor and the attitude of defense afford the best security against those collisions which the ambition, or interest, or some other passion of nations not more justifiable is liable to produce. In many countries it is considered unsafe to put arms into the hands of the people and to instruct them in the elements of military knowledge. That fear can have no place here when it is recollected that the people are the sovereign power. Our Government was instituted and is supported by the ballot box, not by the musket. Whatever changes await it, still greater changes must be made in our social institutions before our political system can yield to physical force. In every aspect, therefore, in which I can view the subject I am impressed with the importance of a prompt and efficient organization of the militia.

The plan of removing the aboriginal people who yet remain within the settled portions of the United States to the country west of the Mississippi River approaches its consummation. It was adopted on the most mature consideration of the condition of this race, and ought to be persisted in till the object is accomplished, and prosecuted with as much vigor as a just regard to their circumstances will permit, and as fast as their consent can be obtained. All preceding experiments for the improvement of the Indians have failed. It seems now to be an established fact that they can not live in contact with a civilized community and prosper. Ages of fruitless endeavors have at length brought us to a knowledge of this principle of intercommunication with them. The past we can not recall, but the future we can provide for. Independently of the treaty stipulations into which we have entered with the various tribes for the usufructuary rights they have ceded to us, no one can doubt the moral duty of the Government of the United States to protect and if possible to preserve and perpetuate the scattered remnants of this race which are left within our borders. In the discharge of this duty an extensive region in the West has been assigned for their permanent residence. It has been divided into districts and allotted among them. Many have already removed and others are preparing to go, and with the exception of two small bands living in Ohio and Indiana, not exceeding 1,500 persons, and of the Cherokees, all the tribes on the east side of the Mississippi, and extending from Lake Michigan to Florida, have entered into engagements which will lead to their transplantation.

The plan for their removal and reestablishment is founded upon the knowledge we have gained of their character and habits, and has been dictated by a spirit of enlarged liberality. A territory exceeding in extent that relinquished has been granted to each tribe. Of its climate, fertility, and capacity to support an Indian population the representations are highly favorable. To these districts the Indians are removed at the expense of the United States, and with certain supplies of clothing, arms, ammunition, and other indispensable articles; they are also furnished gratuitously with provisions for the period of a year after their arrival at their new homes. In that time, from the nature of the country and of the products raised by them, they can subsist themselves by agricultural labor, if they choose to resort to that mode of life; if they do not they are upon the skirts of the great prairies, where countless herds of buffalo roam, and a short time suffices to adapt their own habits to the changes which a change of the animals destined for their food may require. Ample arrangements have also been made for the support of schools; in some instances council houses and churches are to be erected, dwellings constructed for the chiefs, and mills for common use. Funds have been set apart for the maintenance of the poor; the most necessary mechanical arts have been introduced, and blacksmiths, gunsmiths, wheelwrights, millwrights, etc., are supported among them. Steel and iron, and sometimes salt, are purchased for them, and plows and other farming utensils, domestic animals, looms, spinning wheels, cards, etc., are presented to them. And besides these beneficial arrangements, annuities are in all cases paid, amounting in some instances to more than $30 for each individual of the tribe, and in all cases sufficiently great, if justly divided and prudently expended, to enable them, in addition to their own exertions, to live comfortably. And as a stimulus for exertion, it is now provided by law that "in all cases of the appointment of interpreters or other persons employed for the benefit of the Indians a preference shall be given to persons of Indian descent, if such can be found who are properly qualified for the discharge of the duties."

Such are the arrangements for the physical comfort and for the moral improvement of the Indians. The necessary measures for their political advancement and for their separation from our citizens have not been neglected. The pledge of the United States has been given by Congress that the country destined for the residence of this people shall be forever "secured and guaranteed to them." A country west of Missouri and Arkansas has been assigned to them, into which the white settlements are not to be pushed. No political communities can be formed in that extensive region, except those which are established by the Indians themselves or by the United States for them and with their concurrence. A barrier has thus been raised for their protection against the encroachment of our citizens, and guarding the Indians as far as possible from those evils which have brought them to their present condition. Summary authority has been given by law to destroy all ardent spirits found in their country, without waiting the doubtful result and slow process of a legal seizure. I consider the absolute and unconditional interdiction of this article among these people as the first and great step in their melioration. Halfway measures will answer no purpose. These can not successfully contend against the cupidity of the seller and the overpowering appetite of the buyer. And the destructive effects of the traffic are marked in every page of the history of our Indian intercourse.

Some general legislation seems necessary for the regulation of the relations which will exist in this new state of things between the Government and people of the United States and these transplanted Indian tribes, and for the establishment among the latter, and with their own consent, of some principles of intercommunication which their juxtaposition will call for; that moral may be substituted for physical force, the authority of a few and simple laws for the tomahawk, and that an end may be put to those bloody wars whose prosecution seems to have made part of their social system.

After the further details of this arrangement are completed, with a very general supervision over them, they ought to be left to the progress of events. These, I indulge the hope, will secure their prosperity and improvement, and a large portion of the moral debt we owe them will then be paid.

The report from the Secretary of the Navy, shewing the condition of that branch of the public service, is recommended to your special attention. It appears from it that our naval force at present in commission, with all the activity which can be given to it, is inadequate to the protection of our rapidly increasing commerce. This consideration and the more general one which regards this arm of the national defense as our best security against foreign aggressions strongly urge the continuance of the measures which promote its gradual enlargement and a speedy increase of the force which has been heretofore employed abroad and at home. You will perceive from the estimates which appear in the report of the Secretary of the Navy that the expenditures necessary to this increase of its force, though of considerable amount, are small compared with the benefits which they will secure to the country.

As a means of strengthening this national arm I also recommend to your particular attention the propriety of the suggestion which attracted the consideration of Congress at its last session, respecting the enlistment of boys at a suitable age in the service. In this manner a nursery of skillful and able-bodied seamen can be established, which will be of the greatest importance. Next to the capacity to put afloat and arm the requisite number of ships is the possession of the means to man them efficiently, and nothing seems better calculated to aid this object than the measure proposed. As an auxiliary to the advantages derived from our extensive commercial marine, it would furnish us with a resource ample enough for all the exigencies which can be anticipated. Considering the state of our resources, it can not be doubted that whatever provision the liberality and wisdom of Congress may now adopt with a view to the perfect organization of this branch of our service will meet the approbation of all classes of our citizens.

By the report of the Postmaster-General it appears that the revenue of the Department during the year ending on the 30th day of June last exceeded its accruing responsibilities $236,206, and that the surplus of the present fiscal year is estimated at $476,227. It further appears that the debt of the Department on the 1st day of July last, including the amount due to contractors for the quarter then just expired, was about $1,064,381, exceeding the available means about $23,700; and that on the 1st instant about $597,077 of this debt had been paid—$409,991 out of postages accruing before July and $187,086 out of postages accruing since. In these payments are included $67,000 of the old debt due to banks. After making these payments the Department had $73,000 in bank on the 1st instant. The pleasing assurance is given that the Department is entirely free from embarrassment, and that by collection of outstanding balances and using the current surplus the remaining portion of the bank debt and most of the other debt will probably be paid in April next, leaving thereafter a heavy amount to be applied in extending the mail facilities of the country. Reserving a considerable sum for the improvement of existing mail routes, it is stated that the Department will be able to sustain with perfect convenience an annual charge of $300,000 for the support of new routes, to commence as soon as they can be established and put in operation.

The measures adopted by the Postmaster-General to bring the means of the Department into action and to effect a speedy extinguishment of its debt, as well as to produce an efficient administration of its affairs, will be found detailed at length in his able and luminous report. Aided by a reorganization on the principles suggested and such salutary provisions in the laws regulating its administrative duties as the wisdom of Congress may devise or approve, that important Department will soon attain a degree of usefulness proportioned to the increase of our population and the extension of our settlements.

Particular attention is solicited to that portion of the report of the Postmaster-General which relates to the carriage of the mails of the United States upon railroads constructed by private corporations under the authority of the several States. The reliance which the General Government can place on those roads as a means of carrying on its operations and the principles on which the use of them is to be obtained can not too soon be considered and settled. Already does the spirit of monopoly begin to exhibit its natural propensities in attempts to exact from the public, for services which it supposes can not be obtained on other terms, the most extravagant compensation. If these claims be persisted in, the question may arise whether a combination of citizens, acting under charters of incorporation from the States, can, by a direct refusal or the demand of an exorbitant price, exclude the United States from the use of the established channels of communication between the different sections of the country, and whether the United States can not, without transcending their constitutional powers, secure to the Post-Office Department the use of those roads by an act of Congress which shall provide within itself some equitable mode of adjusting the amount of compensation. To obviate, if possible, the necessity of considering this question, it is suggested whether it be not expedient to fix by law the amounts which shall be offered to railroad companies for the conveyance of the mails, graduated according to their average weight, to be ascertained and declared by the Postmaster-General. It is probable that a liberal proposition of that sort would be accepted.

In connection with these provisions in relation to the Post-Office Department, I must also invite your attention to the painful excitement produced in the South by attempts to circulate through the mails inflammatory appeals addressed to the passions of the slaves, in prints and in various sorts of publications, calculated to stimulate them to insurrection and to produce all the horrors of a servile war. There is doubtless no respectable portion of our countrymen who can be so far misled as to feel any other sentiment than that of indignant regret at conduct so destructive of the harmony and peace of the country, and so repugnant to the principles of our national compact and to the dictates of humanity and religion. Our happiness and prosperity essentially depend upon peace within our borders, and peace depends upon the maintenance in good faith of those compromises of the Constitution upon which the Union is founded. It is fortunate for the country that the good sense, the generous feeling, and the deep-rooted attachment of the people of the nonslaveholding States to the Union and to their fellow-citizens of the same blood in the South have given so strong and impressive a tone to the sentiments entertained against the proceedings of the misguided persons who have engaged in these unconstitutional and wicked attempts, and especially against the emissaries from foreign parts who have dared to interfere in this matter, as to authorize the hope that those attempts will no longer be persisted in. But if these expressions of the public will shall not be sufficient to effect so desirable a result, not a doubt can be entertained that the nonslaveholding States, so far from countenancing the slightest interference with the constitutional rights of the South, will be prompt to exercise their authority in suppressing so far as in them lies whatever is calculated to produce this evil.

In leaving the care of other branches of this interesting subject to the State authorities, to whom they properly belong, it is nevertheless proper for Congress to take such measures as will prevent the Post-Office Department, which was designed to foster an amicable intercourse and correspondence between all the members of the Confederacy, from being used as an instrument of an opposite character. The General Government, to which the great trust is confided of preserving inviolate the relations created among the States by the Constitution, is especially bound to avoid in its own action anything that may disturb them. I would therefore call the special attention of Congress to the subject, and respectfully suggest the propriety of passing such a law as will prohibit, under severe penalties, the circulation in the Southern States, through the mail, of incendiary publications intended to instigate the slaves to insurrection.

I felt it to be my duty in the first message which I communicated to Congress to urge upon its attention the propriety of amending that part of the Constitution which provides for the election of the President and the Vice-President of the United States. The leading object which I had in view was the adoption of some new provisions which would secure to the people the performance of this high duty without any intermediate agency. In my annual communications since I have enforced the same views, from a sincere conviction that the best interests of the country would be promoted by their adoption. If the subject were an ordinary one, I should have regarded the failure of Congress to act upon it as an indication of their judgment that the disadvantages which belong to the present system were not so great as those which would result from any attainable substitute that had been submitted to their consideration. Recollecting, however, that propositions to introduce a new feature in our fundamental laws can not be too patiently examined, and ought not to be received with favor until the great body of the people are thoroughly impressed with their necessity and value as a remedy for real evils, I feel that in renewing the recommendation I have heretofore made on this subject I am not transcending the bounds of a just deference to the sense of Congress or to the disposition of the people. However much we may differ in the choice of the measures which should guide the administration of the Government, there can be but little doubt in the minds of those who are really friendly to the republican features of our system that one of its most important securities consists in the separation of the legislative and executive powers at the same time that each is held responsible to the great source of authority, which is acknowledged to be supreme, in the will of the people constitutionally expressed. My reflection and experience satisfy me that the framers of the Constitution, although they were anxious to mark this feature as a settled and fixed principle in the structure of the Government, did not adopt all the precautions that were necessary to secure its practical observance, and that we can not be said to have carried into complete effect their intentions until the evils which arise from this organic defect are remedied.

Considering the great extent of our Confederacy, the rapid increase of its population, and the diversity of their interests and pursuits, it can not be disguised that the contingency by which one branch of the Legislature is to form itself into an electoral college can not become one of ordinary occurrence without producing incalculable mischief. What was intended as the medicine of the Constitution in extreme cases can not be frequently used without changing its character and sooner or later producing incurable disorder.

Every election by the House of Representatives is calculated to lessen the force of that security which is derived from the distinct and separate character of the legislative and executive functions, and while it exposes each to temptations adverse to their efficiency as organs of the Constitution and laws, its tendency will be to unite both in resisting the will of the people, and thus give a direction to the Government antirepublican and dangerous. All history tells us that a free people should be watchful of delegated power, and should never acquiesce in a practice which will diminish their control over it. This obligation, so universal in its application to all the principles of a republic, is peculiarly so in ours, where the formation of parties founded on sectional interests is so much fostered by the extent of our territory. These interests, represented by candidates for the Presidency, are constantly prone, in the zeal of party and selfish objects, to generate influences unmindful of the general good and forgetful of the restraints which the great body of the people would enforce if they were in no contingency to lose the right of expressing their will. The experience of our country from the formation of the Government to the present day demonstrates that the people can not too soon adopt some stronger safeguard for their right to elect the highest officers known to the Constitution than is contained in that sacred instrument as it now stands.

It is my duty to call the particular attention of Congress to the present condition of the District of Columbia. From whatever cause the great depression has arisen which now exists in the pecuniary concerns of this District, it is proper that its situation should be fully understood and such relief or remedies provided as are consistent with the powers of Congress. I earnestly recommend the extension of every political right to the citizens of this District which their true interests require, and which does not conflict with the provisions of the Constitution. It is believed that the laws for the government of the District require revisal and amendment, and that much good may be done by modifying the penal code so as to give uniformity to its provisions.

Your attention is also invited to the defects which exist in the judicial system of the United States. As at present organized the States of the Union derive unequal advantages from the Federal judiciary, which have been so often pointed out that I deem it unnecessary to repeat them here. It is hoped that the present Congress will extend to all the States that equality in respect to the benefits of the laws of the Union which can only be secured by the uniformity and efficiency of the judicial system.

With these observations on the topics of general interest which are deemed worthy of your consideration, I leave them to your care, trusting that the legislative measures they call for will be met as the wants and the best interests of our beloved country demand.

ANDREW JACKSON.

Mr. Livingston to the Duke de Broglie.

LEGATION OF THE UNITED STATES,
Paris, April 25, 1835.

His Excellency the DUC DE BROGLIE, etc.,
Minister Secretary of State for Foreign Affairs.

SIR: About to return to my own country, I am unwilling to leave this without adding one more effort to the many I have heretofore made to restore to both that mutual good understanding which their best interests require, and which probable events may interrupt and perhaps permanently destroy.

From the correspondence and acts of His Majesty's Government since the message of the President of the United States was known at Paris it is evident that an idea is entertained of making the fulfillment of the treaty of 1831 dependent on explanations to be given of the terms used in the message, and withholding payment of an acknowledged debt until satisfaction be given for a supposed indecorum in demanding it. The bare possibility that this opinion might be entertained and acted upon by His Majesty's Government renders it incumbent on me to state explicitly what I understand to be the sentiments of mine on this subject.

Erroneous impressions, arising from the want of a proper attention to the structure of our Government, to the duties of its Chief Magistrate, to the principles it has adopted and its strict adherence to them in similar cases, might raise expectations which could never be realized and lead to measures destructive of all harmony between the parties. This communication is made in full confidence that it is the wish of His Majesty's Government, as it most sincerely is that of the President, to avoid all measures of that description; and it is hoped, therefore, that it will be received in the spirit by which it is dictated—that of conciliation and peace.

The form of our Government and the functions of the President as a component part of it have in their relation to this subject been sufficiently explained in my previous correspondence, especially in my letter to the Comte de Rigny of the 29th of January last. I have therefore little to add to that part of my representation which is drawn from the form of our Government and the duties of the President in administering it. If these are fully understood, the principles of action derived from them can not be mistaken.

The President, as the chief executive power, must have a free and entirely unfettered communication with the coordinate powers of Government. As the organ of intercourse with other nations, he is the only source from which a knowledge of our relations with them can be conveyed to the legislative branches. It results from this that the utmost freedom from all restraint in the details into which he is obliged to enter of international concerns and of the measures in relation to them is essential to the proper performance of this important part of his functions. He must exercise them without having continually before him the fear of offending the susceptibility of the powers whose conduct he is obliged to notice. In the performance of this duty he is subject to public opinion and his own sense of propriety for an indiscreet, to his constituents for a dangerous, and to his constitutional judges for an illegal, exercise of the power, but to no other censure, foreign or domestic. Were any foreign powers permitted to scan the communications of the Executive, their complaints, whether real or affected, would involve the country in continual controversies; for the right being acknowledged, it would be a duty to exercise it by demanding a disavowal of every phrase they might deem offensive and an explanation of every word to which an improper interpretation could be given. The principle, therefore, has been adopted that no foreign power has a right to ask for explanations of anything that the President, in the exercise of his functions, thinks proper to communicate to Congress, or of any course he may advise them to pursue. This rule is not applicable to the Government of the United States alone, but, in common with it, to all those in which the constitutional powers are distributed into different branches. No such nation desirous of avoiding foreign influence or foreign interference in its councils; no such nation possessing a due sense of its dignity and independence, can long submit to the consequences of this interference. When these are felt, as they soon will be, all must unite in repelling it, and acknowledge that the United States are contending in a cause common to them all, and more important to the liberal Governments of Europe than even to themselves; for it is too obvious to escape the slightest attention that the Monarchies of Europe by which they are surrounded will have all the advantage of this supervision of the domestic councils of their neighbors without being subject to it themselves. It is true that in the representative Governments of Europe executive communications to legislative bodies have not the extension that is given to them in the United States, and that they are therefore less liable to attack on that quarter; but they must not imagine themselves safe. In the opening address, guarded as it commonly is, every proposition made by the ministry, every resolution of either chamber, will offer occasions for the jealous interference of national punctilio, for all occupy the same grounds. No intercommunication of the different branches of Government will be safe, and even the courts of justice will afford no sanctuary for freedom of decision and of debate, and the susceptibility of foreign powers must be consulted in all the departments of Government. Occasions for intervention in the affairs of other countries are but too numerous at present, without opening another door to encroachments; and it is no answer to the argument to say that no complaints will be made but for reasonable cause, and that of this, the nation complained of being the judge, no evil can ensue. But this argument concedes the right of examining the communications in question, which is denied. Allow it and you will have frivolous as well as grave complaints to answer, and must not only heal the wounds of a just national pride, but apply a remedy to those of a morbid susceptibility. To show that my fear of the progressive nature of these encroachments is not imaginary, I pray leave to call your excellency's attention to the inclosed report from the Secretary of State to the President. It is offered for illustration, not for complaint; I am instructed to make none. Because the Government of France has taken exceptions to the President's opening message, the chargé d'affaires of France thinks it his duty to protest against a special communication, and to point out the particular passages in a correspondence of an American minister with his own Government to the publication of which he objects. If the principle I contest is just, the chargé d'affaires is right. He has done his duty as a vigilant supervisor of the President's correspondence. If the principle is admitted, every diplomatic agent at Washington will do the same, and we shall have twenty censors of the correspondence of the Government and of the public press. If the principle is correct, every communication which the President makes in relation to our foreign affairs, either to the Congress or to the public, ought in prudence to be previously submitted to these ministers, in order to avoid disputes and troublesome and humiliating explanations. If the principle be submitted to, neither dignity nor independence is left to the nation. To submit even to a discreet exercise of such a privilege would be troublesome and degrading, and the inevitable abuse of it could not be borne. It must therefore be resisted at the threshold, and its entrance forbidden into the sanctuary of domestic consultations. But whatever may be the principles of other governments, those of the United States are fixed; the right will never be acknowledged, and any attempt to enforce it will be repelled by the undivided energy of the nation

I pray your excellency to observe that my argument does not deny a right to all foreign powers of taking proper exceptions to the governmental acts and language of another.   It is to their interference in its consultations, in its proceedings while yet in an inchoate state, that we object.   Should the President do an official executive act affecting a foreign power, or use exceptionable language in addressing it through his minister or through theirs; should a law be passed injurious to the dignity of another nation—in all t iese and other similar cases a demand for explanation would be respectfully received, and answered in the manner that justice and a regard to the dignity of the complaining nation would require.

After stating these principles, let me add that they have not only been theoretically adopted, but that they have been practically asserted.   On two former occasions exceptions of the same nature were taken to the President's message by the Government of France, and in neither did they produce any other explanation than that derived from the nature of our Government, and this seems on those occasions to have been deemed sufficient, for in both cases the objections were virtually abandoned—one when Messrs. Marshall, Gerry, and Pinckney were refused to be received, and again in the negotiation between Prince Polignac and Mr. Rives.   In the former case, although the message of the President was alleged as the cause of the refusal to receive the ministers, yet without any such explanation their successors were honorably accredited.   In the latter case the allusion in the message to an apprehended collision was excepted to, but the reference made by Mr. Rives to the constitutional duties of the President seems to have removed the objection.

Having demonstrated that the United States can not in any case permit their Chief Magistrate to be questioned by any foreign government in relation to his communications with the coordinate branches of his own, it is scarcely necessary to consider the case of such an explanation being required as the condition on which the fulfillment of a treaty or any pecuniary advantage was to depend.   The terms of such a proposition need only be stated to show that it would be not only inadmissible, but rejected as offensive to the nation to which it might be addressed.   In this case it would be unnecessary as well as inadmissible.   France has already received, by the voluntary act of the President, every explanation the nicest sense of national honor could desire.   That which could not have been given to a demand, that which can never be given on the condition now under discussion, a fortunate succession of circumstances, as I shall proceed to shew, has brought about.   Earnestly desirous of restoring the good understanding between the two nations, as soon as a dissatisfaction with the President's message was shewn I suppressed every feeling which the mode of expressing that dissatisfaction was calculated to produce, and without waiting for instructions I hastened on my own responsibility to make a communication to your predecessor in office on the subject.   In this, under the reserve that the President could not be called on for an explanation, I did in fact give one that I thought would have removed all injurious impressions.

This is the first of the fortunate circumstances to which I have alluded—fortunate in being made before any demand implying a right to require it; fortunate in its containing, without any knowledge of the precise parts of the message which gave offense, answers to all that have since come to my knowledge.   I can easily conceive that the communication of which I speak, made, as I expressly stated, without previous authority from my Government, might not have had the effect which its matter was intended to produce, but it has since (as I have now the honor to inform your excellency) received from the President his full and unqualified approbation; but it is necessary to add that this was given before he had any intimation of an intention to attach it as a condition to the payment of the indemnity due by the treaty, given not only when he was ignorant of any such intent, but when he was informed by France that she intended to execute the treaty and saw by the law which was introduced that it was not to be fettered by any such condition.   Thus that is already done by a voluntary act which could not have been done when required as a right, still less when made, what will unquestionably in the United States be considered degrading, as a condition. At this time, sir, I would for no consideration enter into the details I then did. If I could now so far forget what under present circumstances would be due to the dignity of my country, I should be disavowed, and deservedly disavowed, by the President. It is happy, therefore, I repeat, that the good feeling of my country was evinced in the manner I have stated at the only time when it could be done with honor; and though present circumstances would forbid my making the communication I then did, they do not prevent my referring to it for the purpose of shewing that it contains, as I have stated it does, everything that ought to have been satisfactory. Actual circumstances enable me to do this now. Future events, which I need not explain, may hereafter render it improper, and it may be nugatory unless accepted as satisfactory before the occurrence of those events. Let it be examined with the care which the importance of giving it a true construction requires. The objections to the message, as far as I can understand, for they have never been specified, are:

First. That it impeaches the good faith of His Majesty's Government.

Secondly. That it contains a menace of enforcing the performance of the treaty by reprisals.

On the first head, were I now discussing the terms of the message itself, it would be easy to shew that it contains no such charge. The allegation that the stipulations of a treaty have not been complied with, that engagements made by ministers have not been fulfilled, couched in respectful terms, can never be deemed offensive, even when expressly directed to the party whose infractions are complained of, and consequently can never give cause for a demand of explanation; otherwise it is evident that no consideration of national injuries could ever take place. The message, critically examined on this point, contains nothing more than such an enumeration of the causes of complaint. As to its terms, the most fastidious disposition can not fasten on one that could be excepted to. The first refusal and subsequent delay are complained of, but no unworthy motives for either are charged or insinuated. On the whole, if I were commissioned to explain and defend this part of the message, I should say with the conviction of truth that it is impossible to urge a complaint in milder or more temperate terms; but I am not so commissioned. I am endeavoring to shew not only that every proper explanation is given in my letter to M. de Rigny of the 29th of January last, but that in express terms it declares that the sincerity of His Majesty's Government in their desire to execute the treaty was not doubted. Suffer me to draw your excellency's attention to the passages alluded to. In discussing the nature of M. Sérurier's engagement I say:

"It is clear, therefore, that more was required than the expression of a desire on the part of His Majesty's ministers to execute the treaty, *a desire the sincerity of which was never doubted, but which might be unavailing, as its accomplishment depended on the vote of the Chambers.*"

Again, in speaking of the delay which occurred in the month of December, I say:

"It is referred to, I presume, in order to shew that it was produced by a desire on the part of His Majesty's ministers the better to assure the passage of the law. Of this, sir, I never had a doubt, and immediately so advised my Government, and informed it, as was the fact, that I perfectly acquiesced in the delay."

Thus it must be evident, not only that no offensive charge of ill faith is made in the message, but that, as expressly stated in the first extract, full justice was done at Washington to the intentions of the French Government. While the delay is complained of as a wrong, no improper motives are attributed to the Government in causing it. Again, sir, the whole tenor of that part of my letter which relates to the inexecution of the promise made by M. Sérurier, while it asserts the construction put upon it by the President to be the true one, and appeals to facts and circumstances to support that construction, yet it avoids charging the French Government with any intentional violation, by attributing their delay to an erroneous construction only; for in the letter (I again quote literally) I say:

"I have entered into this detail with the object of showing that although the ministers of the King, under the interpretation they seem to have given to M. Sérurier's promise, may have considered themselves at liberty to defer the presentation of the law until the period which they thought would best secure its success, yet the President, interpreting that promise differently, feeling that in consequence of it he had forborne to do what might be strictly called a duty, and seeing that its performance had not taken place, could not avoid stating the whole case clearly and distinctly to Congress."

Thus, sir, the President, in stating the acts of which he thought his country had reason to complain, does not make a single imputation of improper motive, and to avoid all misconstruction he offers a voluntary declaration that none such were entertained.

The part of the message which seems to have caused the greatest sensation in France is that in which, after a statement of the causes of complaint, it enters into a consideration of the measures to obtain redress which in similar cases are sanctioned by the laws of nations. The complaint seems to be that, in a discussion it was impossible to avoid, of the efficacy and convenience of each, a preference was given to reprisals, considered as a remedial, not as a hostile, measure, and this has been construed into a menace. If any explanations were necessary on this head, they are given in the message itself. It is there expressly disavowed, and the power and high character of France are appealed to to shew that it never could be induced by threats to do what its sense of justice denied. If the measure to which I have more than once alluded should be resorted to, and the humiliation attending a compliance with it could be endured; if it were possible under such circumstances to give an explanation, what more could be required than that which is contained in the message itself that it was not intended as a menace? If the measure to which I alluded should be adopted and submitted to, what would His Majesty's Government require? The disavowal of any intent to influence the councils of France by threats? They have it already. It forms a part of the very instrument which caused the offense, and I will not do them the injustice to think that they could form the offensive idea of requiring more. The necessity of discussing the nature of the remedies for the nonexecution of the treaty, the character and spirit in which it was done, are explained in my letter so often referred to, and I pray your excellency to consider the concluding part of it, beginning with the quotation I have last made. But if I wanted any argument to shew that no explanation of this part of the message was necessary or could be required, I should find it in the opinion—certainly a just one—expressed by His Majesty's ministers, that the recommendation of the President not having been adopted by the other branches of the Government it was not a national act, and could not be complained of as such. Nay, in the note presented by M. Sérurier to the Government at Washington and the measures which it announces (his recall and the offer of my passports) the Government of His Majesty seem to have done all that they thought its dignity required, for they at the same time declare that the law providing for the payment will be presented, but give no intimation of any previous condition and annex none to the bill which they present. The account of dignity being thus declared by this demonstration to be settled, it can not be supposed that it will again be introduced as a set-off against an acknowledged pecuniary balance. Before I conclude my observations on this part of the subject it will be well to inquire in what light exceptions are taken to this part of the message, whether as a menace generally or to the particular measure proposed. In the first view, if every measure that a Government having claims on another declares it must pursue if those claims are not allowed (whatever may be the terms employed) is a menace, it is necessary, and not objectionable unless couched in offensive language; it is a fair declaration of what course the party making it intends to pursue, and except in cases where pretexts were wanted for a rupture have rarely been objected to, even when avowedly the act of the nation, not, as in this case, a proposal made by one branch of its Government to another. Instances of this are not wanting, but need not be here enumerated. One, however, ought to be mentioned, because it is intimately connected with the subject now under discussion. While the commerce of the United States was suffering under the aggressions of the two most powerful nations of the world the American Government, in this sense of the word, menaced them both. It passed a law in express terms declaring to them that unless they ceased their aggressions America would hold no intercourse with them; that their ships would be seized if they ventured into American ports; that the productions of their soil or industry should be forfeited. Here was an undisguised menace in clear, unequivocal terms, and of course, according to the argument against which I contend, neither France nor England could deliberate under its pressure without dishonor. Yet the Emperor of France, certainly an unexceptionable judge of what the dignity of his country required, did deliberate, did accept the condition, did repeal the Berlin and Milan decrees, did not make any complaint of the act as a threat, though he called it an injury. Great Britain, too, although at that time on not very friendly terms with the United States, made no complaint that her pride was offended. Her minister on the spot even made a declaration that the obnoxious orders were repealed. It is true he was disavowed, but the disavowal was accompanied by no objections to the law as a threat. Should the objection be to the nature of the remedy proposed, and that the recommendation of reprisals is the offensive part, it would be easy to show that it stands on the same ground with any other remedy; that it is not hostile in its nature; that it has been resorted to by France to procure redress from other powers, and by them against her, without producing war. But such an argument is not necessary. This is not the case of a national measure, either of menace or action; it is a recommendation only of one branch of Government to another, and France has itself shown that a proposal of this nature could not be noticed as an offense. In the year 1808 the Senate of the United States annexed to the bill of nonintercourse a section which not only advised but actually authorized the President to issue letters of marque and reprisal against both France and England, if the one did not repeal the Berlin and Milan decrees and the other did not revoke the orders in council. This clause was not acceded to by the Representatives, but it was complete as the act of the Senate; yet neither France nor England complained of it as an indignity. Both powers had ministers on the spot, and the dignity of neither seems to have been offended.

If the view I have now taken of the subject be correct; if I have succeeded in conveying to His Majesty's ministers the conviction I myself feel that no right exists in any foreign nation to ask explanations of or even to notice any communications between the different branches of our Government; that to admit it even in a single instance would be a dangerous precedent and a derogation from national dignity, and that in the present instance an explanation that ought to be satisfactory has been voluntarily given, I have then demonstrated that any measure founded on such supposed right is not only inadmissible, but is totally unnecessary, and consequently that His Majesty's ministers may at once declare that previous explanations given by the minister of the United States, and subsequently approved by the President, had satisfied them on the subject of the message.

The motives of my Government during the whole course of this controversy have been misunderstood or not properly appreciated, and the question is daily changing its character. A negotiation entered into for procuring compensation to individuals involved no positive obligation on their Governments to prosecute it to extremities. A solemn treaty, ratified by the constitutional organs of the two powers, changed the private into a public right.   The Government acquires by it a perfect right to insist on its stipulations.   All doubts as to their justice seem now to have been removed, and every objection to the payment of a debt acknowledged to be just will be severely scrutinized by the impartial world.   What character will be given to a refusal to pay such a debt on the allegation, whether well or ill founded, of an offense to national honor it does not become me to say.   The French nation are the last that would ever appreciate national honor by any number of millions it could withhold as a compensation for an injury offered to it. The United States, commercial as they are, are the last that would settle such an account.   The proposition I allude to would be unworthy of both, and it is sincerely to be hoped that it will never be made.

To avoid the possibility of misapprehension, I repeat that this communication is made with the single view of apprising His Majesty's Government of the consequences attending a measure which without such notice they might be inclined to pursue; that although I am not authorized to state what measures will be taken by the United States, yet I speak confidently of the principles they have adopted, and have no doubt they will never be abandoned.

This is the last communication I shall have the honor to make.   It is dictated by a sincere desire to restore a good intelligence, which seems to be endangered by the very measure intended to consolidate it.   Whatever be the result, the United States may appeal to the world to bear witness that in the assertion of the rights of their citizens and the dignity of their Government they have never swerved from the respect due to themselves and from that which they owe to the Government of France.

I pray your excellency to receive the assurance of the high consideration with which I have the honor to be, your most obedient servant,

EDW. LIVINGSTON.

Mr. Livingston to Mr. Forsyth.

WASHINGTON, *June 29, 1835.*

Hon. JOHN FORSYTH,
        Secretary of State, etc.

SIR: After having by my note to the Duke de Broglie dated the 25th April last made a final effort to preserve a good understanding between the United States and France by suggesting such means of accommodation as I thought were consistent with the honor of the one country to offer and of the other to accept, I determined to avail myself of the leave to return which was given by your dispatch, No. —, rather than to remain, as I had desired to do, in England waiting the result of my last communication.   This step having been approved by the President, I need not here refer to the reasons which induced me to take it.   Having received my passports, I left Paris on the 29th of April.   At the time of my departure the note, of which a copy has been transmitted to you, asking an explanation of the terms used in Mr. Sérurier's communication to the Department remained unanswered, but I have reason to believe that the answer when given will be satisfactory.

The principal business with which I was charged having thus been brought to a close, I presume that my services can no longer be useful to my country, and I therefore pray that the President will be pleased to accept my resignation of the trust with which I have been honored.   I shall terminate it by transmitting to the Department some papers relating to matters of minor importance which I soon expect to receive, and will add the explanations which may yet be wanting to give a full view of the affairs of the mission up to the time of my leaving France.

I have the honor to be, sir, with perfect respect, your most obedient servant,

EDW. LIVINGSTON.

Mr. Forsyth to Mr. Livingston.

DEPARTMENT OF STATE,
Washington, June 30, 1835.

EDWARD LIVINGSTON, Esq.,
Washington.

SIR: Your letter of the 29th instant has been laid before the President, and I am directed to reply that the President can not allow you, who have been so long and usefully employed in the public service, to leave the trust last confided to you without an expression of his regard and respect, the result of many years of intimate association in peace and war. Although differing on some points of general policy, your singleness of purpose, perfect integrity, and devotion to your country have been always known to him. In the embarrassing and delicate position you have lately occupied your conduct, and especially your last official note in closing your correspondence with the French Government, has met his entire approbation, exhibiting as it does, with truth, the anxious desire of the Government and the people of the United States to maintain the most liberal and pacific relations with the nation to which you were accredited, and a sincere effort to remove ill-founded impressions and to soothe the feelings of national susceptibility, even when they have been unexpectedly excited, while at the same time it discourages with a proper firmness any expectation that the American Government can ever be brought to allow an interference inconsistent with the spirit of its institutions or make concessions incompatible with its self-respect. The President is persuaded that he will be sustained in these opinions by the undivided sentiment of the American people, and that you will carry into a retirement which he trusts may be temporary the consciousness not only of having performed your duty, but of having realized the anticipations of your fellow-citizens and secured for yourself and your country the just appreciation of the world.

I am, sir, very respectfully, your obedient servant,

JOHN FORSYTH.

SPECIAL MESSAGES.

WASHINGTON CITY, *December 8, 1835.*

To the Senate and House of Representatives of the United States:

I transmit herewith a report from the Secretary of the Treasury, exhibiting certain transfers of appropriations that have been made in that Department in pursuance of the power vested in the President by the act of Congress of the 3d of March, 1809, entitled "An act further to amend the several acts for the establishment and regulation of the Treasury, War, and Navy Departments."

ANDREW JACKSON.

WASHINGTON, *December 9, 1835.*

To the Senate and House of Representatives.

GENTLEMEN: I herewith communicate, for the information of Congress, a report of the Secretary of War, with accompanying documents, showing the progress made during the present year in the astronomical observations made under the act of the 14th of July, 1832, relative to the northern boundary of the State of Ohio.

The controversy between the authorities of the State of Ohio and those of the Territory of Michigan in respect to this boundary assumed about the time of the termination of the last session of Congress a very threatening aspect, and much care and exertion were necessary to preserve the jurisdiction of the Territorial government under the acts of Congress and to prevent a forcible collision between the parties. The nature and course of the dispute and the measures taken by the Executive for the purpose of composing it will fully appear in the accompanying report from the Secretary of State and the documents therein referred to.

The formation of a State government by the inhabitants of the Territory of Michigan and their application, now pending, to be admitted into the Union give additional force to the many important reasons which call for the settlement of this question by Congress at their present session.

ANDREW JACKSON.

WASHINGTON, December 9, 1835.

To the Senate and House of Representatives.

GENTLEMEN: By the act of the 11th of January, 1805, all that part of the Indiana Territory lying north of a line drawn due "east from the southerly bend or extreme of Lake Michigan until it shall intersect Lake Erie, and east of a line drawn from the said southerly bend through the middle of said lake to its northern extremity, and thence due north to the northern boundary of the United States," was erected into a separate Territory by the name of Michigan.

The territory comprised within these limits being part of the district of country described in the ordinance of the 13th of July, 1787, which provides that whenever any of the States into which the same should be divided should have 60,000 free inhabitants such State should be admitted by its delegates into the Congress of the United States on an equal footing with the original States in all respects whatever, and shall be at liberty to form a permanent constitution and State government, provided the constitution and State government so to be formed shall be republican, and in conformity to the principles contained in these articles, etc., the inhabitants thereof have during the present year, in pursuance of the right secured by the ordinance, formed a constitution and State government. That instrument, together with various other documents connected therewith, has been transmitted to me for the purpose of being laid before Congress, to whom the power and duty of admitting new States into the Union exclusively appertains; and the whole are herewith communicated for your early decision.

ANDREW JACKSON.

WASHINGTON, *December 17, 1835.*
The VICE-PRESIDENT OF THE UNITED STATES AND PRESIDENT OF THE SENATE:

I transmit, for the consideration of the Senate with a view to its ratification, a convention between the United States and the United Mexican States, concluded and signed by the plenipotentiaries of the respective parties at the City of Mexico on the 3d of April, 1835, and the object of which is to extend the time for the appointment of their commissioners and surveyors provided for by the third article of the treaty of limits between them of the 12th of January, 1835.

ANDREW JACKSON.

WASHINGTON, *December 17, 1835.*
To the Senate and House of Representatives of the United States:

I transmit to Congress a report from the Secretary of State, accompanying copies of certain papers relating to a bequest to the United States by Mr. James Smithson, of London, for the purpose of founding "at Washington an establishment under the name of the Smithsonian Institution, for the increase and diffusion of knowledge among men." The Executive having no authority to take any steps for accepting the trust and obtaining the funds, the papers are communicated with a view to such measures as Congress may deem necessary.

ANDREW JACKSON.

WASHINGTON, *December 22, 1835.*
To the Congress of the United States:

I transmit herewith, for the information of Congress, a report from the War Department, on the condition of the Cumberland road in the States of Illinois and Indiana.

ANDREW JACKSON.

WASHINGTON, *December 22, 1835.*
To the Senate of the United States:

I transmit to the Senate, for their consideration and advice with regard to its ratification, a convention signed at Paris by the plenipotentiaries of the United States and the Swiss Confederation on the 6th of March last. A copy of the convention is also transmitted for the convenience of the Senate.

ANDREW JACKSON.

DECEMBER 23, 1835.
To the Senate of the United States:

I hereby submit, for the advice and sanction of the Senate, the inclosed proposal of the Secretary of the Treasury for the investment of the proceeds of the sales of public lands in behalf of the Chickasaw Indians under the treaties therein mentioned.

ANDREW JACKSON.

WASHINGTON, *January 11, 1836.*

To the Senate and House of Representatives of the United States:

Having laid before Congress on the 9th ultimo the correspondence which had previously taken place relative to the controversy between Ohio and Michigan on the question of boundary between that State and Territory, I now transmit reports from the Secretaries of State and War on the subject, with the papers therein referred to.

ANDREW JACKSON.

WASHINGTON, *January 12, 1836.*

To the Senate:

I transmit herewith, for the consideration and advice of the Senate as to the ratification of the same, the two treaties concluded with the Carmanchee Indians and with the Caddo Indians referred to in the accompanying communication from the War Department.

ANDREW JACKSON.

WASHINGTON, *January 15, 1836.*

To the Senate and House of Representatives.

GENTLEMEN: In my message at the opening of your session I informed you that our chargé d'affaires at Paris had been instructed to ask for the final determination of the French Government in relation to the payment of the indemnification secured by the treaty of the 4th of July, 1831, and that when advices of the result should be received it would be made the subject of a special communication.

In execution of this design I now transmit to you the papers numbered from 1 to 13, inclusive, containing among other things the correspondence on this subject between our chargé d'affaires and the French minister of foreign affairs, from which it will be seen that France requires as a condition precedent to the execution of a treaty unconditionally ratified and to the payment of a debt acknowledged by all the branches of her Government to be due that certain explanations shall be made of which she dictates the terms. These terms are such as that Government has already been officially informed can not be complied with, and if persisted in they must be considered as a deliberate refusal on the part of France to fulfill engagements binding by the laws of nations and held sacred by the whole civilized world. The nature of the act which France requires from this Government is clearly set forth in the letter of the French minister marked No. 4. We will pay the money, says he, when *"the Government of the United States is ready on its part to declare to us, by addressing its claim to us officially in writing, that it regrets the misunderstanding which has arisen between the two countries; that this misunderstanding is founded on a mistake; that it never entered into its intention to call in question the good faith of the French Government nor to take a menacing attitude toward France.*" And he adds: "*If the Government of the United States does not give this assurance we shall be obliged to think that this misunderstanding is not the result of an error.*" In the letter marked No. 6 the French minister also remarks that "*the Government of the United States knows that upon itself depends henceforward the execution of the treaty of July 4, 1831.*"

Obliged by the precise language thus used by the French minister to view it as a peremptory refusal to execute the treaty except on terms incompatible with the honor and independence of the United States, and persuaded that on considering the correspondence now submitted to you you can regard it in no other light, it becomes my duty to call your attention to such measures as the exigency of the case demands if the claim of interfering in the communications between the different branches of our Government shall be persisted in. This pretension is rendered the more unreasonable by the fact that the substance of the required explanation has been repeatedly and voluntarily given before it was insisted on as a condition—a condition the more humiliating because it is demanded as the equivalent of a pecuniary consideration. Does France desire only a declaration that we had no intention to obtain our rights by an address to her fears rather than to her justice? She has already had it, frankly and explicitly given by our minister accredited to her Government, his act ratified by me, and my confirmation of it officially communicated by him in his letter to the French minister of foreign affairs of the 25th of April, 1835, and repeated by my published approval of that letter after the passage of the bill of indemnification. Does France want a degrading, servile repetition of this act, in terms which she shall dictate and which will involve an acknowledgment of her assumed right to interfere in our domestic councils? She will never obtain it. The spirit of the American people, the dignity of the Legislature, and the firm resolve of their executive government forbid it.

As the answer of the French minister to our chargé d'affaires at Paris contains an allusion to a letter addressed by him to the representative of France at this place, it now becomes proper to lay before you the correspondence had between that functionary and the Secretary of State relative to that letter, and to accompany the same with such explanations as will enable you to understand the course of the Executive in regard to it. Recurring to the historical statement made at the commencement of your session, of the origin and progress of our difficulties with France, it will be recollected that on the return of our minister to the United States I caused my official approval of the explanations he had given to the French minister of foreign affairs to be made public. As the French Government had noticed the message without its being officially communicated, it was not doubted that if they were disposed to pay the money due to us they would notice any public explanation of the Government of the United States in the same way. But, contrary to these well-founded expectations, the French ministry did not take this fair opportunity to relieve themselves from their unfortunate position and to do justice to the United States.

Whilst, however, the Government of the United States was awaiting the movements of the French Government in perfect confidence that the difficulty was at an end, the Secretary of State received a call from the French chargé d'affaires in Washington, who desired to read to him a letter he had received from the French minister of foreign affairs. He was asked whether he was instructed or directed to make any official communication, and replied that he was only authorized to read the letter and furnish a copy if requested. The substance of its contents, it is presumed, may be gathered from Nos. 4 and 6, herewith transmitted. It was an attempt to make known to the Government of the United States privately in what manner it could make explanations, apparently voluntary, but really dictated by France, acceptable to her, and thus obtain payment of the 25,000,000 francs. No exception was taken to this mode of communication, which is often used to prepare the way for official intercourse, but the suggestions made in it were in their substance wholly inadmissible. Not being in the shape of an official communication to this Government, it did not admit of reply or official notice, nor could it safely be made the basis of any action by the Executive or the Legislature, and the Secretary of State did not think proper to ask a copy, because he could have no use for it. Copies of papers marked Nos. 9, 10, and 11 shew an attempt on the part of the French chargé d'affaires to place a copy of this letter among the archives of this Government, which for obvious reasons was not allowed to be done; but the assurance before given was repeated, that any official communication which he might be authorized to make in the accustomed form would receive a prompt and just consideration. The indiscretion of this attempt was made more manifest by the subsequent avowal of the French chargé d'affaires that the object was to bring this letter before Congress and the American people. If foreign agents, on a subject of disagreement between their government and this, wish to prefer an appeal to the American people, they will hereafter, it is hoped, better appreciate their own rights and the respect due to others than to attempt to use the Executive as the passive organ of their communications.

It is due to the character of our institutions that the diplomatic intercourse of this Government should be conducted with the utmost directness and simplicity, and that in all cases of importance the communications received or made by the Executive should assume the accustomed official form. It is only by insisting on this form that foreign powers can be held to full responsibility, that their communications can be officially replied to, or that the advice or interference of the Legislature can with propriety be invited by the President. This course is also best calculated, on the one hand, to shield that officer from unjust suspicions, and on the other to subject this portion of his acts to public scrutiny, and, if occasion shall require it, to constitutional animadversion. It was the more necessary to adhere to these principles in the instance in question inasmuch as, in addition to other important interests, it very intimately concerned the national honor—a matter in my judgment much too sacred to be made the subject of private and unofficial negotiation.

It will be perceived that this letter of the French minister of foreign affairs was read to the Secretary of State on the 11th of September last. This was the first authentic indication of the specific views of the French Government received by the Government of the United States after the passage of the bill of indemnification. Inasmuch as the letter had been written before the official notice of my approval of Mr. Livingston's last explanation and remonstrance could have reached Paris, just ground of hope was left, as has been before stated, that the French Government, on receiving that information in the same manner as the alleged offensive message had reached them, would desist from their extraordinary demand and pay the money at once. To give them an opportunity to do so, and, at all events, to elicit their final determination and the ground they intended to occupy, the instructions were given to our chargé d'affaires which were adverted to at the commencement of the present session of Congress. The result, as you have seen, is a demand of an official written expression of regrets and a direct explanation addressed to France with a distinct intimation that this is a *sine qua non*.

Mr. Barton having, in pursuance of his instructions, returned to the United States and the charge d'affaires of France having been recalled, all diplomatic intercourse between the two countries is suspended, a state of things originating in an unreasonable susceptibility on the part of the French Government and rendered necessary on our part by their refusal to perform engagements contained in a treaty from the faithful performance of which by us they are to this day enjoying many important commercial advantages.

It is time that this unequal position of affairs should cease, and that legislative action should be brought to sustain Executive exertion in such measures as the case requires. While France persists in her refusal to comply with the terms of a treaty the object of which was, by removing all causes of mutual complaint, to renew ancient feelings of friendship and to unite the two nations in the bonds of amity and of a mutually beneficial commerce, she can not justly complain if we adopt such peaceful remedies as the law of nations and the circumstances of the case may authorize and demand. Of the nature of these remedies I have heretofore had occasion to speak, and, in reference to a particular contingency, to express my conviction that reprisals would be best adapted to the emergency then contemplated. Since that period France, by all the departments of her Government, has acknowledged the validity of our claims and the obligations of the treaty, and has appropriated the moneys which are necessary to its execution; and though payment is withheld on grounds vitally important to our existence as an independent nation, it is not to be believed that she can have determined permanently to retain a position so utterly indefensible. In the altered state of the questions in controversy, and under all existing circumstances, it appears to me that until such a determination shall have become evident it will be proper and sufficient to retaliate her present refusal to comply with her engagements by prohibiting the introduction of French products and the entry of French vessels into our ports. Between this and the interdiction of all commercial intercourse, or other remedies, you, as the representatives of the people, must determine. I recommend the former in the present posture of our affairs as being the least injurious to our commerce, and as attended with the least difficulty of returning to the usual state of friendly intercourse if the Government of France shall render us the justice that is due, and also as a proper preliminary step to stronger measures should their adoption be rendered necessary by subsequent events.

The return of our chargé d'affaires is attended with public notices of naval preparations on the part of France destined for our seas. Of the cause and intent of these armaments I have no authentic information, nor any other means of judging except such as are common to yourselves and to the public; but whatever may be their object, we are not at liberty to regard them as unconnected with the measures which hostile movements on the part of France may compel us to pursue. They at least deserve to be met by adequate preparation on our part, and I therefore strongly urge large and speedy appropriations for the increase of the Navy and the completion of our coast defenses.

If this array of military force be really designed to affect the action of the Government and people of the United States on the questions now pending between the two nations, then indeed would it be dishonorable to pause a moment on the alternative which such a state of things would present to us. Come what may, the explanation which France demands can never be accorded, and no armament, however powerful and imposing, at a distance or on our coast, will, I trust, deter us from discharging the high duties which we owe to our constituents, our national character, and to the world.

The House of Representatives at the close of the last session of Congress unanimously resolved that the treaty of the 4th of July, 1831, should be maintained and its execution insisted on by the United States. It is due to the welfare of the human race not less than to our own interests and honor that this resolution should at all hazards be adhered to. If after so signal an example as that given by the American people during their long-protracted difficulties with France of forbearance under accumulated wrongs and of generous confidence in her ultimate return to justice she shall now be permitted to withhold from us the tardy and imperfect indemnification which after years of remonstrance and discussion had at length been solemnly agreed on by the treaty of 1831 and to set at naught the obligations it imposes, the United States will not be the only sufferers. The efforts of humanity and religion to substitute the appeals of justice and the arbitrament of reason for the coercive measures usually resorted to by injured nations will receive little encouragement from such an issue. By the selection and enforcement of such lawful and expedient measures as may be necessary to prevent a result so injurious to ourselves and so fatal to the hopes of the philanthropist we shall therefore not only preserve the pecuniary interests of our citizens, the independence of our Government, and the honor of our country, but do much, it may be hoped, to vindicate the faith of treaties and to promote the general interests of peace, civilization, and improvement.

ANDREW JACKSON.

No. 1.

Mr. Forsyth to Mr. Barton.

DEPARTMENT OF STATE,
Washington, June 28, 1835.

THOMAS P. BARTON, Esq., etc.

SIR: Mr. Livingston arrived here the day before yesterday. By the mail of yesterday your letter of the 7th of May, with a copy of Mr. Livingston's last note to the Duke de Broglie, was received.

After an attentive examination of Mr. Livingston's correspondence with this Department and the Government of France, elucidated by his verbal explanations, the President has directed me to say to you that the Messrs. de Rothschild have been authorized by the Treasury Department to receive the money due under the treaty with France. Of this authority they will be directed to give notice to the French Government without demanding payment. For yourself, you will, if the bill of indemnity is rejected, follow Mr. Livingston to the United States. If the money is placed at the disposal of the King, conditionally, by the legislature of France, you will await further orders from the United States, but maintain a guarded silence on the subject of the indemnity. If approached by the Government of France, directly or indirectly, you will hear what is said without reply, state what has occurred in full to the Department, and await its instructions. It is the desire of the President that you will make not even a reference to the subject of the treaty in your intercourse with the French Government until the course intended to be pursued is definitely explained to the United States. Whatever may be said to the Messrs. de Rothschild it will be their duty to report to you as well as to the Treasury Department, and whenever they converse with you they must be reminded that it is expected that they will wait for express notice from the Government of France that it is ready to pay before an application for payment is made.

The course adopted by Mr. Livingston has been fully approved, and the hope is indulged that his representations have had their just influence on the counsels of the King of France. However that may be, the President's determination is that the terms upon which the two Governments are to stand toward each other shall be regulated so far as his constitutional power extends by France.

A packet from the Treasury, addressed to the Messrs. de Rothschild, and containing the instructions of the Secretary, accompanied by a special power appointing them the agents of the United States to receive the payments due under the treaty of 1831, is forwarded herewith. The copy of a letter from this Department to M. Pageot is also inclosed for your perusal.

I am, sir, your obedient servant,   JOHN FORSYTH.

No. 2.

Mr. Forsyth to Mr. Barton.

DEPARTMENT OF STATE,
Washington, September 14, 1835.

THOMAS P. BARTON, Esq., etc.

SIR: So much time will have elapsed before this dispatch can reach you, since the passage of the law by the French Chambers placing at the disposition of the King the funds to fulfill the treaty with the United States, that it is presumed the intention of the French Government will have been by that period disclosed. It is proper therefore, in the opinion of the President, that you should receive your last instructions in relation to it. It has always been his intention that the legation of the United States should leave France if the treaty were not fulfilled. You have been suffered to remain after the departure of Mr. Livingston under the expectation that the Government of France would find in all that has occurred its obligation to proceed forthwith to the fulfillment of it as soon as funds were placed in its hands. If this expectation is disappointed, you must ask for your passports and return to the United States. If no movement has been made on the part of France and no intimation given to you or to the banker of the United States who is the authorized agent of the Treasury to receive the installments due of the time that payment will be made, you are instructed to call upon the Duke de Broglie and request to be informed what are the intentions of the Government in relation to it, stating that you do so by orders of your Government and with a view to regulate your conduct by the information you may receive from him. In the present agitated state of France it is the particular desire of the President that your application should be made in the most conciliatory tone and your interview with the Duke marked by expressions, as coming from your Government, of great personal respect for that minister and of an anxious desire for the safety of the King of France. If the Duke should inform you that the money is to be paid on any fixed day, you will remain in France; otherwise you will apply for your passports, and state the reason to be that the treaty of indemnity has not been executed by France.

The President especially directs that you should comply with these instructions so early that the result may be known here before the meeting of Congress, which takes place on the 7th of December next.

I am, sir, your obedient servant,   JOHN FORSYTH.

No. 3.

Mr. Barton to the Duke de Broglie.

[Translation.]

D.

LEGATION OF THE UNITED STATES OF AMERICA,
Paris, October 24, 1835.

His Excellency the DUKE DE BROGLIE,
Minister of Foreign Affairs, etc.

MONSIEUR LE DUC: Having executed to the letter the last instructions of my Government in the interview which I had the honor to have with your excellency on the 20th of this month, in order further to comply with those instructions I am about to return to the United States. Before leaving France, however, I have thought that it might not be altogether useless to address your excellency and to submit to you the conversation which then took place between us, word for word, as I understood it. In pursuing this course I am prompted by a double motive: First, by a sincere desire to avoid even the slightest misunderstanding as to the precise meaning of any expressions used on either part, and also with a view, in presenting myself to my Government, to furnish indisputable proof of my fidelity in executing the instructions with which I had the honor to be charged. This last motive, Monsieur le Duc, does not interest you personally, but the first, I am sure, will not appear without importance in your eyes.

Having said that I was instructed to employ both language and manner the most conciliatory, I begged you to believe, should anything appear to you not to partake of that character, that the fault must be attributed *to me alone*, and not to my Government, as in that case I should be certain that I neither represented its disposition nor faithfully obeyed its orders.

I began the conversation by informing you that I had requested an interview by order of my Government, and that on the result of that interview would depend my future movements. I said that I was ordered to convey to the French Government assurances of the very lively satisfaction felt by the President on receiving the news and confirmation of the King's safety, and that I was further instructed by the Secretary of State to assure you personally of his high consideration. After an obliging answer of your excellency I had the honor to submit the following question:

"I am instructed by my Government to inquire of your excellency what are the intentions of His Majesty's Government in relation to the funds voted by the Chambers."

And I understood you to make the following answer:

"Having written a dispatch to His Majesty's chargé d'affaires at Washington, with instructions to communicate it to Mr. Forsyth, and M. Pageot having read it to Mr. Forsyth, I have nothing to say in addition to that dispatch."

I said:

"I am also instructed to inquire of your excellency whether His Majesty's Government is ready to pay those funds."

And you returned this answer:

"Yes, in the terms of the dispatch."

I added:

"I am instructed to ask another question: Will His Majesty's Government name any fixed determined period when they will be disposed to pay those funds?"

To this question the following was your excellency's answer, as I understood it:

"To-morrow, if necessary. When the Government of the United States shall by a written official communication have expressed its regret at the misunderstanding which has taken place between the two Governments, assuring us that this misunderstanding was founded on an error—that it did not intend to call in question the good faith of His Majesty's Government—the funds are there; we are ready to pay. In the dispatch to M. Pageot we gave the views of our Government on this question. Mr. Forsyth not having thought proper to accept a copy of that dispatch, and having said that the Government of the United States could not receive a communication in such a form, I have nothing to add. I am forced to retrench myself behind that dispatch. If the Government of the United States does not give this assurance, we shall be obliged to think that this misunderstanding is not the result of an error, and the business will stop there."

To your excellency's offer to communicate to me the dispatch to M. Pageot I replied that as my instructions had no reference to that question I did not think myself authorized to discuss it.

After some minutes I rose and said:

"In a short time I shall have the honor of writing to your excellency."

You answered:

"I shall at all times receive with pleasure any communication addressed to me on the part of the Government of the United States."

And our conversation ended.

Such, Monsieur le Duc, as far as my memory serves me, are the literal expressions employed by both of us. Should you discover any inaccuracies in the relation which I have the honor to submit to you, it will give me pleasure, as it will be my duty, to correct them. If, on the contrary, this relation should appear to you in every respect conformable to the truth, I take the liberty of claiming from your kindness a confirmation of it, for the reasons which I have already, I believe, sufficiently explained.

I eagerly avail myself of this occasion, Monsieur le Duc, to renew the assurances of very high consideration with which I have the honor to be, your excellency's most obedient, humble servant,

THOS. P. BARTON.

No. 4.

The Duke de Broglie to Mr. Barton.

[Translation.]

E.

PARIS, *October 26, 1835.*

T. P. BARTON,

Chargé d' Affaires of the United States.

SIR: I have received the letter which you did me the honor to address to me on the 24th of this month.

You are desirous to give your Government a faithful account of the conversation which you had with me on the 20th. While communicating to me a statement of that conversation you request me to indicate the involuntary errors which I may remark in it. I appreciate the motives which influence you and the importance which you attach to the exactness of this statement, and I therefore hasten to point out three errors which have found their way into your report, acknowledging at the same time its perfect conformity on all other points with the explanations interchanged between us.

In reply to your question *whether the King's Government would name any fixed and determinate period at which it would be disposed to pay the twenty-five millions* you make me say:

"To-morrow, if necessary. When the Government of the United States shall by a written official communication have expressed its regret at the misunderstanding which has taken place between the two Governments, assuring us that this misunderstanding is founded on an error—that it did not intend to call in question the good faith of His Majesty's Government," etc.

Now, this is what I really said:

"To-morrow, to-day, immediately, if the Government of the United States is ready on its part to declare to us, by addressing its claim (*réclamation*) to us officially in writing that it regrets the misunderstanding which has arisen between the two countries; that this misunderstanding is founded upon a mistake, and that it never entered into its intention (*pensée*) to call in question the good faith of the French Government nor to take a menacing attitude toward France."

By the terms of your report I am made to have continued thus:

"In the dispatch to M. Pageot we gave the views of our Government on this question. Mr. Forsyth not having thought proper to accept a copy of that dispatch, and having said that the Government of the United States could not receive the communication in that form," etc.

That was not what I said, because such was not the language of Mr. Forsyth to M. Pageot. On refusing the copy offered to him by that chargé d'affaires Mr. Forsyth gave as the only reason *that it was a document of which he could make no use*, and that was the phrase repeated by me.

Mr. Forsyth made no objection to the form which I had adopted to communicate to the Federal Government the views of the King's Government; in fact, not only is there nothing unusual in that form, not only is it employed in the intercourse between one government and another whenever there is a desire to avoid the irritation which might involuntarily arise from an exchange of contradictory notes in a direct controversy, but reflection on the circumstances and the respective positions of the two countries will clearly show that it was chosen precisely in a spirit of conciliation and regard for the Federal Government.

Finally, sir, after having said, "If the Government of the United States does not give this assurance we shall be obliged to think that this misunderstanding is not the result of an error," I did not add, "and the business will stop there." This last error is, however, of so little importance that I hesitated to notice it.

Receive, sir, the assurances of my high consideration.

V. BROGLIE.

No. 5.

Mr. Barton to the Duke de Broglie.

F.

LEGATION OF THE UNITED STATES OF AMERICA,
Paris, November 6, 1835.

His Excellency the DUKE DE BROGLIE,
Minister of Foreign Affairs, etc.

MONSIEUR LE DUC: Having been recalled by my Government, I have the honor to request that your excellency will be pleased to cause passports to be prepared to enable me to proceed to Havre, thence to embark for the United States, and for my protection during the time I may find it necessary to remain in Paris. I am instructed to give as a reason for my departure the nonexecution on the part of His Majesty's Government of the convention of July 4, 1831.

I avail myself of this opportunity, Monsieur le Duc, to renew the assurances of very high consideration with which I have the honor to be, your excellency's most obedient, humble servant,

THOS. P. BARTON.

No. 6.

The Duke de Broglie to Mr. Barton.

[Translation.]

PARIS, *November 8, 1835.*

Mr. BARTON,
Chargé d'Affaires of the United States of America.

SIR: Having taken His Majesty's orders with regard to your communication of the 6th instant, I have the honor to send you herewith the passports which you requested of me. As to the reasons which you have been charged to advance in explanation of your departure, I have nothing to say (*Je n'ai point à m'y arrêter*). The Government of the United States, sir, knows that upon itself depends henceforward the execution of the treaty of July 4, 1831.

Accept, sir, the assurance of my high consideration.

V. BROGLIE.

No. 7.

Mr. Forsyth to Mr. Pageot.

DEPARTMENT OF STATE,
Washington, June 29, 1835.

M. PAGEOT,
 Chargé d'Affaires, etc.

SIR: I have the honor to acquaint you, for the information of your Government, that the Secretary of the Treasury has, in conformity with the provisions of the act of Congress of 13th July, 1832, designated the Messrs. de Rothschild Brothers, of Paris, as agents to receive the payments from time to time due to this Government under the stipulations of the convention of 4th July, 1831, between the United States and His Majesty the King of the French, and that the President has granted a special power to the said Messrs. de Rothschild Brothers, authorizing and empowering them, upon the due receipt of the same, to give the necessary acquittances to the French Government, according to the provisions of the convention referred to.

The power given to the Messrs. de Rothschild will be presented by them whenever the French Government is ready to make the payments.

I have the honor to be, sir, your obedient servant,

JOHN FORSYTH.

No. 8.

Mr. Pageot to Mr. Forsyth.

[Translation.]

WASHINGTON, *June 29, 1835.*

Hon. Mr. FORSYTH,
 Secretary of State.

SIR: I have received the letter which you did me the honor to address to me this day, and by which you communicate to me, for the information of my Government, that the Secretary of the Treasury, in virtue of the act of Congress of July 13, 1832, has appointed Messrs. de Rothschild Brothers, at Paris, agents for receiving as they become due the several payments of the sum stipulated as indemnification by the convention concluded on the 4th of July, 1831, between His Majesty the King of the French and the United States of America.

I lost no time, sir, in transmitting this communication to my Government, and I embrace this opportunity to offer you the assurance of the high consideration with which I have the honor to be, your most humble and obedient servant,

A. PAGEOT.

No. 9.

Mr. Pageot to Mr. Forsyth.

[Translation.]

WASHINGTON, *December 1, 1835.*

Hon. JOHN FORSYTH,
 Secretary of State of the United States.

SIR: On the 11th of September last I had the honor, as I was authorized, to read to you a dispatch which his excellency the minister of foreign affairs had addressed to me on the 17th of June previous, respecting the state of the relations between France and the United States. The object of this communication was to make known to the Cabinet of Washington, in a form often employed, the point of view from which the King's Government regarded the difficulties between the two countries, and to indicate the means by which, in its opinion, they might be terminated in a manner honorable to both Governments. I was also authorized to allow you, in case you should desire it, to take a copy of this dispatch, but, contrary to the expectation which diplomatic usages in such cases permitted me to entertain, you thought proper to refuse to request it.

I regretted this resolution of yours, sir, at the time, because, in the first place, it appeared to be at variance with (*s'écarter de*) that conciliatory spirit which so particularly characterized the communication just made to you, and, next, as it seemed in a manner to deprive the Cabinet of Washington of the means of knowing in their full extent the views of the King's Government, of which an attentive examination of the Duke de Broglie's letter could alone have enabled it to form a just estimate. These regrets, sir, have not been diminished, and at the moment when the President is about to communicate to Congress the state of the relations between France and the United States I consider it useful and necessary for the interests of all to endeavor to place him in possession of all the facts which may afford him the means of giving an exact account of the real dispositions and views of the King's Government on the subject of the existing difficulties.

With this intention, and from a desire to neglect nothing which, by offering to the American Government another opportunity of making itself acquainted minutely with the highly conciliatory sentiments of His Majesty's Government, may contribute to restore good understanding between the Cabinets of Paris and Washington, I have the honor to transmit to you a copy of the Duke de Broglie's dispatch and to request you to place it under the eye of the President.

I embrace this opportunity, sir, to renew to you the assurance of the high consideration with which I have the honor to be, your most humble and most obedient servant,

A. PAGEOT.

No. 10.

Mr. Forsyth to Mr. Pageot.

DEPARTMENT OF STATE,
Washington, December 3, 1835.

M. PAGEOT,
   Chargé d' Affaires, etc.

SIR: I had yesterday the honor to receive your note of the 1st instant, with the accompanying paper, purporting to be a copy of a letter addressed under date of the 17th of June last by His Excellency the Duke de Broglie, minister of foreign affairs of France, to yourself.

After referring to what occurred in our interview of the 11th September in regard to the original letter, and expressing your regrets at the course I then felt it my duty to take, you request me to place the copy inclosed in your letter under the eye of the President.

In allowing you during that interview to read to me the Duke de Broglie's dispatch, which I cheerfully did, you were enabled to avail yourself of that informal mode of apprising this Department of the views of your Government in the full extent authorized by diplomatic usage. The question whether or not I should ask a copy of that dispatch was of course left, as it should have been, by your Government exclusively to my discretion. My reasons for not making that request were frankly stated to you, founded on a conviction that in the existing state of the relations between the two countries the President would think it most proper that every communication upon the subject in difference between them designed to influence his conduct should, before it was submitted to his consideration, be made to assume the official form belonging to a direct communication from one government to another, by which alone he could be enabled to cause a suitable reply to be given to it and to submit it, should such a step become necessary, to his associates in the Government. I had also the honor at the same time to assure you that any direct communication from yourself as the representative of the King's Government to me, embracing the contents of this dispatch or any other matter you might be authorized to communicate in the accustomed mode, would be laid without delay before the President, and would undoubtedly receive from him an early and just consideration.

It can not have escaped your reflections that my duty required that the circumstances of the interview between us should be reported to the President, and that the discovery of any error on my part in representing his views of the course proper to be pursued on that occasion would without fail have been promptly communicated to you. That duty was performed. The substance of our interview and the reasons by which my course in it had been guided were immediately communicated to and entirely approved by him. I could not, therefore, have anticipated that after so long a period had elapsed, and without any change in the condition of affairs, you should have regarded it as useful or proper to revive the subject at the time and in the form you have seen fit to adopt. Cordially reciprocating, however, the conciliatory sentiments expressed in your note, and in deference to your request, I have again consulted the President on the subject, and am instructed to inform you that the opinion expressed by me in the interview between us, and subsequently confirmed by him, remains unchanged, and I therefore respectfully restore to you the copy of the Duke de Broglie's letter, as I can not make the use of it which you desired.

I am also instructed to say that the President entertains a decided conviction that a departure in the present case from the ordinary and accustomed method of international communication is calculated to increase rather than to diminish the difficulties unhappily existing between France and the United States, and that its observance in their future intercourse will be most likely to bring about the amicable adjustment of those difficulties on terms honorable to both parties. Such a result is sincerely desired by him, and he will omit nothing consistent with the faithful discharge of his duties to the United States by which it may be promoted. In this spirit I am directed by him to repeat to you the assurance made in our interview in September last, that any official communication you may think proper to address to this Government will promptly receive such consideration as may be due to its contents and to the interests involved in the subject to which it may refer.

As the inclosed paper is not considered the subject of reply, you will allow me to add, for the purpose of preventing any misconception in this respect, that my silence in regard to its contents is not to be construed as admitting the accuracy of any of the statements or reasonings contained in it.

I have the honor to renew, etc.

JOHN FORSYTH.

No. 11.

Mr. Pageot to Mr. Forsyth.

[Translation.]

WASHINGTON, *December 5, 1835.*

Hon. JOHN FORSYTH,
Secretary of State of the United States.

SIR: I yesterday evening received the letter which you did me the honor to write to me on the 3d of this month. With it you return to me the copy of a dispatch which I had transmitted to you two days before, and the original of which was addressed to me on the 17th of June last by his excellency the minister of foreign affairs.

I will not seek, sir, to disguise from you the astonishment produced in me by the return of a document so very important in the present state of the relations between the two countries; neither will I undertake to reply to the reasons on which this determination of yours is based. My intention in communicating this document to you in a form not only sanctioned by the diplomatic usages of all nations and all ages, but also the most direct which I could possibly have chosen, was to make known the real dispositions of my Government to the President of the United States, and through him to Congress and the American people, conceiving that in the existing situation of the two countries it was essential that each Government should fully comprehend the intentions of the other. This consideration appeared to me paramount to all others. You have judged otherwise, sir, and you have thought that whatever might be the importance of a communication it was proper before receiving it to examine whether the form in which it came to you were strictly accordant with the usages necessary, in your opinion, to be observed in diplomatic transactions with the Government of the Republic. I will not insist further. I have fulfilled all the duties which appeared to be prescribed for me by the spirit of reconciliation, in conjunction with the respect due by me to all communications from my Government, and nothing more remains for me than to express my deep regret that the misunderstanding between the two Governments, already so serious, should be kept up, not by weighty difficulties which involve the interests and the dignity of the two countries, but by questions of form as uncertain in their principles as doubtful in their application.

I have the honor to renew to you, sir, the assurances of my high consideration.

A. PAGEOT.

No. 12.

Mr. Pageot to Mr. Forsyth.

[Translation.]

WASHINGTON, *January 2, 1836.*

Hon. JOHN FORSYTH,
    Secretary of State of the United States.

SIR: I have the honor to announce to you that, in consequence of the recall of Mr. Barton, the King's Government has given me orders to lay down the character of chargé d'affaires of His Majesty near the Government of the United States. I shall therefore immediately begin the preparations for my return to France; but in the meantime I think proper to claim the protection of the Federal Government during the period which I may consider it necessary to remain in the United States.

I have the honor to be, with the most distinguished consideration, sir, your most humble and obedient servant,

A. PAGEOT.

No. 13.

Mr. Forsyth to Mr. Pageot.

DEPARTMENT OF STATE,
Washington, January 2, 1836.

M. ALPHONSE PAGEOT, etc.

SIR: I have the honor to acknowledge your note of this day's date, in which you announce that you have the orders of your Government, given in consequence of the recall of Mr. Barton, to lay aside the character of chargé d'affaires of the King of France near the Government of the United States. The protection of the Federal Government is due and will of course be extended to you during the time necessary for your preparations to return to France.

I am, sir, with great consideration, your obedient servant,

JOHN FORSYTH.

C.

LEGATION OF THE UNITED STATES,
Paris, January 29, 1835.

His Excellency COUNT DE RIGNY,
Minister Secretary of State of Foreign Affairs.

SIR: Having already had occasion to acknowledge the receipt of your excellency's letter of the 13th instant, and to answer that part of it which most urgently required my attention, I proceed to a consideration of the other matters which it contains. I shall do this with a sincere desire to avoid everything that may excite irritation or increase difficulties which already unfortunately exist. Guided by this disposition, I shall confine myself to an examination of your note, considered only as an exposition of the causes which His Majesty's Government thinks it has to complain of in the message sent by the President of the United States to Congress at the opening of its present session.

Your excellency begins by observing that nothing could have prepared His Majesty's Government for the impressions made upon it by the President's message, and that if the complaints he makes were as just as you think them unfounded, still you would have reason to be astonished at receiving *the first communication of them in such a form.* If His Majesty's Government was not prepared to receive complaints on the part of the United States for nonexecution of the treaty, everything I have said and written since I have had the honor of communicating with your excellency and your predecessors in office must have been misunderstood or forgotten. I can scarcely suppose the first, for if my whole correspondence is referred to and my verbal representations recollected they will be found in the most unequivocal language to express an extreme solicitude for the execution of the treaty, a deep disappointment at the several delays which have intervened, and emphatically the necessity which the President would be under of laying the matter before Congress at the time when in fact he has done so if before that period he did not receive notice that the law had passed for giving effect to the treaty. To urge the obligation of the treaty, to prepare His Majesty's Government for the serious consequences that must result from its breach or an unnecessary delay in executing it, was my duty, and it has been faithfully and unremittingly executed. To my own official representation on the 26th I added on the 29th July last the precise instructions I had received, to inform His Majesty's Government that "the President could not avoid laying before Congress on the 1st of December a full statement of the position of affairs on this interesting subject, or permit the session to end, as it must do on the 3d March, without recommending such measures as the justice and the honor of the country may require."

In this alone, then, there was sufficient, independently of my numerous applications and remonstrances, to prepare His Majesty's Government for the just complaints of the United States and for the "impression" they ought to produce, as well as for the "*mode*" in which they were communicated, a mode clearly pointed out in the passage I have quoted from my note of the 29th of July—that is to say, by the annual message from the President to Congress, which, as I have already had occasion to observe, His Majesty's ministers have erroneously considered as addressed directly to them, and, viewing it in that light, have arraigned this document as containing groundless complaints, couched in language not called for by the occasion, and offering for consideration means of redress offensive to the dignity of France. I shall endeavor by a plain exposition of facts to repel those charges. I shall examine them with the freedom the occasion requires, but, suppressing the feelings which some parts of your excellency's letter naturally excite, will, as far as possible, avoid all those topics for recrimination which press upon my mind. The observation I am about to make will not be deemed a departure from this rule, because it is intended to convey information which seems to have been wanted by His Majesty's minister when on a late occasion he presented a law to the Chamber of Deputies. It is proper, therefore, to state that although the military title of general was gloriously acquired by the present head of the American Government, he is not in official language designated as *General Jackson*, but as "the President of the United States," and that his communication was made in that character.

I proceed now to the examination of that portion of your excellency's letter which attempts to show that the complaints set forth in the President's message are groundless.

It begins by assuming as a principle of argument that after the Chamber of Deputies had rejected the law and His Majesty's Government had promised to present it anew the United States had by receiving that promise given up all right to complain of any anterior delays. I have vainly endeavored, sir, to find any rule of reasoning by which this argument can be supported. It would undoubtedly be much easier to strike off from the case the delays of two years in proposing the law than to justify them.

It is true that the United States, with a moderation and forbearance for which they receive no credit, waited two years, almost without complaint, for the performance of a treaty which engaged the faith of the French nation to pay a just indemnity, for which they had already waited more than twenty years. It is true that His Majesty's Government offered solemn assurances that as soon as the constitution of the country would permit a new attempt would be made to redeem the national pledge given by the treaty. It is true also that the President of the United States gave credit to those assurances; but it is also true—and your excellency seems to lose sight of that important uncontested fact—that formal notice was given that the performance of those promises would be expected according to their letter, and that he could delay no longer than the 1st of December the execution of a duty which those assurances had induced him to postpone. Whatever reasons His Majesty's Government had for not complying with Mr. Sérurier's engagement, or however they may have interpreted it, the President could not be precluded from considering the whole case as open and adding to his statement the wrongs occasioned by the delays anterior to the vote of rejection. Those delays are still unaccounted for, and are rendered more questionable by the preference given to another treaty, although subsequently made, for the guarantee of the Greek loan.

Confining your observations to this second period, you say that the reproaches which the President thinks himself authorized in making to France may be comprised in the following words:

"The Government of the King had promised to present the treaty of July anew to the Chambers as soon as they could be assembled; but they have been assembled on the 31st of July of the last year and the treaty has not yet been presented."

Stating this as the whole of the complaint, you proceed, sir, in your endeavor to refute it.

I am obliged, reluctantly, here to make use of arguments which in the course of this discussion have been often repeated, but which seem to have made no impression on His Majesty's Government. I am obliged, in repelling the reproaches addressed to the President, to bring to your recollection the terms of the promise on which he relied, the circumstances attending it, and the object for which it was given. These must be fully understood and fully waived before the question between us can be resolved.

The circumstances under which Mr. Sérurier's note was written are material in considering its true import. The payment stipulated by a treaty duly ratified on both sides had just been formally refused by a vote of the Chamber of Deputies. More than two years had passed since it had been proclaimed as the law of the land in the United States, and ever since the articles favorable to France had been in constant operation. Notice of this refusal had some time before been received by the President. It would have been his duty, had nothing else occurred, to communicate to Congress this event, so unexpected and so injurious to the interest of the country. One circumstance prevented the performance of this duty and justified the omission. The notice of the rejection was accompanied by information that the minister of France was instructed to make explanations and engagements on the subject, and that a ship of war would be dispatched with his instructions. The President had waited a month for the arrival of this ship. An unusually long session of Congress still afforded an opportunity for making the communication, even after her arrival. If made it would undoubtedly have produced consequences the nature of which may be imagined by considering the events that have since occurred. It was necessary, then, to prevent an interruption of the friendly relations between the two countries, that this communication should be postponed until the subsequent session of Congress; longer than that it was well known that it could not be deferred. This was clearly and explicitly stated in a conference between Mr. Sérurier and the Secretary of State of the United States, in which the former gave the promise in question. But the President desired to have the engagement in a written and official form (and as Mr. Sérurier expresses it in his letter), *"pour des causes prises dans les nécessités de votre Gouvernement."* What governmental necessity does he allude to? Clearly that which obliged the President to communicate these engagements to Congress at the next session.

Here, then, we have a stipulation made under special orders, sent out by a ship dispatched for that express purpose, communicated first verbally in an official conference, afterwards reduced to writing and delivered to the proper officers, for the double purpose of justifying the President for not making an immediate communication at their then session and also to serve as a pledge which he might exhibit if unredeemed at their next. These objects are well stated by Mr. Sérurier to be "that the Government of the Republic may avoid, with a providential solicitude, *in this unsettled state of things* all that may become a cause of new irritation between the two countries, endanger the treaty, and raise obstacles that may become insurmountable to the views of conciliation and harmony which animate the councils of the King." It was, then, to avoid a communication to Congress, which Mr. Sérurier saw would endanger the peace of the two countries, that this engagement was made. Surely, then, every word of a stipulation made under such circumstances and for such important purposes must have been duly considered and its import properly weighed, first by the cabinet who directed, afterwards by the minister who delivered and the Government which received it.

What, then, was this engagement? First, that the Government of the King will use every legal and constitutional effort which its persevering persuasion of the justice and advantages of the treaty authorize the United States to expect from it. "Son intention est" (I quote literally), *"en outre"* (that is, besides using those endeavors above mentioned), "de faire tout ce que *notre constitution permet* pour rapprocher autant que possible l'époque de la présentation nouvelle de la loi rejettée." Your excellency can not fail to have observed two distinct parts in this engagement— one relating to the endeavors the ministry promise to make in order to induce the Chambers to pass the law, for the success of which they could not answer; another relating to the time of presentation of the law, a matter which depended on them alone, restricted only by constitutional forms.

The promise on this point, then, was precise, and could not be misunderstood. Whatever the *constitution of France permitted*, the Government of France promised to do in order to hasten the presentation of the law. What was the cause of this desire to bring the business before the Chambers at an early day? No one can doubt it who knows the situation of the two countries, still less anyone who has read the correspondence. It was to enable the President to make those statements to the next Congress which, relying on the engagements of the French minister, he had omitted to make to this.

It was clear, therefore, that more was required than the expression of a desire on the part of His Majesty's ministers to execute the treaty—a desire the sincerity of which was not doubted, but which might be unavailing, as its accomplishment depended on the vote of the Chambers. For the President's satisfaction, and for his justification too, an engagement was offered and accepted for the performance of an act which depended on His Majesty's Government alone. This engagement was couched in the unequivocal terms I have literally quoted.

This, sir, is not all. That there might be no misunderstanding on the subject, this promise, with the sense in which it was understood, the important object for which it was given, and the serious consequences that might attend a failure to comply with it, were urged in conversation, and repeated in my official letters, particularly those of the 26th and 29th of July and 3d and 9th of August last, in which its performance was strongly pressed.

The answers to these letters left no hope that the question would be submitted to the Chambers in time to have the result known before the adjournment of Congress, and by the refusal to hasten the convocation of the Chambers before the last of December showed unequivocally that, so far from taking all measures permitted by the constitution to *hasten* the period of presenting the law, it was to be left to the most remote period of the ordinary course of legislation.

This decision of His Majesty's Government, contained in your excellency's note to me of the 7th August, was duly transmitted to the President, and it naturally produced upon his mind the impressions which I anticipated in my letters to your excellency that it would produce. He saw with the deepest regret that a positive assurance for convening the Chambers as soon as the constitution would permit was construed to mean only a disposition to do so, and that this disposition had yielded to objections which he could not think of sufficient force to justify a delay even if there had intervened no promise, especially as the serious consequences of that delay had been earnestly and repeatedly brought to the consideration of His Majesty's Government. In fact, sir, what were those objections? I do not speak of those which were made to presenting the law in the session of July last, for although no constitutional impediment offered itself, yet it was not strongly insisted on, because an early session in the autumn would have the same effect; and the President, for the same reason, says that it might have been overlooked if an early call of the Chambers had been made. They are the objections to this call, then, which immediately demand our attention. What, in fact, were they? None derived from the constitutional charter have been or could have been asserted. What, then, were they? Your excellency's letter of the 3d of August to me contains none but this: "His Majesty's Government finds it impossible to make any positive engagement on that point." In that of the 7th of August there are two reasons assigned: First, the general inconvenience to the members. This the President could surely not think of alleging to Congress as a sufficient reason for omitting to lay the matter before them. The next, I confess, has a little more weight, and might have excused a delay if the assurance given by Mr. Sérurier had been, as your excellency construes it, merely of a *disposition* to hasten the presentation of the law. If the engagement had amounted to no more than this, and His Majesty's ministers thought that an early call would endanger the passage of the law, it might possibly justify *them* in not making it. But the President, who relied on the promise he had received, who in consequence of it had deferred the performance of an important duty; the President, who had given timely and official notice that this duty must be performed at the opening of the next Congress; the President, who could see no greater prospect of the passage of the law in a winter than in an autumnal session—how was *he* to justify himself and redeem the pledge *he* had made to his country? He did it in the way he always does—by a strict performance.

From this detail your excellency will, I hope, see that the President's causes of complaint can not, as you suppose, be confined within the narrow limit you have assigned to them. The failure to present the law in the session of July was not the only, nor even the principal, point in which he thought the engagement of Mr. Sérurier uncomplied with; for although he saw no reason for the omission that could be called a constitutional one, yet he expressly says that might have been overlooked. He always (it can not too often be repeated) looked to the promise of Mr. Sérurier as it was given at Washington, not as it was interpreted at Paris, and he had a right to believe that as on previous occasions the Legislature had, in the years 1819, 1822, 1825, and 1830, held their sessions for the transaction of the ordinary business in the months of July and August, he had a right, I say, to believe that there was no insurmountable objection to the consideration of this extraordinary case, enforced by a positive promise. Yet, as I have remarked, he did not make this his principal cause of complaint; it was the omission to call the Chambers at an earlier period than the very end of the year.

On this head your excellency is pleased to observe that the same reasons, drawn from the usual course of administration, which rendered the presentation of the law in the session of July impossible applied with nearly the same force to a call before the end of the year; and you appeal to the President's knowledge of the "fixed principles of a constitutional system" to prove that the administration under such a government is subject to regular and permanent forms, "from which no special interest, however important, should induce it to deviate." For this branch of the argument it unfortunately happens that no regular form of administration, no fixed principle, no usage whatever, would have opposed a call of the Chambers at an early day, and the rule which your excellency states would not be broken "in favor of any interest, however important," has actually been made to yield to one of domestic occurrence. *The Chambers have just been convened before the period which was declared to be the soonest at which they could possibly meet.* Your excellency will also excuse me for remarking that since the first institution of the Chambers, in 1814, there have been convocations for every month of the year, without exception, which I will take the liberty of bringing to your recollection by enumerating the different dates. The Chambers were summoned for the month of January in the years 1823, 1826, and 1829; for February, in the years 1827 and 1829; for March, in 1815, 1824, and 1830; for April, in 1833; for May, in 1814; for June, in 1815, 1822, and 1825; for July, in 1834; for August, in 1830 and 1831; for September, in 1815; for October, in 1816; for November, in 1817, 1818, 1819, 1821, and 1832; and for December, in 1820, 1824, 1826, and 1833. It is, then, clear to demonstration that neither constitutional impediment nor stern, inflexible usage prevented such a call of the Chambers as would have complied with the letter of Mr. Sérurier's engagement. Since I have alluded to the actual meeting of the Chambers on the 1st of December, it is but candid to allow that even this period would not have enabled the President to have attained one of his objects—the presenting of the result of their deliberations to Congress in his opening message. But even that slight concession, if it had been made to my unceasing applications, might have given an opportunity of conveying their decision to Congress before the 4th of March, when they must adjourn, because, had that day been then determined on, everything would have been ready to lay before the Chambers on the opening of the session; but a meeting a month or six weeks earlier would have given ample time for deliberation and decision in season to have it known at Washington on the 1st of December.

The necessity of giving time to the new members to inform themselves of the nature of the question and the old ones to recover from the impression which erroneous statements had made upon their minds I understand to be the remaining motive of His Majesty's ministers for delaying the meeting; but this was a precaution which, relying on the plain obligation of the treaty, the President could not appreciate, and he must, moreover, have thought that if a long discussion was necessary to understand the merits of the question it was an additional reason for hastening the meeting where those merits were to be discussed. The delay that occurred between the meeting of the Chambers and the 1st of January need not have entered into the discussion, because, not long known at Washington, it could not have had any influence on the message. It is referred to, I presume, in order to show that it was produced by a desire on the part of His Majesty's ministers the better to assure the passage of the law. Of this, sir, I never had a doubt, and immediately so advised my Government, and informed it (as was the fact) that I perfectly acquiesced in the delay; first, because of the circumstance to which you allude; secondly, because the statements originally intended to be ready by the 1st of January were not yet prepared. There is a slight error in this part of your excellency's letter; the delay was not made at my request, but was fully approved of, for the reasons which I have stated.

I have entered into this detail, sir, not for the purpose of recrimination, which, in most cases useless, would in this be worse, but with the object, as was my duty, of showing that although the ministers of the King, under the interpretation they seem to have given to Mr. Sérurier's promise, may have considered themselves at liberty to defer the presentation of the law until the period which they thought would best secure its success, yet the President, interpreting that promise differently, feeling that in consequence of it he had forborne to do what might be strictly called a duty, and seeing that its performance had not taken place, could not avoid stating the whole case clearly and distinctly to Congress and detailing to them all the remedies which the law of nations would allow to be applied to the case, leaving to them the choice, leaving to their wisdom and prudence the option, of the alternative of further delay or conditional action. Could he have said less in this branch of his message? If he alluded to the subject at all, he was obliged to detail the circumstances of the case. It is not pretended that this is not done with fidelity as to facts. The ratification of the treaty, its effect in pledging the faith of the nation, the fidelity with which the United States have executed it, the delay that intervened before it was brought before the Chambers, their rejection of the law, the assurances made by Mr. Sérurier, the forbearance of the President to make a communication to Congress in consequence of those assurances, and the adjournment of the question by His Majesty's Government to the end of the year—none of these have ever been denied, and all this the President was obliged to bring before Congress if, as I have said, he spoke on the subject. But he was obliged by a solemn duty to speak of it, and he had given timely and repeated notice of this obligation. The propositions which he submitted to Congress in consequence of those facts were a part of his duty. They were, as I have stated, exclusively addressed to that body, and in offering them he felt and expressed a proper regret, and, doing justice to the character and high feeling of the French nation, he explicitly disavowed any intention of influencing it by a menace.

I have no mission, sir, to offer any modification of the President's communication to Congress, and I beg that what I have said may be considered with the reserve that I do not acknowledge any right to demand or any obligation to give explanations of a document of that nature. But the relations which previously existed between the two countries, a desire that no unnecessary misunderstanding should interrupt them, and the tenor of your excellency's letter (evidently written under excited feeling) all convinced me that it was not incompatible with self-respect and the dignity of my country to enter into the detail I have done. The same reasons induced me to add that the idea erroneously entertained that an injurious menace is contained in the message has prevented your excellency from giving a proper attention to its language. A cooler examination will show that although the President was obliged, as I have demonstrated, to state to Congress the engagements which had been made, and that in his opinion they had not been complied with, yet in a communication not addressed to His Majesty's Government not a disrespectful term is employed, nor a phrase that his own sense of propriety, as well as the regard which one nation owes to another, would induce him to disavow. On the contrary, expressions of sincere regret that circumstances obliged him to complain of acts that disturbed the harmony he wished to preserve with a nation and Government to the high characters of which he did ample justice.

An honorable susceptibility to everything that may in the remotest degree affect the honor of the country is a national sentiment in France; but you will allow, sir, that it is carried too far when it becomes impatient of just complaint, when it will allow none of its acts to be arraigned and considers as an offense a simple and correct examination of injuries received and as an insult a deliberation on the means of redress. If it is forbidden, under the penalties of giving just cause of offense, for the different branches of a foreign government to consult together on the nature of wrongs it has received and review the several remedies which the law of nations present and circumstances justify, then no such consultation can take place in a government like that of the United States, where all the proceedings are public, without at once incurring the risk of war, which it would be the very object of that consultation to avoid.

The measures announced in the close of your letter, as well as the correspondence that it has occasioned between us, have been transmitted to my Government, and I wait the instructions which that communication will produce.

I pray your excellency to receive the renewed assurance of the high consideration with which I have the honor to be, your most obedient, humble servant,

EDW. LIVINGSTON.

[Indorsement.]

This letter was referred to in my message of the 7th of December last, and ought to have been then transmitted with that of the 25th of April, but by some oversight it was omitted.

A. J.

WASHINGTON, *January 18, 1836.*

To the Senate of the United States:

In compliance with the resolution of the Senate of the 12th instant, I transmit a report of the Secretary of State, with the papers therein referred to, which, with those accompanying the special message this day sent to Congress, are believed to contain all the information requested. The papers relative to the letter of the late minister of France have been added to those called for, that the subject may be fully understood.

ANDREW JACKSON.

DEPARTMENT OF STATE,
Washington, January 13, 1836.

The PRESIDENT OF THE UNITED STATES:

The Secretary of State has the honor to lay before the President a copy of a report made to him in June last, and of a letter addressed to this Department by the late minister of the Government of France, with the correspondence connected with that communication, which, together with a late correspondence between the Secretary of State and the French chargé d'affaires and a recent correspondence between the chargé d'affaires of the United States at Paris and the Duke de Broglie, already transmitted to the President to be communicated to Congress with his special message relative thereto, are the only papers in the Department of State supposed to be called for by the resolutions of the Senate of the 12th instant.

It will be seen by the correspondence with the chargé d'affaires of France that a dispatch to him from the Duke de Broglie was read to the Secretary at the Department in September last. It concluded with an authority to permit a copy to be taken if it was desired. That dispatch being an argumentative answer to the last letter of Mr. Livingston to the French Government, and in affirmance of the right of France to expect explanations of the message of the President, which France had been distinctly and timely informed could not be given without a disregard by the Chief Magistrate of his constitutional obligations, no desire was expressed to obtain a copy, it being obviously improper to receive an argument in a form which admitted of no reply, and necessarily unavailing to inquire how much or how little would satisfy France, when her right to any such explanation had been beforehand so distinctly and formally denied.

All which is respectfully submitted.

JOHN FORSYTH.

DEPARTMENT OF STATE,
Washington, June 18, 1835.

The PRESIDENT OF THE UNITED STATES:

I have the honor to present, for the examination of the President, three letters received at the Department from ———, dated at Paris, the 19th, 23d, and 30th of April. The last two I found here on my recent return from Georgia. They were received on the 9th and 10th of June; the last came to my own hand yesterday. Several communications have been previously received from the same quarter, all of them volunteered; none of them have been acknowledged. The unsolicited communications to the Department by citizens of the United States of facts that may come to their knowledge while residing abroad, likely to be interesting to their country, are always received with pleasure and carefully preserved on the files of the Government. Even opinions on foreign topics are received with proper respect for the motives and character of those who may choose to express them.

But holding it both improper and dangerous to countenance any of our citizens occupying no public station in sending confidential communications on our affairs with a foreign government at which we have an accredited agent, upon subjects involving the honor of the country, without the knowledge of such agent, and virtually substituting himself as the channel of communication between that government and his own, I considered it my duty to invite Mr. Pageot to the Department to apprise him of the contents of Mr. ———'s letter of the 23d of April, and at the same time to inform him that he might communicate the fact to the Duke de Broglie that no notice could be taken of Mr. ——— and his communications.

The extreme and culpable indiscretion of Mr. ——— in this transaction was strikingly illustrated by a remark of Mr. Pageot, after a careful examination of the letter of 23d April, that although without instructions from his Government he would venture to assure me that the Duke de Broglie could not have expected Mr. ——— to make such a communication to the Secretary of State. Declining to enter into the consideration of what the Duke might have expected or intended, I was satisfied with the assurances Mr. Pageot gave me that he would immediately state what had occurred to his Government.

All which is respectfully submitted, with the hope, if the course pursued is approved by the President, that this report may be filed in this Department with the letters to which it refers.

JOHN FORSYTH.

Mr. Forsyth to Mr. Livingston.

No. 50.

[Extract.]

DEPARTMENT OF STATE,
Washington, March 5, 1835.

EDWARD LIVINGSTON, Esq.,
　Envoy Extraordinary and Minister Plenipotentiary, Paris.

SIR: In my note No. 49 you were informed that the last letter of M. Sérurier would be made the subject of separate and particular instructions to you. Unwilling to add to the irritation produced by recent incidents in our relations with France, the President will not take for granted that the very exceptionable language of the French minister was used by the orders or will be countenanced by the authority of the King of France. You will therefore, as early as practicable after this reaches you, call the attention of the minister of foreign affairs to the following passage in M. Sérurier's letter:

"Les plaintes que porte M. le Président contre le prétendu non-accomplissement des engagemens pris par le Gouvernement du Roi à la suite du vote du 1er avril 1834, ne sont pas seulement étrangé par l'entière inexactitude des allégations sur lesquelles elles reposent, mais aussi parceque les explications qu'a reçues à Paris M. Livingston, et celles que le soussigné a données directement au cabinet de Washington semblaient ne pas laisser même la possibilité d'un malentendu sur des points aussi délicats."

In all discussions between government and government, whatever may be the differences of opinion on the facts or principles brought into view, the invariable rule of courtesy and justice demands that the sincerity of the opposing party in the views which it entertains should never be called in question. Facts may be denied, deductions examined, disproved, and condemned, without just cause of offense; but no impeachment of the integrity of the Government in its reliance on the correctness of its own views can be permitted without a total forgetfulness of self-respect. In the sentence quoted from M. Sérurier's letter no exception is taken to the assertion that the complaints of this Government are founded upon allegations entirely inexact, nor upon that which declares the explanations given here or in Paris appeared not to have left even the possibility of a misunderstanding on such delicate points. The correctness of these assertions we shall always dispute, and while the records of the two Governments endure we shall find no difficulty in shewing that they are groundless; but when M. Sérurier chooses to qualify the nonaccomplishment of the engagements made by France, to which the President refers, as a *pretended* non-accomplishment, he conveys the idea that the Chief Magistrate knows or believes that he is in error, and acting upon this known error seeks to impose it upon Congress and the world as truth. In this sense it is a direct attack upon the integrity of the Chief Magistrate of the Republic. As such it must be indignantly repelled; and it being a question of moral delinquency between the two Governments, the evidence against France, by whom it is raised, must be sternly arrayed. You will ascertain, therefore, if it has been used by the authority or receives the sanction of the Government of France *in that sense*. Should it be disavowed or explained, as from the note of the Count de Rigny to you, written at the moment of great excitement, and in its matter not differing from M. Sérurier's, it is presumed it will be, you will then use the materials herewith communicated, or already in your power, in a temper of great forbearance, but with a firmness of tone not to be mistaken, to answer the substance of the note itself.

Mr. Sérurier to Mr. Forsyth.

[Translation.]

WASHINGTON, *February 23, 1835.*

Hon. JOHN FORSYTH,
    Secretary of State.

The undersigned, envoy extraordinary and minister plenipotentiary of His Majesty the King of the French at Washington, has received orders to present the following note to the Secretary of State of the Government of the United States:

It would be superfluous to say that the message addressed on the 1st of December, 1834, to the Congress of the United States by President Jackson was received at Paris with a sentiment of painful surprise.

The King's Government is far from supposing that the measures recommended in this message to the attention of Congress can be adopted (*votées*) by that assembly; but even considering the document in question as a mere manifestation of the opinion which the President wishes to express with regard to the course taken in this affair, it is impossible not to consider its publication as a fact of a most serious nature.

The complaints brought forward by the President on account of the pretended nonfulfillment of the engagements entered into by the King's Government after the vote of the 1st of April are strange, not only from the total inaccuracy of the allegations on which they are based, but also because the explanations received by Mr. Livingston at Paris and those which the undersigned has given directly to the Cabinet of Washington seemed not to leave the slightest possibility of misunderstanding on points so delicate.

It appeared, indeed, from these explanations that although the session of the French Chambers, which was opened on the 31st of July last in compliance with an express provision of the charter, was prorogued at the end of a fortnight, before the bill relative to the American claims, announced in the discourse from the throne, could be placed under discussion, this prorogation arose (*tendit*) entirely from the absolute impossibility of commencing at so premature a period the legislative labors belonging to the year 1835.

It also appeared that the motives which had hindered the formal presentation to the Chambers of the bill in question during the first space of a fortnight originated chiefly in the desire more effectually to secure the success of this important affair by choosing the most opportune moment of offering it to the deliberations of the deputies newly elected, who, perhaps, might have been unfavorably impressed by this unusual haste in submitting it to them so long before the period at which they could enter upon an examination of it.

The undersigned will add that it is, moreover, difficult to comprehend what advantage could have resulted from such a measure, since it could not evidently have produced the effect which the President declares that he had in view, of enabling him to state at the opening of Congress that these long-pending negotiations were definitively closed. The President supposes, it is true, that the Chambers might have been called together anew before the last month of 1834; but even though the session had been opened some months earlier—which for several reasons would have been impossible—the simplest calculation will serve to shew that in no case could the decision of the Chambers have been taken, much less made known at Washington, before the 1st of December.

The King's Government had a right (*devait*) to believe that considerations so striking would have proved convincing with the Cabinet of the United States, and the more so as no direct communication made to the undersigned by this Cabinet or transmitted at Paris by Mr. Livingston had given token of the irritation and misunderstandings which the message of December 1 has thus deplorably revealed, and as Mr. Livingston, with that judicious spirit which characterizes him, coinciding with the system of (*ménagemens*) precautions and temporizing prudence adopted by the cabinet of the Tuileries with a view to the common interests, had even requested at the moment of the meeting of the Chambers that the presentation of the bill in question might be deferred, in order that its discussion should not be mingled with debates of another nature, with which its coincidence might place it in jeopardy.

This last obstacle had just been removed and the bill was about to be presented to the Chamber of Deputies when the arrival of the message, by creating in the minds of all a degree of astonishment at least equal to the just irritation which it could not fail to produce, has forced the Government of the King to deliberate on the part which it had to adopt.

Strong in its own right and dignity, it did not conceive that the inexplicable act of the President ought to cause it to renounce absolutely a determination the origin of which had been its respect for engagements (*loyauté*) and its good feelings toward a friendly nation. Although it does not conceal from itself that the provocation given at Washington has materially increased the difficulties of the case, already so great, yet it has determined to ask from the Chambers an appropriation of twenty-five millions to meet the engagements of the treaty of July 4.

But His Majesty has at the same time resolved no longer to expose his minister to hear such language as that held on December 1. The undersigned has received orders to return to France, and the dispatch of this order has been made known to Mr. Livingston.

The undersigned has the honor to present to the Secretary of State the assurance of his high consideration.

SÉRURIER.

Mr. Livingston to the Duke de Broglie.

LEGATION OF THE UNITED STATES OF AMERICA,
Paris, April 18, 1835.

M. LE DUC: I am specially directed to call the attention of His Majesty's Government to the following passage in the note presented by M. Sérurier to the Secretary of State at Washington:

"Les plaintes que porte Monsieur le Président contre le prétendu non-accomplissement des engagemens pris par le Gouvernement du Roi à la suite du vote du 1er avril 1834, ne sont pas seulement étrangé par l'entière inexactitude des allégations sur lesquelles elles reposent, mais aussi parceque les explications qu'a reçues à Paris M. Livingston, et celles que le soussigné a données directement au cabinet de Washington, semblaient ne pas laisser même la possibilité d'un malentendu sur des points aussi délicats."

Each party in a discussion of this nature has an uncontested right to make its own statement of facts and draw its own conclusions from them, to acknowledge or deny the accuracy of counter proof or the force of objecting arguments, with no other restraints than those which respect for his own convictions, the opinion of the world, and the rules of common courtesy impose. This freedom of argument is essential to the discussion of all national concerns, and can not be objected to without showing an improper and irritating susceptibility. It is for this reason that the Government of the United States make no complaint of the assertion in the note presented by M. Sérurier that the statement of facts contained in the President's message is inaccurate, and that the causes assigned for the delay in presenting the law ought to have satisfied them. On their part they contest the facts, deny the accuracy of the conclusions, and appeal to the record, to reason, and to the sense of justice of His Majesty's Government on a more mature consideration of the case for their justification. But I am further instructed to say that there is one expression in the passage I have quoted which in one signification could not be admitted even within the broad limits which are allowed to discussions of this nature, and which, therefore, the President will not believe to have been used in the offensive sense that might be attributed to it. The word "*prétendu*" sometimes, it is believed, in French, and its translation always in English, implies not only that the assertion which it qualifies is untrue, but that the party making it knows it to be so and uses it for the purposes of deception.

Although the President can not believe that the term was employed in this injurious sense, yet the bare possibility of a construction being put upon it which it would be incumbent on him to repel with indignation obliges him to ask for the necessary explanation.

I have the honor to be, etc.,

EDWARD LIVINGSTON.

Mr. Livingston to Mr. Forsyth.

[Extract.]

WASHINGTON, *June 29, 1835.*

* * * Having received my passports, I left Paris on the 29th of April. At the time of my departure the note, of which a copy has been transmitted to you, asking an explanation of the terms used in M. Sérurier's communication to the Department, remained unanswered, but I have reason to believe that the answer when given will be satisfactory.

WASHINGTON, *January 20, 1836.*

Hon. JAMES K. POLK,
    Speaker of the House of Representatives.

SIR: I herewith transmit to the House of Representatives a report from the Director of the Mint, exhibiting the operations of that institution during the year 1835.

The report contains also some very useful suggestions as to certain changes in the laws connected with our coinage and with that establishment, which are recommended to your early and careful attention.

Besides some remarks in it on the progress made in the erection of branch mints and procuring machinery therefor, I inclose a report from the Secretary of the Treasury, submitting more detailed statements as to the new buildings from each of the agents appointed to superintend their erection.

ANDREW JACKSON

WASHINGTON, *February 8, 1836.*

To the Senate and House of Representatives:

The Government of Great Britain has offered its mediation for the adjustment of the dispute between the United States and France. Carefully guarding that point in the controversy which, as it involves our honor and independence, admits of no compromise, I have cheerfully accepted the offer. It will be obviously improper to resort even to the mildest measures of a compulsory character until it is ascertained whether France has declined or accepted the mediation. I therefore recommend a suspension of all proceedings on that part of my special message of the 15th of January last which proposes a partial nonintercourse with France. While we can not too highly appreciate the elevated and disinterested motives of the offer of Great Britain, and have a just reliance upon the great influence of that power to restore the relations of ancient friendship between the United States and France, and know, too, that our own pacific policy will be strictly adhered to until the national honor compels us to depart from it, we should be insensible to the exposed condition of our country and forget the lessons of experience if we did not efficiently and sedulously prepare for an adverse result. The peace of a nation does not depend exclusively upon its own will, nor upon the beneficent policy of neighboring powers; and that nation which is found totally unprepared for the exigencies and dangers of war, although it come without having given warning of its approach, is criminally negligent of its honor and its duty. I can not too strongly repeat the recommendation already made to place the seaboard in a proper state for defense and promptly to provide the means for amply protecting our commerce.

ANDREW JACKSON.

WASHINGTON, *February 9, 1836.*

To the Senate of the United States:

In answer to the call made by the Senate in their resolution of the 3d instant, relative to the Indian hostilities in Florida, I transmit herewith a report from the Secretary of War, accompanied by sundry explanatory papers.

ANDREW JACKSON.

WASHINGTON, *February 10, 1836.*

To the House of Representatives:

I transmit herewith a report from the Secretary of War, with copies of so much of the correspondence relating to Indian affairs called for by the resolution of the House of January 23, 1835, as can be furnished by that Department. I also transmit a report on the same subject from the Treasury Department, from which it appears that without a special appropriation or the suspension for a considerable period of much of the urgent and current business of the General Land Office it is impracticable to take copies of all the papers described in the resolution. Under these circumstances the subject is again respectfully submitted to the consideration of the House of Representatives.

ANDREW JACKSON.

FEBRUARY 11, 1836.

To the Senate of the United States:

I herewith return to the Senate the resolution of the legislature of the State of Indiana requesting the President to suspend from sale a strip of land 10 miles in width, on a line from Munceytown to Fort Wayne, which resolution was referred to me on the 5th instant.

It appears from the memorial to which the resolution is subjoined that the lands embraced therein have been in market for several years past; that the legislature of the State of Indiana have applied to Congress for the passage of a law giving that State the right to purchase at such reduced prices as Congress may fix, and that their suspension from sale is requested as auxiliary to this application.

By the acts of Congress now in force all persons who may choose to make entries for these lands in the manner prescribed by law are entitled to purchase the same, and as the President possesses no dispensing power it will be obvious to the Senate that until authorized by law he can not rightfully act on the subject referred to him.

ANDREW JACKSON.

WASHINGTON, *February 15, 1836.*

To the Senate of the United States:

I transmit to the Senate, in pursuance of the resolutions passed by that body on the 3d instant, a report from the Secretary of State, accompanied by certain papers, relative to the existing relations between the United States and France.

ANDREW JACKSON.

WASHINGTON, *February 18, 1836.*

To the House of Representatives of the United States:

I transmit to the House of Representatives, in answer to their resolutions of the —— February instant, reports from the Secretary of State and the Secretary of the Treasury, with accompanying documents, relating to the relations between the United States and France. For reasons adverted to by the Secretary of State, the resolutions of the House have not been more fully complied with.

ANDREW JACKSON.

FEBRUARY 22, 1836.

To the Senate and House of Representatives:

I transmit herewith to Congress copies of the correspondence between the Secretary of State and the chargé d'affaires of His Britannic Majesty, relative to the mediation of Great Britain in our disagreement with France and to the determination of the French Government to execute the treaty of indemnification without further delay on the application for payment by the agent of the United States.

The grounds upon which the mediation was accepted will be found fully developed in the correspondence. On the part of France the mediation had been publicly accepted before the offer of it could be received here. Whilst each of the two Governments has thus discovered a just solicitude to resort to all honorable means of adjusting amicably the controversy between them, it is a matter of congratulation that the mediation has been rendered unnecessary. Under such circumstances the anticipation may be confidently indulged that the disagreement between the United States and France will not have produced more than a temporary estrangement. The healing effects of time, a just consideration of the powerful motives for a cordial good understanding between the two nations, the strong inducements each has to respect and esteem the other, will no doubt soon obliterate from their remembrance all traces of that disagreement.

Of the elevated and disinterested part the Government of Great Britain has acted and was prepared to act I have already had occasion to express my high sense. Universal respect and the consciousness of meriting it are with Governments as with men the just rewards of those who faithfully exert their power to preserve peace, restore harmony, and perpetuate good will.

I may be permitted, I trust, at this time, without a suspicion of the most remote desire to throw off censure from the Executive or to point it to any other department or branch of the Government, to refer to the want of effective preparation in which our country was found at the late crisis. From the nature of our institutions the movements of the Government in preparation for hostilities must ever be too slow for the exigencies of unexpected war. I submit it, then, to you whether the first duty we owe to the people who have confided to us their power is not to place our country in such an attitude as always to be so amply supplied with the means of self-defense as to afford no inducements to other nations to presume upon our forbearance or to expect important advantages from a sudden assault, either upon our commerce, our seacoast, or our interior frontier. In case of the commencement of hostilities during the recess of Congress, the time inevitably elapsing before that body could be called together, even under the most favorable circumstances, would be pregnant with danger; and if we escaped without signal disaster or national dishonor, the hazard of both unnecessarily incurred could not fail to excite a feeling of deep reproach. I earnestly recommend to you, therefore, to make such provisions that in no future time shall we be found without ample means to repel aggression, even although it may come upon us without a note of warning. We are now, fortunately, so situated that the expenditure for this purpose will not be felt, and if it were it would be approved by those from whom all its means are derived, and for whose benefit only it should be used with a liberal economy and an enlightened forecast.

In behalf of these suggestions I can not forbear repeating the wise precepts of one whose counsels can not be forgotten:

* * * The United States ought not to indulge a persuasion that, contrary to the order of human events, they will forever keep at a distance those painful appeals to arms with which the history of every other nation abounds. There is a rank due to the United States among nations which will be withheld, if not absolutely lost, by the reputation of weakness. If we desire to avoid insult, we must be able to repel it; if we desire to secure peace, one of the most powerful instruments of our rising prosperity, it must be known that we are at all times ready for war.

ANDREW JACKSON.

WASHINGTON, *January 27, 1836.*

The undersigned, His Britannic Majesty's chargé d'affaires, has been instructed to state to Mr. Forsyth, the Secretary of State of the United States, that the British Government has witnessed with the greatest pain and regret the progress of the misunderstanding which has lately grown up between the Governments of France and of the United States. The first object of the undeviating policy of the British cabinet has been to maintain uninterrupted the relations of peace between Great Britain and the other nations of the world, without any abandonment of national interests and without any sacrifice of national honor. The next object to which their anxious and unremitting exertions have been directed has been by an appropriate exercise of the good offices and moral influence of Great Britain to heal dissensions which may have arisen among neighboring powers and to preserve for other nations those blessings of peace which Great Britain is so desirous of securing for herself.

The steady efforts of His Majesty's Government have hitherto been, fortunately, successful in the accomplishment of both these ends, and while Europe during the last five years has passed through a crisis of extraordinary hazard without any disturbance of the general peace, His Majesty's Government has the satisfaction of thinking that it has on more than one occasion been instrumental in reconciling differences which might otherwise have led to quarrels, and in cementing union between friendly powers.

But if ever there could be an occasion on which it would be painful to the British Government to see the relations of amity broken off between two friendly states that occasion is undoubtedly the present, when a rupture is apprehended between two great powers, with both of which Great Britain is united by the closest ties—with one of which she is engaged in active alliance; with the other of which she is joined by community of interests and by the bonds of kindred.

Nor would the grounds of difference on the present occasion reconcile the friends and wellwishers of the differing parties to the misfortune of an open rupture between them.

When the conflicting interests of two nations are so opposed on a particular question as to admit of no possible compromise, the sword may be required to cut the knot which reason is unable to untie.

When passions have been so excited on both sides that no common standard of justice can be found, and what one party insists on as a right the other denounces as a wrong, prejudice may become too headstrong to yield to the voice of equity, and those who can agree on nothing else may consent to abide the fate of arms and to allow that the party which shall prove the weakest in the war shall be deemed to have been wrong in the dispute.

But in the present case there is no question of national interest at issue between France and the United States. In the present case there is no demand of justice made by one party and denied by the other. The disputed claims of America on France, which were founded upon transactions in the early part of the present century and were for many years in litigation, have at length been established by mutual consent and are admitted by a treaty concluded between the two Governments. The money due by France has been provided by the Chambers, and has been placed at the disposal of the French Government for the purpose of being paid to the United States. But questions have arisen between the two Governments in the progress of those transactions affecting on both sides the feelings of national honor, and it is on this ground that the relations between the parties have been for the moment suspended and are in danger of being more seriously interrupted.

In this state of things the British Government is led to think that the good offices of a third power equally the friend of France and of the United States, and prompted by considerations of the highest order most earnestly to wish for the continuance of peace, might be useful in restoring a good understanding between the two parties on a footing consistent with the nicest feelings of national honor in both.

The undersigned has therefore been instructed by His Majesty's Government formally to tender to the Government of the United States the mediation of Great Britain for the settlement of the differences between the United States and France, and to say that a note precisely similar to the present has been delivered to the French Government by His Majesty's ambassador at Paris. The undersigned has, at the same time, to express the confident hope of His Majesty's Government that if the two parties would agree to refer to the British Government the settlement of the point at issue between them, and to abide by the opinion which that Government might after due consideration communicate to the two parties thereupon, means might be found of satisfying the honor of each without incurring those great and manifold evils which a rupture between two such powers must inevitably entail on both.

The undersigned has the honor to renew to Mr. Forsyth the assurance of his most distinguished consideration.

CHARLES BANKHEAD.

DEPARTMENT OF STATE,
Washington, February 3, 1836.

CHARLES BANKHEAD, Esq.:

The undersigned, Secretary of State of the United States, has had the honor to receive the note of the 27th ultimo of Mr. Charles Bankhead, His Britannic Majesty's chargé d'affaires, offering to the Government of the United States the mediation of His Britannic Majesty's Government for the settlement of the differences unhappily existing between the United States and France. That communication having been submitted to the President, and considered with all the care belonging to the importance of the subject and the source from which it emanated, the undersigned has been instructed to assure Mr. Bankhead that the disinterested and honorable motives which have dictated the proposal are fully appreciated. The pacific policy of His Britannic Majesty's cabinet and their efforts to heal dissensions arising among nations are worthy of the character and commanding influence of Great Britain, and the success of those efforts is as honorable to the Government by whose instrumentality it was secured as it has been beneficial to the parties more immediately interested and to the world at large.

The sentiments upon which this policy is founded, and which are so forcibly displayed in the offer that has been made, are deeply impressed upon the mind of the President. They are congenial with the institutions and principles as well as with the interests and habits of the people of the United States, and it has been the constant aim of their Government in its conduct toward other powers to observe and illustrate them. Cordially approving the general views of His Britannic Majesty's Government, the President regards with peculiar satisfaction the enlightened and disinterested solicitude manifested by it for the welfare of the nations to whom its good offices are now tendered, and has seen with great sensibility, in the exhibition of that feeling, the recognition of that community of interests and those ties of kindred by which the United States and Great Britain are united.

If circumstances did not render it certain, it would have been obvious from the language of Mr. Bankhead's note to the undersigned that the Government of His Britannic Majesty, when the instructions under which it was prepared were given, could not have been apprised of all the steps taken in the controversy between the United States and France. It was necessarily ignorant of the tenor of the two recent messages of the President to Congress—the first communicated at the commencement of the present session, under date of the 7th of December, 1835, and the second under that of the 15th of January, 1836. Could these documents have been within the knowledge of His Britannic Majesty's Government, the President does not doubt that it would have been fully satisfied that the disposition of the United States, notwithstanding their well-grounded and serious causes of complaint against France, to restore friendly relations and cultivate a good understanding with the Government of that country was undiminished, and that all had already been done on their part that could in reason be expected of them to secure that result. The first of these documents, although it gave such a history of the origin and progress of the claims of the United States and of the proceedings of France before and since the treaty of 1831 as to vindicate the statements and recommendations of the message of the 1st of December, 1834, yet expressly disclaimed the offensive interpretation put upon it by the Government of France, and while it insisted on the acknowledged rights of the United States and the obligations of the treaty and maintained the honor and independence of the American Government, evinced an anxious desire to do all that constitutional duty and strict justice would permit to remove every cause of irritation and excitement. The special message of the 15th January last being called for by the extraordinary and inadmissible demands of the Government of France as defined in the last official communications at Paris, and by the continued refusal of France to execute a treaty from the faithful performance of which by the United States it was tranquilly enjoying important advantages, it became the duty of the President to recommend such measures as might be adapted to the exigencies of the occasion. Unwilling to believe that a nation distinguished for honor and intelligence could have determined permanently to maintain a ground so indefensible, and anxious still to leave open the door of reconciliation, the President contented himself with proposing to Congress the mildest of the remedies given by the law and practice of nations in connection with such propositions for defense as were evidently required by the condition of the United States and the attitude assumed by France. In all these proceedings, as well as in every stage of these difficulties with France, it is confidently believed that the course of the United States, when duly considered by other Governments and the world, will be found to have been marked not only by a pacific disposition, but by a spirit of forbearance and conciliation.

For a further illustration of this point, as well as for the purpose of presenting a lucid view of the whole subject, the undersigned has the honor to transmit to Mr. Bankhead copies of all that part of the message of December 7, 1835, which relates to it and of the correspondence referred to therein, and also copies of the message and accompanying documents of the 15th of January, 1836, and of another message of the 18th of the same month, transmitting a report of the Secretary of State and certain documents connected with the subject.

These papers, while they will bring down the history of the misunderstanding between the United States and France to the present date, will also remove an erroneous impression which appears to be entertained by His Britannic Majesty's Government. It is suggested in Mr. Bankhead's note that there is no question of national interest at issue between France and the United States, and that there is no demand of justice made by the one party and denied by the other. This suggestion appears to be founded on the facts that the claims of the United States have been admitted by a treaty concluded between the two Governments and that the money due by France has been provided by the Chambers and placed at the disposal of the French Government for the purpose of being paid to the United States. But it is to be observed that the payment of the money thus appropriated is refused by the French Government unless the United States will first comply with a condition not contained in the treaty and not assented to by them. This refusal to make payment is, in the view of the United States, a denial of justice, and has not only been accompanied by acts and language of which they have great reason to complain, but the delay of payment is highly injurious to those American citizens who are entitled to share in the indemnification provided by the treaty and to the interests of the United States, inasmuch as the reduction of the duties levied on French wines in pursuance of that treaty has diminished the public revenue, and has been and yet is enjoyed by France, with all the other benefits of the treaty, without the consideration and equivalents for which they were granted. But there are other national interests, and, in the judgment of this Government, national interests of the highest order, involved in the condition prescribed and insisted on by France which it has been by the President made the duty of the undersigned to bring distinctly into view. That condition proceeds on the assumption that a foreign power whose acts are spoken of by the President of the United States in a message to Congress, transmitted in obedience to his constitutional duties, and which deems itself aggrieved by the language thus held by him, may as a matter of right require from the Government of the United States a direct official explanation of such language, to be given in such form and expressed in such terms as shall meet the requirements and satisfy the feelings of the offended party, and may in default of such explanation annul or suspend a solemn treaty duly executed by its constitutional organ. Whatever may be the responsibility of those nations whose executives possess the power of declaring war and of adopting other coercive remedies without the intervention of the legislative department, for the language held by the Executive in addressing that department, it is obvious that under the Constitution of the United States, which gives to the Executive no such powers, but vests them exclusively in the Legislature, whilst at the same time it imposes on the Executive the duty of laying before the Legislature the state of the nation, with such recommendations as he may deem proper, no such responsibility can be admitted without impairing that freedom of intercommunication which is essential to the system and without surrendering in this important particular the right of self-government. In accordance with this view of the Federal Constitution has been the practice under it. The statements and recommendations of the President to Congress are regarded by this Government as a part of the purely domestic consultations held by its different departments—consultations in which nothing is addressed to foreign powers, and in which they can not be permitted to interfere, and for which, until consummated and carried out by acts emanating from the proper constitutional organs, the nation is not responsible and the Government not liable to account to other States.

It will be seen from the accompanying correspondence that when the condition referred to was first proposed in the Chamber of Deputies the insuperable objections to it were fully communicated by the American minister at Paris to the French Government, and that he distinctly informed it that the condition, if prescribed, could never be complied with. The views expressed by him were approved by the President, and have been since twice asserted and enforced by him in his messages to Congress in terms proportioned in their explicitness and solemnity to the conviction he entertains of the importance and inviolability of the principle involved.

The United States can not yield this principle, nor can they do or consent to any measure by which its influence in the action of their political system can be obstructed or diminished. Under these circumstances the President feels that he may rely on the intelligence and liberality of His Britannic Majesty's Government for a correct estimation of the imperative obligations which leave him no power to subject this point to the control of any foreign state, whatever may be his confidence in its justice and impartiality—a confidence which he has taken pleasure in instructing the undersigned to state is fully reposed by him in the Government of His Britannic Majesty.

So great, however, is the desire of the President for the restoration of a good understanding with the Government of France, provided it can be effected on terms compatible with the honor and independence of the United States, that if, after the frank avowal of his sentiments upon the point last referred to and the explicit reservation of that point, the Government of His Britannic Majesty shall believe that its mediation can be useful in adjusting the differences which exist between the two countries and in restoring all their relations to a friendly footing, he instructs the undersigned to inform Mr. Bankhead that in such case the offer of mediation made in his note is cheerfully accepted.

The United States desire nothing but equal and exact justice, and they can not but hope that the good offices of a third power, friendly to both parties, and prompted by the elevated considerations manifested in Mr. Bankhead's note, may promote the attainment of this end.

Influenced by these motives, the President will cordially cooperate, so far as his constitutional powers may enable him, in such steps as may be requisite on the part of the United States to give effect to the proposed mediation. He trusts that no unnecessary delay will be allowed to occur, and instructs the undersigned to request that the earliest information of the measures taken by Great Britain and of their result may be communicated to this Government.

The undersigned avails himself of the occasion to renew to Mr. Bankhead the assurances of his distinguished consideration.

JOHN FORSYTH.

WASHINGTON, *February 15, 1836.*

Hon. JOHN FORSYTH, etc.:

The undersigned, His Britannic Majesty's chargé d'affaires, with reference to his note of the 27th of last month, has the honor to inform Mr. Forsyth, Secretary of State of the United States, that he has been instructed by his Government to state that the British Government has received a communication from that of France which fulfills the wishes that impelled His Britannic Majesty to offer his mediation for the purpose of effecting an amicable adjustment of the difference between France and the United States.

The French Government has stated to that of His Majesty that the frank and honorable manner in which the President has in his recent message expressed himself with regard to the points of difference between the Governments of France and of the United States has removed those difficulties, upon the score of national honor, which have hitherto stood in the way of the prompt execution by France of the treaty of the 4th July, 1831, and that consequently the French Government is now ready to pay the installment which is due on account of the American indemnity whenever the payment of that installment shall be claimed by the Government of the United States.

The French Government has also stated that it made this communication to that of Great Britain not regarding the British Government as a formal mediator, since its offer of mediation had then reached only the Government of France, by which it had been accepted, but looking upon the British Government as a common friend of the two parties, and therefore as a natural channel of communication between them.

The undersigned is further instructed to express the sincere pleasure which is felt by the British Government at the prospect thus afforded of an amicable termination of a difference which has produced a temporary estrangement between two nations who have so many interests in common, and who are so entitled to the friendship and esteem of each other; and the undersigned has also to assure Mr. Forsyth that it has afforded the British Government the most lively satisfaction to have been upon this occasion the channel of a communication which they trust will lead to the complete restoration of friendly relations between the United States and France.

The undersigned has great pleasure in renewing to Mr. Forsyth the assurances of his most distinguished consideration.

CHARLES BANKHEAD.

DEPARTMENT OF STATE,
Washington, February 16, 1836.

CHARLES BANKHEAD, Esq.:

The undersigned, Secretary of State of the United States, has had the honor to receive Mr. Bankhead's note of the 15th instant, in which he states by the instructions of his Government that the British Government have received a communication from that of France which fulfills the wishes that impelled His Britannic Majesty to offer his mediation for the purpose of effecting an amicable adjustment of the differences between France and the United States; that the French Government, being satisfied with the frank and honorable manner in which the President has in his recent message expressed himself in regard to the points of difference between the two Governments, is ready to pay the installment due on account of the American indemnity whenever it shall be claimed by the Government of the United States, and that this communication is made to the Government of Great Britain not as a formal mediator, but as a common friend of both parties.

The undersigned has submitted this note of His Britannic Majesty's chargé d'affaires to the President, and is instructed to reply that the President has received this information with the highest satisfaction—a satisfaction as sincere as was his regret at the unexpected occurrence of the difficulty created by the erroneous impressions heretofore made upon the national sensibility of France. By the fulfillment of the obligations of the convention between the two Governments the great cause of difference will be removed, and the President anticipates that the benevolent and magnanimous wishes of His Britannic Majesty's Government will be speedily realized, as the temporary estrangement between the two nations who have so many common interests will no doubt be followed by the restoration of their ancient ties of friendship and esteem.

The President has further instructed the undersigned to express to His Britannic Majesty's Government his sensibility at the anxious desire it has displayed to preserve the relations of peace between the United States and France, and the exertions it was prepared to make to effectuate that object, so essential to the prosperity and congenial to the wishes of the two nations and to the repose of the world.

Leaving His Majesty's Government to the consciousness of the elevated motives which have governed its conduct and to the universal respect which must be secured to it, the President is satisfied that no expressions, however strong, of his own feelings can be appropriately used which could add to the gratification afforded to His Majesty's Government at being the channel of communication to preserve peace and restore good will between differing nations, each of whom is its friend.

The undersigned avails himself of this occasion to renew to Mr. Bankhead the assurance of his distinguished consideration.

JOHN FORSYTH.

WASHINGTON, *February 23, 1836.*

To the Senate of the United States:

I transmit herewith a report of the Secretary of War, on the progress of the improvement of Red River, furnishing information in addition to that communicated with my message at the opening of the present session of Congress.

ANDREW JACKSON.

[The same letter was addressed to the Speaker of the House of Representatives.]

WASHINGTON, *February 25, 1836.*

To the Senate:

I transmit to the Senate a report* from the Secretary of State, complying as far as practicable with their resolution of the 16th instant.

ANDREW JACKSON.

WASHINGTON, *February 29, 1836.*

To the Senate and House of Representatives of the United States:

I transmit a report of the Secretary of State, communicating an application from the chargé d'affaires of Portugal for the passage by Congress of a special act abolishing discriminating duties upon the cargoes of Portuguese vessels imported into the United States from those parts of the dominions of Portugal in which no discriminating duties are charged upon the vessels of the United States or their cargoes, and providing for a return of the discriminating duties which have been exacted upon the cargoes of Portuguese vessels thus circumstanced since the 18th of April, 1834. I also transmit a copy of the correspondence which has taken place upon the subject between the Department of State and the chargé d'affaires of Portugal.

The whole matter is submitted to the discretion of Congress, with this suggestion, that if an act should be passed placing the cargoes of Portuguese vessels coming from certain parts of the territories of Portugal on the footing of those imported in vessels of the United States, in deciding upon the propriety of restoring the duties heretofore levied and the time to which they should be restored regard should be had to the fact that the decree of the 18th April, 1834, which is made the basis of the present application, took effect in the islands of Madeira and the Azores many months after its promulgation, and to the more important fact that until the 1st of February instant an indirect advantage was allowed in Portugal to importations from Great Britain over those from other countries, including the United States.

ANDREW JACKSON.

*Relating to claims for spoliations under the French treaty of 1831.

DEPARTMENT OF STATE, *February 27, 1836.*

The PRESIDENT OF THE UNITED STATES:

The undersigned, Secretary of State, has the honor to report to the President that official information was received at this Department some time since from the chargé d'affaires of Portugal of the abolition of all discriminating duties upon the cargoes of foreign vessels, including those of the United States, imported into Lisbon and Oporto, by a decree of the Portuguese Government promulgated on the 18th of April, 1834, the operation of which decree was stated by the chargé to extend to the island of Madeira. Upon the strength of this decree he applied, by order of his Government, for the suspension, under the fourth section of the act of Congress of January 7, 1824, of discriminating duties upon the cargoes of Portuguese vessels imported into the United States; but being informed that the act alluded to was inapplicable by reason that discriminating duties upon the cargoes of American vessels still existed in a part of the dominions of Portugal, he has requested that the principle acted upon in regard to Holland may be extended to Portugal, and that discriminating duties may be abolished in respect to Portugal proper, the Madeira Islands, the Azores, and such other parts of the Portuguese dominions wherein no discriminating duty is levied upon the vessels of the United States or their cargoes. This request is accompanied by a suggestion that unless some such reciprocity is established the benefits of the decree of April, 1834, will be withdrawn so far as respects this country. Application is also made for a return of the discriminating duties which have been collected since the promulgation of the said decree from the vessels of Portugal arriving in the United States from any of the ports embraced by that decree. In reference to this point it is proper to state that it does not appear that the force or operation of the decree referred to of the 18th April, 1834, was extended by any official act of the Portuguese Government to the islands of Madeira or the Azores until February or April, 1835. It is also to be observed that, notwithstanding the abolition by that decree of discriminating duties upon the importation of goods into Portugal from foreign countries, an exemption existed until the 1st of February instant, according to information received from our chargé d'affaires at Lisbon, in favor of various articles when imported from Great Britain, from an excise duty which was exacted upon the same articles when imported from other foreign countries or produced or manufactured at home. This exemption was granted in pursuance of the construction given to a stipulation contained in the late treaty between Portugal and Great Britain, and ceased, together with that treaty, on the 1st day of the present month.

The undersigned has the honor to transmit with this report a copy of the correspondence between the Department and the chargé d'affaires of Portugal upon which it is founded.

JOHN FORSYTH.

WASHINGTON, *February 29, 1836.*

To the Senate of the United States:

I transmit herewith a report from the Secretary of State, correcting an error made in the report recently communicated to the Senate in answer to the resolution of the 16th instant, respecting the number and amount of claims for spoliations presented to the commissioners under the French treaty of 1831 which were rejected.

ANDREW JACKSON.

WASHINGTON, *March 5, 1836.*

To the Senate:

I submit to the Senate, for their advice and consent as to the ratification of the same, the treaty and the supplement to it recently concluded with the Cherokee Indians.

The papers referred to in the accompanying communication from the Secretary of War as necessary to a full view of the whole subject are also herewith submitted.

ANDREW JACKSON.

WASHINGTON, *March 7, 1836.*

To the Senate of the United States:

I transmit to the Senate, for their consideration with a view to its ratification, a treaty of peace, amity, navigation, and commerce between the United States and the Republic of Venezuela, concluded and signed by their plenipotentiaries at the city of Caracas on the 20th of January last.

ANDREW JACKSON.

WASHINGTON, *March 10, 1836.*

To the Senate and House of Representatives:

I transmit herewith a report from the Secretary of State, communicating the proceedings of a convention assembled at Little Rock, in the Territory of Arkansas, for the purpose of forming a constitution and system of government for the State of Arkansas. The constitution adopted by this convention and the documents accompanying it, referred to in the report from the Secretary of State, are respectfully submitted to the consideration of Congress.

ANDREW JACKSON.

WASHINGTON, *April 1, 1836.*

To the Senate:

I transmit herewith to the Senate, for their advice and consent as to its ratification, a treaty concluded with the Ottawa and Chippewa Indians.

ANDREW JACKSON.

WASHINGTON, *April 8, 1836.*

To the Senate:

I transmit herewith reports from the Secretaries of the War and Navy Departments, to whom were referred the resolutions adopted by the Senate on the 18th of February last, requesting information of the probable amount of appropriations that would be necessary to place the land and naval defenses of the country upon a proper footing of strength and respectability.

In respect to that branch of the subject which falls more particularly under the notice of the Secretary of War, and in the consideration of which he has arrived at conclusions differing from those contained in the report from the Engineer Bureau, I think it proper to add my concurrence in the views expressed by the Secretary.

ANDREW JACKSON.

WASHINGTON, *April 12, 1836.*

To the Senate:

I transmit herewith a report* from the Secretary of War, communicating the original letter from Major Davis and the statements which accompany it, referred to in the resolution of the Senate of the 8th instant.

ANDREW JACKSON.

WASHINGTON, *April 27, 1836.*

To the Senate of the United States:

I transmit herewith to the Senate, for their advice and consent as to the ratification of the same, a treaty concluded with the Wyandot Indians for a cession of a portion of their reservation in the State of Ohio.

In order to prevent any abuse of the power granted to the chiefs in the fifth article of the treaty, I recommend the adoption of the suggestion contained in the accompanying letter of the Secretary of War; otherwise I shall not feel satisfied in approving that article.

ANDREW JACKSON.

WASHINGTON, *April 29, 1836.*

To the Senate and House of Representatives:

It affords me pleasure to transmit to Congress a copy of the Catalogue of the Arundel Manuscripts in the British Museum, which has been forwarded to me, as will be perceived from the inclosed letter, on behalf of the trustees of that institution, for the purpose of being placed in the United States Library.

ANDREW JACKSON.

To the Senate and House of Representatives:

Believing that the act of the 12th July, 1832, does not enable the Executive to carry into effect the recently negotiated additional article to the treaty of limits with Mexico, I transmit to Congress copies of that article, that the necessary legislative provision may be made for its faithful execution on the part of the United States.

ANDREW JACKSON.

MAY 6, 1836.

---

* Relating to the treaty of December 29, 1835, with the Cherokee Indians.

WASHINGTON, *May 10, 1836.*

To the Senate and House of Representatives:

Information has been received at the Treasury Department that the four installments under our treaty with France have been paid to the agent of the United States. In communicating this satisfactory termination of our controversy with France, I feel assured that both Houses of Congress will unite with me in desiring and believing that the anticipations of a restoration of the ancient cordial relations between the two countries, expressed in my former messages on this subject, will be speedily realized.

No proper exertion of mine shall be wanting to efface the remembrance of those misconceptions that have temporarily interrupted the accustomed intercourse between them.

ANDREW JACKSON.

To the House of Representatives: WASHINGTON, *May 14, 1836.*

In compliance with a resolution of the House of Representatives of the 10th instant, I transmit reports* from the Secretaries of State and War, with the papers accompanying the same.

ANDREW JACKSON.

To the Senate of the United States: MAY 14, 1836.

I transmit, for the consideration of the Senate, three treaties concluded with certain bands of Pottawatamie Indians in the State of Indiana.

I transmit also a report from the Secretary of War, inclosing the instructions under which these treaties were negotiated.

I would remark that the fourth article of each treaty provides for the appointment of a commissioner and the payment of the debts due by the Indians. There is no limitation upon the amount of these debts, though it is obvious from these instructions that the commissioner should have limited the amount to be applied to this object; otherwise the whole fund might be exhausted and the Indians left without the means of living. I therefore recommend either that the Senate limit the amount at their discretion or that they provide by resolution that the whole purchase money be paid to the Indians, leaving to them the adjustment of their debts.

ANDREW JACKSON.

To the Senate of the United States: WASHINGTON, *May 21, 1836.*

I transmit herewith two treaties concluded with bands of Pottawatamies in the State of Indiana, with accompanying papers, for the consideration and action of the Senate.

ANDREW JACKSON.

*Relating to affairs with Mexico.

WASHINGTON, *May 26, 1836.*

To the House of Representatives:

I transmit, in conformity with a resolution of the House of Representatives of the 21st instant, a report of the Secretary of War, containing the information called for on the subject of the causes of the hostilities of the Seminoles and the measures taken to repress them.

ANDREW JACKSON.

WASHINGTON, *May 27, 1836.*

To the House of Representatives:

In further compliance with so much of the resolution of the House of Representatives of the 21st instant as calls for an account of the causes of the hostilities of the Seminole Indians, I transmit a supplementary report from the Secretary of War.

ANDREW JACKSON.

WASHINGTON, *May 28, 1836.*

To the Senate of the United States:

I transmit herewith, for the consideration and action of the Senate, a treaty concluded on the 24th instant with the Chippewa Indians of Saganaw.

ANDREW JACKSON.

WASHINGTON, *May 31, 1836.*

To the Senate:

I transmit herewith the response of Samuel Gwin, esq.,* to the charges affecting his official conduct and character which were set forth in the evidence taken under the authority of the Senate by the Committee on Public Lands, and which was referred to the President by the resolution of the Senate bearing date the 3d day of March, 1835. This resolution and the evidence it refers to were officially communicated to Mr. Gwin by the Secretary of the Treasury, and the response of Mr. Gwin has been received through the same official channel.

ANDREW JACKSON.

WASHINGTON, *June 1, 1836.*

To the Senate:

I transmit herewith to the Senate a communication which has been received from Mr. B. F. Currey † in answer to a call made upon him by the President, through the War Department, in consequence of the serious charges which were preferred against him by one of the honorable members of the Senate. It seems to be due to justice that the Senate should be furnished, agreeably to the request of Mr. Currey, with the

---

*Register of the land office for the northwestern district of Mississippi.
†Agent for the removal of the Cherokee Indians.

explanations contained in this communication, particularly as they are deemed so far satisfactory as would render his dismissal or even censure undeserved and improper.

ANDREW JACKSON.

WASHINGTON, *June 3, 1836.*

To the Senate:

In compliance with the resolution of the Senate of the 27th ultimo, requesting the President to inform the Senate "whether any increase or improvement of organization is needed in the Ordnance Corps," I have to state that I entertain no doubt of the propriety of increasing the corps, and that I concur in the plan proposed for this purpose in the accompanying report from the Secretary of War.

ANDREW JACKSON.

WASHINGTON, *June 3, 1836.*

To the House of Representatives:

I transmit herewith a supplemental report from the War Department, in answer to the resolution of the House of Representatives of the 21st ultimo, calling for information respecting the causes of the Seminole hostilities and the measures taken to suppress them.

ANDREW JACKSON.

WASHINGTON, *June 3, 1836.*

To the House of Representatives:

I herewith transmit a report from the Secretary of the Treasury, in relation to the injuries sustained by the bridge across the Potomac River during the recent extraordinary rise of water, and would respectfully recommend to the early attention of Congress the legislation therein suggested.

ANDREW JACKSON.

WASHINGTON, *June 14, 1836.*

To the Senate of the United States:

I transmit a report of the Secretary of State, prepared in compliance with the resolution of the Senate of the 11th instant, upon the subject of the depredations of the Mexicans on the property of Messrs. Chouteau and Demun.

ANDREW JACKSON.

WASHINGTON, *June 15, 1836.*

To the Senate of the United States:

I communicate to the Senate a report from the Secretary of State, with a copy of the correspondence requested by a resolution of the 21st ultimo, relative to the northeastern boundary of the United States.

At the last session of Congress I felt it my duty to decline complying with a request made by the House of Representatives for copies of this correspondence, feeling, as I did, that it would be inexpedient to publish it while the negotiation was pending; but as the negotiation was undertaken under the special advice of the Senate, I deem it improper to withhold the information which that body has requested, submitting to them to decide whether it will be expedient to publish the correspondence before the negotiation has been closed.   ANDREW JACKSON.

WASHINGTON, *June 23, 1836.*

To the Senate of the United States:

In compliance with a resolution of the Senate of the 18th instant, I transmit a report* from the Secretary of State, with the papers therewith presented. Not having accurate and detailed information of the civil, military, and political condition of Texas, I have deemed it expedient to take the necessary measures, now in progress, to procure it before deciding upon the course to be pursued in relation to the newly declared government.   ANDREW JACKSON.

JUNE 28, 1836.

To the House of Representatives:

I transmit to the House of Representatives a report from the Secretary of War, conveying the information called for by the House in its resolution of yesterday, concerning the Cherokee treaty recently ratified.

ANDREW JACKSON.

WASHINGTON, *June 28, 1836.*

To the Senate:

As it is probable that it may be proper to send a minister to Paris prior to the next meeting of Congress, I nominate Lewis Cass, now Secretary for the Department of War, to be envoy extraordinary and minister plenipotentiary to France, not to be commissioned until notice has been received here that the Government of France has appointed a minister to the United States who is about to set out for Washington.

ANDREW JACKSON.

WASHINGTON, *June 30, 1836.*

To the Senate and House of Representatives:

It becomes my painful duty to announce to you the melancholy intelligence of the death of James Madison, ex-President of the United States.

---

* Relating to the political condition of Texas, the organization of its Government, and its capacity to maintain its independence, etc.

He departed this life at half past 6 o'clock on the morning of the 28th instant, full of years and full of honors.

I hasten this communication in order that Congress may adopt such measures as may be proper to testify their sense of the respect which is due to the memory of one whose life has contributed so essentially to the happiness and glory of his country and the good of mankind.

ANDREW JACKSON.

To the Senate and House of Representatives:

I transmit to Congress copies of a treaty of peace, friendship, navigation, and commerce between the United States and the Republic of Venezuela, concluded on the 20th of January, and the ratifications of which were exchanged at Caracas on the 31st of May last.

JUNE 30, 1836.

ANDREW JACKSON.

WASHINGTON, *June 30, 1836.*

To the House of Representatives:

I return to the House of Representatives the papers which accompanied their resolution of the 6th of May last, relative to the claim of Don Juan Madrazo, together with a report of the Secretary of State and copies of a correspondence between him and the Attorney-General, showing the grounds upon which that officer declines giving the opinion requested by the resolution.

ANDREW JACKSON.

WASHINGTON, *July 1, 1836.*

To the Senate of the United States:

In answer to the resolution of the Senate of the 21st January last, I transmit a report* of the Secretary of War, containing the copies called for so far as relates to his Department.

ANDREW JACKSON.

VETO MESSAGE.

WASHINGTON, *June 9, 1836.*

To the Senate of the United States:

The act of Congress "to appoint a day for the annual meeting of Congress," which originated in the Senate, has not received my signature. The power of Congress to fix by law a day for the regular annual meeting of Congress is undoubted, but the concluding part of this act, which

---

*Relating to frauds in sales of public lands or Indian reservations.

is intended to fix the adjournment of every succeeding Congress to the second Monday in May after the commencement of the first session, does not appear to me in accordance with the provisions of the Constitution of the United States.

The Constitution provides, Article I, section 5, that—

Neither House, during the session of Congress, shall, without the consent of the other, adjourn for more than three days, nor to any other place than that in which the two Houses shall be sitting.

Article I, section 7, that—

Every order, resolution, or vote to which the concurrence of the Senate and House of Representatives may be necessary (except on a question of adjournment) shall be presented to the President of the United States, and before the same shall take effect shall be approved by him. * * *

Article II, section 3, that—

He [the President] may, on extraordinary occasions, convene both Houses, or either of them, and in case of disagreement between them with respect to the time of adjournment he may adjourn them to such time as he shall think proper. * * *

According to these provisions the day of the adjournment of Congress is not the subject of legislative enactment. Except in the event of disagreement between the Senate and House of Representatives, the President has no right to meddle with the question, and in that event his power is exclusive, but confined to fixing the adjournment of the Congress whose branches have disagreed. The question of adjournment is obviously to be decided by each Congress for itself, by the separate action of each House for the time being, and is one of those subjects upon which the framers of that instrument did not intend one Congress should act, with or without the Executive aid, for its successors. As a substitute for the present rule, which requires the two Houses by consent to fix the day of adjournment, and in the event of disagreement the President to decide, it is proposed to fix a day by law to be binding in all future time unless changed by consent of both Houses of Congress, and to take away the contingent power of the Executive which in anticipated cases of disagreement is vested in him. This substitute is to apply, not to the present Congress and Executive, but to our successors. Considering, therefore, that this subject exclusively belongs to the two Houses of Congress whose day of adjournment is to be fixed, and that each has at that time the right to maintain and insist upon its own opinion, and to require the President to decide in the event of disagreement with the other, I am constrained to deny my sanction to the act herewith respectfully returned to the Senate. I do so with greater reluctance as, apart from this constitutional difficulty, the other provisions of it do not appear to me objectionable.

ANDREW JACKSON.

PROCLAMATION.

[From Statutes at Large (Little, Brown & Co.), Vol. XI, p. 782.]

BY THE PRESIDENT OF THE UNITED STATES OF AMERICA.

A PROCLAMATION.

Whereas by an act of Congress of the United States of the 24th of May, 1828, entitled "An act in addition to an act entitled 'An act concerning discriminating duties of tonnage and impost' and to equalize the duties on Prussian vessels and their cargoes," it is provided that, upon satisfactory evidence being given to the President of the United States by the government of any foreign nation that no discriminating duties of tonnage or impost are imposed or levied in the ports of the said nation upon vessels wholly belonging to citizens of the United States or upon the produce, manufactures, or merchandise imported in the same from the United States or from any foreign country, the President is hereby authorized to issue his proclamation declaring that the foreign discriminating duties of tonnage and impost within the United States are and shall be suspended and discontinued so far as respects the vessels of the said foreign nation and the produce, manufactures, or merchandise imported into the United States in the same from the said foreign nation or from any other foreign country, the said suspension to take effect from the time of such notification being given to the President of the United States and to continue so long as the reciprocal exemption of vessels belonging to citizens of the United States and their cargoes, as aforesaid, shall be continued, and no longer; and

Whereas satisfactory evidence has lately been received by me from the Government of His Imperial and Royal Highness the Grand Duke of Tuscany, through an official communication of Baron Lederer, the consul-general of His Imperial and Royal Highness in the United States, under date of the 6th day of August, 1836, that no discriminating duties of tonnage or impost are imposed or levied in the ports of Tuscany upon vessels wholly belonging to citizens of the United States or upon the produce, manufactures, or merchandise imported in the same from the United States or from any foreign country:

Now, therefore, I, Andrew Jackson, President of the United States of America, do hereby declare and proclaim that the foreign discriminating duties of tonnage and impost within the United States are and shall be suspended and discontinued so far as respects the vessels of the Grand Dukedom of Tuscany and the produce, manufactures, or merchandise imported into the United States in the same from the said Grand Dukedom or from any other foreign country, the said suspension to take effect from the 6th day of August, 1836, above mentioned, and to continue so long as the reciprocal exemption of vessels belonging to citizens of the United States and their cargoes, as aforesaid, shall be continued, and no longer.

Given under my hand, at the city of Washington, the 1st day of September, A. D. 1836, and of the Independence of the United States the sixty-first.

[SEAL.]

ANDREW JACKSON.

By the President:

JOHN FORSYTH,
    Secretary of State.

EXECUTIVE ORDER.

HERMITAGE, *August 7, 1836.*

C. A. HARRIS, Esq.,
    Acting Secretary of War.

SIR: I reached home on the evening of the 4th, and was soon surrounded with the papers and letters which had been sent here in anticipation of my arrival. Amongst other important matters which immediately engaged my attention was the requisition of General Gaines on Tennessee, Kentucky, Mississippi, and Louisiana. Believing that the reasons given for this requisition were not consistent with the neutrality which it is our duty to observe in respect to the contest in Texas, and that it would embarrass the apportionment which had been made of the 10,000 volunteers authorized by the recent act of Congress, I informed Governor Cannon by letter on the 5th instant that it could not receive my sanction. The volunteers authorized by Congress were thought competent, with the aid of the regular force, to terminate the Indian war in the South and protect our western frontier, and they were apportioned in a manner the best calculated to secure these objects. Agreeably to this apportionment, the volunteers raised in Arkansas and Missouri, and ordered to be held in readiness for the defense of the western frontier, should have been called on before any other requisition was made upon Tennessee, who has already more than her proportion in the field. Should an emergency hereafter arise making it necessary to have a greater force on that frontier than was anticipated when the apportionment was made, it will be easy to order the east Tennessee brigade there. All the volunteers under the act are engaged for one year's service, unless sooner discharged. Taking this view of the subject, I regret that as soon as the War Department had information of the requisition made by General Gaines it had not at once notified the governors of the States that the apportionment of the volunteers at first communicated to them would not be departed from, and that of course those in the States nearest to the scene of threatened hostility would be first called on.

I had written thus far when your letter of the 26th of July last, accompanied by one from General Wool of the 15th of July and one from General Towsen of the 25th of July last, was handed to me. The letter from General Wool was unexpected. His guide was the requisition on the State, and I can not well imagine how he could suppose that the Department would authorize a greater number of troops to be mustered and paid than he was specially directed to receive. He was apprised fully of the apportionment which had been made of the 10,000 volunteers, and of the considerations which induced us to require 1,000 from Florida, 2,000 from Georgia, 2,000 from Alabama, and 2,500 from Tennessee. This force was designated in this manner because it was in the country nearest to the Seminoles, Creeks, and Cherokees, and in like manner near the force designated for the western frontier, except a fraction of about 430 men to be hereafter selected when it should be ascertained where it would be most needed. It is therefore unaccountable to me why General Wool would receive and muster into the service a greater number than has been called for and placed under his command, particularly as he knew that Tennessee had already been called upon for more volunteers than her proportion in the general apportionment. He knows that the President can only execute the law, and he ought to have recollected that if the officers charged with the military operations contemplated by the law were to use their own discretion in fixing the number of men to be received and mustered into the service there could be no certainty in the amount of force which would be brought into the field. His guide was the requisition upon Tennessee for 2,500, and he should never have departed from it.

The brave men whose patriotism brought them into the field ought to be paid, but I seriously doubt whether any of the money now appropriated can be used for this purpose, as all the volunteers authorized by the act of Congress have been apportioned, and the appropriations should be first applicable to their payment if they should be ordered into the field. All that we can do is to bring the subject before the next Congress, which I trust will pass an act authorizing the payment. Those men obeyed the summons of their country, and ought not to suffer for the indiscretion of those who caused more of them to turn out than could be received into the service. The excess would have been avoided had the governor of Tennessee apportioned his requisition to each county or regiment, so as to make the proper number. This, however, can now only be regretted. I can not approve the mustering or reception into the service of the excess further than it may have been done to secure them hereafter the justice which it will be in the power of Congress to extend to them. They ought to be paid for their travel and expense to, at, and from the place of rendezvous, and Congress will doubtless pass the necessary law. Their promptness in tendering their services and equipping themselves for the field is a high evidence of patriotism, and deserves the thanks of their country.

I shall inclose a copy of this letter to General Wool, and write to the governors of Kentucky, Mississippi, and Louisiana to withhold for the present the quota called for under General Gaines's requisition, and if they are concentrated to muster and discharge them and wait for further orders.

I am, yours, respectfully,

ANDREW JACKSON.

EIGHTH ANNUAL MESSAGE.

WASHINGTON, *December 5, 1836.*

Fellow-Citizens of the Senate and House of Representatives:

Addressing to you the last annual message I shall ever present to the Congress of the United States, it is a source of the most heartfelt satisfaction to be able to congratulate you on the high state of prosperity which our beloved country has attained. With no causes at home or abroad to lessen the confidence with which we look to the future for continuing proofs of the capacity of our free institutions to produce all the fruits of good government, the general condition of our affairs may well excite our national pride.

I can not avoid congratulating you, and my country particularly, on the success of the efforts made during my Administration by the Executive and Legislature, in conformity with the sincere, constant, and earnest desire of the people, to maintain peace and establish cordial relations with all foreign powers. Our gratitude is due to the Supreme Ruler of the Universe, and I invite you to unite with me in offering to Him fervent supplications that His providential care may ever be extended to those who follow us, enabling them to avoid the dangers and the horrors of war consistently with a just and indispensable regard to the rights and honor of our country. But although the present state of our foreign affairs, standing, without important change, as they did when you separated in July last, is flattering in the extreme, I regret to say that many questions of an interesting character, at issue with other powers, are yet unadjusted. Amongst the most prominent of these is that of our northeastern boundary. With an undiminished confidence in the sincere desire of His Britannic Majesty's Government to adjust that question, I am not yet in possession of the precise grounds upon which it proposes a satisfactory adjustment.

With France our diplomatic relations have been resumed, and under circumstances which attest the disposition of both Governments to preserve a mutually beneficial intercourse and foster those amicable feelings which are so strongly required by the true interests of the two countries. With Russia, Austria, Prussia, Naples, Sweden, and Denmark the best understanding exists, and our commercial intercourse is gradually expanding itself with them. It is encouraged in all these countries, except Naples, by their mutually advantageous and liberal treaty stipulations with us.

The claims of our citizens on Portugal are admitted to be just, but provision for the payment of them has been unfortunately delayed by frequent political changes in that Kingdom.

The blessings of peace have not been secured by Spain. Our connections with that country are on the best footing, with the exception of the burdens still imposed upon our commerce with her possessions out of Europe.

The claims of American citizens for losses sustained at the bombardment of Antwerp have been presented to the Governments of Holland and Belgium, and will be pressed, in due season, to settlement.

With Brazil and all our neighbors of this continent we continue to maintain relations of amity and concord, extending our commerce with them as far as the resources of the people and the policy of their Governments will permit. The just and long-standing claims of our citizens upon some of them are yet sources of dissatisfaction and complaint. No danger is apprehended, however, that they will not be peacefully, although tardily, acknowledged and paid by all, unless the irritating effect of her struggle with Texas should unfortunately make our immediate neighbor, Mexico, an exception.

It is already known to you, by the correspondence between the two Governments communicated at your last session, that our conduct in relation to that struggle is regulated by the same principles that governed us in the dispute between Spain and Mexico herself, and I trust that it will be found on the most severe scrutiny that our acts have strictly corresponded with our professions. That the inhabitants of the United States should feel strong prepossessions for the one party is not surprising. But this circumstance should of itself teach us great caution, lest it lead us into the great error of suffering public policy to be regulated by partiality or prejudice; and there are considerations connected with the possible result of this contest between the two parties of so much delicacy and importance to the United States that our character requires that we should neither anticipate events nor attempt to control them. The known desire of the Texans to become a part of our system, although its gratification depends upon the reconcilement of various and conflicting interests, necessarily a work of time and uncertain in itself, is calculated to expose our conduct to misconstruction in the eyes of the world. There are already those who, indifferent to principle themselves and prone to suspect the want of it in others, charge us with ambitious designs and insidious policy. You will perceive by the accompanying documents that the extraordinary mission from Mexico has been terminated on the sole ground that the obligations of this Government to itself and to Mexico, under treaty stipulations, have compelled me to trust a discretionary authority to a high officer of our Army to advance into territory claimed as part of Texas if necessary to protect our own or the neighboring frontier from Indian depredation. In the opinion of the Mexican functionary who has just left us, the honor of his country will be wounded by American soldiers entering, with the most amicable avowed purposes, upon ground from which the followers of his Government have been expelled, and over which there is at present no certainty of a serious effort on its part being made to reestablish its dominion. The departure of this minister was the more singular as he was apprised that the sufficiency of the causes assigned for the advance of our troops by the commanding general had been seriously doubted by me, and there was every reason to suppose that the troops of the United States, their commander having had time to ascertain the truth or falsehood of the information upon which they had been marched to Nacogdoches, would be either there in perfect accordance with the principles admitted to be just in his conference with the Secretary of State by the Mexican minister himself, or were already withdrawn in consequence of the impressive warnings their commanding officer had received from the Department of War. It is hoped and believed that his Government will take a more dispassionate and just view of this subject, and not be disposed to construe a measure of justifiable precaution, made necessary by its known inability in execution of the stipulations of our treaty to act upon the frontier, into an encroachment upon its rights or a stain upon its honor.

In the meantime the ancient complaints of injustice made on behalf of our citizens are disregarded, and new causes of dissatisfaction have arisen, some of them of a character requiring prompt remonstrance and ample and immediate redress. I trust, however, by tempering firmness with courtesy and acting with great forbearance upon every incident that has occurred or that may happen, to do and to obtain justice, and thus avoid the necessity of again bringing this subject to the view of Congress.

It is my duty to remind you that no provision has been made to execute our treaty with Mexico for tracing the boundary line between the two countries. Whatever may be the prospect of Mexico's being soon able to execute the treaty on its part, it is proper that we should be in anticipation prepared at all times to perform our obligations, without regard to the probable condition of those with whom we have contracted them.

The result of the confidential inquiries made into the condition and prospects of the newly declared Texan Government will be communicated to you in the course of the session.

Commercial treaties promising great advantages to our enterprising merchants and navigators have been formed with the distant Governments of Muscat and Siam. The ratifications have been exchanged, but have not reached the Department of State. Copies of the treaties will be transmitted to you if received before, or published if arriving after, the close of the present session of Congress.

Nothing has occurred to interrupt the good understanding that has long existed with the Barbary Powers, nor to check the good will which is gradually growing up from our intercourse with the dominions of the Government of the distinguished chief of the Ottoman Empire.

Information has been received at the Department of State that a treaty with the Emperor of Morocco has just been negotiated, which, I hope, will be received in time to be laid before the Senate previous to the close of the session.

You will perceive from the report of the Secretary of the Treasury that the financial means of the country continue to keep pace with its improvement in all other respects. The receipts into the Treasury during the present year will amount to about $47,691,898; those from customs being estimated at $22,523,151, those from lands at about $24,000,000, and the residue from miscellaneous sources. The expenditures for all objects during the year are estimated not to exceed $32,000,000, which will leave a balance in the Treasury for public purposes on the 1st day of January next of about $41,723,959. This sum, with the exception of $5,000,000, will be transferred to the several States in accordance with the provisions of the act regulating the deposits of the public money.

The unexpended balances of appropriation on the 1st day of January next are estimated at $14,636,062, exceeding by $9,636,062 the amount which will be left in the deposit banks, subject to the draft of the Treasurer of the United States, after the contemplated transfers to the several States are made. If, therefore, the future receipts should not be sufficient to meet these outstanding and future appropriations, there may be soon a necessity to use a portion of the funds deposited with the States.

The consequences apprehended when the deposit act of the last session received a reluctant approval have been measurably realized. Though an act merely for the deposit of the surplus moneys of the United States in the State treasuries for safe-keeping until they may be wanted for the service of the General Government, it has been extensively spoken of as an act to give the money to the several States, and they have been advised to use it as a gift, without regard to the means of refunding it when called for. Such a suggestion has doubtless been made without a due consideration of the obligations of the deposit act, and without a proper attention to the various principles and interests which are affected by it. It is manifest that the law itself can not sanction such a suggestion, and that as it now stands the States have no more authority to receive and use these deposits without intending to return them than any deposit bank or any individual temporarily charged with the safe-keeping or application of the public money would now have for converting the same to their private use without the consent and against the will of the Government. But independently of the violation of public faith and moral obligation which are involved in this suggestion when examined in reference to the terms of the present deposit act, it is believed that the considerations which should govern the future legislation of Congress on this subject will be equally conclusive against the adoption of any measure recognizing the principles on which the suggestion has been made.

Considering the intimate connection of the subject with the financial interests of the country and its great importance in whatever aspect it can be viewed, I have bestowed upon it the most anxious reflection, and feel it to be my duty to state to Congress such thoughts as have occurred to me, to aid their deliberation in treating it in the manner best calculated to conduce to the common good.

The experience of other nations admonished us to hasten the extinguishment of the public debt; but it will be in vain that we have congratulated each other upon the disappearance of this evil if we do not guard against the equally great one of promoting the unnecessary accumulation of public revenue. No political maxim is better established than that which tells us that an improvident expenditure of money is the parent of profligacy, and that no people can hope to perpetuate their liberties who long acquiesce in a policy which taxes them for objects not necessary to the legitimate and real wants of their Government. Flattering as is the condition of our country at the present period, because of its unexampled advance in all the steps of social and political improvement, it can not be disguised that there is a lurking danger already apparent in the neglect of this warning truth, and that the time has arrived when the representatives of the people should be employed in devising some more appropriate remedy than now exists to avert it.

Under our present revenue system there is every probability that there will continue to be a surplus beyond the wants of the Government, and it has become our duty to decide whether such a result be consistent with the true objects of our Government.

Should a surplus be permitted to accumulate beyond the appropriations, it must be retained in the Treasury, as it now is, or distributed among the people or the States.

To retain it in the Treasury unemployed in any way is impracticable; it is, besides, against the genius of our free institutions to lock up in vaults the treasure of the nation. To take from the people the right of bearing arms and put their weapons of defense in the hands of a standing army would be scarcely more dangerous to their liberties than to permit the Government to accumulate immense amounts of treasure beyond the supplies necessary to its legitimate wants. Such a treasure would doubtless be employed at some time, as it has been in other countries, when opportunity tempted ambition.

To collect it merely for distribution to the States would seem to be highly impolitic, if not as dangerous as the proposition to retain it in the

Treasury. The shortest reflection must satisfy everyone that to require the people to pay taxes to the Government merely that they may be paid back again is sporting with the substantial interests of the country, and no system which produces such a result can be expected to receive the public countenance. Nothing could be gained by it even if each individual who contributed a portion of the tax could receive back promptly the same portion. But it is apparent that no system of the kind can ever be enforced which will not absorb a considerable portion of the money to be distributed in salaries and commissions to the agents employed in the process and in the various losses and depreciations which arise from other causes, and the practical effect of such an attempt must ever be to burden the people with taxes, not for purposes beneficial to them, but to swell the profits of deposit banks and support a band of useless public officers.

A distribution to the people is impracticable and unjust in other respects. It would be taking one man's property and giving it to another. Such would be the unavoidable result of a rule of equality (and none other is spoken of or would be likely to be adopted), inasmuch as there is no mode by which the amount of the individual contributions of our citizens to the public revenue can be ascertained. We know that they contribute *unequally*, and a rule, therefore, that would distribute to them *equally* would be liable to all the objections which apply to the principle of an equal division of property. To make the General Government the instrument of carrying this odious principle into effect would be at once to destroy the means of its usefulness and change the character designed for it by the framers of the Constitution.

But the more extended and injurious consequences likely to result from a policy which would collect a surplus revenue for the purpose of distributing it may be forcibly illustrated by an examination of the effects already produced by the present deposit act. This act, although certainly designed to secure the safe-keeping of the public revenue, is not entirely free in its tendencies from any of the objections which apply to this principle of distribution. The Government had without necessity received from the people a large surplus, which, instead of being employed as heretofore and returned to them by means of the public expenditure, was deposited with sundry banks. The banks proceeded to make loans upon this surplus, and thus converted it into banking capital, and in this manner it has tended to multiply bank charters and has had a great agency in producing a spirit of wild speculation. The possession and use of the property out of which this surplus was created belonged to the people, but the Government has transferred its possession to incorporated banks, whose interest and effort it is to make large profits out of its use. This process need only be stated to show its injustice and bad policy.

And the same observations apply to the influence which is produced by the steps necessary to collect as well as to distribute such a revenue. About three-fifths of all the duties on imports are paid in the city of New York, but it is obvious that the means to pay those duties are drawn from every quarter of the Union. Every citizen in every State who purchases and consumes an article which has paid a duty at that port contributes to the accumulating mass. The surplus collected there must therefore be made up of moneys or property withdrawn from other points and other States. Thus the wealth and business of every region from which these surplus funds proceed must be to some extent injured, while that of the place where the funds are concentrated and are employed in banking are proportionably extended. But both in making the transfer of the funds which are first necessary to pay the duties and collect the surplus and in making the retransfer which becomes necessary when the time arrives for the distribution of that surplus there is a considerable period when the funds can not be brought into use, and it is manifest that, besides the loss inevitable from such an operation, its tendency is to produce fluctuations in the business of the country, which are always productive of speculation and detrimental to the interests of regular trade. Argument can scarcely be necessary to show that a measure of this character ought not to receive further legislative encouragement.

By examining the practical operation of the ratio for distribution adopted in the deposit bill of the last session we shall discover other features that appear equally objectionable. Let it be assumed, for the sake of argument, that the surplus moneys to be deposited with the States have been collected and belong to them in the ratio of their federal representative population—an assumption founded upon the fact that any deficiencies in our future revenue from imposts and public lands must be made up by direct taxes collected from the States in that ratio. It is proposed to distribute this surplus—say $30,000,000—not according to the ratio in which it has been collected and belongs to the people of the States, but in that of their votes in the colleges of electors of President and Vice-President. The effect of a distribution upon that ratio is shown by the annexed table, marked A.

By an examination of that table it will be perceived that in the distribution of a surplus of $30,000,000 upon that basis there is a great departure from the principle which regards representation as the true measure of taxation, and it will be found that the tendency of that departure will be to increase whatever inequalities have been supposed to attend the operation of our federal system in respect to its bearings upon the different interests of the Union. In making the basis of representation the basis of taxation the framers of the Constitution intended to equalize the burdens which are necessary to support the Government, and the adoption of that ratio, while it accomplished this object, was also the means of adjusting other great topics arising out of the conflicting views respecting the political equality of the various members of the Confederacy. Whatever, therefore, disturbs the liberal spirit of the compromises which established a rule of taxation so just and equitable, and which experience has proved to be so well adapted to the genius and habits of our people, should be received with the greatest caution and distrust.

A bare inspection in the annexed table of the differences produced by the ratio used in the deposit act compared with the results of a distribution according to the ratio of direct taxation must satisfy every unprejudiced mind that the former ratio contravenes the spirit of the Constitution and produces a degree of injustice in the operations of the Federal Government which would be fatal to the hope of perpetuating it. By the ratio of direct taxation, for example, the State of Delaware in the collection of $30,000,000 of revenue would pay into the Treasury $188,716, and in a distribution of $30,000,000 she would receive back from the Government, according to the ratio of the deposit bill, the sum of $306,122; and similar results would follow the comparison between the small and the large States throughout the Union, thus realizing to the small States an advantage which would be doubtless as unacceptable to them as a motive for incorporating the principle in any system which would produce it as it would be inconsistent with the rights and expectations of the large States. It was certainly the intention of that provision of the Constitution which declares that "all duties, imposts, and excises" shall "be uniform throughout the United States" to make the burdens of taxation fall equally upon the people in whatever State of the Union they may reside. But what would be the value of such a uniform rule if the moneys raised by it could be immediately returned by a different one which will give to the people of some States much more and to those of others much less than their fair proportions? Were the Federal Government to exempt in express terms the imports, products, and manufactures of some portions of the country from all duties while it imposed heavy ones on others, the injustice could not be greater. It would be easy to show how by the operation of such a principle the large States of the Union would not only have to contribute their just share toward the support of the Federal Government, but also have to bear in some degree the taxes necessary to support the governments of their smaller sisters; but it is deemed unnecessary to state the details where the general principle is so obvious.

A system liable to such objections can never be supposed to have been sanctioned by the framers of the Constitution when they conferred on Congress the taxing power, and I feel persuaded that a mature examination of the subject will satisfy everyone that there are insurmountable difficulties in the operation of any plan which can be devised of collecting revenue for the purpose of distributing it. Congress is only authorized to levy taxes *"to pay the debts and provide for the common defense and general welfare of the United States."* There is no such provision as would authorize Congress to collect together the property of the country, under the name of revenue, for the purpose of dividing it equally or unequally among the States or the people. Indeed, it is not probable that such an idea ever occurred to the States when they adopted the Constitution. But however this may be, the only safe rule for us in interpreting the powers granted to the Federal Government is to regard the absence of express authority to touch a subject so important and delicate as this is as equivalent to a prohibition.

Even if our powers were less doubtful in this respect as the Constitution now stands, there are considerations afforded by recent experience which would seem to make it our duty to avoid a resort to such a system.

All will admit that the simplicity and economy of the State governments mainly depend on the fact that money has to be supplied to support them by the same men, or their agents, who vote it away in appropriations. Hence when there are extravagant and wasteful appropriations there must be a corresponding increase of taxes, and the people, becoming awakened, will necessarily scrutinize the character of measures which thus increase their burdens. By the watchful eye of self-interest the agents of the people in the State governments are repressed and kept within the limits of a just economy. But if the necessity of levying the taxes be taken from those who make the appropriations and thrown upon a more distant and less responsible set of public agents, who have power to approach the people by an indirect and stealthy taxation, there is reason to fear that prodigality will soon supersede those characteristics which have thus far made us look with so much pride and confidence to the State governments as the mainstay of our Union and liberties. The State legislatures, instead of studying to restrict their State expenditures to the smallest possible sum, will claim credit for their profusion, and harass the General Government for increased supplies. Practically there would soon be but one taxing power, and that vested in a body of men far removed from the people, in which the farming and mechanic interests would scarcely be represented. The States would gradually lose their purity as well as their independence; they would not dare to murmur at the proceedings of the General Government, lest they should lose their supplies; all would be merged in a practical consolidation, cemented by widespread corruption, which could only be eradicated by one of those bloody revolutions which occasionally overthrow the despotic systems of the Old World. In all the other aspects in which I have been able to look at the effect of such a principle of distribution upon the best interests of the country I can see nothing to compensate for the disadvantages to which I have adverted. If we consider the protective duties, which are in a great degree the source of the surplus revenue, beneficial to one section of the Union and prejudicial to another, there is no corrective for the evil in such a plan of distribution. On the contrary, there is reason to fear that all the complaints which have sprung from this cause would be aggravated. Everyone must be sensible that a distribution of the surplus must beget a disposition to cherish the means which create it, and any system, therefore, into which it enters must have a powerful tendency to increase rather than diminish the tariff. If it were even admitted that the advantages of such a system could be made equal to all the sections of the Union, the reasons already so urgently calling for a reduction of the revenue would nevertheless lose none of their force, for it will always be improbable that an intelligent and virtuous community can consent to raise a surplus for the mere purpose of dividing it, diminished as it must inevitably be by the expenses of the various machinery necessary to the process.

The safest and simplest mode of obviating all the difficulties which have been mentioned is to collect only revenue enough to meet the wants of the Government, and let the people keep the balance of their property in their own hands, to be used for their own profit. Each State will then support its own government and contribute its due share toward the support of the General Government. There would be no surplus to cramp and lessen the resources of individual wealth and enterprise, and the banks would be left to their ordinary means. Whatever agitations and fluctuations might arise from our unfortunate paper system, they could never be attributed, justly or unjustly, to the action of the Federal Government. There would be some guaranty that the spirit of wild speculation which seeks to convert the surplus revenue into banking capital would be effectually checked, and that the scenes of demoralization which are now so prevalent through the land would disappear.

Without desiring to conceal that the experience and observation of the last two years have operated a partial change in my views upon this interesting subject, it is nevertheless regretted that the suggestions made by me in my annual messages of 1829 and 1830 have been greatly misunderstood. At that time the great struggle was begun against that latitudinarian construction of the Constitution which authorizes the unlimited appropriation of the revenues of the Union to internal improvements within the States, tending to invest in the hands and place under the control of the General Government all the principal roads and canals of the country, in violation of State rights and in derogation of State authority. At the same time the condition of the manufacturing interest was such as to create an apprehension that the duties on imports could not without extensive mischief be reduced in season to prevent the accumulation of a considerable surplus after the payment of the national debt. In view of the dangers of such a surplus, and in preference to its application to internal improvements in derogation of the rights and powers of the States, the suggestion of an amendment of the Constitution to authorize its distribution was made. It was an alternative for what were deemed greater evils—a temporary resort to relieve an overburdened treasury until the Government could, without a sudden and destructive revulsion in the business of the country, gradually return to the just principle of raising no more revenue from the people in taxes than is necessary for its economical support. Even that alternative was not spoken of but in connection with an amendment of the Constitution. No temporary inconvenience can justify the exercise of a prohibited power or a power not granted by that instrument, and it was from a conviction that the power to distribute even a temporary surplus of revenue is of that character that it was suggested only in connection with an appeal to the source of all legal power in the General Government, the States which have established it. No such appeal has been taken, and in my opinion a distribution of the surplus revenue by Congress either to the States or the people is to be considered as among the prohibitions of the Constitution. As already intimated, my views have undergone a change so far as to be convinced that no alteration of the Constitution in this respect is wise or expedient. The influence of an accumulating surplus upon the legislation of the General Government and the States, its effect upon the credit system of the country, producing dangerous extensions and ruinous contractions, fluctuations in the price of property, rash speculation, idleness, extravagance, and a deterioration of morals, have taught us the important lesson that any transient mischief which may attend the reduction of our revenue to the wants of our Government is to be borne in preference to an overflowing treasury.

I beg leave to call your attention to another subject intimately associated with the preceding one—the currency of the country.

It is apparent from the whole context of the Constitution, as well as the history of the times which gave birth to it, that it was the purpose of the Convention to establish a currency consisting of the precious metals. These, from their peculiar properties which rendered them the standard of value in all other countries, were adopted in this as well to establish its commercial standard in reference to foreign countries by a permanent rule as to exclude the use of a mutable medium of exchange, such as of certain agricultural commodities recognized by the statutes of some States as a tender for debts, or the still more pernicious expedient of a paper currency. The last, from the experience of the evils of the issues of paper during the Revolution, had become so justly obnoxious as not only to suggest the clause in the Constitution forbidding the emission of bills of credit by the States, but also to produce that vote in the Convention which negatived the proposition to grant power to Congress to charter corporations—a proposition well understood at the time as intended to authorize the establishment of a national bank, which was to issue a currency of bank notes on a capital to be created to some extent out of Government stocks. Although this proposition was refused by a direct vote of the Convention, the object was afterwards in effect obtained by its ingenious advocates through a strained construction of the Constitution. The debts of the Revolution were funded at prices which formed no equivalent compared with the nominal amount of the stock, and under circumstances which exposed the motives of some of those who participated in the passage of the act to distrust.

The facts that the value of the stock was greatly enhanced by the creation of the bank, that it was well understood that such would be the case, and that some of the advocates of the measure were largely benefited by it belong to the history of the times, and are well calculated to diminish the respect which might otherwise have been due to the action of the Congress which created the institution.

On the establishment of a national bank it became the interest of its creditors that gold should be superseded by the paper of the bank as a general currency. A value was soon attached to the gold coins which made their exportation to foreign countries as a mercantile commodity more profitable than their retention and use at home as money. It followed as a matter of course, if not designed by those who established the bank, that the bank became in effect a substitute for the Mint of the United States.

Such was the origin of a national-bank currency, and such the beginning of those difficulties which now appear in the excessive issues of the banks incorporated by the various States.

Although it may not be possible by any legislative means within our power to change at once the system which has thus been introduced, and has received the acquiescence of all portions of the country, it is certainly our duty to do all that is consistent with our constitutional obligations in preventing the mischiefs which are threatened by its undue extension. That the efforts of the fathers of our Government to guard against it by a constitutional provision were founded on an intimate knowledge of the subject has been frequently attested by the bitter experience of the country. The same causes which led them to refuse their sanction to a power authorizing the establishment of incorporations for banking purposes now exist in a much stronger degree to urge us to exert the utmost vigilance in calling into action the means necessary to correct the evils resulting from the unfortunate exercise of the power, and it is to be hoped that the opportunity for effecting this great good will be improved before the country witnesses new scenes of embarrassment and distress.

Variableness must ever be the characteristic of a currency of which the precious metals are not the chief ingredient, or which can be expanded or contracted without regard to the principles that regulate the value of those metals as a standard in the general trade of the world. With us bank issues constitute such a currency, and must ever do so until they are made dependent on those just proportions of gold and silver as a circulating medium which experience has proved to be necessary not only in this but in all other commercial countries. Where those proportions are not infused into the circulation and do not control it, it is manifest that prices must vary according to the tide of bank issues, and the value and stability of property must stand exposed to all the uncertainty which attends the administration of institutions that are constantly liable to the temptation of an interest distinct from that of the community in which they are established.

The progress of an expansion, or rather a depreciation, of the currency by excessive bank issues is always attended by a loss to the laboring classes. This portion of the community have neither time nor opportunity to watch the ebbs and flows of the money market. Engaged from day to day in their useful toils, they do not perceive that although their wages are nominally the same, or even somewhat higher, they are greatly reduced in fact by the rapid increase of a spurious currency, which, as it appears to make money abound, they are at first inclined to consider a blessing. It is not so with the speculator, by whom this operation is better understood, and is made to contribute to his advantage. It is not until the prices of the necessaries of life become so dear that the laboring classes can not supply their wants out of their wages that the wages rise and gradually reach a justly proportioned rate to that of the products of their labor. When thus, by the depreciation in consequence of the quantity of paper in circulation, wages as well as prices become exorbitant, it is soon found that the whole effect of the adulteration is a tariff on our home industry for the benefit of the countries where gold and silver circulate and maintain uniformity and moderation in prices. It is then perceived that the enhancement of the price of land and labor produces a corresponding increase in the price of products until these products do not sustain a competition with similar ones in other countries, and thus both manufactured and agricultural productions cease to bear exportation from the country of the spurious currency, because they can not be sold for cost. This is the process by which specie is banished by the paper of the banks. Their vaults are soon exhausted to pay for foreign commodities. The next step is a stoppage of specie payment—a total degradation of paper as a currency—unusual depression of prices, the ruin of debtors, and the accumulation of property in the hands of creditors and cautious capitalists.

It was in view of these evils, together with the dangerous power wielded by the Bank of the United States and its repugnance to our Constitution, that I was induced to exert the power conferred upon me by the American people to prevent the continuance of that institution. But although various dangers to our republican institutions have been obviated by the failure of that bank to extort from the Government a renewal of its charter, it is obvious that little has been accomplished except a salutary change of public opinion toward restoring to the country the sound currency provided for in the Constitution. In the acts of several of the States prohibiting the circulation of small notes, and the auxiliary enactments of Congress at the last session forbidding their reception or payment on public account, the true policy of the country has been advanced and a larger portion of the precious metals infused into our circulating medium. These measures will probably be followed up in due time by the enactment of State laws banishing from circulation bank notes of still higher denominations, and the object may be materially promoted by further acts of Congress forbidding the employment as fiscal agents of such banks as continue to issue notes of low denominations and throw impediments in the way of the circulation of gold and silver.

The effects of an extension of bank credits and overissues of bank paper have been strikingly illustrated in the sales of the public lands. From the returns made by the various registers and receivers in the early part of last summer it was perceived that the receipts arising from the sales of the public lands were increasing to an unprecedented amount. In effect, however, these receipts amounted to nothing more than credits in bank. The banks lent out their notes to speculators. They were paid to the receivers and immediately returned to the banks, to be lent out again and again, being mere instruments to transfer to speculators the most valuable public land and pay the Government by a credit on the books of the banks. Those credits on the books of some of the Western banks, usually called deposits, were already greatly beyond their immediate means of payment, and were rapidly increasing. Indeed, each speculation furnished means for another; for no sooner had one individual or company paid in the notes than they were immediately lent to another for a like purpose, and the banks were extending their business and their issues so largely as to alarm considerate men and render it doubtful whether these bank credits if permitted to accumulate would ultimately be of the least value to the Government. The spirit of expansion and speculation was not confined to the deposit banks, but pervaded the whole multitude of banks throughout the Union and was giving rise to new institutions to aggravate the evil.

The safety of the public funds and the interest of the people generally required that these operations should be checked; and it became the duty of every branch of the General and State Governments to adopt all legitimate and proper means to produce that salutary effect. Under this view of my duty I directed the issuing of the order which will be laid before you by the Secretary of the Treasury, requiring payment for the public lands sold to be made in specie, with an exception until the 15th of the present month in favor of actual settlers. This measure has produced many salutary consequences. It checked the career of the Western banks and gave them additional strength in anticipation of the pressure which has since pervaded our Eastern as well as the European commercial cities. By preventing the extension of the credit system it measurably cut off the means of speculation and retarded its progress in monopolizing the most valuable of the public lands. It has tended to save the new States from a nonresident proprietorship, one of the greatest obstacles to the advancement of a new country and the prosperity of an old one. It has tended to keep open the public lands for entry by emigrants at Government prices instead of their being compelled to purchase of speculators at double or triple prices. And it is conveying into the interior large sums in silver and gold, there to enter permanently into the currency of the country and place it on a firmer foundation. It is confidently believed that the country will find in the motives which induced that order and the happy consequences which will have ensued much to commend and nothing to condemn.

It remains for Congress if they approve the policy which dictated this order to follow it up in its various bearings. Much good, in my judgment, would be produced by prohibiting sales of the public lands except to actual settlers at a reasonable reduction of price, and to limit the quantity which shall be sold to them. Although it is believed the General Government never ought to receive anything but the constitutional currency in exchange for the public lands, that point would be of less importance if the lands were sold for immediate settlement and cultivation. Indeed, there is scarcely a mischief arising out of our present land system, including the accumulating surplus of revenues, which would not be remedied at once by a restriction on land sales to actual settlers; and it promises other advantages to the country in general and to the new States in particular which can not fail to receive the most profound consideration of Congress.

Experience continues to realize the expectations entertained as to the capacity of the State banks to perform the duties of fiscal agents for the Government at the time of the removal of the deposits. It was alleged by the advocates of the Bank of the United States that the State banks, whatever might be the regulations of the Treasury Department, could not make the transfers required by the Government or negotiate the domestic exchanges of the country. It is now well ascertained that the real domestic exchanges performed through discounts by the United States Bank and its twenty-five branches were at least one-third less than those of the deposit banks for an equal period of time; and if a comparison be instituted between the amounts of service rendered by these institutions on the broader basis which has been used by the advocates of the United States Bank in estimating what they consider the domestic exchanges transacted by it, the result will be still more favorable to the deposit banks.

The whole amount of public money transferred by the Bank of the United States in 1832 was $16,000,000. The amount transferred and actually paid by the deposit banks in the year ending the 1st of October last was $39,319,899; the amount transferred and paid between that period and the 6th of November was $5,399,000, and the amount of transfer warrants outstanding on that day was $14,450,000, making an aggregate of $59,168,894. These enormous sums of money first mentioned have been transferred with the greatest promptitude and regularity, and the rates at which the exchanges have been negotiated previously to the passage of the deposit act were generally below those charged by the Bank of the United States. Independently of these services, which are far greater than those rendered by the United States Bank and its twenty-five branches, a number of the deposit banks have, with a commendable zeal to aid in the improvement of the currency, imported from abroad, at their own expense, large sums of the precious metals for coinage and circulation.

In the same manner have nearly all the predictions turned out in respect to the effect of the removal of the deposits—a step unquestionably necessary to prevent the evils which it was foreseen the bank itself would endeavor to create in a final struggle to procure a renewal of its charter. It may be thus, too, in some degree with the further steps which may be taken to prevent the excessive issue of other bank paper, but it is to be hoped that nothing will now deter the Federal and State authorities from the firm and vigorous performance of their duties to themselves and to the people in this respect.

In reducing the revenue to the wants of the Government your particular attention is invited to those articles which constitute the necessaries of life. The duty on salt was laid as a war tax, and was no doubt continued to assist in providing for the payment of the war debt. There is no article the release of which from taxation would be felt so generally and so beneficially. To this may be added all kinds of fuel and provisions. Justice and benevolence unite in favor of releasing the poor of our cities from burdens which are not necessary to the support of our Government and tend only to increase the wants of the destitute.

It will be seen by the report of the Secretary of the Treasury and the accompanying documents that the Bank of the United States has made no payment on account of the stock held by the Government in that institution, although urged to pay any portion which might suit its convenience, and that it has given no information when payment may be expected. Nor, although repeatedly requested, has it furnished the information in relation to its condition which Congress authorized the Secretary to collect at their last session. Such measures as are within the power of the Executive have been taken to ascertain the value of the stock and procure the payment as early as possible.

The conduct and present condition of that bank and the great amount of capital vested in it by the United States require your careful attention. Its charter expired on the 3d day of March last, and it has now no power but that given in the twenty-first section, "to use the corporate name, style, and capacity for the purpose of suits for the final settlement and liquidation of the affairs and accounts of the corporation, and for the sale and disposition of their estate—real, personal, and mixed—but not for any other purpose or in any other manner whatsoever, nor for a period exceeding two years after the expiration of the said term of incorporation.'' Before the expiration of the charter the stockholders of the bank obtained an act of incorporation from the legislature of Pennsylvania, excluding only the United States. Instead of proceeding to wind up their concerns and pay over to the United States the amount due on account of the stock held by them, the president and directors of the old bank appear to have transferred the books, papers, notes, obligations, and most or all of its property to this new corporation, which entered upon business as a continuation of the old concern. Amongst other acts of questionable validity, the notes of the expired corporation are known to have been used as its own and again put in circulation. That the old bank had no right to issue or reissue its notes after the expiration of its charter can not be denied, and that it could not confer any such right on its substitute any more than exercise it itself is equally plain. In law and honesty the notes of the bank in circulation at the expiration of its charter should have been called in by public advertisement, paid up as presented, and, together with those on hand, canceled and destroyed. Their reissue is sanctioned by no law and warranted by no necessity. If the United States be responsible in their stock for the payment of these notes, their reissue by the new corporation for their own profit is a fraud on the Government. If the United States is not responsible, then there is no legal responsibility in any quarter, and it is a fraud on the country. They are the redeemed notes of a dissolved partnership, but, contrary to the wishes of the retiring partner and without his consent, are again reissued and circulated.

It is the high and peculiar duty of Congress to decide whether any further legislation be necessary for the security of the large amount of public property now held and in use by the new bank, and for vindicating the rights of the Government and compelling a speedy and honest settlement with all the creditors of the old bank, public and private, or whether the subject shall be left to the power now possessed by the Executive and judiciary. It remains to be seen whether the persons who as managers of the old bank undertook to control the Government, retained the public dividends, shut their doors upon a committee of the House of Representatives, and filled the country with panic to accomplish their own sinister objects may now as managers of a new bank continue with impunity to flood the country with a spurious currency, use the seven millions of Government stock for their own profit, and refuse to the United States all information as to the present condition of their own property and the prospect of recovering it into their own possession.

The lessons taught by the Bank of the United States can not well be lost upon the American people. They will take care never again to place so tremendous a power in irresponsible hands, and it will be fortunate if they seriously consider the consequences which are likely to result on a smaller scale from the facility with which corporate powers are granted by their State governments.

It is believed that the law of the last session regulating the deposit banks operates onerously and unjustly upon them in many respects, and it is hoped that Congress, on proper representations, will adopt the modifications which are necessary to prevent this consequence.

The report of the Secretary of War *ad interim* and the accompanying documents, all which are herewith laid before you, will give you a full view of the diversified and important operations of that Department during the past year.

The military movements rendered necessary by the aggressions of the hostile portions of the Seminole and Creek tribes of Indians, and by other circumstances, have required the active employment of nearly our whole regular force, including the Marine Corps, and of large bodies of militia and volunteers. With all these events so far as they were known at the seat of Government before the termination of your last session you are already acquainted, and it is therefore only needful in this place to lay before you a brief summary of what has since occurred.

The war with the Seminoles during the summer was on our part chiefly confined to the protection of our frontier settlements from the incursions of the enemy, and, as a necessary and important means for the accomplishment of that end, to the maintenance of the posts previously established. In the course of this duty several actions took place, in which the bravery and discipline of both officers and men were conspicuously displayed, and which I have deemed it proper to notice in respect to the former by the granting of brevet rank for gallant services in the field. But as the force of the Indians was not so far weakened by these partial successes as to lead them to submit, and as their savage inroads were frequently repeated, early measures were taken for placing at the disposal of Governor Call, who as commander in chief of the Territorial militia had been temporarily invested with the command, an ample force for the purpose of resuming offensive operations in the most efficient manner so soon as the season should permit. Major-General Jesup was also directed, on the conclusion of his duties in the Creek country, to repair to Florida and assume the command.

The result of the first movement made by the forces under the direction of Governor Call in October last, as detailed in the accompanying papers, excited much surprise and disappointment. A full explanation has been required of the causes which led to the failure of that movement, but has not yet been received. In the meantime, as it was feared that the health of Governor Call, who was understood to have suffered much from sickness, might not be adequate to the crisis, and as Major-General Jesup was known to have reached Florida, that officer was directed to assume the command, and to prosecute all needful operations with the utmost promptitude and vigor. From the force at his disposal and the dispositions he has made and is instructed to make, and from the very efficient measures which it is since ascertained have been taken by Governor Call, there is reason to hope that they will soon be enabled to reduce the enemy to subjection. In the meantime, as you will perceive from the report of the Secretary, there is urgent necessity for further appropriations to suppress these hostilities.

Happily for the interests of humanity, the hostilities with the Creeks were brought to a close soon after your adjournment, without that effusion of blood which at one time was apprehended as inevitable. The unconditional submission of the hostile party was followed by their speedy removal to the country assigned them west of the Mississippi. The inquiry as to alleged frauds in the purchase of the reservations of these Indians and the causes of their hostilities, requested by the resolution of the House of Representatives of the 1st of July last to be made by the President, is now going on through the agency of commissioners appointed for that purpose. Their report may be expected during your present session.

The difficulties apprehended in the Cherokee country have been prevented, and the peace and safety of that region and its vicinity effectually secured, by the timely measures taken by the War Department, and still continued.

The discretionary authority given to General Gaines to cross the Sabine and to occupy a position as far west as Nacogdoches, in case he should deem such a step necessary to the protection of the frontier and to the fulfillment of the stipulations contained in our treaty with Mexico, and the movement subsequently made by that officer have been alluded to in a former part of this message. At the date of the latest intelligence from Nacogdoches our troops were yet at that station, but the officer who has succeeded General Gaines has recently been advised that from the facts known at the seat of Government there would seem to be no adequate cause for any longer maintaining that position, and he was accordingly instructed, in case the troops were not already withdrawn under the discretionary powers before possessed by him, to give the requisite orders for that purpose on the receipt of the instructions, unless he shall then have in his possession such information as shall satisfy him that the maintenance of the post is essential to the protection of our frontiers and to the due execution of our treaty stipulations, as previously explained to him.

Whilst the necessities existing during the present year for the service of militia and volunteers have furnished new proofs of the patriotism of our fellow-citizens, they have also strongly illustrated the importance of an increase in the rank and file of the Regular Army. The views of this subject submitted by the Secretary of War in his report meet my entire concurrence, and are earnestly commended to the deliberate attention of Congress. In this connection it is also proper to remind you that the defects in our present militia system are every day rendered more apparent. The duty of making further provision by law for organizing, arming, and disciplining this arm of defense has been so repeatedly presented to Congress by myself and my predecessors that I deem it sufficient on this occasion to refer to the last annual message and to former Executive communications in which the subject has been discussed.

It appears from the reports of the officers charged with mustering into service the volunteers called for under the act of Congress of the last session that more presented themselves at the place of rendezvous in Tennessee than were sufficient to meet the requisition which had been made by the Secretary of War upon the governor of that State. This was occasioned by the omission of the governor to apportion the requisition to the different regiments of militia so as to obtain the proper number of troops and no more. It seems but just to the patriotic citizens who repaired to the general rendezvous under circumstances authorizing them to believe that their services were needed and would be accepted that the expenses incurred by them while absent from their homes should be paid by the Government. I accordingly recommend that a law to this effect be passed by Congress, giving them a compensation which will cover their expenses on the march to and from the place of rendezvous and while there; in connection with which it will also be proper to make provision for such other equitable claims growing out of the service of the militia as may not be embraced in the existing laws.

On the unexpected breaking out of hostilities in Florida, Alabama, and Georgia it became necessary in some cases to take the property of individuals for public use. Provision should be made by law for indemnifying the owners; and I would also respectfully suggest whether some provision may not be made, consistently with the principles of our Government, for the relief of the sufferers by Indian depredations or by the operations of our own troops.

No time was lost after the making of the requisite appropriations in resuming the great national work of completing the unfinished fortifications on our seaboard and of placing them in a proper state of defense. In consequence, however, of the very late day at which those bills were passed, but little progress could be made during the season which has just closed. A very large amount of the moneys granted at your last session accordingly remains unexpended; but as the work will be again resumed at the earliest moment in the coming spring, the balance of the existing appropriations, and in several cases which will be laid before you, with the proper estimates, further sums for the like objects, may be usefully expended during the next year.

The recommendations of an increase in the Engineer Corps and for a reorganization of the Topographical Corps, submitted to you in my last annual message, derive additional strength from the great embarrassments experienced during the present year in those branches of the service, and under which they are now suffering. Several of the most important surveys and constructions directed by recent laws have been suspended in consequence of the want of adequate force in these corps.

The like observations may be applied to the Ordnance Corps and to the general staff, the operations of which as they are now organized must either be frequently interrupted or performed by officers taken from the line of the Army, to the great prejudice of the service.

For a general view of the condition of the Military Academy and of other branches of the military service not already noticed, as well as for fuller illustrations of those which have been mentioned, I refer you to the accompanying documents, and among the various proposals contained therein for legislative action I would particularly notice the suggestion of the Secretary of War for the revision of the pay of the Army as entitled to your favorable regard.

The national policy, founded alike in interest and in humanity, so long and so steadily pursued by this Government for the removal of the Indian tribes originally settled on this side of the Mississippi to the west of that river, may be said to have been consummated by the conclusion of the late treaty with the Cherokees. The measures taken in the execution of that treaty and in relation to our Indian affairs generally will fully appear by referring to the accompanying papers. Without dwelling on the numerous and important topics embraced in them, I again invite your attention to the importance of providing a well-digested and comprehensive system for the protection, supervision, and improvement of the various tribes now planted in the Indian country. The suggestions submitted by the Commissioner of Indian Affairs, and enforced by the Secretary, on this subject, and also in regard to the establishment of additional military posts in the Indian country, are entitled to your profound consideration. Both measures are necessary, for the double purpose of protecting the Indians from intestine war, and in other respects complying with our engagements to them, and of securing our western frontier against incursions which otherwise will assuredly be made on it. The best hopes of humanity in regard to the aboriginal race, the welfare of our rapidly extending settlements, and the honor of the United States are all deeply involved in the relations existing between this Government and the emigrating tribes. I trust, therefore, that the various matters submitted in the accompanying documents in respect to those relations will receive your early and mature deliberation, and that it may issue in the adoption of legislative measures adapted to the circumstances and duties of the present crisis.

You are referred to the report of the Secretary of the Navy for a satisfactory view of the operations of the Department under his charge during the present year. In the construction of vessels at the different navy-yards and in the employment of our ships and squadrons at sea that branch of the service has been actively and usefully employed. While the situation of our commercial interests in the West Indies required a greater number than usual of armed vessels to be kept on that station, it is gratifying to perceive that the protection due to our commerce in other quarters of the world has not proved insufficient. Every effort has been made to facilitate the equipment of the exploring expedition authorized by the act of the last session, but all the preparation necessary to enable it to sail has not yet been completed. No means will be spared by the Government to fit out the expedition on a scale corresponding with the liberal appropriations for the purpose and with the elevated character of the objects which are to be effected by it.

I beg leave to renew the recommendation made in my last annual message respecting the enlistment of boys in our naval service, and to urge upon your attention the necessity of further appropriations to increase the number of ships afloat and to enlarge generally the capacity and force of the Navy. The increase of our commerce and our position in regard to the other powers of the world will always make it our policy and interest to cherish the great naval resources of our country.

The report of the Postmaster-General presents a gratifying picture of the condition of the Post-Office Department. Its revenues for the year ending the 30th June last were $3,398,455.19, showing an increase of revenue over that of the preceding year of $404,878.53, or more than 13 per cent. The expenditures for the same year were $2,755,623.76, exhibiting a surplus of $642,831.43. The Department has been redeemed from embarrassment and debt, has accumulated a surplus exceeding half a million of dollars, has largely extended and is preparing still further to extend the mail service, and recommends a reduction of postages equal to about 20 per cent. It is practicing upon the great principle which should control every branch of our Government of rendering to the public the greatest good possible with the least possible taxation to the people.

The scale of postages suggested by the Postmaster-General recommends itself, not only by the reduction it proposes, but by the simplicity of its arrangement, its conformity with the Federal currency, and the improvement it will introduce into the accounts of the Department and its agents.

Your particular attention is invited to the subject of mail contracts with railroad companies. The present laws providing for the making of contracts are based upon the presumption that competition among bidders will secure the service at a fair price; but on most of the railroad lines there is no competition in that kind of transportation, and advertising is therefore useless. No contract can now be made with them except such as shall be negotiated before the time of offering or afterwards, and the power of the Postmaster-General to pay them high prices is practically without limitation. It would be a relief to him and no doubt would conduce to the public interest to prescribe by law some equitable basis upon which such contracts shall rest, and restrict him by a fixed rule of allowance. Under a liberal act of that sort he would undoubtedly be able to secure the services of most of the railroad companies, and the interest of the Department would be thus advanced.

The correspondence between the people of the United States and the European nations, and particularly with the British Islands, has become very extensive, and requires the interposition of Congress to give it security. No obstacle is perceived to an interchange of mails between New York and Liverpool or other foreign ports, as proposed by the Postmaster-General. On the contrary, it promises, by the security it will afford, to facilitate commercial transactions and give rise to an enlarged intercourse among the people of different nations, which can not but have a happy effect. Through the city of New York most of the correspondence between the Canadas and Europe is now carried on, and urgent representations have been received from the head of the provincial post-office asking the interposition of the United States to guard it from the accidents and losses to which it is now subjected. Some legislation appears to be called for as well by our own interest as by comity to the adjoining British provinces.

The expediency of providing a fireproof building for the important books and papers of the Post-Office Department is worthy of consideration. In the present condition of our Treasury it is neither necessary nor wise to leave essential public interests exposed to so much danger when they can so readily be made secure. There are weighty considerations in the location of a new building for that Department in favor of placing it near the other executive buildings.

The important subjects of a survey of the coast and the manufacture of a standard of weights and measures for the different custom-houses have been in progress for some years under the general direction of the Executive and the immediate superintendence of a gentleman possessing high scientific attainments. At the last session of Congress the making of a set of weights and measures for each State in the Union was added to the others by a joint resolution.

The care and correspondence as to all these subjects have been devolved on the Treasury Department during the last year. A special report from the Secretary of the Treasury will soon be communicated to Congress, which will show what has been accomplished as to the whole, the number and compensation of the persons now employed in these duties, and the progress expected to be made during the ensuing year, with a copy of the various correspondence deemed necessary to throw light on the subjects which seem to require additional legislation. Claims have been made for retrospective allowances in behalf of the superintendent and some of his assistants, which I did not feel justified in granting. Other claims have been made for large increases in compensation, which, under all the circumstances of the several cases, I declined making without the express sanction of Congress. In order to obtain that sanction the subject was at the last session, on my suggestion and by request of the immediate superintendent, submitted by the Treasury Department to the Committee on Commerce of the House of Representatives. But no legislative action having taken place, the early attention of Congress is now invited to the enactment of some express and detailed provisions in relation to the various claims made for the past, and to the compensation and allowances deemed proper for the future.

It is further respectfully recommended that, such being the inconvenience of attention to these duties by the Chief Magistrate, and such the great pressure of business on the Treasury Department, the general supervision of the coast survey and the completion of the weights and measures, if the works are kept united, should be devolved on a board of officers organized specially for that purpose, or on the Navy Board attached to the Navy Department.

All my experience and reflection confirm the conviction I have so often expressed to Congress in favor of an amendment of the Constitution which will prevent in any event the election of the President and Vice-President of the United States devolving on the House of Representatives and the Senate, and I therefore beg leave again to solicit your attention to the subject. There were various other suggestions in my last annual message not acted upon, particularly that relating to the want of uniformity in the laws of the District of Columbia, that are deemed worthy of your favorable consideration.

Before concluding this paper I think it due to the various Executive Departments to bear testimony to their prosperous condition and to the ability and integrity with which they have been conducted. It has been my aim to enforce in all of them a vigilant and faithful discharge of the public business, and it is gratifying to me to believe that there is no just cause of complaint from any quarter at the manner in which they have fulfilled the objects of their creation.

Having now finished the observations deemed proper on this the last occasion I shall have of communicating with the two Houses of Congress at their meeting, I can not omit an expression of the gratitude which is due to the great body of my fellow-citizens, in whose partiality and indulgence I have found encouragement and support in the many difficult and trying scenes through which it has been my lot to pass during my public career. Though deeply sensible that my exertions have not been crowned with a success corresponding to the degree of favor bestowed upon me, I am sure that they will be considered as having been directed by an earnest desire to promote the good of my country, and I am consoled by the persuasion that whatever errors have been committed will find a corrective in the intelligence and patriotism of those who will succeed us. All that has occurred during my Administration is calculated to inspire me with increased confidence in the stability of our institutions; and should I be spared to enter upon that retirement which is so suitable to my age and infirm health and so much desired by me in other respects, I shall not cease to invoke that beneficent Being to whose providence we are already so signally indebted for the continuance of His blessings on our beloved country. ANDREW JACKSON.

A.—*Statement of distribution of surplus revenue of $30,000,000 among the several States, agreeably to the number of electoral votes for President and according to the constitutional mode of direct taxation by representative population, and the difference arising from those two modes of distribution, as per census of 1830.*

State.	Representative population.	Electoral vote.	Share according to system of direct taxation.	Share according to electoral vote.	Difference in favor of direct-tax mode.	Difference in favor of electoral-vote mode.
Maine	399,454	10	$999,371	$1,020,408	....	$21,037
New Hampshire ..	269,327	7	673,813	714,286	....	40,473
Massachusetts	610,408	14	1,527,144	1,428,571	$98,573	....
Rhode Island	97,192	4	243,159	408,163	....	165,004
Connecticut	297,665	8	744,711	816,327	....	71,616
Vermont	280,652	7	702,147	714,286	....	12,139
New York........	1,918,578	42	4,799,978	4,285,714	514,264	....
New Jersey	319,921	8	800,392	816,427	....	15,935
Pennsylvania	1,348,072	30	3,372,662	3,061,225	311,437	....
Delaware	75,431	3	188,716	306,122	....	117,406
Maryland	405,842	10	1,015,352	1,020,408	....	5,056
Virginia..........	1,023,502	23	2,560,640	2,346,939	213,701	....
North Carolina....	639,747	15	1,600,546	1,530,612	69,934	....
South Carolina....	455,025	11	1,138,400	1,122,449	15,951	....
Georgia	429,811	11	1,075,319	1,122,449	....	47,130
Alabama..........	262,507	7	656,751	714,286	....	57,535
Mississippi	110,357	4	276,096	408,163	....	132,067
Louisiana	171,904	5	430,076	510,204	....	80,128
Tennessee	625,263	15	1,564,309	1,530,612	33,697	....
Kentucky	621,832	15	1,555,725	1,530,612	25,113	....
Ohio..............	937,901	21	2,346,479	2,142,858	203,621	....
Indiana	343,030	9	858,206	918,368	....	60,162
Illinois...........	157,146	5	393,154	510,204	....	117,050
Missouri	130,419	4	326,288	408,163	....	81,875
Arkansas.........	28,557	3	71,445	306,122	....	234,677
Michigan	31,625	3	79,121	306,102	....	227,001
Total........	11,991,168	294	30,000,000	30,000,000	1,486,291	1,486,291

SPECIAL MESSAGES.

WASHINGTON, *December 6, 1836.*

To the Senate and House of Representatives:

I transmit herewith to Congress copies of my correspondence with Mrs. Madison, produced by the resolution adopted at the last session by the Senate and House of Representatives on the decease of her venerated husband. The occasion seems to be appropriate to present a letter from her on the subject of the publication of a work of great political interest and ability, carefully prepared by Mr. Madison's own hand, under circumstances that give it claims to be considered as little less than official.

Congress has already, at considerable expense, published in a variety of forms the naked journals of the Revolutionary Congress and of the Convention that formed the Constitution of the United States. I am persuaded that the work of Mr. Madison, considering the author, the subject-matter of it, and the circumstances under which it was prepared—long withheld from the public, as it has been, by those motives of personal kindness and delicacy that gave tone to his intercourse with his fellow-men, until he and all who had been participators with him in the scenes he describes have passed away—well deserves to become the property of the nation, and can not fail, if published and disseminated at the public charge, to confer the most important of all benefits on the present and all succeeding generations—accurate knowledge of the principles of their Government and the circumstances under which they were recommended and embodied in the Constitution for adoption.

ANDREW JACKSON.

DEPARTMENT OF STATE, *July 9, 1836.*

The Secretary of State has the honor to report to the President that there is no resolution of Congress on the death of Mr. Madison on file in the Department of State. By application at the offices of the Secretary of the Senate and Clerk of the House of Representatives the inclosed certified copy of a set of resolutions has been procured. These resolutions, being joint, should have been enrolled, signed by the presiding officers of the two Houses, and submitted for the Executive approbation. By referring to the proceedings on the death of General Washington such a course appears to have been thought requisite, but in this case it has been deemed unnecessary or has been omitted accidentally. The value of the public expression of sympathy would be so much diminished by postponement to the next session that the Secretary has thought it best to present the papers, incomplete as they are, as the basis of such a letter as the President may think proper to direct to Mrs. Madison.

JOHN FORSYTH,
Secretary of State.

WASHINGTON, *July 9, 1836.*

Mrs. D. P. MADISON,
Montpelier, Va.

MADAM: It appearing to have been the intention of Congress to make me the organ of assuring you of the profound respect entertained by both its branches for your person and character, and of their sincere condolence in the late afflicting dispensation of Providence, which has at once deprived you of a beloved companion and your country of one of its most valued citizens, I perform that duty by transmitting the documents herewith inclosed.

No expression of my own sensibility at the loss sustained by yourself and the nation could add to the consolation to be derived from these high evidences of the public sympathy. Be assured, madam, that there is not one of your countrymen who feels more poignantly the stroke which has fallen upon you or who will cherish with a more endearing constancy the memory of the virtues, the services, and the purity of the illustrious man whose glorious and patriotic life has been just terminated by a tranquil death.

I have the honor to be, madam, your most obedient servant,

ANDREW JACKSON.

The President of the United States having communicated to the two Houses of Congress the melancholy intelligence of the death of their illustrious and beloved fellow-citizen, James Madison, of Virginia, late President of the United States, and the two Houses sharing in the general grief which this distressing event must produce:

Resolved by the Senate and House of Representatives of the United States of America in Congress assembled, That the chairs of the President of the Senate and of the Speaker of the House of Representatives be shrouded in black during the present session, and that the President of the Senate, the Speaker of the House of Representatives, and the members and officers of both Houses wear the usual badge of mourning for thirty days.

Resolved, That it be recommended to the people of the United States to wear crape on the left arm, as mourning, for thirty days.

Resolved, That the President of the United States be requested to transmit a copy of these resolutions to Mrs. Madison, and to assure her of the profound respect of the two Houses of Congress for her person and character and of their sincere condolence on the late afflicting dispensation of Providence.

MONTPELIER, *August 20, 1836.*
The PRESIDENT OF THE UNITED STATES:

I received, sir, in due time, your letter conveying to me the resolutions Congress were pleased to adopt on the occasion of the death of my beloved husband—a communication made the more grateful by the kind expression of your sympathy which it contained.

The high and just estimation of my husband by my countrymen and friends and their generous participation in the sorrow occasioned by our irretrievable loss, expressed through their supreme authorities and otherwise, are the only solace of which my heart is susceptible on the departure of him who had never lost sight of that consistency, symmetry, and beauty of character in all its parts which secured to him the love and admiration of his country, and which must ever be the subject of peculiar and tender reverence to one whose happiness was derived from their daily and constant exercise.

The best return I can make for the sympathy of my country is to fulfill the sacred trust his confidence reposed in me, that of placing before it and the world what his pen prepared for their use—a legacy the importance of which is deeply impressed on my mind.

With great respect,   D. P. MADISON.

MONTPELIER, *November 15, 1836.*
The PRESIDENT OF THE UNITED STATES.

SIR: The will of my late husband, James Madison, contains the following provision:

"Considering the peculiarity and magnitude of the occasion which produced the Convention at Philadelphia in 1787, the characters who composed it, the Constitution which resulted from their deliberations, its effects during a trial of so many years on the prosperity of the people living under it, and the interest it has inspired among the friends of free government, it is not an unreasonable inference that a careful and extended report of the proceedings and discussions of that body, which were with closed doors, by a member who was constant in his attendance, will be particularly gratifying to the people of the United States and to all who take an interest in the progress of political science and the cause of true liberty."

This provision bears evidence of the value he set on his report of the debates in the Convention, and he has charged legacies on them alone to the amount of $1,200 for the benefit of literary institutions and for benevolent purposes, leaving the residuary net proceeds for the use of his widow.

In a paper written by him, and which it is proposed to annex as a preface to the Debates, he traces the formation of confederacies and of the Articles of Confederation, its defects which caused and the steps which led to the Convention, his reasons for taking the debates and the manner in which he executed the task, and his opinion of the framers of the Constitution. From this I extract his description of the manner in which they were taken, as it guarantees their fullness and accuracy:

"In pursuance of the task I had assumed, I chose a seat in front of the presiding member, with the other members on my right and left hands. In this favorable position for hearing all that passed I noted down, in terms legible and in abbreviations and marks intelligible to myself, what was read from the chair or spoken by the members, and losing not a moment unnecessarily between the adjournment and reassembling of the Convention, I was enabled to write out my daily notes during the session, or within a few finishing days after its close, in the extent and form preserved in my own hand on my files.

"In the labor and correctness of this I was not a little aided by practice and by a familiarity with the style and the train of observation and reasoning which characterized the principal speakers. It happened also that I was not absent a single day, nor more than the casual fraction of an hour in any day, so that I could not have lost a single speech, unless a very short one."

However prevailing the restraint which veiled during the life of Mr. Madison this record of the creation of our Constitution, the grave, which has closed over all those who participated in its formation, has separated their acts from all that is personal to him or to them. His anxiety for their early publicity after this was removed may be inferred from his having them transcribed and revised by himself; and, it may be added, the known wishes of his illustrious friend Thomas Jefferson and other distinguished patriots, the important light they would shed for present as well as future usefulness, besides my desire to fulfill the pecuniary obligations imposed by his will, urged their appearance without awaiting the preparation of his other works, and early measures were accordingly adopted by me to ascertain from publishers in various parts of the Union the terms on which their publication could be effected.

It was also intended to publish with these debates those taken by him in the Congress of the Confederation in 1782, 1783, and 1787, of which he was then a member, and selections made by himself and prepared under his eye from his letters narrating the proceedings of that body during the periods of his service in it, prefixing the debates in 1776 on the Declaration of Independence by Thomas Jefferson so as to embody all the memorials in that shape known to exist. This exposé of the situation of the country under the Confederation and the defects of the old system of government evidenced in the proceedings under it seem to convey such preceding information as should accompany the debates on the formation of the Constitution by which it was superseded.

The proposals which have been received, so far from corresponding with the expectations of Mr. Madison when he charged the first of these works with those legacies, have evidenced that their publication could not be engaged in by me without advances of funds and involving of risks which I am not in a situation to make or incur.

Under these circumstances, I have been induced to submit for your consideration whether the publication of these debates be a matter of sufficient interest to the people of the United States to deserve to be brought to the notice of Congress; and should such be the estimation of the utility of these works by the representatives of the nation as to induce them to relieve me individually from the obstacles which impede it, their general circulation will be insured and the people be remunerated by its more economical distribution among them.

With high respect and consideration, D. P. MADISON.

WASHINGTON, *December 6, 1836.*

To the Senate and House of Representatives of the United States:

I transmit to Congress a report from the Commissioner of the Public Buildings, showing the progress made in the construction of the public buildings which by the act of the 4th of July last the President was authorized to cause to be erected.

ANDREW JACKSON.

DECEMBER 20, 1836.

To the Senate and House of Representatives.

GENTLEMEN: Herewith I transmit a report of the Postmaster-General, and recommend the passage of such laws and the making of such appropriations as may be necessary to carry into effect the measures adopted by him for resuming the business of the Department under his charge and securing the public property in the old Post-Office building.

It is understood that the building procured for the temporary use of the Department is far from being fireproof, and that the valuable books and papers saved from the recent conflagration will there be exposed to similar dangers. I therefore feel it my duty to recommend an immediate appropriation for the construction of a fireproof General Post-Office, that the materials may be obtained within the present winter and the buildings erected as rapidly as practicable.

ANDREW JACKSON.

POST-OFFICE DEPARTMENT, *December 20, 1836.*

The PRESIDENT OF THE UNITED STATES.

SIR: On the morning of the 15th instant I performed the painful duty of reporting to you orally the destruction of the General Post-Office building by fire, and received your instructions to inquire into the cause and extent of the calamity, for the purpose of enabling you to make a communication to Congress.

A few hours afterwards I received, through the chairman of the Committee on the Post-Office and Post-Roads of the House of Representatives, an official copy of a resolution adopted by that House, instructing the committee to institute a similar inquiry, and the chairman asked for such information as it was in my power to give. The investigation directed by you was thus rendered unnecessary.

The corporation of the city of Washington with honorable promptitude offered the Department the use of the west wing of the City Hall, now occupied by the mayor and councils and their officers and the officers of the Chesapeake and Ohio Canal Company. The proprietors of the medical college also tendered the use of their building on E street, and offers were made of several other buildings in the central parts of the city. An examination was made of such as promise by their magnitude to afford sufficient room for the force employed in the Department, but none were found equal in the commodiousness of their interior structure and abundant room to Fuller's Hotel, opposite the buildings occupied by the Treasury Department on Pennsylvania avenue. That building has been obtained on terms which the accompanying papers (marked 1 and 2) will fully exhibit. The business of the Department will be immediately resumed in that building.

The agreement with Mr. Fuller will make necessary an immediate appropriation by Congress, and upon that body will devolve also the duty of providing for the payment of the rent, if they shall approve of the arrangement.

In the meantime steps have been taken to secure all that is valuable in the ruins of the Post-Office building, and to protect from the weather the walls of so much of it as was occupied by the General Post-Office which stand firm.

The Department has no fund at command out of which the services necessary in the accomplishment of these objects can be paid for, nor has it the means to replace the furniture which has been lost and must be immediately obtained to enable the clerks to proceed with their current business.

These facts I deem it my duty to report to you, that you may recommend to Congress such measures thereupon as you may deem expedient.

With the highest respect, your obedient servant,

AMOS KENDALL.

WASHINGTON, *December 20, 1836.*

To the Senate of the United States:

I transmit herewith, for the consideration and action of the Senate, treaties concluded with the Ioways and Sacs of Missouri, with the Sioux, with the Sacs and Foxes, and with the Otoes and Missourias and Omahas, by which they have relinquished their rights in the lands lying between the State of Missouri and the Missouri River, ceded in the first article of the treaty with them of July 15, 1830.

ANDREW JACKSON.

WASHINGTON, *December 20, 1836.*

To the Senate of the United States:

I transmit herewith to the Senate, for their consideration in reference to its ratification, a treaty of peace and friendship between the United States of America and the Emperor of Morocco, concluded at Meccanez on the 16th of September, 1836, with a report of the Secretary of State and the documents therein mentioned.

ANDREW JACKSON.

WASHINGTON, *December 21, 1836.*

To the Senate and House of Representatives of the United States:

During the last session information was given to Congress by the Executive that measures had been taken to ascertain "the political, military, and civil condition of Texas." I now submit for your consideration extracts from the report of the agent who had been appointed to collect it relative to the condition of that country.

No steps have been taken by the Executive toward the acknowledgment of the independence of Texas, and the whole subject would have been left without further remark on the information now given to Congress were it not that the two Houses at their last session, acting separately, passed resolutions "that the independence of Texas ought to be acknowledged by the United States whenever satisfactory information should be received that it had in successful operation a civil government capable of performing the duties and fulfilling the obligations of an independent power." This mark of interest in the question of the independence of Texas and indication of the views of Congress make it proper that I should somewhat in detail present the considerations that have governed the Executive in continuing to occupy the ground previously taken in the contest between Mexico and Texas.

The acknowledgment of a new state as independent and entitled to a place in the family of nations is at all times an act of great delicacy and responsibility, but more especially so when such state has forcibly separated itself from another of which it had formed an integral part and which still claims dominion over it. A premature recognition under these circumstances, if not looked upon as justifiable cause of war, is always liable to be regarded as a proof of an unfriendly spirit to one of the contending parties. All questions relative to the government of foreign nations, whether of the Old or the New World, have been treated by the United States as questions of fact only, and our predecessors have cautiously abstained from deciding upon them until the clearest evidence was in their possession to enable them not only to decide correctly, but to shield their decisions from every unworthy imputation. In all the contests that have arisen out of the revolutions of France, out of the disputes relating to the crowns of Portugal and Spain, out of the revolutionary movements of those Kingdoms, out of the separation of the American possessions of both from the European Governments, and out of the numerous and constantly occurring struggles for dominion in Spanish America, so wisely consistent with our just principles has been the action of our Government that we have under the most critical circumstances avoided all censure and encountered no other evil than that produced by a transient estrangement of good will in those against whom we have been by force of evidence compelled to decide.

It has thus been made known to the world that the uniform policy and practice of the United States is to avoid all interference in disputes which merely relate to the internal government of other nations, and eventually to recognize the authority of the prevailing party, without reference to our particular interests and views or to the merits of the original controversy. Public opinion here is so firmly established and well understood in favor of this policy that no serious disagreement has ever arisen among ourselves in relation to it, although brought under review in a variety of forms and at periods when the minds of the people were greatly excited by the agitation of topics purely domestic in their character. Nor has any deliberate inquiry ever been instituted in Congress or in any of our legislative bodies as to whom belonged the power of originally recognizing a new State—a power the exercise of which is equivalent under some circumstances to a declaration of war; a power nowhere expressly delegated, and only granted in the Constitution as it is necessarily involved in some of the great powers given to Congress, in that given to the President and Senate to form treaties with foreign powers and to appoint ambassadors and other public ministers, and in that conferred upon the President to receive ministers from foreign nations.

In the preamble to the resolution of the House of Representatives it is distinctly intimated that the expediency of recognizing the independence of Texas should be left to the decision of Congress. In this view, on the ground of expediency, I am disposed to concur, and do not, therefore, consider it necessary to express any opinion as to the strict constitutional right of the Executive, either apart from or in conjunction with the Senate, over the subject. It is to be presumed that on no future occasion will a dispute arise, as none has heretofore occurred, between the Executive and Legislature in the exercise of the power of recognition. It will always be considered consistent with the spirit of the Constitution, and most safe, that it should be exercised, when probably leading to war, with a previous understanding with that body by whom war can alone be declared, and by whom all the provisions for sustaining its perils must be furnished. Its submission to Congress, which represents in one of its branches the States of this Union and in the other the people of the United States, where there may be reasonable ground to apprehend so grave a consequence, would certainly afford the fullest satisfaction to our own country and a perfect guaranty to all other nations of the justice and prudence of the measures which might be adopted.

In making these suggestions it is not my purpose to relieve myself from the responsibility of expressing my own opinions of the course the interests of our country prescribe and its honor permits us to follow.

It is scarcely to be imagined that a question of this character could be presented in relation to which it would be more difficult for the United States to avoid exciting the suspicion and jealousy of other powers, and maintain their established character for fair and impartial dealing. But on this, as on every trying occasion, safety is to be found in a rigid adherence to principle.

In the contest between Spain and her revolted colonies we stood aloof and waited, not only until the ability of the new States to protect themselves was fully established, but until the danger of their being again subjugated had entirely passed away. Then, and not till then, were they recognized. Such was our course in regard to Mexico herself. The same policy was observed in all the disputes growing out of the separation into distinct governments of those Spanish American States who began or carried on the contest with the parent country united under one form of government. We acknowledged the separate independence of New Granada, of Venezuela, and of Ecuador only after their independent existence was no longer a subject of dispute or was actually acquiesced in by those with whom they had been previously united. It is true that, with regard to Texas, the civil authority of Mexico has been expelled, its invading army defeated, the chief of the Republic himself captured, and all present power to control the newly organized Government of Texas annihilated within its confines. But, on the other hand, there is, in appearance at least, an immense disparity of physical force on the side of Mexico. The Mexican Republic under another executive is rallying its forces under a new leader and menacing a fresh invasion to recover its lost dominion.

Upon the issue of this threatened invasion the independence of Texas may be considered as suspended, and were there nothing peculiar in the relative situation of the United States and Texas our acknowledgment of its independence at such a crisis could scarcely be regarded as consistent with that prudent reserve with which we have heretofore held ourselves bound to treat all similar questions. But there are circumstances in the relations of the two countries which require us to act on this occasion with even more than our wonted caution. Texas was once claimed as a part of our property, and there are those among our citizens who, always reluctant to abandon that claim, can not but regard with solicitude the prospect of the reunion of the territory to this country. A large proportion of its civilized inhabitants are emigrants from the United States, speak the same language with ourselves, cherish the same principles, political and religious, and are bound to many of our citizens by ties of friendship and kindred blood; and, more than all, it is known that the people of that country have instituted the same form of government with our own, and have since the close of your last session openly resolved, on the acknowledgment by us of their independence, to seek admission into the Union as one of the Federal States. This last circumstance is a matter of peculiar delicacy, and forces upon us considerations of the gravest character. The title of Texas to the territory she claims is identified with her independence. She asks us to acknowledge that title to the territory, with an avowed design to treat immediately of its transfer to the United States. It becomes us to beware of a too early movement, as it might subject us, however unjustly, to the imputation of seeking to establish the claim of our neighbors to a territory with a view to its subsequent acquisition by ourselves. Prudence, therefore, seems to dictate that we should still stand aloof and maintain our present attitude, if not until Mexico itself or one of the great foreign powers shall recognize the independence of the new Government, at least until the lapse of time or the course of events shall have proved beyond cavil or dispute the ability of the people of that country to maintain their separate sovereignty and to uphold the Government constituted by them. Neither of the contending parties can justly complain of this course. By pursuing it we are but carrying out the long-established policy of our Government—a policy which has secured to us respect and influence abroad and inspired confidence at home.

Having thus discharged my duty, by presenting with simplicity and directness the views which after much reflection I have been led to take of this important subject, I have only to add the expression of my confidence that if Congress shall differ with me upon it their judgment will be the result of dispassionate, prudent, and wise deliberation, with the assurance that during the short time I shall continue connected with the Government I shall promptly and cordially unite with you in such measures as may be deemed best fitted to increase the prosperity and perpetuate the peace of our favored country.

ANDREW JACKSON.

DECEMBER 26, 1836.

To the Senate of the United States:

I herewith transmit to the Senate the report of the Secretary of the Treasury, giving all the information required by their resolution of the 19th instant, calling for a list of the different appropriations which will leave unexpended balances on the 1st day of January next.

ANDREW JACKSON.

WASHINGTON, *December 26, 1836.*

To the Senate of the United States:

I nominate William Gates, late major of the First Regiment of Artillery, for reappointment in the Army, to be major in the Second Regiment of Artillery, to take rank from the 30th May, 1832, the date of his former commission. This officer was stricken from the rolls of the Army by my order on the 7th of June last, upon a full consideration by me of the proceedings of a court of inquiry held at his request for the purpose of investigating his conduct during and subsequent to the attack on Fort Barnwell, at Volusia, in Florida, in April last, which court, after mature deliberation on the testimony before them, expressed the opinion "that the effective force under the command of Major Gates was much greater than the estimated force of the Indians who attacked him on the morning of the 14th of April, 1836, and that therefore he was capable of meeting the enemy in the field if necessary; also, that the bodies of two volunteers killed were improperly left exposed, and ought to have been brought in on the morning when they were killed, such exposure necessarily operating injuriously on the garrison.'' He is now nominated for a reappointment to the end that he may be brought to trial before a court-martial, such a trial being solicited by him.

ANDREW JACKSON.

Washington, *December, 1836.*

To the Senate and House of Representatives of the United States:

By the second section of the act ''to establish the northern boundary line of the State of Ohio, and to provide for the admission of the State of Michigan into the Union upon the conditions therein expressed,'' approved June 15, 1836, the constitution and State government which the people of Michigan had formed for themselves was ratified and confirmed and the State of Michigan declared to be one of the United States of America, and admitted into the Union upon an equal footing with the original States, but on the express condition that the said State should consist of and have jurisdiction over all the territory included within certain boundaries described in the act, and over none other. It was further enacted by the third section of the same law that, as a compliance with the fundamental condition of admission, the boundaries of the State of Michigan, as thus described, declared, and established, should ''receive the assent of a convention of delegates elected by the people of said State for the sole purpose of giving the assent'' therein required; that as soon as such assent should be given the President of the United States should announce the same by proclamation, and that thereupon, and without any further proceeding on the part of Congress, the admission of the State into the Union as one of the United States of America should be considered as complete, and the Senators and Representatives in the Congress of the United States entitled to take their seats without further delay.

In the month of November last I received a communication inclosing the official proceedings of a convention assembled at Ann Arbor, in Michigan, on the 26th of September, 1836, all which (marked A) are herewith laid before you. It will be seen by these papers that the convention therein referred to was elected by the people of Michigan pursuant to an act of the State legislature passed on the 25th of July last in consequence of the above-mentioned act of Congress, and that it declined giving its assent to the fundamental condition prescribed by Congress, and rejected the same.

On the 24th instant the accompanying paper (marked B), with its inclosure, containing the proceedings of a convention of delegates subsequently elected and held in the State of Michigan, was presented to me. By these papers, which are also herewith submitted for your consideration, it appears that elections were held in all the counties of the State, except two, on the 5th and 6th days of December instant, for the purpose of electing a convention of delegates to give the assent required by Congress; that the delegates then elected assembled in convention on the 14th day of December instant, and that on the following day the assent of the body to the fundamental condition above stated was formally given.

This latter convention was not held or elected by virtue of any act of the Territorial or State legislature; it originated from the people themselves, and was chosen by them in pursuance of resolutions adopted in primary assemblies held in the respective counties. The act of Congress, however, does not prescribe by what authority the convention shall be ordered, or the time when or the manner in which it shall be chosen. Had these latter proceedings come to me during the recess of Congress, I should therefore have felt it my duty, on being satisfied that they emanated from a convention of delegates elected in point of fact by the people of the State for the purpose required, to have issued my proclamation thereon as provided by law; but as the authority conferred on the President was evidently given to him under the expectation that the assent of the convention might be laid before him during the recess of Congress and to avoid the delay of a postponement until the meeting of that body, and as the circumstances which now attend the case are in other respects peculiar and such as could not have been foreseen when the act of June 15, 1836, was passed, I deem it most agreeable to the intent of that law, and proper for other reasons, that the whole subject should be submitted to the decision of Congress. The importance of your early action upon it is too obvious to need remark.

ANDREW JACKSON.

WASHINGTON, *December 28, 1836.*

To the House of Representatives of the United States:

In compliance with the resolution of the House of Representatives of the 23d instant, I herewith transmit a report* from the Secretary of State, to whom the resolution was referred, containing all the information upon the subject which he is now able to communicate.

ANDREW JACKSON.

To the Senate of the United States:

I transmit to the Senate a report † of the Secretary of the Navy, complying with their resolution of the 24th of May, 1836.

ANDREW JACKSON.

DECEMBER 29, 1836.

* Relating to the bequest of James Smithson.
† Relating to the survey of the harbors south of the Chesapeake.

WASHINGTON, *December 30, 1836.*

To the Senate and House of Representatives:

I transmit herewith a communication from the Secretary of War *ad interim*, with certain accompanying papers* from the Engineer Department, required to complete the annual report from that Department.

ANDREW JACKSON.

WASHINGTON, *December 30, 1836.*

To the Senate of the United States:

I transmit herewith, for your consideration and action, four treaties with bands of Potawatamie Indians in Indiana, accompanied by a report from the War Department and sundry other papers.

ANDREW JACKSON.

WASHINGTON, *December 30, 1836.*

To the Senate of the United States:

I transmit herewith, for your consideration and action, a treaty with the Menomonie tribe of Indians, accompanied by a report from the War Department. I recommend the modifications proposed in the report.

ANDREW JACKSON.

WASHINGTON, *January 7, 1837.*

To the House of Representatives of the United States:

I herewith transmit to Congress a report of the Secretary of State, with the accompanying letter, addressed to him by the commission appointed under the act of Congress of the last session for carrying into effect the convention between the United States and Spain.

ANDREW JACKSON.

WASHINGTON, *January 9, 1837.*

To the Senate of the United States:

Immediately after the passage by the Senate, at a former session, of the resolution requesting the President to consider the expediency of opening negotiations with the governments of other nations, and particularly with the Governments of Central America and New Granada, for the purpose of effectually protecting, by equitable treaty stipulations with them, such individuals or companies as might undertake to open a communication between the Atlantic and Pacific oceans by the construction of a ship canal across the isthmus which connects North and South America, and of securing forever by such stipulations the free and equal right of navigating such canal to all such nations on the payment of such

---

*Reports of the superintendents of the Cumberland road in Indiana and Illinois and of the improvement of the Ohio River above the Falls.

reasonable tolls as ought to be established to compensate the capitalists who might engage in such undertaking and complete the work, an agent was employed to obtain information in respect to the situation and character of the country through which the line of communication, if established, would necessarily pass, and the state of the projects which were understood to be contemplated for opening such communication by a canal or a railroad. The agent returned to the United States in September last, and although the information collected by him is not as full as could have been desired, yet it is sufficient to show that the probability of an early execution of any of the projects which have been set on foot for the construction of the communication alluded to is not so great as to render it expedient to open a negotiation at present with any foreign government upon the subject.

ANDREW JACKSON.

WASHINGTON, *January 17, 1837.*

To the House of Representatives of the United States:

I hereby submit to the House of Representatives certain communications from the Secretary of the Treasury and the attorney of the United States for the District of Columbia. They relate to the difficulties which have been interposed under the existing laws in bringing to conviction and punishment the supposed incendiaries of the Treasury buildings in the year 1833.

The peculiar circumstances of this case, so long concealed, and of the flagrant frauds by persons disconnected with the Government, which were still longer concealed, and to screen some of which forever was probably a principal inducement to the burning of the buildings, lead me earnestly to recommend a revision of the laws on this subject. I do this with a wish not only to render the punishment hereafter more severe for the wanton destruction of the public property, but to repeal entirely the statute of limitation in all criminal cases, except small misdemeanors, and in no event to allow a party to avail himself of its benefits during the period the commission of the crime was kept concealed or the persons on trial were not suspected of having perpetrated the offense.

It must be manifest to Congress that the exposed state of the public records here, without fireproof buildings, imperatively requires the most ample remedies for their protection, and the greatest vigilance and fidelity in all officers, whether executive or judicial, in bringing to condign punishment the real offenders.

Without these the public property is in that deplorable situation which depends quite as much on accident and good fortune as the laws, for safety.

ANDREW JACKSON.

[The same message was sent to the Senate.]

WASHINGTON, *January 17, 1837.*

To the Senate and House of Representatives of the United States:

I transmit to Congress herewith the copy of an act of the State of Missouri passed on the 16th ultimo, expressing the assent of that State to the several provisions of the act of Congress entitled "An act to extend the western boundary of the State of Missouri to the Missouri River," approved June 7, 1836. A copy of the act, duly authenticated, has been deposited in the Department of State.   ANDREW JACKSON.

To the Senate of the United States: JANUARY 18, 1837.

In compliance with a resolution of the Senate at their last session, I herewith transmit the inclosed documents, which contain all the information on the subject of the claim of the heirs of George Galphin within the power of the Executive.   ANDREW JACKSON.

WASHINGTON, *January 18, 1837.*

To the Senate of the United States:

In compliance with the resolution of the Senate dated the 16th instant, I transmit a copy and a translation of a letter addressed to me on the 4th of July last by the President of the Mexican Republic, and a copy of my reply to the same on the 4th of September. No other communication on the subject of the resolution referred to has been made to the Executive by any other foreign government, or by any person claiming to act in behalf of Mexico.   ANDREW JACKSON.

The President of the Mexican Republic to the President of the United States.

COLUMBIA, IN TEXAS, *July 4, 1836.*

His Excellency General ANDREW JACKSON,
        President of the United States of America.

MUCH ESTEEMED SIR: In fulfillment of the duties which patriotism and honor impose upon a public man, I came to this country at the head of 6,000 Mexicans. The chances of war, made inevitable by circumstances, reduced me to the condition of a prisoner, in which I still remain, as you may have already learned. The disposition evinced by General Samuel Houston, the commander in chief of the Texan army, and by his successor, General Thomas J. Rusk, for the termination of the war; the decision of the President and cabinet of Texas in favor of a proper compromise between the contending parties, and my own conviction, produced the conventions of which I send you copies inclosed, and the orders given by me to General Filisola, my second in command, to retire from the river Brasos, where he was posted, to the other side of the river Bravo del Norte.

As there was no doubt that General Filisola would religiously comply, as far as concerned himself, the President and cabinet agreed that I should set off for Mexico, in order to fulfill the other engagements, and with that intent I embarked on board the schooner *Invincible*, which was to carry me to the port of Vera Cruz. Unfortunately, however, some indiscreet persons raised a mob, which obliged the authorities to have me landed by force and brought back into strict captivity. This incident has prevented me from going to Mexico, where I should otherwise have arrived early in last month; and in consequence of it the Government of that country, doubtless ignorant of what has occurred, has withdrawn the command of the army from General Filisola and has ordered his successor, General Urrea, to continue its operations, in obedience to which order that general is, according to the latest accounts, already at the river Nueces. In vain have some reflecting and worthy men endeavored to demonstrate the necessity of moderation and of my going to Mexico according to the convention; but the excitement of the public mind has increased with the return of the Mexican army to Texas. Such is the state of things here at present. The continuation of the war and of its disasters is therefore inevitable unless the voice of reason be heard in proper time from the mouth of some powerful individual. It appears to me that you, sir, have it in your power to perform this good office, by interfering in favor of the execution of the said convention, which shall be strictly fulfilled on my part. When I offered to treat with this Government, I was convinced that it was useless for Mexico to continue the war. I have acquired exact information respecting this country which I did not possess four months ago. I have too much zeal for the interests of my country to wish for anything which is not compatible with them. Being always ready to sacrifice myself for its glory and advantage, I never would have hesitated to subject myself to torments or death rather than consent to any compromise if Mexico could thereby have obtained the slightest benefit. I am firmly convinced that it is proper to terminate this question by political negotiation. That conviction alone determined me sincerely to agree to what has been stipulated, and in the same spirit I make to you this frank declaration. Be pleased, sir, to favor me by a like confidence on your part. Afford me the satisfaction of avoiding approaching evils and of contributing to that good which my heart advises. Let us enter into negotiations by which the friendship between your nation and the Mexican may be strengthened, both being amicably engaged in giving being and stability to a people who are desirous of appearing in the political world, and who, under the protection of the two nations, will attain its object within a few years.

The Mexicans are magnanimous when treated with consideration. I will clearly set before them the proper and humane reasons which require noble and frank conduct on their part, and I doubt not that they will act thus as soon as they have been convinced.

By what I have here submitted you will see the sentiments which animate me, and with which I remain, your most humble and obedient servant,

ANTONIO LOPEZ DE SANTA ANNA.

The President of the United States to the President of the Mexican Republic.

HERMITAGE, *September 4, 1836.*

General ANTONIO LOPEZ DE SANTA ANNA.

SIR: I have the honor to acknowledge the receipt of your letter of the 4th day of July last, which has been forwarded to me by General Samuel Houston, under cover of one from him, transmitted by an express from General Gaines, who is in command of the United States forces on the Texan frontier. The great object of these communications appears to be to put an end to the disasters which necessarily attend the civil war now raging in Texas, and asking the interposition of the United States in furthering so humane and desirable a purpose. That any well-intended effort of yours in aid of this object should have been defeated is calculated to excite the regret of all who justly appreciate the blessings of peace, and who take an interest in the causes which contribute to the prosperity of Mexico in her domestic as well as her foreign relations.

The Government of the United States is ever anxious to cultivate peace and friendship with all nations; but it proceeds on the principle that all nations have the right to alter, amend, or change their own government as the sovereign power—the people— may direct. In this respect it never interferes with the policy of other powers, nor can it permit any on the part of others with its internal policy. Consistently with this principle, whatever we can do to restore peace between contending nations or remove the causes of misunderstanding is cheerfully at the service of those who are willing to rely upon our good offices as a friend or mediator.

In reference, however, to the agreement which you, as the representative of Mexico, have made with Texas, and which invites the interposition of the United States, you will at once see that we are forbidden by the character of the communications made to us through the Mexican minister from considering it. That Government has notified us that as long as you are a prisoner no act of yours will be regarded as binding by the Mexican authorities. Under these circumstances it will be manifest to you that good faith to Mexico, as well as the general principle to which I have adverted as forming the basis of our intercourse with all foreign powers, make it impossible for me to take any step like that you have anticipated. If, however, Mexico should signify her willingness to avail herself of our good offices in bringing about the desirable result you have described, nothing could give me more pleasure than to devote my best services to it. To be instrumental in terminating the evils of civil war and in substituting in their stead the blessings of peace is a divine privilege. Every government and the people of all countries should feel it their highest happiness to enjoy an opportunity of thus manifesting their love of each other and their interest in the general principles which apply to them all as members of the common family of man.

Your letter, and that of General Houston, commander in chief of the Texan army, will be made the basis of an early interview with the Mexican minister at Washington. They will hasten my return to Washington, to which place I will set out in a few days, expecting to reach it by the 1st of October. In the meantime I hope Mexico and Texas, feeling that war is the greatest of calamities, will pause before another campaign is undertaken and can add to the number of those scenes of bloodshed which have already marked the progress of their contest and have given so much pain to their Christian friends throughout the world.

This is sent under cover to General Houston, who will give it a safe conveyance to you.

I am, very respectfully, your obedient servant,

ANDREW JACKSON.

JANUARY 19, 1837.

To the Senate and House of Representatives of the United States:

I herewith transmit a copy of the annual report of the Director of the Mint, showing the operations of the institution during the past year and also the progress made toward completion of the branch mints in North Carolina, Georgia, and Louisiana.

ANDREW JACKSON.

WASHINGTON, *January 20, 1837.*

To the Senate and House of Representatives:

In compliance with the act of Congress of the 3d of March, 1829, I herewith transmit to Congress the report of the board of inspectors of the penitentiary of Washington, and beg leave to draw their attention to the fact presented with the report, "that the inspectors have received no compensation for their services for two years, viz, 1829 and 1830," and request that an appropriation be made for the same.

ANDREW JACKSON.

WASHINGTON, *January 21, 1837.*

To the Senate of the United States:

I transmit, for your constitutional action, a report from the War Department, accompanied by a treaty with the Stockbridge and Munsee Indians.

ANDREW JACKSON.

WASHINGTON, *January 21, 1837.*

To the Senate of the United States:

I transmit, for your constitutional action, a report from the War Department, accompanied by a treaty with a portion of the New York Indians.

ANDREW JACKSON.

WASHINGTON, *January 25, 1837.*

To the House of Representatives of the United States:

In compliance with the resolution of the House of Representatives of the 17th instant, I transmit a report * from the Secretary of State, together with the documents by which it was accompanied.

ANDREW JACKSON.

WASHINGTON, *January 27, 1837.*

To the Senate and House of Representatives:

I transmit herewith certain papers from the War Department, relative to the improvement of Brunswick Harbor, Georgia.

ANDREW JACKSON.

WASHINGTON, *January 30, 1837.*

To the House of Representatives of the United States:

I herewith transmit to the House the copy of a letter addressed to me by the governor of the State of Maine on the 30th of June last, communicating sundry resolutions of the legislature of that State and claiming the reimbursement of certain moneys paid to John and Phineas R. Harford for losses and expenses incurred by them under circumstances explained in the accompanying papers.

ANDREW JACKSON.

WASHINGTON, *February 6, 1837.*

The SPEAKER OF THE HOUSE OF REPRESENTATIVES:

In compliance with the resolution of the House of Representatives of the 3d instant, I herewith transmit the report † of the Secretary of the Navy, which affords all the information required by said resolution. The

---

* Relating to the condition of the political relations between the United States and Mexico, and to the condition of Texas.

† Relating to the South Sea exploring expedition.

President begs leave to add that he trusts that all facilities will be given to this exploring expedition that Congress can bestow and the honor of the nation demands.

ANDREW JACKSON.

WASHINGTON, *February 6, 1837.*

To the Senate and House of Representatives of the United States:

At the beginning of this session Congress was informed that our claims upon Mexico had not been adjusted, but that notwithstanding the irritating effect upon her councils of the movements in Texas, I hoped, by great forbearance, to avoid the necessity of again bringing the subject of them to your notice. That hope has been disappointed. Having in vain urged upon that Government the justice of those claims and my indispensable obligation to insist that there should be ''no further delay in the acknowledgment, if not in the redress, of the injuries complained of,'' my duty requires that the whole subject should be presented, as it now is, for the action of Congress, whose exclusive right it is to decide on the further measures of redress to be employed. The length of time since some of the injuries have been committed, the repeated and unavailing applications for redress, the wanton character of some of the outrages upon the property and persons of our citizens, upon the officers and flag of the United States, independent of recent insults to this Government and people by the late extraordinary Mexican minister, would justify in the eyes of all nations immediate war. That remedy, however, should not be used by just and generous nations, confiding in their strength for injuries committed, if it can be honorably avoided; and it has occurred to me that, considering the present embarrassed condition of that country, we should act with both wisdom and moderation by giving to Mexico one more opportunity to atone for the past before we take redress into our own hands. To avoid all misconception on the part of Mexico, as well as to protect our own national character from reproach, this opportunity should be given with the avowed design and full preparation to take immediate satisfaction if it should not be obtained on a repetition of the demand for it. To this end I recommend that an act be passed authorizing reprisals, and the use of the naval force of the United States by the Executive against Mexico to enforce them, in the event of a refusal by the Mexican Government to come to an amicable adjustment of the matters in controversy between us upon another demand thereof made from on board one of our vessels of war on the coast of Mexico.

The documents herewith transmitted, with those accompanying my message in answer to a call of the House of Representatives of the 17th ultimo, will enable Congress to judge of the propriety of the course heretofore pursued and to decide upon the necessity of that now recommended.

If these views should fail to meet the concurrence of Congress, and that body be able to find in the condition of the affairs between the two countries, as disclosed by the accompanying documents, with those referred to, any well-grounded reasons to hope that an adjustment of the controversy between them can be effected without a resort to the measures I have felt it my duty to recommend, they may be assured of my cooperation in any other course that shall be deemed honorable and proper. ANDREW JACKSON.

WASHINGTON, *February 7, 1837.*

To the Senate of the United States:

I transmit communications from the War Department relating to the treaty with the Sacs and Foxes recently submitted to the Senate.

ANDREW JACKSON.

WASHINGTON, *February 7, 1837.*

To the Senate of the United States:

I transmit herewith, for the constitutional action of the Senate, a report from the War Department, accompanied by a treaty with the Saganaw tribe of Chippewa Indians. ANDREW JACKSON.

WASHINGTON, *February, 1837.*

To the Senate of the United States:

I transmit, for your consideration and action, a treaty with certain Potawatamie Indians, accompanied by a report from the War Department.

ANDREW JACKSON.

WASHINGTON, *February 9, 1837.*

To the Senate and House of Representatives of the United States:

I communicate to Congress printed copies of the treaty of peace and commerce between the United States and the Empire of Morocco, concluded at Meccanez on the 16th day of September last, and duly ratified by the respective Governments. ANDREW JACKSON.

WASHINGTON, *February 11, 1837.*

To the House of Representatives of the United States:

I herewith transmit to the House of Representatives a letter addressed to me on the 30th ultimo by the governor of the State of New Hampshire, communicating several resolutions of the legislature of that Commonwealth and claiming the reimbursement of certain expenses incurred by that State in maintaining jurisdiction over that portion of its territory north of the forty-fifth degree of north latitude, known by the name of Indian Stream, under circumstances explained in his excellency's letter.

ANDREW JACKSON.

WASHINGTON, *February 13, 1837.*

To the Senate of the United States:

I herewith transmit to the Senate a report * from the Secretary of State, with accompanying papers, embracing a copy of the correspondence requested by the resolution of the 7th instant, and such additional documents as were deemed necessary to a correct understanding of the whole subject.

ANDREW JACKSON.

WASHINGTON CITY, *February 14, 1837.*

To the House of Representatives:

I transmit herewith a copy of the instructions, prepared under my direction by the War Department, for the commissioners appointed by me, in pursuance of the request contained in the resolution adopted by the House of Representatives on the 1st of July last, to investigate the causes of the hostilities then existing with the Creek Indians, and also copies of the reports on that subject received from the commissioners.

ANDREW JACKSON.

To the Senate of the United States: FEBRUARY 15, 1837.

I herewith transmit to the Senate a report of the Postmaster-General, on the subject of the claims of Messrs. Stockton and Stokes, with a review of that report by the Solicitor of the Treasury, to whom, under a law of the last session of Congress, all the suspended debts of those contractors had been submitted; also a supplemental rejoinder by the Postmaster-General since the report of the Solicitor of the Treasury was made, with the papers accompanying the same, all of which are respectfully submitted for the consideration of the Senate.

ANDREW JACKSON.

WASHINGTON, *February 15, 1837.*

To the Senate of the United States:

I transmit herewith, for your consideration and action, a treaty lately made with the Sioux of the Mississippi, accompanied by a report from the War Department.

ANDREW JACKSON.

WASHINGTON, *February, 1837.*

To the Senate of the United States:

I transmit herewith a convention between the Choctaws and Chickasaws, which meets my approbation, and for which I ask your favorable consideration and action.

ANDREW JACKSON.

---

* Relating to the seizure of slaves on board the brigs *Encomium* and *Enterprise* by the authorities of Bermuda and New Providence.

WASHINGTON, *February 20, 1837.*

To the House of Representatives of the United States:

In compliance with the resolution of the House of Representatives of the 9th ultimo, I transmit a report from the Secretary of State and the documents* by which it was accompanied.

ANDREW JACKSON.

WASHINGTON, *February 24, 1837.*

To the House of Representatives:

I transmit a letter from the Secretary of War *ad interim*, accompanied by various documents, in relation to a survey recently made of the mouths of the Mississippi River under a law of the last session of Congress.

ANDREW JACKSON.

WASHINGTON, *March 3, 1837.*

To the Senate of the United States:

In the month of October last, the office of Secretary of War being vacant, I appointed Benjamin F. Butler, of the State of New York, to perform the duties thereof during the pleasure of the President, but with the expectation that the office would be otherwise filled, on the nomination of my successor, immediately on the commencement of his term of service. This expectation I have reason to believe will be fulfilled, but as it is necessary in the present state of the public service that the vacancy should actually occur, and as it is doubtful whether Mr. Butler can act under his present appointment after the expiration of the present session of the Senate, I hereby nominate the said Benjamin F. Butler to be Secretary of War of the United States, to hold the said office during the pleasure of the President until a successor duly appointed shall accept such office and enter on the duties thereof.

ANDREW JACKSON.

WASHINGTON, *March 3, 1837.*

To the Senate of the United States:

In my message to Congress of the 21st of December last I laid before that body, without reserve, my views concerning the recognition of the independence of Texas, with a report of the agent employed by the Executive to obtain information in respect to the condition of that country. Since that time the subject has been repeatedly discussed in both branches of the Legislature. These discussions have resulted in the insertion of a clause in the general appropriation law passed by both Houses providing

*Correspondence of William Tudor, jr., while consul, etc., of the United States to Peru and chargé d'affaires at Rio de Janeiro.

for the outfit and salary of a diplomatic agent to be sent to the Republic of Texas whenever the President of the United States may receive satisfactory evidence that Texas is an independent power and shall deem it expedient to appoint such minister, and in the adoption of a resolution by the Senate, the constitutional advisers of the Executive on the diplomatic intercourse of the United States with foreign powers, expressing the opinion that "the State of Texas having established and maintained an independent government capable of performing those duties, foreign and domestic, which appertain to independent governments, and it appearing that there is no longer any reasonable prospect of the successful prosecution of the war by Mexico against said State, it is expedient and proper and in conformity with the laws of nations and the practice of this Government in like cases that the independent political existence of said State be acknowledged by the Government of the United States." Regarding these proceedings as a virtual decision of the question submitted by me to Congress, I think it my duty to acquiesce therein, and therefore I nominate Alcée La Branche, of Louisiana, to be chargé d'affaires to the Republic of Texas.

ANDREW JACKSON.

VETO MESSAGE.*

MARCH 3, 1837—11.45 p. m.

The bill from the Senate entitled "An act designating and limiting the funds receivable for the revenues of the United States" came to my hands yesterday at 2 o'clock p. m. On perusing it I found its provisions so complex and uncertain that I deemed it necessary to obtain the opinion of the Attorney-General of the United States on several important questions touching its construction and effect before I could decide on the disposition to be made of it. The Attorney-General took up the subject immediately, and his reply was reported to me this day at 5 o'clock p. m., and is hereunto annexed. As this officer, after a careful and laborious examination of the bill and a distinct expression of his opinion on the points proposed to him still came to the conclusion that the construction of the bill, should it become a law, would yet be a subject of much perplexity and doubt (a view of the bill entirely coincident with my own), and as I can not think it proper, in a matter of such vital interest and of such constant application, to approve a bill so liable to diversity of interpretations, and more especially as I have not had time, amid the duties

* Pocket veto. This message was never sent to Congress, but was deposited in the Department of State.

constantly pressing on me, to give the subject that deliberate consideration which its importance demands, I am constrained to retain the bill,
without acting definitively thereon; and to the end that my reasons for
this step may be fully understood I shall cause this paper, with the opinion of the Attorney-General and the bill in question, to be deposited in
the Department of State.

ANDREW JACKSON.

ATTORNEY-GENERAL'S OFFICE, *March 3, 1837.*

The PRESIDENT OF THE UNITED STATES.

SIR: I have had the honor to receive the several questions proposed to me by
you on the bill which has just passed the two Houses of Congress, entitled "An
act designating and limiting the funds receivable for the revenues of the United
States," and which is now before you for consideration. These questions may be
arranged under three general heads, and in that order I shall proceed to reply to
them.

I. Will the proposed bill, if approved, repeal or alter the laws now in force designating the currency required to be received in payment of the public dues, for lands
or otherwise?

Will it compel the Treasury officers to receive the notes of specie-paying banks
having the characteristics described in its first and second sections?

In what respect does it differ from and how far will it change the joint resolution
of April 30, 1816?

Answer. In order to a correct reply to this question, and indeed to any other
question arising on this obscurely penned bill, we must first obtain a general view
of all its provisions.

The first section requires the Secretary of the Treasury to take measures for collecting the public revenue, first, in the legal currency of the United States (i. e.,
gold and silver), or, second, in the notes of such specie-paying banks as shall from
time to time conform to certain conditions in regard to small bills, described in the
section. This section does not expressly give the Secretary power to direct that any
particular notes *shall* be received for lands or for duties, but it *forbids* the receipt
of any paper currency other than such bank notes as are described in the section;
and it requires the Secretary to adopt measures, in his discretion, to effectuate that
prohibition.

The second section extends the prohibition still further, by forbidding the receipt
of any notes which the banks in which they are to be deposited shall not, under the
supervision and control of the Secretary of the Treasury, agree to pass to the credit
of the United States as *cash;* to which is added a proviso authorizing the Secretary
to withdraw the public deposits from any bank which shall refuse to receive as cash
from the United States any notes receivable under the law which such bank receives
in the ordinary course of business on general deposit.

The third and last section allows the receipt, as heretofore, of land scrip and
Treasury certificates for public lands, and forbids the Secretary of the Treasury to
make any discrimination in the funds receivable (other than such as results from
the receipt of land scrip or Treasury certificates) between the different branches
of the public revenue.

From this analysis of the bill it appears that, so far as regards bank notes, the bill
designates and limits their receivableness for the revenues of the United States, first,
by forbidding the receipts of any except such as have all the characteristics described
in the first and second sections of the bill, and, secondly, by restraining the Secretary

of the Treasury from making any discrimination in this respect between the different branches of the public revenue. In this way the bill performs, to a certain extent, the office of "designating and limiting the funds receivable for the revenues of the United States," as mentioned in its title; but it would seem from what has been stated that it is only in this way that any such office is performed. This impression will be fully confirmed as we proceed.

The bill, should it be approved, will be supplementary to the laws now in force relating to the same subject, but as it contains no repealing clause no provision of those former laws, except such as may be plainly repugnant to the present bill, will be repealed by it.

The existing laws embraced in the above question, and applicable to the subject, are:

First. As to duties on goods imported.—The seventy-fourth section of the collection law of the 2d of March, 1799, the first of which, reenacting in this respect the act of the 31st of July, 1789, provides "that all duties and fees to be collected shall be *payable in money of the United States or in foreign gold and silver coins* at the following rates," etc. The residue of the section, as to rates, has been altered by subsequent laws, and the clause quoted was varied during the existence of the Bank of the United States, the notes of which were expressly made receivable in all payments to the United States, and during the existence of the act making Treasury notes receivable by such act; but in no other respects has it ever been repealed.

Second. As to public lands.—The general land law of the 10th of May, 1800, section 5, provided that no lands should be sold, "at either public or private sale, for less than $2 per acre, and payment may be made for the same by all purchasers *either in specie or in evidences of the public debt of the United States*, at the rates prescribed" by a prior law. This provision was varied by the acts relative to Treasury notes and the Bank of the United States in like manner as above mentioned. The second section of the general land law of the 24th of April, 1820, abrogated the allowance of credits on the sale of public lands after the 1st day of July then next; required every purchaser at public sale to make complete payment on the day of purchase, and the purchaser at private sale to produce to the register a receipt from the Treasurer of the United States or from the receiver of the district for the amount of the purchase money. The proviso to the fourth section of the same law enacted, in respect to reverted lands and lands remaining unsold, that they should not be sold for less price than $1.25 per acre, "nor on any other terms than that of *cash* payment." This latter act has been further modified by the allowing Virginia land scrip to be received in payment for public lands.

Third. As to both duties and lands.—The joint resolution of the 30th of April, 1816, provides that the Secretary of the Treasury "be required and directed to adopt such measures as he may deem necessary to cause, as soon as may be, all duties, taxes, debts, or sums of money accruing or becoming payable to the United States to be collected and paid in the legal currency of the United States, or Treasury notes, or notes of the Bank of the United States, *as by law provided and declared*, or in notes of banks which are payable and paid on demand in the said legal currency of the United States, and that from and after the 20th day of February next no such duties, taxes, debts, or sums of money accruing or becoming payable to the United States as aforesaid ought to be collected or received otherwise than in the legal currency of the United States, or Treasury notes, or notes of the Bank of the United States, or in notes of banks which are payable and paid on demand in the legal currency of the United States." According to the opinion given by me as a member of your Cabinet in the month of July last, and to which I still adhere, this resolution was mandatory only as it respected the legal currency of the United States, Treasury notes, and notes of the Bank of the United States, and in respect to the notes of the

State banks, though payable and paid in specie, was permissive merely in the discretion of the Secretary; and in accordance with this opinion has been the practical construction given to the resolution by the Treasury Department. It is known to you, however, that distinguished names have been vouched for the opinion that the resolution was mandatory as to the notes of all specie-paying banks; that the debtor had the right, at his option, to make payment in such notes, and that if tendered by him the Treasury officers had no discretion to refuse them.

It is thus seen that the laws now in force, so far as they *positively enjoin* the receipt of any particular currency in payment of public dues, are confined to gold and silver, except that in certain cases Virginia land scrip and Treasury certificates are directed to be received on the sale of public lands. In my opinion, there is nothing in the bill before me repugnant to those laws. The bill does not *expressly* declare and enact that any particular species of currency *shall be receivable* in payment of the public revenue. On the contrary, as the provisions of the first and second sections are chiefly of a *negative* character, I think they do not take away the power of the Secretary, previously possessed under the acts of Congress, and as the agent of the President, to *forbid* the receipt of any bank notes which are not by some act of Congress expressly made absolutely receivable in payment of the public dues.

The above view will, I think, be confirmed by a closer examination of the bill. It sets out with the assumption that there is a currency established by law (i. e., gold and silver); and it further assumes that the public revenue of all descriptions ought to be collected exclusively in such legal currency, or in bank notes of a certain character; and therefore it provides that the Secretary of the Treasury *shall* take measures to effect a collection of the revenue "in the legal currency of the United States, *or* in notes of banks which are payable and paid on demand in the said legal currency," under certain restrictions, afterwards mentioned in the act.

The question then arises: Are bank notes having the requisite characteristics placed by the clause just quoted on the same footing with the legal currency, so as to make it the duty of the Secretary of the Treasury to allow the receipt of them when tendered by the debtor? In my judgment, such is not the effect of the provision.

If Congress had intended to make so important an alteration of the existing law as to compel the receiving officers to take payment in the bank notes described in the bill, the natural phraseology would have been, "in the legal currency of the United States *and* in notes of banks which are payable and paid in the legal currency," etc. And it is reasonable to presume that Congress would have used such phraseology, or would have gone on to make a distinct provision expressly declaring that such bank notes *should be receivable*, as was done in the bank charters of 1790 and 1816, and as was also done by the acts relative to evidences of debt, Treasury notes, and Virginia land scrip. The form of one of these provisions (the fourteenth section of the act incorporating the late Bank of the United States) will illustrate the idea I desire to present:

"SEC. 14. *And be it further enacted*, That the bills or notes of the said corporation, originally made payable, or which shall have become payable, on demand, *shall be receivable* in all payments to the United States, unless otherwise directed by act of Congress."

The difference between the language there used and that employed in the present bill is too obvious to require comment. It is true that the word "or," when it occurs in wills and agreements, is sometimes construed to mean "and," in order to give effect to the plain intent of the parties; and such a construction of the word may sometimes be given when it occurs in statutes, where the general intent of the lawmakers evidently requires it. But this construction of the word in the present case is not only unnecessary, but, in my opinion, repugnant to the whole scope of the bill, which, so far from commanding the public officers to receive bank notes in cases not required by the existing laws, introduces several new prohibitions on the receipt of such notes.

Nor do I think this one of those cases in which a choice is given to the debtor to pay in one or other of two descriptions of currency, both of which are receivable by law. Such a choice was given by the land law of the 10th of May, 1800, section 5, between specie and the evidences of the public debt of the United States then receivable by law, and also by the joint resolution of the 30th of April, 1816, between "the legal currency of the United States, or Treasury notes, or notes of the Bank of the United States, as by law provided and declared." The option given by that resolution continued in force so long as the laws providing and declaring that Treasury notes and notes of the Bank of the United States should be receivable in payments to the United States, and ceased when those laws expired. The distinction between that description of paper currency which is by law expressly made receivable in payment of public dues, and the notes of the State banks, which were only *permitted* to be received, is plainly marked in the resolution of 1816. While the former are placed on the same footing with the legal currency, because by previous laws it had been so "*provided and declared*," the latter were left to be received or not received, at the discretion of the Secretary of the Treasury, except that he was restricted from allowing any to be received which were not payable and paid on demand in the legal currency. The bank notes spoken of in the bill before me, having never been made receivable by law, must be regarded as belonging to the latter class, and not to the former; and there can therefore be no greater obligation under the present bill, should it become a law, to receive them in payment than there was to receive the paper of the State banks under the resolution of 1816.

As to the difference between this bill and the joint resolution of 1816, the bill differs from that resolution in the following particulars:

First. It says nothing of Treasury notes and the notes of the Bank of the United States, which by the resolution of 1816 are recognized as having been made receivable by laws then in force in payment of public dues of all descriptions.

Second. It abridges the discretion left with the Secretary of the Treasury by that resolution, by positively forbidding the receipt of bank notes not having the characteristics described in the first and second sections of the bill; whereas the receipt of some of the notes so forbidden might, under the resolution of 1816, have been allowed by the Secretary.

Third. It forbids the making of any discrimination in respect to the receipt of bank notes between the different branches of the public revenue; whereas the Secretary of the Treasury, under the resolution of 1816, was subject to no such restraint, and had the power to make the discrimination forbidden by the bill, except as to the notes of the Bank of the United States and Treasury notes.

This bill, if approved, will change the resolution of 1816, so far as it now remains in force, in the second and third particulars just mentioned, but in my opinion, as already suggested, will change it in no other respect.

II. What is the extent of the supervision and control allowed by this bill to the Secretary of the Treasury over the notes to be received by the deposit banks?

And does it allow him to direct what particular notes shall or shall not be received for lands or for duties?

Answer. After maturely considering, so far as time has been allowed me, the several provisions of the bill, I think the following conclusions may fairly be drawn from them when taken in connection with the laws now in force, and above referred to, and that should it become a law they will probably express its legal effect.

First. That the Secretary of the Treasury *can not direct* the receipt of any notes except such as are issued by banks which conform to the first section of the law and such as will be passed by the proper deposit bank to the credit of the United States as *cash.*

Second. That he *may direct* the receipt of notes issued by banks which conform to the first section, provided the deposit bank in which the notes are to be deposited shall agree to credit them as cash.

Third. That if the deposit bank in which the money is to be deposited shall refuse to receive as cash the notes designated by the Secretary, and which such bank receives in the ordinary course of business on general deposit, he may withdraw the public deposits and select another depository which will agree to receive them.

Fourth. That if he can not find a depository which will so agree, then that the Secretary can not direct or authorize the receipt of any notes except such as the deposit bank primarily entitled to the deposits will agree to receive and deposit as cash.

Fifth. That although a deposit bank might be willing to receive from the collectors and receivers, and to credit as *cash*, notes of certain banks which conform to the first section, yet, for the reasons before stated, I am of opinion that the Secretary is not *obliged* to allow the receipt of such notes.

Sixth. The Secretary is forbidden to make any discrimination in the *funds receivable* "between the different branches of the public revenue," and therefore, though he may forbid the receipt of the notes of any particular bank or class of banks not excluded by the bill, and may forbid the receipt of notes of denominations larger than those named in the bill, yet when he issues any such prohibition it must apply to *all* the branches of the public revenue.

Seventh. If I am right in the foregoing propositions, the result will be that the proposed law will leave in the Secretary of the Treasury power to *prohibit* the receipt of particular notes *provided his prohibition apply to both lands and duties*, and power to *direct* what particular notes allowed by the law shall be received *provided he can find a deposit bank which will agree to receive and* [*credit*] *them as cash.*

III. Are the deposit banks the sole judges under this bill of what notes they will receive, or are they bound to receive the notes of every specie-paying bank, chartered or unchartered, wherever situated, in any part of the United States?

Answer. In my opinion the deposit banks, under the bill in question, will be the sole judges of the notes to be received by them from any collector or receiver of public money, and they will not be bound to receive the notes of any other bank whose notes they may choose to reject, provided they apply the same rule to the United States which they apply to their own depositors. In other words, the general rule as to what notes are to be received as cash, prescribed by each deposit bank for the regulation of its ordinary business, must be complied with by the collectors and receivers whose moneys are to be deposited with that bank. But it will not therefore follow that those officers will be bound to receive what the bank generally receives, because, as already stated, they may refuse of their own accord, or under the direction of the Secretary of the Treasury, any bank notes not expressly directed by act of Congress to be received in payment of the public dues.

I have thus answered the several questions proposed on the bill before me; and though I have been necessarily obliged to examine the subject with much haste, I have no other doubts as to the soundness of the construction above given than such as belong to discussions of this nature and to a proper sense of the fallibility of human judgment. It is, however, my duty to remind you that very different opinions were expressed in the course of the debates on the proposed law by some of the members who took part therein. It would seem from these debates that the bill, in some instances at least, was supported under the impression that it would compel the Treasury officers to receive all bank notes possessing all the characteristics described in the first and second sections, and that the Secretary of the Treasury would have no power to forbid their receipt. It must be confessed that the language is sufficiently ambiguous to give some plausibility to such a construction, and that it seems to derive some support from the refusal of the House of Representatives to consider an amendment reported by the Committee of Ways and Means of that

House, which would substantially have given the bill, in explicit terms, the interpretation I have put on it, and have removed the uncertainty which now pervades it. Under these circumstances it may reasonably be expected that the true meaning of the bill, should it be passed into a law, will become a subject of discussion and controversy, and probably remain involved in much perplexity and doubt until it shall have been settled by a judicial decision. How far these latter considerations are to be regarded by you in your decision on the bill is a question which belongs to another place, and on which, therefore, I forbear to enlarge in this communication.

I have the honor to be, sir, with high respect, your obedient servant,

B. F. BUTLER.

AN ACT designating and limiting the funds receivable for the revenues of the United States.

Be it enacted by the Senate and House of Representatives of the United States of America in Congress assembled, That the Secretary of the Treasury be, and hereby is, required to adopt such measures as he may deem necessary to effect a collection of the public revenue of the United States, whether arising from duties, taxes, debts, or sales of lands, in the manner and on the principles herein provided; that is, that no such duties, taxes, debts, or sums of money, payable for lands, shall be collected or received otherwise than in the legal currency of the United States, or in notes of banks which are payable and paid on demand in the said legal currency of the United States under the following restrictions and conditions in regard to such notes, to wit: From and after the passage of this act the notes of no bank which shall issue or circulate bills or notes of a less denomination than five dollars shall be received on account of the public dues; and from and after the thirtieth day of December, eighteen hundred and thirty-nine, the notes of no bank which shall issue or circulate bills or notes of a less denomination than ten dollars shall be so receivable; and from and after the thirtieth day of December, one thousand eight hundred and forty-one, the like prohibition shall be extended to the notes of all banks issuing bills or notes of a less denomination than twenty dollars.

SEC. 2. *And be it further enacted,* That no notes shall be received by the collectors or receivers of the public money which the banks in which they are to be deposited shall not, under the supervision and control of the Secretary of the Treasury, agree to pass to the credit of the United States as cash: *Provided,* That if any deposit bank shall refuse to receive and pass to the credit of the United States as cash any notes receivable under the provisions of this act, which said bank, in the ordinary course of business, receives on general deposit, the Secretary of the Treasury is hereby authorized to withdraw the public deposits from said bank.

SEC. 3. *And be it further enacted,* That this act shall not be so construed as to prohibit receivers or collectors of the dues of the Government from receiving for the public lands any kind of land scrip or Treasury certificates now authorized by law, but the same shall hereafter be received for the public lands in the same way and manner as has heretofore been practiced; and it shall not be lawful for the Secretary of the Treasury to make any discrimination in the funds receivable between the different branches of the public revenue, except as is provided in this section.

JAMES K. POLK,
Speaker of the House of Representatives.

W. R. KING,
President of the Senate pro tempore.

I certify that this act did originate in the Senate.

ASBURY DICKINS, *Secretary.*

PROCLAMATION.

[From Senate Journal, Twenty-fourth Congress, second session, p. 355.]

DECEMBER 20, 1836.

The President of the United States to ——, *Senator for the State of* ——:

By virtue of the power vested in me by the Constitution, I hereby convene the Senate of the United States to meet in the Senate Chamber on the 4th day of March next, at 10 o'clock in the forenoon, to receive any communication the President of the United States may think it his duty to make.

ANDREW JACKSON.

EXECUTIVE ORDERS.

WAR DEPARTMENT, *February 15, 1837.*

Major-General ALEXANDER MACOMB,
    President of the Court of Inquiry, etc.

SIR: I have the honor to inclose a copy of the opinion of the President of the United States on the proceedings of the court of inquiry of which you are president, relative to the campaign against the Creek Indians, and, in compliance with the direction at the close thereof, to transmit herewith those proceedings, with the documentary evidence referred to therein, for the further action of the court.

Very respectfully, your most obedient servant,

B. F. BUTLER,
Secretary of War ad interim.

P. S.—The proceedings and a portion of the documents accompany this. The balance of the documents (except Nos. 204 and 209, which will be sent to-morrow) are in a separate package, and sent by the same mail.

WASHINGTON, *February 14, 1837.*

The President has carefully examined the proceedings of the court of inquiry recently held at the city of Frederick, by virtue of Orders Nos. 65 and 68, so far as the same relate to the causes of the delay in opening and prosecuting the campaign in Georgia and Alabama against the hostile Creek Indians in the year 1836, and has maturely considered the opinion of the court on this part of the subject referred to it.

The order constituting the court directs it, among other things—

To inquire and examine into the causes of the delay in opening and prosecuting the campaign in Georgia and Alabama against the hostile Creek Indians in the year

1836, and into every subject connected with the military operations in the campaign aforesaid, and, after fully investigating the same, to report the facts, together with its opinion on the whole subject, for the information of the President.

It appears from the proceedings that after the testimony of nine witnesses had been received by the court, and after more than one hundred documents bearing on the subject had also been produced in evidence, and after Major-General Scott had addressed the court on the subject, the court proceeded to pronounce its opinion, as follows:

Upon a careful examination of the abundant testimony taken in the foregoing case the court is of opinion that no delay which it was practicable to have avoided was made by Major-General Scott in opening the campaign against the Creek Indians. On the contrary, it appears that he took the earliest measures to provide arms, munitions, and provisions for his forces, who were found almost wholly destitute; and as soon as arms could be put into the hands of the volunteers they were, in succession, detached and placed in position to prevent the enemy from retiring upon Florida, and whence they could move against the main body of the enemy as soon as equipped for offensive operations.

From the testimony of the governor of Georgia, of Major-General Sanford, commander of the Georgia volunteers, and many other witnesses of high rank and standing who were acquainted with the topography of the country and the position and strength of the enemy, the court is of opinion that the plan of campaign adopted by Major-General Scott was well calculated to lead to successful results, and that it was prosecuted by him, as far as practicable, with zeal and ability, until recalled from the command upon representations made by Major-General Jesup, his second in command, from Fort Mitchell, in a letter bearing date the 20th of June, 1836, addressed to F. P. Blair, esq., at Washington, marked "private," containing a request that it be shown to the President; which letter was exposed and brought to light by the dignified and magnanimous act of the President in causing it to be placed on file in the Department of War as an official document, and which forms part of the proceedings. (See Document No. 214.) Conduct so extraordinary and inexplicable on the part of Major-General Jesup, in reference to the character of said letter, should, in the opinion of the court, be investigated.

The foregoing opinion is not accompanied by any report of the *facts* in the case, as required by the order constituting the court; on the contrary, the facts are left to be gathered from the mass of oral and documentary evidence contained in the proceedings, and thus a most important part of the duty assigned to the court remains unexecuted. Had the court stated the facts of the case as established to its satisfaction by the evidence before it, the President, on comparing such state of facts found by the court with its opinion, would have distinctly understood the views entertained by the court in respect to the degree of promptitude and energy which ought to be displayed in a campaign against Indians— a point manifestly indispensable to a correct appreciation of the opinion, and one which the President's examination of the evidence has not supplied, inasmuch as he has no means of knowing whether the conclusions drawn by him from the evidence agree with those of the court.

The opinion of the court is also argumentative, and wanting in requisite precision, inasmuch as it states that "no delay *which it was practicable to have avoided was made by Major-General Scott* in opening the campaign against the Creek Indians,'' etc.; thus leaving it to be inferred, but not distinctly finding, that there was some delay, and that it was made by some person other than Major-General Scott, without specifying in what such delay consisted, when it occurred, how long it continued, nor by whom it was occasioned. Had the court found a state of facts, as required by the order constituting it, the uncertainty now existing in this part of the opinion would have been obviated and the justice of the opinion itself readily determined.

That part of the opinion of the court which animadverts on the letter addressed by Major-General Jesup to F. P. Blair, esq., bearing date the 20th of June, 1836, and which presents the same as a subject demanding investigation, appears to the President to be wholly unauthorized by the order constituting the court, and by which its jurisdiction was confined to an inquiry into the causes of the delay in opening and prosecuting the campaign against the hostile Creeks and into such subjects as were connected with the military operations in that campaign. The causes of the recall of Major-General Scott from the command and the propriety or impropriety of the conduct of General Jesup in writing the letter referred to were not submitted to the court as subjects of inquiry. The court itself appears to have been of this opinion, inasmuch as no notice was given to General Jesup of the pendency of the proceedings, nor had he any opportunity to cross-examine and interrogate the witnesses, nor to be heard in respect to his conduct in the matter remarked on by the court.

For the several reasons above assigned, the President disapproves the opinion of the court, and remits to it the proceedings in question, to the end that the court may resume the consideration of the evidence and from the same, and from such further evidence as shall be taken (in case the court shall deem it necessary to take further evidence), may ascertain and report with distinctness and precision, especially as to time, place, distances, and other circumstances, all the facts touching the opening and prosecuting of the campaign in Georgia and Alabama against the hostile Creek Indians in the year 1836, and the military operations in the said campaign, and touching the delay, if any there was, in the opening or prosecuting of said campaign, and the causes of such delay; and to the end, also, that the court, whilst confining its opinion to the subject-matters submitted to it, may fully and distinctly express its opinion on those matters for the information of the President.

The Secretary of War *ad interim* will cause the proceedings of the court on the subject of the campaign against the Creek Indians, with the documentary evidence referred to therein and a copy of the foregoing opinion, to be transmitted to Major-General Alexander Macomb, president of the court, for the proper action thereon.

ANDREW JACKSON.

WASHINGTON, *February 18, 1837.*

The proceedings of the court of inquiry recently assembled and still sitting at Frederick by virtue of Orders Nos. 65 and 68, so far as the same relate to the causes of the failure of the campaign of Major-General Scott against the Seminole Indians in 1836, were heretofore submitted to the President, and the examination thereof suspended in consequence of the necessary connection between the case of Major-General Scott and that of Major-General Gaines, also referred to the same court, and not yet reported on. Certain other proceedings of the same court having been since examined by the President, and having been found defective, and therefore remitted to the court for reconsideration, the President has deemed it proper, in order to expedite the matter, to look into the first-mentioned proceedings for the purpose of ascertaining whether or not the like defects existed therein. On this inspection of the record he perceives that the court has not reported, except in a few instances, the facts of the case, as required by the order constituting the court, and in those instances the facts found by the court are stated in a very general form and without sufficient minuteness and precision; and he therefore remits the said proceedings to the court, to the end that the court may resume the consideration of the evidence, and from the same, and from such further evidence as may be taken (in case the court shall deem it necessary to take further evidence), may ascertain and report with distinctness and precision all the facts touching the subject to be inquired of, established to the satisfaction of the court by the evidence before it, and especially the times when and places where the several occurrences which are deemed material by the court in the formation of its opinion actually took place, with the amount of force on both sides at the different periods of time embraced in the transactions, and the positions thereof, and such other circumstances as are deemed material by the court; together with its opinion on the whole subject, for the information of the President.

The Secretary of War *ad interim* will cause the proceedings of the court in the case of Major-General Scott, first above mentioned, with the documentary evidence referred to therein and a copy hereof, to be transmitted to Major-General Alexander Macomb, president of the court, for the proper action thereon.

ANDREW JACKSON.

FAREWELL ADDRESS.

MARCH 4, 1837.

FELLOW-CITIZENS: Being about to retire finally from public life, I beg leave to offer you my grateful thanks for the many proofs of kindness and confidence which I have received at your hands. It has been my fortune in the discharge of public duties, civil and military, frequently to have found myself in difficult and trying situations, where prompt decision and energetic action were necessary, and where the interest of the country required that high responsibilities should be fearlessly encountered; and it is with the deepest emotions of gratitude that I acknowledge the continued and unbroken confidence with which you have sustained me in every trial. My public life has been a long one, and I can not hope that it has at all times been free from errors; but I have the consolation of knowing that if mistakes have been committed they have not seriously injured the country I so anxiously endeavored to serve, and at the moment when I surrender my last public trust I leave this great people prosperous and happy, in the full enjoyment of liberty and peace, and honored and respected by every nation of the world.

If my humble efforts have in any degree contributed to preserve to you these blessings, I have been more than rewarded by the honors you have heaped upon me, and, above all, by the generous confidence with which you have supported me in every peril, and with which you have continued to animate and cheer my path to the closing hour of my political life. The time has now come when advanced age and a broken frame warn me to retire from public concerns, but the recollection of the many favors you have bestowed upon me is engraven upon my heart, and I have felt that I could not part from your service without making this public acknowledgment of the gratitude I owe you. And if I use the occasion to offer to you the counsels of age and experience, you will, I trust, receive them with the same indulgent kindness which you have so often extended to me, and will at least see in them an earnest desire to perpetuate in this favored land the blessings of liberty and equal law.

We have now lived almost fifty years under the Constitution framed by the sages and patriots of the Revolution. The conflicts in which the nations of Europe were engaged during a great part of this period, the spirit in which they waged war against each other, and our intimate commercial connections with every part of the civilized world rendered it a time of much difficulty for the Government of the United States. We have had our seasons of peace and of war, with all the evils which precede or follow a state of hostility with powerful nations. We encountered these trials with our Constitution yet in its infancy, and under the disadvantages which a new and untried government must always feel when it is called upon to put forth its whole strength without the lights of experience to guide it or the weight of precedents to justify its measures. But we have passed triumphantly through all these difficulties. Our Constitution is no longer a doubtful experiment, and at the end of nearly half a century we find that it has preserved unimpaired the liberties of the people, secured the rights of property, and that our country has improved and is flourishing beyond any former example in the history of nations.

In our domestic concerns there is everything to encourage us, and if you are true to yourselves nothing can impede your march to the highest point of national prosperity. The States which had so long been retarded in their improvement by the Indian tribes residing in the midst of them are at length relieved from the evil, and this unhappy race—the original dwellers in our land—are now placed in a situation where we may well hope that they will share in the blessings of civilization and be saved from that degradation and destruction to which they were rapidly hastening while they remained in the States; and while the safety and comfort of our own citizens have been greatly promoted by their removal, the philanthropist will rejoice that the remnant of that ill-fated race has been at length placed beyond the reach of injury or oppression, and that the paternal care of the General Government will hereafter watch over them and protect them.

If we turn to our relations with foreign powers, we find our condition equally gratifying. Actuated by the sincere desire to do justice to every nation and to preserve the blessings of peace, our intercourse with them has been conducted on the part of this Government in the spirit of frankness; and I take pleasure in saying that it has generally been met in a corresponding temper. Difficulties of old standing have been surmounted by friendly discussion and the mutual desire to be just, and the claims of our citizens, which had been long withheld, have at length been acknowledged and adjusted and satisfactory arrangements made for their final payment; and with a limited, and I trust a temporary, exception, our relations with every foreign power are now of the most friendly character, our commerce continually expanding, and our flag respected in every quarter of the world.

These cheering and grateful prospects and these multiplied favors we owe, under Providence, to the adoption of the Federal Constitution. It is no longer a question whether this great country can remain happily united and flourish under our present form of government. Experience, the unerring test of all human undertakings, has shown the wisdom and foresight of those who formed it, and has proved that in the union of these States there is a sure foundation for the brightest hopes of freedom and for the happiness of the people. At every hazard and by every sacrifice this Union must be preserved.

The necessity of watching with jealous anxiety for the preservation of the Union was earnestly pressed upon his fellow-citizens by the Father of his Country in his Farewell Address. He has there told us that "while experience shall not have demonstrated its impracticability, there will always be reason to distrust the patriotism of those who in any quarter may endeavor to weaken its bands;" and he has cautioned us in the strongest terms against the formation of parties on geographical discriminations, as one of the means which might disturb our Union and to which designing men would be likely to resort.

The lessons contained in this invaluable legacy of Washington to his countrymen should be cherished in the heart of every citizen to the latest generation; and perhaps at no period of time could they be more usefully remembered than at the present moment; for when we look upon the scenes that are passing around us and dwell upon the pages of his parting address, his paternal counsels would seem to be not merely the offspring of wisdom and foresight, but the voice of prophecy, foretelling events and warning us of the evil to come. Forty years have passed since this imperishable document was given to his countrymen. The Federal Constitution was then regarded by him as an experiment—and he so speaks of it in his Address—but an experiment upon the success of which the best hopes of his country depended; and we all know that he was prepared to lay down his life, if necessary, to secure to it a full and a fair trial. The trial has been made. It has succeeded beyond the proudest hopes of those who framed it. Every quarter of this widely extended nation has felt its blessings and shared in the general prosperity produced by its adoption. But amid this general prosperity and splendid success the dangers of which he warned us are becoming every day more evident, and the signs of evil are sufficiently apparent to awaken the deepest anxiety in the bosom of the patriot. We behold systematic efforts publicly made to sow the seeds of discord between different parts of the United States and to place party divisions directly upon geographical distinctions; to excite the *South* against the *North* and the *North* against the *South*, and to force into the controversy the most delicate and exciting topics—topics upon which it is impossible that a large portion of the Union can ever speak without strong emotion. Appeals, too, are constantly made to sectional interests in order to influence the election of the Chief Magistrate, as if it were desired that he should favor a particular quarter of the country instead of fulfilling the duties of his station with impartial justice to all; and the possible dissolution of the Union has at length become an ordinary and familiar subject of discussion. Has the warning voice of Washington been forgotten, or have designs already been formed to sever the Union? Let it not be supposed that I impute to all of those who have taken an active part in these unwise and unprofitable discussions a want of patriotism or of public virtue. The honorable feeling of State pride and local attachments finds a place in the bosoms of the most enlightened and pure. But while such men are conscious of their own integrity and honesty of purpose, they ought never to forget that the citizens of other States are their political brethren, and that however mistaken they may be in their views, the great body of them are equally honest and upright with themselves. Mutual suspicions and reproaches may in time create mutual hostility, and artful and designing men will always be found who are ready to foment these fatal divisions and to inflame the natural jealousies of different sections of the country. The history of the world is full of such examples, and especially the history of republics.

What have you to gain by division and dissension? Delude not yourselves with the belief that a breach once made may be afterwards repaired. If the Union is once severed, the line of separation will grow wider and wider, and the controversies which are now debated and settled in the halls of legislation will then be tried in fields of battle and determined by the sword. Neither should you deceive yourselves with the hope that the first line of separation would be the permanent one, and that nothing but harmony and concord would be found in the new associations formed upon the dissolution of this Union. Local interests would still be found there, and unchastened ambition. And if the recollection of common dangers, in which the people of these United States stood side by side against the common foe, the memory of victories won by their united valor, the prosperity and happiness they have enjoyed under the present Constitution, the proud name they bear as citizens of this great Republic— if all these recollections and proofs of common interest are not strong enough to bind us together as one people, what tie will hold united the new divisions of empire when these bonds have been broken and this Union dissevered? The first line of separation would not last for a single generation; new fragments would be torn off, new leaders would spring up, and this great and glorious Republic would soon be broken into a multitude of petty States, without commerce, without credit, jealous of one another, armed for mutual aggression, loaded with taxes to pay armies and leaders, seeking aid against each other from foreign powers, insulted and trampled upon by the nations of Europe, until, harassed with conflicts and humbled and debased in spirit, they would be ready to submit to the absolute dominion of any military adventurer and to surrender their liberty for the sake of repose. It is impossible to look on the consequences that would inevitably follow the destruction of this Government and not feel indignant when we hear cold calculations about the value of the Union and have so constantly before us a line of conduct so well calculated to weaken its ties.

There is too much at stake to allow pride or passion to influence your decision. Never for a moment believe that the great body of the citizens of any State or States can deliberately intend to do wrong. They may, under the influence of temporary excitement or misguided opinions, commit mistakes; they may be misled for a time by the suggestions of self-interest; but in a community so enlightened and patriotic as the people of the United States argument will soon make them sensible of their errors, and when convinced they will be ready to repair them. If they have no higher or better motives to govern them, they will at least perceive that their own interest requires them to be just to others, as they hope to receive justice at their hands.

But in order to maintain the Union unimpaired it is absolutely necessary that the laws passed by the constituted authorities should be faithfully executed in every part of the country, and that every good citizen should at all times stand ready to put down, with the combined force of the nation, every attempt at unlawful resistance, under whatever pretext it may be made or whatever shape it may assume. Unconstitutional or oppressive laws may no doubt be passed by Congress, either from erroneous views or the want of due consideration; if they are within the reach of judicial authority, the remedy is easy and peaceful; and if, from the character of the law, it is an abuse of power not within the control of the judiciary, then free discussion and calm appeals to reason and to the justice of the people will not fail to redress the wrong. But until the law shall be declared void by the courts or repealed by Congress no individual or combination of individuals can be justified in forcibly resisting its execution. It is impossible that any government can continue to exist upon any other principles. It would cease to be a government and be unworthy of the name if it had not the power to enforce the execution of its own laws within its own sphere of action.

It is true that cases may be imagined disclosing such a settled purpose of usurpation and oppression on the part of the Government as would justify an appeal to arms. These, however, are extreme cases, which we have no reason to apprehend in a government where the power is in the hands of a patriotic people. And no citizen who loves his country would in any case whatever resort to forcible resistance unless he clearly saw that the time had come when a freeman should prefer death to submission; for if such a struggle is once begun, and the citizens of one section of the country arrayed in arms against those of another in doubtful conflict, let the battle result as it may, there will be an end of the Union and with it an end to the hopes of freedom. The victory of the injured would not secure to them the blessings of liberty; it would avenge their wrongs, but they would themselves share in the common ruin.

But the Constitution can not be maintained nor the Union preserved, in opposition to public feeling, by the mere exertion of the coercive powers confided to the General Government. The foundations must be laid in the affections of the people, in the security it gives to life, liberty, character, and property in every quarter of the country, and in the fraternal attachment which the citizens of the several States bear to one another as members of one political family, mutually contributing to promote the happiness of each other. Hence the citizens of every State should studiously avoid everything calculated to wound the sensibility or offend the just pride of the people of other States, and they should frown upon any proceedings within their own borders likely to disturb the tranquillity of their political brethren in other portions of the Union. In a country so extensive as the United States, and with pursuits so varied, the internal regulations of the several States must frequently differ from one another in important particulars, and this difference is unavoidably increased by the varying principles upon which the American colonies were originally planted—principles which had taken deep root in their social relations before the Revolution, and therefore of necessity influencing their policy since they became free and independent States. But each State has the unquestionable right to regulate its own internal concerns according to its own pleasure, and while it does not interfere with the rights of the people of other States or the rights of the Union, every State must be the sole judge of the measures proper to secure the safety of its citizens and promote their happiness; and all efforts on the part of people of other States to cast odium upon their institutions, and all measures calculated to disturb their rights of property or to put in jeopardy their peace and internal tranquillity, are in direct opposition to the spirit in which the Union was formed, and must endanger its safety. Motives of philanthropy may be assigned for this unwarrantable interference, and weak men may persuade themselves for a moment that they are laboring in the cause of humanity and asserting the rights of the human race; but everyone, upon sober reflection, will see that nothing but mischief can come from these improper assaults upon the feelings and rights of others. Rest assured that the men found busy in this work of discord are not worthy of your confidence, and deserve your strongest reprobation.

In the legislation of Congress also, and in every measure of the General Government, justice to every portion of the United States should be faithfully observed. No free government can stand without virtue in the people and a lofty spirit of patriotism, and if the sordid feelings of mere selfishness shall usurp the place which ought to be filled by public spirit, the legislation of Congress will soon be converted into a scramble for personal and sectional advantages. Under our free institutions the citizens of every quarter of our country are capable of attaining a high degree of prosperity and happiness without seeking to profit themselves at the expense of others; and every such attempt must in the end fail to succeed, for the people in every part of the United States are too enlightened not to understand their own rights and interests and to detect and defeat every effort to gain undue advantages over them; and when such designs are discovered it naturally provokes resentments which can not always be easily allayed. Justice—full and ample justice—to every portion of the United States should be the ruling principle of every freeman, and should guide the deliberations of every public body, whether it be State or national.

It is well known that there have always been those amongst us who wish to enlarge the powers of the General Government, and experience would seem to indicate that there is a tendency on the part of this Government to overstep the boundaries marked out for it by the Constitution. Its legitimate authority is abundantly sufficient for all the purposes for which it was created, and its powers being expressly enumerated, there can be no justification for claiming anything beyond them. Every attempt to exercise power beyond these limits should be promptly and firmly opposed, for one evil example will lead to other measures still more mischievous; and if the principle of constructive powers or supposed advantages or temporary circumstances shall ever be permitted to justify the assumption of a power not given by the Constitution, the General Government will before long absorb all the powers of legislation, and you will have in effect but one consolidated government. From the extent of our country, its diversified interests, different pursuits, and different habits, it is too obvious for argument that a single consolidated government would be wholly inadequate to watch over and protect its interests; and every friend of our free institutions should be always prepared to maintain unimpaired and in full vigor the rights and sovereignty of the States and to confine the action of the General Government strictly to the sphere of its appropriate duties.

There is, perhaps, no one of the powers conferred on the Federal Government so liable to abuse as the taxing power. The most productive and convenient sources of revenue were necessarily given to it, that it might be able to perform the important duties imposed upon it; and the taxes which it lays upon commerce being concealed from the real payer in the price of the article, they do not so readily attract the attention of the people as smaller sums demanded from them directly by the taxgatherer. But the tax imposed on goods enhances by so much the price of the commodity to the consumer, and as many of these duties are imposed on articles of necessity which are daily used by the great body of the people, the money raised by these imposts is drawn from their pockets. Congress has no right under the Constitution to take money from the people unless it is required to execute some one of the specific powers intrusted to the Government; and if they raise more than is necessary for such purposes, it is an abuse of the power of taxation, and unjust and oppressive. It may indeed happen that the revenue will sometimes exceed the amount anticipated when the taxes were laid. When, however, this is ascertained, it is easy to reduce them, and in such a case it is unquestionably the duty of the Government to reduce them, for no circumstances can justify it in assuming a power not given to it by the Constitution nor in taking away the money of the people when it is not needed for the legitimate wants of the Government.

Plain as these principles appear to be, you will yet find there is a constant effort to induce the General Government to go beyond the limits of its taxing power and to impose unnecessary burdens upon the people. Many powerful interests are continually at work to procure heavy duties on commerce and to swell the revenue beyond the real necessities of the public service, and the country has already felt the injurious effects of their combined influence. They succeeded in obtaining a tariff of duties bearing most oppressively on the agricultural and laboring classes of society and producing a revenue that could not be usefully employed within the range of the powers conferred upon Congress, and in order to fasten upon the people this unjust and unequal system of taxation extravagant schemes of internal improvement were got up in various quarters to squander the money and to purchase support. Thus one unconstitutional measure was intended to be upheld by another, and the abuse of the power of taxation was to be maintained by usurping the power of expending the money in internal improvements. You can not have forgotten the severe and doubtful struggle through which we passed when the executive department of the Government by its veto endeavored to arrest this prodigal scheme of injustice and to bring back the legislation of Congress to the boundaries prescribed by the Constitution. The good sense and practical judgment of the people when the subject was brought before them sustained the course of the Executive, and this plan of unconstitutional expenditures for the purposes of corrupt influence is, I trust, finally overthrown.

The result of this decision has been felt in the rapid extinguishment of the public debt and the large accumulation of a surplus in the Treasury, notwithstanding the tariff was reduced and is now very far below the amount originally contemplated by its advocates. But, rely upon it, the design to collect an extravagant revenue and to burden you with taxes beyond the economical wants of the Government is not yet abandoned. The various interests which have combined together to impose a heavy tariff and to produce an overflowing Treasury are too strong and have too much at stake to surrender the contest. The corporations and wealthy individuals who are engaged in large manufacturing establishments desire a high tariff to increase their gains. Designing politicians will support it to conciliate their favor and to obtain the means of profuse expenditure for the purpose of purchasing influence in other quarters; and since the people have decided that the Federal Government can not be permitted to employ its income in internal improvements, efforts will be made to seduce and mislead the citizens of the several States by holding out to them the deceitful prospect of benefits to be derived from a surplus revenue collected by the General Government and annually divided among the States; and if, encouraged by these fallacious hopes, the States should disregard the principles of economy which ought to characterize every republican government, and should indulge in lavish expenditures exceeding their resources, they will before long find themselves oppressed with debts which they are unable to pay, and the temptation will become irresistible to support a high tariff in order to obtain a surplus for distribution. Do not allow yourselves, my fellow-citizens, to be misled on this subject. The Federal Government can not collect a surplus for such purposes without violating the principles of the Constitution and assuming powers which have not been granted. It is, moreover, a system of injustice, and if persisted in will inevitably lead to corruption, and must end in ruin. The surplus revenue will be drawn from the pockets of the people—from the farmer, the mechanic, and the laboring classes of society; but who will receive it when distributed among the States, where it is to be disposed of by leading State politicians, who have friends to favor and political partisans to gratify? It will certainly not be returned to those who paid it and who have most need of it and are honestly entitled to it. There is but one safe rule, and that is to confine the General Government rigidly within the sphere of its appropriate duties. It has no power to raise a revenue or impose taxes except for the purposes enumerated in the Constitution, and if its income is found to exceed these wants it should be forthwith reduced and the burden of the people so far lightened.

In reviewing the conflicts which have taken place between different interests in the United States and the policy pursued since the adoption of our present form of Government, we find nothing that has produced such deep-seated evil as the course of legislation in relation to the currency. The Constitution of the United States unquestionably intended to secure to the people a circulating medium of gold and silver. But the establishment of a national bank by Congress, with the privilege of issuing paper money receivable in the payment of the public dues, and the unfortunate course of legislation in the several States upon the same subject, drove from general circulation the constitutional currency and substituted one of paper in its place.

It was not easy for men engaged in the ordinary pursuits of business, whose attention had not been particularly drawn to the subject, to foresee all the consequences of a currency exclusively of paper, and we ought not on that account to be surprised at the facility with which laws were obtained to carry into effect the paper system. Honest and even enlightened men are sometimes misled by the specious and plausible statements of the designing. But experience has now proved the mischiefs and dangers of a paper currency, and it rests with you to determine whether the proper remedy shall be applied.

The paper system being founded on public confidence and having of itself no intrinsic value, it is liable to great and sudden fluctuations, thereby rendering property insecure and the wages of labor unsteady and uncertain. The corporations which create the paper money can not be relied upon to keep the circulating medium uniform in amount. In times of prosperity, when confidence is high, they are tempted by the prospect of gain or by the influence of those who hope to profit by it to extend their issues of paper beyond the bounds of discretion and the reasonable demands of business; and when these issues have been pushed on from day to day, until public confidence is at length shaken, then a reaction takes place, and they immediately withdraw the credits they have given, suddenly curtail their issues, and produce an unexpected and ruinous contraction of the circulating medium, which is felt by the whole community. The banks by this means save themselves, and the mischievous consequences of their imprudence or cupidity are visited upon the public. Nor does the evil stop here. These ebbs and flows in the currency and these indiscreet extensions of credit naturally engender a spirit of speculation injurious to the habits and character of the people. We have already seen its effects in the wild spirit of speculation in the public lands and various kinds of stock which within the last year or two seized upon such a multitude of our citizens and threatened to pervade all classes of society and to withdraw their attention from the sober pursuits of honest industry. It is not by encouraging this spirit that we shall best preserve public virtue and promote the true interests of our country; but if your currency continues as exclusively paper as it now is, it will foster this eager desire to amass wealth without labor; it will multiply the number of dependents on bank accommodations and bank favors; the temptation to obtain money at any sacrifice will become stronger and stronger, and inevitably lead to corruption, which will find its way into your public councils and destroy at no distant day the purity of your Government. Some of the evils which arise from this system of paper press with peculiar hardship upon the class of society least able to bear it. A portion of this currency frequently becomes depreciated or worthless, and all of it is easily counterfeited in such a manner as to require peculiar skill and much experience to distinguish the counterfeit from the genuine note. These frauds are most generally perpetrated in the smaller notes, which are used in the daily transactions of ordinary business, and the losses occasioned by them are commonly thrown upon the laboring classes of society, whose situation and pursuits put it out of their power to guard themselves from these impositions, and whose daily wages are necessary for their subsistence. It is the duty of every government so to regulate its currency as to protect this numerous class, as far as practicable, from the impositions of avarice and fraud. It is more especially the duty of the United States, where the Government is emphatically the Government of the people, and where this respectable portion of our citizens are so proudly distinguished from the laboring classes of all other nations by their independent spirit, their love of liberty, their intelligence, and their high tone of moral character. Their industry in peace is the source of our wealth and their bravery in war has covered us with glory; and the Government of the United States will but ill discharge its duties if it leaves them a prey to such dishonest impositions. Yet it is evident that their interests can not be effectually protected unless silver and gold are restored to circulation.

These views alone of the paper currency are sufficient to call for immediate reform; but there is another consideration which should still more strongly press it upon your attention.

Recent events have proved that the paper-money system of this country may be used as an engine to undermine your free institutions, and that those who desire to engross all power in the hands of the few and to govern by corruption or force are aware of its power and prepared to employ it. Your banks now furnish your only circulating medium, and money is plenty or scarce according to the quantity of notes issued by them. While they have capitals not greatly disproportioned to each other, they are competitors in business, and no one of them can exercise dominion over the rest; and although in the present state of the currency these banks may and do operate injuriously upon the habits of business, the pecuniary concerns, and the moral tone of society, yet, from their number and dispersed situation, they can not combine for the purposes of political influence, and whatever may be the dispositions of some of them their power of mischief must necessarily be confined to a narrow space and felt only in their immediate neighborhoods.

But when the charter for the Bank of the United States was obtained from Congress it perfected the schemes of the paper system and gave to its advocates the position they have struggled to obtain from the commencement of the Federal Government to the present hour. The immense capital and peculiar privileges bestowed upon it enabled it to exercise despotic sway over the other banks in every part of the country. From its superior strength it could seriously injure, if not destroy, the business of any one of them which might incur its resentment; and it openly claimed for itself the power of regulating the currency throughout the United States. In other words, it asserted (and it undoubtedly possessed) the power to make money plenty or scarce at its pleasure, at any time and in any quarter of the Union, by controlling the issues of other banks and permitting an expansion or compelling a general contraction of the circulating medium, according to its own will. The other banking institutions were sensible of its strength, and they soon generally became its obedient instruments, ready at all times to execute its mandates; and with the banks necessarily went also that numerous class of persons in our commercial cities who depend altogether on bank credits for their solvency and means of business, and who are therefore obliged, for their own safety, to propitiate the favor of the money power by distinguished zeal and devotion in its service. The result of the ill-advised legislation which established this great monopoly was to concentrate the whole moneyed power of the Union, with its boundless means of corruption and its numerous dependents, under the direction and command of one acknowledged head, thus organizing this particular interest as one body and securing to it unity and concert of action throughout the United States, and enabling it to bring forward upon any occasion its entire and undivided strength to support or defeat any measure of the Government. In the hands of this formidable power, thus perfectly organized, was also placed unlimited dominion over the amount of the circulating medium, giving it the power to regulate the value of property and the fruits of labor in every quarter of the Union, and to bestow prosperity or bring ruin upon any city or section of the country as might best comport with its own interest or policy.

We are not left to conjecture how the moneyed power, thus organized and with such a weapon in its hands, would be likely to use it. The distress and alarm which pervaded and agitated the whole country when the Bank of the United States waged war upon the people in order to compel them to submit to its demands can not yet be forgotten. The ruthless and unsparing temper with which whole cities and communities were oppressed, individuals impoverished and ruined, and a scene of cheerful prosperity suddenly changed into one of gloom and despondency ought to be indelibly impressed on the memory of the people of the United States. If such was its power in a time of peace, what would it not have been in a season of war, with an enemy at your doors? No nation but the freemen of the United States could have come out victorious from such a contest; yet, if you had not conquered, the Government would have passed from the hands of the many to the hands of the few, and this organized money power from its secret conclave would have dictated the choice of your highest officers and compelled you to make peace or war, as best suited their own wishes. The forms of your Government might for a time have remained, but its living spirit would have departed from it.

The distress and sufferings inflicted on the people by the bank are some of the fruits of that system of policy which is continually striving to enlarge the authority of the Federal Government beyond the limits fixed by the Constitution. The powers enumerated in that instrument do not confer on Congress the right to establish such a corporation as the Bank of the United States, and the evil consequences which followed may warn us of the danger of departing from the true rule of construction and of permitting temporary circumstances or the hope of better promoting the public welfare to influence in any degree our decisions upon the extent of the authority of the General Government. Let us abide by the Constitution as it is written, or amend it in the constitutional mode if it is found to be defective.

The severe lessons of experience will, I doubt not, be sufficient to prevent Congress from again chartering such a monopoly, even if the Constitution did not present an insuperable objection to it. But you must remember, my fellow-citizens, that eternal vigilance by the people is the price of liberty, and that you must pay the price if you wish to secure the blessing. It behooves you, therefore, to be watchful in your States as well as in the Federal Government. The power which the moneyed interest can exercise, when concentrated under a single head and with our present system of currency, was sufficiently demonstrated in the struggle made by the Bank of the United States. Defeated in the General Government, the same class of intriguers and politicians will now resort to the States and endeavor to obtain there the same organization which they failed to perpetuate in the Union; and with specious and deceitful plans of public advantages and State interests and State pride they will endeavor to establish in the different States one moneyed institution with overgrown capital and exclusive privileges sufficient to enable it to control the operations of the other banks. Such an institution will be pregnant with the same evils produced by the Bank of the United States, although its sphere of action is more confined, and in the State in which it is chartered the money power will be able to embody its whole strength and to move together with undivided force to accomplish any object it may wish to attain. You have already had abundant evidence of its power to inflict injury upon the agricultural, mechanical, and laboring classes of society, and over those whose engagements in trade or speculation render them dependent on bank facilities the dominion of the State monopoly will be absolute and their obedience unlimited. With such a bank and a paper currency the money power would in a few years govern the State and control its measures, and if a sufficient number of States can be induced to create such establishments the time will soon come when it will again take the field against the United States and succeed in perfecting and perpetuating its organization by a charter from Congress.

It is one of the serious evils of our present system of banking that it enables one class of society—and that by no means a numerous one—by its control over the currency, to act injuriously upon the interests of all the others and to exercise more than its just proportion of influence in political affairs. The agricultural, the mechanical, and the laboring classes have little or no share in the direction of the great moneyed corporations, and from their habits and the nature of their pursuits they are incapable of forming extensive combinations to act together with united force. Such concert of action may sometimes be produced in a single city or in a small district of country by means of personal communications with each other, but they have no regular or active correspondence with those who are engaged in similar pursuits in distant places; they have but little patronage to give to the press, and exercise but a small share of influence over it; they have no crowd of dependents about them who hope to grow rich without labor by their countenance and favor, and who are therefore always ready to execute their wishes. The planter, the farmer, the mechanic, and the laborer all know that their success depends upon their own industry and economy, and that they must not expect to become suddenly rich by the fruits of their toil. Yet these classes of society form the great body of the people of the United States; they are the bone and sinew of the country—men who love liberty and desire nothing but equal rights and equal laws, and who, moreover, hold the great mass of our national wealth, although it is distributed in moderate amounts among the millions of freemen who possess it. But with overwhelming numbers and wealth on their side they are in constant danger of losing their fair influence in the Government, and with difficulty maintain their just rights against the incessant efforts daily made to encroach upon them. The mischief springs from the power which the moneyed interest derives from a paper currency which they are able to control, from the multitude of corporations with exclusive privileges which they have succeeded in obtaining in the different States, and which are employed altogether for their benefit; and unless you become more watchful in your States and check this spirit of monopoly and thirst for exclusive privileges you will in the end find that the most important powers of Government have been given or bartered away, and the control over your dearest interests has passed into the hands of these corporations.

The paper-money system and its natural associations—monopoly and exclusive privileges—have already struck their roots too deep in the soil, and it will require all your efforts to check its further growth and to eradicate the evil. The men who profit by the abuses and desire to perpetuate them will continue to besiege the halls of legislation in the General Government as well as in the States, and will seek by every artifice to mislead and deceive the public servants. It is to yourselves that you must look for safety and the means of guarding and perpetuating your free institutions. In your hands is rightfully placed the sovereignty of the country, and to you everyone placed in authority is ultimately responsible. It is always in your power to see that the wishes of the people are carried into faithful execution, and their will, when once made known, must sooner or later be obeyed; and while the people remain, as I trust they ever will, uncorrupted and incorruptible, and continue watchful and jealous of their rights, the Government is safe, and the cause of freedom will continue to triumph over all its enemies.

But it will require steady and persevering exertions on your part to rid yourselves of the iniquities and mischiefs of the paper system and to check the spirit of monopoly and other abuses which have sprung up with it, and of which it is the main support. So many interests are united to resist all reform on this subject that you must not hope the conflict will be a short one nor success easy. My humble efforts have not been spared during my administration of the Government to restore the constitutional currency of gold and silver, and something, I trust, has been done toward the accomplishment of this most desirable object; but enough yet remains to require all your energy and perseverance. The power, however, is in your hands, and the remedy must and will be applied if you determine upon it.

While I am thus endeavoring to press upon your attention the principles which I deem of vital importance in the domestic concerns of the country, I ought not to pass over without notice the important considerations which should govern your policy toward foreign powers. It is unquestionably our true interest to cultivate the most friendly understanding with every nation and to avoid by every honorable means the calamities of war, and we shall best attain this object by frankness and sincerity in our foreign intercourse, by the prompt and faithful execution of treaties, and by justice and impartiality in our conduct to all. But no nation, however desirous of peace, can hope to escape occasional collisions with other powers, and the soundest dictates of policy require that we should place ourselves in a condition to assert our rights if a resort to force should ever become necessary. Our local situation, our long line of seacoast, indented by numerous bays, with deep rivers opening into the interior, as well as our extended and still increasing commerce, point to the Navy as our natural means of defense. It will in the end be found to be the cheapest and most effectual, and now is the time, in a season of peace and with an overflowing revenue, that we can year after year add to its strength without increasing the burdens of the people. It is your true policy, for your Navy will not only protect your rich and flourishing commerce in distant seas, but will enable you to reach and annoy the enemy and will give to defense its greatest efficiency by meeting danger at a distance from home. It is impossible by any line of fortifications to guard every point from attack against a hostile force advancing from the ocean and selecting its object, but they are indispensable to protect cities from bombardment, dockyards and naval arsenals from destruction, to give shelter to merchant vessels in time of war and to single ships or weaker squadrons when pressed by superior force. Fortifications of this description can not be too soon completed and armed and placed in a condition of the most perfect preparation. The abundant means we now possess can not be applied in any manner more useful to the country, and when this is done and our naval force sufficiently strengthened and our militia armed we need not fear that any nation will wantonly insult us or needlessly provoke hostilities. We shall more certainly preserve peace when it is well understood that we are prepared for war.

In presenting to you, my fellow-citizens, these parting counsels, I have brought before you the leading principles upon which I endeavored to administer the Government in the high office with which you twice honored me. Knowing that the path of freedom is continually beset by enemies who often assume the disguise of friends, I have devoted the last hours of my public life to warn you of the dangers. The progress of the United States under our free and happy institutions has surpassed the most sanguine hopes of the founders of the Republic. Our growth has been rapid beyond all former example in numbers, in wealth, in knowledge, and all the useful arts which contribute to the comforts and convenience of man, and from the earliest ages of history to the present day there never have been thirteen millions of people associated in one political body who enjoyed so much freedom and happiness as the people of these United States. You have no longer any cause to fear danger from abroad; your strength and power are well known throughout the civilized world, as well as the high and gallant bearing of your sons. It is from within, among yourselves—from cupidity, from corruption, from disappointed ambition and inordinate thirst for power—that factions will be formed and liberty endangered. It is against such designs, whatever disguise the actors may assume, that you have especially to guard yourselves. You have the highest of human trusts committed to your care. Providence has showered on this favored land blessings without number, and has chosen you as the guardians of freedom, to preserve it for the benefit of the human race. May He who holds in His hands the destinies of nations make you worthy of the favors He has bestowed and enable you, with pure hearts and pure hands and sleepless vigilance, to guard and defend to the end of time the great charge He has committed to your keeping.

My own race is nearly run; advanced age and failing health warn me that before long I must pass beyond the reach of human events and cease to feel the vicissitudes of human affairs. I thank God that my life has been spent in a land of liberty and that He has given me a heart to love my country with the affection of a son. And filled with gratitude for your constant and unwavering kindness, I bid you a last and affectionate farewell.

ANDREW JACKSON.

Martin Van Buren

March 4, 1837, to March 4, 1841

HOME AT KINDERHOOK, NEW YORK, OF

MARTIN VAN BUREN

With official portrait engraved from copy of original in steel

VAN BUREN.

Martin Van Buren

MARTIN VAN BUREN was born in Kinderhook, Columbia County, N. Y., December 5, 1782. He was the eldest son of Abraham Van Buren, a small farmer, and of Mary Hoes (originally spelled Goes), whose first husband was named Van Alen. He studied the rudiments of English and Latin in the schools of his native village. At the age of 14 years commenced reading law in the office of Francis Sylvester, and pursued his legal novitiate for seven years. Combining with his professional studies a fondness for extemporaneous debate, he was early noted for his intelligent observation of public events and for his interest in politics; was chosen to participate in a nominating convention when only 18 years old. In 1802 went to New York City and studied law with William P. Van Ness, a friend of Aaron Burr; was admitted to the bar in 1803, returned to Kinderhook, and associated himself in practice with his half-brother, James I. Van Alen. He was a zealous adherent of Jefferson, and supported Morgan Lewis for governor of New York in 1803 against Aaron Burr. In February, 1807, he married Hannah Hoes, a distant kinswoman. In the winter of 1806–7 removed to Hudson, the county seat of Columbia County, and in the same year was admitted to practice in the supreme court. In 1807 supported Daniel D. Tompkins for governor against Morgan Lewis, the latter having come to be considered less true than the former to the measures of Jefferson. In 1808 became surrogate of Columbia County, displacing his half-brother and partner, who belonged to the defeated faction. In 1813, on a change of party predominance at Albany, his half-brother was restored to the office. Early in 1811 he figured in the councils of his party at a convention held in Albany, when the proposed recharter of the United States Bank was the leading question of Federal politics. Though Albert Gallatin, Secretary of the Treasury, had recommended a recharter, the predominant sentiment of the Republican party was adverse to the measure. Van Buren shared in this hostility, and publicly lauded the "Spartan firmness" of George Clinton when as Vice-President he gave his casting vote in the United States Senate against the bank bill, February 20, 1811. In 1812 was elected to the senate of New York from the middle district as a Clinton Republican, defeating Edward P. Livingston; took his seat in November of that year, and became thereby a member of the court of errors, then composed of senators in connection with the chancellor and the supreme court. As senator he strenuously opposed the charter of "The Bank of America," which was then seeking to establish itself in New York and to take the place of the United States Bank. Though counted among the adherents of Madison's Administration, and though committed to the policy of declaring war against Great Britain, he sided with the Republican members of the New York legislature in 1812, and supported De Witt Clinton for the Presidency. In the following year, however, he dissolved his political relations with Clinton and resumed the *entente cordiale* with Madison's Administration. In 1815, while still a member of the senate, was appointed attorney-general of the State, superseding the venerable Abraham Van Vechten. In 1816 was reelected to the State senate, and, removing to Albany, formed a partnership with his life-long friend, Benjamin F. Butler. In the same year was appointed a regent of the University of New York. Supported De Witt Clinton for governor of New York in 1817, but opposed his reelection in 1820. In 1819 was removed from the office of attorney-general. February 6, 1821, was elected United States Senator. In the same year was chosen from Otsego County as a member of the convention to revise the constitution of the State. Took his seat in the United States Senate December 3, 1821, and was at once made a member of its Committees on the Judiciary and Finance. For many years was chairman of the former. Supported William H. Crawford for the Presidency in 1824. Was reelected to the Senate in 1827, but soon resigned his seat to accept the office of governor of New York, to which he was elected in 1828. Was a zealous supporter of Andrew Jackson in the Presidential election of 1828, and in 1829 became premier of the new Administration. As Secretary of State he brought to a favorable close the long-standing feud between the United States and England with regard to the West India trade. Resigned his Secretaryship in June, 1831, and was sent as minister to England. The Senate refused in 1832 to confirm his nomination by the casting vote of John C. Calhoun, the Vice-President. In 1832 was elected Vice-President of the United States, and in 1833 came to preside over the body which a year before had rejected him as a foreign minister. On May 20, 1835, was formally nominated for the Presidency, and was elected in 1836 over his three competitors, William H. Harrison, Hugh L. White, and Daniel Webster, by a majority of 57 in the electoral college, but of only 25,000 in the popular vote. On May 5, 1840, was nominated for the Presidency by the Democratic national convention at Baltimore, Md. At the election on November 10 was defeated by William Henry Harrison, who received 234 electoral votes and a popular majority of nearly 140,000. Van Buren received but 60 votes in the electoral college. Retired to his country seat, Lindenwald, in his native county. Was a candidate for the Presidential nomination at the Democratic national convention at Baltimore, Md., May 27, 1844, but was defeated by James K. Polk. Was nominated for the Presidency by a Barnburner convention at Utica, N. Y., June

22, 1848, a nomination which he had declined by letter in advance. He was also nominated for the Presidency by the Free Soil national convention of Buffalo, August 9, 1848. At the election, November 7, received only a popular vote of 291,263, and no electoral vote. Supported Franklin Pierce for the Presidency in 1852 and James Buchanan in 1856. In 1860 voted the fusion ticket of Breckinridge, Douglas, and Bell in New York against Mr. Lincoln, but when the civil war began gave to the Administration his zealous support. Died at Kinderhook July 24, 1862, and was buried there.

INAUGURAL ADDRESS.

FELLOW-CITIZENS: The practice of all my predecessors imposes on me an obligation I cheerfully fulfill—to accompany the first and solemn act of my public trust with an avowal of the principles that will guide me in performing it and an expression of my feelings on assuming a charge so responsible and vast. In imitating their example I tread in the footsteps of illustrious men, whose superiors it is our happiness to believe are not found on the executive calendar of any country. Among them we recognize the earliest and firmest pillars of the Republic—those by whom our national independence was first declared, him who above all others contributed to establish it on the field of battle, and those whose expanded intellect and patriotism constructed, improved, and perfected the inestimable institutions under which we live. If such men in the position I now occupy felt themselves overwhelmed by a sense of gratitude for this the highest of all marks of their country's confidence, and by a consciousness of their inability adequately to discharge the duties of an office so difficult and exalted, how much more must these considerations affect one who can rely on no such claims for favor or forbearance! Unlike all who have preceded me, the Revolution that gave us existence as one people was achieved at the period of my birth; and whilst I contemplate with grateful reverence that memorable event, I feel that I belong to a later age and that I may not expect my countrymen to weigh my actions with the same kind and partial hand.

So sensibly, fellow-citizens, do these circumstances press themselves upon me that I should not dare to enter upon my path of duty did I not look for the generous aid of those who will be associated with me in the various and coordinate branches of the Government; did I not repose with unwavering reliance on the patriotism, the intelligence, and the kindness of a people who never yet deserted a public servant honestly laboring in their cause; and, above all, did I not permit myself humbly to hope for the sustaining support of an ever-watchful and beneficent Providence.

To the confidence and consolation derived from these sources it would be ungrateful not to add those which spring from our present fortunate condition. Though not altogether exempt from embarrassments that disturb our tranquillity at home and threaten it abroad, yet in all the attributes of a great, happy, and flourishing people we stand without a parallel in the world. Abroad we enjoy the respect and, with scarcely an exception, the friendship of every nation; at home, while our Government quietly but efficiently performs the sole legitimate end of political institutions—in doing the greatest good to the greatest number—we present an aggregate of human prosperity surely not elsewhere to be found.

How imperious, then, is the obligation imposed upon every citizen, in his own sphere of action, whether limited or extended, to exert himself in perpetuating a condition of things so singularly happy! All the lessons of history and experience must be lost upon us if we are content to trust alone to the peculiar advantages we happen to possess. Position and climate and the bounteous resources that nature has scattered with so liberal a hand—even the diffused intelligence and elevated character of our people—will avail us nothing if we fail sacredly to uphold those political institutions that were wisely and deliberately formed with reference to every circumstance that could preserve or might endanger the blessings we enjoy. The thoughtful framers of our Constitution legislated for our country as they found it. Looking upon it with the eyes of statesmen and patriots, they saw all the sources of rapid and wonderful prosperity; but they saw also that various habits, opinions, and institutions peculiar to the various portions of so vast a region were deeply fixed. Distinct sovereignties were in actual existence, whose cordial union was essential to the welfare and happiness of all. Between many of them there was, at least to some extent, a real diversity of interests, liable to be exaggerated through sinister designs; they differed in size, in population, in wealth, and in actual and prospective resources and power; they varied in the character of their industry and staple productions, and [in some] existed domestic institutions which, unwisely disturbed, might endanger the harmony of the whole. Most carefully were all these circumstances weighed, and the foundations of the new Government laid upon principles of reciprocal concession and equitable compromise. The jealousies which the smaller States might entertain of the power of the rest were allayed by a rule of representation confessedly unequal at the time, and designed forever to remain so. A natural fear that the broad scope of general legislation might bear upon and unwisely control particular interests was counteracted by limits strictly drawn around the action of the Federal authority, and to the people and the States was left unimpaired their sovereign power over the innumerable subjects embraced in the internal government of a just republic, excepting such only as necessarily appertain to the concerns of the whole confederacy or its intercourse as a united community with the other nations of the world.

This provident forecast has been verified by time. Half a century, teeming with extraordinary events, and elsewhere producing astonishing results, has passed along, but on our institutions it has left no injurious mark. From a small community we have risen to a people powerful in numbers and in strength; but with our increase has gone hand in hand the progress of just principles. The privileges, civil and religious, of the humblest individual are still sacredly protected at home, and while the valor and fortitude of our people have removed far from us the slightest apprehension of foreign power, they have not yet induced us in a single instance to forget what is right. Our commerce has been extended to the remotest nations; the value and even nature of our productions have been greatly changed; a wide difference has arisen in the relative wealth and resources of every portion of our country; yet the spirit of mutual regard and of faithful adherence to existing compacts has continued to prevail in our councils and never long been absent from our conduct. We have learned by experience a fruitful lesson—that an implicit and undeviating adherence to the principles on which we set out can carry us prosperously onward through all the conflicts of circumstances and vicissitudes inseparable from the lapse of years.

The success that has thus attended our great experiment is in itself a sufficient cause for gratitude, on account of the happiness it has actually conferred and the example it has unanswerably given. But to me, my fellow-citizens, looking forward to the far-distant future with ardent prayers and confiding hopes, this retrospect presents a ground for still deeper delight. It impresses on my mind a firm belief that the perpetuity of our institutions depends upon ourselves; that if we maintain the principles on which they were established they are destined to confer their benefits on countless generations yet to come, and that America will present to every friend of mankind the cheering proof that a popular government, wisely formed, is wanting in no element of endurance or strength. Fifty years ago its rapid failure was boldly predicted. Latent and uncontrollable causes of dissolution were supposed to exist even by the wise and good, and not only did unfriendly or speculative theorists anticipate for us the fate of past republics, but the fears of many an honest patriot overbalanced his sanguine hopes. Look back on these forebodings, not hastily but reluctantly made, and see how in every instance they have completely failed.

An imperfect experience during the struggles of the Revolution was supposed to warrant the belief that the people would not bear the taxation requisite to discharge an immense public debt already incurred and to pay the necessary expenses of the Government. The cost of two wars has been paid, not only without a murmur, but with unequaled alacrity. No one is now left to doubt that every burden will be cheerfully borne that may be necessary to sustain our civil institutions or guard our honor or welfare. Indeed, all experience has shown that the willingness of the people to contribute to these ends in cases of emergency has uniformly outrun the confidence of their representatives.

In the early stages of the new Government, when all felt the imposing influence as they recognized the unequaled services of the first President, it was a common sentiment that the great weight of his character could alone bind the discordant materials of our Government together and save us from the violence of contending factions. Since his death nearly forty years are gone. Party exasperation has been often carried to its highest point; the virtue and fortitude of the people have sometimes been greatly tried; yet our system, purified and enhanced in value by all it has encountered, still preserves its spirit of free and fearless discussion, blended with unimpaired fraternal feeling.

The capacity of the people for self-government, and their willingness, from a high sense of duty and without those exhibitions of coercive power so generally employed in other countries, to submit to all needful restraints and exactions of municipal law, have also been favorably exemplified in the history of the American States. Occasionally, it is true, the ardor of public sentiment, outrunning the regular progress of the judicial tribunals or seeking to reach cases not denounced as criminal by the existing law, has displayed itself in a manner calculated to give pain to the friends of free government and to encourage the hopes of those who wish for its overthrow. These occurrences, however, have been far less frequent in our country than in any other of equal population on the globe, and with the diffusion of intelligence it may well be hoped that they will constantly diminish in frequency and violence. The generous patriotism and sound common sense of the great mass of our fellow-citizens will assuredly in time produce this result; for as every assumption of illegal power not only wounds the majesty of the law, but furnishes a pretext for abridging the liberties of the people, the latter have the most direct and permanent interest in preserving the landmarks of social order and maintaining on all occasions the inviolability of those constitutional and legal provisions which they themselves have made.

In a supposed unfitness of our institutions for those hostile emergencies which no country can always avoid their friends found a fruitful source of apprehension, their enemies of hope. While they foresaw less promptness of action than in governments differently formed, they overlooked the far more important consideration that with us war could never be the result of individual or irresponsible will, but must be a measure of redress for injuries sustained, voluntarily resorted to by those who were to bear the necessary sacrifice, who would consequently feel an individual interest in the contest, and whose energy would be commensurate with the difficulties to be encountered. Actual events have proved their error; the last war, far from impairing, gave new confidence to our Government, and amid recent apprehensions of a similar conflict we saw that the energies of our country would not be wanting in ample season to vindicate its rights. We may not possess, as we should not desire to possess, the extended and ever-ready military organization of other nations; we may occasionally suffer in the outset for the want of it; but among ourselves all doubt upon this great point has ceased, while a salutary experience will prevent a contrary opinion from inviting aggression from abroad.

Certain danger was foretold from the extension of our territory, the multiplication of States, and the increase of population. Our system was supposed to be adapted only to boundaries comparatively narrow. These have been widened beyond conjecture; the members of our Confederacy are already doubled, and the numbers of our people are incredibly augmented. The alleged causes of danger have long surpassed anticipation, but none of the consequences have followed. The power and influence of the Republic have risen to a height obvious to all mankind; respect for its authority was not more apparent at its ancient than it is at its present limits; new and inexhaustible sources of general prosperity have been opened; the effects of distance have been averted by the inventive genius of our people, developed and fostered by the spirit of our institutions; and the enlarged variety and amount of interests, productions, and pursuits have strengthened the chain of mutual dependence and formed a circle of mutual benefits too apparent ever to be overlooked.

In justly balancing the powers of the Federal and State authorities difficulties nearly insurmountable arose at the outset, and subsequent collisions were deemed inevitable. Amid these it was scarcely believed possible that a scheme of government so complex in construction could remain uninjured. From time to time embarrassments have certainly occurred; but how just is the confidence of future safety imparted by the knowledge that each in succession has been happily removed! Overlooking partial and temporary evils as inseparable from the practical operation of all human institutions, and looking only to the general result, every patriot has reason to be satisfied. While the Federal Government has successfully performed its appropriate functions in relation to foreign affairs and concerns evidently national, that of every State has remarkably improved in protecting and developing local interests and individual welfare; and if the vibrations of authority have occasionally tended too much toward one or the other, it is unquestionably certain that the ultimate operation of the entire system has been to strengthen all the existing institutions and to elevate our whole country in prosperity and renown.

The last, perhaps the greatest, of the prominent sources of discord and disaster supposed to lurk in our political condition was the institution of domestic slavery. Our forefathers were deeply impressed with the delicacy of this subject, and they treated it with a forbearance so evidently wise that in spite of every sinister foreboding it never until the present period disturbed the tranquillity of our common country. Such a result is sufficient evidence of the justice and the patriotism of their course; it is evidence not to be mistaken that an adherence to it can prevent all embarrassment from this as well as from every other anticipated cause of difficulty or danger. Have not recent events made it obvious to the slightest reflection that the least deviation from this spirit of forbearance is injurious to every interest, that of humanity included? Amidst the violence of excited passions this generous and fraternal feeling has been sometimes disregarded; and standing as I now do before my countrymen, in this high place of honor and of trust, I can not refrain from anxiously invoking my fellow-citizens never to be deaf to its dictates. Perceiving before my election the deep interest this subject was beginning to excite, I believed it a solemn duty fully to make known my sentiments in regard to it, and now, when every motive for misrepresentation has passed away, I trust that they will be candidly weighed and understood. At least they will be my standard of conduct in the path before me. I then declared that if the desire of those of my countrymen who were favorable to my election was gratified ''I must go into the Presidential chair the inflexible and uncompromising opponent of every attempt on the part of Congress to abolish slavery in the District of Columbia against the wishes of the slaveholding States, and also with a determination equally decided to resist the slightest interference with it in the States where it exists.'' I submitted also to my fellow-citizens, with fullness and frankness, the reasons which led me to this determination. The result authorizes me to believe that they have been approved and are confided in by a majority of the people of the United States, including those whom they most immediately affect. It now only remains to add that no bill conflicting with these views can ever receive my constitutional sanction. These opinions have been adopted in the firm belief that they are in accordance with the spirit that actuated the venerated fathers of the Republic, and that succeeding experience has proved them to be humane, patriotic, expedient, honorable, and just. If the agitation of this subject was intended to reach the stability of our institutions, enough has occurred to show that it has signally failed, and that in this as in every other instance the apprehensions of the timid and the hopes of the wicked for the destruction of our Government are again destined to be disappointed. Here and there, indeed, scenes of dangerous excitement have occurred, terrifying instances of local violence have been witnessed, and a reckless disregard of the consequences of their conduct has exposed individuals to popular indignation; but neither masses of the people nor sections of the country have been swerved from their devotion to the bond of union and the principles it has made sacred. It will be ever thus. Such attempts at dangerous agitation may periodically return, but with each the object will be better understood. That predominating affection for our political system which prevails throughout our territorial limits, that calm and enlightened judgment which ultimately governs our people as one vast body, will always be at hand to resist and control every effort, foreign or domestic, which aims or would lead to overthrow our institutions.

What can be more gratifying than such a retrospect as this? We look back on obstacles avoided and dangers overcome, on expectations more than realized and prosperity perfectly secured. To the hopes of the hostile, the fears of the timid, and the doubts of the anxious actual experience has given the conclusive reply. We have seen time gradually dispel every unfavorable foreboding and our Constitution surmount every adverse circumstance dreaded at the outset as beyond control. Present excitement will at all times magnify present dangers, but true philosophy must teach us that none more threatening than the past can remain to be overcome; and we ought (for we have just reason) to entertain an abiding confidence in the stability of our institutions and an entire conviction that if administered in the true form, character, and spirit in which they were established they are abundantly adequate to preserve to us and our children the rich blessings already derived from them, to make our beloved land for a thousand generations that chosen spot where happiness springs from a perfect equality of political rights.

For myself, therefore, I desire to declare that the principle that will govern me in the high duty to which my country calls me is a strict adherence to the letter and spirit of the Constitution as it was designed by those who framed it. Looking back to it as a sacred instrument carefully and not easily framed; remembering that it was throughout a work of concession and compromise; viewing it as limited to national objects; regarding it as leaving to the people and the States all power not explicitly parted with, I shall endeavor to preserve, protect, and defend it by anxiously referring to its provision for direction in every action. To matters of domestic concernment which it has intrusted to the Federal Government and to such as relate to our intercourse with foreign nations I shall zealously devote myself; beyond those limits I shall never pass.

To enter on this occasion into a further or more minute exposition of my views on the various questions of domestic policy would be as obtrusive as it is probably unexpected. Before the suffrages of my countrymen were conferred upon me I submitted to them, with great precision, my opinions on all the most prominent of these subjects. Those opinions I shall endeavor to carry out with my utmost ability.

Our course of foreign policy has been so uniform and intelligible as to constitute a rule of Executive conduct which leaves little to my discretion, unless, indeed, I were willing to run counter to the lights of experience and the known opinions of my constituents. We sedulously cultivate the friendship of all nations as the condition most compatible with our welfare and the principles of our Government. We decline alliances as adverse to our peace. We desire commercial relations on equal terms, being ever willing to give a fair equivalent for advantages received   We endeavor to conduct our intercourse with openness and sincerity, promptly avowing our objects and seeking to establish that mutual frankness which is as beneficial in the dealings of nations as of men.   We have no disposition and we disclaim all right to meddle in disputes, whether internal or foreign, that may molest other countries, regarding them in their actual state as social communities, and preserving a strict neutrality in all their controversies.   Well knowing the tried valor of our people and our exhaustless resources, we neither anticipate nor fear any designed aggression; and in the consciousness of our own just conduct we feel a security that we shall never be called upon to exert our determination never to permit an invasion of our rights without punishment or redress.

In approaching, then, in the presence of my assembled countrymen, to make the solemn promise that yet remains, and to pledge myself that I will faithfully execute the office I am about to fill, I bring with me a settled purpose to maintain the institutions of my country, which I trust will atone for the errors I commit.

In receiving from the people the sacred trust twice confided to my illustrious predecessor, and which he has discharged so faithfully and so well, I know that I can not expect to perform the arduous task with equal ability and success.   But united as I have been in his counsels, a daily witness of his exclusive and unsurpassed devotion to his country's welfare, agreeing with him in sentiments which his countrymen have warmly supported, and permitted to partake largely of his confidence, I may hope that somewhat of the same cheering approbation will be found to attend upon my path.   For him I but express with my own the wishes of all, that he may yet long live to enjoy the brilliant evening of his well-spent life; and for myself, conscious of but one desire, faithfully to serve my country, I throw myself without fear on its justice and its kindness.   Beyond that I only look to the gracious protection of the Divine Being whose strengthening support I humbly solicit, and whom I fervently pray to look down upon us all.   May it be among the dispensations of His providence to bless our beloved country with honors and with length of days.   May her ways be ways of pleasantness and all her paths be peace!

MARCH 4, 1837.

SPECIAL MESSAGE.

WASHINGTON, *March 6, 1837.*

To the Senate of the United States:

I nominate to the Senate Powhatan Ellis, of Mississippi, to be envoy extraordinary and minister plenipotentiary of the United States to the United Mexican States, to be sent whenever circumstances will permit a renewal of diplomatic intercourse honorably with that power.

M. VAN BUREN.

PROCLAMATIONS.

[From Statutes at Large (Little & Brown), Vol. V, p. 802.]

By the President of the United States of America.

A PROCLAMATION.

Whereas by an act of Congress of the 7th of June, 1836, it was enacted that when the Indian title to all the lands lying between the State of Missouri and the Missouri River should be extinguished the jurisdiction over said land should be ceded by the said act to the State of Missouri and the western boundary of said State should be then extended to the Missouri River, reserving to the United States the original right of soil in said lands and of disposing of the same; and

Whereas it was in and by the said act provided that the same should not take effect until the President should by proclamation declare that the Indian title to said lands had been extinguished, nor until the State of Missouri should have assented to the provisions of the said act; and

Whereas an act was passed by the general assembly of the State of Missouri on the 16th of December, 1836, expressing the assent of the said State to the provisions of the said act of Congress, a copy of which act of the general assembly, duly authenticated, has been officially communicated to this Government and is now on file in the Department of State:

Now, therefore, I, Martin Van Buren, President of the United States of America, do by this my proclamation declare and make known that the Indian title to all the said lands lying between the State of Missouri and the Missouri River has been extinguished and that the said act of Congress of the 7th of June, 1836, takes effect from the date hereof.

Given under my hand, at the city of Washington, this 28th day of March, A. D. 1837, and of the Independence of the United States of America the sixty-first.

By the President: MARTIN VAN BUREN.

John Forsyth,
Secretary of State.

[From Statutes at Large (Little, Brown & Co.), Vol. XI, p. 783.]

By the President of the United States of America.

A PROCLAMATION.

Whereas great and weighty matters ciaiming the consideration of the Congress of the United States form an extraordinary occasion for convening them, I do by these presents appoint the first Monday of September next for their meeting at the city of Washington, hereby requiring the respective Senators and Representatives then and there to assemble in Congress in order to receive such communications as may then be made to them and to consult and determine on such measures as in their wisdom may be deemed meet for the welfare of the United States.

In testimony whereof I have caused the seal of the United States to be hereunto affixed, and signed the same with my hand.

[SEAL.]   Done at the city of Washington, the 15th day of May, A. D. 1837, and of the Independence of the United States the sixty-first.

MARTIN VAN BUREN.

By the President:
    JOHN FORSYTH,
        Secretary of State.

BY THE PRESIDENT OF THE UNITED STATES OF AMERICA.

A PROCLAMATION.

Whereas by the third section of the act of Congress of the United States of the 13th of July, 1832, entitled "An act concerning tonnage duty on Spanish vessels," it is provided that whenever the President shall be satisfied that the discriminating or countervailing duties of tonnage levied by any foreign nation on the ships or vessels of the United States shall have been abolished he may direct that the tonnage duty on the vessels of such nation shall cease to be levied in the ports of the United States; and

Whereas satisfactory evidence has lately been received from His Majesty the King of Greece that the discriminating duties of tonnage levied by said nation on the ships or vessels of the United States have been abolished:

Now, therefore, I, Martin Van Buren, President of the United States, do hereby declare and proclaim that the tonnage duty on the vessels of the Kingdom of Greece shall from this date cease to be levied in the ports of the United States.

Given under my hand, at the city of Washington, the 14th day of June, A. D. 1837, and of the Independence of the United States the sixty-first.

M. VAN BUREN.

By the President:
    JOHN FORSYTH,
        Secretary of State.

By the President of the United States of America

A Proclamation

Whereas, by the third section of the Act of Congress of the United States of the thirteenth of July, one thousand eight hundred and thirty two, entitled, "An Act concerning tonnage duty on Spanish vessels," it is provided, that whenever the President shall be satisfied that the discriminating or countervailing duties of tonnage levied by any foreign nation on the ships or vessels of the United States, shall have been abolished, he may direct that the tonnage duty on the vessels of such nation shall cease to be levied in the ports of the United States, —

And, whereas, satisfactory evidence has lately been received from His Majesty, the King of Greece, that the discriminating duties of tonnage levied by by said nation on the ships or vessels of the United States, have been abolished. —

Now, therefore, I, Martin Van Buren, President of the United States, do hereby declare, and proclaim that the tonnage duty on the vessels of the Kingdom of Greece shall from this date cease to be levied in the ports of the United States.

Given—

PRESIDENT VAN BUREN'S PROCLAMATION REVOKING TON-
NAGE DUTIES ON VESSELS OF GREECE.

Given under my hand, at the City
of Washington, the fourteenth day of
June, in the year of our
Lord, one thousand eight
hundred and thirty seven,
and of the Independence
of the United States the
Sixty first.

M Van Buren

By the President.

Jno Forsyth
Secretary of State.

EXECUTIVE ORDER.

HEADQUARTERS OF THE ARMY,
ADJUTANT-GENERAL'S OFFICE,
Washington, March 7, 1837.

GENERAL ORDER No. 6.

I. The Major-General Commanding in Chief has received from the War Department the following order:

WASHINGTON, *March 6, 1837.*

General Andrew Jackson, ex-President of the United States, being about to depart from this city for his home in Tennessee, and the state of his health rendering it important that he should be accompanied by a medical attendant, the President directs that the Surgeon-General of the Army accompany the ex-President to Wheeling, in the State of Virginia, there to be relieved, in case the ex-President's health shall be such as to allow it, by some officer of the Medical Department, who will attend the ex-President from that place to his residence.

In giving this order the President feels assured that this mark of attention to the venerable soldier, patriot, and statesman now retiring in infirm health from the cares of office to the repose of private life will be as grateful to the feelings of the American people as it appears to the President to be suitable in itself.

M. VAN BUREN.

The Major-General Commanding in Chief will carry into effect the foregoing directions of the President of the United States.

B. F. BUTLER,
Secretary of War ad interim.

II. Pursuant to the above order, Surgeon-General Lawson will immediately join the ex-President, and will accompany him as his medical attendant to Wheeling, in the State of Virginia, and, at his discretion, to the residence of the ex-President, at the Hermitage, near Nashville, in the State of Tennessee.

III. Assistant Surgeon Reynolds will join the ex-President at Wheeling, Va., and from that place, either alone or in conjunction with the Surgeon-General, as the latter may direct, will proceed with the ex-President to his residence in Tennessee.

IV. The officers above named, on the conclusion of the duties above assigned to them, will repair to their respective stations.

By order of Alexander Macomb, Major-General Commanding in Chief:

R. JONES, *Adjutant-General.*

SPECIAL SESSION MESSAGE.

WASHINGTON, *September 4, 1837.*

Fellow-Citizens of the Senate and House of Representatives:

The act of the 23d of June, 1836, regulating the deposits of the public money and directing the employment of State, District, and Territorial banks for that purpose, made it the duty of the Secretary of the Treasury to discontinue the use of such of them as should at any time refuse to redeem their notes in specie, and to substitute other banks, provided a sufficient number could be obtained to receive the public deposits upon the terms and conditions therein prescribed. The general and almost simultaneous suspension of specie payments by the banks in May last rendered the performance of this duty imperative in respect to those which had been selected under the act, and made it at the same time impracticable to employ the requisite number of others upon the prescribed conditions. The specific regulations established by Congress for the deposit and safe-keeping of the public moneys having thus unexpectedly become inoperative, I felt it to be my duty to afford you an early opportunity for the exercise of your supervisory powers over the subject.

I was also led to apprehend that the suspension of specie payments, increasing the embarrassments before existing in the pecuniary affairs of the country, would so far diminish the public revenue that the accruing receipts into the Treasury would not, with the reserved five millions, be sufficient to defray the unavoidable expenses of the Government until the usual period for the meeting of Congress, whilst the authority to call upon the States for a portion of the sums deposited with them was too restricted to enable the Department to realize a sufficient amount from that source. These apprehensions have been justified by subsequent results, which render it certain that this deficiency will occur if additional means be not provided by Congress.

The difficulties experienced by the mercantile interest in meeting their engagements induced them to apply to me previously to the actual suspension of specie payments for indulgence upon their bonds for duties, and all the relief authorized by law was promptly and cheerfully granted. The dependence of the Treasury upon the avails of these bonds to enable it to make the deposits with the States required by law led me in the outset to limit this indulgence to the 1st of September, but it has since been extended to the 1st of October, that the matter might be submitted to your further direction.

Questions were also expected to arise in the recess in respect to the October installment of those deposits requiring the interposition of Congress.

A provision of another act, passed about the same time, and intended to secure a faithful compliance with the obligation of the United States to satisfy all demands upon them in specie or its equivalent, prohibited the offer of any bank note not convertible on the spot into gold or silver at the will of the holder; and the ability of the Government, with millions on deposit, to meet its engagements in the manner thus required by law was rendered very doubtful by the event to which I have referred.

Sensible that adequate provisions for these unexpected exigencies could only be made by Congress; convinced that some of them would be indispensably necessary to the public service before the regular period of your meeting, and desirous also to enable you to exercise at the earliest moment your full constitutional powers for the relief of the country, I could not with propriety avoid subjecting you to the inconvenience of assembling at as early a day as the state of the popular representation would permit. I am sure that I have done but justice to your feelings in believing that this inconvenience will be cheerfully encountered in the hope of rendering your meeting conducive to the good of the country.

During the earlier stages of the revulsion through which we have just passed much acrimonious discussion arose and great diversity of opinion existed as to its real causes. This was not surprising. The operations of credit are so diversified and the influences which affect them so numerous, and often so subtle, that even impartial and well-informed persons are seldom found to agree in respect to them. To inherent difficulties were also added other tendencies which were by no means favorable to the discovery of truth. It was hardly to be expected that those who disapproved the policy of the Government in relation to the currency would, in the excited state of public feeling produced by the occasion, fail to attribute to that policy any extensive embarrassment in the monetary affairs of the country. The matter thus became connected with the passions and conflicts of party; opinions were more or less affected by political considerations, and differences were prolonged which might otherwise have been determined by an appeal to facts, by the exercise of reason, or by mutual concession. It is, however, a cheering reflection that circumstances of this nature can not prevent a community so intelligent as ours from ultimately arriving at correct conclusions. Encouraged by the firm belief of this truth, I proceed to state my views, so far as may be necessary to a clear understanding of the remedies I feel it my duty to propose and of the reasons by which I have been led to recommend them.

The history of trade in the United States for the last three or four years affords the most convincing evidence that our present condition is chiefly to be attributed to overaction in all the departments of business—an overaction deriving, perhaps, its first impulses from antecedent causes, but stimulated to its destructive consequences by excessive issues of bank paper and by other facilities for the acquisition and enlargement of credit. At the commencement of the year 1834 the banking capital of the United States, including that of the national bank, then existing, amounted to about $200,000,000, the bank notes then in circulation to about ninety-five millions, and the loans and discounts of the banks to three hundred and twenty-four millions. Between that time and the 1st of January, 1836, being the latest period to which accurate accounts have been received, our banking capital was increased to more than two hundred and fifty-one millions, our paper circulation to more than one hundred and forty millions, and the loans and discounts to more than four hundred and fifty-seven millions. To this vast increase are to be added the many millions of credit acquired by means of foreign loans, contracted by the States and State institutions, and, above all, by the lavish accommodations extended by foreign dealers to our merchants.

The consequences of this redundancy of credit and of the spirit of reckless speculation engendered by it were a foreign debt contracted by our citizens estimated in March last at more than $30,000,000; the extension to traders in the interior of our country of credits for supplies greatly beyond the wants of the people; the investment of $39,500,000 in unproductive public lands in the years 1835 and 1836, whilst in the preceding year the sales amounted to only four and a half millions; the creation of debts, to an almost countless amount, for real estate in existing or anticipated cities and villages, equally unproductive, and at prices now seen to have been greatly disproportionate to their real value; the expenditure of immense sums in improvements which in many cases have been found to be ruinously improvident; the diversion to other pursuits of much of the labor that should have been applied to agriculture, thereby contributing to the expenditure of large sums in the importation of grain from Europe—an expenditure which, amounting in 1834 to about $250,000, was in the first two quarters of the present year increased to more than $2,000,000; and finally, without enumerating other injurious results, the rapid growth among all classes, and especially in our great commercial towns, of luxurious habits founded too often on merely fancied wealth, and detrimental alike to the industry, the resources, and the morals of our people.

It was so impossible that such a state of things could long continue that the prospect of revulsion was present to the minds of considerate men before it actually came. None, however, had correctly anticipated its severity. A concurrence of circumstances inadequate of themselves to produce such widespread and calamitous embarrassments tended so greatly to aggravate them that they can not be overlooked in considering their history. Among these may be mentioned, as most prominent, the great loss of capital sustained by our commercial emporium in the fire of December, 1835—a loss the effects of which were underrated at the time because postponed for a season by the great facilities of credit then existing; the disturbing effects in our commercial cities of the transfers of the public moneys required by the deposit law of June, 1836, and the measures adopted by the foreign creditors of our merchants to reduce their debts and to withdraw from the United States a large portion of our specie.

However unwilling any of our citizens may heretofore have been to assign to these causes the chief instrumentality in producing the present state of things, the developments subsequently made and the actual condition of other commercial countries must, as it seems to me, dispel all remaining doubts upon the subject. It has since appeared that evils similar to those suffered by ourselves have been experienced in Great Britain, on the Continent, and, indeed, throughout the commercial world, and that in other countries as well as in our own they have been uniformly preceded by an undue enlargement of the boundaries of trade, prompted, as with us, by unprecedented expansions of the systems of credit. A reference to the amount of banking capital and the issues of paper credits put in circulation in Great Britain, by banks and in other ways, during the years 1834, 1835, and 1836 will show an augmentation of the paper currency there as much disproportioned to the real wants of trade as in the United States. With this redundancy of the paper currency there arose in that country also a spirit of adventurous speculation embracing the whole range of human enterprise. Aid was profusely given to projected improvements; large investments were made in foreign stocks and loans; credits for goods were granted with unbounded liberality to merchants in foreign countries, and all the means of acquiring and employing credit were put in active operation and extended in their effects to every department of business and to every quarter of the globe. The reaction was proportioned in its violence to the extraordinary character of the events which preceded it. The commercial community of Great Britain were subjected to the greatest difficulties, and their debtors in this country were not only suddenly deprived of accustomed and expected credits, but called upon for payments which in the actual posture of things here could only be made through a general pressure and at the most ruinous sacrifices.

In view of these facts it would seem impossible for sincere inquirers after truth to resist the conviction that the causes of the revulsion in both countries have been substantially the same. Two nations, the most commercial in the world, enjoying but recently the highest degree of apparent prosperity and maintaining with each other the closest relations, are suddenly, in a time of profound peace and without any great national disaster, arrested in their career and plunged into a state of embarrassment and distress. In both countries we have witnessed the same redundancy of paper money and other facilities of credit; the same spirit of speculation; the same partial successes; the same difficulties and reverses, and at length nearly the same overwhelming catastrophe. The most material difference between the results in the two countries has only been that with us there has also occurred an extensive derangement in the fiscal affairs of the Federal and State Governments, occasioned by the suspension of specie payments by the banks.

The history of these causes and effects in Great Britain and the United States is substantially the history of the revulsion in all other commercial countries.

The present and visible effects of these circumstances on the operations of the Government and on the industry of the people point out the objects which call for your immediate attention.

They are, to regulate by law the safe-keeping, transfer, and disbursement of the public moneys; to designate the funds to be received and paid by the Government; to enable the Treasury to meet promptly every demand upon it; to prescribe the terms of indulgence and the mode of settlement to be adopted, as well in collecting from individuals the revenue that has accrued as in withdrawing it from former depositories; and to devise and adopt such further measures, within the constitutional competency of Congress, as will be best calculated to revive the enterprise and to promote the prosperity of the country.

For the deposit, transfer, and disbursement of the revenue national and State banks have always, with temporary and limited exceptions, been heretofore employed; but although advocates of each system are still to be found, it is apparent that the events of the last few months have greatly augmented the desire, long existing among the people of the United States, to separate the fiscal operations of the Government from those of individuals or corporations.

Again to create a national bank as a fiscal agent would be to disregard the popular will, twice solemnly and unequivocally expressed. On no question of domestic policy is there stronger evidence that the sentiments of a large majority are deliberately fixed, and I can not concur with those who think they see in recent events a proof that these sentiments are, or a reason that they should be, changed.

Events similar in their origin and character have heretofore frequently occurred without producing any such change, and the lessons of experience must be forgotten if we suppose that the present overthrow of credit would have been prevented by the existence of a national bank. Proneness to excessive issues has ever been the vice of the banking system—a vice as prominent in national as in State institutions. This propensity is as subservient to the advancement of private interests in the one as in the other, and those who direct them both, being principally guided by the same views and influenced by the same motives, will be equally ready to stimulate extravagance of enterprise by improvidence of credit. How strikingly is this conclusion sustained by experience! The Bank of the United States, with the vast powers conferred on it by Congress, did not or could not prevent former and similar embarrassments, nor has the still greater strength it has been said to possess under its present charter enabled it in the existing emergency to check other institutions or even to save itself. In Great Britain, where it has been seen the same causes have been attended with the same effects, a national bank possessing powers far greater than are asked for by the warmest advocates of such an institution here has also proved unable to prevent an undue expansion of credit and the evils that flow from it. Nor can I find any tenable ground for the reestablishment of a national bank in the derangement alleged at present to exist in the domestic exchanges of the country or in the facilities it may be capable of affording them. Although advantages of this sort were anticipated when the first Bank of the United States was created, they were regarded as an incidental accommodation, not one which the Federal Government was bound or could be called upon to furnish. This accommodation is now, indeed, after the lapse of not many years, demanded from it as among its first duties, and an omission to aid and regulate commercial exchange is treated as a ground of loud and serious complaint. Such results only serve to exemplify the constant desire among some of our citizens to enlarge the powers of the Government and extend its control to subjects with which it should not interfere. They can never justify the creation of an institution to promote such objects. On the contrary, they justly excite among the community a more diligent inquiry into the character of those operations of trade toward which it is desired to extend such peculiar favors.

The various transactions which bear the name of domestic exchanges differ essentially in their nature, operation, and utility. One class of them consists of bills of exchange drawn for the purpose of transferring actual capital from one part of the country to another, or to anticipate the proceeds of property actually transmitted. Bills of this description are highly useful in the movements of trade and well deserve all the encouragement which can rightfully be given to them. Another class is made up of bills of exchange not drawn to transfer actual capital nor on the credit of property transmitted, but to create fictitious capital, partaking at once of the character of notes discounted in bank and of bank notes in circulation, and swelling the mass of paper credits to a vast extent in the most objectionable manner. These bills have formed for the last few years a large proportion of what are termed the domestic exchanges of the country, serving as the means of usurious profit and constituting the most unsafe and precarious paper in circulation. This species of traffic, instead of being upheld, ought to be discountenanced by the Government and the people.

In transferring its funds from place to place the Government is on the same footing with the private citizen and may resort to the same legal means. It may do so through the medium of bills drawn by itself or purchased from others; and in these operations it may, in a manner undoubtedly constitutional and legitimate, facilitate and assist exchanges of individuals founded on real transactions of trade. The extent to which this may be done and the best means of effecting it are entitled to the fullest consideration. This has been bestowed by the Secretary of the Treasury, and his views will be submitted to you in his report,

But it was not designed by the Constitution that the Government should assume the management of domestic or foreign exchange. It is indeed authorized to regulate by law the commerce between the States and to provide a general standard of value or medium of exchange in gold and silver, but it is not its province to aid individuals in the transfer of their funds otherwise than through the facilities afforded by the Post-Office Department. As justly might it be called on to provide for the transportation of their merchandise. These are operations of trade. They ought to be conducted by those who are interested in them in the same manner that the incidental difficulties of other pursuits are encountered by other classes of citizens. Such aid has not been deemed necessary in other countries. Throughout Europe the domestic as well as the foreign exchanges are carried on by private houses, often, if not generally, without the assistance of banks; yet they extend throughout distinct sovereignties, and far exceed in amount the real exchanges of the United States. There is no reason why our own may not be conducted in the same manner with equal cheapness and safety. Certainly this might be accomplished if it were favored by those most deeply interested; and few can doubt that their own interest, as well as the general welfare of the country, would be promoted by leaving such a subject in the hands of those to whom it properly belongs. A system founded on private interest, enterprise, and competition, without the aid of legislative grants or regulations by law, would rapidly prosper; it would be free from the influence of political agitation and extend the same exemption to trade itself, and it would put an end to those complaints of neglect, partiality, injustice, and oppression which are the unavoidable results of interference by the Government in the proper concerns of individuals. All former attempts on the part of the Government to carry its legislation in this respect further than was designed by the Constitution have in the end proved injurious, and have served only to convince the great body of the people more and more of the certain dangers of blending private interests with the operations of public business; and there is no reason to suppose that a repetition of them now would be more successful.

It can not be concealed that there exists in our community opinions and feelings on this subject in direct opposition to each other. A large portion of them, combining great intelligence, activity, and influence, are no doubt sincere in their belief that the operations of trade ought to be assisted by such a connection; they regard a national bank as necessary for this purpose, and they are disinclined to every measure that does not tend sooner or later to the establishment of such an institution. On the other hand, a majority of the people are believed to be irreconcilably opposed to that measure; they consider such a concentration of power dangerous to their liberties, and many of them regard it as a violation of the Constitution. This collision of opinion has doubtless caused much of the embarrassment to which the commercial transactions of the country have lately been exposed. Banking has become a political topic of the highest interest, and trade has suffered in the conflict of parties. A speedy termination of this state of things, however desirable, is scarcely to be expected. We have seen for nearly half a century that those who advocate a national bank, by whatever motive they may be influenced, constitute a portion of our community too numerous to allow us to hope for an early abandonment of their favorite plan. On the other hand, they must indeed form an erroneous estimate of the intelligence and temper of the American people who suppose that they have continued on slight or insufficient grounds their persevering opposition to such an institution, or that they can be induced by pecuniary pressure or by any other combination of circumstances to surrender principles they have so long and so inflexibly maintained

My own views of the subject are unchanged. They have been repeatedly and unreservedly announced to my fellow-citizens, who with full knowledge of them conferred upon me the two highest offices of the Government. On the last of these occasions I felt it due to the people to apprise them distinctly that in the event of my election I would not be able to cooperate in the reestablishment of a national bank. To these sentiments I have now only to add the expression of an increased conviction that the reestablishment of such a bank in any form, whilst it would not accomplish the beneficial purpose promised by its advocates, would impair the rightful supremacy of the popular will, injure the character and diminish the influence of our political system, and bring once more into existence a concentrated moneyed power, hostile to the spirit and threatening the permanency of our republican institutions.

Local banks have been employed for the deposit and distribution of the revenue at all times partially and on three different occasions exclusively: First, anterior to the establishment of the first Bank of the United States; secondly, in the interval between the termination of that institution and the charter of its successor; and thirdly, during the limited period which has now so abruptly closed. The connection thus repeatedly attempted proved unsatisfactory on each successive occasion, notwithstanding the various measures which were adopted to facilitate or insure its success. On the last occasion, in the year 1833, the employment of the State banks was guarded especially, in every way which experience and caution could suggest. Personal security was required for the safe-keeping and prompt payment of the moneys to be received, and full returns of their condition were from time to time to be made by the depositories. In the first stages the measure was eminently successful, notwithstanding the violent opposition of the Bank of the United States and the unceasing efforts made to overthrow it. The selected banks performed with fidelity and without any embarrassment to themselves or to the community their engagements to the Government, and the system promised to be permanently useful; but when it became necessary, under the act of June, 1836, to withdraw from them the public money for the purpose of placing it in additional institutions or of transferring it to the States, they found it in many cases inconvenient to comply with the demands of the Treasury, and numerous and pressing applications were made for indulgence or relief. As the installments under the deposit law became payable their own embarrassments and the necessity under which they lay of curtailing their discounts and calling in their debts increased the general distress and contributed, with other causes, to hasten the revulsion in which at length they, in common with the other banks, were fatally involved.

Under these circumstances it becomes our solemn duty to inquire whether there are not in any connection between the Government and banks of issue evils of great magnitude, inherent in its very nature and against which no precautions can effectually guard.

Unforeseen in the organization of the Government and forced on the Treasury by early necessities, the practice of employing banks was in truth from the beginning more a measure of emergency than of sound policy. When we started into existence as a nation, in addition to the burdens of the new Government we assumed all the large but honorable load of debt which was the price of our liberty; but we hesitated to weigh down the infant industry of the country by resorting to adequate taxation for the necessary revenue. The facilities of banks, in return for the privileges they acquired, were promptly offered, and perhaps too readily received by an embarrassed Treasury. During the long continuance of a national debt and the intervening difficulties of a foreign war the connection was continued from motives of convenience; but these causes have long since passed away. We have no emergencies that make banks necessary to aid the wants of the Treasury; we have no load of national debt to provide for, and we have on actual deposit a large surplus. No public interest, therefore, now requires the renewal of a connection that circumstances have dissolved. The complete organization of our Government, the abundance of our resources, the general harmony which prevails between the different States and with foreign powers, all enable us now to select the system most consistent with the Constitution and most conducive to the public welfare. Should we, then, connect the Treasury for a fourth time with the local banks, it can only be under a conviction that past failures have arisen from accidental, not inherent, defects.

A danger difficult, if not impossible, to be avoided in such an arrangement is made strikingly evident in the very event by which it has now been defeated. A sudden act of the banks intrusted with the funds of the people deprives the Treasury, without fault or agency of the Government, of the ability to pay its creditors in the currency they have by law a right to demand. This circumstance no fluctuation of commerce could have produced if the public revenue had been collected in the legal currency and kept in that form by the officers of the Treasury. The citizen whose money was in bank receives it back since the suspension at a sacrifice in its amount, whilst he who kept it in the legal currency of the country and in his own possession pursues without loss the current of his business. The Government, placed in the situation of the former, is involved in embarrassments it could not have suffered had it pursued the course of the latter. These embarrassments are, moreover, augmented by those salutary and just laws which forbid it to use a depreciated currency, and by so doing take from the Government the ability which individuals have of accommodating their transactions to such a catastrophe.

A system which can in a time of profound peace, when there is a large revenue laid by, thus suddenly prevent the application and the use of the money of the people in the manner and for the objects they have directed can not be wise; but who can think without painful reflection that under it the same unforeseen events might have befallen us in the midst of a war and taken from us at the moment when most wanted the use of those very means which were treasured up to promote the national welfare and guard our national rights? To such embarrassments and to such dangers will this Government be always exposed whilst it takes the moneys raised for and necessary to the public service out of the hands of its own officers and converts them into a mere right of action against corporations intrusted with the possession of them. Nor can such results be effectually guarded against in such a system without investing the Executive with a control over the banks themselves, whether State or national, that might with reason be objected to. Ours is probably the only Government in the world that is liable in the management of its fiscal concerns to occurrences like these.

But this imminent risk is not the only danger attendant on the surrender of the public money to the custody and control of local corporations. Though the object is aid to the Treasury, its effect may be to introduce into the operations of the Government influences the most subtle, founded on interests the most selfish.

The use by the banks, for their own benefit, of the money deposited with them has received the sanction of the Government from the commencement of this connection. The money received from the people, instead of being kept till it is needed for their use, is, in consequence of this authority, a fund on which discounts are made for the profit of those who happen to be owners of stock in the banks selected as depositories. The supposed and often exaggerated advantages of such a boon will always cause it to be sought for with avidity. I will not stop to consider on whom the patronage incident to it is to be conferred. Whether the selection and control be trusted to Congress or to the Executive, either will be subjected to appeals made in every form which the sagacity of interest can suggest. The banks under such a system are stimulated to make the most of their fortunate acquisition; the deposits are treated as an increase of capital; loans and circulation are rashly augmented, and when the public exigencies require a return it is attended with embarrassments not provided for nor foreseen. Thus banks that thought themselves most fortunate when the public funds were received find themselves most embarrassed when the season of payment suddenly arrives.

Unfortunately, too, the evils of the system are not limited to the banks. It stimulates a general rashness of enterprise and aggravates the fluctuations of commerce and the currency. This result was strikingly exhibited during the operations of the late deposit system, and especially in the purchases of public lands. The order which ultimately directed the payment of gold and silver in such purchases greatly checked, but could not altogether prevent, the evil. Specie was indeed more difficult to be procured than the notes which the banks could themselves create at pleasure; but still, being obtained from them as a loan and returned as a deposit, which they were again at liberty to use, it only passed round the circle with diminished speed. This operation could not have been performed had the funds of the Government gone into the Treasury to be regularly disbursed, and not into banks to be loaned out for their own profit while they were permitted to substitute for it a credit in account.

In expressing these sentiments I desire not to undervalue the benefits of a salutary credit to any branch of enterprise. The credit bestowed on probity and industry is the just reward of merit and an honorable incentive to further acquisition. None oppose it who love their country and understand its welfare. But when it is unduly encouraged; when it is made to inflame the public mind with the temptations of sudden and unsubstantial wealth; when it turns industry into paths that lead sooner or later to disappointment and distress, it becomes liable to censure and needs correction. Far from helping probity and industry, the ruin to which it leads falls most severely on the great laboring classes, who are thrown suddenly out of employment, and by the failure of magnificent schemes never intended to enrich them are deprived in a moment of their only resource. Abuses of credit and excesses in speculation will happen in despite of the most salutary laws; no government, perhaps, can altogether prevent them, but surely every government can refrain from contributing the stimulus that calls them into life.

Since, therefore, experience has shown that to lend the public money to the local banks is hazardous to the operations of the Government, at least of doubtful benefit to the institutions themselves, and productive of disastrous derangement in the business and currency of the country, is it the part of wisdom again to renew the connection?

It is true that such an agency is in many respects convenient to the Treasury, but it is not indispensable. A limitation of the expenses of the Government to its actual wants, and of the revenue to those expenses, with convenient means for its prompt application to the purposes for which it was raised, are the objects which we should seek to accomplish. The collection, safe-keeping, transfer, and disbursement of the public money can, it is believed, be well managed by officers of the Government. Its collection, and to a great extent its disbursement also, have indeed been hitherto conducted solely by them, neither national nor State banks, when employed, being required to do more than keep it safely while in their custody, and transfer and pay it in such portions and at such times as the Treasury shall direct.

Surely banks are not more able than the Government to secure the money in their possession against accident, violence, or fraud. The assertion that they are so must assume that a vault in a bank is stronger than a vault in the Treasury, and that directors, cashiers, and clerks not selected by the Government nor under its control are more worthy of confidence than officers selected from the people and responsible to the Government—officers bound by official oaths and bonds for a faithful performance of their duties, and constantly subject to the supervision of Congress.

The difficulties of transfer and the aid heretofore rendered by banks have been less than is usually supposed. The actual accounts show that by far the larger portion of payments is made within short or convenient distances from the places of collection; and the whole number of warrants issued at the Treasury in the year 1834—a year the result of which will, it is believed, afford a safe test for the future—fell short of 5,000, or an average of less than 1 daily for each State; in the city of New York they did not average more than 2 a day, and at the city of Washington only 4.

The difficulties heretofore existing are, moreover, daily lessened by an increase in the cheapness and facility of communication, and it may be asserted with confidence that the necessary transfers, as well as the safe-keeping and disbursements of the public moneys, can be with safety and convenience accomplished through the agencies of Treasury officers. This opinion has been in some degree confirmed by actual experience since the discontinuance of the banks as fiscal agents in May last—a period which from the embarrassments in commercial intercourse presented obstacles as great as any that may be hereafter apprehended.

The manner of keeping the public money since that period is fully stated in the report of the Secretary of the Treasury. That officer also suggests the propriety of assigning by law certain additional duties to existing establishments and officers, which, with the modifications and safeguards referred to by him, will, he thinks, enable the Department to continue to perform this branch of the public service without any material addition either to their number or to the present expense. The extent of the business to be transacted has already been stated; and in respect to the amount of money with which the officers employed would be intrusted at any one time, it appears that, assuming a balance of five millions to be at all times kept in the Treasury, and the whole of it left in the hands of the collectors and receivers, the proportion of each would not exceed an average of $30,000; but that, deducting one million for the use of the Mint and assuming the remaining four millions to be in the hands of one-half of the present number of officers—a supposition deemed more likely to correspond with the fact—the sum in the hands of each would still be less than the amount of most of the bonds now taken from the receivers of public money. Every apprehension, however, on the subject, either in respect to the safety of the money or the faithful discharge of these fiscal transactions, may, it appears to me, be effectually removed by adding to the present means of the Treasury the establishment by law at a few important points of offices for the deposit and disbursement of such portions of the public revenue as can not with obvious safety and convenience be left in the possession of the collecting officers until paid over by them to the public creditors. Neither the amounts retained in their hands nor those deposited in the offices would in an ordinary condition of the revenue be larger in most cases than those often under the control of disbursing officers of the Army and Navy, and might be made entirely safe by requiring such securities and exercising such controlling supervision as Congress may by law prescribe. The principal officers whose appointments would become necessary under this plan, taking the largest number suggested by the Secretary of the Treasury, would not exceed ten, nor the additional expenses, at the same estimate, $60,000 a year.

There can be no doubt of the obligation of those who are intrusted with the affairs of Government to conduct them with as little cost to the nation as is consistent with the public interest; and it is for Congress, and ultimately for the people, to decide whether the benefits to be derived from keeping our fiscal concerns apart and severing the connection which has hitherto existed between the Government and banks offer sufficient advantages to justify the necessary expenses. If the object to be accomplished is deemed important to the future welfare of the country, I can not allow myself to believe that the addition to the public expenditure of comparatively so small an amount as will be necessary to effect it will be objected to by the people.

It will be seen by the report of the Postmaster-General herewith communicated that the fiscal affairs of that Department have been successfully conducted since May last upon the principle of dealing only in the legal currency of the United States, and that it needs no legislation to maintain its credit and facilitate the management of its concerns, the existing laws being, in the opinion of that officer, ample for those objects.

Difficulties will doubtless be encountered for a season and increased services required from the public functionaries; such are usually incident to the commencement of every system, but they will be greatly lessened in the progress of its operations.

The power and influence supposed to be connected with the custody and disbursement of the public money are topics on which the public mind is naturally, and with great propriety, peculiarly sensitive. Much has been said on them in reference to the proposed separation of the Government from the banking institutions; and surely no one can object to any appeals or animadversions on the subject which are consistent with facts and evince a proper respect for the intelligence of the people. If a Chief Magistrate may be allowed to speak for himself on such a point, I can truly say that to me nothing would be more acceptable than the withdrawal from the Executive, to the greatest practicable extent, of all concern in the custody and disbursement of the public revenue; not that I would shrink from any responsibility cast upon me by the duties of my office, but because it is my firm belief that its capacity for usefulness is in no degree promoted by the possession of any patronage not actually necessary to the performance of those duties. But under our present form of government the intervention of the executive officers in the custody and disbursement of the public money seems to be unavoidable; and before it can be admitted that the influence and power of the Executive would be increased by dispensing with the agency of banks the nature of that intervention in such an agency must be carefully regarded, and a comparison must be instituted between its extent in the two cases.

The revenue can only be collected by officers appointed by the President with the advice and consent of the Senate. The public moneys in the first instance must therefore in all cases pass through hands selected by the Executive. Other officers appointed in the same way, or, as in some cases, by the President alone, must also be intrusted with them when drawn for the purpose of disbursement. It is thus seen that even when banks are employed the public funds must twice pass through the hands of executive officers. Besides this, the head of the Treasury Department, who also holds office at the pleasure of the President, and some other officers of the same Department, must necessarily be invested with more or less power in the selection, continuance, and supervision of the banks that may be employed. The question is then narrowed to the single point whether in the intermediate stage between the collection and disbursement of the public money the agency of banks is necessary to avoid a dangerous extension of the patronage and influence of the Executive. But is it clear that the connection of the Executive with powerful moneyed institutions, capable of ministering to the interests of men in points where they are most accessible to corruption, is less liable to abuse than his constitutional agency in the appointment and control of the few public officers required by the proposed plan? Will the public money when in their hands be necessarily exposed to any improper interference on the part of the Executive? May it not be hoped that a prudent fear of public jealousy and disapprobation in a matter so peculiarly exposed to them will deter him from any such interference, even if higher motives be found inoperative? May not Congress so regulate by law the duty of those officers and subject it to such supervision and publicity as to prevent the possibility of any serious abuse on the part of the Executive? And is there equal room for such supervision and publicity in a connection with banks, acting under the shield of corporate immunities and conducted by persons irresponsible to the Government and the people? It is believed that a considerate and candid investigation of these questions will result in the conviction that the proposed plan is far less liable to objection on the score of Executive patronage and control than any bank agency that has been or can be devised.

With these views I leave to Congress the measures necessary to regulate in the present emergency the safe-keeping and transfer of the public moneys. In the performance of constitutional duty I have stated to them without reserve the result of my own reflections. The subject is of great importance, and one on which we can scarcely expect to be as united in sentiment as we are in interest. It deserves a full and free discussion, and can not fail to be benefited by a dispassionate comparison of opinions. Well aware myself of the duty of reciprocal concession among the coordinate branches of the Government, I can promise a reasonable spirit of cooperation, so far as it can be indulged in without the surrender of constitutional objections which I believe to be well founded. Any system that may be adopted should be subjected to the fullest legal provision, so as to leave nothing to the Executive but what is necessary to the discharge of the duties imposed on him; and whatever plan may be ultimately established, my own part shall be so discharged as to give to it a fair trial and the best prospect of success.

The character of the funds to be received and disbursed in the transactions of the Government likewise demands your most careful consideration.

There can be no doubt that those who framed and adopted the Constitution, having in immediate view the depreciated paper of the Confederacy—of which $500 in paper were at times only equal to $1 in coin—intended to prevent the recurrence of similar evils, so far at least as related to the transactions of the new Government. They gave to Congress express powers to coin money and to regulate the value thereof and of foreign coin; they refused to give it power to establish corporations—the agents then as now chiefly employed to create a paper currency; they prohibited the States from making anything but gold and silver a legal tender in payment of debts; and the First Congress directed by positive law that the revenue should be received in nothing but gold and silver.

Public exigency at the outset of the Government, without direct legislative authority, led to the use of banks as fiscal aids to the Treasury. In admitted deviation from the law, at the same period and under the

CARTOON ON "THE TIMES."

CARTOON ON "TROUBLED TREASURES."

same exigency, the Secretary of the Treasury received their notes in payment of duties. The sole ground on which the practice thus commenced was then or has since been justified is the certain, immediate, and convenient exchange of such notes for specie. The Government did, indeed, receive the inconvertible notes of State banks during the difficulties of war, and the community submitted without a murmur to the unequal taxation and multiplied evils of which such a course was productive. With the war this indulgence ceased, and the banks were obliged again to redeem their notes in gold and silver. The Treasury, in accordance with previous practice, continued to dispense with the currency required by the act of 1789, and took the notes of banks in full confidence of their being paid in specie on demand; and Congress, to guard against the slightest violation of this principle, have declared by law that if notes are paid in the transactions of the Government it must be under such circumstances as to enable the holder to convert them into specie without depreciation or delay.

Of my own duties under the existing laws, when the banks suspended specie payments, I could not doubt. Directions were immediately given to prevent the reception into the Treasury of anything but gold and silver, or its equivalent, and every practicable arrangement was made to preserve the public faith by similar or equivalent payments to the public creditors. The revenue from lands had been for some time substantially so collected under the order issued by directions of my predecessor. The effects of that order had been so salutary and its forecast in regard to the increasing insecurity of bank paper had become so apparent that even before the catastrophe I had resolved not to interfere with its operation. Congress is now to decide whether the revenue shall continue to be so collected or not.

The receipt into the Treasury of bank notes not redeemed in specie on demand will not, I presume, be sanctioned. It would destroy without the excuse of war or public distress that equality of imposts and identity of commercial regulation which lie at the foundation of our Confederacy, and would offer to each State a direct temptation to increase its foreign trade by depreciating the currency received for duties in its ports. Such a proceeding would also in a great degree frustrate the policy so highly cherished of infusing into our circulation a larger proportion of the precious metals—a policy the wisdom of which none can doubt, though there may be different opinions as to the extent to which it should be carried. Its results have been already too auspicious and its success is too closely interwoven with the future prosperity of the country to permit us for a moment to contemplate its abandonment. We have seen under its influence our specie augmented beyond eighty millions, our coinage increased so as to make that of gold amount, between August, 1834, and December, 1836, to $10,000,000, exceeding the whole coinage at the Mint during the thirty-one previous years.

The prospect of further improvement continued without abatement until the moment of the suspension of specie payments. This policy has now, indeed, been suddenly checked, but is still far from being overthrown. Amidst all conflicting theories, one position is undeniable—the precious metals will invariably disappear when there ceases to be a necessity for their use as a circulating medium. It was in strict accordance with this truth that whilst in the month of May last they were everywhere seen and were current for all ordinary purposes they disappeared from circulation the moment the payment of specie was refused by the banks and the community tacitly agreed to dispense with its employment. Their place was supplied by a currency exclusively of paper, and in many cases of the worst description. Already are the bank notes now in circulation greatly depreciated, and they fluctuate in value between one place and another, thus diminishing and making uncertain the worth of property and the price of labor, and failing to subserve, except at a heavy loss, the purposes of business. With each succeeding day the metallic currency decreases; by some it is hoarded in the natural fear that once parted with it can not be replaced, while by others it is diverted from its more legitimate uses for the sake of gain. Should Congress sanction this condition of things by making irredeemable paper money receivable in payment of public dues, a temporary check to a wise and salutary policy will in all probability be converted into its absolute destruction.

It is true that bank notes actually convertible into specie may be received in payment of the revenue without being liable to all these objections, and that such a course may to some extent promote individual convenience—an object always to be considered where it does not conflict with the principles of our Government or the general welfare of the country. If such notes only were received, and always under circumstances allowing their early presentation for payment, and if at short and fixed periods they were converted into specie to be kept by the officers of the Treasury, some of the most serious obstacles to their reception would perhaps be removed. To retain the notes in the Treasury would be to renew under another form the loans of public money to the banks, and the evils consequent thereon.

It is, however, a mistaken impression that any large amount of specie is required for public payments. Of the seventy or eighty millions now estimated to be in the country, ten millions would be abundantly sufficient for that purpose provided an accumulation of a large amount of revenue beyond the necessary wants of the Government be hereafter prevented. If to these considerations be added the facilities which will arise from enabling the Treasury to satisfy the public creditors by its drafts or notes receivable in payment of the public dues, it may be safely assumed that no motive of convenience to the citizen requires the reception of bank paper.

To say that the refusal of paper money by the Government introduces an unjust discrimination between the currency received by it and that used by individuals in their ordinary affairs is, in my judgment, to view it in a very erroneous light. The Constitution prohibits the States from making anything but gold and silver a tender in the payment of debts, and thus secures to every citizen a right to demand payment in the legal currency. To provide by law that the Government will only receive its dues in gold and silver is not to confer on it any peculiar privilege, but merely to place it on an equality with the citizen by reserving to it a right secured to him by the Constitution. It is doubtless for this reason that the principle has been sanctioned by successive laws from the time of the first Congress under the Constitution down to the last. Such precedents, never objected to and proceeding from such sources, afford a decisive answer to the imputation of inequality or injustice.

But in fact the measure is one of restriction, not of favor. To forbid the public agent to receive in payment any other than a certain kind of money is to refuse him a discretion possessed by every citizen. It may be left to those who have the management of their own transactions to make their own terms, but no such discretion should be given to him who acts merely as an agent of the people—who is to collect what the law requires and to pay the appropriations it makes. When bank notes are redeemed on demand, there is then no discrimination in reality, for the individual who receives them may at his option substitute the specie for them; he takes them from convenience or choice. When they are not so redeemed, it will scarcely be contended that their receipt and payment by a public officer should be permitted, though none deny that right to an individual; if it were, the effect would be most injurious to the public, since their officer could make none of those arrangements to meet or guard against the depreciation which an individual is at liberty to do. Nor can inconvenience to the community be alleged as an objection to such a regulation. Its object and motive are their convenience and welfare.

If at a moment of simultaneous and unexpected suspension by the banks it adds something to the many embarrassments of that proceeding, yet these are far overbalanced by its direct tendency to produce a wider circulation of gold and silver, to increase the safety of bank paper, to improve the general currency, and thus to prevent altogether such occurrences and the other and far greater evils that attend them.

It may indeed be questioned whether it is not for the interest of the banks themselves that the Government should not receive their paper. They would be conducted with more caution and on sounder principles. By using specie only in its transactions the Government would create a demand for it, which would to a great extent prevent its exportation, and by keeping it in circulation maintain a broader and safer basis for the paper currency. That the banks would thus be rendered more sound and the community more safe can not admit of a doubt.

The foregoing views, it seems to me, do but fairly carry out the provisions of the Federal Constitution in relation to the currency, as far as relates to the public revenue. At the time that instrument was framed there were but three or four banks in the United States, and had the extension of the banking system and the evils growing out of it been foreseen they would probably have been specially guarded against. The same policy which led to the prohibition of bills of credit by the States would doubtless in that event have also interdicted their issue as a currency in any other form. The Constitution, however, contains no such prohibition; and since the States have exercised for nearly half a century the power to regulate the business of banking, it is not to be expected that it will be abandoned. The whole matter is now under discussion before the proper tribunal—the people of the States. Never before has the public mind been so thoroughly awakened to a proper sense of its importance; never has the subject in all its bearings been submitted to so searching an inquiry. It would be distrusting the intelligence and virtue of the people to doubt the speedy and efficient adoption of such measures of reform as the public good demands. All that can rightfully be done by the Federal Government to promote the accomplishment of that important object will without doubt be performed.

In the meantime it is our duty to provide all the remedies against a depreciated paper currency which the Constitution enables us to afford. The Treasury Department on several former occasions has suggested the propriety and importance of a uniform law concerning bankruptcies of corporations and other bankers. Through the instrumentality of such a law a salutary check may doubtless be imposed on the issues of paper money and an effectual remedy given to the citizen in a way at once equal in all parts of the Union and fully authorized by the Constitution.

The indulgence granted by Executive authority in the payment of bonds for duties has been already mentioned. Seeing that the immediate enforcement of these obligations would subject a large and highly respectable portion of our citizens to great sacrifices, and believing that a temporary postponement could be made without detriment to other interests and with increased certainty of ultimate payment, I did not hesitate to comply with the request that was made of me. The terms allowed are to the full extent as liberal as any that are to be found in the practice of the executive department. It remains for Congress to decide whether a further postponement may not with propriety be allowed; and if so, their legislation upon the subject is respectfully invited.

The report of the Secretary of the Treasury will exhibit the condition of these debts, the extent and effect of the present indulgence, the probable result of its further extension on the state of the Treasury, and every other fact necessary to a full consideration of the subject. Similar information is communicated in regard to such depositories of the public moneys as are indebted to the Government, in order that Congress may also adopt the proper measures in regard to them.

The receipts and expenditures for the first half of the year and an estimate of those for the residue will be laid before you by the Secretary of the Treasury. In his report of December last it was estimated that the current receipts would fall short of the expenditures by about $3,000,000. It will be seen that the difference will be much greater. This is to be attributed not only to the occurrence of greater pecuniary embarrassments in the business of the country than those which were then predicted, and consequently a greater diminution in the revenue, but also to the fact that the appropriations exceeded by nearly six millions the amount which was asked for in the estimates then submitted. The sum necessary for the service of the year, beyond the probable receipts and the amount which it was intended should be reserved in the Treasury at the commencement of the year, will be about six millions. If the whole of the reserved balance be not at once applied to the current expenditures, but four millions be still kept in the Treasury, as seems most expedient for the uses of the Mint and to meet contingencies, the sum needed will be ten millions.

In making this estimate the receipts are calculated on the supposition of some further extension of the indulgence granted in the payment of bonds for duties, which will affect the amount of the revenue for the present year to the extent of two and a half millions.

It is not proposed to procure the required amount by loans or increased taxation. There are now in the Treasury $9,367,214, directed by the act of the 23d of June, 1836, to be deposited with the States in October next. This sum, if so deposited, will be subject under the law to be recalled if needed to defray existing appropriations; and as it is now evident that the whole, or the principal part, of it will be wanted for that purpose, it appears most proper that the deposit should be withheld. Until the amount can be collected from the banks, Treasury notes may be temporarily issued, to be gradually redeemed as it is received.

I am aware that this course may be productive of inconvenience to many of the States. Relying upon the acts of Congress which held out to them the strong probability, if not the certainty, of receiving this installment, they have in some instances adopted measures with which its retention may seriously interfere. That such a condition of things should have occurred is much to be regretted. It is not the least among the unfortunate results of the disasters of the times; and it is for Congress to devise a fit remedy, if there be one. The money being indispensable to the wants of the Treasury, it is difficult to conceive upon what principle of justice or expediency its application to that object can be avoided. To recall any portion of the sums already deposited with the States would be more inconvenient and less efficient. To burden the country with increased taxation when there is in fact a large surplus revenue would be unjust and unwise; to raise moneys by loans under such circumstances, and thus to commence a new national debt, would scarcely be sanctioned by the American people.

The plan proposed will be adequate to all our fiscal operations during the remainder of the year. Should it be adopted, the Treasury, aided by the ample resources of the country, will be able to discharge punctually every pecuniary obligation. For the future all that is needed will be that caution and forbearance in appropriations which the diminution of the revenue requires and which the complete accomplishment or great forwardness of many expensive national undertakings renders equally consistent with prudence and patriotic liberality.

The preceding suggestions and recommendations are submitted in the belief that their adoption by Congress will enable the executive department to conduct our fiscal concerns with success so far as their management has been committed to it. Whilst the objects and the means proposed to attain them are within its constitutional powers and appropriate duties, they will at the same time, it is hoped, by their necessary operation, afford essential aid in the transaction of individual concerns, and thus yield relief to the people at large in a form adapted to the nature of our Government. Those who look to the action of this Government for specific aid to the citizen to relieve embarrassments arising from losses by revulsions in commerce and credit lose sight of the ends for which it was created and the powers with which it is clothed. It was established to give security to us all in our lawful and honorable pursuits, under the lasting safeguard of republican institutions. It was not intended to confer special favors on individuals or on any classes of them, to create systems of agriculture, manufactures, or trade, or to engage in them either separately or in connection with individual citizens or organized associations. If its operations were to be directed for the benefit of any one class, equivalent favors must in justice be extended to the rest, and the attempt to bestow such favors with an equal hand, or even to select those who should most deserve them, would never be successful.

All communities are apt to look to government for too much. Even in our own country, where its powers and duties are so strictly limited, we are prone to do so, especially at periods of sudden embarrassment and distress. But this ought not to be. The framers of our excellent Constitution and the people who approved it with calm and sagacious deliberation acted at the time on a sounder principle. They wisely judged that the less government interferes with private pursuits the better for the general prosperity. It is not its legitimate object to make men rich or to repair by direct grants of money or legislation in favor of particular pursuits losses not incurred in the public service. This would be substantially to use the property of some for the benefit of others. But its real duty—that duty the performance of which makes a good government the most precious of human blessings—is to enact and enforce a system of general laws commensurate with, but not exceeding, the objects of its establishment, and to leave every citizen and every interest to reap under its benign protection the rewards of virtue, industry, and prudence.

FINANCIAL CRISIS OF VAN BUREN'S ADMINISTRATION, FOL-
LOWING RETIRING OF INFLATED PAPER CURRENCY
AND RESUMPTION OF SPECIE PAYMENTS.

CARTOON ON VAN BUREN'S POLICY OF PAYMENTS IN COIN
WHICH PARTISANS AT THAT TIME CLAIMED
THROTTLED "THE POOR MAN."

I can not doubt that on this as on all similar occasions the Federal Government will find its agency most conducive to the security and happiness of the people when limited to the exercise of its conceded powers. In never assuming, even for a well-meant object, such powers as were not designed to be conferred upon it, we shall in reality do most for the general welfare. To avoid every unnecessary interference with the pursuits of the citizen will result in more benefit than to adopt measures which could only assist limited interests, and are eagerly, but perhaps naturally, sought for under the pressure of temporary circumstances. If, therefore, I refrain from suggesting to Congress any specific plan for regulating the exchanges of the country, relieving mercantile embarrassments, or interfering with the ordinary operations of foreign or domestic commerce, it is from a conviction that such measures are not within the constitutional province of the General Government, and that their adoption would not promote the real and permanent welfare of those they might be designed to aid.

The difficulties and distresses of the times, though unquestionably great, are limited in their extent, and can not be regarded as affecting the permanent prosperity of the nation. Arising in a great degree from the transactions of foreign and domestic commerce, it is upon them that they have chiefly fallen. The great agricultural interest has in many parts of the country suffered comparatively little, and, as if Providence intended to display the munificence of its goodness at the moment of our greatest need, and in direct contrast to the evils occasioned by the waywardness of man, we have been blessed throughout our extended territory with a season of general health and of uncommon fruitfulness. The proceeds of our great staples will soon furnish the means of liquidating debts at home and abroad, and contribute equally to the revival of commercial activity and the restoration of commercial credit. The banks, established avowedly for its support, deriving their profits from it, and resting under obligations to it which can not be overlooked, will feel at once the necessity and justice of uniting their energies with those of the mercantile interest.

The suspension of specie payments at such a time and under such circumstances as we have lately witnessed could not be other than a temporary measure, and we can scarcely err in believing that the period must soon arrive when all that are solvent will redeem their issues in gold and silver. Dealings abroad naturally depend on resources and prosperity at home. If the debt of our merchants has accumulated or their credit is impaired, these are fluctuations always incident to extensive or extravagant mercantile transactions. But the ultimate security of such obligations does not admit of question. They are guaranteed by the resources of a country the fruits of whose industry afford abundant means of ample liquidation, and by the evident interest of every merchant to sustain a credit hitherto high by promptly applying these means for its preservation.

I deeply regret that events have occurred which require me to ask your consideration of such serious topics. I could have wished that in making my first communication to the assembled representatives of my country I had nothing to dwell upon but the history of her unalloyed prosperity. Since it is otherwise, we can only feel more deeply the responsibility of the respective trusts that have been confided to us, and under the pressure of difficulties unite in invoking the guidance and aid of the Supreme Ruler of Nations and in laboring with zealous resolution to overcome the difficulties by which we are environed.

It is under such circumstances a high gratification to know by long experience that we act for a people to whom the truth, however unpromising, can always be spoken with safety; for the trial of whose patriotism no emergency is too severe, and who are sure never to desert a public functionary honestly laboring for the public good. It seems just that they should receive without delay any aid in their embarrassments which your deliberations can afford. Coming directly from the midst of them, and knowing the course of events in every section of our country, from you may best be learnt as well the extent and nature of these embarrassments as the most desirable measures of relief.

I am aware, however, that it is not proper to detain you at present longer than may be demanded by the special objects for which you are convened. To them, therefore, I have confined my communication; and believing it will not be your own wish now to extend your deliberations beyond them, I reserve till the usual period of your annual meeting that general information on the state of the Union which the Constitution requires me to give.

M. VAN BUREN.

SPECIAL MESSAGES.

WASHINGTON, *September 7, 1837.*

To the Senate of the United States:

I transmit, for the consideration of the Senate with a view to its ratification, a general convention of peace, friendship, commerce, and navigation between the United States and the Peru-Bolivian Confederation, signed at Lima on the 30th of November, 1836, by Samuel Larned, the chargé d'affaires of the United States, and J. Garcia del Rio, minister of state in the department of finance of the North Peruvian State.

M. VAN BUREN.

Hon. R. M. JOHNSON. WASHINGTON, *September 19, 1837.*

SIR: I have the honor to inclose a report of the Secretary of War, on the subject of the resolution of the Senate of the 2d of March, 1837.*

Very respectfully, your obedient servant,

M. VAN BUREN.

* Whether the works at Black Rock raise the waters of Lake Erie to the injury of property on its southern and western shores.

WASHINGTON, *September 26, 1837.*

To the House of Representatives of the United States:

I herewith transmit to the House of Representatives a report from the Secretary of State, accompanied by copies of the correspondence requested by their resolution of the 13th instant.

M. VAN BUREN.

DEPARTMENT OF STATE,
Washington, September 25, 1837.

The Secretary of State, to whom was referred the resolution of the House of Representatives dated the 13th instant, requesting the President to communicate to that body, "so far as the public interest will permit, the correspondence between the Government of the United States and that of Great Britain relating to the northeastern boundary of the United States since the message of the late President to the Senate of the United States of the 15th of June, 1836, and all the correspondence which has taken place since that period between the Government of the United States and the governor of the State of Maine on the subject of alleged aggressions upon the rights of Maine by the British authorities," has the honor respectfully to submit to the President copies of the letters and documents requested by that resolution.

JOHN FORSYTH.

STATE OF MAINE, EXECUTIVE DEPARTMENT,
Augusta, March 30, 1837.

SIR: In compliance with a request of the legislature of this State, I have the honor to transmit to you the accompanying report and resolutions.

I am, very respectfully, your obedient servant,

ROBERT P. DUNLAP.

STATE OF MAINE, HOUSE OF REPRESENTATIVES,
March 29, 1837.

The joint select committee who had under consideration the order relating to the expediency of calling the attention of Congress to the subject of fortifying our maritime and interior frontier have attended to that duty, and ask leave to present the following report:

One object of the federal compact is "to provide for the common defense and general welfare."

In accordance with these objects of the compact, the General Government has from time to time made liberal appropriations for fortifying and defending the several States along our extended maritime frontier west and south of the western boundary line of this State. East of that line a mere trifle has as yet been appropriated for these objects.

Maine has a maritime frontier of about 500 miles in extent, following the indentations of her shores, and our interior frontier, bounding on New Brunswick on the east and the Canadas on the north, is about 600 miles in extent.

Considering this great extent of seacoast, her numerous excellent harbors, her noble rivers and great advantages for shipbuilding, and her proximity to the fishing grounds, probably no State in the Union possesses the natural advantages for carrying on this branch of industry that Maine does.

It is a fact worthy of consideration that all maritime nations have looked to their fisheries as the nursery of hardy seamen for the merchant service in time of peace and for the navy in time of war, and as a great question of national policy (aside from the inducement to encourage this branch of business as an unfailing source of natural wealth) it is deemed worthy of the fostering care of all commercial nations.

Already the navigation of Maine is estimated at more than 300,000 tons, and exceeded by only two States in the Union, and her increase annually of tonnage is greater than that of any other State.

The abundance of building materials, believed to be inexhaustible, her great conveniences for shipbuilding along her extended seacoast, her numerous bays, rivers, and harbors, render it highly probable that the day is not far distant when the maritime interests of Maine will exceed that of any of her sister States; and if reliance can be placed upon the statements of a scientific engineer of high respectability and standing, who has during the past year, under the direction of the government of this State and our parent Commonwealth, made a geological survey of a portion of our State, it may be doubted whether the same extent of territory on the continent contains more real value viewed in all its bearings (the facilities of quarrying, manufacturing, exporting, and its influence upon the great interests of the State and nation) than is contained in our inexhaustible quarries of granite, lime, marble, slate, etc., mines and minerals in which large and profitable investments are already made. Some of these branches of business have been carried on for many years, and others to a large extent are commencing under the most favorable auspices.

These, together with our agricultural, commercial, and manufacturing interests, our immense forests of invaluable timber, with a water power of vast extent and value, giving us the means of laying the seaports of the Union under a contribution for ages to come, and warranting the belief that our present shipping interest will be sustained and employed and a great increase required.

About one-third of the most valuable portion of our territory is claimed by Great Britain, and the history of this protracted controversy from its commencement to the present time is such as to awaken general anxiety. We are admonished by recent events that we have not yet reached the termination of our toils and embarrassments, and they have awakened the painful apprehension that our just rights may not be secured by honorable negotiation or patient submission to unprovoked injuries. These considerations, in the opinion of your committee, call loudly for the interposition of the General Government, and require at their hands all needful preparation for possible contingencies. The late Governor Lincoln nearly ten years since called the attention of the Government to the importance of erecting a strong fortification in some eligible position on the confines of that portion of our territory to which an adverse claim is set up by Great Britain. In the opinion of your committee, the subject has lost none of its interest since that period, but, on the contrary, the events to which we have alluded give to it vastly augmented importance; and to our view, irrespective of any conditions growing out of the present controversy, a strong fortification upon the northeastern boundary of the United States, situated far in the interior and upon the confines of a foreign country, and surrounded by millions of acres of fertile land, destined soon to be peopled with a numerous population of hardy yeomanry, is of high importance.

Our isolated situation, being the northeastern boundary of the nation, with an interior frontier upward of 600 miles upon a foreign country and a large proportion of our territory lying between two Provinces of Great Britain and so situated as to render it greatly to the advantage of that nation to possess it; the inflexible determination which she manifests to pursue the course which interest dictates should not be forgotten; the extent of our seacoast; the exposed situation of our seaport towns, lying within a few hours' sail of the British naval depot in the neighborhood of Maine; the disastrous consequences of our defenseless situation during the last war; the great and increasing maritime interests which we have at stake without one single point where a ship, if dependent upon the United States fortifications, would be safe from the attacks of a frigate—these and the consideration that little, comparatively, has yet been done for Maine seem to our view to constitute irresistible reasons why Maine should no longer be forgotten or neglected in the common defense of the country.

Through all the long-protracted struggles, difficulties, and embarrassments of our infant Republic this portion of our Union has never been urgent or importunate in pressing its claims, but has submitted patiently to the force of circumstances which rendered it necessary to defer them.

But in the present altered condition of the country—the national debt paid off at a season of universal peace and unexampled prosperity, with an overburthened Treasury, and when it is deemed necessary to dispose of it to resort to measures which many eminent statesmen consider unwarranted by the Constitution and which a great portion of the people of the Union consider of doubtful policy—at such a period and under such circumstances it is difficult to perceive the justice of longer withholding suitable appropriations for the defense of Maine, and to our view it can only be withheld by doing violence to the principles of equal rights and by neglecting a plain constitutional duty.

Your committee therefore submit the following resolutions.

STEPHEN C. FOSTER, *Chairman.*

STATE OF MAINE.

RESOLVE relating to the fortification of frontier States.

Resolved, That the obligation of the Federal Government, under the Constitution, when it has the means to erect suitable fortifications for the defense of the frontier of the States, is a practical duty not justly to be denied, evaded, neglected, or delayed.

Resolved, That our Senators in Congress be instructed and our Representatives requested to use their influence to obtain liberal appropriations for the defense of Maine and the Union.

Resolved, That the governor be requested to transmit copies of the above report and resolutions to the President and Vice-President, the Secretaries of State, Navy, and War, and to each of our Senators and Representatives in Congress.

[Passed by both Houses and approved March 30, 1837.]

STATE OF MAINE, EXECUTIVE DEPARTMENT,
Augusta, April 30, 1837.

His Excellency MARTIN VAN BUREN,
President of the United States.

SIR: In compliance with a request of the legislature of this State, I have the honor to transmit to Your Excellency the accompanying report and resolutions:

In behalf of the State of Maine, I would respectfully, yet urgently, call on the President of the United States to cause the northeastern boundary of this State to be explored and surveyed and monuments erected in accordance with the request contained in the resolutions which are herewith communicated. As the subject is one in which the people of Maine have a deep interest, I feel a confidence it will commend itself to your early attention.

With high consideration, I have the honor to be, your obedient servant,

ROBERT P. DUNLAP.

STATE OF MAINE, IN HOUSE OF REPRESENTATIVES,
February 2, 1837.

The joint committee to whom was referred so much of the governor's message as relates to the northeastern boundary, and the documents and evidence, together with an order of the two houses instructing the committee "to inquire into the expediency of providing by law for the appointment of commissioners on the part of this

State, by the consent of the Government of the United States, to survey the line between this State and the Province of New Brunswick according to the treaty of 1783, to establish monuments in such places as shall be fixed by said commissioners and by commissioners to be appointed on the part of the Government of Great Britain," have attended to the duties assigned them with the industry and solicitude which the importance of the subject demanded. Could the committee have spared the time and had the means to obtain documents not within the jurisdiction of the State, and consequently out of its power, a more clear, methodical, and perfect view of the subject would have been presented; but as there had been hitherto so much procrastination and the impatience of the public, already great, was becoming more and more intense, your committee without further preamble or apology ask leave to present the following report:

The legislature and people of Maine, we believe, will not contend that the treaty-making power of the United States does not extend to a final adjustment of a disputed and undefined line of boundary between a State and a foreign nation; *but we do insist* that no power is granted by the Constitution of the United States to *limit* or *change the boundary of a State or cede a part of its territory without its consent.* It is even by no means certain how far *such consent* would enable the treaty authority to exert its powers. *Citizens* might be made the subjects of a treaty transfer, and these citizens owing allegiance to the State and to the Union, and allegiance and protection being reciprocally binding, the right to transfer a citizen to a foreign government, to *sell* him, might well be questioned as being inconsistent with the spirit of our free institutions. But be this as it may, Maine will never concede the principle that the President and two-thirds of the Senate can transfer its territory, much less its citizens, without its permission, given by its constitutional organs.

Your committee, however, deem it but fair to admit that they have discovered no inclination in the General Government, or any department of it, to assume this power. On the contrary, the President has repeatedly declined the adoption of a conventional line deviating from the treaty of 1783, upon the express ground that it could not be done without the consent of Maine.

It is due, nevertheless, to the State of Maine to say that the committee have no evidence that any conventional line has been proposed to them for their consent. It indeed appears that the consent of Maine had not been given to the adoption of any other boundary than that prescribed by the treaty of 1783 up to the 29th February, 1836, and we are well assured that no proposition for a different boundary has since that time been made to any department of the government of this State.

The President of the United States on the 15th June last communicated to the Senate, in compliance with their resolution, a copy of the correspondence relative to the northeastern boundary. This correspondence embraced a period from the 21st July, 1832, to the 5th March, 1836.

The opinion and advice of the King of the Netherlands, to whom the controversy was referred by the provisions of the treaty of Ghent, was made on the 10th January, 1831, and of the three questions submitted, viz, *the northeastern boundary, the northwesternmost head of Connecticut River*, and *the forty-fifth parallel of latitude*, he seems to have determined *but one*. He did decide that the source of the stream running into and through Connecticut Lake is the true northwest head of that river as intended by the treaty of 1783; and as to the rest, he *advises* that it will be *convenient (il conviendra)* to adopt the "Thalweg," the deepest channel of the St. John and St. Francis, for the north line, and that the forty-fifth degree is to be measured in order to mark out the boundary to the St. Lawrence, with a deviation so as to include Rouses Point within the United States. As to *the convenience* of establishing the St. John and St. Francis as the northern boundary of Maine, we have only to observe that however "convenient" it may be to Great Britain to obtain so large a portion of our territory and waters, it would certainly be very *inconvenient* to us, and inasmuch as we are probably capable of judging of our own "convenience," and have never solicited *the advice* of anyone on this point, it is scarcely to be expected that we shall be *advised* to adopt a line so preposterous and injurious.

It was in this view and in strict conformity with the Constitution conferring the treaty power that the President on the 7th December, 1831, submitted to the Senate this "award" and "advice" of the King of the Netherlands. Senators were divided on a principal point, some insisting that to carry the award or opinion into effect was only *in execution* of the treaty, and it therefore belonged exclusively to the President "to take care" that this "supreme law" was faithfully executed or to reject it altogether.

But the prevailing opinion was that this "award" or "advice" was *perfecting an unfinished* treaty, and that therefore it could not be effected by the President without " the advice and consent of the Senate, two-thirds of the members present concurring therein." So far from the concurrence of two-thirds *for* the measure, there were *thirty-four* to *eight against* it, and it was consequently rejected, and a recommendation to the President was adopted to open a new negotiation to determine the line of boundary according to the treaty of 1783.

It is insisted by the British ministers that a due north line from the monument at the source of the St. Croix will intersect no highlands described in the treaty of 1783. Now this is an assumption by Great Britain totally unwarranted by any evidence. The boundaries bearing upon the question are thus given: "From the northwest angle of Nova Scotia, to wit, that angle which is formed by a line drawn due north from the source of the St. Croix River to the highlands; along the said highlands which divide *the rivers* that empty themselves into the St. Lawrence from those which fall into the Atlantic Ocean, to the northwesternmost head of Connecticut River;" "east by a line to be drawn along the middle of the river St. Croix from its mouth, in the Bay of Fundy, to its source, and from its source directly north to the aforesaid highlands which divide the rivers that fall into the Atlantic Ocean from those which fall into the St. Lawrence."

The first object, starting place, or *terminus a quo*, is this *northwest angle of Nova Scotia*. It is the corner of the British Province *designated by themselves*. It was presumed, and it is still believed, that they knew the identical spot; we have a right to demand of them to define it. In the treaty of 1783 they were disposed to define it, and hence they say it is *that angle which is formed by a line drawn due north from the source of the St. Croix to those highlands which divide the rivers that flow into the St. Lawrence from those which flow into the Atlantic Ocean.*

Nothing can be more clear than that the British negotiators of the treaty of 1783 had reference to their east and west line between Canada and Nova Scotia. This in 1755–56 was matter of controversy between France and England, the French claiming that it was far south and the British strenuously contending that these very highlands were even more north than we have endeavored to fix them.

The controversy resulted in a war, which, after the capture of Quebec, was terminated by the peace of 1763, whereby Great Britain obtained both sides of the line, and she then established the north line of Nova Scotia about where we contend it should be. So far from admitting that a due north line from the monument will not intersect the highlands intended by the treaty of 1783, the State of Maine has always insisted, and still insists, that no known obstacle exists to the ascertaining and accurately defining them, and thus establishing the *terminus a quo, to wit, the northwest angle of Nova Scotia*. It would seem strange, indeed, that this line, so fully discussed and controverted between the English and French in 1755–56, should have been left unsettled still when both Provinces became British. It is impossible to imagine such ignorance of so important a point as this northwest angle, so often referred to and spoken of as a notorious monument.

The peace of 1783 was considered by Great Britain as *a grant by metes and bounds*. The boundaries were prescribed, and this northwest angle was *the commencement*. Twenty years only before this (1763) Nova Scotia had been organized as a distinct Province, then including what are now Nova Scotia and New Brunswick, and this angle was referred to as a boundary without hesitancy or doubt. Indeed, the treaty itself, as if to make assurance doubly sure, fixed it where a due north line from the source of the St. Croix will intersect those highlands which divide the rivers which flow into the *river* St. Lawrence from those which flow into the Atlantic Ocean. This source of the St. Croix has been determined and a monument fixed there by the commissioners under the fifth article of the treaty of 1795 (Jay's). Now the assumption that the north line from this monument will intersect or meet no such highlands is entirely gratuitous.

The treaty does not speak of mountains nor even hills, but of "highlands" that divide rivers flowing different ways. It was well known that rivers did fall into the St. Lawrence and into the Atlantic, that these rivers would run *down* and not *up*, and it was consequently inferred that the *land* from whence these *rivers* flowed must of necessity be *high*, and unless there are to be found in that region *geological phenomena* which exist nowhere else on the face of the globe this inference is irresistible.

The truth is that these highlands have been known and well understood by the British themselves ever since the grant of James I to Sir William Alexander, in 1621. The portion of the boundary there given which relates to this controversy is "from the western spring head of the St. Croix, by an imaginary line conceived to run through the land northward to the next road of Ships River or Spring discharging itself into the great river of Canada, and proceeding thence *eastward* along the shores of the sea of the said river of Canada to the road, haven, or shore commonly called *Gaspeck*" (Gaspé).

The cession of Canada by France made it necessary to define the limits of the Province of Quebec, and accordingly His Britannic Majesty, by his proclamation of 7th October, 1763, is thus explicit as to what affects this question: "Passing along the highlands which divide *the rivers* that empty themselves into the said *river* St. Lawrence from those which fall into *the* sea, and also *along the north coast of the Bay de Chaleurs* and the coast of the *Gulf* of the St. Lawrence to *Cape Rosiers*," etc.

The act of Parliament of the fourteenth George III (1774) defines thus the south line of Canada: "South by a line from the Bay de Chaleurs along the highlands which divide the rivers that empty themselves into the river St. Lawrence from those which flow into *the sea*." The north line of the grant to Alexander is from the source of the St. Croix to the "spring head" or source of some river or stream which falls into the river St. Lawrence, and thence *eastward* to Gaspé Bay, which communicates with the Gulf of St. Lawrence in latitude 49° 30', and would make nearly an east and west line. The proclamation of 1763 defines the *south* line of the Province of Quebec as passing along the highlands which divide the rivers that fall into the St. Lawrence from those which fall into the sea, and also along the north coast of the Bay de Chaleurs to *the Gulf* of St. Lawrence. This is the *south* boundary, and consequently in an *east* and *west direction;* but it passes *north* of Bay de Chaleurs, wherefore the south boundary of the Province must of necessity be north of Bay de Chaleurs. The eastern boundary is northerly by the Gulf of *Cape Rosiers*, in about latitude 50°, longitude 64° north of Gaspé Bay, and at the mouth of the river St. Lawrence, where it communicates with the gulf or sea. And the act of Parliament makes *this south side* from this same bay along those highlands, and it must *inevitably run west* or *it is no south* boundary. Now no one can doubt that in the proclamation of 1763 it was the intent to adopt Sir William Alexander's *northern* for this *southern* boundary of the Province of Quebec.

Indeed, it appears in every commission to the governor of Novia Scotia and New

Brunswick from 1763 to 1784, and after the treaty of peace of 1783, that the Province of Nova Scotia extended to the southern boundary of the Province of Quebec. It then irresistibly and inevitably follows that a west line from the Bay de Chaleurs, intersecting a due north line from the monument, is the identical northwest angle. Now a line from Mars Hill direct to Cape Rosiers, instead of being *easterly*, would be north of northeast, *crossing* the Bay de Chaleurs. But passing along its north coast, as the proclamation provides, the line from this Mars Hill must be more northerly still. Indeed, the pretense that a pyramidal spur or peak, such as this hill, should constitute the range of highlands mentioned in the treaty is so utterly visionary that it is entitled to *no sort of respect*.

We may now by these facts and reflections give this inquiry a right direction, *to wit*, to the ascertainment of the north boundary of Nova Scotia, which is the southern boundary of Canada. We have always been lured from this by the British negotiators to the *left* or *west* of this north line from the monument.

No one who is in the least conversant with the subject can suppose for a moment that this northwest angle can be found in such a direction. The question for us is, Are there any highlands north of the Bay de Chaleurs extending *in a western direction toward* a north line drawn from the monument? If this line westerly from the bay be not distinctly marked so far as to intersect this north line, the principle is to extend it in the same direction to the place of intersection; that is, if the line between Nova Scotia and Canada is *west* to within, say, 30 miles of the north line from the monument, and the rest of the way is indefinite or obscure, extend it on in the same direction until you form a point of intersection, and this will be the northwest angle of Nova Scotia. But the truth is, *the highlands are there*, and have been found in running due north from the monument. The elevations were taken by the British surveyor from the source of the St. Croix, at the monument, to the first waters of the Restigouche; and at Mars Hill, 40 miles, the summit of this isolated sugar loaf was 1,100 feet; and at the termination of the survey at the Restigouche waters, 100 miles farther, the elevation was 1,600 feet; consequently the summit of Mars Hill, 1,100 feet above the waters of the St. Croix, is 500 feet lower than the lands at the Restigouche. And yet the pretense is that there are no highlands but this detached spur, Mars Hill! Still further, the highest position surveyed is nearly 50 miles short of the Melis, which falls into the St. Lawrence, and we do not perceive that the elevations have been taken there at all, but we do find it is here that *the waters separate*, and consequently the land must be still higher.

In failure of highlands (*assumed* not to exist), the British negotiators claim a line which, instead of dividing the St. Lawrence and Atlantic waters, would actually extend between two rivers, *both of which fall into the Atlantic*.

To say nothing of the absurdity, not to say ignorance, of such a claim, it is enough that it is in the teeth of the treaty itself. It is painful to repeat the argument that no other highlands were intended, for all others were expressly excluded but those which divide the waters that flow in those different directions. The effect of their construction, as we all know, is to give them the whole of the St. John, with all its tributaries, and a tract of territory south of that river equal at least to 75 miles square.

Whether from the peaceful spirit of our Government, the Christian patience of Maine, or the "modest assurance" of the British negotiators—any or all—certain it is that His Britannic Majesty's pretensions *are growing every day*. It is not only an afterthought, but one very recently conceived, that we were to be driven south of the St. John.

His Britannic Majesty's agent, Mr. Chipman, who has been lately urging us south of that river, was also agent to the commission, under the treaty of 1795, to ascertain the true St. Croix, and in insisting on a more *western* branch of this river gives as a reason that a line due north will cross the St. John *farther up*, whereas if you

take an *eastern* branch such line will cross near Frederickton, the seat of gov
ment of New Brunswick, and materially infringe upon His Majesty's Province.
not only admits, but contends, that this north line *must* cross the river. Here
his words: "This north line must of necessity cross the river St. John." Mr.
ton, the British minister, in a private letter to Mr. Chipman of 23d October, r
recommends a modification of the powers of the commissioners for the reason
it might give Great Britain a greater extent of navigation on the St. John Ri
The same agent, Mr. Chipman, was also agent under the fourth article of the tr
of Ghent, and we find him contending there "that the northwest angle of Nova Sc
is the same designated in the grant to Sir William Alexander in 1621, subject
to such alterations as were occasioned by the erection of the Province of Qu
in 1763." Now we have already seen that this south line of the Province of (
bec, so far from *altering* this northwest angle, in fact confirms it.

In perfect accordance with this disposition to encroach is a proposition of the Bri
minister (Mr. Vaughan) that inasmuch as the highlands can not be found by a
north direction from the monument we should *vary west* until we should inter
them, *but not* EAST. Now that in case a monument can not be found in the co
prescribed you should look for it *at the left, but not to the right*, seems to us a
sinister proposition. We have shown, and, as we think, conclusively, that the ra
of highlands is to be looked for on British ground, and nowhere else, because it is t
own boundary, and a line which must, with an ascertained north line, form the a
of one of their own Provinces. And yet we are not to examine there at all; we
never explored the country there, and are expected to yield to such arrogant, ext
agant, and baseless pretensions!

We would ask why, in what justice, if we can not find the object in the route
scribed, are we to be thus trammeled? Where is the *reciprocity* of such a proposit
so degrading to the dignity and insulting to the rights and liberties of this St
No; the people of Maine will not now, and we trust they never will, tamely sul
to such a *one-sided* measure.

The next restriction or limitation with which this negotiation is to be clogge
an admission that the Restigouche and St. John are not Atlantic rivers, because
flows into the Bay de Chaleurs and the other into the Bay of Fundy; yet neither
into the river St. Lawrence. They would then find those highlands between the
John and the Penobscot. There can not be a more arrogant pretension or palp
absurdity. Suppose the waters of both these rivers are excluded as flowing nei
way, still the waters that flow *each way* are so far separated as to leave a trac
country which, if equally divided, would carry us far beyond the St. John.
we admit no such hypothesis. The *Atlantic* and the *sea* are used in the charter
synonymous terms. The Restigouche, uniting with the Bay de Chaleurs, which c
municates with the sea, and the St. John, uniting with the Bay of Fundy, which
communicates with the sea, and that, too, by a mouth 90 miles wide, are
Atlantic rivers. These rivers were known by the negotiators not to be *St. Lawr*
rivers; they were known to exist, for they were rivers of the first class. If they
neither St. Lawrence nor Atlantic, why were they not excepted? They were
of the former, therefore they must be included in the latter description. Ind
if rivers uniting with Atlantic bays are not Atlantic rivers, the Penobscot and I
nebec, which unite with the respective bays of Penobscot and Sagadahock, we
not be Atlantic rivers, and then where are those highlands which divide the wa
referred to in the treaty of 1783? Should we leave this question unsettled a l
longer, and the British claims continue to increase, we might very soon find t
highlands south of the Connecticut, and all the intermediate country would be r
onized by "construction." We therefore invoke the sympathy of all New Engl
with New York besides, to unite against this progressive claim—this avalanche w
threatens to overwhelm *them as well as ourselves.*

Again, if this Mars Hill (and we confess we can not speak of the pretension with any patience) *is the northwest angle*, and the north boundary of Nova Scotia and the south boundary of the Province of Quebec are the same, and north of the Bay de Chaleurs, then there is indeed *no* northwest angle, for a line due north from the monument, passing by Mars Hill, must pursue nearly the same direction to get to the north of that bay without crossing it; and who ever thought of an angle at the side of a continuous line? Now, according to the British maps taken in this very case, you must run a course of north about 14° east to obtain the north side of the bay without crossing it, and the distance would be in this almost due north direction more than 100 miles, while that from the monument to Mars Hill would be little more than 40. Now when we consider that this northerly line must form nearly a right angle to pass along the north shore of the Bay de Chaleurs, that this is 100 miles farther north than Mars Hill, where instead of an angle there can be only an inclination of 14°, can there be a greater absurdity than the British claim founded on these facts?

We will now present some facts and remarks in regard to the surveys and explorings made by the commission under the fifth article of the treaty of Ghent, and the first fact that occurs is that the elevations taken by the British surveyor stop far short of where the waters divide, and we find no proof that these elevations were carried through by our own surveyors. If the British surveyor, after ascertaining *he was still ascending* and had in fact arrived at the lands at *a branch of a river* elevated 500 feet above the summit of Mars Hill, *found it prudent to stop short*, we see no good reason why the American agent did not *proceed on* and take accurate elevations at a place where the waters divide. If such a survey was made, the committee have not been able to obtain the evidence. It is not in the maps or documents in the library or office of the Secretary of State, and the committee believe that no such elevations have been taken northerly of the first waters of the Restigouche. It is, indeed, a little singular that we have so little evidence, not only in regard to this height of land, but also of the rivers which flow into the St. Lawrence *to the left*, and *especially to the right*, of the north line from the monument.

We know some of them, to be sure, such as the *Oelle Kamouska*, *Verte*, *Trois Pistoles*, *Remouskey*, and *Metis* on the left, and the *Blanche*, *Louis*, *Magdalen*, and others on the right of this line, but we know them chiefly as *on maps* and as transcribed from older maps, but very little from actual survey or even exploration. An examination of the sources of those rivers at the right of this north line, with the important natural boundary, the north shore of the Bay de Chaleurs, would accurately define the divisional line between the Province of Quebec and Nova Scotia, which extending west would intersect the due north line and thus form the northwest angle of Nova Scotia.

It moreover appears that little or no exploration has been made of the lands *east* of the due north line. It seems strange to us, although it may be satisfactorily explained, why we should have been drawn away from this very important region. It is, indeed, the true source of inquiry. In this direction the evidence is to be found, and Maine can never be satisfied until it is looked for here.

An extraordinary method of adjusting this question, though in perfect accordance with other pretensions, has been proposed by Great Britain—that the disputed territory should be divided in equal portions, each party being satisfied of the justice of its claims. To this proposition we can not subscribe. It is equally unjust between nations and individuals. Whether a party in controversy is satisfied or not with the justice of his claims is what is only known to himself, and consequently the one whose claims are most exorbitant, however unjust, will always get the best end of the bargain. But such a rule would in this case apply most unfortunately to Maine. We are limited at farthest to the St. Lawrence, and to a very narrow point there, while the British may extend their claims to the south and west indefinitely.

Establish this principle and we shall soon find their claims, already so progressive, stretched over to the Piscataqua, and then if we are to divide equally both as to *quantity and quality* the divisional line then would fall south of the Kennebec. If the want of the consent of Maine is the obstacle to such an adjustment, we trust it will always remain an insuperable one. Indeed, we protest against the application to us of such a rule as manifestly unequal and unjust.

We come now to the recent transactions of the British colonial authorities, sanctioned, as it appears, by the Government at home, and we regret to perceive in them also those strong indications of continual and rapid encroachment which have characterized that Government in the whole of this controversy. Mr. Livingston, in his letter of 21st July, 1832, proposes that "until the matter be brought to a final conclusion both parties should refrain from the exercise of jurisdiction," and Mr. Vaughan, in reply of 14th April, 1833, in behalf of his Government, "entirely concurs." Here, then, the faith of the two Governments is *pledged* to abstain from acts of jurisdiction until all is settled. Now, how are the facts? We understand, and indeed it appears by documents herewith exhibited, that an act has passed the legislature of New Brunswick "incorporating the St. Andrews and Quebec Railroad Company," that the King has granted £10,000 to aid the enterprise, and that the legislature of Lower Canada, by its resolutions of both houses, has approved the scheme and promised its cooperation. It may be that the Government at home was not aware that this railroad must inevitably cross the disputed territory.

But this ignorance of the subject seems incredible. A railroad from St. Andrews to Quebec would be *impossible* unless it crossed the territory in question, even next to impossible and totally useless were it to pass at the north of the St. John. It seems, therefore, extraordinary indeed that the British Government, even in the incipient stages of this enterprise, should make an appropriation which is in direct violation of its solemn pledge. To give to a railroad corporation powers over our rights and property is the strongest act of sovereignty. It is an act of delegated power which we ourselves give to our own citizens with extreme caution and with guarded restrictions and reservations. This railroad *must* not only cross the disputed territory, but it crosses it 50 miles south of the St. John and almost to the southerly extremity of the British claim, extravagant as it is. By the map herewith exhibited of the survey of the route it appears that the road crosses our due north line at Mars Hill, thence doubling round it toward the south it crosses the *Roostic* between the Great and Little *Machias*, the *Alleguash* at the outlet of *First Lake*, a branch of the St. John south of *Black River*, and passes into Canada between "Spruce Hills" on the right and "Three Hills" on the left, thus crossing a tract of country south of the St. John 100 by 50 miles. We have not a copy of the act of incorporation of New Brunswick, and can not, therefore, say that the route there defined is the same as on the map. Be this as it may, certain it is, as anyone will see, that no possible route can be devised which will not cross the territory in question. It is, then, a deliberate act of power, palpable and direct, claiming and exercising sovereignty far south even of the line recommended by the King of the Netherlands.

In all our inquiries and examinations of this subject there has been great negligence in regard to this northwest angle. Judge Benson, one of the commissioners under Jay's treaty, in a letter to the President of the United States expressly and clearly defines this angle. He states distinctly that the due north line from the source of the St. Croix is *the west-side line*, and the highlands are *the north-side line* which form this angle, and this had never been questioned by the British themselves. This due north line, viz, the west-side line, was established by the commission of which Judge Benson was a member, and the British have made the north-side line to be north of the Bay de Chaleurs, and yet with these postulates to pretend that the points of intersection can not be found is one of the greatest of their absurdities; and another absurdity quite equal is that after passing west along the north shore of this bay they would fall down nearly south more than 100 miles to Mars Hill, about 60 miles from the south shore of the Province, at the Bay of Passamaquoddy, which is part of the Bay of Fundy, and this point, too, of so little inclination that it is a palpable perversion of language to call it *an angle,* much more a northwest angle.

It is, indeed, time for us to begin to search, and in the right places, too, in order to put a stop to these perpetual encroachments upon our territory and rights. Our first object should be to ascertain and trace the north boundary of Nova Scotia, which is the south boundary of the Province of Quebec, and see if Canada comes as far down as Mars Hill. And we should proceed to finish taking the elevations on the due north line to some point where the waters divide. The General Government should be immediately called on to execute the work, with the cooperation of Massachusetts and Maine. Notice should be given to the British authorities to unite in the undertaking, and if they refuse our Government ought to proceed *ex parte.* The act would be entirely pacific, as the object would be *to ascertain facts*—much more pacific than the survey, *without notice,* of the St. Andrews and Quebec Railroad through our territory, not for the purpose of ascertaining a boundary, but to assume jurisdiction.

Your committee have gone through this tedious investigation with all the deliberation, exactness, and candor which our time, means, and feelings would allow. Our animadversions may in some instances have been strong, and even severe, but we think we have expressed the sentiments and feelings of the people of Maine, suffering under protracted injuries. This State should take a firm, deliberate, and dignified stand, and one which it will not retract. While it awards to the General Government all its legitimate powers, it will not be forgetful of its own. We call upon the President and Congress. We invoke that aid and sympathy of our sister States which Maine has always accorded to them. We ask, nay we demand, in the name of justice, how long we are to be thus trampled down by a foreign people? And we trust we shall meet a cordial and patriotic response in the heart of every republican of the Union.

Your committee therefore submit the following resolutions:

STATE OF MAINE.

RESOLVES relative to the northeastern boundary.

Resolved, That we view with much solicitude the British usurpations and encroachments on the northeastern part of the territory of this State.

Resolved, That pretensions so groundless and extravagant indicate a spirit of hostility which we had no reason to expect from a nation with whom we are at peace.

Resolved, That vigilance, resolution, firmness, and union on the part of this State are necessary in this state of the controversy.

Resolved, That the governor be authorized and requested to call on the President of the United States to cause the northeastern boundary of this State to be explored and surveyed and monuments erected according to the *treaty* of 1783.

Resolved, That the cooperation of Massachusetts be requested.

Resolved, That our Senators in Congress be *instructed* and our Representatives *requested* to endeavor to obtain a *speedy* adjustment of the controversy.

Resolved, That copies of this report and resolution be transmitted to the governor of Massachusetts, the President of the United States, to each of our Senators and Representatives in Congress, and other Senators in Congress, and the governors of the several States.

[Passed house March 24, 1837; passed Senate and approved March 25, 1837.]

STATE OF MAINE, EXECUTIVE DEPARTMENT,
Augusta, June 27, 1837.

His Excellency MARTIN VAN BUREN,
President of the United States.

SIR: I lose no time in communicating to Your Excellency a copy of a letter from Sir John Harvey, lieutenant-governor of the Province of New Brunswick, and also of a letter from J. A. Maclauchlan to Sir John Harvey, in relation to the arrest and imprisonment of Ebenezer S. Greely.

I have the honor to be, with high consideration, your obedient servant,

ROBERT P. DUNLAP.

GOVERNMENT HOUSE,
Frederickton, New Brunswick, June 12, 1837.

His Excellency the GOVERNOR OF THE STATE OF MAINE.

SIR: Since I had the honor of addressing your excellency under date the 6th instant, announcing my assumption of the administration of this government, a report has been laid before me by the warden of the disputed territory, copy of which I feel it to be an act of courtesy toward your excellency to lose no time in communicating to you.

In including the territory within the limits of the British claim in the census which "Ebenezer Greely" appears to have been instructed to take of the population of the county of "Penobscot" he has evidently acted in ignorance or under a misconception of the subsisting relations betwixt England and the United States of America, which I can not allow myself to doubt that your excellency will lose no time in causing to be explained and removed. Though necessarily committed to confinement, I have desired that every regard may be shown to Greely's personal convenience consistent with the position in which he has *voluntarily* placed himself. I use this expression because, as your excellency will observe, Greely was informed by the warden that if he would desist from the act in which he was engaged and the language which he was holding to the people of the Madawaska settlement (acts constituting not only an interference with the acknowledged rights of jurisdiction of this Province, but the positive exercise within its limits of actual jurisdiction, however unauthorized on the part of the State of Maine) and would withdraw from this district he should be allowed to do so; otherwise that in the discharge of the duties imposed upon him by his office he (the warden), who is in the commission of the peace, must be under the necessity of apprehending, in order to make him amenable to the laws of the Province. This proposal Greely rejected, and was accordingly committed to jail to be dealt with according to law. In the meantime, as an evidence of my desire to cultivate the most friendly understanding with the government of the State of which Greely is a citizen, I lose no time in saying that upon receiving an assurance from your excellency that your authority shall be exerted in restraining this or any other citizen of the State of Maine from adopting proceedings within the British limits (as claimed) calculated to infringe the authority and jurisdiction of this Province and to disturb and unsettle the minds of that portion of its inhabitants residing in the disputed territories until the question in dispute be brought to a final settlement Greely shall immediately be enlarged.

Trusting that your excellency will see in this proposition an anxious desire on my part to redeem the pledge given in my communication of the 6th instant, I have the honor to be, your excellency's most obedient, humble servant,

J. HARVEY,
Major-General, Lieutenant-Governor, etc.

FREDERICKTON, NEW BRUNSWICK, *June 10, 1837.*

Excellency Major-General SIR JOHN HARVEY, K. C. H.,
Lieutenant-Governor, etc.:

May it please your excellency: In obedience to your excellency's instructions, communicated to me through the advocate-general in the absence of the attorney and solicitor generals, I have now the honor to report for the information of your excellency that I proceeded with the least possible delay to the Madawaska settlement. On my arrival at the Great Falls, 130 miles from hence, I was informed the American citizen Ebenezer S. Greely had passed up the day previous for the purpose of again proceeding with the census of the inhabitants of Madawaska under authority from the State of Maine. Aware of the probable excitement that would naturally arise between the two governments from this circumstance, and at the same time fully convinced that His Majesty's Government would but regret any unnecessary misunderstanding during the pending negotiation, I thought it advisable to call on Mr. Coombs, a magistrate residing 12 miles above the Falls, and request him to accompany me, which he readily did, to witness the conversation between Mr. Greely and myself.

We then proceeded and overtook Mr. Greely a short distance above Green River, about 24 miles from the Falls, having ascertained by the inhabitants, as he passed up the river, that Mr. Greely was the whole of the previous day employed in taking down their names, number of each family, and stating they would shortly receive from the State of Maine a sum of money not exceeding $3 for each head of family out of the surplus revenue of the United States.

I required Mr. Greely to show me his instructions for exercising authority in Madawaska, when he handed me a document, a copy of which I beg to inclose your excellency, and after perusing the same I returned it with my opinion that I really thought he (Mr. Greely) had mistaken the intention of his instructions, as no allusion was made either to that settlement or the territory in dispute, and therefore if he would then desist in taking the census I would take no notice of what had passed. Moreover, in reply to my advice and request, he (Mr. Greely) remonstrated and attempted to make it appear that he would be fully borne out by his government in what he had done, and it was also his intention to complete the census if he was not prevented; this reply I regret having left me no alternative but to make him a prisoner, which I did on Wednesday, the 7th instant. On Friday evening I arrived in Frederickton, and this morning (Saturday), by the advice of the advocate-generals, committed him to the gaol of the county of York.

I have the honor to be, your excellency's most obedient, humble servant.

J. A. MACLAUCHLAN,
Warden of the Disputed Territory.

STATE OF MAINE, EXECUTIVE DEPARTMENT,
June 19, 1837.

His Excellency MARTIN VAN BUREN,
President of the United States.

SIR: I have the honor to inclose to Your Excellency the copy of a letter which came to hand by the last mail, by which it appears that Ebenezer S. Greely, esq., the agent employed by the county commissioners for the county of Penobscot to take the census of the town of Madawaska, has been arrested by the authorities of the Province of New Brunswick and is now incarcerated in the jail at Frederickton.

In this state of things it becomes my painful duty to make this communication to Your Excellency and to insist that prompt measures be adopted by the Government of the United States to effect the early release of the aforementioned citizen.

I have the honor to be, with great respect, your obedient servant,

ROBERT P. DUNLAP.

FREDERICKTON, PROVINCE OF NEW BRUNSWICK,
June 12, 1837.

ROBERT P. DUNLAP, Esq.,
Governor of Maine.

SIR: On the 15th of May last I was appointed by the county commissioners of Penobscot County to take the census of Madawaska. On the 6th of June instant I was arrested by Mr. Maclauchlan, from this place, and committed to jail by him, and there I now remain—in the prison at Frederickton. I was committed on the 10th instant. I addressed a letter to you on the 10th, which has gone by the way of St. Andrews. Fearing that letter will not arrive soon, I write again to-day by way of Houlton. I have described my arrest more particularly in my first letter, which you will undoubtedly receive before long; therefore I only give the facts in this, having a chance, by the assistance of Mr. Lombard, of Hallowell, of forwarding this to Houlton privately. I was employed in business of the State, and do expect my Government will intercede and liberate me from prison in a foreign and adjacent Province. I shall be pleased to receive a line from you expressing your opinion, direction, etc.

I remain, sir, respectfully, your obedient servant,

EBEN'R S. GREELY.

DEPARTMENT OF STATE,
Washington, June 26, 1837.

His Excellency ROBERT P. DUNLAP, Esq.,
Governor of Maine.

SIR: I have the honor, by direction of the President, to acknowledge the receipt of your letter to him of the 19th instant, inclosing the copy of a communication dated the 12th of the same month addressed to you by Ebenezer S. Greely, esq., the agent employed by the county commissioners for the county of Penobscot to take the census of the town of Madawaska, from which it appears that he has been arrested by the authorities of the Province of New Brunswick and is now in confinement in the jail at Frederickton, and insisting that prompt measures be adopted by the Government of the United States to effect the early release of the above-named citizen.

The circumstances attending this outrage as given in Mr. Greely's letter are not sufficient, in the view of the President, to warrant the interference of the Government at present. For what cause, at what place, and by what authority the arrest was made is not stated. The necessary explanations may be found, perhaps, in the previous communication which Mr. Greely refers to as having been addressed to you by him on the 10th June; if not, it is probable that you will easily be able to obtain explicit information from other sources and communicate it to this Department. It is indispensable that a full knowledge of all the facts illustrative of the case should be in possession of the Government before any formal application for redress can be properly preferred.

In the meantime I have in conversation unofficially called the attention of Mr. Fox, the British minister at Washington, to this complaint, and he has given me an assurance that he will immediately address a representation on the subject to the governor of New Brunswick requesting, unless there shall be some very extraordinary reasons against it, that Mr. Greely may be set at liberty.

I am, sir, your obedient servant,

JOHN FORSYTH.

STATE OF MAINE, EXECUTIVE DEPARTMENT,
Augusta, June 27, 1837.

Hon. JOHN FORSYTH,
Secretary of State of the United States.

SIR: I would respectfully solicit copies of all documents and papers in the Department of State of the United States in relation to the subject of the northeastern boundary, with the exception of such as were furnished this department by the General Government in the year 1827. It is understood that copies have been furnished relative to this subject down to the respective statements submitted by the two Governments to the King of the Netherlands, but the arguments we have not been furnished with.

I am, very respectfully, your obedient servant,

ROBERT P. DUNLAP.

STATE OF MAINE, EXECUTIVE DEPARTMENT,
July 3, 1837.

Hon. JOHN FORSYTH,
Secretary of State of United States.

SIR: I have had the honor to receive yours of the 26th of June last, in which, by direction of the President, you indicate that the circumstances detailed in Mr. Greely's letter relative to his arrest and imprisonment are not of themselves without further explanation sufficient to justify the interference of the Government of the United States. This information is received with some surprise and much regret—surprise because I had understood Mr. Greely's communication to show that while employed within the limits of this State and under its authority on a business intrusted to him by the laws of the State he was, without being charged or suspected of any other offense, seized and transported to a foreign jail; regret inasmuch as the feelings of the people of this State have been strongly excited by this outrage upon the honor and sovereignty of Maine, and each additional day's confinement which that unoffending citizen endures is adding to the indignation of our citizens. I therefore hasten to lay before you a summary of the transactions connected with this subject as they are gathered from Mr. Greely's communications to this department. The facts are to be considered the less indisputable because they are in the main confirmed by the statements contained in the letter of the lieutenant-governor of the Province of New Brunswick, by whose order the imprisonment was made, and a copy of which I recently had the honor of transmitting to the President.

On the 8th day of March last the legislature of this State passed an act relative to the surplus revenue, a copy of which is inclosed,* to the eleventh, twelfth, and thirteenth sections of which I beg leave to refer your attention. An additional act was passed on the 29th day of March last, a copy of which I also inclose.* By this last-named act it became the duty of the county commissioners of Penobscot County to cause an enumeration to be taken of the inhabitants of said county residing north of the surveyed and located townships. The tract thus defined comprised the town of Madawaska, which was incorporated by this State on the 15th of March, 1831. Pursuant to that requirement, the county commissioners of said county appointed Ebenezer S. Greely to perform that service, and, being duly commissioned, he forthwith proceeded to the place designated and entered upon the required operations. Being thus employed, he was on the 29th day of May last arrested by the authorities of the Province of New Brunswick and conveyed to Woodstock, in the county of Carleton, in said Province, but the sheriff of the county refused to commit him to jail, and he was accordingly discharged. He immediately returned to the

* Omitted.

Madawaska settlements to enter again upon the duty intrusted to him. On the 6th day of June last he was arrested a second time by the same authorities and committed to the jail at Frederickton. It is for this act of obedience to the laws of his government that Mr. Greely now lies incarcerated in a public jail in the Province of New Brunswick. Is not redress urgently called for? Must not this unoffending citizen be immediately released?

Permit me, sir, to add my confident belief that the President on this presentation of the facts relative to this outrage upon the national as well as the State rights will not fail to demand the immediate release of Ebenezer S. Greely and to interpose suitable claims of indemnity for the wrongs so wantonly enforced upon him.

I am, very respectfully, your obedient servant,

ROBERT P. DUNLAP.

DEPARTMENT OF STATE,
Washington, July 14, 1837.

Hon. ROBERT P. DUNLAP,
   Governor of the State of Maine.

SIR: Your letter of the 3d instant has been received. The surprise you express that the information contained in the letter of Mr. Greely which accompanied your former communication was not considered sufficient to enable the President to make a formal application to the British Government for his release has probably arisen from your not having adverted particularly to the defects of his statement. It was not expressly mentioned for what offense the arrest was made nor where it took place—upon the territory in dispute between the United States and Great Britain or beyond it. The character of the charge and the place at which the offense was committed might have been inferred from what was stated, but you must perceive the impropriety of a formal complaint from one government to another founded upon inference when the means of ascertaining and presenting the facts distinctly were within the power of the party complaining; but although this Department felt itself constrained by these considerations to delay a formal application to the British Government for the release of Mr. Greely, it lost no time, as has been already stated, in procuring the interference to that end of the British minister near this Government; and I have now the satisfaction to inform you that I have learnt from him that he has opened a correspondence with the lieutenant-governor of New Brunswick, which it is expected will lead to the release of Greely from confinement without waiting for the decision of His Britannic Majesty's Government on the whole question.

The information communicated to the Department since the receipt of your letter of the 3d instant is sufficiently explicit, and a note founded upon it has been, by direction of the President, addressed to Mr. Stevenson, instructing him to demand the immediate liberation of Mr. Greely and indemnity for his imprisonment.

I have the honor to be, sir, your obedient servant,

JOHN FORSYTH.

P. S.—The papers asked for in your letter of the 27th ultimo will be sent to you.

DEPARTMENT OF STATE,
Washington, July 19, 1837.

Hon. ROBERT P. DUNLAP,
   Governor of Maine.

SIR: In compliance with the request contained in your letter of the 27th ultimo, I have the honor to transmit to you a printed volume containing a statement on the part of the United States of the case referred, in pursuance of the convention of the 29th September, 1827, between the said States and Great Britain to the King

he Netherlands for his decision thereon, and to refer you for such other papers
documents in relation to the northeastern boundary as have not been specially
ished by this Department to the executive of Maine to the following numbers
he volumes of documents of the Senate and House of Representatives distributed
er a resolution of Congress, and which have been from time to time transmitted
he several State governments, including that of Maine:'
ocuments of the House of Representatives: First session Twentieth Congress,
. 217, 218; second session Twentieth Congress, No. 90; second session Twenty-
d Congress, No. 62. Documents of the Senate: First session Twenty-fourth
gress, No. 414.

I have the honor to be, sir, your obedient servant,

JOHN FORSYTH.

STATE OF MAINE, EXECUTIVE DEPARTMENT,
July 28, 1837.

Excellency MARTIN VAN BUREN,
President of the United States.

IR: Impelled by a sense of duty arising from the oversight committed to me of
rights and interests of this State, I beg leave to invite the attention of Your
cellency to the subject of the northeastern boundary of Maine. By the federal
pact the obligation of defending each State against foreign invasion and of pro-
ing it in the exercise of its jurisdictional rights up to its extreme line of boundary
evolved upon the National Government. Permit me respectfully to inform the
sident that in the opinion of the people of Maine the justice due to this State in
 respect has not been rendered.
et it not be suspected that the discontents which are moving strongly and deeply
ough the public mind flow from any deficiency of attachment or practical adhesion
ur National Government. Without appealing to the blood so freely poured out
war by the citizens of Maine, to the privations so cheerfully endured while the
trictive measures of the Government were prostrating the most important inter-
 of this commercial people, or to the support of the Union so cordially given
ough every vicissitude up to the present hour, such a suspicion, if it could arise,
uld be sufficiently refuted by merely adverting to the forbearance with which they
ve so long endured the aggressions by a foreign government upon their sover-
nty, their citizens, and their soil.
 would be easy to prove that the territory of Maine extends to the highlands north
he St. John; but that point, having been not only admitted, but successfully dem-
strated, by the Federal Government, needs not now to be discussed. Candor, how-
r, requires me to say that this conceded and undeniable position ill accords with
 proceedings in which the British authorities have for many years been indulged,
 by which the rightful jurisdiction of Maine has been subverted, her lands rav-
d of their most valuable products, and her citizens dragged beyond the limits of
 State to undergo the sufferings and ignominies of a foreign jail. These outrages
ve been made known to the Federal Government; they have been the subject of
eated remonstrances by the State, and these remonstrances seem as often to have
n contemned. It can not be deemed irrelevant for me here to ask, amid all these
rious impositions, and while Maine has been vigorously employed in sustaining
 Union and in training her children to the same high standard of devotion to
 political institutions of the country, what relief has been brought to us by the
deral Government. The invaders have not been expelled. The sovereignty and
l of the State are yet stained by the hostile machinations of resident emissaries
 a foreign government. The territory and the jurisdiction of 6,000,000 acres, our
le to which the Government of the United States has pronounced to be perfect,
ve, without the knowledge of Maine, been once put entirely at hazard. Grave

discussions, treaty arrangements, and sovereign arbitration have been resorted to, in which Maine was not permitted to speak, and they have resulted not in removing the fictitious pretensions, but in supplying new encouragements to the aggressors. Diplomatic ingenuity, the only foundation of the British claim, has been arrayed against the perfect right. In the meantime a stipulation made by the Executive of the nation, without the knowledge of Maine, purported to preclude her from reclaiming her rightful jurisdiction until the slow process of a negotiation should be brought to a close. Whatever the real force of that stipulation might be, made as it was without the concurrence of the two branches of the treaty-making power, it was hoped when it expired by the closing up of that negotiation that a measure fraught with such hurtful consequences to Maine would not again be attempted; but that hope was to be disappointed, and now, by a compact of similar character, a writ of protection appears to have been spread by our own Government over the whole mass of British aggressions. What, then, has the Federal Government done for this State? May it not be said, in the language of another, " Maine has not been treated as she endeavored to deserve "?

On the 22d day of April last I had the honor to transmit to Your Excellency certain resolves passed by the legislature of this State relative to the northeastern boundary, and in behalf of the State to call upon the President of the United States to cause the line to be explored and surveyed and monuments thereof erected. That this call, made by direction of the legislature, did not extend to the expulsion of invaders, but merely to the ascertainment of the treaty line, will, I trust, be viewed as it was designed to be, not only as an evidence of the continued forbearance of Maine, but as a testimonial of the confidence she cherished that the Federal Executive would protect the territory after its limitation should be ascertained. That this application would meet with favor from the Federal Executive was expected, more especially as Congress had made a specific appropriation for the purpose. I will not attempt to conceal the mortification I have realized that no reply has been made to that communication nor any measures taken, so far as my information extends, for effecting the object proposed.

It now remains that in the exercise of that faithfulness for which I stand solemnly pledged to the people of Maine I should again commend to the attention of the National Executive this apparently unwelcome but really important subject.

I have, therefore, the honor again to request that the President will cause the treaty line upon the northeastern limits of Maine to be run and marked, and I can not but hope that on a reexamination of the subject Your Excellency will concur with this State in relation to the rightfulness and the necessity of the measure proposed, as well as to all the remedies to be adopted for restoring to Maine the invaluable rights from which she has so long been debarred.

I have the honor to be, with high consideration, your obedient servant,

ROBERT P. DUNLAP.

DEPARTMENT OF STATE,
Washington, August 17, 1837.

His Excellency ROBERT P. DUNLAP,
Governor of the State of Maine.

SIR: Your letter of the 28th ultimo to the President was duly received. It has been referred to this Department with instructions to make a suitable reply.

Your excellency is of opinion that the Federal Government has for a series of years failed to protect the State of Maine in the exercise of her jurisdictional rights to the extent of her boundary, and complains that these rights have been in consequence thereof subverted, the lands of the State ravaged of their most valuable productions, and her citizens subjected to imprisonment in a foreign jail. Your excellency particularly objects to the course of the Federal Government for having, without the knowledge of the State, put entirely at hazard the title of Maine, admitted by the Government of the United States to be perfect, to the territory in question by the resort to diplomatic discussions, treaty arrangements, and foreign arbitration in which Maine was not permitted to speak; for having entered into a stipulation without her consent purporting to preclude the State from retaining her rightful jurisdiction pending a negotiation, and for the continuance of it after that negotiation was supposed to have been concluded, and for an omission on the part of the Executive of the United States to comply with an application of the State made through her legislature to have the boundary line between Maine and the British North American possessions explored, surveyed, and monuments erected thereon in pursuance of the authority conferred on the President by Congress and of a request made by your excellency, which is now renewed.

The views which your excellency has been pleased to take of the subject at this time embrace measures some of which have long since ceased to be operative and reach back to the propriety of the stipulations entered into by the treaty of Ghent, also of the subsequent negotiation designed to bring those stipulations to a satisfactory result in the mode prescribed by that treaty—that of arbitrament. It being, as your excellency states, the opinion of Maine that those proceedings were unjust and unwise, it is, in a matter in which she is so deeply interested, her undoubted right to say so; yet the President thinks that he can not be mistaken in believing that no practical good can at this time be expected from discussion between the Federal and State Governments upon those points. That the measures referred to have not been as fortunate in their results as was hoped is entirely true, but your excellency may nevertheless be assured that they had their origin in a sincere desire on the part of the Federal Government to discharge all its duties toward the State of Maine as a member of the Union, and were resorted to in the full belief that her just rights would be promoted by their adoption.

In speaking of the restrictions imposed upon Maine in reclaiming her rightful jurisdiction your excellency doubtlessly refers to the understanding between the Federal Government and that of Great Britain that each party should abstain from the exercise of jurisdiction over the disputed territory during the pendency of negotiation. Unless it be correct to say that the controversy was one that did not admit of negotiation, and that the duty of the Federal Government consisted only in an immediate resort to maintain the construction put by itself upon its own rights and those of the State of Maine, there would seem to be no reasonable objection to such an arrangement as that alluded to, whether it be viewed in respect to the interests or the pacific and just characters of the respective Governments. That this arrangement was not abrogated at the period at which your excellency is understood to suppose that it ought to have been done, viz, upon the failure of a settlement of the controversy by arbitration, is explained by events of subsequent occurrence. When the award of the arbitrator was submitted by the late President to the Senate of the United States, that body refused its advice and consent to the execution of the award, and passed a resolution recommending to him to open a new negotiation with Great Britain for the ascertainment of the boundary according to the treaty of peace of 1783. That negotiation was forthwith entered upon by the Executive, is still pending, and has been prosecuted with unremitting assiduity. It is under such circumstances that the Federal Executive has decided upon a continued compliance with the arrangement referred to, and has insisted also upon its observance on the part of Great Britain.

Considerations of a similar nature have induced the President to refrain hitherto from exercising the discretionary authority with which he is invested to cause the boundary line in dispute to be explored, surveyed, and monuments to be erected thereon. Coinciding with the government of Maine on the question of the true boundary between the British Provinces and the State, the President is yet bound by

duty to consider the claim which has been set up by a foreign power in amity w
the United States and the circumstances under which the negotiation for the adj
ment of that claim has been transmitted to him. It could not be useful to exam
the foundation of the British claim in a letter to your excellency. Respect for
authorities of a friendly nation compels us to admit that they have persuaded th
selves that their claim is justly grounded. However that may be, the present Pr
dent of the United States upon entering on the discharge of the duties of his off
found that a distinct proposition had been made by his predecessor for the purp
of amicably settling this long-disputed controversy, to which no answer has yet be
received. Under such circumstances the President was not able to satisfy hims
however anxious to gratify the people and the legislature of Maine, that a step l
that recommended by them could be usefully or properly taken.

The clause containing the specific appropriation made by the last Congress
exploring, surveying, and marking certain portions of the northeastern boundary
the United States, to which your excellency alludes, is by no means imperative
its character. The simple legislative act of placing a sum of money under the c
trol of the Executive for a designated object is not understood to be a direction t
it must in any event be immediately applied to the prosecution of that object.
the contrary, so far from implying that the end in view is to be attained at all h
ards, it is believed that it merely vests a discretionary power in the President
carry out the views of Congress on his own responsibility should contingencies ar
to render expedient the proposed expenditure.

Under existing circumstances the President deems it proper to wait for the defi
tive answer of the British Government to the last proposition offered by the Unit
States. When received, a further communication to your excellency may be fou
proper, and if so will be made without unnecessary delay.

It can not be necessary to assure your excellency that the omission to reply
your communication forwarding to this Department the resolutions of the legislatu
of Maine did not in any degree arise either from a want of respect for their wishes
for the wishes of your excellency, or from indifference to the interests of the Sta
When these resolutions were received, there was every reason at no distant day
expect what is now daily looked for—a definitive answer to the proposition ju
alluded to, to which the attention of the British Government had been again forcib
invited about the time those resolutions were on their passage. Under this expect
tion a reply to the application from Maine was temporarily delayed; the more readi
as about the time of its reception the Representatives of Maine, acting in referen
to one of those resolutions, had a full and free conversation with the President. T
most recent proceedings relative to the question of boundary were shewn to the
in this Department by his directions, and the occasion thus afforded was cheerful
embraced of offering frank and unreserved explanations of the President's views.

Of the recent events which have called the attention of the State of Maine to t
question of the northeastern boundary, and which have been brought by it
the notice of the President, one—the arrest and imprisonment of Mr. Greely—h
already been made the subject of communication with your excellency. All th
it was competent for the Federal Executive to do has been done. Redress has bee
demanded, will be insisted upon, and is expected from that authority from who
alone redress can properly be sought. The President has followed the same cour
that was pursued by one of his predecessors and which was understood to be sati
factory to the State of Maine under circumstances of a somewhat similar characte
In respect to the other—the projected construction of a railroad between St. Andre
and Quebec—a representation has been addressed to the British Government statir
that the proposed measure is inconsistent with the understanding between the tw
Governments to preserve the *status quo* in the disputed territory until the questio
of boundary be satisfactorily adjusted, remonstrating against the project as contrar

to the American claim and demanding a suspension of all further movements in execution of it. No answer has yet been received to this communication. From an informal conversation between the British minister at Washington and myself at the Department of State, the President is, however, firm in the conviction that the attempt to make the road in question will not be further prosecuted.

I am, in conclusion, directed to inform you that however unbounded may be the confidence of the legislature and people of Maine in the justice of their claim to the boundary contended for by the United States, the President's is not less so; and your excellency may rest assured that no exertions have been or shall be spared on his part to bring to a favorable and speedy termination a question involving interests so highly important to Maine and to the Union.

I have the honor to be, with high consideration, your excellency's obedient servant,

JOHN FORSYTH.

DEPARTMENT OF STATE,
Washington, August 25, 1837.

His Excellency ROBERT P. DUNLAP,
   Governor of Maine.

SIR: I have the honor to transmit to your excellency, by direction of the President, the copy of a note from the British minister at Washington, dated yesterday, stating that the Government of Her Britannic Majesty has been pleased to direct the immediate discontinuance by the colonial authorities of Lower Canada and New Brunswick, respectively, of all operations connected with the projected railroad between the cities of Quebec and St. Andrews.

Mr. Fox took occasion on Wednesday last to inform me that Mr. Greely had been discharged from imprisonment at Frederickton, a fact of which doubtlessly your excellency has been some time since apprised.

I have the honor to be, with high consideration, your excellency's obedient servant,

JOHN FORSYTH.

DEPARTMENT OF STATE,
Washington, March 23, 1837.

HENRY S. FOX, Esq., etc.:

The undersigned, Secretary of State of the United States, has the honor, by direction of the President, to invite the attention of Mr. Fox, His Britannic Majesty's envoy extraordinary and minister plenipotentiary, to a subject which from its high importance demands the prompt consideration of His Majesty's Government.

It appears from representations and documents recently received at the Department of State that a number of inhabitants of the town of St. Andrews, in New Brunswick, associated themselves together in the year 1835, by the name of the St. Andrews and Quebec Railroad Association, for the purpose of bringing into public notice the practicability of constructing a railway between those ports, and that sundry resolutions were passed in furtherance of this object; that the project was sanctioned and patronized by the governor in chief of British North America, the lieutenant-governors of New Brunswick and Nova Scotia, and the legislatures and people of the Provinces of Lower Canada and New Brunswick; that the route of the proposed railroad had been explored as far as the head waters of the St. John River by surveyors employed by the association; that an act has actually passed the legislature of New Brunswick incorporating this company, and that a similar act was expected to be passed in Lower Canada; that letters were addressed to the boards of trade of Quebec and Montreal requesting their cooperation; that these communications were favorably received, and that petitions had been forwarded to His Britannic Majesty, signed by committees of the association and by inhabitants of the cities of Quebec and

Montreal, soliciting the construction of a railway between the ports above named, or the extension of royal aid and protection to the petitioners in the proposed undertaking.

Without allowing himself for a moment to believe that His Britannic Majesty's Government will in any manner countenance the projected railroad from St. Andrews to Quebec when the slightest inspection of the map of the country which it crosses will show that its intended location would be for a great portion of the route an encroachment upon the territory in dispute between the United States and Great Britain, the President yet sees cause for painful surprise and deep regret in the fact that the civil authorities of His Majesty's Provinces on our northeastern borders should have lent their encouragement to or should in any wise have promoted an undertaking which if persevered in will inevitably lead to the most disastrous consequences. The object of the association from its inception was objectionable, since it could only be effected by entering upon territory the title to which was controverted and unsettled—a proceeding which could not fail to be offensive to the Government and people of the United States. Still more unjustifiable was the act of sovereignty giving to this company corporate powers over property known to be claimed by citizens of a friendly and neighboring State, and which constituted at the time the subject of an amicable negotiation between the Government of His Majesty and that of the United States. The President regrets to see in this step on the part of His Majesty's provincial authorities and subjects a most exceptionable departure from the principle of continuing to abstain during the progress of negotiation from any extension of the exercise of jurisdiction within the disputed territory on either side, the propriety of which has been hitherto so sedulously inculcated and so distinctly acquiesced in by both parties. An understanding that this principle should be observed by them was the natural result of the respective positions and pacific intentions of the two Governments, and could alone prevent the exercise of asserted rights by force. Without it the end of all negotiation on the subject would have been defeated. If, therefore, nothing had been said by either party relative to such an understanding, it would have been proper to infer that a tacit agreement to that effect existed between the two Governments. But the correspondence between them is sufficiently full and explicit to prevent all misconception. The views of both Governments in respect to it will be found in the letters of the Secretary of State to the minister of Great Britain dated the 18th of January, 1826, 9th of January, 11th of March, and 11th of May, 1829, and of the British minister to the Secretary of State dated 15th of November and 2d of December, 1825; 16th of January, 1827; 18th of February and 25th of March, 1828, and 14th of April, 1833, as well as in other communications, which it is deemed needless now to designate.

The undersigned is directed by the President to inform Mr. Fox that the prosecution of the enterprise above referred to will be regarded by this Government as a deliberate infringement of the rights of the United States to the territory in question and as an unwarrantable assumption of jurisdiction therein by the British Government, and the undersigned is instructed to urge the prompt adoption of such measures as may be deemed most appropriate by His Majesty's Government to suspend any further movements in execution of the proposed railroad from St. Andrews to Quebec during the continuance of the pending negotiations between the two Governments relative to the northeastern boundary of the United States.

The proceedings above alluded to, considered in connection with incidents on other parts of the disputed boundary line well known to His Majesty's ministers, would seem to render it indispensable to the maintenance of those liberal and friendly relations between the two countries which both Governments are so sincerely anxious to preserve that they should come to a speedy adjustment of the subject. The recent resolutions of the State of Maine, to which the projected railroad from St. Andrews to Quebec gave rise, requesting the President of the United States to cause the line established by the treaty of 1783 to be run and monuments to be established thereon, and the appropriation of $20,000 by Congress at their late session to enable the Executive to carry that request into effect, with a subsequent earnest application from the Representatives of Maine for an immediate compliance with it, afford additional incentives to exertion to bring this controversy to a conclusion not to be disregarded by the President of the United States.

The President therefore awaits with great anxiety the decision of His Majesty's Government on the proposition made by the undersigned to His Majesty's chargé d'affaires at Washington in February, 1836, suggesting the river St. John, from its mouth to its source, as an eligible and convenient line of boundary. No small degree of disappointment has been felt that this decision, already long expected, has not been given, but the hope is entertained that the result of this protracted deliberation will prove favorable to the wishes of the President, and that even if that proposition be not acceded to by His Britannic Majesty some definitive offer looking to a prompt termination of the controversy will be made without further delay.

The undersigned avails himself of this occasion to renew to Mr. Fox the assurance of his distinguished consideration.

JOHN FORSYTH.

WASHINGTON, *March 28, 1837.*

Hon. JOHN FORSYTH, etc.:

The undersigned, His Britannic Majesty's envoy extraordinary and minister plenipotentiary, has had the honor to receive the official note addressed to him under date of the 23d instant by Mr. Forsyth, Secretary of State of the United States, upon the subject of information received by the United States Government of a projected railroad between the cities of Quebec and St. Andrews, and upon certain other matters connected with the question of the boundary line between the United States and the British possessions in North America.

The undersigned, in accordance with the wishes of the President signified in Mr. Forsyth's official note, will not fail immediately to convey that note to the knowledge of his Government at home; and he entertains no doubt that His Majesty's Government will proceed to the consideration of the several matters therein contained with the serious and ready attention that their importance deserves.

The undersigned avails himself of this occasion to renew to Mr. Forsyth the assurance of his high esteem and consideration.

H. S. FOX.

WASHINGTON, *August 24, 1837.*

Hon. JOHN FORSYTH, etc.

SIR: With reference to the official note which, by direction of the President, you addressed to me on the 23d of March last, respecting a projected railroad between the cities of Quebec and St. Andrews, which it was apprehended would, if carried into effect, traverse a part of the territory at present in dispute between Great Britain and the United States, I am now enabled to inform you that, in consideration of the arguments and observations contained in your note, Her Majesty's Government has been pleased to direct the colonial authorities of Lower Canada and New Brunswick, respectively, to cause all operations connected with the above-mentioned project within the limits of the disputed territory to be immediately discontinued.

I have the honor to be, sir, with high respect and consideration, your most obedient and humble servant,

H. S. FOX.

Mr. Stevenson to Lord Palmerston.

[Extract.]

23 PORTLAND PLACE, *August 10, 1837.*

*   *   *   *   *   *   *

The undersigned will avail himself of the occasion to remind Lord Palmerston of the urgency which exists for the immediate and final adjustment of this long-pending controversy [respecting the northeastern boundary] and the increased obstacles which will be thrown in the way of its harmonious settlement by these repeated collisions of authority and the exercise of exclusive jurisdiction by either party within the disputed territory.

He begs leave also to repeat to his lordship assurances of the earnest and unabated desire which the President feels that the controversy should be speedily and amicably settled, and to express the anxiety with which the Government of the United States is waiting the promised decision of Her Majesty's Government upon the proposition submitted to it as far back as July, 1836, and which the undersigned had been led to believe would long since have been given; and he has been further directed to say that should this proposition be disapproved the President entertains the hope that some new one, on the part of Her Majesty's Government, will immediately be made for the final and favorable termination of this protracted and deeply exciting controversy.

The undersigned begs Lord Palmerston to receive renewed assurances of his distinguished consideration.

A. STEVENSON.

WASHINGTON, *September 26, 1837.*

To the House of Representatives of the United States:

In compliance with that part of the resolution of the House of Representatives of the 9th of January last which relates to the diplomatic correspondence of the late William Tudor while chargé d'affaires of the United States to Brazil, I transmit a report from the Secretary of State, together with the documents by which it was accompanied.

M. VAN BUREN.

WASHINGTON, *September 30, 1837.*

To the House of Representatives of the United States:

In compliance with the resolution of the House of Representatives of the United States of the 13th instant, respecting an annexation of Texas to the United States, I transmit a report from the Secretary of State and the documents by which it was accompanied.

M. VAN BUREN.

WASHINGTON, *September 30, 1837.*

To the House of Representatives of the United States:

I transmit to the House of Representatives a report of the Secretary of State, containing the information requested by their resolution of the 19th instant, together with the documents by which the report was accompanied.

M. VAN BUREN.

DEPARTMENT OF STATE,
Washington, September 29, 1837.

The PRESIDENT OF THE UNITED STATES:

The Secretary of State, to whom was referred a resolution of the House of Representatives of the 19th instant, requesting the President to communicate to that House what measures have been adopted since the adjournment of the last Congress in relation to the tobacco trade between the United States and foreign countries, also such information as he may have received from our ministers or other agents abroad in relation to the same, has the honor to report that since the adjournment of the last Congress instructions have been given to the diplomatic representatives of this country at the Courts of Great Britain, France, Russia, Prussia, Sweden, Denmark, Holland, and Belgium directing them to endeavor to procure from the respective Governments to which they are accredited the abolition or modification of the existing duties and restrictions upon tobacco imported from the United States, and that special agents have been appointed to collect information respecting the importation, the cultivation, the manufacture, and consumption of tobacco in the various States of Germany to which the United States have not accredited representatives, and to prepare the way for negotiations for the promotion of the interests of the tobacco trade with those countries. A copy of the dispatches of the representatives of the United States received upon this subject is herewith communicated.*

The special agents have proceeded to the execution of their duties, but no report has as yet been received from either of them.

All which is respectfully submitted.

JOHN FORSYTH.

WASHINGTON CITY, *October 2, 1837.*
To the Senate of the United States:

I transmit herewith, for the consideration of the Senate, a treaty concluded with the Miami tribe of Indians by General Marshall in 1834, with explanatory documents from the Department of War, and ask its advice in regard to the ratification of the original treaty with the amendments proposed by the Secretary of War; the treaty, with the amendments, in the event of its ratification by the United States, to be again submitted to the chiefs and warriors of the Miami tribes for their sanction or rejection.

M. VAN BUREN.

'WASHINGTON, *October 2, 1837.*
To the House of Representatives of the United States:

In compliance with the resolution of the House of Representatives of the 13th ultimo, concerning the boundary between the United States and the Mexican Republic and a cession of territory belonging to the Mexican Confederation to the United States, I transmit a report from the Secretary of State and the documents by which it was accompanied.

M. VAN BUREN.

[*Omitted.

WASHINGTON, *October, 1837.*

To the House of Representatives of the United States:

I have the honor, in compliance with the resolution of the House of Representatives of the 4th instant, to transmit the proceedings of the court of inquiry in the case of Brevet Brigadier-General Wool.*

M. VAN BUREN.

PROCLAMATION.

BY THE PRESIDENT OF THE UNITED STATES OF AMERICA.

A PROCLAMATION.

Whereas by an act of Congress of the United States of the 25th of May, 1832, entitled "An act to exempt the vessels of Portugal from the payment of duties of tonnage," it was enacted as follows: "No duties upon tonnage shall be hereafter levied or collected of the vessels of the Kingdom of Portugal: *Provided, always,* That whenever the President of the United States shall be satisfied that the vessels of the United States are subjected in the ports of the Kingdom of Portugal to payment of any duties of tonnage, he shall by proclamation declare the fact, and the duties now payable by vessels of that Kingdom shall be levied and paid as if this act had not been passed;" and

Whereas satisfactory evidence has been received by me not only that the vessels of the United States are subjected in the ports of the said Kingdom of Portugal to payment of duties of tonnage, but that a discrimination exists in respect to those duties against the vessels of the United States:

Now, therefore, I, Martin Van Buren, President of the United States of America, do hereby declare that fact and proclaim that the duties payable by vessels of the said Kingdom of Portugal on the 25th day of May, 1832, shall henceforth be levied and paid as if the said act of the 25th of May, 1832, had not been passed.

Given under my hand, at the city of Washington, the 11th day of October, 1837, and of the Independence of the United States the sixty-second.

M. VAN BUREN.

By the President:
JOHN FORSYTH,
Secretary of State.

---

* Respecting transactions in the Cherokee country.

FIRST ANNUAL MESSAGE.

WASHINGTON, *December 5, 1837.*

Fellow-Citizens of the Senate and House of Representatives:

We have reason to renew the expression of our devout gratitude to the Giver of All Good for His benign protection. Our country presents on every side the evidences of that continued favor under whose auspices it has gradually risen from a few feeble and dependent colonies to a prosperous and powerful confederacy. We are blessed with domestic tranquillity and all the elements of national prosperity. The pestilence which, invading for a time some flourishing portions of the Union, interrupted the general prevalence of unusual health has happily been limited in extent and arrested in its fatal career. The industry and prudence of our citizens are gradually relieving them from the pecuniary embarrassments under which portions of them have labored; judicious legislation and the natural and boundless resources of the country have afforded wise and timely aid to private enterprise, and the activity always characteristic of our people has already in a great degree resumed its usual and profitable channels.

The condition of our foreign relations has not materially changed since the last annual message of my predecessor. We remain at peace with all nations, and no efforts on my part consistent with the preservation of our rights and the honor of the country shall be spared to maintain a position so consonant to our institutions. We have faithfully sustained the foreign policy with which the United States, under the guidance of their first President, took their stand in the family of nations—that of regulating their intercourse with other powers by the approved principles of private life; asking and according equal rights and equal privileges; rendering and demanding justice in all cases; advancing their own and discussing the pretensions of others with candor, directness, and sincerity; appealing at all times to reason, but never yielding to force nor seeking to acquire anything for themselves by its exercise.

A rigid adherence to this policy has left this Government with scarcely a claim upon its justice for injuries arising from acts committed by its authority. The most imposing and perplexing of those of the United States upon foreign governments for aggressions upon our citizens were disposed of by my predecessor. Independently of the benefits conferred upon our citizens by restoring to the mercantile community so many millions of which they had been wrongfully divested, a great service was also rendered to his country by the satisfactory adjustment of so many ancient and irritating subjects of contention; and it reflects no ordinary credit on his successful administration of public affairs that this great object was accomplished without compromising on any occasion either the honor or the peace of the nation.

With European powers no new subjects of difficulty have arisen, and those which were under discussion, although not terminated, do not present a more unfavorable aspect for the future preservation of that good understanding which it has ever been our desire to cultivate.

Of pending questions the most important is that which exists with the Government of Great Britain in respect to our northeastern boundary. It is with unfeigned regret that the people of the United States must look back upon the abortive efforts made by the Executive, for a period of more than half a century, to determine what no nation should suffer long to remain in dispute—the true line which divides its possessions from those of other powers. The nature of the settlements on the borders of the United States and of the neighboring territory was for a season such that this, perhaps, was not indispensable to a faithful performance of the duties of the Federal Government. Time has, however, changed this state of things, and has brought about a condition of affairs in which the true interests of both countries imperatively require that this question should be put at rest. It is not to be disguised that, with full confidence, often expressed, in the desire of the British Government to terminate it, we are apparently as far from its adjustment as we were at the time of signing the treaty of peace in 1783. The sole result of long-pending negotiations and a perplexing arbitration appears to be a conviction on its part that a conventional line must be adopted, from the impossibility of ascertaining the true one according to the description contained in that treaty. Without coinciding in this opinion, which is not thought to be well founded, my predecessor gave the strongest proof of the earnest desire of the United States to terminate satisfactorily this dispute by proposing the substitution of a conventional line if the consent of the States interested in the question could be obtained. To this proposition no answer has as yet been received. The attention of the British Government has, however, been urgently invited to the subject, and its reply can not, I am confident, be much longer delayed. The general relations between Great Britain and the United States are of the most friendly character, and I am well satisfied of the sincere disposition of that Government to maintain them upon their present footing. This disposition has also, I am persuaded, become more general with the people of England than at any previous period. It is scarcely necessary to say to you how cordially it is reciprocated by the Government and people of the United States. The conviction, which must be common to all, of the injurious consequences that result from keeping open this irritating question, and the certainty that its final settlement can not be much longer deferred, will, I trust, lead to an early and satisfactory adjustment. At your last session I laid before you the recent communications between the two Governments and between this Government and that of the State of Maine, in whose solicitude concerning a subject in which she has so deep an interest every portion of the Union participates.

The feelings produced by a temporary interruption of those harmonious relations between France and the United States which are due as well to the recollections of former times as to a correct appreciation of existing interests have been happily succeeded by a cordial disposition on both sides to cultivate an active friendship in their future intercourse. The opinion, undoubtedly correct, and steadily entertained by us, that the commercial relations at present existing between the two countries are susceptible of great and reciprocally beneficial improvements is obviously gaining ground in France, and I am assured of the disposition of that Government to favor the accomplishment of such an object. This disposition shall be met in a proper spirit on our part. The few and comparatively unimportant questions that remain to be adjusted between us can, I have no doubt, be settled with entire satisfaction and without difficulty.

Between Russia and the United States sentiments of good will continue to be mutually cherished. Our minister recently accredited to that Court has been received with a frankness and cordiality and with evidences of respect for his country which leave us no room to doubt the preservation in future of those amicable and liberal relations which have so long and so uninterruptedly existed between the two countries. On the few subjects under discussion between us an early and just decision is confidently anticipated.

A correspondence has been opened with the Government of Austria for the establishment of diplomatic relations, in conformity with the wishes of Congress as indicated by an appropriation act of the session of 1837, and arrangements made for the purpose, which will be duly carried into effect.

With Austria and Prussia and with the States of the German Empire (now composing with the latter the Commercial League) our political relations are of the most friendly character, whilst our commercial intercourse is gradually extending, with benefit to all who are engaged in it.

Civil war yet rages in Spain, producing intense suffering to its own people, and to other nations inconvenience and regret. Our citizens who have claims upon that country will be prejudiced for a time by the condition of its treasury, the inevitable consequence of long-continued and exhausting internal wars. The last installment of the interest of the debt due under the convention with the Queen of Spain has not been paid and similar failures may be expected to happen until a portion of the resources of her Kingdom can be devoted to the extinguishment of its foreign debt.

Having received satisfactory evidence that discriminating tonnage duties were charged upon the vessels of the United States in the ports of Portugal, a proclamation was issued on the 11th day of October last, in compliance with the act of May 25, 1832, declaring that fact, and the duties on foreign tonnage which were levied upon Portuguese vessels in the United States previously to the passage of that act are accordingly revived.

The act of July 4, 1836, suspending the discriminating duties upon the produce of Portugal imported into this country in Portuguese vessels, was passed, upon the application of that Government through its representative here, under the belief that no similar discrimination existed in Portugal to the prejudice of the United States. I regret to state that such duties are now exacted in that country upon the cargoes of American vessels, and as the act referred to vests no discretion in the Executive, it is for Congress to determine upon the expediency of further legislation on the subject. Against these discriminations affecting the vessels of this country and their cargoes seasonable remonstrance was made, and notice was given to the Portuguese Government that unless they should be discontinued the adoption of countervailing measures on the part of the United States would become necessary; but the reply of that Government, received at the Department of State through our chargé d'affaires at Lisbon in the month of September last, afforded no ground to hope for the abandonment of a system so little in harmony with the treatment shown to the vessels of Portugal and their cargoes in the ports of this country and so contrary to the expectations we had a right to entertain.

With Holland, Sweden, Denmark, Naples, and Belgium a friendly intercourse has been uninterruptedly maintained.

With the Government of the Ottoman Porte and its dependencies on the coast of the Mediterranean peace and good will are carefully cultivated, and have been fostered by such good offices as the relative distance and the condition of those countries would permit.

Our commerce with Greece is carried on under the laws of the two Governments, reciprocally beneficial to the navigating interests of both; and I have reason to look forward to the adoption of other measures which will be more extensively and permanently advantageous.

Copies of the treaties concluded with the Governments of Siam and Muscat are transmitted for the information of Congress, the ratifications having been received and the treaties made public since the close of the last annual session. Already have we reason to congratulate ourselves on the prospect of considerable commercial benefit; and we have, besides, received from the Sultan of Muscat prompt evidence of his desire to cultivate the most friendly feelings, by liberal acts toward one of our vessels, bestowed in a manner so striking as to require on our part a grateful acknowledgment.

Our commerce with the islands of Cuba and Porto Rico still labors under heavy restrictions, the continuance of which is a subject of regret. The only effect of an adherence to them will be to benefit the navigation of other countries at the expense of both the United States and Spain.

The independent nations of this continent have ever since they emerged from the colonial state experienced severe trials in their progress to the permanent establishment of liberal political institutions. Their unsettled condition not only interrupts their own advances to prosperity, but has often seriously injured the other powers of the world. The claims of our citizens upon Peru, Chili, Brazil, the Argentine Republic, the Governments formed out of the Republics of Colombia and Mexico, are still pending, although many of them have been presented for examination more than twenty years. New Granada, Venezuela, and Ecuador have recently formed a convention for the purpose of ascertaining and adjusting claims upon the Republic of Colombia, from which it is earnestly hoped our citizens will ere long receive full compensation for the injuries inflicted upon them and for the delay in affording it.

An advantageous treaty of commerce has been concluded by the United States with the Peru-Bolivian Confederation, which wants only the ratification of that Government. The progress of a subsequent negotiation for the settlement of claims upon Peru has been unfavorably affected by the war between that power and Chili and the Argentine Republic, and the same event is also likely to produce delays in the settlement of our demands on those powers.

The aggravating circumstances connected with our claims upon Mexico and a variety of events touching the honor and integrity of our Government led my predecessor to make at the second session of the last Congress a special recommendation of the course to be pursued to obtain a speedy and final satisfaction of the injuries complained of by this Government and by our citizens. He recommended a final demand of redress, with a contingent authority to the Executive to make reprisals if that demand should be made in vain. From the proceedings of Congress on that recommendation it appeared that the opinion of both branches of the Legislature coincided with that of the Executive, that any mode of redress known to the law of nations might justifiably be used. It was obvious, too, that Congress believed with the President that another demand should be made, in order to give undeniable and satisfactory proof of our desire to avoid extremities with a neighboring power, but that there was an indisposition to vest a discretionary authority in the Executive to take redress should it unfortunately be either denied or unreasonably delayed by the Mexican Government.

So soon as the necessary documents were prepared, after entering upon the duties of my office, a special messenger was sent to Mexico to make a final demand of redress, with the documents required by the provisions of our treaty. The demand was made on the 20th of July last. The reply, which bears date the 29th of the same month, contains assurances of a desire on the part of that Government to give a prompt and explicit answer respecting each of the complaints, but that the examination of them would necessarily be deliberate; that in this examination it would be guided by the principles of public law and the obligation of treaties; that nothing should be left undone that might lead to the most speedy and equitable adjustment of our demands, and that its determination in respect to each case should be communicated through the Mexican minister here.

Since that time an envoy extraordinary and minister plenipotentiary has been accredited to this Government by that of the Mexican Republic. He brought with him assurances of a sincere desire that the pending differences between the two Governments should be terminated in a manner satisfactory to both. He was received with reciprocal assurances, and a hope was entertained that his mission would lead to a speedy, satisfactory, and final adjustment of all existing subjects of complaint. A sincere believer in the wisdom of the pacific policy by which the United States have always been governed in their intercourse with foreign nations, it was my particular desire, from the proximity of the Mexican Republic and well-known occurrences on our frontier, to be instrumental in obviating all existing difficulties with that Government and in restoring to the intercourse between the two Republics that liberal and friendly character by which they should always be distinguished. I regret, therefore, the more deeply to have found in the recent communications of that Government so little reason to hope that any future efforts of mine for the accomplishment of those desirable objects would be successful.

Although the larger number—and many of them aggravated cases of personal wrongs—have been now for years before the Mexican Government, and some of the causes of national complaint, and those of the most offensive character, admitted of immediate, simple, and satisfactory replies, it is only within a few days past that any specific communication in answer to our last demand, made five months ago, has been received from the Mexican minister. By the report of the Secretary of State herewith presented and the accompanying documents it will be seen that for not one of our public complaints has satisfaction been given or offered, that but one of the cases of personal wrong has been favorably considered, and that but four cases of both descriptions out of all those formally presented and earnestly pressed have as yet been decided upon by the Mexican Government.

Not perceiving in what manner any of the powers given to the Executive alone could be further usefully employed in bringing this unfortunate controversy to a satisfactory termination, the subject was by my predecessor referred to Congress as one calling for its interposition. In accordance with the clearly understood wishes of the Legislature, another and formal demand for satisfaction has been made upon the Mexican Government, with what success the documents now communicated will show. On a careful and deliberate examination of their contents, and considering the spirit manifested by the Mexican Government, it has become my painful duty to return the subject as it now stands to Congress, to whom it belongs to decide upon the time, the mode, and the measure of redress. Whatever may be your decision, it shall be faithfully executed, confident that it will be characterized by that moderation and justice which will, I trust, under all circumstances govern the councils of our country.

The balance in the Treasury on the 1st January, 1837, was $45,968,523. The receipts during the present year from all sources, including the amount of Treasury notes issued, are estimated at $23,499,981, constituting an aggregate of $69,468,504. Of this amount about $35,281,361 will have been expended at the end of the year on appropriations made by Congress, and the residue, amounting to $34,187,143, will be the nominal balance in the Treasury on the 1st of January next; but of that sum only $1,085,498 is considered as immediately available for and applicable to public purposes. Those portions of it which will be for some time unavailable consist chiefly of sums deposited with the States and due from the former deposit banks. The details upon this subject will be found in the annual report of the Secretary of the Treasury. The amount of Treasury notes which it will be necessary to issue during the year on account of those funds being unavailable will, it is supposed, not exceed four and a half millions. It seemed proper, in the condition of the country, to have the estimates on all subjects made as low as practicable without prejudice to any great public measures. The Departments were therefore desired to prepare their estimates accordingly, and I am happy to find that they have been able to graduate them on so economical a scale. In the great and often unexpected fluctuations to which the revenue is subjected it is not possible to compute the receipts beforehand with great certainty, but should they not differ essentially from present anticipations, and should the appropriations not much exceed the estimates, no difficulty seems likely to happen in defraying the current expenses with promptitude and fidelity.

Notwithstanding the great embarrassments which have recently occurred in commercial affairs, and the liberal indulgence which in consequence of these embarrassments has been extended to both the merchants and the banks, it is gratifying to be able to anticipate that the Treasury notes which have been issued during the present year will be redeemed and that the resources of the Treasury, without any resort to loans or increased taxes, will prove ample for defraying all charges imposed on it during 1838.

The report of the Secretary of the Treasury will afford you a more minute exposition of all matters connected with the administration of the finances during the current year—a period which for the amount of public moneys disbursed and deposited with the States, as well as the financial difficulties encountered and overcome, has few parallels in our history.

Your attention was at the last session invited to the necessity of additional legislative provisions in respect to the collection, safe-keeping, and transfer of the public money. No law having been then matured, and not understanding the proceedings of Congress as intended to be final, it becomes my duty again to bring the subject to your notice.

On that occasion three modes of performing this branch of the public service were presented for consideration. These were, the creation of a national bank; the revival, with modifications, of the deposit system established by the act of the 23d of June, 1836, permitting the use of the public moneys by the banks; and the discontinuance of the use of such institutions for the purposes referred to, with suitable provisions for their accomplishment through the agency of public officers. Considering the opinions of both Houses of Congress on the first two propositions as expressed in the negative, in which I entirely concur, it is unnecessary for me again to recur to them. In respect to the last, you have had an opportunity since your adjournment not only to test still further the expediency of the measure by the continued practical operation of such parts of it as are now in force, but also to discover what should ever be sought for and regarded with the utmost deference—the opinions and wishes of the people.

The national will is the supreme law of the Republic, and on all subjects within the limits of his constitutional powers should be faithfully obeyed by the public servant. Since the measure in question was submitted to your consideration most of you have enjoyed the advantage of personal communication with your constituents. For one State only has an election been held for the Federal Government; but the early day at which it took place deprived the measure under consideration of much of the support it might otherwise have derived from the result. Local elections for State officers have, however, been held in several of the States, at which the expediency of the plan proposed by the Executive has been more or less discussed. You will, I am confident, yield to their results the respect due to every expression of the public voice. Desiring, however, to arrive at truth and a just view of the subject in all its bearings, you will at the same time remember that questions of far deeper and more immediate local interest than the fiscal plans of the National Treasury were involved in those elections. Above all, we can not overlook the striking fact that there were at the time in those States more than one hundred and sixty millions of bank capital, of which large portions were subject to actual forfeiture, other large portions upheld only by special and limited legislative indulgences, and most of it, if not all, to a greater or less extent dependent for a continuance of its corporate existence upon the will of the State legislatures to be then chosen. Apprised of this circumstance, you will judge whether it is not most probable that the peculiar condition of that vast interest in these respects, the extent to which it has been spread through all the ramifications of society, its direct connection with the then pending elections, and the feelings it was calculated to infuse into the canvass have exercised a far greater influence over the result than any which could possibly have been produced by a conflict of opinion in respect to a question in the administration of the General Government more remote and far less important in its bearings upon that interest.

I have found no reason to change my own opinion as to the expediency of adopting the system proposed, being perfectly satisfied that there will be neither stability nor safety either in the fiscal affairs of the Government or in the pecuniary transactions of individuals and corporations so long as a connection exists between them which, like the past, offers such strong inducements to make them the subjects of political agitation. Indeed, I am more than ever convinced of the dangers to which the free and unbiased exercise of political opinion—the only sure foundation and safeguard of republican government—would be exposed by any further increase of the already overgrown influence of corporate authorities. I can not, therefore, consistently with my views of duty, advise a renewal of a connection which circumstances have dissolved.

The discontinuance of the use of State banks for fiscal purposes ought not, to be regarded as a measure of hostility toward those institutions. Banks properly established and conducted are highly useful to the business of the country, and will doubtless continue to exist in the States so long as they conform to their laws and are found to be safe and beneficial. How they should be created, what privileges they should enjoy, under what responsibilities they should act, and to what restrictions they should be subject are questions which, as I observed on a previous occasion, belong to the States to decide. Upon their rights or the exercise of them the General Government can have no motive to encroach. Its duty toward them is well performed when it refrains from legislating for their special benefit, because such legislation would violate the spirit of the Constitution and be unjust to other interests; when it takes no steps to impair their usefulness, but so manages its own affairs as to make it the interest of those institutions to strengthen and improve their condition for the security and welfare of the community at large. They have no right to insist on a connection with the Federal Government, nor on the use of the public money for their own benefit. The object of the measure under consideration is to avoid for the future a compulsory connection of this kind. It proposes to place the General Government, in regard to the essential points of the collection, safe-keeping, and transfer of the public money, in a situation which shall relieve it from all dependence on the will of irresponsible individuals or corporations; to withdraw those moneys from the uses of private trade and confide them to agents constitutionally selected and controlled by law; to abstain from improper interference with the industry of the people and withhold inducements to improvident dealings on the part of individuals; to give stability to the concerns of the Treasury; to preserve the measures of the Government from the unavoidable reproaches that flow from such a connection, and

the banks themselves from the injurious effects of a supposed participation in the political conflicts of the day, from which they will otherwise
find it difficult to escape.

These are my views upon this important subject, formed after careful
reflection and with no desire but to arrive at what is most likely to promote the public interest. They are now, as they were before, submitted
with unfeigned deference for the opinions of others. It was hardly to
be hoped that changes so important on a subject so interesting could be
made without producing a serious diversity of opinion; but so long as
those conflicting views are kept above the influence of individual or local
interests, so long as they pursue only the general good and are discussed
with moderation and candor, such diversity is a benefit, not an injury.
If a majority of Congress see the public welfare in a different light, and
more especially if they should be satisfied that the measure proposed
would not be acceptable to the people, I shall look to their wisdom to
substitute such as may be more conducive to the one and more satisfactory to the other. In any event, they may confidently rely on my hearty
cooperation to the fullest extent to which my views of the Constitution
and my sense of duty will permit.

It is obviously important to this branch of the public service and to
the business and quiet of the country that the whole subject should in
some way be settled and regulated by law, and, if possible, at your present
session. Besides the plans above referred to, I am not aware that any
one has been suggested except that of keeping the public money in the
State banks in special deposit. This plan is to some extent in accordance with the practice of the Government and with the present arrangements of the Treasury Department, which, except, perhaps, during the
operation of the late deposit act, has always been allowed, even during
the existence of a national bank, to make a temporary use of the State
banks in particular places for the safe-keeping of portions of the revenue.
This discretionary power might be continued if Congress deem it desirable, whatever general system be adopted. So long as the connection is
voluntary we need, perhaps, anticipate few of those difficulties and little
of that dependence on the banks which must attend every such connection when compulsory in its nature and when so arranged as to make the
banks a fixed part of the machinery of government. It is undoubtedly
in the power of Congress so to regulate and guard it as to prevent the public money from being applied to the use or intermingled with the affairs
of individuals. Thus arranged, although it would not give to the Government that entire control over its own funds which I desire to secure
to it by the plan I have proposed, it would, it must be admitted, in a
great degree accomplish one of the objects which has recommended that
plan to my judgment—the separation of the fiscal concerns of the Government from those of individuals or corporations.

With these observations I recommend the whole matter to your dispassionate reflection, confidently hoping that some conclusion may be reached by your deliberations which on the one hand shall give safety and stability to the fiscal operations of the Government, and be consistent, on the other, with the genius of our institutions and with the interests and wishes of the great mass of our constituents.

It was my hope that nothing would occur to make necessary on this occasion any allusion to the late national bank. There are circumstances, however, connected with the present state of its affairs that bear so directly on the character of the Government and the welfare of the citizen that I should not feel myself excused in neglecting to notice them. The charter which terminated its banking privileges on the 4th of March, 1836, continued its corporate power two years more for the sole purpose of closing its affairs, with authority "to use the corporate name, style, and capacity for the purpose of suits for a final settlement and liquidation of the affairs and acts of the corporation, and for the sale and disposition of their estate—real, personal, and mixed—but for no other purpose or in any other manner whatsoever." Just before the banking privileges ceased, its effects were transferred by the bank to a new State institution, then recently incorporated, in trust, for the discharge of its debts and the settlement of its affairs. With this trustee, by authority of Congress, an adjustment was subsequently made of the large interest which the Government had in the stock of the institution. The manner in which a trust unexpectedly created upon the act granting the charter, and involving such great public interests, has been executed would under any circumstances be a fit subject of inquiry; but much more does it deserve your attention when it embraces the redemption of obligations to which the authority and credit of the United States have given value. The two years allowed are now nearly at an end. It is well understood that the trustee has not redeemed and canceled the outstanding notes of the bank, but has reissued and is actually reissuing, since the 3d of March, 1836, the notes which have been received by it to a vast amount. According to its own official statement, so late as the 1st of October last, nineteen months after the banking privileges given by the charter had expired, it had under its control uncanceled notes of the late Bank of the United States to the amount of $27,561,866, of which $6,175,861 were in actual circulation, $1,468,627 at State bank agencies, and $3,002,390 *in transitu*, thus showing that upward of ten millions and a half of the notes of the old bank were then still kept outstanding.

The impropriety of this procedure is obvious, it being the duty of the trustee to cancel and not to put forth the notes of an institution whose concerns it had undertaken to wind up. If the trustee has a right to reissue these notes now, I can see no reason why it may not continue to do so after the expiration of the two years. As no one could have anticipated a course so extraordinary, the prohibitory clause of the charter above quoted was not accompanied by any penalty or other special provision for enforcing it, nor have we any general law for the prevention of similar acts in future.

But it is not in this view of the subject alone that your interposition is required. The United States in settling with the trustee for their stock have withdrawn their funds from their former direct liability to the creditors of the old bank, yet notes of the institution continue to be sent forth in its name, and apparently upon the authority of the United States. The transactions connected with the employment of the bills of the old bank are of vast extent, and should they result unfortunately the interests of individuals may be deeply compromised. Without undertaking to decide how far or in what form, if any, the trustee could be made liable for notes which contain no obligation on its part, or the old bank for such as are put in circulation after the expiration of its charter and without its authority, or the Government for indemnity in case of loss, the question still presses itself upon your consideration whether it is consistent with duty and good faith on the part of the Government to witness this proceeding without a single effort to arrest it.

The report of the Commissioner of the General Land Office, which will be laid before you by the Secretary of the Treasury, will show how the affairs of that office have been conducted for the past year. The disposition of the public lands is one of the most important trusts confided to Congress. The practicability of retaining the title and control of such extensive domains in the General Government, and at the same time admitting the Territories embracing them into the Federal Union as coequals with the original States, was seriously doubted by many of our wisest statesmen. All feared that they would become a source of discord, and many carried their apprehensions so far as to see in them the seeds of a future dissolution of the Confederacy. But happily our experience has already been sufficient to quiet in a great degree all such apprehensions. The position at one time assumed, that the admission of new States into the Union on the same footing with the original States was incompatible with a right of soil in the United States and operated as a surrender thereof, notwithstanding the terms of the compacts by which their admission was designed to be regulated, has been wisely abandoned. Whether in the new or the old States, all now agree that the right of soil to the public lands remains in the Federal Government, and that these lands constitute a common property, to be disposed of for the common benefit of all the States, old and new. Acquiescence in this just principle by the people of the new States has naturally promoted a disposition to adopt the most liberal policy in the sale of the public lands. A policy which should be limited to the mere object of selling the lands for the greatest possible sum of money, without regard to higher considerations, finds but few advocates. On the contrary, it is generally conceded that whilst the mode of disposition adopted by the Government should always be a prudent one, yet its leading object ought to be the early settlement and cultivation of the lands sold, and that it should discountenance, if it can not prevent, the accumulation of large tracts in the same hands, which must necessarily retard the growth of the new States or entail upon them a dependent tenantry and its attendant evils.

A question embracing such important interests and so well calculated to enlist the feelings of the people in every quarter of the Union has very naturally given rise to numerous plans for the improvement of the existing system. The distinctive features of the policy that has hitherto prevailed are to dispose of the public lands at moderate prices, thus enabling a greater number to enter into competition for their purchase and accomplishing a double object—of promoting their rapid settlement by the purchasers and at the same time increasing the receipts of the Treasury; to sell for cash, thereby preventing the disturbing influence of a large mass of private citizens indebted to the Government which they have a voice in controlling; to bring them into market no faster than good lands are supposed to be wanted for improvement, thereby preventing the accumulation of large tracts in few hands; and to apply the proceeds of the sales to the general purposes of the Government, thus diminishing the amount to be raised from the people of the States by taxation and giving each State its portion of the benefits to be derived from this common fund in a manner the most quiet, and at the same time, perhaps, the most equitable, that can be devised. These provisions, with occasional enactments in behalf of special interests deemed entitled to the favor of the Government, have in their execution produced results as beneficial upon the whole as could reasonably be expected in a matter so vast, so complicated, and so exciting. Upward of 70,000,000 acres have been sold, the greater part of which is believed to have been purchased for actual settlement. The population of the new States and Territories created out of the public domain increased between 1800 and 1830 from less than 60,000 to upward of 2,300,000 souls, constituting at the latter period about one-fifth of the whole people of the United States. The increase since can not be accurately known, but the whole may now be safely estimated at over three and a half millions of souls, composing nine States, the representatives of which constitute above one-third of the Senate and over one-sixth of the House of Representatives of the United States.

Thus has been formed a body of free and independent landholders with a rapidity unequaled in the history of mankind; and this great result has been produced without leaving anything for future adjustment between the Government and its citizens. The system under which so much has been accomplished can not be intrinsically bad, and with occasional modifications to correct abuses and adapt it to changes of circumstances may, I think, be safely trusted for the future. There is in the management of such extensive interests much virtue in stability; and although great and obvious improvements should not be declined, changes should never be made without the fullest examination and the clearest demonstration of their practical utility. In the history of the past we have an assurance that this safe rule of action will not be departed from in relation to the public lands; nor is it believed that any necessity exists for interfering with the fundamental principles of the system, or that the public mind, even in the new States, is desirous of any radical alterations. On the contrary, the general disposition appears to be to make such modifications and additions only as will the more effectually carry out the original policy of filling our new States and Territories with an industrious and independent population.

The modification most perseveringly pressed upon Congress, which has occupied so much of its time for years past, and will probably do so for a long time to come, if not sooner satisfactorily adjusted, is a reduction in the cost of such portions of the public lands as are ascertained to be unsalable at the rate now established by law, and a graduation according to their relative value of the prices at which they may hereafter be sold. It is worthy of consideration whether justice may not be done to every interest in this matter, and a vexed question set at rest, perhaps forever, by a reasonable compromise of conflicting opinions. Hitherto, after being offered at public sale, lands have been disposed of at one uniform price, whatever difference there might be in their intrinsic value. The leading considerations urged in favor of the measure referred to are that in almost all the land districts, and particularly in those in which the lands have been long surveyed and exposed to sale, there are still remaining numerous and large tracts of every gradation of value, from the Government price downward; that these lands will not be purchased at the Government price so long as better can be conveniently obtained for the same amount; that there are large tracts which even the improvements of the adjacent lands will never raise to that price, and that the present uniform price, combined with their irregular value, operates to prevent a desirable compactness of settlements in the new States and to retard the full development of that wise policy on which our land system is founded, to the injury not only of the several States where the lands lie, but of the United States as a whole.

The remedy proposed has been a reduction of the prices according to the length of time the lands have been in market, without reference to any other circumstances. The certainty that the efflux of time would not always in such cases, and perhaps not even generally, furnish a true criterion of value, and the probability that persons residing in the vicinity, as the period for the reduction of prices approached, would postpone purchases they would otherwise make, for the purpose of availing themselves of the lower price, with other considerations of a similar character, have hitherto been successfully urged to defeat the graduation upon time.

May not all reasonable desires upon this subject be satisfied without encountering any of these objections? All will concede the abstract principle that the price of the public lands should be proportioned to their relative value, so far as can be accomplished without departing from the rule heretofore observed requiring fixed prices in cases of private entries. The difficulty of the subject seems to lie in the mode of ascertaining what that value is. Would not the safest plan be that which has been adopted by many of the States as the basis of taxation—an actual valuation of lands and classification of them into different rates? Would it not be practicable and expedient to cause the relative value of the public lands in the old districts which have been for a certain length of time in market to be appraised and classed into two or more rates below the present minimum price by the officers now employed in this branch of the public service or in any other mode deemed preferable, and to make those prices permanent if upon the coming in of the report they shall prove satisfactory to Congress? Could not all the objects of graduation be accomplished in this way, and the objections which have hitherto been urged against it avoided? It would seem to me that such a step, with a restriction of the sales to limited quantities and for actual improvement, would be free from all just exception.

By the full exposition of the value of the lands thus furnished and extensively promulgated persons living at a distance would be informed of their true condition and enabled to enter into competition with those residing in the vicinity; the means of acquiring an independent home would be brought within the reach of many who are unable to purchase at present prices; the population of the new States would be made more compact, and large tracts would be sold which would otherwise remain on hand. Not only would the land be brought within the means of a larger number of purchasers, but many persons possessed of greater means would be content to settle on a larger quantity of the poorer lands rather than emigrate farther west in pursuit of a smaller quantity of better lands. Such a measure would also seem to be more consistent with the policy of the existing laws—that of converting the public domain into cultivated farms owned by their occupants. That policy is not best promoted by sending emigration up the almost interminable streams of the West to occupy in groups the best spots of land, leaving immense wastes behind them and enlarging the frontier beyond the means of the Government to afford it adequate protection, but in encouraging it to occupy with reasonable denseness the territory over which it advances, and find its best defense in the compact front which it presents to the Indian tribes. Many of you will bring to the consideration of the subject the advantages of local knowledge and greater experience, and all will be desirous of making an early and final disposition of every disturbing question in regard to this important interest. If these suggestions shall in any degree contribute to the accomplishment of so important a result, it will afford me sincere satisfaction.

In some sections of the country most of the public lands have been sold, and the registers and receivers have very little to do. It is a subject worthy of inquiry whether in many cases two or more districts may not be consolidated and the number of persons employed in this business considerably reduced. Indeed, the time will come when it will be the true policy of the General Government, as to some of the States, to transfer to them for a reasonable equivalent all the refuse and unsold lands and to withdraw the machinery of the Federal land offices altogether. All who take a comprehensive view of our federal system and believe that one of its greatest excellences consists in interfering as little as possible with the internal concerns of the States look forward with great interest to this result.

A modification of the existing laws in respect to the prices of the public lands might also have a favorable influence on the legislation of Congress in relation to another branch of the subject. Many who have not the ability to buy at present prices settle on those lands with the hope of acquiring from their cultivation the means of purchasing under preemption laws from time to time passed by Congress. For this encroachment on the rights of the United States they excuse themselves under the plea of their own necessities; the fact that they dispossess nobody and only enter upon the waste domain: that they give additional value to the public lands in their vicinity, and their intention ultimately to pay the Government price. So much weight has from time to time been attached to these considerations that Congress have passed laws giving actual settlers on the public lands a right of preemption to the tracts occupied by them at the minimum price. These laws have in all instances been retrospective in their operation, but in a few years after their passage crowds of new settlers have been found on the public lands for similar reasons and under like expectations, who have been indulged with the same privilege. This course of legislation tends to impair public respect for the laws of the country. Either the laws to prevent intrusion upon the public lands should be executed, or, if that should be impracticable or inexpedient, they should be modified or repealed. If the public lands are to be considered as open to be occupied by any, they should by law be thrown open to all. That which is intended in all instances to be legalized should at once be made legal, that those who are disposed to conform to the laws may enjoy at least equal privileges with those who are not. But it is not believed to be the disposition of Congress to open the public lands to occupancy without regular entry and payment of the Government price, as such a course must tend to worse evils than the credit system, which it was found necessary to abolish.

It would seem, therefore, to be the part of wisdom and sound policy to remove as far as practicable the causes which produce intrusions upon the public lands, and then take efficient steps to prevent them in future. Would any single measure be so effective in removing all plausible grounds for these intrusions as the graduation of price already suggested? A short period of industry and economy in any part of our country would enable the poorest citizen to accumulate the means to buy him a home at the lower prices, and leave him without apology for settling on lands not his own. If he did not under such circumstances, he would enlist no sympathy in his favor, and the laws would be readily executed without doing violence to public opinion.

A large portion of our citizens have seated themselves on the public lands without authority since the passage of the last preemption law, and now ask the enactment of another to enable them to retain the lands occupied upon payment of the minimum Government price. They ask that which has been repeatedly granted before. If the future may be judged of by the past, little harm can be done to the interests of the Treasury by yielding to their request. Upon a critical examination it is found that the lands sold at the public sales since the introduction of cash payments, in 1820, have produced on an average the net revenue of only 6 cents an acre more than the minimum Government price. There is no reason to suppose that future sales will be more productive. The Government, therefore, has no adequate pecuniary interest to induce it to drive these people from the lands they occupy for the purpose of selling them to others.

Entertaining these views, I recommend the passage of a preemption law for their benefit in connection with the preparatory steps toward the graduation of the price of the public lands, and further and more effectual provisions to prevent intrusions hereafter. Indulgence to those who have settled on these lands with expectations that past legislation would be made a rule for the future, and at the same time removing the most plausible ground on which intrusions are excused and adopting more efficient means to prevent them hereafter, appears to me the most judicious disposition which can be made of this difficult subject. The limitations and restrictions to guard against abuses in the execution of a preemption law will necessarily attract the careful attention of Congress, but under no circumstances is it considered expedient to authorize floating claims in any shape. They have been heretofore, and doubtless would be hereafter, most prolific sources of fraud and oppression, and instead of operating to confer the favor of the Government on industrious settlers are often used only to minister to a spirit of cupidity at the expense of the most meritorious of that class.

The accompanying report of the Secretary of War will bring to your view the state of the Army and all the various subjects confided to the superintendence of that officer.

The principal part of the Army has been concentrated in Florida, with a view and in the expectation of bringing the war in that Territory to a speedy close. The necessity of stripping the posts on the maritime and inland frontiers of their entire garrisons for the purpose of assembling in the field an army of less than 4,000 men would seem to indicate the necessity of increasing our regular forces; and the superior efficiency, as well as greatly diminished expense of that description of troops, recommend this measure as one of economy as well as of expediency. I refer to the report for the reasons which have induced the Secretary of War to urge the reorganization and enlargement of the staff of the Army, and of the Ordnance Corps, in which I fully concur.

It is not, however, compatible with the interests of the people to maintain in time of peace a regular force adequate to the defense of our extensive frontiers. In periods of danger and alarm we must rely principally upon a well-organized militia, and some general arrangement that will render this description of force more efficient has long been a subject of anxious solicitude. It was recommended to the First Congress by General Washington, and has been since frequently brought to your notice, and recently its importance strongly urged by my immediate predecessor. The provision in the Constitution that renders it necessary to adopt a uniform system of organization for the militia throughout the United States presents an insurmountable obstacle to an efficient arrangement by the classification heretofore proposed, and I invite your attention to the plan which will be submitted by the Secretary of War, for the organization of volunteer corps and the instruction of militia officers, as more simple and practicable, if not equally advantageous, as a general arrangement of the whole militia of the United States.

A moderate increase of the corps both of military and topographical engineers has been more than once recommended by my predecessor, and my conviction of the propriety, not to say necessity, of the measure, in order to enable them to perform the various and important duties imposed upon them, induces me to repeat the recommendation.

The Military Academy continues to answer all the purposes of its establishment, and not only furnishes well-educated officers to the Army, but serves to diffuse throughout the mass of our citizens individuals possessed of military knowledge and the scientific attainments of civil and military engineering. At present the cadet is bound, with consent of his parents or guardians, to remain in service five years from the period of his enlistment, unless sooner discharged, thus exacting only one year's service in the Army after his education is completed. This does not appear to me sufficient. Government ought to command for a longer period the services of those who are educated at the public expense, and I recommend that the time of enlistment be extended to seven years, and the terms of the engagement strictly enforced.

The creation of a national foundry for cannon, to be common to the service of the Army and Navy of the United States, has been heretofore recommended, and appears to be required in order to place our ordnance on an equal footing with that of other countries and to enable that branch of the service to control the prices of those articles and graduate the supplies to the wants of the Government, as well as to regulate their quality and insure their uniformity. The same reasons induce me to recommend the erection of a manufactory of gunpowder, to be under the direction of the Ordnance Office. The establishment of a manufactory of small arms west of the Alleghany Mountains, upon the plan proposed by the Secretary of War, will contribute to extend throughout that country the improvements which exist in establishments of a similar description in the Atlantic States, and tend to a much more economical distribution of the armament required in the western portion of our Union.

The system of removing the Indians west of the Mississippi, commenced by Mr. Jefferson in 1804, has been steadily persevered in by every succeeding President, and may be considered the settled policy of the country. Unconnected at first with any well-defined system for their improvement, the inducements held out to the Indians were confined to the greater abundance of game to be found in the West; but when the beneficial effects of their removal were made apparent a more philanthropic and enlightened policy was adopted in purchasing their lands east of the Mississippi. Liberal prices were given and provisions inserted in all the treaties with them for the application of the funds they received in exchange to such purposes as were best calculated to promote their present welfare and advance their future civilization. These measures have been attended thus far with the happiest results.

It will be seen by referring to the report of the Commissioner of Indian Affairs that the most sanguine expectations of the friends and promoters of this system have been realized. The Choctaws, Cherokees, and other tribes that first emigrated beyond the Mississippi have for the most part abandoned the hunter state and become cultivators of the soil. The improvement in their condition has been rapid, and it is believed that they are now fitted to enjoy the advantages of a simple form of government, which has been submitted to them and received their sanction; and I can not too strongly urge this subject upon the attention of Congress.

Stipulations have been made with all the Indian tribes to remove them beyond the Mississippi, except with the bands of the Wyandots, the Six Nations in New York, the Menomonees, Munsees, and Stockbridges in Wisconsin, and Miamies in Indiana. With all but the Menomonees it is expected that arrangements for their emigration will be completed the present year. The resistance which has been opposed to their removal by some of the tribes even after treaties had been made with them to that effect has arisen from various causes, operating differently on each of them. In most instances they have been instigated to resistance by persons to whom the trade with them and the acquisition of their annuities were important, and in some by the personal influence of interested chiefs. These obstacles must be overcome, for the Government can not relinquish the execution of this policy without sacrificing important interests and abandoning the tribes remaining east of the Mississippi to certain destruction.

The decrease in numbers of the tribes within the limits of the States and Territories has been most rapid. If they be removed, they can be protected from those associations and evil practices which exert so pernicious and destructive an influence over their destinies. They can be induced to labor and to acquire property, and its acquisition will inspire them with a feeling of independence. Their minds can be cultivated, and they can be taught the value of salutary and uniform laws and be made sensible of the blessings of free government and capable of enjoying its advantages. In the possession of property, knowledge, and a good government, free to give what direction they please to their labor, and sharers in the legislation by which their persons and the profits of their industry are to be protected and secured, they will have an ever-present conviction of the importance of union and peace among themselves and of the preservation of amicable relations with us. The interests of the United States would also be greatly promoted by freeing the relations between the General and State Governments from what has proved a most embarrassing incumbrance by a satisfactory adjustment of conflicting titles to lands caused by the occupation of the Indians, and by causing the resources of the whole country to be developed by the power of the State and General Governments and improved by the enterprise of a white population.

Intimately connected with this subject is the obligation of the Government to fulfill its treaty stipulations and to protect the Indians thus assembled "at their new residences from all interruptions and disturbances from any other tribes or nations of Indians or from any other person or persons whatsoever," and the equally solemn obligation to guard from Indian hostility its own border settlements, stretching along a line of more than 1,000 miles. To enable the Government to redeem this pledge to the Indians and to afford adequate protection to its own citizens will require the continual presence of a considerable regular force on the frontiers and the establishment of a chain of permanent posts. Examinations of the country are now making, with a view to decide on the most suitable points for the erection of fortresses and other works of defense, the results of which will be presented to you by the Secretary of War at an early day, together with a plan for the effectual protection of the friendly Indians and the permanent defense of the frontier States.

By the report of the Secretary of the Navy herewith communicated it appears that unremitted exertions have been made at the different navy-yards to carry into effect all authorized measures for the extension and employment of our naval force. The launching and preparation of the ship of the line *Pennsylvania* and the complete repairs of the ships of the line *Ohio*, *Delaware*, and *Columbus* may be noticed as forming a respectable addition to this important arm of our national defense. Our commerce and navigation have received increased aid and protection during the present year. Our squadrons in the Pacific and on the Brazilian station have been much increased, and that in the Mediterranean, although small, is adequate to the present wants of our commerce in that sea. Additions have been made to our squadron on the West India station, where the large force under Commodore Dallas has been most actively and efficiently employed in protecting our commerce, in preventing the importation of slaves, and in cooperating with the officers of the Army in carrying on the war in Florida.

The satisfactory condition of our naval force abroad leaves at our disposal the means of conveniently providing for a home squadron for the protection of commerce upon our extensive coast. The amount of appropriations required for such a squadron will be found in the general estimates for the naval service for the year 1838.

The naval officers engaged upon our coast survey have rendered important service to our navigation. The discovery of a new channel into the harbor of New York, through which our largest ships may pass without danger, must afford important commercial advantages to that harbor and add greatly to its value as a naval station. The accurate survey of Georges Shoals, off the coast of Massachusetts, lately completed, will render comparatively safe a navigation hitherto considered dangerous.

Considerable additions have been made to the number of captains, commanders, lieutenants, surgeons, and assistant surgeons in the Navy. These additions were rendered necessary by the increased number of vessels put in commission to answer the exigencies of our growing commerce.

Your attention is respectfully invited to the various suggestions of the Secretary for the improvement of the naval service.

The report of the Postmaster-General exhibits the progress and condition of the mail service. The operations of the Post-Office Department constitute one of the most active elements of our national prosperity, and it is gratifying to observe with what vigor they are conducted. The mail routes of the United States cover an extent of about 142,877 miles, having been increased about 37,103 miles within the last two years. The annual mail transportation on these routes is about 36,228,962 miles, having been increased about 10,359,476 miles within the same period. The number of post-offices has also been increased from 10,770 to 12,099, very few of which receive the mails less than once a week, and a large portion of them daily. Contractors and postmasters in general are represented as attending to their duties with most commendable zeal and fidelity. The revenue of the Department within the year ending on the 30th of June last was $4,137,056.59, and its liabilities accruing within the same time were $3,380,847.75. The increase of revenue over that of the preceding year was $708,166.41.

For many interesting details I refer you to the report of the Postmaster-General, with the accompanying papers. Your particular attention is invited to the necessity of providing a more safe and convenient building for the accommodation of that Department.

I lay before Congress copies of reports submitted in pursuance of a call made by me upon the heads of Departments for such suggestions as their experience might enable them to make as to what further legislative provisions may be advantageously adopted to secure the faithful application of public moneys to the objects for which they are appropriated, to prevent their misapplication or embezzlement by those intrusted with the expenditure of them, and generally to increase the security of the Government against losses in their disbursement. It is needless to dilate on the importance of providing such new safeguards as are within the power of legislation to promote these ends, and I have little to add to the recommendations submitted in the accompanying papers.

By law the terms of service of our most important collecting and disbursing officers in the civil departments are limited to four years, and when reappointed their bonds are required to be renewed. The safety of the public is much increased by this feature of the law, and there can be no doubt that its application to all officers intrusted with the collection or disbursement of the public money, whatever may be the tenure of their offices, would be equally beneficial. I therefore recommend, in addition to such of the suggestions presented by the heads of Departments as you may think useful, a general provision that all officers of the Army or Navy, or in the civil departments, intrusted with the receipt or payment of public money, and whose term of service is either unlimited or for a longer time than four years, be required to give new bonds, with good and sufficient sureties, at the expiration of every such period.

A change in the period of terminating the fiscal year, from the 1st of October to the 1st of April, has been frequently recommended, and appears to be desirable.

The distressing casualties in steamboats which have so frequently happened during the year seem to evince the necessity of attempting to prevent them by means of severe provisions connected with their custom-house papers. This subject was submitted to the attention of Congress by the Secretary of the Treasury in his last annual report, and will be again noticed at the present session, with additional details. It will doubtless receive that early and careful consideration which its pressing importance appears to require.

Your attention has heretofore been frequently called to the affairs of the District of Columbia, and I should not again ask it did not their entire dependence on Congress give them a constant claim upon its notice. Separated by the Constitution from the rest of the Union, limited in extent, and aided by no legislature of its own, it would seem to be a spot where a wise and uniform system of local government might have been easily adopted. This District has, however, unfortunately been left to linger behind the rest of the Union. Its codes, civil and

AGITATION AGAINST DUELING IN WASHINGTON IN MARTIN
VAN BUREN'S ADMINISTRATION.

criminal, are not only very defective, but full of obsolete or inconvenient provisions. Being formed of portions of two States, discrepancies in the laws prevail in different parts of the territory, small as it is; and although it was selected as the seat of the General Government, the site of its public edifices, the depository of its archives, and the residence of officers intrusted with large amounts of public property and the management of public business, yet it has never been subjected to or received that special and comprehensive legislation which these circumstances peculiarly demand. I am well aware of the various subjects of greater magnitude and immediate interest that press themselves on the consideration of Congress, but I believe there is not one that appeals more directly to its justice than a liberal and even generous attention to the interests of the District of Columbia and a thorough and careful revision of its local government.

M. VAN BUREN.

SPECIAL MESSAGES.

WASHINGTON, *December 6, 1837.*

To the Senate and House of Representatives of the United States:

I transmit herewith a report from the Secretary of the Treasury, exhibiting a transfer of appropriation that has been made in that Department in pursuance of the power vested in the President by the first section of the act of Congress of the 3d of March, 1809, entitled "An act further to amend the several acts for the establishment and regulation of the Treasury, War, and Navy Departments."

M. VAN BUREN.

WASHINGTON, *December, 1837.*

To the Senate:

I transmit, for the action of the Senate, treaties negotiated with the following Indian tribes, viz:

(1) The Chippewas of the Mississippi; (2) the Kioways, Ka-ta-kas, and Ta-wa-ka-ros; (3) the Sioux of the Mississippi; (4) the Sacs and Foxes of the Mississippi; (5) the Sioux of the Missouri; (6) the Sacs and Foxes of the Missouri; (7) the Winnebagoes; (8) the Ioways.

M. VAN BUREN.

WASHINGTON, *December 11, 1837.*

To the Senate of the United States:

I herewith transmit to the Senate a report* from the Secretary of State, with accompanying documents, in pursuance of their resolution of the 12th of October last.

M. VAN BUREN.

---

*Relating to the capture and sequestration of the ship *Mary*, of Baltimore, and her cargo by the Dutch Government at the island of Curaçoa in 1800.

WASHINGTON, *December, 1837.*
To the Senate of the United States:

In compliance with the resolution of the Senate of the 13th of October last, relative to claims of citizens of the United States on the Government of the Mexican Republic, I transmit a report from the Secretary of State and the documents by which it was accompanied.

M. VAN BUREN.

WASHINGTON, *December 15, 1837.*
To the Senate and House of Representatives:

I transmit herewith a communication from the Secretary of War and the plans for marine hospitals on the Western waters, referred to by him, which are connected with the annual report from the War Department.

M. VAN BUREN.

WASHINGTON, *December 18, 1837.*
To the Senate of the United States:

I transmit herewith a report and accompanying documents* from the Secretary of War, which contain the information called for by a resolution of the 13th of October last.

M. VAN BUREN.

WASHINGTON, *December 21, 1837.*
To the House of Representatives of the United States:

In compliance with a resolution of the House of Representatives of the last session, I transmit a report made to me by the architect of the public buildings, with the accompanying documents, exhibiting a plan of the Treasury building now in process of erection, showing its location in reference to the adjacent streets and public square on which it is located, its elevation, the number and size of the rooms it will afford suitable for office business and the number and size of those suitable only for the deposit of records, with a statement of the sum expended on said building and an estimate of the sum that will be required to complete the same. As the fifth section of the act of July 4, 1836, under the authority of which this building has been commenced, provides only for the erection of an edifice of such dimensions as may be required for the present and future accommodation of the Treasury Department, the size of the structure has been adapted to that purpose; and it is not contemplated to appropriate any part of the building to the use of any other Department. As it is understood, however, that the plan of the edifice admits of its

* Relating to adjustment of claims to reservations of land under the fourteenth article of the treaty of 1830 with the Choctaw Indians.

being completed either with or without wings, and that if Congress should think proper accommodation may be provided by means of wings consistently with the harmony of the original design for the Department of State and the General Post-Office, it is not thought that the public interest requires any change in the location or plan, although it is believed that the convenience of the public business would be promoted by including in the building the proposed accommodations for the two other Departments just mentioned. The report of the architect shows the supposed difference of the expense that would be incurred in the event of the construction of the building with wings, in taking down the edifice now occupied by the Department of State, or repairing it so as to render it fireproof and make its outside conform to the other parts of the new building.

I also transmit statements from the heads of the several Departments of the number and size of the rooms that are necessary for their respective Departments for office business and for the deposit of records.

M. VAN BUREN.

WASHINGTON, *December 22, 1837.*

To the Senate of the United States:

I herewith transmit to the Senate a report from the Secretary of State, in answer to their resolution of the 16th of October last.

M. VAN BUREN.

DEPARTMENT OF STATE,
Washington, December 22, 1837.

The PRESIDENT OF THE UNITED STATES:

The Secretary of State, to whom has been referred the resolution of the Senate of the 16th of October last, requesting the President of the United States to communicate to that body "at the next session of Congress (if not inconsistent with the public interest) any correspondence between the Government of the United States and any foreign government relative to the occupation of the territory of the United States west of the Rocky Mountains and bordering on the Pacific Ocean, and whether any, and, if so, what, portion of the said territory is in the possession of any foreign power," has the honor to report to the President that no correspondence between this and any foreign government on the subject referred to has passed since the negotiation of the existing convention of 1827 with Great Britain, by which the provisions of the third article of the convention of the 20th of October, 1818, with His Britannic Majesty, leaving the territory claimed by either power westward of the Rocky Mountains free and open to the citizens and subjects of both, were extended and continued in force indefinitely, but liable to be annulled at the will of either party, on due notice of twelve months, at any time after the 20th of October, 1828, and that the papers relating to the negotiation to which allusion has just been made were communicated to the Senate in confidence in the early part of the first session of the Twentieth Congress.

With regard to the second clause of the resolution above cited, the Secretary has to state that the trading establishment called "Astoria," at the mouth of the Columbia River, formerly belonging to John Jacob Astor, of New York, was sold to, and therefore left in the possession of, the British Northwest Company, which subsequently united with the British Hudson Bay Company; that this company has now several depots in the country, the principal of which is at Fort Vancouver, on the north bank of the Columbia River, and about 80 or 100 miles from its mouth. It appears that these posts have not been considered as being in contravention of the third article of the convention of 1818, before referred to; and if not, there is no portion of the territory claimed by the United States west of the Stony Mountains known to be in the exclusive possession of a foreign power. It is known, by information recently obtained, that the English company have a steamboat on the Columbia, and have erected a sawmill and are cutting timber on the territory claimed by the United States, and shipping it in considerable quantities to the Sandwich Islands.

Respectfully submitted.

JOHN FORSYTH.

WASHINGTON, *December 26, 1837.*

To the House of Representatives of the United States:

I herewith transmit to the House of Representatives a report from the Secretary of State, in answer to their resolution of the 9th of October last.

M. VAN BUREN.

DEPARTMENT OF STATE,
Washington, December 23, 1837.

The PRESIDENT OF THE UNITED STATES:

The Secretary of State, to whom has been referred the resolution of the House of Representatives of the 9th of October last, requesting the President to communicate to that House "at its next session, so far as in his judgment is consistent with the public interest, whether any foreign power, or the subjects of any foreign power, have possession of any portion of the territory of the United States on the Columbia River, or are in the occupancy of the same, and, if so, in what way, by what authority, and how long such possession or occupancy has been kept by such persons," has the honor to report to the President that a trading establishment called "Astoria" was founded at the mouth of the Columbia River about the year 1811 by J. J. Astor, of New York; that his interest was sold to the British Northwest Company during the late war between the United States and Great Britain; that this company held it, and were left in possession at the time the country was formally delivered to the American commissioners, and that this company afterwards united with and became a part of the Hudson Bay Company under that name, which company, it is believed, have from the period of such union occupied the post in question, now commonly called "Fort George." The Hudson Bay Company have also several depots situated on water courses in the interior of the country. The principal one is at Fort Vancouver, on the northern bank of the Columbia River, about 80 or 100 miles from its mouth. It is known by information recently obtained that the English company have a steamboat on this river, and that they have erected a sawmill and are cutting timber on the territory claimed by the United States, and are shipping it in considerable quantities to the Sandwich Islands.

The original occupation was under the authority of the purchase of J. J. Astor's interest, and it has been continued under the provisions of the conventions of 1818 and 1827 with Great Britain. By the third article of the first of these conventions it is stipulated that the territory claimed by either power westward of the Rocky Mountains shall be free and open for a term of years to the citizens and subjects of both. By the second convention this stipulation is extended and continued in force indefinitely, liable, however, to be annulled at any time after the 20th of October, 1828, at the will of either party, on due notice of twelve months.

Respectfully submitted.

JOHN FORSYTH.

WASHINGTON, *January 5, 1838.*

To the Senate and House of Representatives of the United States:

Recent experience on the southern boundary of the United States and the events now daily occurring on our northern frontier have abundantly shown that the existing laws are insufficient to guard against hostile invasion from the United States of the territory of friendly and neighboring nations.

The laws in force provide sufficient penalties for the punishment of such offenses after they have been committed, and provided the parties can be found, but the Executive is powerless in many cases to prevent the commission of them, even when in possession of ample evidence of an intention on the part of evil-disposed persons to violate our laws.

Your attention is called to this defect in our legislation. It is apparent that the Executive ought to be clothed with adequate power effectually to restrain all persons within our jurisdiction from the commission of acts of this character. They tend to disturb the peace of the country and inevitably involve the Government in perplexing controversies with foreign powers. I recommend a careful revision of all the laws now in force and such additional enactments as may be necessary to vest in the Executive full power to prevent injuries being inflicted upon neighboring nations by the unauthorized and unlawful acts of citizens of the United States or of other persons who may be within our jurisdiction and subject to our control.

In illustration of these views and to show the necessity of early action on the part of Congress, I submit herewith a copy of a letter received from the marshal of the northern district of New York, who had been directed to repair to the frontier and take all authorized measures to secure the faithful execution of existing laws.

M. VAN BUREN.

BUFFALO, *December 28, 1837.*

His Excellency M. VAN BUREN.

SIR: This frontier is in a state of commotion. I came to this city on the 22d instant, by direction of the United States attorney for the northern district of this State, for the purpose of serving process upon individuals suspected of violating the laws of the United States enacted with a view to maintain our neutrality. I learned on my arrival that some 200 or 300 men, mostly from the district of country adjoining this frontier and from this side of the Niagara, had congregated upon Navy Island (Upper Canada), and were there in arms, with Rensselaer van Rensselaer, of Albany, at their head as commander in chief. From that time to the present they have received constant accessions of men, munitions of war, provisions, etc., from persons residing within the States. Their whole force is now about 1,000 strong, and, as is said, are well supplied with arms, etc.

Warrants have been issued in some cases, but no arrests have as yet been effected. This expedition was got up in this city soon after McKenzie's arrival upon this side of the river, and the first company that landed upon the island were organized, partially at least, before they crossed from this side to the island.

From all that I can see and learn I am satisfied that if the Government deem it their duty to prevent supplies being furnished from this side to the army on the island, and also the augmentation of their forces from among the citizens of the States, that an armed force stationed along upon the line of the Niagara will be absolutely necessary to its accomplishment.

I have just received a communication from Colonel McNab, commanding His Majesty's forces now at Chippewa, in which he strongly urges the public authorities here to prevent supplies being furnished to the army on the island, at the same time stating that if this can be effected the whole affair could be closed without any effusion of blood.

McNab is about 2,500 strong and constantly increasing. I replied to him that I should communicate with you immediately, as also with the governor of this State, and that everything which could would be done to maintain a strict neutrality.

I learn that persons here are engaged in dislodging one or more steamboats from the ice, and, as is supposed, with a view to aid in the patriot expedition.

I am, sir, with great consideration, your obedient servant,

N. GANON,
United States Marshal, Northern District of New York.

WASHINGTON, *January 8, 1838.*
To the House of Representatives of the United States:

In answer to the resolution of the House of Representatives of the 5th instant, respecting the capture* and restoration of the Mexican brig of war the *General Urrea*, I transmit reports from the Secretaries of State and the Navy.

M. VAN BUREN.

WASHINGTON, *January 8, 1838.*
To the House of Representatives of the United States:

I herewith transmit to the House of Representatives a report,† and accompanying documents, from the Secretary of State, in compliance with a resolution of that body dated the 5th instant.

M. VAN BUREN.

WASHINGTON, *January 8, 1838.*
To the House of Representatives of the United States:

I herewith transmit to the House of Representatives a report from the Secretary of State, in answer to a resolution ‡ of that body dated the 5th instant.

M. VAN BUREN.

---

* By the United States sloop of war *Natchez* off the coast of Texas.

† Transmitting instructions and correspondence concerning the preservation of the neutrality of the United States in the civil wars and insurrections in Mexico and in any of the British Provinces north of the United States since 1829.

‡ Calling for information of any acts endangering the amicable relations with Great Britain.

WASHINGTON, *January 8, 1838.*

To the Senate and House of Representatives of the United States:

In the highly excited state of feeling on the northern frontier, occasioned by the disturbances in Canada, it was to be apprehended that causes of complaint might arise on the line dividing the United States from Her Britannic Majesty's dominions. Every precaution was therefore taken on our part authorized by the existing laws, and as the troops of the Provinces were embodied on the Canadian side it was hoped that no serious violation of the rights of the United States would be permitted to occur. I regret, however, to inform you that an outrage of a most aggravated character has been committed, accompanied by a hostile though temporary invasion of our territory, producing the strongest feelings of resentment on the part of our citizens in the neighborhood and on the whole border line, and that the excitement previously existing has been alarmingly increased. To guard against the possible recurrence of any similar act I have thought it indispensable to call out a portion of the militia, to be posted on that frontier. The documents herewith presented to Congress show the character of the outrage committed, the measures taken in consequence of its occurrence, and the necessity for resorting to them.

It will also be seen that the subject was immediately brought to the notice of the British minister accredited to this country, and the proper steps taken on our part to obtain the fullest information of all the circumstances leading to and attendant upon the transaction, preparatory to a demand for reparation. I ask such appropriations as the circumstances in which our country is thus unexpectedly placed require.

M. VAN BUREN.

Mr. Rogers to the President.

BUFFALO, *December 30, 1837.*

His Excellency MARTIN VAN BUREN,
President of the United States.

SIR: Inclosed are copies of affidavits which I have prepared in great haste, and which contain all that is material in relation to the gross and extraordinary transaction to which they relate. Our whole frontier is in commotion, and I fear it will be difficult to restrain our citizens from revenging by a resort to arms this flagrant invasion of our territory. Everything that can be done will be by the public authorities to prevent so injudicious a movement. The respective sheriffs of Erie and Niagara have taken the responsibility of calling out the militia to guard the frontier and prevent any further depredations.

I am, sir, with great consideration, your obedient servant,

H. W. ROGERS,
District Attorney for Erie County, and Acting for the United States.

STATE OF NEW YORK, *Niagara County, ss:*

Gilman Appleby, of the city of Buffalo, being sworn, says that he left the port of Buffalo on the morning of the 29th instant in the steamboat *Caroline*, owned by William Wells, of Buffalo, and bound for Schlosser, upon the east side of the Niagara

River and within the United States; that this deponent commanded the said *Caroline*, and that she was cleared from Buffalo with a view to run between said Buffalo and Schlosser, carrying passengers, freight, etc.; that this deponent caused the said *Caroline* to be landed at Black Rock on her way down, and that while at Black Rock this deponent caused the American flag to be run up, and that soon after leaving Black Rock Harbor a volley of musketry was discharged at the *Caroline* from the Canada shore, but without injury; that the said *Caroline* continued her course down the Niagara River unmolested and landed outside of certain scows or boats attached to Navy Island, where a number of passengers disembarked and, as this deponent supposes, certain articles of freight were landed; that from this point the *Caroline* ran to Schlosser, arriving there at 3 o'clock in the afternoon; that between this time and dark the *Caroline* made two trips to Navy Island, landing as before; that at about 6 o'clock in the evening this deponent caused the said *Caroline* to be landed at Schlosser and made fast with chains to the dock at that place; that the crew and officers of the *Caroline* numbered ten, and that in the course of the evening twenty-three individuals, all of whom were citizens of the United States, came on board of the *Caroline* and requested this deponent and other officers of the boat to permit them to remain on board during the night, as they were unable to get lodgings at the tavern near by; these requests were acceded to, and the persons thus coming on board retired to rest, as did also the crew and officers of the *Caroline*, except such as were stationed to watch during the night; that about midnight this deponent was informed by one of the watch that several boats filled with men were making toward the *Caroline* from the river, and this deponent immediately gave the alarm, and before he was able to reach the dock the *Caroline* was boarded by some seventy or eighty men, all of whom were armed; that they immediately commenced a warfare with muskets, swords, and cutlasses upon the defenseless crew and passengers of the *Caroline* under a fierce cry of "G—d d—n them, give them no quarters; kill every man. Fire! fire!"; that the *Caroline* was abandoned without resistance, and the only effort made by either the crew or passengers seemed to be to escape slaughter; that this deponent narrowly escaped, having received several wounds, none of which, however, are of a serious character; that immediately after the *Caroline* fell into the hands of the armed force who boarded her she was set on fire, cut loose from the dock, was towed into the current of the river, there abandoned, and soon after descended the Niagara Falls; that this deponent has made vigilant search after the individuals, thirty-three in number, who are known to have been on the *Caroline* at the time she was boarded, and twenty-one only are to be found, one of which, to wit, Amos Durfee, of Buffalo, was found dead upon the dock, having received a shot from a musket, the ball of which penetrated the back part of the head and came out at the forehead; James H. King and Captain C. F. Harding were seriously though not mortally wounded; several others received slight wounds; the twelve individuals who are missing, this deponent has no doubt, were either murdered upon the steamboat or found a watery grave in the cataract of the Falls; and this deponent further says that immediately after the *Caroline* was got into the current of the stream and abandoned, as before stated, beacon lights were discovered upon the Canada shore near Chippewa, and after sufficient time had elapsed to enable the boats to reach that shore this deponent distinctly heard loud and vociferous cheering at that point; that this deponent has no doubt that the individuals who boarded the *Caroline* were a part of the British forces now stationed at Chippewa.

[Subscribed and sworn to before a commissioner, etc.]

STATE OF NEW YORK, *Niagara County, ss:*

Charles F. Harding, James H. King, Joshua H. Smith, William Seaman, William Kennedy, William Wells, John Leonard, Sylvanus Staring, and John Haggarty, being sworn, severally depose and say that they have heard the foregoing affidavit of Gilman Appleby read; that they were on the *Caroline* at the time she was boarded as stated in said affidavit, and that all the facts sworn to by said Appleby as occurring after the said *Caroline* was so boarded as aforesaid are correct and true.

[Subscribed and sworn to before a commissioner, etc.]

Mr. Poinsett to General Scott.

DEPARTMENT OF WAR, *January 5, 1838.*

Brevet Major-General WINFIELD SCOTT,
   Washington City.

SIR: You will repair without delay to the Canada frontier of the United States and assume the military command there.

Herewith you will receive duplicate letters to the governors of the States of New York and Vermont, requesting them to call into the service of the United States such a militia force as you may deem necessary for the defense of that frontier of the United States.

This power has been confided to you in the full persuasion that you will use it discreetly and extend the call only so far as circumstances may seem to require.

It is important that the troops called into the service should be, if possible, exempt from that state of excitement which the late violation of our territory has created, and you will therefore impress upon the governors of these border States the propriety of selecting troops from a portion of the State distant from the theater of action.

The Executive possesses no legal authority to employ the military force to restrain persons within our jurisdiction and who ought to be under our control from violating the laws by making incursions into the territory of neighboring and friendly nations with hostile intent. I can give you, therefore, no instructions on that subject, but request that you will use your influence to prevent such excesses and to preserve the character of this Government for good faith and a proper regard for the rights of friendly powers.

The militia will be called into the service for three months, unless sooner discharged, and in your requisitions you will designate the number of men and take care that the officers do not exceed a due proportion.

It is deemed important that the administrative branch of the service should be conducted wherever practicable by officers of the Regular Army.

The disposition of the force with regard to the points to be occupied is confided to your discretion, military skill, and intimate knowledge of the country; and the amount of that force must depend upon the character and duration of the contest now going on in Canada and the disposition manifested by the people and the public authorities of that colony.

The President indulges a hope that outrages similar to that which lately occurred at Schlosser will not be repeated, and that you will be able to maintain the peace of that frontier without being called upon to use the force which has been confided to you.

  Very respectfully, your most obedient servant,

           J. R. POINSETT.

Mr. Poinsett to Governor Marcy.

DEPARTMENT OF WAR, *January 5, 1838.*

His Excellency W. L. MARCY,
  Governor of New York, Albany, N. Y.

SIR: The territory of the United States having been violated by a party of armed men from the Canada shore, and apprehensions being entertained from the highly excited feelings of both parties that similar outrages may lead to an invasion of our soil, the President has thought proper to exercise the authority vested in him by law and call out such militia force as may be deemed necessary to protect the frontiers of the United States.

I am, in consequence, instructed by the President to request you will call into the service of the United States and place under the command of Brevet Major-General Scott such militia force as he may require, to be employed on the Canada frontier for the purpose herein set forth.

Very respectfully, your most obedient servant,

J. R. POINSETT.

[Same to His Excellency Silas H. Jennison, governor of Vermont, Montpelier, Vt.]

Mr. Forsyth to Mr. Fox.

DEPARTMENT OF STATE,
Washington, January 5, 1838.

HENRY S. FOX, Esq., etc.

SIR: By the direction of the President of the United States I have the honor to communicate to you a copy of the evidence furnished to this Department of an extraordinary outrage committed from Her Britannic Majesty's Province of Upper Canada on the persons and property of citizens of the United States within the jurisdiction of the State of New York. The destruction of the property and assassination of citizens of the United States on the soil of New York at the moment when, as is well known to you, the President was anxiously endeavoring to allay the excitement and earnestly seeking to prevent any unfortunate occurrence on the frontier of Canada has produced upon his mind the most painful emotions of surprise and regret. It will necessarily form the subject of a demand for redress upon Her Majesty's Government. This communication is made to you under the expectation that through your instrumentality an early explanation may be obtained from the authorities of Upper Canada of all the circumstances of the transaction, and that by your advice to those authorities such decisive precautions may be used as will render the perpetration of similar acts hereafter impossible. Not doubting the disposition of the government of Upper Canada to do its duty in punishing the aggressors and preventing future outrage, the President, notwithstanding, has deemed it necessary to order a sufficient force on the frontier to repel any attempt of a like character, and to make known to you that if it should occur he can not be answerable for the effects of the indignation of the neighboring people of the United States.

I take this occasion to renew to you the assurance of my distinguished consideration.

JOHN FORSYTH.

WASHINGTON, *January 12, 1838.*

To the Senate and House of Representatives of the United States:

I transmit to Congress copies of a representation from a late grand jury of the county of Washington, in this District, concurred in by two of the judges of the circuit court, of the necessity of the erection of a new jail and a lunatic asylum in this city. I also transmit copies of certain proceedings of the circuit court for the county of Alexandria at the last October term, and of a representation of the grand jury, made with the approbation of the court, showing the unsafe condition of the court-house of that county and the necessity for a new one.

I recommend these objects to the favorable consideration of Congress.

M. VAN BUREN.

WASHINGTON, *January 12, 1838.*

The SPEAKER OF THE HOUSE OF REPRESENTATIVES:

In answer to a resolution of the House of Representatives of the 2d instant, I transmit herewith a report* of the Secretary of War, explanatory of the causes which have prevented a compliance with a resolution of that branch of Congress of February 24, 1837.

M. VAN BUREN.

WASHINGTON, *January 13, 1838.*

To the Senate:

I transmit to the Senate, for its constitutional action, a treaty made with the Chippewa Indians of Saganaw on the 20th of December, 1837.

M. VAN BUREN.

WASHINGTON, *January 26, 1838.*

To the House of Representatives of the United States:

I herewith communicate to the House of Representatives a report from the Secretary of State, with accompanying documents, in answer to their resolution of the 9th instant.

M. VAN BUREN.

DEPARTMENT OF STATE,
Washington, January 25, 1838.

The PRESIDENT OF THE UNITED STATES:

The Secretary of State, to whom has been referred a resolution of the House of Representatives, dated the 9th instant, requesting the President to communicate to that body "what measures, if any, have been taken by the Executive for the release of Mr. Greely, a citizen of Maine, now imprisoned in the provincial jail of New Brunswick at Frederickton for an alleged violation of the jurisdiction of said Province over the territory claimed by the British Government; and also to communicate any correspondence which the executive department may have had with the British Government or the executive of Maine upon the subject of said Greely's imprisonment, so far as a communication of the same may be deemed by him not incompatible with the public interest;" and likewise requesting the President, if not incompatible with the public interests, to communicate to that House "any correspondence or communication held between the Government of the United States and that of Great Britain at different times respecting the wardenship, occupation, or actual possession of that part of the territory of the State of Maine which is claimed by Great Britain," has the honor to report to the President the accompanying documents, which embrace the information and correspondence not heretofore published by Congress called for by the above-cited resolution.

Respectfully submitted.

JOHN FORSYTH.

The governor of Maine to the President of the United States.

STATE OF MAINE, EXECUTIVE DEPARTMENT,
September 18, 1837.

His Excellency MARTIN VAN BUREN,
President of the United States.

SIR: I lose no time in advising Your Excellency that Ebenezer S. Greely, esq., a citizen of this State, while employed within its limits and under its authority in taking an enumeration of the inhabitants of the county of Penobscot residing north

*Relating to alleged frauds upon the Creek Indians in the sale and purchase of their lands, etc.

of the surveyed and located townships, has been arrested a second time by the provincial authorities of New Brunswick, and is now in confinement in the jail of Frederickton.

It becomes my duty to request that prompt measures be adopted by the Government of the United States to effect the release of Mr. Greely.

I have the honor to be, etc.,

ROBERT P. DUNLAP.

Mr. Forsyth to Mr. Dunlap.

DEPARTMENT OF STATE,
Washington, September 26, 1837.

His Excellency ROBERT P. DUNLAP,
Governor of Maine.

SIR: I have the honor, by direction of the President, to acknowledge the receipt of the letter addressed to him by your excellency on the 18th instant, advising him that Ebenezer S. Greely, esq., a citizen of Maine, while employed within its limits and under its authority in taking an enumeration of the inhabitants of the county of Penobscot, has been arrested a second time by the provincial authorities of New Brunswick, and is now in confinement in the jail at Frederickton; and requesting that prompt measures be adopted by the Government of the United States to effect the release of Mr. Greely.

I hasten to assure you in reply that Mr. Stevenson, the minister of the United States at London, will be immediately instructed to renew his application to the British Government for the release of Mr. Greely, and that the result, when obtained and communicated to this Department, will be made known to your excellency without unnecessary delay.

Information was given at an early day to the executive of Maine of the informal arrangement between the United States and Great Britain in regard to the exercise of jurisdiction within the disputed territory, and the President's desire was then expressed that the government and people of that State would cooperate with the Federal Government in carrying it into effect. In the letter addressed to your excellency from this Department on the 17th ultimo you were informed of the continuance of that arrangement and of the reasons for it. I am now instructed by the President (who indulges the confident expectation that the executive of Maine will still see in the gravity of the interests involved a sufficient motive for his cordial concurrence in an arrangement which offers the best prospect of an amicable and satisfactory adjustment of the general question of boundary) to request your excellency's cooperation in the conciliatory course adopted by the two Governments, an adherence to which seems the more important at this time from the consideration that an answer to the President's last proposition is daily looked for, and to renew to you the assurance that no efforts shall be spared on his part to bring the negotiation to a speedy conclusion.

I have the honor to be, etc.,

JOHN FORSYTH.

Mr. Forsyth to Mr. Stevenson.

[Extract.]

DEPARTMENT OF STATE,
Washington, July 12, 1837.

ANDREW STEVENSON, Esq., etc.

SIR: I inclose an extract* of a letter received at this Department from the governor of Maine, by which you will perceive that a citizen of that State, named Ebenezer S. Greely, while employed, in virtue of an appointment under one of its laws, in making an enumeration of the inhabitants upon a part of the territory claimed as being within the limits of the State, was seized by order of the authorities of the Province of New Brunswick on the 6th of June last and imprisoned in the public jail of

*Omitted.

Frederickton, where he still remains. I also transmit a copy of sundry documents relating to his arrest and detention.* This outrage upon the personal liberty of one of its citizens has actually caused great excitement in Maine, and has produced an urgent appeal to the General Government for its intervention in procuring redress for what is considered an unprovoked and unjustifiable aggression. This arrest was made on a part of the territory in dispute between the United States and Great Britain, and could only have been justified in the existing state of that controversy by some plain infringement of the understanding which exists between the parties, that until the settlement of the question of right there shall be no extension of jurisdiction on either side within the disputed limits. It is not perceived how the simple enumeration of the inhabitants, about which Mr. Greely was employed, could be construed as a breach of that understanding, and it is expected that the Government of Great Britain will promptly mark its disapproval of this act of violence committed by the provincial authorities, so inconsistent with those amicable feelings under which the negotiation respecting the controverted boundary has been hitherto conducted, and so essential to bring it to a happy termination. You are directed immediately upon the receipt of this dispatch to bring the subject to the notice of His Majesty's Government, and to demand as a matter of justice and right the prompt release of Mr. Greely and a suitable indemnity for his imprisonment.

Mr. Stevenson to Mr. Forsyth.

[Extract.]

LEGATION OF THE UNITED STATES,
London, August 21, 1837.

SIR: I received by the last packet to Liverpool your dispatch of the 12th of July (No. 21), transmitting copies of the documents and correspondence in relation to the arrest and imprisonment of Mr. Greely, a citizen of Maine, by the authorities of New Brunswick.

In pursuance of your instructions, I lost no time in presenting the subject to the consideration of the Government, and herewith transmit to you a copy of my note to Lord Palmerston, to which no answer has yet been received.

You will see that I waived for the present the discussion of the question of right and jurisdiction, and contented myself with presenting the facts of the case and demanding the immediate release of Mr. Greely and indemnity for the injuries which he had sustained.

Mr. Stevenson to Lord Palmerston.

23 PORTLAND PLACE, *August 10, 1837.*

LORD PALMERSTON, etc.:

The undersigned, envoy extraordinary and minister plenipotentiary from the United States, has the honor, in pursuance of instructions from his Government, to transmit to Lord Palmerston, Her Majesty's principal secretary of state for foreign affairs, copies of sundry official documents detailing the circumstances under which a most unwarrantable outrage has recently been committed by the authorities of the Province of New Brunswick upon the rights and liberty of a citizen of the United States.

From these papers it appears that Ebenezer S. Greely, a citizen of the State of Maine, was duly appointed for the purpose of taking an enumeration of the inhabitants of that State by an act of its legislature; that on the 6th of June last, whilst Mr. Greely was engaged in performing this duty and taking down the names of the inhabitants residing in that part of the disputed territory claimed by the United States as lying within the limits of Maine, he was forcibly arrested by the authorities

* Omitted.

of New Brunswick, immediately transported in custody to the town of Frederickton, and imprisoned in the public jail, where he still remains. This proceeding by the authorities of New Brunswick, having produced, as might justly have been expected, very deep excitement in Maine, was followed by an immediate appeal from the governor of that State to the Government of the United States for intervention and redress.

This application on the part of Maine having received the special consideration of the President, the undersigned has been instructed to lose no time in presenting the subject to the early and earnest attention of Her Majesty's Government, and demanding not only the immediate liberation of Mr. Greely from imprisonment, but indemnity for the injuries that he has sustained.

In fulfilling these instructions of his Government it is not the purpose of the undersigned to open the general discussion of the respective claims of Great Britain and the United States to the disputed territory (within which Mr. Greely was arrested), or the right of either Government to exercise jurisdiction within its limits. Whatever opinion the undersigned may entertain as to the rightful claim of the State of Maine to the territory in dispute, and however unanswerable he may regard the arguments by which the claim may be sustained, he deems it neither proper nor needful to urge them upon the consideration of Her Majesty's Government in the decision of the present case; more especially as the whole subject is elsewhere, and in another form, matter of negotiation between the two Governments, where the discussion of the question of right more appropriately belongs. The undersigned, moreover, does not presume that pending the negotiation, and whilst efforts are making for the peaceable and final adjustment of these delicate and exciting questions, Her Majesty's Government can claim the right of exclusive jurisdiction and sovereignty over the disputed territory or the persons residing within its limits. In such a claim of power on the part of Great Britain or its provincial authorities, the undersigned need not repeat to Lord Palmerston (what he is already fully apprised of) the Government of the United States can never consent to acquiesce in the existing state of the controversy. On the contrary, the mutual understanding which exists between the two Governments on the subject and the moderation which both Governments have heretofore manifested forbid the exercise by either of such high acts of sovereign power as that which has been exerted in the present case by the authorities of Her Majesty's provincial government.

The undersigned must therefore suppose that this arrest and imprisonment of an American citizen under such circumstances and in the existing state of the controversy could only have been justified by some supposed infringement of the understanding existing between the parties in relation to the question of jurisdiction within the disputed territory. Such, however, was not the case. The correspondence between the governor of Maine and the lieutenant-governor of New Brunswick shows that the only act done by Mr. Greely was the simple enumeration of the inhabitants, and it is not perceived how such an act could be construed into a breach of the understanding between the two Governments.

It is proper also to remark that this was not the first time that the inhabitants within this particular settlement had been enumerated under the authority of the United States. It was done in the census of 1820 (as a portion of the State of Maine), and was at the time neither objected to nor remonstrated against by the British Government or that of New Brunswick.

Wherever, then, the right of jurisdiction and sovereignty over this territory may dwell, the undersigned feels satisfied that Her Majesty's Government can not fail to perceive that the arrest and imprisonment of Mr. Greely under the circumstances of the case was not only a violation of the rights of the United States, but was wholly irreconcilable with that moderation and forbearance which it is peculiarly the duty of both Governments to maintain until the question of right shall be definitively settled.

It becomes the duty of the undersigned, therefore, in pursuance of special instructions from his Government, to invite the early and favorable consideration of Her Majesty's Government to the subject, and to demand, as a matter of justice and right, the immediate discharge of Mr. Greely from imprisonment, and a suitable indemnity for the wrongs he has sustained.

Before closing this note the undersigned will avail himself of the occasion to remind Lord Palmerston of the urgency which exists for the immediate and final adjustment of this long-pending controversy, and the increased obstacles which will be thrown in the way of its harmonious settlement by these repeated collisions of authority and the exercise of exclusive jurisdiction by either party within the disputed territory.

He begs leave also to repeat to his lordship assurances of the earnest and unabated desire which the President feels that the controversy should be speedily and amicably settled, and to express the anxiety with which the Government of the United States is waiting the promised decision of Her Majesty's Government upon the proposition submitted to it as far back as July, 1836, and which the undersigned had been led to believe would long since have been given; and he has been further directed to say that should this proposition be disapproved the President entertains the hope that some new one on the part of Her Majesty's Government will immediately be made for the final and favorable termination of this protracted and deeply exciting controversy.

The undersigned begs Lord Palmerston to receive renewed assurances of his distinguished consideration.

A. STEVENSON.

Mr. Forsyth to Mr. Stevenson.

DEPARTMENT OF STATE,
Washington, September 28, 1837.

ANDREW STEVENSON, Esq., etc.

SIR: You will receive herewith the copy of a note, dated the 18th instant, recently received by the President from the governor of Maine, who alleges that Ebenezer S. Greely, esq., a citizen of that State, while employed within its limits and under its authority in enumerating the inhabitants of Penobscot County, has been again arrested and imprisoned by the provincial authorities of New Brunswick, and requests that speedy measures be adopted by the Government of the United States to procure the release of Mr. Greely.

Governor Dunlap has been assured, by the President's direction, that steps would be immediately taken to effect that object, and you are accordingly instructed, on the receipt of this dispatch, to bring the subject without delay to the attention of the British secretary of state for foreign affairs. You will remonstrate in a respectful but earnest manner against this second violation of the rights of Maine in the person of her agent, and demand the prompt release of Mr. Greely, with such additional indemnification as the nature of the outrage calls for.

I am, etc.,
JOHN FORSYTH.

Mr. Stevenson to Mr. Forsyth.

[Extracts.]

LEGATION OF THE UNITED STATES,
London, November 22, 1837.

On my return to London, after an absence of a few weeks, I found your dispatches Nos. 26 and 27, under date of the 8th and 28th of September. In pursuance of your instructions I addressed an official note to Lord Palmerston on the subject of the second arrest and imprisonment of Mr. Greely by the provincial authority of New Brunswick, a copy of which I have now the honor of transmitting to you.

No answer has yet been received to my first note, but I presume a decision of the case may be soon expected.

Mr. Stevenson to Lord Palmerston.

23 PORTLAND PLACE, *November 8, 1837.*

The undersigned, envoy extraordinary and minister plenipotentiary from the United States, had the honor on the 10th of August last of addressing to Lord Viscount Palmerston, Her Majesty's principal secretary of state for foreign affairs, an official note complaining of the arrest and imprisonment of Ebenezer S. Greely, a citizen of the United States, by the provincial authorities of New Brunswick, and demanding, by order of his Government, the immediate release of Mr. Greely from imprisonment, with suitable indemnity for the wrongs he had sustained. To this communication a note was received from his lordship, under date of the 22d of the same month, in which an assurance was given that an early answer to the complaint might be expected. No answer, however, has yet been received, and it is with unfeigned regret that the undersigned finds himself constrained, in again inviting the attention of Her Majesty's Government to the subject, to accompany it with another complaint of a second outrage committed by the authorities of New Brunswick upon the rights and liberty of this individual.

From recent information received it appears that shortly after the first arrest and imprisonment of Mr. Greely he was, by the orders of the lieutenant-governor of New Brunswick, released from confinement, but was immediately thereafter again taken into custody by his authority and recommitted to the jail of Frederickton, where he is now detained. This fact having been communicated by the governor of Maine to the President of the United States (in an official communication setting forth the circumstances under which it was done, a copy of which is herewith transmitted), the undersigned has received the special instructions of his Government to bring the subject without delay to the notice of Her Majesty's Government, in order that immediate steps may be taken for the liberation of Mr. Greely and indemnity made for the injuries he has suffered.

Having in the first note which he had the honor of addressing to Lord Palmerston stated the grounds upon which the release of this individual was demanded and the expectations of his Government in relation to the subject, and having waived the discussion of the questions of right and jurisdiction, which he still intends doing, it will not be needful to do more on this occasion than express to his lordship the painful surprise and regret with which the President has received information of this second outrage on the part of the authorities of New Brunswick, and to repeat the assurances heretofore given that such proceeding can be regarded in no other light than a violation of the rights and sovereignty of the United States, and entirely irreconcilable with that mutual forbearance which it was understood would be practiced by both Governments pending the negotiation.

The circumstances under which these recent attempts to enforce jurisdiction have been made show that in the most favorable aspect in which they can be regarded they were wholly indefensible.

The act for which Greely was arrested and imprisoned, so far from having been committed within the acknowledged dominions of the British Crown, and beyond the limits of the disputed territory, and therefore liable to be treated as a violation of territorial jurisdiction, took place, as appears by the statement of the governor of Maine, whilst he was employed within the limits of that State, and under its authority, in enumerating the inhabitants of the county of Penobscot.

By what authority, then, the provincial government of New Brunswick felt itself justified in exercising such acts of sovereign power the undersigned is at a loss to conceive, unless, indeed, upon the ground that the jurisdiction and sovereignty over the disputed territory pending the controversy rests exclusively with Great Britain. If such should turn out to be the fact, it can hardly be necessary again to repeat the assurances which have been heretofore given that in any such claim of power the Government of the United States can not acquiesce.

Upon the consequences which would unavoidably result from attempting to exercise such jurisdiction it is needless to enlarge. It must now be apparent that all such attempts, if persevered in, can produce only feuds and collisions of the most painful character, and besides increasing the feelings of international discord which have already been excited between the contending parties, they will close every avenue to an amicable adjustment of a controversy which it is so much the desire and interest of both Governments to accomplish. Ought it not, then, to be the earnest endeavor of the two Governments to avoid doing anything which can have a tendency to lead to such mischievous consequences?

It is under this view of the subject that the undersigned has been instructed again to remonstrate against these proceedings of the authorities of New Brunswick, as a violation of the rights of Maine in the person of her agent, and to protest in the most solemn manner against the future exercise of all such acts of jurisdiction and sovereignty over the disputed territory or the citizens of the United States residing within its limits until a final adjustment of the controversy takes place.

The undersigned, therefore, can not and ought not to close this note without again invoking the early and earnest attention of Lord Palmerston and that of Her Majesty's Government to this painful subject.

It is one of deep and mutual interest to the parties concerned, and the delicacy and embarrassments which surround it are justly appreciated by the Government of the United States. Deeply regretting, as that Government does, the collisions of authority to which both countries have been so repeatedly exposed by the delay that has taken place in the final settlement of the main question, it is sincerely desirous, as the undersigned has taken occasion repeatedly to assure Lord Palmerston, to have it brought to a speedy and amicable termination. This can only be done by measures of mutual forbearance and moderation on the part of both Governments. To this end the efforts of the American Government have been earnest, persevering, and constant. It has done, as it will continue to do, everything in its power to induce the State of Maine to pursue a course best calculated to avoid all excitement and collision between the citizens of that State and the inhabitants of New Brunswick, or which would tend in any manner to embarrass the mediatorial action of their two Governments on the subject; but it can not be expected, if the authorities of New Brunswick still persevere in attempting to exercise jurisdiction over the disputed territory by the arrest and imprisonment in foreign jails of citizens of Maine for performing their duty under the laws of their own State, and within what is believed to be her territorial limits, that measures of retaliation will not be resorted to by Maine, and great mischief ensue.

Indeed, under existing circumstances and in the nature of human connections, it is not possible, should such a course of violence be continued, to avoid collisions of the most painful character, for which the Government of the United States can not be responsible, but which both Governments would equally deplore.

It was doubtless with a view of guarding against these consequences that the understanding took place that each Government should abstain from exercising jurisdiction within the limits of the disputed territory pending the settlement of the main question.

The undersigned therefore persuades himself that these proceedings of the colonial government may have taken place without a careful examination of the important questions involved in them or the consequences to which they might lead, rather than under instructions from Her Majesty's Government or with a deliberate view of asserting and enforcing territorial and jurisdictional rights over the contested territory.

In looking back, as he does with satisfaction, to the conciliatory spirit in which the negotiation has heretofore been conducted and the moderation which both Governments have observed, the undersigned can not permit himself to doubt but that upon a careful review of the whole subject Her Majesty's Government will see fit not only to mark with its disapprobation this last proceeding of her colonial government, and direct the immediate liberation of Mr. Greely from imprisonment, with ample indemnity for the wrongs he may have sustained, but that it will see the propriety of giving suitable instructions to the authorities of New Brunswick to abstain for the future from all acts of that character, which can have no other tendency than to increase the excitement and jealousies which already prevail and retard the final and amicable adjustment of this painful controversy.

The undersigned requests Lord Palmerston to accept assurances of his distinguished consideration.

A. STEVENSON.

Mr. Clay to Mr. Vaughan.

DEPARTMENT OF STATE,
Washington, January 9, 1829.

Right Hon. CHARLES R. VAUGHAN, etc.

SIR: I have this day received a letter from the governor of the State of Massachusetts, transmitting an extract from a letter addressed by George W. Coffin, esq., land agent of Massachusetts, to his excellency, a copy of which is herewith communicated, and to which I request your immediate and particular attention.

It appears from this document that "mills are now erecting on the grant formerly made to General Eaton, on the Aroostook River, for the avowed purpose of getting their supply of timber from our forests;" that the proprietor of these mills "says he has assurances from the authorities of New Brunswick that he may cut timber without hindrance from them, provided he will engage to pay them for it if they succeed in obtaining their right to the territory;" "that mills are also erected at Fish River, and to supply them the growth in that section is fast diminishing, and that the inhabitants of St. John River obtain from the Province of New Brunswick permits to cut on the Crown lands. But it is evident that many having such permits do not confine themselves to Crown lands, for in my travels across the interior country logging roads and the chips where timber had been hewn were seen in every direction, also many stumps of trees newly cut." I need scarcely remark that the proceedings thus described are in opposition to the understanding which has existed between the Governments of the United States and Great Britain that during the pendency of the arbitration which is to settle the question of boundary neither party should exercise any jurisdiction or perform any act on the disputed territory to strengthen his own claims or to affect the state of the property in issue. The governor of Massachusetts observes in his letter to me that, "in relation to the lands on Fish River, it must be recollected that the survey of a road by the joint commissioners of Massachusetts and Maine a short time since was made matter of complaint by the British minister resident at Washington on the express ground that the territory was within the scope of the dispute. From courtesy to his Government and a respectful regard to a suggestion from the Department of State, the making of the road was suspended." The governor justly concludes: "But it will be an ill requital for this voluntary forbearance on our part if the land is to be plundered of its timber and the value of the property destroyed before it shall be determined that it does not belong to us."

If the government of New Brunswick will authorize or countenance such trespasses as have been stated by Mr. Coffin on the disputed territory, it can not be expected that the State of Maine will abstain from the adoption of preventive measures or from the performance of similar or other acts of jurisdiction and proprietorship. The consequence would be immediate and disagreeable collision. To prevent this state of things, I am directed by the President again to demand through you the effectual interposition of the British Government. Without that the friendly, if not the peaceful, relations between the two countries may be interrupted or endangered.

I request your acceptance on this occasion of assurances of my distinguished consideration.
H. CLAY.

Mr. Vaughan to Mr. Clay.

WASHINGTON, *January 13, 1829.*

Hon. HENRY CLAY, etc.:

The undersigned, His Britannic Majesty's envoy extraordinary and minister plenipotentiary, has the honor to acknowledge the receipt of Mr. Clay's note containing a representation which has been made by his excellency the governor of the State of Massachusetts respecting the cutting down of timber upon the disputed territory in the Province of New Brunswick.

The undersigned will immediately transmit a copy of Mr. Clay's note to His Majesty's lieutenant-governor of New Brunswick, in order to obtain an explanation of the transaction which has given rise to the remonstrance made by the governor of Massachusetts.

The undersigned takes this opportunity of renewing to the Secretary of State the assurances of his highest consideration.
CHS. R. VAUGHAN.

Mr. Vaughan to Mr. Hamilton.

WASHINGTON, *March 7, 1829.*

JAMES A. HAMILTON, Esq., etc.:

The undersigned, His Britannic Majesty's envoy extraordinary and minister plenipotentiary, had the honor to receive from the Secretary of State of the United States a note, dated the 9th January last, containing a representation made by his excellency the governor of Massachusetts respecting some trespasses committed on the disputed territory in the Province of New Brunswick.

A copy of the note of the Secretary of State having been transmitted to Sir Howard Douglas, His Majesty's lieutenant-governor of that Province, the undersigned has lately received an answer, which he has the honor to communicate to Mr. Hamilton by inclosing an extract* of his excellency's letter, which shews in the most satisfactory manner that, so far from the proceedings complained of by the governor of Massachusetts having been authorized or countenanced in any shape by the government of New Brunswick, every precaution has been taken to prevent and restrain depredations in the disputed territory.

Mr. Hamilton will see by the inclosed letter that Sir Howard Douglas has sent a magistrate to report upon the mills which have been established without license or authority, to inspect minutely the stations of the cutters of lumber, and to seize any timber brought into the acknowledged boundaries of New Brunswick from the disputed territory, and to hold the proceeds of the sale of it for the benefit of the party to whom that territory may be ultimately awarded.

As the time is approaching when Sir Howard Douglas will be absent from his government, he will leave injunctions strictly to observe the understanding between the two governments during his absence. The undersigned has great satisfaction in being able to offer to the Government of the United States the unequivocal testimony

*Omitted.

contained in the inclosed letter from Sir Howard Douglas of the conciliatory spirit in which the government of New Brunswick is administered, and trusting that a simi- lar spirit will animate the government of the American States which border on that Province, he confidently anticipates a cessation of that excitement which has unfor- tunately prevailed in the neighborhood of the disputed territory.

The undersigned takes this occasion to offer to Mr. Hamilton the assurances of his high consideration.

CHAS. R. VAUGHAN.

Mr. Hamilton to Mr. Vaughan.

DEPARTMENT OF STATE,
Washington, March 11, 1829.

Right Hon. CHARLES RICHARD VAUGHAN,

Envoy Extraordinary and Minister Plenipotentiary from Great Britain.

SIR: I have received and laid before the President of the United States the note, with its inclosures, which you did me the honor to write to me on the 7th of this month in answer to a representation which was made to you by Mr. Clay on the 9th of January last, at the instance of the governor of Massachusetts, concerning dep- redations complained of by him against inhabitants of the Province of New Bruns- wick in cutting timber, preparing lumber for market, and erecting mills upon the soil of the territory in dispute between the United States and Great Britain, and I am directed by the President to state in reply, as I have much pleasure in doing, that he derives great satisfaction from the information contained in your communica- tion, as he especially perceives in the prompt and energetic measures adopted by Sir Howard Douglas, lieutenant-governor of the Province in question, and detailed in the inclosure referred to, a pledge of the same disposition on the part of the authori- ties of that Province which animates this Government—to enforce a strict observance of the understanding between the two Governments that the citizens or subjects of neither shall exercise any acts of ownership in the disputed territory whilst the title to it remains unsettled. I will lose no time in making known to the governors of Mas- sachusetts and Maine the measures which have been thus adopted by the lieutenant- governor of New Brunswick to guard against all depredations upon the disputed territory, and will at the same time inform their excellencies of the just and confi- dent expectation entertained by the President that the conciliatory understanding or arrangement between the two Governments of the United States and Great Britain already referred to should not be disturbed by the citizens of these two States.

I am directed likewise by the President expressly to use this first occasion of an official communication with you under his orders to request the favor of you to make known to your Government the sincere regret he feels at the existence of any differ- ence or misunderstanding between the United States and Great Britain upon the subject-matter of this letter, or any other whatever, and that in all the measures which may be adopted on his part toward their adjustment he will be entirely actu- ated and governed by a sincere desire to promote the kindest and best feelings on both sides and secure the mutual and lasting interests of the parties.

I pray you, sir, to accept the renewed assurances of the high and distinguished consideration with which I have the honor to be, your obedient, humble servant,

JAMES A. HAMILTON.

Mr. Vaughan to Mr. Hamilton.

WASHINGTON, *March 12, 1829.*

Mr. J. A. HAMILTON, etc.:

It is with great satisfaction that the undersigned, His Britannic Majesty's envoy extraordinary and minister plenipotentiary, acknowledges the receipt of Mr. Hamil- ton's note of the 11th instant, containing a prompt acknowledgment of the efficacious measures adopted by the lieutenant-governor of New Brunswick to investigate and to restrain the proceedings complained of in the disputed territory; and he begs leave to assure the President that he derives great satisfaction from being requested to communicate to His Majesty's Government that in the adjustment of differences between Great Britain and the United States the President will be entirely actuated and governed by a sincere desire to promote the kindest and best feelings on both sides and secure the mutual and lasting interests of the parties.

The undersigned begs Mr. Hamilton to accept the assurances of his highest consideration.

CHS. R. VAUGHAN.

Mr. Vaughan to Mr. Van Buren.

WASHINGTON, *April 10, 1829.*

Hon. MARTIN VAN BUREN, etc.:

The undersigned, His Britannic Majesty's envoy extraordinary and minister plenipotentiary, has the honor to inform the Secretary of State of the United States that he has received an intimation from His Majesty's lieutenant-governor of New Brunswick that, apparently, it is the intention of the Government of the United States to carry the road now making through the State of Maine to Mars Hill over the point, and to occupy it as a military station.

The undersigned begs leave to remind Mr. Van Buren that Mars Hill is situated upon the northeastern line of boundary which is in dispute between the two Governments; and he is called upon to protest against the occupation of it by American troops upon the ground that the line drawn by the commissioners of boundary under the treaty of Ghent due north from the monument which marks the sources of the river St. Croix was not considered by them as correctly laid down, and it yet remains to be determined whether Mars Hill lies eastward or westward of a line drawn upon scientific principles. For a better explanation of the motives for this protest the undersigned has the honor to refer the Secretary of State to a copy of a letter, which is inclosed,* from Sir Howard Douglas.

A joint resolution of both Houses of Congress passed during the last session tends to confirm the intentions of the Government of the United States as inferred by Sir Howard Douglas from the information which he has received. That resolution authorized the making of a road from and beyond Mars Hill to the mouth of the Madawaska River; but as the carrying into effect that resolution was left entirely to the discretion of the President, the undersigned can not entertain any apprehension of a forcible seizure of a large portion of the disputed territory, which a compliance with the resolution of Congress would imply.

The undersigned acknowledges with great satisfaction the assurances which he has received of the kind feelings which will actuate the President of the United States in the adjustment of any differences which may exist with Great Britain. He submits, therefore, the representation of the lieutenant-governor of New Brunswick respecting the occupation of Mars Hill, relying confidently on the manifest propriety of restraining the aggression which it is supposed is meditated from the frontier of the State of Maine, and of both parties mutually abstaining from any acts which can affect the disputed territory, as the question of possession is now in the course of arbitration.

The undersigned reiterates to the Secretary of State the assurances of his highest consideration.

CHAS. R. VAUGHAN.

* Omitted.

Mr. Van Buren to Mr. Vaughan.

DEPARTMENT OF STATE,
Washington, May 11, 1829.

Right Hon. CHARLES R. VAUGHAN, etc.:

The undersigned, Secretary of State of the United States, has the honor to acknowledge the receipt of the note which Mr. Vaughan, His Britannic Majesty's envoy extraordinary and minister plenipotentiary, addressed to him on the 10th of April, stating upon the authority of a letter from the governor of New Brunswick, whereof a copy came inclosed in Mr. Vaughan's note, that it was apparently the intention of the Government of the United States to carry the road now making through the State of Maine to Mars Hill over that point, and to occupy Mars Hill as a military station; and protesting against such occupation upon the ground that the line drawn by the commissioners of boundary under the treaty of Ghent due north from the monument which marks the source of the river St. Croix was not considered by them as correctly laid down, and that it yet remains to be determined whether Mars Hill is eastward or westward of the true line.

The undersigned deems it unnecessary upon the present occasion to enter into an elaborate discussion of the point stated by Sir Howard Douglas, the lieutenant-governor of New Brunswick, concerning the line referred to by him, inasmuch as the relative position of Mars Hill to that line is already designated upon map A, and the line itself mutually agreed to and sufficiently understood for all present purposes, though not definitively settled by the convention of London of the 29th September, 1827.

The undersigned will therefore merely state that he finds nothing in the record of the proceedings of the commissioners under the fifth article of the treaty of Ghent to warrant the doubt suggested by the lieutenant-governor of New Brunswick whether Mars Hill lies to the westward of the line to be drawn due north from the monument at the source of the St. Croix to the highlands which divide the waters that empty into the river St. Lawrence from those which empty into the Atlantic Ocean; that the joint surveys and explorations made under that commission place the hill about a mile due west of that line; and that the agent of His Britannic Majesty before the commissioners, so far from intimating any doubt on the point, made it one ground of argument that the true line, when correctly laid down, would necessarily, on account of the ascertained progressive westerly variation of the needle, fall still farther westward.

The undersigned can not acquiesce in the supposition that, because the agent of His Britannic Majesty thought proper in the proceedings before the commissioners to lay claim to all that portion of the State of Maine which lies north of a line running westerly from Mars Hill, and designated as the limit or boundary of the British claim, thereby the United States or the State of Maine ceased to have jurisdiction in the territory thus claimed. In the view of this Government His Britannic Majesty's agent might with equal justice have extended his claim to any other undisputed part of the State as to claim the portion of it which he has drawn in question, and in such case the lieutenant-governor of New Brunswick could surely not have considered a continuance on the part of the United States and of the State of Maine to exercise their accustomed jurisdiction and authority to be an encroachment. If so, in what light are we to regard the continued acts of jurisdiction now exercised by him in the Madawaska settlement? More than twenty years ago large tracts of land lying westward of Mars Hill, and northward on the river Restook, were granted by the State of Massachusetts, which tracts are held and possessed under those grants to this day, and the United States and the States of Massachusetts and Maine, in succession, have never ceased to exercise that jurisdiction which the unsettled condition of the country in that region and other circumstances admitted and required.

The undersigned, therefore, can not discover in the facts and circumstances of the case any just principles upon which Sir Howard Douglas could predicate his protest. He has, however, submitted the note which he had the honor to receive from Mr. Vaughan to the President of the United States, and is by him directed to say in reply that although this Government could feel no difficulty in the exercise of what it deems an unquestionable right, and could not allow itself to be restrained by the protest of the lieutenant-governor of New Brunswick, yet, as a further proof of the spirit of amity, forbearance, and conciliation which the President is desirous of cultivating between the two Governments, he has decided to postpone for the present the exercise of the authority vested in him by the Congress of the United States to cause to be surveyed and laid out a military road to be continued from Mars Hill, or such other point on the military road laid out in the State of Maine as he may think proper, to the mouth of the river Madawaska, and to add that the lieutenant-governor of New Brunswick is under a misapprehension as to the design of this Government to occupy Mars Hill as a military station, no such intention being entertained by the President, nor have any measures been taken by this Government with an ulterior view to that object.

The undersigned indulges the hope that Mr. Vaughan will perceive in the manner in which the President, discriminating between the rights of this Government and their present exercise, has used the discretion conferred upon him an additional evidence of the desire which he sincerely entertains, and which he has heretofore caused to be communicated to Mr. Vaughan, that both Governments should, as far as practicable, abstain from all acts of authority over the territory in dispute which are not of immediate and indispensable necessity, and which would serve to create or increase excitement whilst the matter is in course of arbitration; and he feels well persuaded that Mr. Vaughan will not fail to inculcate the same spirit and to recommend in the strongest terms the observance of the same course on the part of the provincial government of New Brunswick.

The undersigned offers to Mr. Vaughan the renewed assurances of his high consideration.

M. VAN BUREN.

Mr. Vaughan to Mr. Van Buren.

WASHINGTON, *May 14, 1829.*

Hon. MARTIN VAN BUREN, etc.:

The undersigned, His Britannic Majesty's envoy extraordinary and minister plenipotentiary, has the honor to acknowledge the receipt of Mr. Van Buren's note dated the 11th instant, and he derives great satisfaction from being able to communicate to His Majesty's Government the assurances which it contains that the Government of the United States has never entertained the design of occupying Mars Hill, and that the President, in the spirit of amity, forbearance, and conciliation which he is desirous of cultivating between the two Governments, has decided to postpone for the present the exercise of the authority vested in him by the Congress of the United States to cause to be surveyed and laid out a military road to be continued from Mars Hill to the river Madawaska.

The undersigned will transmit immediately a copy of Mr. Van Buren's note to His Majesty's Government, and he forbears, therefore, from taking notice of the observations which it contains relative to the exact position of Mars Hill and to the exercise of jurisdiction in the district on the northwest of it.

The undersigned begs leave to renew to Mr. Van Buren the assurances of his highest consideration.

CHAS. R. VAUGHAN.

Mr. Vaughan to Mr. Van Buren.

WASHINGTON, *June 8, 1829.*

Hon. MARTIN VAN BUREN, etc.:

The undersigned, His Britannic Majesty's envoy extraordinary and minister pleni-potentiary, had the honor on the 7th March last to lay before the Government of the United States a letter from Sir Howard Douglas, His Majesty's lieutenant-governor of New Brunswick, in explanation of trespasses alleged by the governor of the State of Massachusetts to have been committed by British subjects in the disputed territory within that Province. The lieutenant-governor announced his intention in that letter of sending a magistrate into the district where the proceedings complained of had taken place to ascertain the nature and extent of the alleged trespasses and afterwards to make a report to his excellency.

The report of the magistrate having been received by Mr. Black, who has been commissioned by His Majesty to administer the government of New Brunswick during the temporary absence of Sir Howard Douglas, a copy of it has been transmitted to the undersigned, and he begs leave to submit it * to the consideration of the Secretary of State of the United States, together with an extract* of the letter of Mr. Black which accompanied it. As it appears by the report of Mr. Maclauchlan, the magistrate, that some American citizens settled in the disputed territory are implicated in the trespasses which have been committed, Mr. Black, the president and commissioner in chief of the government of New Brunswick, suggests the propriety of an officer being appointed by the Government of the United States to act in concert with the British magistrate in preventing further depredations.

The undersigned has received from Mr. Black the most satisfactory assurances that it will be his earnest study to adhere scrupulously to the good feeling and conciliatory conduct toward the United States which has been observed by Sir Howard Douglas.

The undersigned seizes this opportunity to renew to Mr. Van Buren the assurances of his distinguished consideration.

CHAS. R. VAUGHAN.

Mr. Bankhead to Mr. Livingston.

WASHINGTON, *October 1, 1831.*

Hon. EDWARD LIVINGSTON, etc.:

The undersigned, His Britannic Majesty's chargé d'affaires, has the honor to acquaint Mr. Livingston, Secretary of State of the United States, that he has received a communication from His Majesty's lieutenant-governor of New Brunswick, stating that the authorities of Maine have endeavored to exercise a jurisdiction over part of the territory at present in dispute between His Majesty and the United States, and, further, that an order has been issued by a justice of the peace for the county of Penobscot to the inhabitants of the town of Madawaska to assemble for the purpose of choosing municipal officers.

The undersigned regrets sincerely that these irregular proceedings should have been had recourse to during a period when the question of boundary is in a course of settlement, and in opposition to the desire expressed by the President that pending the discussion of that question the State of Maine should refrain from committing any act which could be construed into a violation of the neighboring territory.

The undersigned begs leave to submit to the Secretary of State several documents* which he has received from Sir Archibald Campbell in support of his complaint of a violation of territory; and the undersigned entertains a confident hope that such measures will be adopted as shall prevent a recurrence of acts on the part of the authorities of the State of Maine which are productive of so much inconvenience

*Omitted.

and which tend to disturb that harmony and good will so necessary to be preserved between the two countries.

The undersigned has the honor to renew to Mr. Livingston the assurances of his distinguished consideration.

CHARLES BANKHEAD.

Mr. Livingston to Mr. Bankhead.

DEPARTMENT OF STATE,
Washington, October 17, 1831.

CHARLES BANKHEAD, Esq., etc.

SIR: Immediately after receiving your note of the 1st instant I wrote to the governor of the State of Maine for information on the subject of it. I have just received his answer, of which I have the honor to inclose two extracts.* By the first you will perceive that the election of town officers in the settlement of Madawaska, of which complaint was made in the papers inclosed in your letter, was made under color of a general law, which was not intended by either the executive or legislative authority of that State to be executed in that settlement, and that the whole was the work of inconsiderate individuals.

By the second extract it will appear that the individuals said to have been most prominent in setting up the authority of the State have been arrested by order of the lieutenant-governor of the Province of New Brunswick, and were on their way to be imprisoned at Frederickton.

The innovation on the existing state of things in the disputed territory being distinctly disavowed by the executive authority of the State, no act of authority or exercise of jurisdiction having followed the election, I would respectfully suggest the propriety of your recommending to the lieutenant-governor of New Brunswick the release of the prisoners who were arrested for exercising this act of authority in the territory mutually claimed by the two nations, contrary to the understanding between their Governments. It is their avowed object to avoid any collision until the intention of both parties in relation to the award shall be fully known. All subjects calculated to produce irritation, therefore, ought evidently to be avoided. The arrest of the persons concerned in the election must produce that feeling in a high degree. A conviction can not take place without eliciting a decision from the bench declaratory of and enforcing the jurisdiction over the territory in dispute, which it is the present policy of both powers to avoid, at least for the short time that must elapse before the question can be finally settled. If punishment should follow conviction, the passions that would be excited must inevitably be hostile to that spirit of conciliation so necessary where sacrifices of national feeling and individual interest are required for the common good. It would be absurd here to enter into the question of title. Both parties claim it. No act that either can do is necessary to assist its right while there is hope of an amicable arrangement; and it was with this view of the subject that a mutual understanding has been had to leave things in the state in which they are until the question of the award is settled.

On the part of the Americans some individuals, in contravention of this understanding, have proceeded to do acts which if followed out would change the political state of part of the disputed land. But it has not been so followed out; it is disavowed by the power whose assent is necessary to carry it into execution. It is therefore of no avail, and can have no more effect than if the same number of men had met at Madawaska and declared themselves duly elected members of the British Parliament. The act interferes with no right; it comes in actual collision with no established power. Not so the punishment of the individuals concerned. This is at once

*.Omitted.

a practical decision of the question, and may lead to retaliating legal measures; for if the lieutenant-governor of New Brunswick feels himself obliged, as he says he does, to impose the authority of the law within which he thinks the boundaries of his Province, will not the same feeling incite the governor of Maine, under the same sense of duty, to pursue the like measures? And thus the fruits of moderation and mutual forbearance during so long a period will be lost for the want of perseverance in them for the short time that is now wanting to bring the controversy to an amicable close. It is therefore, sir, that I invite your interposition with his excellency the lieutenant-governor of New Brunswick to induce him to set at liberty the persons arrested, on their engagement to make no change in the state of things until the business shall be finally decided between the two Governments.

On our part, the desire of the General Government to avoid any measures tending to a change in the existing state of things on our northeast boundary has been fully and, it is believed, efficaciously expressed to the executive of the State of Maine, so that the actual relation of the State with the neighboring Province will not in future suffer any change.

I have great pleasure, sir, in renewing on this occasion the assurance of my high consideration.

EDWD. LIVINGSTON.

Mr. Bankhead to Mr. Livingston.

WASHINGTON, *October 20, 1831.*

Hon. EDWARD LIVINGSTON, Esq., etc.:

The undersigned, His Britannic Majesty's chargé d'affaires, has the honor to acknowledge the receipt of Mr. Livingston's note of the 17th instant, in answer to a representation which the undersigned thought it his duty to make to the Government of the United States upon a violation committed upon the territory at present in dispute between the two countries.

The friendly tone assumed by the Secretary of State in this communication, the discountenance on the part of the General Government of the proceedings which were complained of, and the determination of the President to cause the strictest forbearance to be maintained until the question of boundary shall be settled have been received by the undersigned with great satisfaction, and it is in the same spirit of harmony that he has addressed a letter to His Majesty's lieutenant-governor of New Brunswick, inclosing a copy of Mr. Livingston's note, for his excellency's serious consideration.

The undersigned has the honor to renew to Mr. Livingston the assurance of his distinguished consideration.

CHARLES BANKHEAD.

Mr. Bankhead to Mr. Livingston.

WASHINGTON, *October 22, 1831.*

Hon. EDWARD LIVINGSTON, etc.:

The undersigned, His Britannic Majesty's chargé d'affaires, has the honor to transmit to the Secretary of State of the United States the copy of a letter* from His Majesty's lieutenant-governor of New Brunswick, inclosing a deposition* made before a justice of the peace of that Province in support of a charge against certain inhabitants of Houlton, in the State of Maine, for having made a forcible inroad on the territory of His Majesty in search of an Irishman (an inhabitant of Woodstock, New Brunswick) who committed a most violent outrage against the constituted authorities at Houlton.

*Omitted.

The lieutenant-governor deprecates in the strongest manner the infamous conduct of the individual in question, and is perfectly ready to exert the utmost rigor of the laws against him; but his excellency at the same time protests against the conduct of those persons who have thus attempted to interfere with the jurisdiction of the laws in His Majesty's possessions.

Under these circumstances the undersigned has to request that Mr. Livingston will be good enough to cause the necessary inquiries to be instituted into this transaction, and upon the charges being clearly proved that he will make such a representation to the authorities of the State of Maine as shall prevent the recurrence of a similar irregularity in future.

The undersigned has the honor to renew to Mr. Livingston the assurances of his distinguished consideration.

CHARLES BANKHEAD.

Mr. Bankhead to Mr. Livingston.

WASHINGTON, *November 25, 1831.*

Hon. EDWARD LIVINGSTON, etc.:

The undersigned, His Britannic Majesty's chargé d'affaires, has the honor to refer the Secretary of State of the United States to the correspondence which took place in the month of October upon the subject of violations which had been committed upon the territory at present in dispute between Great Britain and the United States, and the measures which His Majesty's lieutenant-governor of New Brunswick deemed it expedient to adopt thereupon.

The trial of these persons took place at Frederickton, and they were sentenced by the supreme court of the Province to fine and imprisonment.

At the time the undersigned communicated to the Government of the United States the decision which the authorities of New Brunswick had felt it necessary to adopt upon this occasion he expressed the deep regret of the governor of that Province that the conduct of these individuals was such as to compel his excellency to pursue a course so uncongenial to his own feelings and at variance with the harmony which subsists between the Governments of Great Britain and the United States.

The Secretary of State upon receiving this communication expressed to the undersigned the earnest desire of the President, upon a total disavowal on the part of the General Government of the proceedings of the persons implicated in this transaction, that His Majesty's lieutenant-governor might consider himself authorized to exercise a prerogative in their favor and to remit the sentence which had been pronounced against them.

No time was lost in submitting Mr. Livingston's note to the consideration of Sir Archibald Campbell, and the undersigned has the greatest satisfaction in acquainting him that his excellency fully acquiesced in the desire manifested by the President of the United States. The undersigned can not better fulfill the wishes of Sir Archibald Campbell, which are so much in accordance with that spirit of good will which happily subsists between the two countries and which characterizes their relations with each other, than by transmitting to the Secretary of State a copy of the dispatch which he yesterday received from that officer, and which he feels assured will be received by the President as an earnest of his uninterrupted good feeling toward the Government and people of the United States.

The undersigned has the honor to renew to Mr. Livingston the assurance of his highest consideration.

CHARLES BANKHEAD.

Sir Archibald Campbell to Mr. Bankhead.

GOVERNMENT HOUSE,
Frederickton, November 8, 1831.

SIR: I had this morning the honor to receive your letter of the 20th ultimo, which, with its inclosures, are in every respect so satisfactory that I did not lose a moment in giving effect to the wishes therein expressed by exercising that prerogative so congenial to my own feelings, whether viewed in the extension of mercy or in the gratifying anticipation of such a measure being received as an earnest of my most anxious desire, as far as rests with me (consistent with my public duties), to preserve inviolate the harmony and good understanding so happily existing between the two Governments. The prisoners, Barnabas Hunnewell, Jesse Wheelock, and Daniel Savage, are released; and I have taken it upon myself, knowing that such a measure will be fully sanctioned by my Government, to remit the fines imposed by the supreme court of this Province, as already communicated to you by Lieutenant-Colonel Snodgrass—an act that I trust will not fail in being duly appreciated *when it is known* that the above-mentioned individuals did, with several others, follow up their first proceedings by acts of much more serious aggression, for which they stood charged under another (untried) indictment. However, everything connected therewith is now corrected.

You will see with what readiness and satisfaction I have received and adopted your kind advice, for which accept of my sincere thanks, and believe me to remain, sir, etc.,

ARCHIBALD CAMPBELL,
Lieutenant-Governor.

Mr. Livingston to Mr. Bankhead.

DEPARTMENT OF STATE,
Washington, November 28, 1831.

CHARLES BANKHEAD, Esq., etc.:

The undersigned, Secretary of State, etc., has the honor to acknowledge the receipt of a note from Mr. Bankhead, His Britannic Majesty's chargé d'affaires, under date of the 25th instant, accompanied by a copy of a letter from Sir A. Campbell, the lieutenant-governor of the Province of New Brunswick, by both of which the Secretary of State is informed that the citizens of the United States lately under prosecution at Frederickton for acts done in the territory now possessed by Great Britain within the country claimed both by that power and the United States, have been set at liberty, in accordance with the suggestions made in the former correspondence between Mr. Bankhead and the Secretary of State.

Mr. Bankhead's note, with its inclosure, has been laid before the President, who has instructed the undersigned to express his satisfaction at the prompt manner in which his suggestions have been complied with, and to say that he considers it as a proof of the disposition of His Britannic Majesty's officers to preserve the harmony that so happily subsists between the two Governments.

The undersigned renews to Mr. Bankhead the assurance of his high consideration.

EDWARD LIVINGSTON.

Sir Charles R. Vaughan to Mr. McLane.

WASHINGTON, *October 20, 1833.*

Hon. LOUIS MCLANE, etc.:

The undersigned, His Britannic Majesty's envoy extraordinary and minister plenipotentiary, has the honor to lay before the Secretary of State of the United States a copy of a letter* which he has received from His Excellency Sir Archibald Campbell, His Majesty's lieutenant-governor of New Brunswick, and to call his attention to the conduct of certain land agents of the States of Maine and Massachusetts in the territory in dispute between Great Britain and the United States.

It appears by the report contained in Sir Archibald Campbell's letter that land agents of Maine and Massachusetts have been holding out inducements to persons of both countries to cut pine timber on the disputed territory on condition of paying to them 2 shillings and 6 pence the ton, and that they have entered into contracts for opening two roads which will intersect the Roostook River.

As it is the declared will and mutual interest of the Governments of Great Britain and of the United States to preserve the disputed territory in its present state and to avoid all collision pending the settlement of the boundary question, the undersigned is convinced that it is sufficient to insure the prompt interference of the Government of the United States to put a stop to the proceedings of these land agents to state the conduct complained of.

The undersigned has the honor to renew to Mr. McLane the assurance of his most distinguished consideration. CHAS. R. VAUGHAN.

Mr. McLane to Sir Charles R. Vaughan.

DEPARTMENT OF STATE,
Washington, October 23, 1833.

Right Hon. SIR CHARLES R. VAUGHAN, G. C. H.,
Envoy Extraordinary and Minister Plenipotentiary of His Britannic Majesty:

The undersigned, Secretary of State of the United States, has the honor to acknowledge the receipt of the note of Sir Charles R. Vaughan, envoy extraordinary and minister plenipotentiary of His Britannic Majesty, of the 20th instant, accompanied by a copy of a letter from Sir Archibald Campbell, lieutenant-governor of New Brunswick, to Sir Charles R. Vaughan, and also a letter from J. A. Maclauchlan to the lieutenant-governor of New Brunswick, complaining of the "conduct of certain land agents of the States of Maine and Massachusetts in the territory in dispute between the United States and Great Britain."

The undersigned is instructed to state that it would be a source of regret to the President should this complaint prove to be well founded, and that he has caused a copy of Sir Charles's note and of the accompanying papers promptly to be communicated to the governors of Maine and Massachusetts, in order that the necessary steps may be taken to enforce a due observance of the terms of the existing arrangement between the Government of the United States and that of Great Britain in regard to the disputed territory.

The undersigned avails himself of the occasion to renew to Sir Charles R. Vaughan the assurance of his distinguished consideration. LOUIS McLANE.

Sir Charles R. Vaughan to Mr. McLane.

WASHINGTON, *December 17, 1833.*

Hon. LOUIS McLANE, etc.:

The undersigned, His Britannic Majesty's envoy extraordinary and minister plenipotentiary, regrets that a letter received from His Majesty's lieutenant-governor of New Brunswick should again require him to ask the intervention of the General Government of the United States to put a stop to certain proceedings of the State of Maine in the territory still in dispute between Great Britain and the United States.

*Omitted.

The inclosed letter, with the report which accompanies it,* shows that the State of Maine has opened a road beyond the conventional frontier, with the avowed intention of carrying it to the bank of the river St. John.

The undersigned is convinced that the Secretary of State of the United States will agree with him that the State of Maine must not be allowed to take upon herself the right to define the meaning of the treaty of 1783, and, by aggressions such as those against which the undersigned is called upon to remonstrate, to take possession, without reference to the General Government of the United States, of territory which has been so long in abeyance between the two Governments. Such conduct is calculated to lead to collisions of a distressing nature between the subjects of His Britannic Majesty and the citizens of the United States employed to assert a futile and hazardous possession which so entirely depends upon the arrangements in progress between the two Governments.

The undersigned trusts that the representation made in this note will be received by the Secretary of State in the same spirit of good will and conciliation which has hitherto characterized the conduct of the Government of the United States in all occurrences of a similar nature.

The undersigned has the honor to renew to Mr. McLane the assurance of his most distinguished consideration.

CHAS. R. VAUGHAN.

Mr. McLane to Sir Charles R. Vaughan.

DEPARTMENT OF STATE,
Washington, December 21, 1833.

Right Hon. SIR CHARLES R. VAUGHAN, G. C. H.,
Envoy Extraordinary and Minister Plenipotentiary of His Britannic Majesty:

The undersigned, Secretary of State, has the honor to acknowledge the receipt of the note addressed to him on the 17th instant by Sir Charles R. Vaughan, His Britannic Majesty's envoy extraordinary and minister plenipotentiary, requesting the intervention of the Government of the United States to put a stop to certain proceedings of the State of Maine in the territory still in dispute between Great Britain and the United States.

The proceedings referred to appear, by the letter of the lieutenant-governor of New Brunswick and the report of the officer acting on the part of Great Britain as warden of the disputed territory (copies of which accompanied Sir Charles R. Vaughan's note), to be the construction of a road to the Restook River, passing, as is alleged, through 15 miles of the disputed territory, and supposed by the warden to be intended to intersect the St. John River in the Madawaska settlement.

The undersigned is happy to have it in his power to afford at once such explanations upon this subject as he trusts may be satisfactory. By a communication received from the governor of Maine, in answer to a representation recently made by Sir Charles R. Vaughan concerning other alleged encroachments on the disputed territory, it will be seen that no part of the road now constructing by that State is believed to be within the territory of which the British Government has ever been in the actual possession since the treaty of 1783, and that it is not designed to extend the road beyond the Aroostook. The apprehensions entertained of its being extended to the St. John River in the Madawaska settlement appear, therefore, to be groundless, and, if the views of the governor of Maine as to the locality of the road be correct, it would seem that its construction can afford no just cause of complaint, as it is not supposed that such improvements made by either party within that part of the territory which has been in its possession, or so considered, since the treaty of 1783 are

*Omitted.

contrary to the spirit of the existing understanding between the two Governments. It will be seen, moreover, as well by the communication from the governor of Maine as by one received from the governor of Massachusetts on the same occasion, that a conciliatory and forbearing disposition prevails on their part, and that no measures will be taken or any acts authorized by them which may justly be considered as a violation of the understanding in regard to the disputed territory.

The undersigned has nevertheless been directed by the President to transmit copies of Sir Charles R. Vaughan's note and its inclosures to the governors of Maine and Massachusetts, and to repeat to their excellencies his earnest desire that as far as depends on them no departure from the understanding between the two Governments may be permitted.

In regard to the complaint heretofore made by Sir Charles R. Vaughan, upon the representations of the lieutenant-governor of New Brunswick and the warden of the disputed territory, as to the cutting and sale of timber under the authority of the land agents of Maine and Massachusetts, the undersigned begs leave to refer to the communications from the governors of those States already mentioned, copies of which are now transmitted, by which it appears that the conduct of those agents has furnished no just cause of dissatisfaction, but that, on the contrary, it is alleged that His Britannic Majesty's officers of the Province of New Brunswick, by the seizure and sale of timber cut by trespassers on the Aroostook, and afterwards in the rightful custody of the agent of the State of Massachusetts, have been the first to violate the existing understanding upon this subject.

These complaints on both sides, arising, as the undersigned believes, from acts which do not on either side indicate an intention to disregard the existing understanding, but are attributable to the unsettled state of the boundary question, and which should therefore be viewed with mutual forbearance, furnish increased reason for a speedy adjustment of that interesting matter; and the President looks with great solicitude for the answer, which is daily expected, from the British Government to the proposition submitted on the part of the United States, in the hope that it may soon set all those difficulties at rest.

The undersigned has the honor to renew to Sir Charles R. Vaughan the assurance of his distinguished consideration.

LOUIS McLANE.

EXECUTIVE DEPARTMENT OF MASSACHUSETTS,

November 1, 1833.

Hon. LOUIS McLANE,
     Secretary of State of the United States.

SIR: I have to acknowledge the honor of the receipt of your letter of the 23d of October, covering a copy of a note addressed to you by Sir Charles R. Vaughan, envoy extraordinary and minister plenipotentiary of His Britannic Majesty, accompanied also by copies of certain documents conveying complaints on the part of the authorities of His Majesty's Province of New Brunswick "of the conduct of certain land agents of the States of Maine and Massachusetts on the territory in dispute between the United States and Great Britain."

Permit me to assure you that I shall lose no time in making inquiry of the land agent of this Commonwealth into the supposed occasion of the complaints of His Majesty's provincial officers, and in transmitting to the Department of State such information as I may receive in reply.

Prejudicial as the delay in the settlement of this long-vexed subject of boundary is to the rights of property which Massachusetts claims in the disputed territory, and impatient as both the government and the people have become at the unreasonableness and pertinacity of the adversary pretensions and with the present state of the question, yet the executive of this Commonwealth will not cease to respect the understanding which has been had between the Governments of the two countries, *that no act of wrong to the property of either* shall be committed during the pending of measures to produce an amicable adjustment of the controversy.

In the meantime, I can not but earnestly protest against the authority of any appointment on the behalf of His Majesty's Government which may be regarded as a claim to the executive protection of this property or be deemed an acquiescence on the part of the United States in an interference, *under color* of a "wardenship of the disputed territory," with the direction to its improvement which the governments of Massachusetts and Maine, respectively, may see fit to give to their agents. The rights of soil and jurisdiction over it are in the States, and forbearance to the exercise of these rights for a season, from mere prudential considerations, a respectful regard to the wishes of the General Government, or amity toward a foreign nation is not to be construed into a readiness to surrender them upon the issue of any proposed negotiation.

I have the honor to be, sir, with sentiments of the highest respect, your obedient servant,

LEVI LINCOLN.

EXECUTIVE DEPARTMENT OF MAINE,
Augusta, November 23, 1833.

Hon. LOUIS MCLANE,
    Secretary of State of the United States, Washington.

SIR: I have the honor to acknowledge the receipt of your letter of the 23d of October last, communicating a copy of a note from Sir Charles R. Vaughan, accompanied with a copy of a letter from Sir Archibald Campbell, lieutenant-governor of New Brunswick, to Sir Charles R. Vaughan, and also of a letter from Lieutenant J. A. Maclauchlan to Sir Archibald Campbell, complaining of the conduct of the land agents of the States of Maine and Massachusetts in the territory in dispute between the United States and Great Britain.

In compliance with your request to be furnished with information in relation to this subject, I reply that by a resolve of the legislature of this State passed March 30, 1831, "the land agent of this State, in conjunction with the land agent of the Commonwealth of Massachusetts, is authorized and empowered to survey, lay out, and make a suitable winter road, or cause the same to be done, from the mouth of the Matawamkeag, a branch of the Penobscot River, in a northerly direction, so as to strike the Aroostook River on or near the line dividing the sixth and seventh ranges of townships." The same resolve authorizes the land agents to lay out and make, or cause to be made, a winter road from the village of Houlton, in a westerly direction, to intersect the road to the Aroostook River at some point most convenient for traveling and most for the interest of the State. By a subsequent resolve, passed March 8, 1832, the authority given to the land agents was enlarged so as to authorize them "to locate and survey the Aroostook road so that it may strike the Aroostook River at any place between the west line of the third range and the east line of the sixth range of townships west of the east line of the State." The first of these roads has been surveyed and located, and much the greater part of it lies within the undisputed limits of this State south of the sources of the Penobscot River, and it is believed that no part of it lies within territory of which the British Government has ever been in the actual possession since the treaty of 1783. A portion of this road only has yet been opened, and I have no information that any part of it has been opened over territory *claimed* by the British, although it is contemplated to extend it to the Aroostook when it can be done consistently with the public interest. The second road described in the resolve of March 30, 1831, is wholly within the undisputed limits of this State.

A report of the recent proceedings of the land agent in making these roads and disposing of the timber on the lands of the State has not been received, and his late sickness and death have rendered it impossible at this time to obtain a detailed statement of all that has been done in his official capacity. But it can not be presumed that he has in any particular exceeded his instructions (copies of which are herewith transmitted*), or, in the discharge of his official duties, taken any measures or authorized any acts to be done which could justly be considered as a violation of any known provision of the existing arrangement between the Governments of the United States and Great Britain in regard to the disputed territory.

With high consideration, I have the honor to be, sir, your obedient servant,

SAML. E. SMITH.

Sir Charles R. Vaughan to Mr. McLane.

WASHINGTON, *December 23, 1833.*

Hon. LOUIS McLANE, etc.:

The undersigned, His Britannic Majesty's envoy extraordinary and minister plenipotentiary, has the honor to acknowledge the receipt of the note of the Secretary of State of the United States, in answer to the representation which he was called upon to make respecting proceedings of the States of Massachusetts and Maine in the disputed territory.

To understand correctly the bearings of the roads which those States have resolved to construct requires a more accurate knowledge of the topography of the country through which they are to pass than the undersigned possesses, but he will not fail to transmit a copy of Mr. McLane's note, together with its inclosures, to His Majesty's lieutenant-governor of New Brunswick. In the meantime the undersigned begs leave to observe that the letter from the executive of Maine states that one of the roads surveyed and located lies, for the greater part of it, within the undisputed limits of that State, although it is contemplated to extend it to the Aroostook River. The land agent of Massachusetts is aware that the road from the river Matawamkeag to the Aroostook is the one that has given rise to complaint, and which, he observes, "is now nearly completed." As the Aroostook River, from its source till it falls into the St. John, flows exclusively through the disputed territory, to reach it by a road from the State of Maine must cause an encroachment and be considered an attempt to assume a right of possession in territory which has never yet been set apart from the original possession of Great Britain, on account of the difficulties of ascertaining the boundary according to the treaty of 1783.

With regard to the cutting down and sale of timber, the justification of the land agent at Boston will be submitted to Sir Archibald Campbell, and the undersigned is sure that the grievance complained of (taking away timber which had been seized by the agent from Massachusetts) will be attended to.

The undersigned receives with great satisfaction the assurances of Mr. McLane that "a conciliatory and forbearing disposition prevails on the part of Massachusetts and Maine, and that no measure will be taken or any acts authorized by them which may justly be considered as a violation of the understanding in regard to the disputed territory;" and he can not conclude without begging leave to acknowledge the readiness with which the President directed inquiries to be made and the desire which he has shewn on this and every similar occasion to prevent any encroachment on the disputed territory pending the settlement of the boundary now in progress between the two Governments.

The undersigned has the honor to assure Mr. McLane of his most distinguished consideration.

CHAS. R. VAUGHAN.

*Omitted.

Sir Charles R. Vaughan to Mr. McLane.

Hon. LOUIS McLANE, etc.:

WASHINGTON, *February 28, 1834.*

The undersigned, His Britannic Majesty's envoy extraordinary and minister pleni-potentiary, has the honor to communicate to the Secretary of State of the United States the explanation which he has received from the lieutenant-governor of New Brunswick of a transaction complained of by the land agent of Massachusetts in a report communicated to the undersigned in a note from Mr. McLane dated 21st December last.

The complaint arose out of the seizure of timber cut down without authority upon the disputed territory, and which, after having been seized in the first instance by the land agent of Massachusetts, was taken possession of and sold by the British agent intrusted with the preservation of the disputed territory on the northeastern frontier of the United States.

The explanation of this transaction is contained in an extract of a letter to the undersigned from the lieutenant-governor of New Brunswick and the report of Mr. Beckwith, the surveyor-general of that Province, which the undersigned has the honor to inclose in this note.*

The seizure of the timber in the first instance by Mr. Coffin, the land agent of Maine [Massachusetts], was the exercise of authority within the conventional fron-tier of the Province of New Brunswick, which could not be admitted so long as the northeastern boundary of the United States remains a subject of negotiation; and it appears that the proceeds of the sale of timber unlawfully cut down are carried to account, and the possession of them will be appropriated to the party to which the territory may be adjudged by the settlement of the boundary question.

The undersigned trusts that the explanation which he is now able to give of this transaction will prove satisfactory to the Government of the United States.

The undersigned has the honor to renew to Mr. McLane the assurance of his most distinguished consideration.

CHAS. R. VAUGHAN.

Mr. McLane to Sir Charles R. Vaughan.

DEPARTMENT OF STATE,
Washington, March 4, 1834.

Right Hon. SIR CHARLES R. VAUGHAN, G. C. H.,
Envoy Extraordinary, etc.

SIR: I have the honor to acknowledge the receipt of your note of the 28th ultimo, furnishing the explanation of the lieutenant-governor of New Brunswick of a trans-action referred to by the land agent of Massachusetts in a letter addressed to his excellency the governor of that Commonwealth, and subsequently communicated to you by this Department in a note dated 21st December last, and to inform you that copies of your communication, together with the documents which accompanied it, will, by direction of the President, be transmitted without unnecessary delay to the executive of the State of Massachusetts.

I pray you to accept the assurance of my distinguished consideration.

LOUIS McLANE.

Hon. R. M. JOHNSON,
President of the Senate.

WASHINGTON, *January 27, 1838.*

SIR: I transmit herewith, in compliance with the requirements of the second section of the act of March 3, 1837, making appropriations for

*Omitted.

the Indian Department, a communication from the War Department, accompanied by a copy of the report of the agents appointed to inquire what depredations had been committed by the Seminole and Creek Indians on the property of citizens of Florida, Georgia, and Alabama.

M. VAN BUREN.

[The same message was addressed to the Speaker of the House of Representatives.]

WASHINGTON CITY, *February 5, 1838.*

Hon. JAMES K. POLK,
   Speaker of the House of Representatives.

SIR: I have the honor to transmit to you a report from the Secretary of the Navy, prepared in obedience to a resolution of the House of Representatives of the 7th December last, requiring information as to the causes which have delayed the outfit and preparation of the South Sea surveying and exploring expedition.

M. VAN BUREN.

WASHINGTON, *February, 1838.*

To the House of Representatives of the United States:

In compliance with the resolution of the House of Representatives of the 20th instant, I transmit a report from the Secretary of State, which is accompanied by a copy and translation of the pamphlet* requested in that resolution.

M. VAN BUREN.

WASHINGTON, *February 17, 1838.*

To the Senate:

I transmit for your constitutional action articles of a treaty concluded on the 23d ultimo with the Chippewas of Saganaw, accompanied by a communication from the Secretary of War.

M. VAN BUREN.

WASHINGTON, *February 17, 1838.*

To the Senate:

I transmit for your consideration a communication from the Secretary of War, respecting a treaty now before you with the Stockbridge and Munsee Indians.

M. VAN BUREN.

* Issued by Manuel E. de Gorostiza, formerly minister from Mexico, before his departure from the United States, containing the correspondence between the Department of State and the Mexican legation relative to the passage of the Sabine River by troops under the command of General Gaines.

Hon. J. K. Polk,   WASHINGTON, *March, 1838.*
  Speaker of the House of Representatives.

Sir: The inclosed report and accompanying papers from the Secretary of War contain all the information required by the resolution of the House of Representatives of the 5th instant, respecting the present state of the campaign in Florida and the disposition of the Indians to treat for peace.
  Very respectfully, your most obedient servant,

M. VAN BUREN.

WASHINGTON, *March 12, 1838.*
To the House of Representatives:

  I transmit for the consideration of Congress a report from the Secretary of State, with the accompanying documents, relative to an application made by the minister of France in behalf of Captain Beziers for remuneration for services in saving the captain and crew of an American vessel wrecked in the bay of Cadiz in the year 1825.

  I am happy to evince my high sense of the humane and intrepid conduct of Captain Beziers by presenting his case to Congress, to whom alone it belongs to determine upon the expediency of granting his request.

M. VAN BUREN.

WASHINGTON, *March 13, 1838.*
The SPEAKER OF THE HOUSE OF REPRESENTATIVES:

  In compliance with a resolution of the House of Representatives of the 17th of February, I transmit a report* of the Secretary of State, with the accompanying documents, which contain the information requested.

M. VAN BUREN.

WASHINGTON, *March 14, 1838.*
The PRESIDENT OF THE SENATE:

  I transmit to the Senate a treaty of commerce and navigation between the United States and His Majesty the King of Greece, concluded at London on the 22d day of December last, together with a copy of the documents relating to the negotiation of the same, for the constitutional consideration of the Senate in reference to its ratification.

M. VAN BUREN.

WASHINGTON, *March 15, 1838.*
To the House of Representatives of the United States:

  In compliance with the resolution of the House of Representatives of the 5th instant, I transmit a report† from the Secretary of State, to whom the resolution was referred, with the documents by which the said report was accompanied.

M. VAN BUREN.

---

* Relating to a ship canal across the Isthmus of Darien.
  † Relating to the prosecution of the claim of the United States to the bequest made by James Smithson.

WASHINGTON, *March, 1838.*

To the House of Representatives of the United States:

I transmit a copy and translation of a letter from Mr. Pontois, the minister plenipotentiary from France to this Government, addressed to the Secretary of State, and communicating a memorial to me from the trustees of the former house of Lafitte & Co., of Paris, complaining of the rejection of a claim preferred in behalf of that house before the commissioners under the convention with France of the 4th of July, 1831, and asking redress.

The commission created by the act for carrying that convention into effect has expired. The fund provided by it has been distributed among those whose claims were admitted. The Executive has no power over the subject. If the memorialists are entitled to relief, it can be granted by Congress alone, to whom, in compliance with the request of the trustees, that question is now submitted for decision.

M. VAN BUREN.

WASHINGTON, *March 19, 1838.*

To the House of Representatives of the United States:

I transmit a report* from the Secretary of State, to whom the resolution of the House of Representatives of the 5th instant was referred, with the documents by which the said report was accompanied.

M. VAN BUREN.

WASHINGTON, *March 20, 1838.*

To the Senate of the United States:

I herewith transmit to the Senate of the United States a report from the Secretary of State, accompanied by a copy of the correspondence requested by their resolution of the 5th ultimo.

M. VAN BUREN.

DEPARTMENT OF STATE,
Washington, March 7, 1838.

The PRESIDENT OF THE UNITED STATES:

The Secretary of State, to whom has been referred the resolution of the Senate of the 5th of February, requesting the President of the United States to communicate to that body, in such manner as he shall deem proper, all the correspondence recently received and had between this and the Governments of Great Britain and the State of Maine on the subject of the northeastern boundary, has the honor to report to the President the accompanying copy of letters, which comprise all the correspondence in the Department asked for by the resolution.

Respectfully submitted.

JOHN FORSYTH.

* Relating to high duties and restrictions on tobacco imported into foreign countries from the United States, etc.

Mr. Fox to Mr. Forsyth.

Hon. JOHN FORSYTH, etc.:

WASHINGTON, *January 10, 1838.*

The undersigned, Her Britannic Majesty's envoy extraordinary and minister plenipotentiary, is directed by his Government to make the following observations to Mr. Forsyth, Secretary of State of the United States, with reference to certain points connected with the question of the northeastern boundary, which question forms the subject of the accompanying note, which the undersigned has the honor this day to address to Mr. Forsyth:

The British Government, with a view to prevail upon that of the United States to come to an understanding with Great Britain upon the river question, had stated that the King of the Netherlands in his award had decided that question according to the British interpretation of it and had expressed his opinion that the rivers which fall into the Bay of Fundy are not to be considered as Atlantic rivers for the purposes of the treaty.

Mr. Forsyth, however, in his note to Sir Charles Vaughan of the 28th of April, 1835, controverts this assertion and maintains that the King of the Netherlands did not in his award express such an opinion, and Mr. Forsyth quotes a passage from the award in support of this proposition.

But it appears to Her Majesty's Government that Mr. Forsyth has not correctly perceived the] meaning of the passage which he quotes, for in the passage in question Mr. Forsyth apprehends that the word *"alone"* is governed by the verb *"include,"* whereas an attentive examination of the context will show that the word *"alone"* is governed by the verb *"divide,"* and that the real meaning of the passage is this: That the rivers flowing north and south from the highlands claimed by the United States may be arranged in two genera, the first genus comprehending the rivers which fall into the St. Lawrence, the second genus comprehending those whose waters in some manner or other find their way into the Atlantic; but that even if, according to this general classification and in contradistinction from rivers flowing into the St. Lawrence, the rivers which fall into the bays of Chaleurs and Fundy might be comprised in the same genus with the rivers which fall directly into the Atlantic, still the St. John and the Restigouche form a distinct species by themselves and do not belong to the species of rivers which fall *directly* into the Atlantic, for the St. John and Restigouche are not divided in company with any such last-mentioned rivers. And the award goes on to say that, moreover, if this distinction between the two species were confounded an erroneous interpretation would be applied to a treaty in which every separate word must be supposed to have a meaning, and a generic distinction would be given to cases which are purely specific.

The above appears to be the true meaning of the passage quoted by Mr. Forsyth; but if that passage had not been in itself sufficiently explicit, which Her Majesty's Government think it is, the passage which immediately follows it would remove all doubt as to what the opinion of the King of the Netherlands was upon the river question, for that passage, setting forth reasons against the line of boundary claimed by the United States, goes on to say that such line would not even separate the St. Lawrence rivers immediately from the St. John and Restigouche, and that thus the rivers which this line would separate from the St. Lawrence rivers would need, *in order to reach the Atlantic*, the aid of *two intermediaries—*first, the rivers St. John and Restigouche, and, *secondly, the bays of Chaleurs and Fundy.*

Now it is evident from this passage that the King of the Netherlands deemed the bays of Fundy and Chaleurs to be, for the purposes of the treaty, as distinct and separate from the Atlantic Ocean as are the rivers St. John and Restigouche, for he specifically mentions those rivers and those bays as the channels through which certain rivers would have to pass in their way from the northern range of dividing highlands down to the Atlantic Ocean; and it is clear that he considers that the waters of those highland rivers would not reach the Atlantic Ocean until after they had traveled through the whole extent either of the Restigouche and the Bay of Chaleurs or of the St. John and the Bay of Fundy, as the case might be; and for this reason, among others, the King of the Netherlands declared it to be his opinion that the line north of the St. John claimed by the United States is not the line intended by the treaty.

The undersigned avails himself of this occasion to renew to Mr. Forsyth the assurances of his high respect and consideration.

H. S. FOX.

Mr. Fox to Mr. Forsyth.

WASHINGTON, *January 10, 1838.*

Hon. JOHN FORSYTH, etc.:

The undersigned, Her Britannic Majesty's envoy extraordinary and minister plenipotentiary, has received the orders of his Government to make the following communication to the Secretary of State of the United States with reference to the question pending between the two Governments upon the subject of the northeastern boundary:

The undersigned is, in the first instance, directed to express to Mr. Forsyth the sincere regret of Her Majesty's Government that the long-continued endeavors of both parties to come to a settlement of this important matter have hitherto been unavailing. Her Majesty's Government feel an undiminished desire to cooperate with the Cabinet of Washington for the attainment of an object of so much mutual interest, and they learn with satisfaction that their sentiments upon this point are fully shared by the actual President of the United States.

The communications which during the last few years have taken place between the two Governments with reference to the present subject, if they have not led to the solution of the questions at issue, have at least narrowed the field of future discussion.

Both Governments have agreed to consider the award of the King of the Netherlands as binding upon neither party, and the two Governments, therefore, are as free in this respect as they were before the reference to that Sovereign was made. The British Government, despairing of the possibility of drawing a line that shall be in literal conformity with the words of the treaty of 1783, has suggested that a conventional boundary should be substituted for the line described by the treaty, and has proposed that in accordance with the principles of equity and in pursuance of the general practice of mankind in similar cases the object of difference should be equally divided between the two differing parties, each of whom is alike convinced of the justice of its own claim.

The United States Government has replied that to such an arrangement it has no power to agree; that until the line of the treaty shall have been otherwise determined the State of Maine will continue to assume that the line which it claims is the true line of 1783, and will assert that all the land up to that line is territory of Maine; that consequently such a division of the disputed territory as is proposed by Great Britain would be considered by Maine as tantamount to a cession of what that State regards as a part of its own territory, and that the Federal Government has no power to agree to such an arrangement without the consent of the State concerned.

Her Majesty's Government exceedingly regrets that such an obstacle should exist to prevent that settlement which under all the circumstances of the case appears to be the simplest, the readiest, the most satisfactory, and the most just. Nor can Her Majesty's Government admit that the objection of the State of Maine is well founded, for the principle on which that objection rests is as good for Great Britain as it is for Maine. If Maine thinks itself entitled to contend that until the true line described in the treaty is determined the boundary claimed by Maine must be regarded as the right one, Great Britain is surely still more entitled to insist upon a similar pretension, and to assert that until the line of the treaty shall be established to the satisfaction of both parties the whole of the disputed territory ought to be considered as belonging to the British Crown, because Great Britain is the original possessor, and all the territory which has not been proved to have been by treaty ceded by her must be looked upon as belonging to her still. But the very existence of such conflicting pretensions seems to point out the expediency of a compromise, and what compromise can be more fair than that which would give to each party one-half of the subject-matter of dispute?

A conventional line different from that described in the treaty was agreed to, as stated by Mr. Forsyth in his note of the 28th of April, 1835, with respect to the boundary westward from the Lake of the Woods. Why should such a line not be agreed to likewise for the boundary eastward from the river Connecticut?

Her Majesty's Government can not refrain from again pressing this proposition upon the serious consideration of the Government of the United States as the arrangement which would be best calculated to effect a prompt and satisfactory settlement between the two powers.

The Government of the United States, indeed, while it expressed a doubt of its being able to obtain the assent of Maine to the above-mentioned proposal, did, nevertheless, express its readiness to apply to the State of Maine for the assent of that State to the adoption of another conventional line, which should make the river St. John from its source to its mouth the boundary between the two countries. But it is difficult to understand upon what grounds any expectation could have been formed that such a proposal could be entertained by the British Government, for such an arrangement would give to the United States even greater advantages than they would obtain by an unconditional acquiescence in their claim to the whole of the disputed territory, because such an arrangement would, in the first place, give to Maine all that part of the disputed territory which lies to the south of the St. John, and would, in the next place, in exchange for the remaining part of the disputed territory which lies to the north of the St. John, add to the State of Maine a large district of New Brunswick lying between the United States boundary and the southern part of the course of the St. John—a district smaller, indeed, in extent, but much more considerable in value, than the portion of the disputed territory which lies to the north of the St. John.

But with respect to a conventional line generally, the Government of Washington has stated that it has not at present the powers constitutionally requisite for treating for such a line and has no hopes of obtaining such powers until the impossibility of establishing the line described by the treaty shall have been completely demonstrated by the failure of another attempt to trace that line by a local survey.

Under these circumstances it appears that a conventional line can not at present be agreed upon, and that such a mode of settlement is in the existing state of the negotiation impossible.

Thus, then, the award of the King of the Netherlands has been abandoned by both parties in consequence of its rejection by the American Senate, and a negotiation between the two Governments for a conventional line suited to the interests and convenience of the two parties has for the present been rendered impossible by difficulties arising on the part of the United States; and both Governments are alike averse to a new arbitration. In this state of things the Government of the United States has proposed to the British cabinet that another attempt should be made to trace out a boundary according to the letter of the treaty, and that a commission of exploration and survey should be appointed for that purpose.

Her Majesty's Government have little expectation that such a commission could lead to any useful result, and on that account would be disposed to object to the measure; but at the same time they are so unwilling to reject the only plan now left which seems to afford a chance of making any further advance in this long-pending matter that they will not withhold their consent to such a commission if the principle upon which it is to be formed and the manner in which it is to proceed can be satisfactorily settled.

The United States Government have proposed two modes in which such a commission might be constituted: First, that it might consist of commissioners named in equal numbers by each of the two Governments, with an umpire to be selected by some friendly European power; secondly, that it might be entirely composed of scientific Europeans, to be selected by a friendly sovereign, and might be accompanied in its operations by agents of the two different parties, in order that such agents might give to the commissioners assistance and information.

If such a commission were to be appointed, Her Majesty's Government think that the first of these two modes of constructing it would be the best, and that it should consist of members chosen in equal numbers by each of the two Governments. It might, however, be better that the umpire should be selected by the members of the commission themselves rather than that the two Governments should apply to a third power to make such a choice.

The object of this commission, as understood by Her Majesty's Government, would be to explore the disputed territory in order to find within its limits dividing highlands which may answer the description of the treaty, the search being first to be made in the due north line from the monument at the head of the St. Croix, and if no such highlands should be found in that meridian the search to be then continued to the westward thereof; and Her Majesty's Government have stated their opinion that in order to avoid all fruitless disputes as to the character of such highlands the commissioners should be instructed to look for highlands which both parties might acknowledge as fulfilling the conditions of the treaty.

The United States Secretary of State, in his note of the 5th of March, 1836, expresses a wish to know how the report of the commissioners would, according to the views of Her Majesty's Government, be likely when rendered to lead to an ultimate settlement of the question of boundary between the two Governments.

In reply to this inquiry Her Majesty's Government would beg to observe that the proposal to appoint a commission originated not with them, but with the Government of the United States, and that it is therefore rather for the Government of the United States than for that of Great Britain to answer this question.

Her Majesty's Government have themselves already stated that they have little expectation that such a commission could lead to any useful result, and that they would on that account be disposed to object to it; and if Her Majesty's Government were now to agree to appoint such a commission it would be only in compliance with the desire so strongly expressed by the Government of the United States, and in spite of doubts (which Her Majesty's Government still continue to entertain) of the efficacy of the measure.

But with respect to the way in which the report of the commission might be likely to lead to an ultimate settlement of the question, Her Majesty's Government, in the first place, conceive that it was meant by the Government of the United States that if the commission should discover highlands answering to the description of the treaty a connecting line drawn from these highlands to the head of the St. Croix should be deemed to be a portion of the boundary line between the two countries. But Her Majesty's Government would further beg to refer the United States Secretary of State to the notes of Mr. McLane of the 5th of June, 1833, and of the 11th and 28th of March, 1834, on this subject, in which it will be seen that the Government of the United States appears to have contemplated as one of the possible results of the proposed commission of exploration that such additional information might possibly be obtained respecting the features of the country in the district to which the treaty relates as might remove all doubt as to the impracticability of laying down a boundary in accordance with the letter of the treaty.

And if the investigations of the proposed commission should show that there is no reasonable prospect of finding a line strictly conformable with the description contained in the treaty of 1783, the constitutional difficulties which now prevent the United States from agreeing to a conventional line may possibly be removed, and the way may thus be prepared for the satisfactory settlement of the difference by an equitable division of the disputed territory.

But if the two Governments should agree to the appointment of such a commission it would be necessary that their agreement should be first recorded in a convention, and it would obviously be indispensable that the State of Maine should be an assenting party to the arrangement.

The undersigned, in making the above communication by order of Her Majesty's Government to the United States Secretary of State, Mr. Forsyth, has the honor to renew to him the assurance of his high respect and consideration.

H. S. FOX.

Mr. Forsyth to Mr. Fox.

DEPARTMENT OF STATE,
Washington, February 6, 1838.

HENRY S. FOX, Esq., etc.:

The undersigned, Secretary of State of the United States, has the honor to acknowledge the receipt of the note of Mr. Fox, envoy extraordinary and minister plenipotentiary of Her Britannic Majesty, of the 10th ultimo, in which he presents, by direction of his Government, certain observations in respect to the construction to be given to that part of the award of the arbiter on the question of the northeastern boundary which relates to the character in which the rivers St. John and Restigouche are to be regarded in reference to that question. Sir Charles Vaughan, in his note to Mr. McLane of February 10, 1834, alleged that although the arbiter had not decided the first of the three main questions proposed to him, yet that he had determined certain subordinate points connected with that question upon which the parties had entertained different views, and among others that the rivers St. John and Restigouche could not be considered, according to the meaning of the treaty, as " rivers flowing into the Atlantic." The undersigned, in his note to Sir Charles R. Vaughan of the 28th of April, 1835, questioned the correctness of the interpretation which had been given by Sir Charles to the award of the arbiter in this particular, and after quoting that part of the award to which Sir Charles was supposed to refer as containing the determination by the arbiter of the point just mentioned observed that it could not but appear from further reflection to Sir Charles that the declaration that the rivers St. John and Restigouche could not be *alone* taken into view without hazard in determining the disputed boundary was not the expression of an opinion that they should be altogether excluded in determining that question; or, in other words, that they could not be looked upon as rivers emptying into the Atlantic. The remarks presented by Mr. Fox in the note to which this is a reply are designed to shew a misconception on the part of the undersigned of the true meaning of the passage cited by him from the award and to support the construction which was given to it by Sir Charles Vaughan. Whether the apprehension entertained by the one party or the other of the opinion of the arbiter upon this minor point be correct is regarded by the undersigned as a matter of no consequence in the settlement of the main question. The Government of the United States, never having acquiesced in the decision of the arbiter that " the nature of the difference and the vague and not sufficiently determinate stipulations of the treaty of 1783 do not permit the adjudication of either of the two lines respectively claimed by the interested parties to one of the said parties without wounding the principles of law and equity with regard to the other," can not consent to be governed in the prosecution of the existing negotiation by the opinion of the arbiter upon any of the preliminary points about which there was a previous difference between the parties, and the adverse decision of which has led to so unsatisfactory and, in the view of this Government, so errone- ous a conclusion. This determination on the part of the United States not to adopt the premises of the arbiter while rejecting his conclusion has been heretofore made known to Her Majesty's Government, and while it remains must necessarily render the discussion of the question what those premises were unavailing, if not irrelevant. The few observations which the undersigned was led to make in the course of his note to Sir Charles Vaughan upon one of the points alleged to have been thus deter- mined were prompted only by a respect for the arbiter and a consequent anxiety to remove a misinterpretation of his meaning, which alone, it was believed, could induce the supposition that the arbiter, in searching for the rivers referred to in the treaty as designating the boundary, could have come to the opinion that the two great rivers whose waters pervaded the whole district in which the search was made and consti- tuted the most striking objects of the country had been entirely unnoticed by the negotiators of the treaty and were to be passed over unheeded in determining the line, while others were to be sought for which he himself asserts could not be found. That the imputation of such an opinion to the respected arbiter could only be the result of misinterpretation seemed the more evident, as he had himself declared that "it could not be sufficiently explained how, if the high contracting parties intended in 1783 to establish the boundary at the south of the river St. John, that river, to which the territory in dispute was in a great measure indebted for its distinctive character, had been neutralized and set aside." It is under the influence of the same motives that the undersigned now proceeds to make a brief comment upon the obser- vations contained in Mr. Fox's note of the 10th ultimo, and thus to close a discussion which it can answer no purpose to prolong.

The passage from the award of the arbiter quoted by the undersigned in his note of the 28th April, 1835, to Sir Charles Vaughan, and the true meaning of which Mr. Fox supposes to have been misconceived, is the following: "If in contradistinction to the rivers that empty themselves into the river St. Lawrence it had been proper, agreeably to the language ordinarily used in geography, to comprehend the rivers falling into the bays Fundy and Des Chaleurs with those emptying themselves directly into the Atlantic Ocean in the generical denomination of rivers falling into the Atlantic Ocean it would be hazardous to include into the species belonging to that class the rivers St. John and Restigouche, which the line claimed at the north of the river St. John divides *immediately* from rivers emptying themselves into the river St. Lawrence, not with other rivers falling into the Atlantic Ocean, but *alone*, and thus to apply in interpreting the delimitation established by a treaty, where each word must have a meaning, to two exclusively special cases, and where no men- tion is made of the genus (*genre*), a generical expression which would ascribe to them a broader meaning," etc.

It was observed by the undersigned that this passage did not appear to contain an expression of opinion by the arbiter that the rivers St. John and Restigouche should be altogether excluded in determining the question of disputed boundary, or, in other words, that they could not be looked upon as "rivers emptying into the Atlantic." Mr. Fox alleges this to be a misconception of the meaning of the arbiter, and sup- poses it to have arisen from an erroneous apprehension by the undersigned that the word "*alone*" is governed by the verb "*include*," whereas he thinks that an atten- tive examination of the context will shew that the word "*alone*" is governed by the verb "*divide*," and that the real meaning of the passage is this: "That the rivers flowing north and south from the highlands claimed by the United States may be arranged in two genera, the first genus comprehending the rivers which fall into the St. Lawrence, the second genus comprehending those whose waters in some manner or other find their way into the Atlantic; but that even if, according to the general classification and in contradistinction from rivers flowing into the St. Lawrence, the rivers which fall into the bays of Chaleurs and Fundy might be comprised in the same genus with the rivers which fall directly into the Atlantic, still the St. John and the Restigouche form a distinct species by themselves and do not belong to the species of rivers which fall *directly* into the Atlantic, for the St. John and Restigouche are not divided in company with any *such last-mentioned rivers.*" The undersigned considers it unnecessary to enter into the question whether according to the context the circumstance expressed by the adverb "alone" has reference to the verb "divide" or to the verb "include," because even allowing it to refer to the former it does not appear to the undersigned that his interpretation of the passage is thereby impaired or that of Mr. Fox sustained. The undersigned conceives that the arbiter contemplated two different *species* of rivers as admissible into the *genus* of those which "fall into the Atlantic," to wit, those which fall *directly* into the Atlantic and those which fall into it *indirectly;* that the arbiter was further of opinion, though at variance with the idea entertained in that respect by the United States, that the rivers St. John and Restigouche, emptying their waters into the bays of Fundy and Des Chaleurs, did not belong to the species of rivers falling *directly* into the Atlantic; that if they were considered *alone,* therefore, the appellation of "rivers falling into the Atlantic Ocean" could not be regarded as applicable to them, because, to use the language of the award, it would be "applying to two exclusively special cases, where no mention was made of the genus, a generical expression which would ascribe to them a broader meaning;" but it is not conceived that the arbiter intended to express an opinion that these rivers *might not be included with others* in forming the *genus* of rivers described by the treaty as those which "fall into the Atlantic," and that upon this ground they should be wholly excluded in determining the question of the disputed boundary. While, therefore, the undersigned agrees with Mr. Fox that the arbiter did not consider these rivers as falling directly into the Atlantic Ocean, the undersigned can not concur in Mr. Fox's construction when he supposes the arbiter to give as a reason for this that they are not divided in company with any *such last-mentioned rivers*—that is, with rivers falling *directly* into the Atlantic. Conceding as a point which it is deemed unnecessary for the present purpose to discuss that the grammatical construction of the sentence contended for by Mr. Fox is the correct one, the arbiter is understood to say only that those rivers are not divided *immediately* with others falling into the Atlantic, either directly or indirectly, but he does not allege this to be a sufficient reason for excluding them when connected with other rivers divided mediately from those emptying into the St. Lawrence from the genus of rivers "falling into the Atlantic." On the contrary, it is admitted in the award that the line claimed to the north of the St. John divides the St. John and Restigouche in company with the Schoodic Lakes, the Penobscot, and the Kennebec, which are stated as emptying themselves *directly* into the Atlantic; and it is strongly implied in the language used by the arbiter that the first-named rivers might, in his opinion, be classed for the purposes of the treaty with those last named, though not in the same *species,* yet in the same *genus* of "Atlantic rivers."

The reason why the St. John and Restigouche were not permitted to determine the question of boundary in favor of the United States is understood to have been, not that they were to be wholly excluded as rivers not falling into the Atlantic Ocean, as Mr. Fox appears to suppose, but because in order to include them in that genus of rivers they must be considered in connection with other rivers which were not divided *immediately,* like themselves, from the rivers falling into the St. Lawrence, but *mediately* only; which would introduce the principle that the treaty of 1783 meant highlands that divide as well mediately as immediately the rivers that empty themselves into the river St. Lawrence from those which fall into the Atlantic Ocean— a principle which the arbiter did not reject as unfounded or erroneous, but which, considered in connection with the other points which he had decided, he regarded as *equally realized by both lines,* and therefore as constituting an equal weight in either scale, and consequently affording him no assistance in determining the dispute between the respective parties.

The arbiter appears to the undersigned to have viewed the rivers St. John and Restigouche as possessing both a specific and a generic character; that considered *alone* they were *specific,* and the designation in the treaty of "rivers falling into the Atlantic" was inapplicable to them; that considered *in connection with other rivers* they were *generic* and were embraced in the terms of the treaty, but that as their connection with other rivers would bring them within a principle which, according to the views taken by him of other parts of the question, was equally realized by both lines, it would be hazardous to allow them any weight in deciding the disputed boundary. It has always been contended by this Government that the rivers St. John and Restigouche were to be considered in connection with the Penobscot and Kennebec in determining the highlands called for by the treaty, and the arbiter is not understood to deny to them, when thus connected, the character of "rivers falling into the Atlantic Ocean."

This construction of the arbiter's meaning, derived from the general tenor of the context, it will be perceived, is not invalidated by the next succeeding paragraph cited by Mr. Fox, in which the bays of Fundy and Des Chaleurs are spoken of as *intermediaries* whereby the rivers flowing into the St. John and Restigouche reach the Atlantic Ocean, inasmuch as such construction admits the opinion of the arbiter to have been that the St. John and Restigouche do not fall *directly* into the Atlantic, and that they thus constitute a *species* by themselves, while it denies that they are therefore excluded by the arbiter from the genus of "rivers falling into the Atlantic."

The undersigned avails himself of this opportunity to renew to Mr. Fox the assurance of his distinguished consideration.

JOHN FORSYTH.

Mr. Forsyth to Mr. Fox.

DEPARTMENT OF STATE,
Washington, February 7, 1838.

HENRY S. FOX, Esq., etc.:

The undersigned, Secretary of State of the United States, has the honor to acknowledge the receipt of the note addressed to him on the 10th ultimo by Mr. Fox, Her Britannic Majesty's envoy extraordinary and minister plenipotentiary at Washington, with regard to the question pending between the two Governments upon the subject of the northeastern boundary, and to inform him that his communication has been submitted to the President. It has received from him the attentive examination due to a paper expected to embody the views of Her Britannic Majesty's Government in reference to interests of primary importance to both countries. But whilst the President sees with satisfaction the expression it contains of a continued desire on the part of Her Majesty's Government to cooperate with this in its earnest endeavors to arrange the matter of dispute between them, he perceives with feelings of deep disappointment that the answer now presented to the propositions made by this Government with the view of effecting that object, after having been so long delayed, notwithstanding the repeated intimations that it was looked for here with much anxiety, is so indefinite in its terms as to render it impracticable to ascertain without further discussion what are the real wishes and intentions of Her Majesty's Government respecting the proposed appointment of a commission of exploration and survey to trace out a boundary according to the letter of the treaty of 1783. The President, however, for the purpose of placing in the possession of the State of Maine the views of Her Majesty's Government as exhibited in Mr. Fox's note, and of ascertaining the sense of the State authorities upon the expediency of meeting those views so far as they are developed therein, has directed the undersigned to transmit a copy of it to Governor Kent for their consideration. This will be accordingly done without unnecessary delay, and the result when obtained may form the occasion of a further communication to Her Majesty's minister.

In the meantime the undersigned avails himself of the present occasion to offer a few remarks upon certain parts of Mr. Fox's note of the 10th ultimo. After adverting to the suggestion heretofore made by the British Government that a conventional line equally dividing the territory in dispute between the two parties should be substituted for the line described by the treaty, and regretting the constitutional incompetency of the Federal Government to agree to such an arrangement without the consent of the State of Maine, Mr. Fox refers to the conventional line adopted, although different from that designated by the treaty, with respect to the boundary westward from the Lake of the Woods, and asks, "Why should such a line not be agreed to likewise for the boundary eastward from the river Connecticut?" The reply to this question is obvious. The parallel of latitude adopted on the occasion referred to as a conventional substitute for the treaty line passed over territory within the exclusive jurisdiction of the General Government without trenching upon the rights or claims of any individual member of the Union, and the legitimate power of the Government, therefore, to agree to such line was perfect and unquestioned. Now in consenting to a conventional line for the boundary eastward from the river Connecticut the Government of the United States would transcend its constitutional powers, since such a measure could only be carried into effect by violating the jurisdiction of a sovereign State of the Union and by assuming to alienate, without the color of rightful authority to do so, a portion of the territory claimed by the State.

With regard to the suggestion made by the undersigned in his note of the 29th of February, 1836, of the readiness of the President to apply to the State of Maine for her assent to the adoption of a conventional line making the river St. John, from its source to its mouth, the boundary between the United States and the adjacent British Provinces, Mr. Fox thinks it difficult to understand upon what grounds an expectation could have been formed that such a proposal could be entertained by the British Government, since such an arrangement would give to the United States even greater advantages than would be obtained by an unconditional acquiescence in their claim to the whole territory in dispute. In making the suggestion referred to, the undersigned expressly stated to Mr. Bankhead that it was offered, as the proposition on the part of Great Britain that led to it was supposed to have been, without regard to the mere question of acres—the extent of territory lost or acquired by the respective parties. The suggestion was submitted in the hope that the preponderating importance of terminating at once and forever this controversy by establishing an unchangeable and definite and indisputable boundary would be seen and acknowledged by Her Majesty's Government, and have a correspondent weight in influencing its decision. That the advantages of substituting a river for a highland boundary could not fail to be recognized was apparent from the fact that Mr. Bankhead's note of 28th December, 1835, suggested the river St. John from the point in which it is intersected by a due north line drawn from the monument at the head of the St. Croix to the southernmost source of that river as a part of the general outline of a conventional boundary. No difficulty was anticipated on the part of Her Majesty's Government in understanding the grounds upon which such a proposal was expected to be entertained by it, since the precedent proposition of Mr. Bankhead, just adverted to, although professedly based on the principle of an equal division between the parties, could not be justified by it, as it would have given nearly two-thirds of the disputed territory to Her Majesty's Government. It was therefore fairly presumed that the river line presented, in the opinion of Her Majesty's Government, advantages sufficient to counterbalance any loss of territory by either party that would follow its adoption as a boundary. Another recommendation of the river line, it was supposed, would be found by Her Majesty's Government in the fact that whilst by its adoption the right of jurisdiction alone would have been yielded to the United States over that portion of New Brunswick south of the St. John, Great Britain would have acquired the right of soil as well as of jurisdiction of the whole portion of the disputed territory north of the river. It is to be lamented that the imposing considerations alluded to have failed in their desired effect—that the hopes of the President in regard to them have not been realized, and consequently that Her Britannic Majesty's Government is not prepared at present to enter into an arrangement of the existing difference between the two nations upon the basis proposed.

It would seem to the undersigned, from an expression used in Mr. Fox's late communication, that some misapprehension exists on his part either as to the object of this Government in asking for information relative to the manner in which the report of a commission of exploration and survey might tend to a practical result in the settlement of the boundary question or as to the distinctive difference between the American proposal for the appointment of such a commission and the same proposition when modified to meet the wishes of Her Majesty's Government. Of the two modes suggested, by direction of the President, for constituting such a commission, the first is that which is regarded by Her Majesty's Government with most favor, viz, the commissioners to be chosen in equal numbers by each of the two parties, with an umpire selected by some friendly European sovereign to decide on all points on which they might disagree, with instructions to explore the disputed territory in order to find within its limits dividing highlands answering to the description of the treaty of 1783, in a due north or northwesterly direction from the monument at the head of the St. Croix, and that a right line drawn between such highlands and said monument should form so far as it extends a part of the boundary between the two countries, etc. It is now intimated that Her Majesty's Government will not withhold its consent to such a commission "if the principle upon which it is to be formed and the manner in which it is to proceed can be satisfactorily settled." This condition is partially explained by the suggestion afterwards made that instead of leaving the umpire to be chosen by some friendly European power it might be better that he should be elected by the members of the commission themselves, and a modification is then proposed that "the commission shall be instructed to look for highlands which both parties might acknowledge as fulfilling the conditions of the treaty." The American proposition is intended—and if agreed to would doubtless be successful—to decide the question of boundary definitively by the adoption of the highlands reported by the commissioners of survey, and would thus secure the treaty line. The British modification looks to no such object. It merely contemplates a commission of boundary analogous to that appointed under the fifth article of the treaty of Ghent, and would in all probability prove equally unsatisfactory in practice. Whether highlands such as are described in the treaty do or do not exist, it can scarcely be hoped that those called for by the modified instructions could be found. The fact that this question is still pending, although more than half a century has elapsed since the conclusion of the treaty in which it originated, renders it in the highest degree improbable that the two Governments can unite in believing that either the one or the other of the ranges of highlands claimed by the respective parties fulfills the required conditions of that instrument. The opinions of the parties have been over and over again expressed on this point and are well known to differ widely. The commission can neither reconcile nor change these variant opinions resting on conviction, nor will it be authorized to decide the difference. Under these impressions of the inefficiency of such a commission was the inquiry made in the letter of the undersigned of 5th March, 1836, as to the manner in which the report of the commission, as proposed to be constituted and instructed by Her Majesty's Government, was expected to lead to an ultimate settlement of the question of boundary. The results which the American proposition promised to secure were fully and frankly explained in previous notes from the Department of State, and had its advantages not been clearly understood this Government would not have devolved upon that of Her Majesty the task of illustrating them. Mr. Fox will therefore see that although the proposal to appoint a commission had its origin with this Government the modification of the American proposition was, as understood by the undersigned, so fundamentally important that it entirely changed its nature, and that the supposition, therefore, that it was rather for the Government of the United States than for that of Great Britain to answer the inquiry referred to is founded in misapprehension. Any decision made by a commission constituted in the manner proposed by the United States and instructed to seek for the highlands of the treaty of 1783 would be binding upon this Government and could without unnecessary delay be carried into effect; but if the substitute presented by Her Majesty's Government be insisted on and its principles be adopted, a resort will then be necessary to the State of Maine for her assent to all proceedings hereafter in relation to this matter, since if any arrangement can be made under it it can only be for a conventional line, to which she must of course be a party.

The undersigned, in conclusion, is instructed to inform Mr. Fox that if a negotiation be entertained at all upon the inconclusive and unsatisfactory basis afforded by the British counter proposition or substitute, which possesses hardly a feature in common with the American proposition, the President will not venture to invite it unless the authorities of the State of Maine, to whom, as before stated, it will be forthwith submitted, shall think it more likely to lead to a final adjustment of the question of boundary than the General Government deems it to be, though predisposed to see it in the most favorable light.

The undersigned avails himself of the occasion to renew to Mr. Fox the assurance of his distinguished consideration.

JOHN FORSYTH.

DEPARTMENT OF STATE,
Washington, March 1, 1838.

His Excellency EDWARD KENT,
    Governor of the State of Maine.

SIR: The discussions between the Federal Government and that of Great Britain in respect to the northeastern boundary of the United States have arrived at a stage in which the President thinks it due to the State of Maine and necessary to the intelligent action of the General Government to take the sense of that State in regard to the expediency of opening a direct negotiation for the establishment of a conventional line, and if it should deem an attempt to adjust the matter of controversy in that form advisable, then to ask its assent to the same. With this view and to place the government of Maine in full possession of the present state of the negotiation and of all the discussions that have been had upon the subject, the accompanying documents are communicated, which, taken in connection with those heretofore transmitted, will be found to contain that information.

The principles which have hitherto governed every successive Administration of the Federal Government in respect to its powers and duties in the matter are—

First. That it has power to settle the boundary line in question with Great Britain upon the principles and according to the stipulations of the treaty of 1783, either by direct negotiation or, in case of ascertained inability to do so, by arbitration, and that it is its duty to make all proper efforts to accomplish this object by one or the other of those means.

Second. That the General Government is not competent to negotiate, unless, perhaps, on grounds of imperious public necessity, a conventional line involving a cession of territory to which the State of Maine is entitled, or the exchange thereof for other territory not included within the limits of that State according to the true construction of the treaty, without the consent of the State.

In these views of his predecessors in office the President fully concurs, and it is his design to continue to act upon them.

The attention of the Federal Government has, of course, in the first instance been directed to efforts to settle the treaty line. A historical outline of the measures which have been successively taken by it to that end may be useful to the government of Maine in coming to a conclusion on the proposition now submitted. It will, however, be unnecessary here to do more than advert to the cardinal features of this protracted negotiation.

The treaty of peace between the United States of America and His Britannic Majesty, concluded at Paris in September, 1783, defines the boundaries of the said States, and the following words, taken from the second article of that instrument, are intended to designate a part of the boundary between those States and the British North American Provinces, viz: "From the northwest angle of Nova Scotia, viz, that angle which is formed by a line drawn due north from the source of the St. Croix River to the highlands; along the said highlands which divide those rivers that empty themselves into the river St. Lawrence from those which fall into the Atlantic Ocean to the northwesternmost head of Connecticut River;" * * * "east by a line to be drawn along the middle of the river St. Croix from its mouth in the Bay of Fundy to its source, and from its source directly north to the aforesaid highlands which divide the rivers that fall into the Atlantic Ocean from those which fall into the river St. Lawrence." An immediate execution of some of the provisions of this treaty was, however, delayed by circumstances on which it is now unnecessary to dwell, and in November, 1794, a second treaty was concluded between the two powers. In the meantime, doubts having arisen as to what river was truly intended under the name of the St. Croix mentioned in the treaty of peace and forming a part of the boundary therein described, this question was referred by virtue of the fifth article of the new treaty to the decision of a commission appointed in the manner therein prescribed, both parties agreeing to consider such decision final and conclusive. The commissioners appointed in pursuance of the fifth article of the treaty of 1794 decided by their declaration of October 25, 1798, that the northern branch (Cheputnaticook) of a river called Scoodiac was the true river St. Croix intended by the treaty of peace.

At the date of the treaty of Ghent, December 24, 1814, the whole of the boundary line from the source of the river St. Croix to the most northwesternmost point of the Lake of the Woods still remained unascertained, and it was therefore agreed to provide for a final adjustment thereof. For this purpose the appointment of commissioners was authorized by the fifth article of the treaty of Ghent, with power to ascertain and determine the northwest angle of Nova Scotia and the northwesternmost head of Connecticut River, in conformity with the provisions of the treaty of 1783, and to cause the boundary from the source of the river St. Croix to the river Iroquois or Cateraguy to be surveyed and marked according to the said provisions, etc. In the event of the commissioners differing, or both or either of them failing to act, the same article made provision for a reference to a friendly sovereign or state. Commissioners were appointed under this article in 1815–16, but although their sessions continued several years, they were unable to agree on any of the matters referred to them. Separate reports were accordingly made to both Governments of the two commissioners in 1822, stating the points on which they differed and the grounds upon which their respective opinions had been formed. The case having thus happened which made it necessary to refer the points of difference to a friendly sovereign or state, it was deemed expedient by the parties to regulate this reference by a formal arrangement. A convention for the purpose was therefore concluded on the 29th of September, 1827, and the two Governments subsequently agreed in the choice of His Majesty the King of the Netherlands as arbiter, who consented to act as such. The submission of the points of difference, three in number, was accordingly made to that Sovereign, and his award, or rather written opinion on the questions submitted to him, was rendered on the 10th of January, 1831. On the 7th of December following the President communicated the award of the arbiter to the Senate of the United States for the advice and consent of that body as to its execution, and at the same time intimated the willingness of the British Government to abide by it. The result was a determination on the part of the Senate not to consider the decision of His Netherland Majesty obligatory and a refusal to advise and consent to its execution. They, however, passed a resolution in June, 1832, advising the President to open a new negotiation with His Britannic Majesty's Government for the ascertainment of the boundary between the possessions of the two powers on the northeastern frontier of the United States according to the definitive treaty of peace. Of the negotiation subsequent to this event it is deemed proper to take a more particular notice.

In July the result of the action of the Senate in relation to the award was communicated to Mr. Bankhead, the British chargé d'affaires, and he was informed that the resolution had been adopted in the conviction that the sovereign arbiter, instead of deciding the questions submitted to him, had recommended a specified compromise of them. The Secretary of State at the same time expressed the desire of the President to enter into further negotiation in pursuance of the resolution of the Senate, and proposed that the discussion should be carried on at Washington. He also said that if the plenipotentiaries of the two parties should fail in this new attempt to agree upon the line intended by the treaty of 1783 there would probably be less difficulty than before in fixing a convenient boundary, as measures were in progress to obtain from the State of Maine more extensive powers than were before possessed, with a view of overcoming the constitutional obstacles which had opposed themselves to such an arrangement; and he further intimated that the new negotiation would naturally embrace the important question of the navigation of the river St. John.

In April, 1833, Sir Charles R. Vaughan, the British minister, addressed a note to the Department of State, in which, hopeless of finding out by a new negotiation an assumed line of boundary which so many attempts had been fruitlessly made to discover, he wished to ascertain, first, the principle of the plan of boundary which the American Government appeared to contemplate as likely to be more convenient to both parties than those hitherto discussed, and, secondly, whether any, and what, arrangement for avoiding the constitutional difficulty alluded to had yet been concluded with the State of Maine. Satisfactory answers on these points, he said, would enable the British Government to decide whether it would entertain the proposition, but His Majesty's Government could not consent to embarrass the negotiation respecting the boundary by mixing up with it a discussion regarding the navigation of the St. John as an integral part of the same question or as necessarily connected with it.

In reply to this note, Mr. Livingston, under date of the 30th of April, stated that the arrangement spoken of in his previous communication, by which the Government of the United States expected to be enabled to treat for a more convenient boundary, had not been effected, and that as the suggestion in regard to the navigation of the St. John was introduced merely to form a part of the system of compensations in negotiating for such a boundary if that of the treaty should be abandoned, it would not be insisted on.

The proposition of the President for the appointment of a joint commission, with an umpire, to decide upon all points on which the two Governments disagree was then presented. It was accompanied by a suggestion that the controversy might be terminated by the application to it of the rule for surveying and laying down the boundaries of tracts and of countries designated by natural objects, the precise situation of which is not known, viz, that the natural objects called for as terminating points should first be found, and that the lines should then be drawn to them from the given points with the least possible departure from the course prescribed in the instrument describing the boundary. Two modes were suggested in which such commission might be constituted: First, that it should consist of commissioners to be chosen in equal numbers by the two parties, with an umpire selected by some friendly sovereign from among the most skillful men in Europe; or, secondly, that it should be entirely composed of such men so selected, to be attended in the survey and view of the country by agents appointed by the parties. This commission, it was afterwards proposed, should be restricted to the simple question of determining the point designated by the treaty as the highlands which divide the waters that fall into the Atlantic from those which flow into the St. Lawrence; that these highlands should be sought for in a north or northwest direction from the source of the St. Croix, and that a straight line to be drawn from the monument at the head of that river to those highlands should be considered, so far as it extends, as a part of the boundary in question. The commissioners were then to designate the course of the line along the highlands and to fix on the northwesternmost head of the Connecticut River.

In a note of 31st May the British minister suggested that this perplexed and hitherto interminable question could only be set at rest by an abandonment of the defective description of boundary contained in the treaty, by the two Governments mutually agreeing upon a conventional line more convenient to both parties than those insisted upon by the commissioners under the fifth article of the treaty of Ghent, or that suggested by the King of the Netherlands.

Mr. McLane remarked in reply (June 5) that the embarrassments in tracing the treaty boundary had arisen more from the principles assumed and from the manner of seeking for it than from any real defect in the description when properly understood; that in the present state of the business the suggestion of Sir Charles R. Vaughan would add to the existing difficulties growing out of a want of power in the General Government under the Constitution of the United States to dispose of territory belonging to either of the States of the Union without the consent of the State; that as a conventional line to the south of and confessedly variant from that of the treaty would deprive the State of Maine of a portion of the territory she claims, it was not probable that her consent to it would be given while there remained a reasonable prospect of discovering the line of the treaty of 1783, and that the President would not be authorized, after the recent proceedings in the Senate, to venture now to agree upon a conventional line without such consent, whilst the proposition submitted in April afforded not only a fair prospect, but in his opinion the certain means, of ascertaining the boundary called for by the treaty of 1783 and of finally terminating all the perplexities which have encompassed that subject.

In February, 1834, Sir Charles R. Vaughan, after submitting certain observations intended to controvert the positions assumed by the United States on the subject of the constitutional difficulty by which the American Government was prevented from acquiescing in the arrangement recommended by the King of the Netherlands for the settlement of the boundary in the neighborhood of the St. John, asserted that the two Governments bound themselves by the convention of September, 1827, to submit to an arbiter certain points of difference relative to the boundary between the American and British dominions; that the arbiter was called on to determine certain questions, and that if he has determined the greater part of the points submitted to him his decision on them ought not to be set aside merely because he declares that one remaining point can not be decided in conformity with the words of the treaty of 1783, and therefore recommends to the parties a compromise on that particular point; that the main points referred to the arbiter were three in number; that upon the second and third of these he made a plain and positive decision; that upon the remaining point he has declared that it is impossible to find a spot or to trace a line which shall fulfill all the conditions required by the words of the treaty for the northwest angle of Nova Scotia and for the highlands along which the boundary from that angle is to be drawn; yet that in the course of his reasoning upon this point he has decided several questions connected with it upon which the two parties had entertained different views, viz:

"First. The arbiter expresses his opinion that the term 'highlands' may properly be applied not only to a hilly and elevated country, but to a tract of land which, without being hilly, divides waters flowing in different directions, and consequently, according to this opinion, the highlands to be sought for are not necessarily a range of mountains, but rather the summit level of the country.

"Second. The arbiter expresses his opinion that an inquiry as to what were the ancient boundaries of the North American Provinces can be of no use for the present purpose, because those boundaries were not maintained by the treaty of 1783 and had in truth never been distinctly ascertained and laid down.

"Third. The arbiter declares that the northwest angle of Nova Scotia mentioned in the treaty of 1783 is not a point which was then known and ascertained; that it is not an angle which is created by the intersection of any lines of boundary at that time acknowledged as existing, but that it is an angle still to be found and to be created by the intersection of new lines, which are hereafter to be drawn in pursuance of the stipulations of the treaty; and further, that the nature of the country eastward of the said angle affords no argument for laying that angle down in one place rather than in another.

"Fourth. He states that no just argument can be deduced for the settlement of this question from the exercise of the rights of sovereignty over the fief of Madawaska and over the Madawaska settlement.

"Fifth. He declares that the highlands contemplated in the treaty should divide immediately, and not mediately, rivers flowing into the St. Lawrence and rivers flowing into the Atlantic, and that the word 'divide' requires contiguity of the things to be divided.

"Sixth. He declares that rivers falling into the Bay of Chaleurs and the Bay of Fundy can not be considered according to the meaning of the treaty as rivers flowing into the Atlantic, and specifically that the rivers St. John and Restigouche can not be looked upon as answerable to the latter description.

"Seventh. He declares that neither the line of boundary claimed by Great Britain nor that claimed by the United States can be adjudged as the true line without departing from the principles of equity and justice as between the two parties."

It was the opinion of His Majesty's Government, Sir Charles alleged, that the decisions of the arbiter upon the second and third points referred to him, as well as upon the subordinate questions, ought to be acquiesced in by the two Governments, and that in any future attempt to establish a boundary, whether in strict conformity with the words of the treaty of 1783 or by agreeing to the mode of settlement recommended by the arbiter, it would be necessary to adopt these seven decisions as a groundwork for further proceedings; that the British Government, therefore, previously to any further negotiation, claimed from the Government of the United States an acquiescence in the decisions pronounced by the arbiter upon all those points which he had decided, and as a preliminary to any attempt to settle the remaining point by negotiation to be satisfied that the Federal Government was possessed of the necessary powers to carry into effect any arrangement upon which the two parties might agree.

With respect to the proposition made by the American Government, Sir Charles thought that the difficulty which was found insurmountable as against the line recommended by the King of the Netherlands, viz, the want of authority to agree to any line which might imply a cession of any part of the territory to which the treaty as hitherto interpreted by the United States might appear to entitle one of the component States of the Union, would be equally fatal to that suggested by Mr. Livingston, since a line drawn from the head of the St. Croix to highlands found to the westward of the meridian of that spot would not be the boundary of the treaty and might be more justly objected to by Maine and with more appearance of reason than that proposed by the arbiter.

The reply of Mr. McLane to the preceding note is dated on the 11th of March. He expressed his regret that His Britannic Majesty's Government should still consider any part of the opinion of the arbiter obligatory on either party. Those opinions, the Secretary stated, could not have been carried into effect by the President without the concurrence of the Senate, who, regarding them not only as not determining the principal object of the reference, but as in fact deciding that object to be impracticable, and therefore recommending to the two parties a boundary not even contemplated either by the treaty or by the reference nor within the power of the General Government to take, declined to give their advice and consent to the execution of the measures recommended by the arbiter, but did advise the Executive to open a new negotiation for the ascertainment of the boundary in pursuance of the treaty of 1783, and the proposition of Mr. Livingston, submitted in his letter of 30th of April, 1833, accordingly proceeded upon that basis. Mr. McLane denied that a decision, much less the expression of an opinion, by the arbiter upon some of the disputed points, but of a character not to settle the real controversy, was binding upon either party, and he alleged that the most material point in the line of the true boundary, both as it respects the difficulty of the subject and the extent of territory and dominions of the respective Governments, the arbiter not only failed to decide, but acknowledged his inability to decide, thereby imposing upon both Governments the unavoidable necessity of resorting to further negotiation to ascertain the treaty boundary and absolving each party from any obligation to adopt his recommendations. The Secretary also declined to admit that of the three main points referred to the arbiter as necessary to ascertain the boundary of the treaty he had decided two. On the first point, Mr. McLane said, it was not contended a decision was made or that either the angle or the highlands called for by the treaty was found, and on the third point an opinion merely was expressed that it would be suitable to proceed to fresh operations to measure the observed latitude, etc.

The Secretary admitted that if the American proposition should be acceded to by His Majesty's Government and the commission hereafter to be appointed should result in ascertaining the true situation of the boundary called for by the treaty of 1783, that it would be afterwards necessary, in order to ascertain the true line, to settle the other two points according to which it should be traced. He therefore offered, if the American proposition should be acceded to, notwithstanding the obligatory effect of the decision of the arbiter on the point is denied, "to take the stream situated farthest to the northwest among those which fall into the northernmost of the three lakes, the last of which bears the name of Connecticut Lake, as the northwesternmost head of the Connecticut River according to the treaty of 1783;" and as it respects the third point referred to the arbiter, the line of boundary on the forty-fifth degree of latitude, but upon which he failed to decide, the President would agree, if the proposition as to the first point was embraced, to adopt the old line surveyed and marked by Valentine and Collins in 1771 and 1772.

The Secretary then proceeded to state further and insuperable objections to an acquiescence by the United States in the opinions supposed to have been pronounced by the arbiter in the course of his reasoning upon the first point submitted to him. He remarked that the views expressed by the arbiter on these subordinate matters could not be regarded as decisions within the meaning of the reference, but rather as postulates or premises, by which he arrived at the opinion expressed in regard to the point in dispute. By an acquiescence in them, therefore, as required by Great Britain, the United States would reject as erroneous the conclusion of the arbiter, whilst they would adopt the premises and reasoning by which it was attained—that the seven postulates or premises presented as necessary to be considered by the United

States are but part of those on which the arbiter was equally explicit in the expression of his views, that on others his reasoning might be considered as more favorable to the pretensions of this Government, and that no reason was perceived why an acquiescence in his opinions upon them should not equally apply to all the premises assumed by him and be binding upon both parties. Mr. McLane was, however, persuaded that there was no obligation on either Government to acquiesce in the opinion of the arbiter on any of the matters involved in his premises; that such acquiescence would defeat the end of the present negotiation, and that as it appeared to be mutually conceded that the arbiter had not been able to decide upon the first and most material point so as to make a binding decision, there could certainly be no greater obligation to yield to his opinions on subordinate matters merely. The Secretary further observed that the most material point of the three submitted to the arbiter was that of the highlands, to which the President's proposition directly applies, and which are designated in the treaty of peace as the northwest angle of Nova Scotia, formed by a line drawn due north from the source of the St. Croix River to the highlands dividing the rivers, etc.; that the arbiter found it impossible to decide this point, and therefore recommended a new line, different from that called for by the treaty of 1783, and which could only be established by a conventional arrangement between the two Governments; that the Government of the United States could not adopt this recommendation nor agree upon a new and conventional line without the consent of the State of Maine; that the present negotiation proposed to ascertain the boundary according to the treaty of 1783, and for this purpose, however attained, the authority of the Government of the United States was complete; that the proposition offered by the Government of the United States promised, in the opinion of the President, the means of ascertaining the true line by discovering the highlands of the treaty, but the British Government asked the United States as a preliminary concession to acquiesce in the opinion of the arbiter upon certain subordinate facts—a concession which would in effect defeat the sole object, not only of the proposition, but of the negotiation, viz, the determination of the boundary according to the treaty of 1783 by confining the negotiation to a conventional line, to which this Government had not the authority to agree. Mr. McLane also said that if by a resort to the plain rule now recommended it should be found impracticable to trace the boundary according to the definitive treaty, it would then be time enough to enter upon a negotiation for a conventional substitute for it. He stated in answer to the suggestion of Sir Charles R. Vaughan that the objection urged against the line of the arbiter would equally lie against that suggested by Mr. Livingston; that the authority of the Government to ascertain the true line of the treaty was unquestionable, and that the American proposition, by confining the course to the natural object, would be a legitimate ascertainment of that line.

In a note dated 16th March Sir Charles R. Vaughan offered some observations upon the objections on the part of the United States to acquiesce in the points previously submitted to the American Government. He said that the adoption of the views of the British Government by the Government of the United States was meant to be the groundwork of future proceedings, whether those proceedings were to be directed to another attempt to trace the boundary as proposed by the latter or to a division of the territory depending upon the conventional line. He maintained that the arbiter had decided, as the British Government asserted, two out of the three main points submitted for his decision, viz, what ought to be considered as the northwesternmost head of the Connecticut (but which the Government of the United States is only willing to admit conditionally) and the point relative to tracing the boundary along the forty-fifth degree of latitude. This point, he observed, Mr. McLane wished to dispose of by adopting the old line of Collins and Valentine, which was suspected of great inaccuracy by both parties, and the only motive for retaining which was because some American citizens have made settlements upon territory that a new survey might throw into the possession of Great Britain. Sir Charles denied that the acquiescence of the United States in the seven subordinate points lately submitted by His Majesty's Government would confine the negotiation to a conventional line, to which the President had no authority to agree, and affirmed that not a step could be taken by the commissioners to be appointed according to Mr. Livingston's proposition, notwithstanding the unlimited discretion which it was proposed to give them, unless the two Governments agreed upon two of the seven subordinate points—"the character of the land they are to discover as dividing waters according to the treaty of 1783 and what are to be considered as Atlantic rivers." In answer to Mr. McLane's observation that on many points the reasoning of the arbiter had been more favorable to the United States than to Great Britain, and that therefore acquiescence should equally apply to all the premises assumed, Sir Charles expressed his confidence that if acquiescence in them could facilitate the object which now occupied both Governments they would meet with the most favored consideration. Sir Charles adverted to the obligations contracted under the seventh article of the convention, to the opinion of His Majesty's Government that they were binding and its willingness to abide by the award of the arbiter. He referred to the small majority by which he supposed the award to have been defeated in the Senate of the United States and a new negotiation advised to be opened, to the complicated nature of the plan proposed by the United States for another attempt to trace the boundary of the treaty, to the rejection of the points proposed by the British Government to render that plan more practicable, etc., and regretted sincerely that the award of the arbiter, which conferred upon the United States three-fifths of the disputed territory, together with Rouses Point—a much greater concession than is ever likely to be obtained by a protracted negotiation—was set aside. An alleged insuperable constitutional difficulty having occasioned the rejection of the award, Sir Charles wished to ascertain previously to any further proceedings how far the General Government had the power to carry into effect any arrangement resulting from a new negotiation, the answer of Mr. McLane upon this point having been confined to stating that should a new commission of survey, freed from the restriction of following the due north line of the treaty, find anywhere westward of that line highlands separating rivers according to the treaty of 1783, a line drawn from the monument at the source of the St. Croix would be such a fulfillment of the terms of that treaty that the President could agree to make it the boundary without reference to the State of Maine.

Mr. McLane, under date of 21st March, corrected the error into which Sir Charles had fallen in regard to the proceedings on the award in the Senate of the United States, and showed that that body not only failed, but by two repeated votes of 35 and 34 to 8 refused, to consent to the execution of the award, and by necessary implication denied its binding effect upon the United States, thus putting it out of the power of the President to carry it into effect and leaving the high parties to the submission situated precisely as they were prior to the selection of the arbiter.

The President had perceived, Mr. McLane said, in all the previous efforts to adjust the boundary in accordance with the terms of the treaty of 1783 that a natural and uniform rule in the settlement of disputed questions of location had been quite overlooked; that the chief, if not only, difficulty arose from a supposed necessity of finding highlands corresponding with the treaty description in a due north line from the monument, but it was plain that if such highlands could be anywhere discovered it would be a legal execution of the treaty to draw a line to them from the head of the St. Croix without regard to the precise course given in the treaty. It therefore became his duty to urge the adoption of this principle upon the Government of His Britannic Majesty as perhaps the best expedient which remained for ascertaining the boundary of the treaty of 1783. The Secretary could not perceive in the plan proposed anything so complicated as Sir Charles appeared to suppose. On the contrary, it was recommended to approbation and confidence by its entire simplicity. It chiefly required the discovery of the highlands called for by the treaty, and the mode of reaching them upon the principle suggested was so simple that no observations could make it plainer. The difficulty of discovering such highlands, Mr. McLane said, was presumed not to be insuperable. The arbiter himself was not understood to have found it impracticable to discover highlands answering the description of the highlands of the treaty, though unable to find them due north from the monument; and certainly it could not be more difficult for commissioners on the spot to arrive at a conclusion satisfactory to their own judgment as to the locality of the highlands.

Mr. McLane, in answer to Sir Charles's request for information on the subject, stated that the difficulty in the way of the adoption of the line recommended by the arbiter was the want of authority in the Government of the United States to agree to a line not only confessedly different from the line called for by the treaty, but which would deprive the State of Maine of a portion of territory to which she would be entitled according to the line of the definitive treaty; that by the President's proposition a commission would be raised, not to establish a new line differing from the treaty of 1783, but to determine what the true and original boundary was and in which of the two disagreeing parties the right to the disputed territory originally was; that for this purpose the authority of the original commissioners, if they could have agreed, was complete under the Ghent treaty, and that of the new commission proposed to be constituted could not be less.

Sir Charles R. Vaughan explained, under date of the 24th of March, with regard to his observation "that the mode in which it was proposed by the United States to settle the boundary was complicated; that he did not mean to apply it to the adoption of a rule in the settlement of disputed questions of location, but to the manner in which it is proposed by the United States that the new commission of survey shall be selected and constituted."

On the 8th of December, 1834, Sir Charles R. Vaughan transmitted a note to the Department of State, in which, after a passing expression of the regret of His Majesty's Government that the American Government still declined to come to a separate understanding on the several points of difference with respect to which the elements of decision were fully before both Governments, but without abandoning the argument contained in his note of 10th February last, he addressed himself exclusively to the American proposition for the appointment of a new commission to be empowered to seek westward of the meridian of the St. Croix highlands answering to the description of those mentioned in the treaty of 1783. He stated with regard to the rule of surveying on which the proposition was founded that however just and reasonable it might be, His Majesty's Government did not consider it so generally established and recognized as Mr. McLane assumed it to be; that, indeed, no similar case was recollected in which the principle asserted had been put in practice; yet, on the contrary, one was remembered not only analogous to that under discussion, but arising out of the same article of the same treaty, in which the supposed rule was invested by the agents of the American Government itself; that the treaty of 1783 declared that the line of boundary was to proceed from the Lake of the Woods "in a due west course to the Mississippi," but it being ascertained that such a line could never reach that river, since its sources lie south of the latitude of the Lake of the Woods, the commissioners, instead of adhering to the natural object—the source of the Mississippi—and drawing a new connecting line to it from the Lake of the Woods, adhered to the arbitrary line to be drawn due west from the lake and abandoned the Mississippi, the specific landmark mentioned in the treaty.

Sir Charles further stated that if the President was persuaded that he could carry out the principle of surveying he had proposed without the consent of Maine, and if no hope remained, as was alleged by Mr. McLane, of overcoming the constitutional difficulty in any other way until at least this proposition should have been tried and have failed, His Majesty's Government, foregoing their own doubts on the subject, were ready to acquiesce in the proceeding proposed by the President if that proceeding could be carried into effect in a manner not otherwise objectionable; that "His Majesty's Government would consider it desirable that the principles on which the new commissioners would have to conduct their survey should be settled beforehand by a special convention between the two Governments;" that there was, indeed, one preliminary question upon which it was obviously necessary the two Governments should agree before the commission could begin their survey with any chance of success, viz, What is the precise meaning to be attached to the words employed in the treaty to define the highlands which the commissioners are to seek for? that those highlands are to be distinguished from other highlands by the rivers flowing from them, and those distinguishing rivers to be known from others by the situation of their mouths; that with respect to the rivers flowing south into the Atlantic Ocean a difference of opinion existed between the two Governments; that whilst the American Government contended that rivers falling into the Bay of Fundy were, the British Government contended that they were not, for the purposes of the treaty, rivers falling into the Atlantic Ocean, and that the views and arguments of the British Government on this point had been confirmed by an impartial authority selected by the common consent of the two Governments, who was of opinion that the rivers St. John and Restigouche were not Atlantic rivers within the meaning of the treaty, and that His Majesty's Government therefore trusted that the American Cabinet would concur with that of His Majesty in deciding "that the Atlantic rivers which are to guide the commissioners in searching for the highlands described in the treaty are those which fall into the sea to the westward of the mouth of the river St. Croix;" that a clear agreement on this point must be an indispensable preliminary to the establishment of any new commission of survey; that till this point be decided no survey of commissioners could lead to a useful result, but that its decision turns upon the interpretation of the words of a treaty, and not upon the operations of surveyors; and His Majesty's Government, having once submitted it, in common with other points, to the judgment of an impartial arbiter, by whose award they had declared themselves ready to abide, could not consent to refer it to any other arbitration.

In a note from the Department of State dated 28th April, 1835, Sir Charles R. Vaughan was assured that his prompt suggestion, as His Britannic Majesty's minister, that a negotiation should be opened for the establishment of a conventional boundary between the two countries was duly appreciated by the President, who, had he possessed like powers with His Majesty's Government over the subject, would have met the suggestion in a favorable spirit.

The Secretary observed that the submission of the whole subject or any part of it to a new arbitrator promised too little to attract the favorable consideration of either party; that the desired adjustment of the controversy was consequently to be sought for in the application of some new principle to the controverted question, and that the President thought that by a faithful prosecution of the plan submitted by his direction a settlement of the boundary in dispute according to the terms of the treaty of 1783 was attainable.

With regard to the rule of practical surveying offered as the basis of the American proposition, he said if it should become material to do so—which was not to be anticipated—he would find no difficulty either in fortifying the ground occupied by this Government in this regard or in satisfying Sir Charles that the instance brought into notice by His Britannic Majesty's Government of a supposed departure from the rule was not at variance with the assertion of Mr. Livingston repeated by Mr. McLane. The Secretary therefore limited himself to the remark that the line of demarcation referred to by Sir Charles was not established as the true boundary prescribed by the treaty of 1783, but was a conventional substitute for it, the result of a new negotiation controlled by other considerations than those to be drawn from that instrument only.

The Secretary expressed the President's unfeigned regret upon learning the decision of His Majesty's Government not to agree to the proposition made on the part of the United States without a precedent compliance by them with inadmissible conditions. He said that the views of this Government in regard to this proposal of His Majesty's Government had been already communicated to Sir Charles R. Vaughan, and the President perceived with pain that the reasons upon which these opinions were founded had not been found to possess sufficient force and justice to induce the entire withdrawal of the objectionable conditions, but that, on the contrary, while His Majesty's Government had been pleased to waive for the present six of the seven opinions referred to, the remaining one, amongst the most important of them all, was still insisted upon, viz, that the St. John and Restigouche should be treated by the supposed commission as not being Atlantic rivers according to the meaning of those terms in the treaty. With reference to that part of Sir Charles's communication which seeks to strengthen the ground heretofore taken on this point by the British Government by calling to its aid the supposed confirmation of the arbiter, the Secretary felt himself warranted in questioning whether the arbiter had ever given his opinion that the rivers St. John and Restigouche can not be considered according to the meaning of the treaty as rivers falling into the Atlantic, and he insisted that it was not the intention of the arbiter to express the opinion imputed to him.

The Secretary also informed Sir Charles that the President could not consent to clog the submission with the condition proposed by Her Majesty's Government; that a just regard to the rights of the parties and a proper consideration of his own duties required that the new submission, if made, should be made without restriction or qualification upon the discretion of the commissioners other than such as resulted from established facts and the just interpretation of the definitive treaty, and such as had been heretofore and were now again tendered to His Britannic Majesty's Government; that he despaired of obtaining a better constituted tribunal than the one proposed; that he saw nothing unfit or improper in submitting the question as to the character in which the St. John and Restigouche were to be regarded to the decision of an impartial commission; that the parties had heretofore thought it proper so to submit it, and that it by no means followed that because commissioners chosen by the parties themselves, without an umpire, had failed to come to an agreement respecting it, that the same result would attend the efforts of a commission differently selected. The Secretary closed his note by stating that the President had no new proposal to offer, but would be happy to receive any such proposition as His Britannic Majesty's Government might think it expedient to make, and by intimating that he was authorized to confer with Sir Charles whenever it might suit his convenience and comport with the instructions of his Government with respect to the treaty boundary or a conventional substitute for it.

On the 4th of May, 1835, Sir Charles R. Vaughan expressed his regret that the condition which His Majesty's Government had brought forward as an essential preliminary to the adoption of the President's proposal had been declared to be inadmissible by the American Government.

Sir Charles confidently appealed to the tenor of the language of the award of the arbiter to justify the inference drawn from it by His Majesty's Government in regard to that point in the dispute which respects the rivers which are to be considered as falling directly into the Atlantic. The acquiescence of the United States in what was understood to be the opinion of the arbiter was invited, he said, because the new commission could not enter upon their survey in search of the highlands of the treaty without a previous agreement between the two Governments what rivers ought to be considered as falling into the Atlantic, and that if the character in which the

Restigouche and St. John were to be regarded was a question to be submitted to the commissioners the President's proposition would assume the character of a new arbitration, which had been already objected to by the Secretary. Sir Charles also stated that while His Majesty's Government had wished to maintain the decisions of the arbiter on subordinate points, their mention had not been confined to those decided in favor of British claims; that the decisions were nearly balanced in favor of either party, and the general result of the arbitration was so manifestly in favor of the United States that to them were assigned three-fifths of the territory in dispute and Rouses Point, to which they had voluntarily resigned all claim.

Sir Charles acknowledged with much satisfaction the Secretary's assurance that if the President possessed the same power as His Majesty's Government over the question of boundary he would have met the suggestion of a conventional line, contained in Sir Charles's note of 31st May, 1833, in a favorable spirit. He lamented that the two Governments could not coincide in the opinion that the removal of the only difficulty in the relations between them was attainable by the last proposal of the President, as it was the only one in his power to offer in alleviation of the task of tracing the treaty line, to which the Senate had advised that any further negotiation should be restricted. He said that he was ready to confer with the Secretary whenever it might be convenient to receive him, and stated that as to any proposition which it might be the wish of the United States to receive from His Majesty's Government respecting a conventional substitute for the treaty of 1783, it would in the first instance, to avoid constitutional difficulties in the way of the Executive, be necessary to obtain the consent of Maine, an object which must be undertaken exclusively by the General Government of the United States.

Mr. Bankhead, the British chargé d'affaires, in a note to the Department dated 28th December, 1835, stated that during the three years which had elapsed since the refusal of the Senate to agree to the award of the King of the Netherlands, although the British Government had more than once declared its readiness to abide by its offer to accept the award, the Government of the United States had as often replied that on its part that award could not be agreed to; that the British Government now considered itself by this refusal of the United States fully and entirely released from the conditional offer which it had made, and that he was instructed distinctly to announce to the President that the British Government withdrew its consent to accept the territorial compromise recommended by the King of the Netherlands.

With regard to the American proposition for the appointment of a new commission of exploration and survey, Mr. Bankhead could not see, since the President found himself unable to admit the distinction between the Bay of Fundy and the Atlantic Ocean, how any useful result could arise out of the proposed survey. He thought, on the contrary, that if it did not furnish fresh subjects of difference between the two Governments it could at best only bring the subject back to the same point at which it now stood.

To the suggestion of the President that the commission of survey should be empowered to decide the river question Mr. Bankhead said it was not in the power of His Majesty's Government to assent; that this question could not properly be referred to such a commission, because it turned upon the interpretation to be put upon the words of the treaty of 1783, and upon the application of that interpretation to geographical facts already well known and ascertained, and that therefore a commission of survey had no peculiar competency to decide such a question; that to refer it to any authority would be to submit it to a fresh arbitration, and that if His Majesty's Government were prepared to agree to a fresh arbitration, which was not the case, such arbitration ought necessarily, instead of being confined to one particular point alone, to include all the points in dispute between the two Governments; that His Majesty's Government could therefore only agree to such a commission provided there were a previous understanding between the two Governments; that although neither should be required to give up its own interpretation of the river question, yet "the commissioners should be instructed to search for highlands upon the character of which no doubt could exist on either side."

If this modification of the President's proposal should not prove acceptable, Mr. Bankhead observed, the only remaining way of adjusting the difference would be to abandon altogether the attempt to draw a line in conformity with the words of the treaty and to fix upon a convenient line, to be drawn according to equitable principles and with a view to the respective interests and the convenience of the two parties. He stated that His Majesty's Government were perfectly ready to treat for such a line, and conceived that the natural features of the disputed territory would afford peculiar facilities for drawing it; that His Majesty's Government would therefore propose an equal division of the territory in dispute between Great Britain and the United States, and that the general outline of such a division would be that the boundary between the two States should be drawn due north from the head of St. Croix River till it intersected the St. John; thence up the bed of the St. John to the southernmost source of that river, and from that point it should be drawn to the head of the Connecticut River in such manner as to make the northern and southern allotments of the divided territory as nearly as possible equal to each other in extent.

In reply to the preceding note the Secretary, under date of February 29, 1836, expressed the President's regret to find that His Britannic Majesty's Government adhered to its objection to the appointment of a commission to be chosen in either of the modes heretofore proposed by the United States and his conviction that the proposition on which it was founded, "that the river question was a treaty construction only," although repeated on various occasions by Great Britain, was demonstrably untenable, and, indeed, only plausible when material and most important words of description in the treaty are omitted in quoting from that instrument. He said that while His Majesty's Government maintain their position agreement between the United States and Great Britain on this point was impossible; that the President was therefore constrained to look to the new and conventional line offered in Mr. Bankhead's note, but that in such a line the wishes and interests of Maine were to be consulted, and that the President could not in justice to himself or that State make any proposition utterly irreconcilable with her previously well-known opinions on the subject; that the principle of compromise and equitable division was adopted by the King of the Netherlands in the line recommended by him, a line rejected by the United States because unjust to Maine; and yet that line gave to Great Britain little more than 2,000,000, while the proposition now made by His Majesty's Government secured to Great Britain of the disputed land more than 4,000,000 acres; that the division offered by Mr. Bankhead's note was not in harmony with the equitable rule from which it is said to spring, and if it were in conformity with it could not be accepted without disrespect to the previous decisions and just expectations of Maine. The President was far from attributing this proposition, the Secretary said, to the desire of His Majesty's Government to acquire territory. He doubted not that the offer, without regard to the extent of territory falling to the north or south of the St. John, was made by His Majesty's Government from a belief that the substitution of a river for a highland boundary would be useful in preventing territorial disputes in future; but although the President coincided in this view of the subject he was compelled to decline the boundary proposed as inconsistent with the known wishes, rights, and decisions of the State.

The Secretary concluded by stating that the President, with a view to terminate at once all controversy, and without regard to the extent of territory lost by one party or acquired by the other, to establish a definite and indisputable line, would, if His Majesty's Government assented to it, apply to the State of Maine for its consent to make the river St. John from its source to its mouth the boundary between Maine and His Britannic Majesty's dominions in that part of North America.

Mr. Bankhead acknowledged on the 4th March, 1836, the receipt of this note from the Department, and said that the rejection of the conventional line proposed in his previous note would cause His Majesty's Government much regret. He referred the Secretary to that part of his note of the 28th December last wherein the proposition of the President for a commission of exploration and survey was fully discussed, as it appeared to Mr. Bankhead that the Secretary had not given the modification on the part of His Majesty's Government of the American proposition the weight to which it was entitled. He said that it was offered with the view of meeting as far as practicable the wishes of the President and of endeavoring by such a preliminary measure to bring about a settlement of the boundary upon a basis satisfactory to both parties; that with this view he again submitted to the Secretary the modified proposal of His Majesty's Government, remarking that the commissioners who might be appointed were not to *decide* upon points of difference, but merely to present to the respective Governments the result of their labors, which, it was hoped and believed, would pave the way for an ultimate settlement of the question.

Mr. Bankhead considered it proper to state frankly and clearly that the proposition offered in the last note from the Department to make the river St. John from its source to its mouth the boundary between the United States and His Majesty's Province of New Brunswick was one to which the British Government, he was co vinced, would never agree.

On the 5th March the Secretary expressed regret that his proposition to make the river St. John the boundary between Maine and New Brunswick would, in the opinion of Mr. Bankhead, be declined by his Government; that the Government of the United States could not, however, relinquish the hope that the proposal, when brought before His Majesty's cabinet and considered with the attention and deliberation due to its merits, would be viewed in a more favorable light than that in which it appeared to have presented itself to Mr. Bankhead. If, however, the Secretary added, this expectation should be disappointed, it would be necessary before the President consented to the modification of his previous proposition for the appointment of a commission of exploration and survey to be informed more fully of the views of the British Government in offering the modification, so that he might be enabled to judge how the report of the commission (which as now proposed to be constituted was not to decide upon points of difference) would be likely to lead to an ultimate settlement of the question of boundary, and also which of the modes proposed for the selection of commissioners was the one intended to be accepted, with the modification suggested by His Britannic Majesty's Government.

In January last Mr. Fox, the British minister at Washington, made a communication to the Department of State, in which, with reference to the objection preferred by the American Government that it had no power without the consent of Maine to agree to the arrangement proposed by Great Britain, since it would be considered by that State as equivalent to a cession of what she regarded as a part of her territory, he observed that the objection of the State could not be admitted as valid, for the principle on which it rested was as good for Great Britain as it was for Maine; that if the State was entitled to contend that until the treaty line was determined the boundary claimed by Maine must be regarded as the right one, Great Britain was still more entitled to insist on a similar pretension and to assert that until the line of the treaty shall be established satisfactorily the whole of the disputed territory ought to be considered as belonging to the British Crown, since Great Britain was the original possessor, and all the territory which had not been proved to have been by treaty ceded by her must be deemed to belong to her still. But Mr. Fox said the existence of these conflicting pretensions pointed out the expediency of a compromise; and why, he asked, as a conventional line different from that described in the treaty was agreed to with respect to the boundary westward from the Lake of the Woods, should such a line not be agreed to likewise for the boundary eastward from the Connecticut? Her Majesty's Government could not, he added, refrain from again pressing this proposition upon the serious consideration of the United States as the arrangement best calculated to effect a prompt and satisfactory settlement between the two powers.

With reference to the American proposition to make the river St. John from its mouth to its source the boundary, Mr. Fox remarked that it was difficult to understand upon what grounds any expectation could have been formed that such a proposal could be entertained by the British Government, for such an arrangement would give to the United States even greater advantages than they would obtain by an unconditional acquiescence in their claim to the whole of the disputed territory, because it would give to Maine all the disputed territory lying south of the St. John, and in exchange for the remaining part of the territory lying to the north of the St. John would add to the State of Maine a large district of New Brunswick—a district smaller in extent, but much more considerable in value, than the portion of the disputed territory which lies to the north of the St. John.

With regard to the proposition for the appointment of a commission of exploration and survey, Mr. Fox stated that Her Majesty's Government, with little expectation that it could lead to a useful result, but unwilling to reject the only plan left which seemed to afford a chance of making a further advance in this matter, would not withhold their consent to such a commission if the principle upon which it was to be formed and the manner in which it was to proceed could be satisfactorily settled; that of the two modes proposed in which such a commission might be constituted Her Majesty's Government thought the first, viz, that it might consist of commissioners named in equal numbers by each of the two Governments, with an umpire to be selected by some friendly European power, would be the best, but suggested that it might be better that the umpire should be selected by the members of the commission themselves rather than that the two Governments should apply to a third power to make such a choice; that the object of this commission should be to explore the disputed territory in order to find within its limits dividing highlands which might answer the description of the treaty, the search to be made in a north and northwest line from the monument at the head of the St. Croix; and that Her Majesty's Government had given their opinion that the commissioners should be instructed to look for highlands which both parties might acknowledge as fulfilling the conditions of the treaty.

In answer to the inquiry how the report of the commission would, according to the views of Her Majesty's Government, be likely when rendered to lead to an ultimate settlement of the boundary question, Mr. Fox observed that since the proposal for the appointment of a commission originated with the Government of the United States, it was rather for that Government than the Government of Great Britain to answer this question. Her Majesty's Government had already stated they had little expectation that such a commission could lead to any useful result, etc., but that Her Majesty's Government, in the first place, conceived that it was meant by the Government of the United States that if the commission should discover highlands answering to the description of the treaty a connecting line from them to the head of the St. Croix should be deemed to be a portion of the boundary between the two countries. Mr. Fox further referred the Secretary to the previous notes of Mr. McLane on the subject, in which it was contemplated as one of the possible results of the proposed commission that such additional information might be obtained of the features of the country as might remove all doubt as to the impracticability of laying down a boundary in accordance with the letter of the treaty. Mr. Fox said that if the investigations of the commission should show that there was no reasonable prospect of finding the line described in the treaty of 1783 the constitutional difficulties which now prevented the United States from agreeing to a conventional line might possibly be removed, and the way be thus prepared for a satisfactory settlement of the difference by equitable division of the territory; but, he added in conclusion, if the two Governments should agree to the appointment of such a commission, it would be necessary that their agreement should be by a convention, and it would be obviously indispensable that the State of Maine should be an assenting party to the arrangement.

In acknowledging the receipt of Mr. Fox's communication at the Department he was informed (7th February) that the President experienced deep disappointment in finding that the answer just presented on the part of the British Government to the proposition made by this Government with the view of effecting the settlement of the boundary question was so indefinite in its terms as to render it impracticable to ascertain without further discussion what were the real wishes and intentions of Her Majesty's Government respecting the appointment of a commission of exploration and survey, but that a copy of it would be transmitted to the executive of Maine for the purpose of ascertaining the sense of the State authorities upon the expediency of meeting the views of Her Majesty's Government so far as they were therein developed.

Occasion was taken at the same time to explain to Mr. Fox, in answer to the suggestion in his note of the 10th of January last, that the parallel of latitude adopted as a conventional substitute for the line designated in the treaty for the boundary westward from the Lake of the Woods passed over territory within the exclusive jurisdiction of the General Government, without trenching upon the rights or claims of any member of the Union, and the legitimate power of the Government, therefore, to agree to such line was held to be perfect, but that in acceding to a conventional line for the boundary eastward from the river Connecticut it would transcend its constitutional powers, since such a measure could only be carried into effect by violating the jurisdiction of a sovereign State and assuming to alienate a portion of the territory claimed by such State.

In reply to the observation of Mr. Fox that it was difficult to understand upon what ground an expectation could have been entertained that the proposition to make the St. John the boundary would be received by Her Majesty's Government, he was informed that the suggestion had been offered, as the proposition on the part of Great Britain that led to it was supposed to have been, with regard to the extent of territory lost or acquired by the respective parties, and in the hope that the great importance of terminating this controversy by establishing a definite and indisputable boundary would be seen and acknowledged by the British Government, and have a correspondent weight in influencing its decision; that the suggestion in Mr. Bankhead's note of 28th December, 1835, of a part of the river St. John as a portion of the general outline of a conventional boundary, apparently recognized the superior advantages of a river over a highland boundary, and that no difficulty was anticipated on the part of Her Majesty's Government in understanding the grounds upon which such a proposal was expected to be entertained by it, since the precedent proposition of Mr. Bankhead just alluded to, although based upon the principle of an equal division between the parties, could not be justified by it, as it would have given nearly two-thirds of the disputed territory to Great Britain; that it was therefore fair to presume that the river line, in the opinion of His Majesty's Government, presented advantages sufficient to counterbalance any loss of territory by either party that might accrue from its adoption; and it was also supposed that another recommendation of this line would be seen by Great Britain in the fact that whilst by its adoption the right of jurisdiction alone would have been yielded to the United States over that portion of New Brunswick south of the St. John, Great Britain would have acquired the right of soil and jurisdiction of all the disputed territory north of that river.

To correct a misapprehension into which Mr. Fox appeared to have fallen, the distinctive difference between the American proposition for a commission and that proposition as subsequently modified by Great Britain was pointed out, and he was informed that although the proposal originated with this Government, the modification was so fundamentally important that it entirely changed the nature of the proposition, and that the supposition, therefore, that it was rather for the Government of the United States than for that of Great Britain to answer the inquiry preferred by the Secretary of State for information relative to the manner in which the report of the commission as proposed to be constituted and instructed by the British Government might tend to a practical result was unfounded. Mr. Fox was also given to understand that any decision made by a commission constituted in the manner proposed by the United States and instructed to seek for the highlands of the treaty of 1783 would be binding upon this Government and could be carried into effect without unnecessary delay; but if the substitute presented by Her Majesty's Government should be insisted on and its principles be adopted, it would then be necessary to resort to the State of Maine for her assent in all proceedings relative to the matter, since any arrangement under it can only be for a conventional line to which she must be a party.

In conclusion, it was intimated to Mr. Fox that if a negotiation be entertained by this Government at all upon the unsatisfactory basis afforded by the British counter proposition or substitute, the President will not invite it unless the authorities of the State of Maine shall think it more likely to lead to an adjustment of the question of boundary than the General Government deemed it to be, although predisposed to see it in the most favorable light.

Your excellency will perceive that in the course of these proceedings, but without abandoning the attempt to adjust the treaty line, steps necessary, from the want of power in the Federal Government, of an informal character, have been taken to test the dispositions of the respective Governments upon the subject of substituting a conventional for the treaty line. It will also be seen from the correspondence that the British Government, despairing of a satisfactory adjustment of the line of the treaty, avows its willingness to enter upon a direct negotiation for the settlement of a conventional line if the assent of the State of Maine to that course can be obtained.

Whilst the obligations of the Federal Government to do all in its power to effect a settlement of this boundary are fully recognized on its part, it has in the event of its being unable to do so specifically by mutual consent no other means to accomplish the object amicably than by another arbitration, or a commission, with an umpire, in the nature of an arbitration. In the contingency of all other measures failing the President will feel it to be his duty to submit another proposition to the Government of Great Britain to refer the decision of the question to a third party. He would not, however, be satisfied in taking this final step without having first ascertained the opinion and wishes of the State of Maine upon the subject of a negotiation for the establishment of a conventional line, and he conceives the present the proper time to seek it.

I am therefore directed by the President to invite your excellency to adopt such measures as you may deem necessary to ascertain the sense of the State of Maine with respect to the expediency of attempting to establish a conventional line of boundary between that State and the British possessions by direct negotiation between the Governments of the United States and Great Britain, and whether the State of Maine will agree, and upon what conditions, if she elects to prescribe any, to abide by such settlement if the same be made. Should the State of Maine be of opinion that additional surveys and explorations might be useful either in leading to a satisfactory adjustment of the controversy according to the terms of the treaty or in enabling the parties to decide more understandingly upon the expediency of opening a negotiation for the establishment of a line that would suit their mutual convenience and be reconcilable to their conflicting interests, and desire the creation for that purpose of a commission upon the principles and with the limited powers described in the letter of Mr. Fox, the President will without hesitation open a negotiation with Great Britain for the accomplishment of that object.

I have the honor to be, with high consideration, your excellency's obedient servant, JOHN FORSYTH.

WASHINGTON, *April 5, 1838.*

To the House of Representatives of the United States:

I herewith transmit to the House of Representatives a report from the Secretary of State, with accompanying papers, in answer to their resolution of the 21st ultimo.

M. VAN BUREN.

DEPARTMENT OF STATE,
Washington, April 4, 1838.

The PRESIDENT OF THE UNITED STATES:

The Secretary of State, to whom has been referred the resolution of the House of Representatives of the 21st ultimo, requesting the President, "if not incompatible with the public interests, to communicate to that House any information possessed by him respecting the capture and destruction of the steamboat *Caroline* at Schlosser during the night of the 29th December last, and the murder of citizens of the United States on board, and all the particulars thereof not heretofore communicated, and especially to inform the House whether said capture was authorized, commanded, or sanctioned or has been avowed by the British authorities or officers, or any of them, and also what steps have been taken by him to obtain satisfaction from the Government of Great Britain on account of said outrage, and to communicate to the House all correspondence or communications relative thereto which have passed between the Government of the United States and Great Britain, or any of the public authorities of either," has the honor to lay before the President the accompanying documents, which contain all the information in the possession of this Department relative to the subject of the resolution; and to state, moreover, that instructions have been transmitted to the minister of the United States in London to make a full representation to Her Britannic Majesty's Government of the facts connected with this lamentable occurrence, to remonstrate against the unwarrantable course pursued on the occasion by the British troops from Canada, and to express the expectation of this Government that such redress as the nature of the case obviously requires will be promptly given.

Respectfully submitted. JOHN FORSYTH.

Mr. Forsyth to Mr. Fox.

DEPARTMENT OF STATE,
Washington, January 5, 1838.

HENRY S. FOX, Esq., etc.

SIR: By the direction of the President of the United States, I have the honor to communicate to you a copy of the evidence furnished to this Department of an extraordinary outrage committed from Her Britannic Majesty's Province of Upper Canada on the persons and property of citizens of the United States within the jurisdiction of the State of New York. The destruction of the property and the assassination of citizens of the United States on the soil of New York at the moment when, as is well known to you, the President was anxiously endeavoring to allay the excitement and earnestly seeking to prevent any unfortunate occurrence on the frontier of Canada have produced upon his mind the most painful emotions of surprise and regret. It will necessarily form the subject of a demand for redress upon Her

Majesty's Government. This communication is made to you under the expectation that through your instrumentality an early explanation may be obtained from the authorities of Upper Canada of all the circumstances of the transaction, and that by your advice to those authorities such decisive precautions may be used as will render the perpetration of similar acts hereafter impossible. Not doubting the disposition of the government of Upper Canada to do its duty in punishing the aggressors and preventing future outrage, the President nevertheless has deemed it necessary to order a sufficient force on the frontier to repel any attempt of a like character and to make known to you that if it should occur he can not be answerable for the effects of the indignation of the neighboring people of the United States.

I avail myself of this occasion, etc.

JOHN FORSYTH.

Mr. Forsyth to Mr. Fox.

DEPARTMENT OF STATE,
Washington, January 19, 1838.

HENRY S. FOX, Esq., etc.

SIR: With reference to my note of the 5th instant, communicating to you evidence of an extraordinary outrage committed from Her Britannic Majesty's Province of Upper Canada on the persons and property of certain citizens of the United States at Schlosser, within the jurisdiction of the State of New York, on the night of the 29th ultimo, I have now the honor to transmit to you the copy of a letter* recently received from the attorney of the United States for the northern district of New York, dated the 8th of the current month, with transcripts of sundry depositions* which accompanied it, containing additional information in regard to that most disastrous occurrence. A letter from Mr. George W. Pratt of the 10th of January, with inclosures relating to the same subject, is also sent.

I avail myself of this occasion to renew to you the assurance of my distinguished consideration.

JOHN FORSYTH.

The PRESIDENT.

ROCHESTER, *January 10, 1838.*

SIR: Colonel McNab, having avowed that the steamboat *Caroline* was destroyed by his orders, justifies himself by the plea, sustained by affidavits, that hostilities were commenced from the American shore.

I inclose you the affidavits* of four respectable citizens of Rochester, who were present at the time, who contradict the assertions of Colonel McNab.

I have the honor to be, your obedient servant,

GEO. W. PRATT.

Mr. Fox to Mr. Forsyth.

WASHINGTON, *February 6, 1838.*

Hon. JOHN FORSYTH, etc.

SIR: With reference to the letters which, by direction of the President, you addressed to me on the 5th and 19th ultimo, respecting the capture and destruction of the steamboat *Caroline* by a Canadian force on the American side of the Niagara River, within the jurisdiction of the State of New York, I have now the honor to communicate to you the copy of a letter upon that subject which I have received from Sir Francis Head, lieutenant-governor of the Province of Upper Canada, with divers reports and depositions annexed.

The piratical character of the steamboat *Caroline* and the necessity of self-defense and self-preservation under which Her Majesty's subjects acted in destroying that vessel would seem to be sufficiently established.

At the time when the event happened the ordinary laws of the United States were

*Omitted.

not enforced within the frontier district of the State of New York. The authority of the law was overborne publicly by piratical violence. Through such violence Her Majesty's subjects in Upper Canada had already severely suffered, and they were threatened with still further injury and outrage. This extraordinary state of things appears naturally and necessarily to have impelled them to consult their own security by pursuing and destroying the vessel of their piratical enemy wheresoever they might find her.

I avail myself of this occasion to renew to you the assurance of my high respect and consideration. H. S. FOX.

TORONTO, UPPER CANADA, *January 8, 1838.*

His Excellency HENRY S. FOX,
Her Majesty's Minister, Washington.

SIR: I have the honor to inclose you the copy of a special message sent by His Excellency Governor Marcy to the legislature of the State of New York, in relation to a matter on which your excellency will desire the earliest and most authentic information. The message only reached this place yesterday, and I lose no time in communicating with your excellency on the subject.

The governor of the State of New York complains of the cutting out and burning of the steamboat *Caroline* by order of Colonel McNab, commanding Her Majesty's forces at Chippewa, in the Province of Upper Canada, and of the destruction of the lives of some American citizens who were on board of the boat at the time she was attacked.

The act complained of was done under the following circumstances:

In Upper Canada, which contains a population of about 450,000 souls, the most perfect tranquillity prevailed up to the 4th day of December last, although in the adjoining Province of Lower Canada many of the French Canadian inhabitants had been in open rebellion against the Government for about a month preceding.

At no time since the treaty of peace with the United States in 1815 had Upper Canada been more undisturbed. The real causes of the insurrection in Lower Canada, namely, the national antipathy of the French inhabitants, did not in any degree apply in the upper Province, whose population, like the British and American inhabitants of Lower Canada, were wholly opposed to the revolt and anxious to render every service in their power in support of the Queen's authority.

It had been reported to the Government some time before the 4th of December that in a remote portion of the home district a number of persons occasionally met and drilled with arms under leaders known to be disaffected, but it was not believed by the Government that anything more could be intended than to make a show of threatened revolt in order to create a diversion in favor of the rebels in Lower Canada.

The feeling of loyalty throughout this Province was known to be so prevalent and decided that it was not thought unsafe to forbear, for the time at least, to take any notice of the proceedings of this party.

On the night of the 4th December the inhabitants of the city of Toronto were alarmed by the intelligence that about 500 persons armed with rifles were approaching the city; that they had murdered a gentleman of great respectability in the highway, and had made several persons prisoners. The inhabitants rushed immediately to arms; there were no soldiers in the Province and no militia had been called out. The home district, from which this party of armed men came, contains 60,000 inhabitants; the city of Toronto 10,000. In a few hours a respectable force, although undisciplined, was collected and armed in self-defense, and awaited the threatened attack. It seems now to admit of no doubt that if they had at once advanced against the insurgents they would have met with no formidable resistance, but it was thought more prudent to wait until a sufficient force should be collected to put the success of an attack beyond question.   In the meantime people poured in from all quarters to oppose the insurgents, who obtained no increase of numbers, but, on the contrary, were deserted by many of their body in consequence of the acts of devastation and plunder into which their leader had forced them.

On the 7th of December an overwhelming force of militia went against them and dispersed them without losing a man, taking many prisoners, who were instantly by my order released and suffered to depart to their homes.   The rest, with their leaders, fled; some have since surrendered themselves to justice; many have been taken, and some have escaped from the Province.

It was reported about this time that in the district of London a similar disposition to rise had been observed, and in consequence a militia force of about 400 men was sent into that district, where it was speedily joined by three times as many of the inhabitants of the district, who assembled voluntarily and came to their aid with the greatest alacrity.

It was discovered that about 300 persons under Dr. Duncombe, an American by birth, were assembled with arms, but before the militia could reach them they dispersed themselves and fled.   Of these by far the greater came in immediately and submitted themselves to the Government, declaring that they had been misled and deceived, and praying for forgiveness.

In about a week perfect tranquillity was restored, and from that moment not a man has been seen in arms against the Government in any part of the Province, with the exception of the hostile aggression upon Navy Island, which I shall presently notice; nor has there been the slightest resistance offered to the execution of legal process in a single instance.

After the dispersion of the armed insurgents near Toronto Mr. McKenzie, their leader, escaped in disguise to the Niagara River and crossed over to Buffalo. Reports had been spread there and elsewhere along the American frontier that Toronto had been burnt and that the rebels were completely successful, but the falsehood of these absurd rumors was well known before McKenzie arrived on the American side.   It was known also that the ridiculous attempt of 400 men to revolutionize a country containing nearly half a million inhabitants had been put down by the people instantly and decidedly without the loss of a man.

Nevertheless, a number of American citizens in Buffalo and other towns on the frontier of the State of New York enlisted as soldiers, with the avowed object of invading Canada and establishing a provisional government.   Public meetings were held to forward this design of invading a country with which the United States were at peace.   Volunteers were called for, and arms, ammunition, and provisions were supplied by contributions openly made.   All this was in direct and flagrant violation of the express laws of the United States, as well as of the law of nations.

The civil authority of Buffalo offered some slight shew of resistance to the movement, being urged to interpose by many of the most respectable citizens.   But no real impediment was offered, and on the 13th of December some hundreds of the citizens of the State of New York, as an armed body under the command of a Mr. Van Rensselaer, an American citizen, openly invaded and took possession of Navy Island, a part of Upper Canada, situate in the Niagara River.

Not believing that such an outrage would really be committed, no force whatever was assembled at the time to counteract this hostile movement.

In a very short time this lawless band obtained from some of the arsenals of the State of New York (clandestinely, as it is said) several pieces of artillery and other arms, which in broad daylight were openly transported to Navy Island without resistance from the American authorities.   The people of Buffalo and the adjacent country continued to supply them with stores of various kinds, and additional men enlisted in their ranks.

In a few days their force was variously stated from 500 to 1,500, of whom a small proportion were rebels who had fled from Upper Canada. They began to intrench themselves, and threatened that they would in a short time make a landing on the Canadian side of the Niagara River.

To prevent this and to keep them in check a body of militia was hastily collected and stationed on the frontier, under the command of Colonel Cameron, assistant adjutant-general of militia, who was succeeded in this command by Colonel McNab, the speaker of the house of assembly, an officer whose humanity and discretion, as well as his activity, have been proved by his conduct in putting down the insurrection in the London district and have been acknowledged in warm terms of gratitude by the misguided persons who had surrendered themselves into his hands. He received orders to act on the defensive only, and to be careful not to do any act which the American Government could justly complain of as a breach of neutrality.

An official statement of the unfriendly proceedings at Buffalo was without delay (on the 13th December) made by me to his excellency the governor of the State of New York, to which no answer has been received. And after this open invasion of our territory, and when it became evident that nothing was effected at Buffalo for preventing the violation of neutrality, a special messenger was sent to your excellency at Washington to urge your interposition in the matter. Sufficient time has not yet elapsed to admit of his return. Soon after his departure this band of outlaws on Navy Island, acting in defiance of the laws and Government of both countries, opened a fire from several pieces of ordnance upon the Canadian shore, which in this part is thickly settled, the distance from the island being about 600 yards and within sight of the populous village of Chippewa. They put several balls (6-pound shot) through a house in which a party of militiamen were quartered and which is the dwelling house of Captain Usher, a respectable inhabitant. They killed a horse on which a man at the time was riding, but happily did no further mischief, though they fired also repeatedly with cannon and musketry upon our boats.

They continued daily to render their position more formidable, receiving constant supplies of men and warlike stores from the State of New York, which were chiefly embarked at a landing place on the American main shore, called Fort Schlosser, nearly opposite to Navy Island. This place was once, I believe, a military position, before the conquest of Canada from the French, but there is now neither fort nor village there, but merely a single house occupied as a tavern, and a wharf in front of it, to which boats and vessels are moored. The tavern had been during these lawless proceedings a rendezvous for the band (who can not be called by any name more appropriate than pirates), and was in fact openly and notoriously resorted to as their headquarters on the mainland, and is so to this time. On the 28th December positive information was given to Colonel McNab by persons from Buffalo that a small steamboat called the *Caroline*, of about 50 tons burthen, had been hired by the pirates, who called themselves "patriots," and was to be employed in carrying down cannon and other stores and in transporting men and anything else that might be required between Fort Schlosser and Navy Island.

He resolved if she came down and engaged in this service to take or destroy her. She did come down agreeably to the information he received. She transported a piece of artillery and other stores to the island, and made repeated passages during the day between the island and the main shore.

In the night he sent a party of militia in boats, with orders to take or destroy her. They proceeded to execute the order. They found the *Caroline* moored to the wharf opposite to the inn at Fort Schlosser. In the inn there was a guard of armed men to protect her—part of the pirate force, or acting in their support. On her deck there was an armed party and a sentinel, who demanded the countersign.

Thus identified as she was with the force which in defiance of the law of nations and every principle of natural justice had invaded Upper Canada and made war upon its unoffending inhabitants, she was boarded, and after a resistance in which some desperate wounds were inflicted upon the assailants she was carried. If any peaceable citizens of the United States perished in the conflict, it was and is unknown to the captors, and it was and is equally unknown to them whether any such were there. Before this vessel was thus taken not a gun had been fired by the force under the orders of Colonel McNab, even upon this gang of pirates, much less upon any peaceable citizen of the United States. It must therefore have been a consciousness of the guilty service she was engaged in that led those who were employing her to think an armed guard necessary for her defense. Peaceable citizens of the United States were not likely to be found in a vessel so employed at such a place and in such a juncture, and if they were there their presence, especially unknown as it was to the captors, could not prevent, in law or reason, this necessary act of self-defense.

Fifteen days had elapsed since the invasion of Upper Canada by a force enlisted, armed, and equipped openly in the State of New York. The country where this outrage upon the law of nations was committed is populous. Buffalo also contains 15,000 inhabitants. The public authorities, it is true, gave no countenance to those flagrant acts, but it did not prevent them or in the slightest degree obstruct them further than by issuing proclamations, which were disregarded.

Perhaps they could not, but in either case the insult and injury to the inhabitants of Canada were the same and their right to defend themselves equally unquestionable.

No wanton injury was committed by the party who gallantly effected this service. They loosed the vessel from the wharf, and finding they could not tow her against the rapid current of the Niagara, they abandoned the effort to secure her, set her on fire, and let her drift down the stream.

The prisoners taken were a man who, it will be seen by the documents accompanying this dispatch, avowed himself to be a subject of Her Majesty, inhabiting Upper Canada, who had lately been traitorously in arms in that Province, and, having fled to the United States, was then on board for the purpose of going to the camp at Navy Island; and a boy, who, being born in Lower Canada, was probably residing in the United States, and who, being afraid to land from the boat in consequence of the firing kept up by the guard on the shore, was placed in one of the boats under Captain Drew and taken over to our side, from whence he was sent home the next day by the Falls ferry with money given him to bear his expenses.

I send with this letter, first, a copy of my first communication to His Excellency Governor Marcy,* to which no reply has reached me; second, the official reports, correspondence, and militia general order respecting the destruction of the *Caroline*, with other documents;* third, the correspondence between Commissary-General Arcularius, of the State of New York, respecting the artillery belonging to the government of the State of New York, which has been and is still used in making war upon this Province;* fourth, other correspondence arising out of the present state of things on the Niagara frontier;* fifth, the special message of Governor Marcy.*

It will be seen from these documents that a high officer of the government of the State of New York has been sent by his excellency the governor for the express purpose of regaining possession of the artillery of that State which is now employed in hostile aggressions upon this portion of Her Majesty's dominions, and that, being aided and favored, as he acknowledges, by the most friendly cooperation which the commanding officer of Her Majesty's forces could give him, he has been successfully defied by this army of American citizens, and has abandoned the object of his mission in despair.

It can hardly fail also to be observed by your excellency that in the course of this negotiation between Mr. Van Rensselaer and the commissary-general of the State of New York this individual, Mr. Van Rensselaer, has not hesitated to place himself within the immediate jurisdiction of the government whose laws he had violated and in direct personal communication with the officer of that government, and has, nevertheless, been allowed to return unmolested to continue in command of American citizens engaged in open hostilities against Great Britain.

* Omitted.

The exact position, then, of affairs on our frontier may be thus described:

An army of American citizens, joined to a very few traitors from Upper Canada, and under the command of a subject of the United States, has been raised and equipped in the State of New York against the laws of the United States and the treaties now subsisting, and are using artillery plundered from the arsenals of the State of New York in carrying on this piratical warfare against a friendly country.

The officers and Government of the United States and of the State of New York have attempted to arrest these proceedings and to control their citizens, but they have failed. Although this piratical assemblage are thus defying the civil authorities of both countries, Upper Canada alone is the object of their hostilities. The Government of the United States has failed to enforce its authority by any means, civil or military, and the single question (if it be a question) is whether Upper Canada was bound to refrain from necessary acts of self-defense against a people whom their own Government either could not or would not control.

In perusing the message of His Excellency Governor Marcy to the legislature of the State of New York your excellency will probably feel some degree of surprise that after three weeks' continued hostility carried on by the citizens of New York against the people of Upper Canada his excellency seems to have considered himself not called upon to make this aggression the subject of remark for any other purpose than to complain of a solitary act of self-defense on the part of Her Majesty's Province of Upper Canada, to which such unprovoked hostilities have unavoidably led.

I have the honor to be, sir, your excellency's most obedient, humble servant,

F. B. HEAD.

Mr. Forsyth to Mr. Fox.

DEPARTMENT OF STATE,
Washington, February 13, 1838.

HENRY S. FOX, Esq., etc.

SIR: I have the honor to acknowledge the receipt of your note of the 6th instant, communicating a copy of a letter from Sir Francis Head, lieutenant-governor of the Province of Upper Canada, respecting the capture and destruction of the steamboat *Caroline* by a Canadian force on the American side of the Niagara River within the jurisdiction of the State of New York, together with the reports and depositions thereto annexed.

The statement of the facts which these papers present is at variance with the information communicated to this Government respecting that transaction; but it is not intended to enter at present upon an examination of the details of the case, as steps have been taken to obtain the fullest evidence that can be had of the particulars of the outrage, upon the receipt of which it will be made the subject of a formal complaint to the British Government for redress. Even admitting that the documents transmitted with your note contain a correct statement of the occurrence, they furnish no justification of the aggression committed upon the territory of the United States—an aggression which was the more unexpected as Sir Francis Head, in his speech at the opening of the parliament of Upper Canada, had expressed his confidence in the disposition of this Government to restrain its citizens from taking part in the conflict which was waging in that Province, and added that, having communicated with the governor of the State of New York and yourself, he was then waiting for replies.

It is not necessary to remind you that his expectations have been met by the adoption of measures on the part of the United States as prompt and vigorous as they have been successful in repressing every attempt of the inhabitants of the frontier States to interfere unlawfully in that contest. The most serious obstacle thrown in the way of those measures was the burning of the *Caroline*, which, while it was of no service to Her Britannic Majesty's cause in Canada, had the natural effect of increasing the excitement on the border, which this Government was endeavoring to allay.

I avail myself of this occasion to renew to you the assurance of my distinguished consideration.

JOHN FORSYTH.

His Excellency MARTIN VAN BUREN,   BUFFALO, *December 30, 1837.*
   President of the United States.

SIR: Inclosed are copies of affidavits* which I have prepared in great haste, and which contain all that is material in relation to the gross and extraordinary transaction to which they relate. Our whole frontier is in commotion, and I fear it will be difficult to restrain our citizens from avenging by a resort to arms this flagrant invasion of our territory. Everything that can be done will be by the public authorities to prevent so injudicious a movement. The respective sheriffs of Erie and Niagara have taken the responsibility of calling out the militia to guard the frontier and prevent any further depredations.

I am, sir, with great consideration, your obedient servant,

H. W. ROGERS,
District Attorney for Erie County, and Acting for the United States.

To the Senate: WASHINGTON, *April, 1838.*

I transmit a communication from the Department of War, on the subject of the treaty with the Stockbridge and Munsee Indians of September, 1836, which is now before the Senate.

M. VAN BUREN.

WASHINGTON, *April 15, 1838.*
The PRESIDENT OF THE SENATE OF THE UNITED STATES.

SIR: I transmit to you a report from the Secretary of the Navy, accompanied with the papers relating to surveys, examinations and surveys of light-houses, sites for light-houses, and improvements in the light-house system, called for by the resolution of the Senate of the 8th of March last.

M. VAN BUREN.

Hon. JAMES K. POLK,   WASHINGTON, *April 16, 1838.*
   Speaker of the House of Representatives.

SIR: I have the honor to transmit to you copies of the letters, documents, and communications called for by a resolution of the House of Representatives of the 7th of December last, received from the Secretary of the Navy, to be annexed to his report of the 5th day of February last, in relation to the delay of the sailing of the exploring expedition.†

M. VAN BUREN.

WASHINGTON, *April 18, 1838.*
To the Senate of the United States:

I return the petition and papers of Econchatta Nico,‡ referred to me by a resolution of the Senate of February 7, 1837, and transmit a com-

----

*Omitted.
†South Sea surveying and exploring expedition.
‡A chief of the Apalachicola Indians, for indemnification for losses sustained by depredations on his property by white persons.

munication and accompanying papers from the Acting Secretary of War, showing the failure of the attempt made, in conformity with the resolution, to obtain indemnity for the petitioner by prosecuting the depredators on his property, and also the causes of the failure. The papers are returned and the report and documents of the Acting Secretary of War submitted in order that Congress may devise such other mode of relief as may seem proper.

M. VAN BUREN.

WASHINGTON, *April 23, 1838.*
To the House of Representatives of the United States:

In compliance with the resolution of the House of Representatives of the 16th instant, relative to an attack on the steamboat *Columbia* in the Gulf of Mexico by a Mexican armed vessel, I transmit a report from the Secretary of State, to whom the resolution was referred.

M. VAN BUREN.

WASHINGTON, *April 23, 1838.*
To the Senate:

I transmit, for the consideration and action of the Senate, communications from the Department of War, accompanying treaties with the Indians in the State of New York, with the St. Regis band, and with the Oneidas residing at Green Bay.

M. VAN BUREN.

WASHINGTON, *April 26, 1838.*
To the House of Representatives of the United States:

In partial compliance with the resolution of the House of Representatives of the 21st ultimo, calling for further information on the relations between the United States and the Mexican Republic, I transmit a report from the Secretary of State, to whom the resolution was referred.

M. VAN BUREN.

WASHINGTON, *April 27, 1838.*
To the Senate of the United States:

I transmit to the Senate, for their consideration with a view to its ratification, a convention between the United States and the Republic of Texas for marking the boundary between them, signed in this city by the plenipotentiaries of the parties on the 25th instant.

M. VAN BUREN.

WASHINGTON, *April 30, 1838.*
To the House of Representatives of the United States:

I herewith transmit to the House of Representatives a report from the Secretary of State, in answer to that part of their resolution of the 19th ultimo requesting the communication of all correspondence with any foreign government in regard to the title or occupation of the territory of the United States beyond the Rocky Mountains.

M. VAN BUREN.

DEPARTMENT OF STATE,
Washington, April 25, 1838.

The PRESIDENT OF THE UNITED STATES:

The Secretary of State, to whom has been referred so much of the resolution of the House of Representatives dated the 19th ultimo as requests the President, if not incompatible with the public interest, to communicate to that body all correspondence had with any foreign government respecting the title or occupation of the territory of the United States beyond the Rocky Mountains, has the honor to report to the President that no recent communication on this subject has passed between this Government and any foreign power, and that copies of the correspondence growing out of previous discussions in which the question of title or occupation of this territory was involved have been heretofore communicated to the House and will be found among the documents printed by their order. Document No. 65 of the House of Representatives, contained in the fourth volume of State Papers of the first session of the Nineteenth Congress, and that numbered 199, in the fifth volume of State Papers of the first session of the Twentieth Congress, are particularly referred to as immediately connected with this subject.

Respectfully submitted.

JOHN FORSYTH.

WASHINGTON, *May 1, 1838.*

To the House of Representatives of the United States:

I transmit herewith a report, and accompanying documents, from the Acting Secretary of War, which contains the information* required by the resolution of the 16th ultimo, respecting the officers of the Corps of Engineers, the works upon which they were engaged during the last year, and the other matters embraced in the resolution.

M. VAN BUREN.

WASHINGTON, *May 2, 1838.*

To the House of Representatives of the United States:

The report of the Secretary of State transmitted by me to the House of Representatives in compliance with their resolution of the 16th ultimo, respecting an attack alleged to have been made by a Mexican armed vessel upon an American steamboat, having stated that no information on the subject had at that time reached the Department, I now transmit another report from the same officer, communicating a copy of a note from the Mexican minister, with an accompanying document, in reference to the act alluded to, which have been received at the Department since the date of the former report.

M. VAN BUREN.

* List of officers of the Corps of Engineers and of the works upon which they were employed during the year 1837.

WASHINGTON, *May 7, 1838.*

To the Senate of the United States:

I transmit to the Senate, for their consideration with a view to its ratification, a convention signed at Houston on the 11th ultimo by Alcée La Branche, chargé d'affaires of the United States, and R. A. Irion, secretary of state of the Republic of Texas, stipulating for the adjustment and satisfaction of claims of citizens of the United States on that Government in the cases of the brigs *Pocket* and *Durango.* This convention having been concluded in anticipation of the receipt from the Department of a formal power for that purpose, an extract from a dispatch of Mr. La Branche to the Secretary of State explanatory of his motives for that act is also transmitted for the information of the Senate.

M. VAN BUREN.

WASHINGTON, *May 10, 1838.*

To the Senate and House of Representatives:

I submit to the consideration of Congress a statement prepared by the Secretary of the Treasury, by which it appears that the United States, with over twenty-eight millions in deposit with the States and over fifteen millions due from individuals and banks, are, from the situation in which those funds are placed, in immediate danger of being rendered unable to discharge with good faith and promptitude the various pecuniary obligations of the Government. The occurrence of this result has for some time been apprehended, and efforts made to avert it. As the principal difficulty arises from a prohibition in the present law to reissue such Treasury notes as might be paid in before they fell due, and may be effectually obviated by giving the Treasury during the whole year the benefit of the full amount originally authorized, the remedy would seem to be obvious and easy.

The serious embarrassments likely to arise from a longer continuance of the present state of things induces me respectfully to invite the earliest attention of Congress to the subject which may be consistent with a due regard to other public interests.

M. VAN BUREN.

WASHINGTON, *May 11, 1838.*

To the House of Representatives of the United States:

I herewith transmit to the House of Representatives reports from the Secretary of State and the Secretary of the Treasury, with accompanying papers, in answer to the resolution of the House of the 30th ultimo, relating to the introduction of foreign paupers into the United States.

M. VAN BUREN.

WASHINGTON, *May 19, 1838.*

To the Senate of the United States:

I herewith transmit to the Senate the copy of a letter addressed to me on the 28th ultimo by the governor of Maine, inclosing several resolves of the legislature of that State, and claiming reimbursement from the General Government of certain moneys paid to Ebenezer S. Greely, John Baker, and others in compensation for losses and sufferings experienced by them respectively under circumstances more fully explained in his excellency's letter.

In the absence of any authority on the part of the Executive to satisfy these claims, they are now submitted to Congress for consideration; and I deem it proper at the same time, with reference to the observations contained in Governor Kent's note above mentioned, to communicate to the Senate copies of other papers connected with the subject of the northeastern boundary of the United States, which, with the documents already made public, will show the actual state of the negotiations with Great Britain on the general question.

M. VAN BUREN.

[The same message was sent to the House of Representatives.]

STATE OF MAINE, EXECUTIVE DEPARTMENT,
Augusta, April 28, 1838.

His Excellency MARTIN VAN BUREN,
President of the United States.

SIR: I have the honor to inclose to you a copy of a resolve* of the legislature of this State in favor of Ebenezer S. Greely, also a copy of a resolve* in favor of John Baker and others; and in compliance with the request of the legislature I ask of the Government of the United States a reimbursement of the several sums allowed thereby, which several sums have been paid by this State to the individuals named in the resolves.

The justice and propriety of granting this request, I can have no doubt, will be apparent to you and to Congress when the circumstances under which the allowances were made are called to mind.

Mr. Greely, acting as agent under a law of this State authorizing and directing a census to be taken in unincorporated places, was forcibly seized and imprisoned for several months, and then, without trial, released.

John Baker and his associates named in the other resolve suffered by imprisonment and otherwise for acting under a law of this State incorporating the town of Madawaska in 1831. The State of Maine has acknowledged by these and other resolves its sense of obligation to remunerate in the first instance these sufferers in its cause and to satisfy as far as it is able their claims upon its justice. But the wrongs by which they suffered were committed by a foreign power with whom we are now at peace. The State of Maine has no power to make war or authorize reprisals. She can only look to the General Government to assume the payment as an act of justice to a member of the Union under the provisions of the Constitution and to demand redress and remuneration from the authors of the wrong in the name of the United States.

A minute recapitulation of the facts upon which these resolves are founded is deemed entirely unnecessary and superfluous, as they have heretofore been communicated and are well known to the Executive and to Congress.

* Omitted.

Maine has suffered too many repetitions of similar attempts to prevent her from enjoying her rightful possessions and enforcing her just claims to feel indifferent on the subject, and we look with confidence to the General Government for protection and support. The amount of money, although considerable, is of comparatively small importance when contrasted with the principles involved and the effect which must result from an immediate and ready assumption of the liability on the part of the United States. Such an act would be highly gratifying to the people of this State as evidence that their just claims and rights are fully recognized by the United States, and that the strong arm of the Union will be stretched out for their protection in every lawful effort to maintain and enforce their claims, which they know and feel to be just and unimpeachable and which they are determined to maintain.

I trust I shall be pardoned for earnestly urging immediate action on the subject.

I had the honor to inclose to you, under date of the 28th of March last, a copy of my message to the legislature and of the resolves of the legislature of Maine in relation to the northeastern boundary, which I have no doubt have received and will receive all the attention the importance of the subjects therein discussed and acted on demands. You will perceive that in accordance with your wishes I communicated the proposition in relation to a conventional line of boundary, with the letter of Mr. Forsyth addressed to the executive of Maine. The views and wishes and determination of the executive and legislature, and I think I may safely add of the people, of Maine are fully and distinctly set forth in the documents referred to, communicated to you heretofore by me. The proposition was distinct and definite, and the answer is equally so, and I consider that it may be regarded as the fixed determination of Maine to consent to no proposition on our part to vary the treaty line, but to stand by that line as a definite, a practicable, and a fair one until its impracticability is demonstrated. It is needless for me to recapitulate the reasons upon which this determination is founded. I refer you to the documents before alluded to for my own views on this topic, sanctioned fully by the legislature. The duty devolving upon me by your request I have endeavored to discharge in a spirit of profound respect for the constituted officers of the General Government, and with a single eye to the interest and honor of the United States and of the State of Maine. The attitude assumed by Maine in relation to the survey of the line of the treaty of 1783 has doubtless attracted your attention. I feel it due to the State to say to you frankly and unequivocally that this position was taken deliberately and with a full consideration of all the circumstances of the case; but it was assumed in no spirit of defiance or resistance and with no design to embarrass the action of the General Government. Maine feels no desire to act alone or independently on this question. She knows and feels that it is a national question, and that it is the right and duty of the General Government to move forward in effecting the object proposed.

I feel fully warranted in saying that Maine does not intend by this expression of her determination to run the line in a certain contingency to waive in the least degree her well-founded claim upon the General Government to run, mark, and establish it. On the contrary, she will most reluctantly yield the hope she now so strongly feels that it is the intention of that Government to relieve her from the necessity of throwing herself upon her own resources to assert and defend her most unquestionable right. The wish of this State is that the first act should be to run the line of the treaty of 1783 to ascertain the facts in relation to the topography of the country and the exact spot where the northwest angle of Nova Scotia may be found according to our construction of the treaty language, and to place suitable monuments along the whole line. Such a survey would not settle or determine any rights, but it would express and declare our views and intentions. Such a survey is not a warlike or offensive movement, and can not justly give offense to the other party in the controversy. It is the unquestionable right of litigants in a court of justice to make explorations of land in dispute, and if either party declines a joint survey it may be made *ex parte*, and surely the United States have never so far yielded the actual possession to Great Britain as to preclude the right on our part to ascertain for ourselves the absolute facts and to mark out the limits of our claim and our alleged right. This act Maine asks, and asks earnestly, the General Government to perform without delay. Such an assumption of the controversy on the part of the United States would be to Maine an assurance that her rights were duly regarded, and would be steadily and perseveringly maintained. We want the name and the authority of the United States, and there can be no doubt that an act emanating from that source would be regarded by those interested on both sides as of more importance than any act of an individual State. So far, then, from any indifference on the part of Maine as to the action of the General Government, or any desire to be driven to assume the performance of the duty alluded to, she looks with intense anxiety and confident hope to be relieved from this position. She believes it is alike due to the honor of the United States and the rights of Maine that the General Government should go forward in the work, and that there is less to apprehend in the result from such a course than any other. But Maine feels that the time for decisive action has come, that she can not be satisfied to have the claim to absolute and exclusive jurisdiction of a large part of her territory longer tolerated and acquiesced in. She knows that it rightfully belongs to her jurisdiction, that it is hers by a clear, perfect, and honest title—as clear, as perfect, and rightful as her title to any portion of the State—and she can not consent to have this title impaired or weakened by bold encroachments and unscrupulous demands. She can not consent that a title transmitted by the fathers of the Revolution shall be destroyed or defeated by acquiescence in the adverse occupation of a foreign state, and that what was once fairly yielded shall be reclaimed in utter defiance of a solemn deed of cession. I am confident I am not mistaken in stating that the legislature of Maine considered the question as fairly and plainly before the National Government, and that if the present session of Congress should close with a denial or postponement of the proposed survey and no commission should be created by the Executive, as contemplated in the resolution referred to, we should have a right and be bound to regard such a delay or refusal as evidence of an indisposition on the part of the General Government to accede to our expressed views and wishes, and a denial of justice, and that Maine in that event owed it to herself to cause the survey to be made under her own authority. The duty of the executive of Maine is plainly pointed out and made imperative and absolute by the resolves of the legislature, and I certainly can not hesitate, so far as I have the means and power, to execute their declared will.

The people of Maine, sir, are not desirous of conflict or war. Both in their habits and their principles they love and wish for peace and quiet within their borders. They are not ambitious to win laurels or to acquire military glory by waging war with their neighbors, and least of all are they desirous of a *border* warfare, which may be the means of sacrificing human life and engendering ill will and bad passions, without bringing the controversy to a conclusion. They are scattered over our thousand hills, engaged in their quiet and peaceful labors, and it is the first wish of their hearts to live peaceably with all men and all nations. They have no anxiety to extend our limits or to gain territory by conquest, but there is a firm and determined spirit in this people which can not brook insult and will not submit to intentional injury. "They know their rights, and knowing dare maintain them" with calm determination and deliberate purpose, and they appeal with unshrinking confidence to their sister States and to the Government which binds them together for effective support in this their purpose.

The crisis, as we believe, demands firm and decided language and the expression of a determined design. Maine has never refused to acquiesce in any fair and honorable mode of fixing the line *according to the treaty of 1783*. I have no doubt (but upon this point I speak according to my individual belief) that the mode proposed by Great Britain of establishing the treaty line upon the face of the earth by a commission composed of impartial and scientific men, to be selected by a friendly power, would be satisfactory and acquiesced in by this State, but that we should neither ask nor agree that any preliminary points should be yielded by either party. We should only ask that the treaty should be placed in their hands with directions to ascertain and run and fix the line according to its plain language and obvious meaning.

Maine can never consent, as I apprehend, to yield the main points of the case and then refer it to enable the judges to divide the subject-matter of the controversy.

We feel that we now stand on the high vantage ground of truth and justice, and that it can not be that any nation professing to act on the principles of right and equity can stand up before the civilized world and contest with unyielding pertinacity our claim. We have too much respect for the nation from which we descended to believe that she will sully her reputation by such persevering resistance.

I am conscious that the language and style of this communication are unusual and probably undiplomatic; that there is more of the fervor of feeling and the plain language of direct appeal than is usual in such papers; but it is a subject of such vast importance to the State whose interests have been in part intrusted to me and whose organ I am that I can not speak in measured terms or indefinite language. On this subject we have no ulterior views and no concealed objects. Our plans and our policy are open and exposed to the view of all men. Maine has nothing in either to conceal or disguise. She plainly and distinctly asks for specific and definite action. In performing what I conceive to be my duty I have been actuated by entire respect toward the General Government and by the single desire to explain and enforce as well as I was able our wishes and our rights. I can only add that we trust the General Government will assume the performance of the act specified in the resolution and relieve Maine from the necessity of independent action.

With great respect, I have the honor to be, your most obedient servant,

EDWARD KENT.

DEPARTMENT OF STATE,
Washington, April 27, 1838.

HENRY S. FOX, Esq., etc.:

The undersigned, Secretary of State of the United States, has the honor, by the directions of the President, to communicate to Mr. Fox, Her Britannic Majesty's envoy extraordinary and minister plenipotentiary, the result of the application of the General Government to the State of Maine on the subject of the northeastern boundary line and the resolution which the President has formed upon a careful consideration thereof. By the accompanying papers,* received from the executive of Maine, Mr. Fox will perceive that Maine declines to give a consent to the negotiation for a conventional boundary, is disinclined to the reference of the points in dispute to a new arbitration, but is yet firmly persuaded that the line described in the treaty of 1783 can be found and traced whenever the Governments of the United States and Great Britain shall proceed to make the requisite investigations with a predisposition to effect that very desirable object. Confidently relying, as the President does, upon the assurances frequently repeated by the British Government of the earnest desire to reach that result if it is practicable, he has instructed the undersigned to announce to Mr. Fox the willingness of this Government to enter into an arrangement with Great Britain for the establishment of a joint commission of survey and exploration upon the basis of the original American proposition and the modifications offered by Her Majesty's Government.

The Secretary of State is therefore authorized to invite Mr. Fox to a conference upon the subject at as early a day as his convenience will permit, and the

*Omitted.

undersigned will be immediately furnished with a requisite full power by the President to conclude a convention embracing that object if Her Majesty's minister is duly empowered to proceed to the negotiation of it on the part of Great Britain.

The undersigned avails himself of this occasion to renew to Mr. Fox the expression of his distinguished consideration.

JOHN FORSYTH.

WASHINGTON, *May 1, 1838.*

Hon. JOHN FORSYTH, etc.

SIR: I have the honor to acknowledge the receipt of your official note of the 27th ultimo, in which you inclose to me a communication received by the Federal Government from the executive of Maine upon the subject of the northeastern boundary line, and in which you inform me that the President is willing to enter into an arrangement with Her Majesty's Government for the establishment of a joint commission of survey and exploration upon the basis of the original American proposition and of the modifications offered by Her Majesty's Government, as communicated to you in my note of the 10th of January last, and you invite me to a conference for the purpose of negotiating a convention that shall embrace the above object if I am duly empowered by my Government to proceed to such negotiation.

I have the honor to state to you in reply that my actual instructions were fulfilled by the delivery of the communication which I addressed to you on the 10th of January, and that I am not at present provided with full powers for negotiating the proposed convention. I will forthwith, however, transmit to Her Majesty's Government the note which I have had the honor to receive from you in order that such fresh instructions may be furnished to me or such other steps taken as the present situation of the question may appear to Her Majesty's Government to require.

I avail myself of this occasion to renew to you the assurance of my high respect and consideration.

H. S. FOX.

DEPARTMENT OF STATE,
Washington, May 8, 1838.

His Excellency EDWARD KENT,
Governor of Maine.

SIR: I have the honor to acknowledge the receipt on the 22d ultimo of the communication addressed to this Department by your excellency on the 28th of March last, transmitting a printed copy of your message of the 14th of the same month to the legislature of Maine, together with certain resolves passed by that body, in relation to the northeastern boundary of the State.

Although the answer thus given to the application made to you, by direction of the President, under date of the 1st of March last, to ascertain the sense of the State of Maine in regard to a conventional line of boundary may be regarded as conclusive, I still deem it proper, with reference to your excellency's message, to mark a misconception which appears to have existed on your part when communicating to the legislature the letter and documents received from this Department. This is done with the greater freedom since the frank and liberal manner in which your excellency invited the attention of that body to the subject is highly appreciated by the President. The question therein presented for consideration was not, as your excellency supposed, whether the State of Maine should "take the lead in abandoning the treaty and volunteer propositions for a conventional line," but simply whether the government of Maine would consent that the General Government should entertain a direct negotiation with the British Government for a conventional line of boundary on the northeastern frontier of the United States. Had that consent been given it would have been reasonable to expect the proposition of a line from Great Britain, as it was that power which particularly desired the resort to that mode of settling the controversy. It was also the intention of the President so to arrange the negotiation that the approbation of Maine to the boundary line agreed upon should have been secured. It was with this view that in the application to the State of Maine for its assent to a negotiation for a conventional line express reference was made to such conditions as she might think proper to prescribe. To all such as were, in the opinion of the President, required by a proper regard for the security of Maine and consistent with the Constitution he would have yielded a ready assent. Of that character was he disposed to regard a condition that in a negotiation for the final establishment of a new line, with power on the part of the negotiators to stipulate for the cession or exchange of territory as the interests and convenience of the parties might be found to require, the State of Maine should be represented by commissioners of her own selection and that their previous assent should be requisite to make any treaty containing such stipulation binding upon her.

These suggestions are not now made as matter of complaint at the decision which the State of Maine has come to on a matter in which she was at perfect liberty to pursue the course she has adopted, but in justice to the views of the President in making the application.

I am instructed to announce to your excellency that by direction of the President, upon due consideration of the result of the late application of the General Government to the State of Maine on the subject of the northeastern boundary and in accordance with the expressed wishes of her legislature, I have informed Mr. Fox of the willingness of this Government to enter into an arrangement with that of Great Britain for the establishment of a joint commission of survey and exploration upon the basis of the original American proposition and the modifications offered by Her Majesty's Government, and to apprise you that Mr. Fox, being at present unprovided with full powers for negotiating the proposed convention, has transmitted my communication to his Government in order that such fresh instructions may be furnished to him or such other steps taken as may be deemed expedient on its part.

I have the honor to be, with great respect, your excellency's obedient servant,

JOHN FORSYTH.

WASHINGTON, *May 21, 1838.*

To the Senate and House of Representatives of the United States:

The accompanying copy of a communication addressed by the Secretary of War to the Cherokee delegation is submitted to Congress in order that such measures may be adopted as are required to carry into effect the benevolent intentions of the Government toward the Cherokee Nation, and which it is hoped will induce them to remove peaceably and contentedly to their new homes in the West.

M. VAN BUREN.

WASHINGTON, *May 24, 1838.*

To the House of Representatives of the United States:

I herewith submit a report from the Secretary of the Treasury, explanatory of the manner in which extracts from certain newspapers relating to the introduction of foreign paupers into this country, and the steps taken to prevent it, became connected with his communication to me on that subject, accompanying my message of the 11th instant. Sensible that those extracts are of a character which would, if attention had been directed to them, have prevented their transmission to the House, I request permission to withdraw them.

M. VAN BUREN.

WASHINGTON, *May 30, 1838.*
To the House of Representatives of the United States:

I herewith transmit to the House of Representatives a report from the Secretary of State, in answer to their resolution of the 28th instant, relative to the claim* in the case of the ship *Mary* and cargo, of Baltimore.

M. VAN BUREN.

WASHINGTON, *May 31, 1838.*
To the House of Representatives of the United States:

In compliance with the resolution of the House of Representatives of the 28th instant, regarding the annexation of the Republic of Texas to the United States, I transmit a report from the Secretary of State, to whom the resolution was referred.

M. VAN BUREN.

WASHINGTON, *June 1, 1838.*
To the Senate of the United States:

Negotiations have been opened with the Osage and Delaware Indians, in compliance with the resolution of the Senate of the 19th of January last, for the relinquishment of certain school lands secured to them by treaty. These relinquishments have been obtained on the terms authorized by the resolution, and copies of them are herewith transmitted for the information of the Senate.

M. VAN BUREN.

WASHINGTON, *June 4, 1838.*
To the House of Representatives of the United States:

I transmit herewith to the House of Representatives a report from the Secretary of State, with accompanying papers, relating to the claim of the orphan children of Peter Shackerly,† in answer to their resolution of the 28th ultimo.

M. VAN BUREN.

---

*Against the Government of Holland.

† Killed on board of the United States ship *Chesapeake* when attacked by the British ship of war *Leopard*, June 22, 1807.

WASHINGTON, *June 6, 1838.*

To the House of Representatives of the United States:

In compliance with the resolution of the 4th instant, calling for any communication received from the governors of the States of Georgia, North Carolina, Tennessee, and Alabama in reference to the proposed modification of the Cherokee treaty of 1835, I herewith inclose a report of the Secretary of War, accompanied by a copy of a letter addressed by him to the governor of Georgia and of his reply thereto. As stated by the Secretary, no communication on that subject has been received from either of the other executives mentioned.

M. VAN BUREN.

WASHINGTON, *June 7, 1838.*

To the House of Representatives of the United States:

I transmit to the House of Representatives an account against the United States, presented by Heman Cady, of Plattsburg, in the State of New York, for services alleged to have been rendered as deputy marshal for the northern district of New York from the 20th December, 1837, to the 9th February, 1838, by direction of the attorney and marshal of the United States for that district, in endeavoring to prevent the arming and enlisting of men for the invasion of Canada. I also transmit certain documents which were exhibited in support of the said account. I recommend to the consideration of Congress the expediency of an appropriation for the payment of this claim and of some general provision for the liquidation and payment of others which may be expected to be presented hereafter for services of a similar character rendered before and after the passage of the act of the 20th March last, for preserving the neutrality of the United States on the northern frontier, which act imposes important duties upon the marshals and other civil officers, but omits to provide for their remuneration or for the reimbursement of their expenses.

M. VAN BUREN.

To the Senate of the United States: WASHINGTON, *June 7, 1838.*

Having received satisfactory assurances from the Government of Ecuador of its desire to negotiate a treaty of commerce on the most liberal principles in place of the expired treaty made with the Republic of Colombia, heretofore regulating our intercourse with Ecuador, it is my design to give the requisite authority for that purpose to the chargé d'affaires of the United States about to be appointed for Peru, with instructions to stop in Ecuador on his way to Lima as the agent of the United States to accomplish that object. The only additional charges to be incurred will be the expense of his journey from Panama to Quito, and from thence to the place of embarkation for Lima, to be paid out of the foreign-intercourse fund. I make this communication to the Senate that an opportunity may be afforded for the expression of an opinion, if it shall be deemed necessary, on the exercise of such a power by the Executive without applying to the Senate for its approbation and consent. In debate it has been sometimes asserted that this power, frequently exercised without question or complaint, and leading to no practical evil, as no arrangement made under such circumstances can be obligatory upon the United States without being submitted to the approbation of the Senate, is an encroachment upon its rightful authority. It appears to have been considered that the annual appropriation of a gross sum for the expenses of foreign intercourse is intended, among other objects, to provide for the cost of such agencies, and that the authority granted is the same as that frequently given to the Secretary of State to form treaties with the representatives or agents of foreign governments, upon the granting of which the Senate never have been consulted.

Desiring in this and in all other instances to act with the most cautious respect to the claims of other branches of the Government, I bring this subject to the notice of the Senate that if it shall be deemed proper to raise any question it may be discussed and decided before and not after the power shall have been exercised.

M. VAN BUREN.

WASHINGTON CITY, *June 11, 1838.*

To the Senate of the United States:

I submit herewith, for consideration and action, a communication from the Secretary of War and the treaty with the Otoe, Missouria, and Omaha Indians therein referred to.

M. VAN BUREN.

WASHINGTON, *June 20, 1838.*

To the House of Representatives of the United States:

I transmit, in compliance with a resolution of the House of Representatives of the 11th instant, reports from the Secretaries of State, Treasury, and War, with the documents referred to by them respectively. It will be seen that the outrage committed on the steamboat *Sir Robert Peel*, under the British flag, within the waters of the United States, and on the steamboat *Telegraph*, under the American flag, at Brockville, in Upper Canada, have not been followed by any demand by either Government on the other for redress. These acts have been so far treated on each side as criminal offenses committed within the jurisdiction of tribunals competent to inquire into the facts and to punish the persons concerned in them. Investigations have been made, some of the individuals inculpated have been arrested, and prosecutions are in progress, the result of which can not be doubted. The excited state of public feeling on the borders of Canada on both sides of the line has occasioned the most painful anxiety to this Government. ·Every effort has been and will be made to prevent the success of the design, apparently formed and in the course of execution by Canadians who have found a refuge within the territory, aided by a few reckless persons of our own country, to involve the nation in a war with a neighboring and friendly power. Such design can not succeed while the two Governments appreciate and confidently rely upon the good faith of each other in the performance of their respective duties. With a fixed determination to use all the means in my power to put a speedy and satisfactory termination to these border troubles, I have the most confident assurances of the cordial cooperation of the British authorities, at home and in the North American possessions, in the accomplishment of a purpose so sincerely and earnestly desired by the Governments and people both of the United States and Great Britain.

M. VAN BUREN.

WASHINGTON, *June 28, 1838.*

To the House of Representatives of the United States:

In compliance with a resolution passed by the House of Representatives on the 23d instant, in respect to the new Treasury building, I submit the inclosed report from the commissioners charged with a general superintendence of the work, and which, with the documents annexed, is believed to contain all the information desired.

M. VAN BUREN.

WASHINGTON, *June 28, 1838.*

To the Senate of the United States:

I nominate Lieutenant-Colonel Thayer, of the Corps of Engineers, for the brevet of colonel in the Army, agreeably to the recommendation of the Secretary of War.

M. VAN BUREN.

WAR DEPARTMENT, *June 28, 1838.*

The PRESIDENT OF THE UNITED STATES.

SIR: In submitting the name of Brevet Lieutenant-Colonel S. Thayer, of the Corps of Engineers, for the brevet of colonel for ten years' faithful service in one grade it may be proper to state the circumstances of his case.

When the law of 1812 regulating brevets was repealed by the act of June 30, 1834, all the officers of the Army who were known to be entitled to the ordinary brevet promotion for ten years' faithful service in one grade received on that day, by and with the advice and consent of the Senate, the brevet promotion to which they were respectively entitled. The regulation which governed the subject under the law had reference only to service with regularly organized bodies of troops, and valid claims arising under it were generally known and easily understood at the Adjutant-General's Office. If incidental cases occurred for which the written regulations could not provide the rule, although equally valid, such, nevertheless, may not in every instance have been known at the War Department until specially represented by the party interested. The case of Brevet Lieutenant-Colonel Thayer happened to be one of those incidental claims, and as soon as it was submitted for consideration its validity was clearly seen and acknowledged. Had it been submitted to the Department when the list was made out in June, 1834, it may not be doubted that this highly meritorious and deserving officer would at the time have received the brevet of colonel for "having served faithfully as brevet lieutenant-colonel and performed the appropriate duties of that grade for ten years," which, it may be seen, was due more than *a year before the passage of the act repealing the law.*

In presenting now this deferred case for your favorable consideration justice requires that I should advert to the valuable services rendered to the Army and the country by Lieutenant-Colonel Thayer as Superintendent of the Military Academy at West Point. In 1817 he found that institution defective in all its branches, and without order; in 1833 he left it established upon a basis alike honorable to himself and useful to the nation. These meritorious services constitute *another* claim which entitles this officer to the notice of the Government, and as they come fairly within one of the conditions of the law which yet open the way to brevet promotion, the incentive it provides is fully realized by the services that have been rendered.

I am, sir, with great respect, your obedient servant,

J. R. POINSETT.

WASHINGTON, *July 2, 1838.*

To the House of Representatives of the United States:

I herewith transmit to the House of Representatives a report* from the Secretary of State, together with the documents therein referred to in answer to their resolution of the 28th of May last.

M. VAN BUREN.

WASHINGTON, *July 3, 1838.*

To the House of Representatives of the United States:

I transmit a report from the War Department, in relation to the investigations of the allegations of fraud committed on the Creek Indians in the sales of their reservations authorized by the resolution of that body of the 1st of July, 1836.

M. VAN BUREN.

WASHINGTON, *July 4, 1838.*

To the House of Representatives of the United States:

In further compliance with the resolution of the House of Representatives of the 21st of March last, requesting papers on the subject of the relations between the United States and Mexico, I transmit a report from the Secretary of State, to whom the resolution was referred, supplementary to the report of that officer communicated with my message to the House of Representatives of the 27th of April last.

M. VAN BUREN.

WASHINGTON, *July 7, 1838.*

The PRESIDENT OF THE SENATE.

SIR: In conformity with the resolution of the Senate, I transmit herewith the report of Major-General Jesup,† together with a letter from the Secretary of War.

M. VAN BUREN.

---

* Transmitting reports of the commissioners appointed under the sixth and seventh articles of the treaty of Ghent to ascertain and fix the boundary between the United States and the British possessions in North America, etc.

† Relating to operations while commanding the army in Florida.

PROCLAMATIONS.

[From Statutes at Large (Little, Brown & Co.), Vol. XI, p. 784.]

BY THE PRESIDENT OF THE UNITED STATES OF AMERICA.

A PROCLAMATION.

Whereas information having been received of a dangerous excitement on the northern frontier of the United States in consequence of the civil war begun in Canada, and instructions having been given to the United States officers on that frontier and applications having been made to the governors of the adjoining States to prevent any unlawful interference on the part of our citizens in the contest unfortunately commenced in the British Provinces, additional information has just been received that, notwithstanding the proclamations of the governors of the States of New York and Vermont exhorting their citizens to refrain from any unlawful acts within the territory of the United States, and notwithstanding the presence of the civil officers of the United States, who by my directions have visited the scenes of commotion with a view of impressing the citizens with a proper sense of their duty, the excitement, instead of being appeased, is every day increasing in degree; that arms and munitions of war and other supplies have been procured by the insurgents in the United States; that a military force, consisting in part, at least, of citizens of the United States, had been actually organized, had congregated at Navy Island, and were still in arms under the command of a citizen of the United States, and that they were constantly receiving accessions and aid:

Now, therefore, to the end that the authority of the laws may be maintained and the faith of treaties observed, I, Martin Van Buren, do most earnestly exhort all citizens of the United States who have thus violated their duties to return peaceably to their respective homes; and I hereby warn them that any persons who shall compromit the neutrality of this Government by interfering in an unlawful manner with the affairs of the neighboring British Provinces will render themselves liable to arrest and punishment under the laws of the United States, which will be rigidly enforced; and, also, that they will receive no aid or countenance from their Government, into whatever difficulties they may be thrown by the violation of the laws of their country and the territory of a neighboring and friendly nation.

Given under my hand, at the city of Washington, the 5th day of January, A. D. 1838, and the sixty-second of the Independence of the United States.

[SEAL.]

M. VAN BUREN.

By the President:
JOHN FORSYTH,
    Secretary of State.

[From Statutes at Large (Little, Brown & Co.), Vol. XI, p. 785.]

BY THE PRESIDENT OF THE UNITED STATES OF AMERICA.

A PROCLAMATION.

Whereas there is too much reason to believe that citizens of the United States, in disregard to the solemn warning heretofore given to them by the proclamations issued by the Executive of the General Government and by some of the governors of the States, have combined to disturb the peace of the dominions of a neighboring and friendly nation; and

Whereas information has been given to me, derived from official and other sources, that many citizens in different parts of the United States are associated or associating for the same purpose; and

Whereas disturbances have actually broken out anew in different parts of the two Canadas; and

Whereas a hostile invasion has been made by citizens of the United States, in conjunction with Canadians and others, who, after forcibly seizing upon the property of their peaceful neighbor for the purpose of effecting their unlawful designs, are now in arms against the authorities of Canada, in perfect disregard of their obligations as American citizens and of the obligations of the Government of their country to foreign nations:

Now, therefore, I have thought it necessary and proper to issue this proclamation, calling upon every citizen of the United States neither to give countenance nor encouragement of any kind to those who have thus forfeited their claim to the protection of their country; upon those misguided or deluded persons who are engaged in them to abandon projects dangerous to their own country, fatal to those whom they profess a desire to relieve, impracticable of execution without foreign aid, which they can not rationally expect to obtain, and giving rise to imputations (however unfounded) upon the honor and good faith of their own Government; upon every officer, civil or military, and upon every citizen, by the veneration due by all freemen to the laws which they have assisted to enact for their own government, by his regard for the honor and reputation of his country, by his love of order and respect for the sacred code of laws by which national intercourse is regulated, to use every effort in his power to arrest for trial and punishment every offender against the laws providing for the performance of our obligations to the other powers of the world. And I hereby warn all those who have engaged in these criminal enterprises, if persisted in, that, whatever may be the condition to which they may be reduced, they must not expect the interference of this Government in any form on their behalf, but will be left, reproached by every virtuous fellow-citizen, to be dealt with according to the policy and justice of that Government whose dominions they have, in defiance of the known wishes of their own Government and without the shadow of justification or excuse, nefariously invaded.

Given under my hand, at the city of Washington, the 21st day of November, A. D. 1838, and the sixty-third of the Independence of the United States.

[SEAL.]

M. VAN BUREN.

By the President:
JOHN FORSYTH,
    Secretary of State.

SECOND ANNUAL MESSAGE.

WASHINGTON, *December 3, 1838.*

Fellow-Citizens of the Senate and House of Representatives:

I congratulate you on the favorable circumstances in the condition of our country under which you reassemble for the performance of your official duties. Though the anticipations of an abundant harvest have not everywhere been realized, yet on the whole the labors of the husbandman are rewarded with a bountiful return; industry prospers in its various channels of business and enterprise; general health again prevails through our vast diversity of climate; nothing threatens from abroad the continuance of external peace; nor has anything at home impaired the strength of those fraternal and domestic ties which constitute the only guaranty to the success and permanency of our happy Union, and which, formed in the hour of peril, have hitherto been honorably sustained through every vicissitude in our national affairs. These blessings, which evince the care and beneficence of Providence, call for our devout and fervent gratitude.

We have not less reason to be grateful for other bounties bestowed by the same munificent hand, and more exclusively our own.

The present year closes the first half century of our Federal institutions, and our system, differing from all others in the acknowledged practical and unlimited operation which it has for so long a period given to the sovereignty of the people, has now been fully tested by experience.

The Constitution devised by our forefathers as the framework and bond of that system, then untried, has become a settled form of government; not only preserving and protecting the great principles upon which it was founded, but wonderfully promoting individual happiness and private interests. Though subject to change and entire revocation whenever deemed inadequate to all these purposes, yet such is the wisdom of its construction and so stable has been the public sentiment that it remains unaltered except in matters of detail comparatively unimportant. It has proved amply sufficient for the various emergencies incident to our condition as a nation. A formidable foreign war; agitating collisions between domestic, and in some respects rival, sovereignties; temptations to interfere in the intestine commotions of neighboring countries; the dangerous influences that arise in periods of excessive prosperity, and the antirepublican tendencies of associated wealth—these, with other trials not less formidable, have all been encountered, and thus far successfully resisted.

It was reserved for the American Union to test the advantages of a government entirely dependent on the continual exercise of the popular will, and our experience has shown that it is as beneficent in practice as it is just in theory. Each successive change made in our local institutions has contributed to extend the right of suffrage, has increased the direct influence of the mass of the community, given greater freedom to individual exertion, and restricted more and more the powers of Government; yet the intelligence, prudence, and patriotism of the people have kept pace with this augmented responsibility. In no country has education been so widely diffused. Domestic peace has nowhere so largely reigned. The close bonds of social intercourse have in no instance prevailed with such harmony over a space so vast. All forms of religion have united for the first time to diffuse charity and piety, because for the first time in the history of nations all have been totally untrammeled and absolutely free. The deepest recesses of the wilderness have been penetrated; yet instead of the rudeness in the social condition consequent upon such adventures elsewhere, numerous communities have sprung up, already unrivaled in prosperity, general intelligence, internal tranquillity, and the wisdom of their political institutions. Internal improvement, the fruit of individual enterprise, fostered by the protection of the States, has added new links to the Confederation and fresh rewards to provident industry. Doubtful questions of domestic policy have been quietly settled by mutual forbearance, and agriculture, commerce, and manufactures minister to each other. Taxation and public debt, the burdens which bear so heavily upon all other countries, have pressed with comparative lightness upon us. Without one entangling alliance, our friendship is prized by every nation, and the rights of our citizens are everywhere respected, because they are known to be guarded by a united, sensitive, and watchful people.

To this practical operation of our institutions, so evident and successful, we owe that increased attachment to them which is among the most cheering exhibitions of popular sentiment and will prove their best security in time to come against foreign or domestic assault.

This review of the results of our institutions for half a century, without exciting a spirit of vain exultation, should serve to impress upon us the great principles from which they have sprung—constant and direct supervision by the people over every public measure. strict forbearance on the part of the Government from exercising any doubtful or disputed powers, and a cautious abstinence from all interference with concerns which properly belong and are best left to State regulations and individual enterprise.

Full information of the state of our foreign affairs having been recently on different occasions submitted to Congress, I deem it necessary now to bring to your notice only such events as have subsequently occurred or are of such importance as to require particular attention.

The most amicable dispositions continue to be exhibited by all the nations with whom the Government and citizens of the United States have an habitual intercourse. At the date of my last annual message Mexico was the only nation which could not be included in so gratifying a reference to our foreign relations.

I am happy to be now able to inform you that an advance has been made toward the adjustment of our differences with that Republic and the restoration of the customary good feeling between the two nations. This important change has been effected by conciliatory negotiations that have resulted in the conclusion of a treaty between the two Governments, which, when ratified, will refer to the arbitrament of a friendly power all the subjects of controversy between us growing out of injuries to individuals. There is at present also reason to believe that an equitable settlement of all disputed points will be attained without further difficulty or unnecessary delay, and thus authorize the free resumption of diplomatic intercourse with our sister Republic.

With respect to the northeastern boundary of the United States, no official correspondence between this Government and that of Great Britain has passed since that communicated to Congress toward the close of their last session. The offer to negotiate a convention for the appointment of a joint commission of survey and exploration I am, however, assured will be met by Her Majesty's Government in a conciliatory and friendly spirit, and instructions to enable the British minister here to conclude such an arrangement will be transmitted to him without needless delay. It is hoped and expected that these instructions will be of a liberal character, and that this negotiation, if successful, will prove to be an important step toward the satisfactory and final adjustment of the controversy.

I had hoped that the respect for the laws and regard for the peace and honor of their own country which have ever characterized the citizens of the United States would have prevented any portion of them from using any means to promote insurrection in the territory of a power with which we are at peace, and with which the United States are desirous of maintaining the most friendly relations. I regret deeply, however, to be obliged to inform you that this has not been the case. Information has been given to me, derived from official and other sources, that many citizens of the United States have associated together to make hostile incursions from our territory into Canada and to aid and abet insurrection there, in violation of the obligations and laws of the United States and in open disregard of their own duties as citizens. This information has been in part confirmed by a hostile invasion actually made by citizens of the United States, in conjunction with Canadians and others, and accompanied by a forcible seizure of the property of our citizens and an application thereof to the prosecution of military operations against the authorities and people of Canada.

The results of these criminal assaults upon the peace and order of a neighboring country have been, as was to be expected, fatally destructive to the misguided or deluded persons engaged in them and highly injurious to those in whose behalf they are professed to have been undertaken. The authorities in Canada, from intelligence received of such intended movements among our citizens, have felt themselves obliged to take precautionary measures against them; have actually embodied the militia and assumed an attitude to repel the invasion to which they believed the colonies were exposed from the United States. A state of feeling on both sides of the frontier has thus been produced which called for prompt and vigorous interference. If an insurrection existed in Canada, the amicable dispositions of the United States toward Great Britain, as well as their duty to themselves, would lead them to maintain a strict neutrality and to restrain their citizens from all violations of the laws which have been passed for its enforcement. But this Government recognizes a still higher obligation to repress all attempts on the part of its citizens to disturb the peace of a country where order prevails or has been reestablished. Depredations by our citizens upon nations at peace with the United States, or combinations for committing them, have at all times been regarded by the American Government and people with the greatest abhorrence. Military incursions by our citizens into countries so situated, and the commission of acts of violence on the members thereof, in order to effect a change in their government, or under any pretext whatever, have from the commencement of our Government been held equally criminal on the part of those engaged in them, and as much deserving of punishment as would be the disturbance of the public peace by the perpetration of similar acts within our own territory.

By no country or persons have these invaluable principles of international law—principles the strict observance of which is so indispensable to the preservation of social order in the world—been more earnestly cherished or sacredly respected than by those great and good men who first declared and finally established the independence of our own country. They promulgated and maintained them at an early and critical period in our history; they were subsequently embodied in legislative enactments of a highly penal character, the faithful enforcement of which has hitherto been, and will, I trust, always continue to be, regarded as a duty inseparably associated with the maintenance of our national honor. That the people of the United States should feel an interest in the spread of political institutions as free as they regard their own to be is natural, nor can a sincere solicitude for the success of all those who are at any time in good faith struggling for their acquisition be imputed to our citizens as a crime. With the entire freedom of opinion and an undisguised expression thereof on their part the Government has neither the right nor, I trust, the disposition to interfere. But whether the interest or the honor of the United States requires that they should be made a party to any such struggle, and by inevitable consequence to the war which is waged in its support, is a question which by our Constitution is wisely left to Congress alone to decide. It is by the laws already made criminal in our citizens to embarrass or anticipate that decision by unauthorized military operations on their part. Offenses of this character, in addition to their criminality as violations of the laws of our country, have a direct tendency to draw down upon our own citizens at large the multiplied evils of a foreign war and expose to injurious imputations the good faith and honor of the country. As such they deserve to be put down with promptitude and decision. I can not be mistaken, I am confident, in counting on the cordial and general concurrence of our fellow-citizens in this sentiment. A copy of the proclamation which I have felt it my duty to issue is herewith communicated. I can not but hope that the good sense and patriotism, the regard for the honor and reputation of their country, the respect for the laws which they have themselves enacted for their own government, and the love of order for which the mass of our people have been so long and so justly distinguished will deter the comparatively few who are engaged in them from a further prosecution of such desperate enterprises. In the meantime the existing laws have been and will continue to be faithfully executed, and every effort will be made to carry them out in their full extent. Whether they are sufficient or not to meet the actual state of things on the Canadian frontier it is for Congress to decide.

It will appear from the correspondence herewith submitted that the Government of Russia declines a renewal of the fourth article of the convention of April, 1824, between the United States and His Imperial Majesty, by the third article of which it is agreed that ''hereafter there shall not be formed by the citizens of the United States or under the authority of the said States any establishment upon the northwest coast of America, nor in any of the islands adjacent, to the north of 54° 40' of north latitude, and that in the same manner there shall be none formed by Russian subjects or under the authority of Russia south of the same parallel;'' and by the fourth article, ''that during a term of ten years, counting from the signature of the present convention, the ships of both powers, or which belong to their citizens or subjects, respectively, may reciprocally frequent, without any hindrance whatever, the interior seas, gulfs, harbors, and creeks upon the coast mentioned in the preceding article, for the purpose of fishing and trading with the natives of the country.'' The reasons assigned for declining to renew the provisions of this article are, briefly, that the only use made by our citizens of the privileges it secures to them has been to supply the Indians with spirituous liquors, ammunition, and firearms; that this traffic has been excluded from the Russian trade; and as the supplies furnished from the United States are injurious to the Russian establishments on the northwest coast and calculated to produce complaints between the two Governments, His Imperial Majesty thinks it for the interest of both countries not to accede to the proposition made by the American Government for the renewal of the article last referred to.

The correspondence herewith communicated will show the grounds upon which we contend that the citizens of the United States have, independent of the provisions of the convention of 1824, a right to trade with the natives upon the coast in question at unoccupied places, liable, however, it is admitted, to be at any time extinguished by the creation of Russian establishments at such points. This right is denied by the Russian Government, which asserts that by the operation of the treaty of 1824 each party agreed to waive the general right to land on the vacant coasts on the respective sides of the degree of latitude referred to, and accepted in lieu thereof the mutual privileges mentioned in the fourth article. The capital and tonnage employed by our citizens in their trade with the northwest coast of America will, perhaps, on adverting to the official statements of the commerce and navigation of the United States for the last few years, be deemed too inconsiderable in amount to attract much attention; yet the subject may in other respects deserve the careful consideration of Congress.

I regret to state that the blockade of the principal ports on the eastern coast of Mexico, which, in consequence of differences between that Republic and France, was instituted in May last, unfortunately still continues, enforced by a competent French naval armament, and is necessarily embarrassing to our own trade in the Gulf, in common with that of other nations. Every disposition, however, is believed to exist on the part of the French Government to render this measure as little onerous as practicable to the interests of the citizens of the United States and to those of neutral commerce, and it is to be hoped that an early settlement of the difficulties between France and Mexico will soon reestablish the harmonious relations formerly subsisting between them and again open the ports of that Republic to the vessels of all friendly nations.

A convention for marking that part of the boundary between the United States and the Republic of Texas which extends from the mouth of the Sabine to the Red River was concluded and signed at this city on the 25th of April last. It has since been ratified by both Governments, and seasonable measures will be taken to carry it into effect on the part of the United States.

The application of that Republic for admission into this Union, made in August, 1837, and which was declined for reasons already made known to you, has been formally withdrawn, as will appear from the accompanying copy of the note of the minister plenipotentiary of Texas, which was presented to the Secretary of State on the occasion of the exchange of the ratifications of the convention above mentioned.

Copies of the convention with Texas, of a commercial treaty concluded with the King of Greece, and of a similar treaty with the Peru-Bolivian Confederation, the ratifications of which have been recently exchanged, accompany this message, for the information of Congress and for such legislative enactments as may be found necessary or expedient in relation to either of them.

To watch over and foster the interests of a gradually increasing and widely extended commerce, to guard the rights of American citizens whom business or pleasure or other motives may tempt into distant climes, and at the same time to cultivate those sentiments of mutual respect and good will which experience has proved so beneficial in international intercourse, the Government of the United States has deemed it expedient from time to time to establish diplomatic connections with different foreign states, by the appointment of representatives to reside within their respective territories. I am gratified to be enabled to announce to you that since the close of your last session these relations have been opened under the happiest auspices with Austria and the Two Sicilies, that new nominations have been made in the respective missions of Russia, Brazil, Belgium, and Sweden and Norway in this country, and that a minister extraordinary has been received, accredited to this Government, from the Argentine Confederation.

An exposition of the fiscal affairs of the Government and of their condition for the past year will be made to you by the Secretary of the Treasury.

The available balance in the Treasury on the 1st of January next is estimated at $2,765,342. The receipts of the year from customs and lands will probably amount to $20,615,598. These usual sources of revenue have been increased by an issue of Treasury notes, of which less than $8,000,000, including interest and principal, will be outstanding at the end of the year, and by the sale of one of the bonds of the Bank of the United States for $2,254,871. The aggregate of means from these and other sources, with the balance on hand on the 1st of January last, has been applied to the payment of appropriations by Congress. The whole expenditure for the year on their account, including the redemption of more than eight millions of Treasury notes, constitutes an aggregate of about $40,000,000, and will still leave in the Treasury the balance before stated.

Nearly $8,000,000 of Treasury notes are to be paid during the coming year in addition to the ordinary appropriations for the support of Government. For both these purposes the resources of the Treasury will undoubtedly be sufficient if the charges upon it are not increased beyond the annual estimates. No excess, however, is likely to exist. Nor can the postponed installment of the surplus revenue be deposited with the States nor any considerable appropriations beyond the estimates be made without causing a deficiency in the Treasury. The great caution, advisable at all times, of limiting appropriations to the wants of the public service is rendered necessary at present by the prospective and rapid reduction of the tariff, while the vigilant jealousy evidently excited among the people by the occurrences of the last few years assures us that they expect from their representatives, and will sustain them in the exercise of, the most rigid economy. Much can be effected by postponing appropriations not immediately required for the ordinary public service or for any pressing emergency, and much by reducing the expenditures where the entire and immediate accomplishment of the objects in view is not indispensable.

When we call to mind the recent and extreme embarrassments produced by excessive issues of bank paper, aggravated by the unforeseen withdrawal of much foreign capital and the inevitable derangement arising from the distribution of the surplus revenue among the States as required by Congress, and consider the heavy expenses incurred by the removal of Indian tribes, by the military operations in Florida, and on account of the unusually large appropriations made at the last two annual sessions of Congress for other objects, we have striking evidence in the present efficient state of our finances of the abundant resources of the country to fulfill all its obligations. Nor is it less gratifying to find that the general business of the community, deeply affected as it has been, is reviving with additional vigor, chastened by the lessons of the past and animated by the hopes of the future. By the curtailment of paper issues, by curbing the sanguine and adventurous spirit of speculation, and by the honorable application of all available means to the fulfillment of obligations, confidence has been restored both at home and abroad, and ease and facility secured to all the operations of trade.

The agency of the Government in producing these results has been as efficient as its powers and means permitted. By withholding from the States the deposit of the fourth installment, and leaving several millions at long credits with the banks, principally in one section of the country, and more immediately beneficial to it, and at the same time aiding the banks and commercial communities in other sections by postponing the payment of bonds for duties to the amount of between four and five millions of dollars; by an issue of Treasury notes as a means to enable the Government to meet the consequences of their indulgences, but affording at the same time facilities for remittance and exchange; and by steadily declining to employ as general depositories of the public revenues, or receive the notes of, all banks which refused to redeem them with specie— by these measures, aided by the favorable action of some of the banks and by the support and cooperation of a large portion of the community, we have witnessed an early resumption of specie payments in our great commercial capital, promptly followed in almost every part of the United States. This result has been alike salutary to the true interests of agriculture, commerce, and manufactures; to public morals, respect for the laws, and that confidence between man and man which is so essential in all our social relations.

The contrast between the suspension of 1814 and that of 1837 is most striking. The short duration of the latter, the prompt restoration of business, the evident benefits resulting from an adherence by the Government to the constitutional standard of value instead of sanctioning the suspension by the receipt of irredeemable paper, and the advantages derived from the large amount of specie introduced into the country previous to 1837 afford a valuable illustration of the true policy of the Government in such a crisis. Nor can the comparison fail to remove the impression that a national bank is necessary in such emergencies. Not only were specie payments resumed without its aid, but exchanges have also been more rapidly restored than when it existed, thereby showing that private capital, enterprise, and prudence are fully adequate to these ends. On all these points experience seems to have confirmed the views heretofore submitted to Congress. We have been saved the mortification of seeing the distresses of the community for the third time seized on to fasten upon the country so dangerous an institution, and we may also hope that the business of individuals will hereafter be relieved from the injurious effects of a continued agitation of that disturbing subject. The limited influence of a national bank in averting derangement in the exchanges of the country or in compelling the resumption of specie payments is now not less apparent than its tendency to increase inordinate speculation by sudden expansions and contractions; its disposition to create panic and embarrassment for the promotion of its own designs; its interference with politics, and its far greater power for evil than for good, either in regard to the local institutions or the operations of Government itself. What was in these respects but apprehension or opinion when a national bank was first established now stands confirmed by humiliating experience. The scenes through which we have passed conclusively prove how little our commerce, agriculture, manufactures, or finances require such an institution, and what dangers are attendant on its power—a power, I trust, never to be conferred by the American people upon their Government, and still less upon individuals not responsible to them for its unavoidable abuses.

My conviction of the necessity of further legislative provisions for the safe-keeping and disbursement of the public moneys and my opinion in regard to the measures best adapted to the accomplishment of those objects have been already submitted to you. These have been strengthened by recent events, and in the full conviction that time and experience must still further demonstrate their propriety I feel it my duty, with respectful deference to the conflicting views of others, again to invite your attention to them.

With the exception of limited sums deposited in the few banks still employed under the act of 1836, the amounts received for duties, and, with very inconsiderable exceptions, those accruing from lands also, have since the general suspension of specie payments by the deposit banks been kept and disbursed by the Treasurer under his general legal powers, subject to the superintendence of the Secretary of the Treasury. The propriety of defining more specifically and of regulating by law the exercise of this wide scope of Executive discretion has been already submitted to Congress.

A change in the office of collector at one of our principal ports has brought to light a defalcation of the gravest character, the particulars of which will be laid before you in a special report from the Secretary of the Treasury. By his report and the accompanying documents it will be seen that the weekly returns of the defaulting officer apparently exhibited throughout a faithful administration of the affairs intrusted to his management. It, however, now appears that he commenced abstracting the public moneys shortly after his appointment and continued to do so, progressively increasing the amount, for the term of more than seven years, embracing a portion of the period during which the public moneys were deposited in the Bank of the United States, the whole of that of the State bank deposit system, and concluding only on his retirement from office, after that system had substantially failed in consequence of the suspension of specie payments.

The way in which this defalcation was so long concealed and the steps taken to indemnify the United States, as far as practicable, against loss will also be presented to you. The case is one which imperatively claims the attention of Congress and furnishes the strongest motive for the establishment of a more severe and secure system for the safe-keeping and disbursement of the public moneys than any that has heretofore existed.

It seems proper, at all events, that by an early enactment similar to that of other countries the application of public money by an officer of Government to private uses should be made a felony and visited with severe and ignominious punishment. This is already in effect the law in respect to the Mint, and has been productive of the most salutary results. Whatever system is adopted, such an enactment would be wise as an independent measure, since much of the public moneys must in their collection and ultimate disbursement pass twice through the hands of public officers, in whatever manner they are intermediately kept. The Government, it must be admitted, has been from its commencement comparatively fortunate in this respect. But the appointing power can not always be well advised in its selections, and the experience of every country has shown that public officers are not at all times proof against temptation. It is a duty, therefore, which the Government owes, as well to the interests committed to its care as to the officers themselves, to provide every guard against transgressions of this character that is consistent with reason and humanity. Congress can not be too jealous of the conduct of those who are intrusted with the public money, and I shall at all times be disposed to encourage a watchful discharge of this duty.

If a more direct cooperation on the part of Congress in the supervision of the conduct of the officers intrusted with the custody and application of the public money is deemed desirable, it will give me pleasure to assist in the establishment of any judicious and constitutional plan by which that object may be accomplished. You will in your wisdom determine upon the propriety of adopting such a plan and upon the measures necessary to its effectual execution. When the late Bank of the United States was incorporated and made the depository of the public moneys, a right was reserved to Congress to inspect at its pleasure, by a committee of that body, the books and the proceedings of the bank. In one of the States, whose banking institutions are supposed to rank amongst the first in point of stability, they are subjected to constant examination by commissioners appointed for that purpose, and much of the success of its banking system is attributed to this watchful supervision.

The same course has also, in view of its beneficial operation, been adopted by an adjoining State, favorably known for the care it has always bestowed upon whatever relates to its financial concerns. I submit to your consideration whether a committee of Congress might not be profitably employed in inspecting, at such intervals as might be deemed proper, the affairs and accounts of officers intrusted with the custody of the public moneys. The frequent performance of this duty might be made obligatory on the committee in respect to those officers who have large sums in their possession, and left discretionary in respect to others. They might report to the Executive such defalcations as were found to exist, with a view to a prompt removal from office unless the default was satisfactorily accounted for, and report also to Congress, at the commencement of each session, the result of their examinations and proceedings. It does appear to me that with a subjection of this class of public officers to the general supervision of the Executive, to examinations by a committee of Congress at periods of which they should have no previous notice, and to prosecution and punishment as for felony for every breach of trust, the safe-keeping of the public moneys might under the system proposed be placed on a surer foundation than it has ever occupied since the establishment of the Government.

The Secretary of the Treasury will lay before you additional information containing new details on this interesting subject. To these I ask your early attention. That it should have given rise to great diversity of opinion can not be a subject of surprise. After the collection and custody of the public moneys had been for so many years connected with and made subsidiary to the advancement of private interests, a return to the simple self-denying ordinances of the Constitution could not but be difficult. But time and free discussion, eliciting the sentiments of the people, and aided by that conciliatory spirit which has ever characterized their course on great emergencies, were relied upon for a satisfactory settlement of the question. Already has this anticipation, on one important point at least—the impropriety of diverting public money to private purposes—been fully realized. There is no reason to suppose that legislation upon that branch of the subject would now be embarrassed by a difference of opinion, or fail to receive the cordial support of a large majority of our constituents.

The connection which formerly existed between the Government and banks was in reality injurious to both, as well as to the general interests of the community at large. It aggravated the disasters of trade and the derangements of commercial intercourse, and administered new excitements and additional means to wild and reckless speculations, the disappointment of which threw the country into convulsions of panic, and all but produced violence and bloodshed. The imprudent expansion of bank credits, which was the natural result of the command of the revenues of the State, furnished the resources for unbounded license in every species of adventure, seduced industry from its regular and salutary occupations by the hope of abundance without labor, and deranged the social state by tempting all trades and professions into the vortex of speculation on remote contingencies.

The same wide-spreading influence impeded also the resources of the Government, curtailed its useful operations, embarrassed the fulfillment of its obligations, and seriously interfered with the execution of the laws. Large appropriations and oppressive taxes are the natural consequences of such a connection, since they increase the profits of those who are allowed to use the public funds, and make it their interest that money should be accumulated and expenditures multiplied. It is thus that a concentrated money power is tempted to become an active agent in political affairs; and all past experience has shown on which side that influence will be arrayed. We deceive ourselves if we suppose that it will ever be found asserting and supporting the rights of the community at large in opposition to the claims of the few.

In a government whose distinguishing characteristic should be a diffusion and equalization of its benefits and burdens the advantage of individuals will be augmented at the expense of the community at large. Nor is it the nature of combinations for the acquisition of legislative influence to confine their interference to the single object for which they were originally formed. The temptation to extend it to other matters is, on the contrary, not unfrequently too strong to be resisted. The rightful influence in the direction of public affairs of the mass of the people is therefore in no slight danger of being sensibly and injuriously affected by giving to a comparatively small but very efficient class a direct and exclusive personal interest in so important a portion of the legislation of Congress as that which relates to the custody of the public moneys. If laws acting upon private interests can not always be avoided, they should be confined within the narrowest limits, and left wherever possible to the legislatures of the States. When not thus restricted they lead to combinations of powerful associations, foster an influence necessarily selfish, and turn the fair course of legislation to sinister ends rather than to objects that advance public liberty and promote the general good.

The whole subject now rests with you, and I can not but express a hope that some definite measure will be adopted at the present session.

It will not, I am sure, be deemed out of place for me here to remark that the declaration of my views in opposition to the policy of employing banks as depositories of the Government funds can not justly be construed as indicative of hostility, official or personal, to those institutions; or to repeat in this form and in connection with this subject opinions which I have uniformly entertained and on all proper occasions expressed. Though always opposed to their creation in the form of exclusive privileges, and, as a State magistrate, aiming by appropriate legislation to secure the community against the consequences of their occasional mismanagement, I have yet ever wished to see them protected in the exercise of rights conferred by law, and have never doubted their utility when properly managed in promoting the interests of trade, and through that channel the other interests of the community. To the General Government they present themselves merely as State institutions, having no necessary connection with its legislation or its administration. Like other State establishments, they may be used or not in conducting the affairs of the Government, as public policy and the general interests of the Union may seem to require. The only safe or proper principle upon which their intercourse with the Government can be regulated is that which regulates their intercourse with the private citizen—the conferring of mutual benefits. When the Government can accomplish a financial operation better with the aid of the banks than without it, it should be at liberty to seek that aid as it would the services of a private banker or other capitalist or agent, giving the preference to those who will serve it on the best terms. Nor can there ever exist an interest in the officers of the General Government, as such, inducing them to embarrass or annoy the State banks any more than to incur the hostility of any other class of State institutions or of private citizens. It is not in the nature of things that hostility to these institutions can spring from this source, or any opposition to their course of business, except when they themselves depart from the objects of their creation and attempt to usurp powers not conferred upon them or to subvert the standard of value established by the Constitution. While opposition to their regular operations can not exist in this quarter, resistance to any attempt to make the Government dependent upon them for the successful administration of public affairs is a matter of duty, as I trust it ever will be of inclination, no matter from what motive or consideration the attempt may originate.

It is no more than just to the banks to say that in the late emergency most of them firmly resisted the strongest temptations to extend their paper issues when apparently sustained in a suspension of specie payments by public opinion, even though in some cases invited by legislative enactments. To this honorable course, aided by the resistance of the General Government, acting in obedience to the Constitution and laws of the United States, to the introduction of an irredeemable paper medium, may be attributed in a great degree the speedy restoration of our currency to a sound state and the business of the country to its wonted prosperity.

The banks have but to continue in the same safe course and be content in their appropriate sphere to avoid all interference from the General Government and to derive from it all the protection and benefits which it bestows on other State establishments, on the people of the States, and on the States themselves. In this, their true position, they can not but secure the confidence and good will of the people and the Government, which they can only lose when, leaping from their legitimate sphere, they attempt to control the legislation of the country and pervert the operations of the Government to their own purposes.

Our experience under the act, passed at the last session, to grant preemption rights to settlers on the public lands has as yet been too limited to enable us to pronounce with safety upon the efficacy of its provisions to carry out the wise and liberal policy of the Government in that respect. There is, however, the best reason to anticipate favorable results from its operation. The recommendations formerly submitted to you in respect to a graduation of the price of the public lands remain to be finally acted upon. Having found no reason to change the views then expressed, your attention to them is again respectfully requested.

Every proper exertion has been made and will be continued to carry out the wishes of Congress in relation to the tobacco trade, as indicated in the several resolutions of the House of Representatives and the legislation of the two branches. A favorable impression has, I trust, been made in the different foreign countries to which particular attention has been directed; and although we can not hope for an early change in their policy, as in many of them a convenient and large revenue is derived from monopolies in the fabrication and sale of this article, yet, as these monopolies are really injurious to the people where they are established, and the revenue derived from them may be less injuriously and with equal facility obtained from another and a liberal system of administration, we can not doubt that our efforts will be eventually crowned with success if persisted in with temperate firmness and sustained by prudent legislation.

In recommending to Congress the adoption of the necessary provisions at this session for taking the next census or enumeration of the inhabitants of the United States, the suggestion presents itself whether the scope of the measure might not be usefully extended by causing it to embrace authentic statistical returns of the great interests specially intrusted to or necessarily affected by the legislation of Congress.

The accompanying report of the Secretary of War presents a satisfactory account of the state of the Army and of the several branches of the public service confided to the superintendence of that officer.

The law increasing and organizing the military establishment of the United States has been nearly carried into effect, and the Army has been extensively and usefully employed during the past season.

I would again call to your notice the subjects connected with and essential to the military defenses of the country which were submitted to you at the last session, but which were not acted upon, as is supposed, for want of time. The most important of them is the organization of the militia on the maritime and inland frontiers. This measure is deemed important, as it is believed that it will furnish an effective volunteer force in aid of the Regular Army, and may form the basis of a general system of organization for the entire militia of the United States. The erection of a national foundry and gunpowder manufactory, and one for making small arms, the latter to be situated at some point west of the Allegany Mountains, all appear to be of sufficient importance to be again urged upon your attention.

The plan proposed by the Secretary of War for the distribution of the forces of the United States in time of peace is well calculated to promote regularity and economy in the fiscal administration of the service, to preserve the discipline of the troops, and to render them available for the maintenance of the peace and tranquillity of the country. With this view, likewise, I recommend the adoption of the plan presented by that officer for the defense of the western frontier. The preservation of the lives and property of our fellow-citizens who are settled upon that border country, as well as the existence of the Indian population, which might be tempted by our want of preparation to rush on their own destruction and attack the white settlements, all seem to require that this subject should be acted upon without delay, and the War Department authorized to place that country in a state of complete defense against any assault from the numerous and warlike tribes which are congregated on that border.

It affords me sincere pleasure to be able to apprise you of the entire removal of the Cherokee Nation of Indians to their new homes west of the Mississippi. The measures authorized by Congress at its last session, with a view to the long-standing controversy with them, have had the happiest effects. By an agreement concluded with them by the commanding general in that country, who has performed the duties assigned to him on the occasion with commendable energy and humanity, their removal has been principally under the conduct of their own chiefs, and they have emigrated without any apparent reluctance.

The successful accomplishment of this important object, the removal also of the entire Creek Nation with the exception of a small number of fugitives amongst the Seminoles in Florida, the progress already made toward a speedy completion of the removal of the Chickasaws, the Choctaws, the Pottawatamies, the Ottawas, and the Chippewas, with the extensive purchases of Indian lands during the present year, have rendered the speedy and successful result of the long-established policy of the Government upon the subject of Indian affairs entirely certain. The occasion is therefore deemed a proper one to place this policy in such a point of view as will exonerate the Government of the United States from the undeserved reproach which has been cast upon it through several successive Administrations. That a mixed occupancy of the same territory by the white and red man is incompatible with the safety or happiness of either is a position in respect to which there has long since ceased to be room for a difference of opinion. Reason and experience have alike demonstrated its impracticability. The bitter fruits of every attempt heretofore to overcome the barriers interposed by nature have only been destruction, both physical and moral, to the Indian, dangerous conflicts of authority between the Federal and State Governments, and detriment to the individual prosperity of the citizen as well as to the general improvement of the country. The remedial policy, the principles of which were settled more than thirty years ago under the Administration of Mr. Jefferson, consists in an extinction, for a fair consideration, of the title to all the lands still occupied by the Indians within the States and Territories of the United States; their removal to a country west of the Mississippi much more extensive and better adapted to their condition than that on which they then resided; the guarantee to them by the United States of their exclusive possession of that country forever, exempt from all intrusions by white men, with ample provisions for their security against external violence and internal dissensions, and the extension to them of suitable facilities for their advancement in civilization. This has not been the policy of particular Administrations only, but of each in succession since the first attempt to carry it out under that of Mr. Monroe. All have labored for its accomplishment, only with different degrees of success. The manner of its execution has, it is true, from time to time given rise to conflicts of opinion and unjust imputations; but in respect to the wisdom and necessity of the policy itself there has not from the beginning existed a doubt in the mind of any calm, judicious, disinterested friend of the Indian race accustomed to reflection and enlightened by experience.

Occupying the double character of contractor on its own account and guardian for the parties contracted with, it was hardly to be expected that the dealings of the Federal Government with the Indian tribes would escape misrepresentation. That there occurred in the early settlement of this country, as in all others where the civilized race has succeeded to the possessions of the savage, instances of oppression and fraud on the part of the former there is too much reason to believe. No such offenses can, however, be justly charged upon this Government since it became free to pursue its own course. Its dealings with the Indian tribes have been just and friendly throughout; its efforts for their civilization constant, and directed by the best feelings of humanity; its watchfulness in protecting them from individual frauds unremitting; its forbearance under the keenest provocations, the deepest injuries, and the most flagrant outrages may challenge at least a comparison with any nation, ancient or modern, in similar circumstances; and if in future times a powerful, civilized, and happy nation of Indians shall be found to exist within the limits of this northern continent it will be owing to the consummation of that policy which has been so unjustly assailed. Only a very brief reference to facts in confirmation of this assertion can in this form be given, and you are therefore necessarily referred to the report of the Secretary of War for further details. To the Cherokees, whose case has perhaps excited the greatest share of attention and sympathy, the United States have granted in fee, with a perpetual guaranty of exclusive and peaceable possession, 13,554,135 acres of land on the west side of the Mississippi, eligibly situated, in a healthy climate, and in all respects better suited to their condition than the country they have left, in exchange for only 9,492,160 acres on the east side of the same river. The United States have in addition stipulated to pay them $5,600,000 for their interest in and improvements on the lands thus relinquished, and $1,160,000 for subsistence and other beneficial purposes, thereby putting it in their power to become one of the most wealthy and independent separate communities of the same extent in the world.

By the treaties made and ratified with the Miamies, the Chippewas, the Sioux, the Sacs and Foxes, and the Winnebagoes during the last year the Indian title to 18,458,000 acres has been extinguished. These purchases have been much more extensive than those of any previous year, and have, with other Indian expenses, borne very heavily upon the Treasury. They leave, however, but a small quantity of unbought Indian lands within the States and Territories, and the Legislature and Executive were equally sensible of the propriety of a final and more speedy extinction of Indian titles within those limits. The treaties, which were with a single exception made in pursuance of previous appropriations for defraying the expenses, have subsequently been ratified by the Senate, and received the sanction of Congress by the appropriations necessary to

carry them into effect.   Of the terms upon which these important negotiations were concluded I can speak from direct knowledge, and I feel no
difficulty in affirming that the interest of the Indians in the extensive
territory embraced by them is to be paid for at its fair value, and that
no more favorable terms have been granted to the United States than
would have been reasonably expected in a negotiation with civilized men
fully capable of appreciating and protecting their own rights.   For the
Indian title to 116,349,897 acres acquired since the 4th of March, 1829,
the United States have paid $72,560,056 in permanent annuities, lands,
reservations for Indians, expenses of removal and subsistence, merchandise, mechanical and agricultural establishments and implements.   When
the heavy expenses incurred by the United States and the circumstance
that so large a portion of the entire territory will be forever unsalable
are considered, and this price is compared with that for which the United
States sell their own lands, no one can doubt that justice has been done
to the Indians in these purchases also.   Certain it is that the transactions
of the Federal Government with the Indians have been uniformly characterized by a sincere and paramount desire to promote their welfare;
and it must be a source of the highest gratification to every friend to
justice and humanity to learn that notwithstanding the obstructions
from time to time thrown in its way and the difficulties which have
arisen from the peculiar and impracticable nature of the Indian character, the wise, humane, and undeviating policy of the Government in this
the most difficult of all our relations, foreign or domestic, has at length
been justified to the world in its near approach to a happy and certain
consummation.

The condition of the tribes which occupy the country set apart for
them in the West is highly prosperous, and encourages the hope of their
early civilization.   They have for the most part abandoned the hunter
state and turned their attention to agricultural pursuits.   All those who
have been established for any length of time in that fertile region maintain themselves by their own industry.   There are among them traders
of no inconsiderable capital, and planters exporting cotton to some extent,
but the greater number are small agriculturists, living in comfort upon
the produce of their farms.   The recent emigrants, although they have
in some instances removed reluctantly, have readily acquiesced in their
unavoidable destiny.   They have found at once a recompense for past
sufferings and an incentive to industrious habits in the abundance and
comforts around them.   There is reason to believe that all these tribes
are friendly in their feelings toward the United States; and it is to be
hoped that the acquisition of individual wealth, the pursuits of agriculture, and habits of industry will gradually subdue their warlike propensities and incline them to maintain peace among themselves.   To effect
this desirable object the attention of Congress is solicited to the measures
recommended by the Secretary of War for their future government and

protection, as well from each other as from the hostility of the warlike tribes around them and the intrusions of the whites. The policy of the Government has given them a permanent home and guaranteed to them its peaceful and undisturbed possession. It only remains to give them a government and laws which will encourage industry and secure to them the rewards of their exertions. The importance of some form of government can not be too much insisted upon. The earliest effects will be to diminish the causes and occasions for hostilities among the tribes, to inspire an interest in the observance of laws to which they will have themselves assented, and to multiply the securities of property and the motives for self-improvement. Intimately connected with this subject is the establishment of the military defenses recommended by the Secretary of War, which have been already referred to. Without them the Government will be powerless to redeem its pledge of protection to the emigrating Indians against the numerous warlike tribes that surround them and to provide for the safety of the frontier settlers of the bordering States.

The case of the Seminoles constitutes at present the only exception to the successful efforts of the Government to remove the Indians to the homes assigned them west of the Mississippi. Four hundred of this tribe emigrated in 1836 and 1,500 in 1837 and 1838, leaving in the country, it is supposed, about 2,000 Indians. The continued treacherous conduct of these people; the savage and unprovoked murders they have lately committed, butchering whole families of the settlers of the Territory without distinction of age or sex, and making their way into the very center and heart of the country, so that no part of it is free from their ravages; their frequent attacks on the light-houses along that dangerous coast, and the barbarity with which they have murdered the passengers and crews of such vessels as have been wrecked upon the reefs and keys which border the Gulf, leave the Government no alternative but to continue the military operations against them until they are totally expelled from Florida. There are other motives which would urge the Government to pursue this course toward the Seminoles. The United States have fulfilled in good faith all their treaty stipulations with the Indian tribes, and have in every other instance insisted upon a like performance of their obligations. To relax from this salutary rule because the Seminoles have maintained themselves so long in the territory they had relinquished, and in defiance of their frequent and solemn engagements still continue to wage a ruthless war against the United States, would not only evince a want of constancy on our part, but be of evil example in our intercourse with other tribes. Experience has shown that but little is to be gained by the march of armies through a country so intersected with inaccessible swamps and marshes, and which, from the fatal character of the climate, must be abandoned at the end of the winter. I recommend, therefore, to your attention the plan submitted by the Secretary of War in the accompanying report, for the permanent occupation of the portion of the Territory freed from the Indians and the more efficient protection of the people of Florida from their inhuman warfare.

From the report of the Secretary of the Navy herewith transmitted it will appear that a large portion of the disposable naval force is either actively employed or in a state of preparation for the purposes of experience and discipline and the protection of our commerce. So effectual has been this protection that so far as the information of Government extends not a single outrage has been attempted on a vessel carrying the flag of the United States within the present year, in any quarter, however distant or exposed.

The exploring expedition sailed from Norfolk on the 19th of August last, and information has been received of its safe arrival at the island of Madeira. The best spirit animates the officers and crews, and there is every reason to anticipate from its efforts results beneficial to commerce and honorable to the nation.

It will also be seen that no reduction of the force now in commission is contemplated. The unsettled state of a portion of South America renders it indispensable that our commerce should receive protection in that quarter; the vast and increasing interests embarked in the trade of the Indian and China seas, in the whale fisheries of the Pacific Ocean, and in the Gulf of Mexico require equal attention to their safety, and a small squadron may be employed to great advantage on our Atlantic coast in meeting sudden demands for the reenforcement of other stations, in aiding merchant vessels in distress, in affording active service to an additional number of officers, and in visiting the different ports of the United States, an accurate knowledge of which is obviously of the highest importance.

The attention of Congress is respectfully called to that portion of the report recommending an increase in the number of smaller vessels, and to other suggestions contained in that document. The rapid increase and wide expansion of our commerce, which is every day seeking new avenues of profitable adventure; the absolute necessity of a naval force for its protection precisely in the degree of its extension; a due regard to the national rights and honor; the recollection of its former exploits, and the anticipation of its future triumphs whenever opportunity presents itself, which we may rightfully indulge from the experience of the past—all seem to point to the Navy as a most efficient arm of our national defense and a proper object of legislative encouragement.

The progress and condition of the Post-Office Department will be seen by reference to the report of the Postmaster-General. The extent of post-roads covered by mail contracts is stated to be 134,818 miles, and the annual transportation upon them 34,580,202 miles. The number of post-offices in the United States is 12,553, and rapidly increasing. The gross revenue for the year ending on the 30th day of June last was $4,262,145; the accruing expenditures, $4,680,068; excess of expenditures, $417,923. This has been made up out of the surplus previously on hand. The cash on hand on the 1st instant was $314,068. The revenue for the year ending June 30, 1838, was $161,540 more than that for the year ending June 30, 1837. The expenditures of the Department had been graduated upon the anticipation of a largely increased revenue. A moderate curtailment of mail service consequently became necessary, and has been effected, to shield the Department against the danger of embarrassment. Its revenue is now improving, and it will soon resume its onward course in the march of improvement.

Your particular attention is requested to so much of the Postmaster-General's report as relates to the transportation of the mails upon railroads. The laws on that subject do not seem adequate to secure that service, now become almost essential to the public interests, and at the same time protect the Department from combinations and unreasonable demands.

Nor can I too earnestly request your attention to the necessity of providing a more secure building for this Department. The danger of destruction to which its important books and papers are continually exposed, as well from the highly combustible character of the building occupied as from that of others in the vicinity, calls loudly for prompt action.

Your attention is again earnestly invited to the suggestions and recommendations submitted at the last session in respect to the District of Columbia.

I feel it my duty also to bring to your notice certain proceedings at law which have recently been prosecuted in this District in the name of the United States, on the relation of Messrs. Stockton & Stokes, of the State of Maryland, against the Postmaster-General, and which have resulted in the payment of money out of the National Treasury, for the first time since the establishment of the Government, by judicial compulsion exercised by the common-law writ of mandamus issued by the circuit court of this District.

The facts of the case and the grounds of the proceedings will be found fully stated in the report of the decision, and any additional information which you may desire will be supplied by the proper Department. No interference in the particular case is contemplated. The money has been paid, the claims of the prosecutors have been satisfied, and the whole subject, so far as they are concerned, is finally disposed of; but it is on the supposition that the case may be regarded as an authoritative exposition of the law as it now stands that I have thought it necessary to present it to your consideration.

The object of the application to the circuit court was to compel the Postmaster-General to carry into effect an award made by the Solicitor of the Treasury, under a special act of Congress for the settlement of certain claims of the relators on the Post-Office Department, which award the Postmaster-General declined to execute in full until he should receive further legislative direction on the subject. If the duty imposed on the Postmaster-General by that law was to be regarded as one of an official nature, belonging to his office as a branch of the executive, then it is obvious that the constitutional competency of the judiciary to direct and control him in its discharge was necessarily drawn in question; and if the duty so imposed on the Postmaster-General was to be considered as merely ministerial, and not executive, it yet remained to be shown that the circuit court of this District had authority to interfere by mandamus, such a power having never before been asserted or claimed by that court. With a view to the settlement of these important questions, the judgment of the circuit court was carried by a writ of error to the Supreme Court of the United States. In the opinion of that tribunal the duty imposed on the Postmaster-General was not an official executive duty, but one of a merely ministerial nature. The grave constitutional questions which had been discussed were therefore excluded from the decision of the case, the court, indeed, expressly admitting that with powers and duties properly belonging to the executive no other department can interfere by the writ of mandamus; and the question therefore resolved itself into this: Has Congress conferred upon the circuit court of this District the power to issue such a writ to an officer of the General Government commanding him to perform a ministerial act? A majority of the court have decided that it has, but have founded their decision upon a process of reasoning which in my judgment renders further legislative provision indispensable to the public interests and the equal administration of justice.

It has long since been decided by the Supreme Court that neither that tribunal nor the circuit courts of the United States, held within the respective States, possess the power in question; but it is now held that this power, denied to both of these high tribunals (to the former by the Constitution and to the latter by Congress), has been by its legislation vested in the circuit court of this District. No such direct grant of power to the circuit court of this District is claimed, but it has been held to result by necessary implication from several sections of the law establishing the court. One of these sections declares that the laws of Maryland, as they existed at the time of the cession, should be in force in that part of the District ceded by that State, and by this provision the common law in civil and criminal cases, as it prevailed in Maryland in 1801, was established in that part of the District.

In England the court of king's bench—because the Sovereign, who, according to the theory of the constitution, is the fountain of justice, originally sat there in person, and is still deemed to be present in construction of law—alone possesses the high power of issuing the writ of mandamus, not only to inferior jurisdictions and corporations, but also to magistrates and others, commanding them in the King's name to do what their duty requires in cases where there is a vested right and no other specific remedy. It has been held in the case referred to that as the Supreme Court of the United States is by the Constitution rendered incompetent to exercise this power, and as the circuit court of this District is a court of general jurisdiction in cases at common law, and the highest court of original jurisdiction in the District, the right to issue the writ of mandamus is incident to its common-law powers. Another ground relied upon to maintain the power in question is that it was included by fair construction in the powers granted to the circuit courts of the United States by the act "to provide for the more convenient organization of the courts of the United States," passed 13th February, 1801; that the act establishing the circuit court of this District, passed the 27th day of February, 1801, conferred upon that court and the judges thereof the same powers as were by law vested in the circuit courts of the United States and in the judges of the said courts; that the repeal of the first-mentioned act, which took place in the next year, did not divest the circuit court of this District of the authority in dispute, but left it still clothed with the powers over the subject which, it is conceded, were taken away from the circuit courts of the United States by the repeal of the act of 13th February, 1801.

Admitting that the adoption of the laws of Maryland for a portion of this District confers on the circuit court thereof, in that portion, the transcendent extrajudicial prerogative powers of the court of king's bench in England, or that either of the acts of Congress by necessary implication authorizes the former court to issue a writ of mandamus to an officer of the United States to compel him to perform a ministerial duty, the consequences are in one respect the same. The result in either case is that the officers of the United States stationed in different parts of the United States are, in respect to the performance of their official duties, subject to different laws and a different supervision—those in the States to one rule, and those in the District of Columbia to another and a very different one. In the District their official conduct is subject to a judicial control from which in the States they are exempt.

Whatever difference of opinion may exist as to the expediency of vesting such a power in the judiciary in a system of government constituted like that of the United States, all must agree that these disparaging discrepancies in the law and in the administration of justice ought not to be permitted to continue; and as Congress alone can provide the remedy, the subject is unavoidably presented to your consideration.

M. VAN BUREN.

SPECIAL MESSAGES.

WASHINGTON, *December 6, 1838.*
To the Senate and House of Representatives of the United States:

The act of the 1st July, 1836, to enable the Executive to assert and prosecute with effect the claim of the United States to the legacy bequeathed to them by James Smithson, late of London, having received its entire execution, and the amount recovered and paid into the Treasury having, agreeably to an act of the last session, been invested in State stocks, I deem it proper to invite the attention of Congress to the obligation now devolving upon the United States to fulfill the object of the bequest. In order to obtain such information as might serve to facilitate its attainment, the Secretary of State was directed in July last to apply to persons versed in science and familiar with the subject of public education for their views as to the mode of disposing of the fund best calculated to meet the intentions of the testator and prove most beneficial to mankind. Copies of the circular letter written in compliance with these directions, and of the answers to it received at the Department of State, are herewith communicated for the consideration of Congress.

M. VAN BUREN.

WASHINGTON, *December 7, 1838.*
To the House of Representatives of the United States:

I herewith transmit to the House of Representatives reports* from the Secretary of State and the Secretary of the Treasury, with accompanying documents, in answer to the resolution of the House of the 9th of July last.

M. VAN BUREN.

WASHINGTON, *December 8, 1838.*
To the Senate and House of Representatives of the United States:

I herewith transmit a special report made to me by the Secretary of the Treasury, for your consideration, in relation to the recently discovered default of Samuel Swartwout, late collector of the customs at the port of New York.

I would respectfully invite the early attention of Congress to the adoption of the legal provisions therein suggested, or such other measures as may appear more expedient, for increasing the public security against similar defalcations hereafter.

M. VAN BUREN.

*Transmitting communications, papers, documents, etc., elucidating the origin and objects of the Smithsonian bequest and the origin, progress, and consummation of the process by which that bequest was recovered, etc.

WASHINGTON, *December 14, 1838.*

To the Senate of the United States:

With the accompanying communication of the Secretary of War I transmit, for the consideration and constitutional action of the Senate. a treaty concluded with the Miami tribe of Indians on the 6th ultimo. Your attention is invited to that section which reserves a tract of land for the use of certain Indians, and to other reservations contained in the treaty. All such reservations are objectionable, but for the reasons given by the Secretary of War I submit to your consideration whether the circumstances attending this negotiation, and the great importance of removing the Miamies from the State of Indiana, will warrant a departure in this instance from the salutary rule of excluding all reservations from Indian treaties.

M. VAN BUREN.

WAR DEPARTMENT, *December 14, 1838.*

The PRESIDENT OF THE UNITED STATES.

SIR: I have the honor to lay before you, for submission to the Senate for its action if approved by you, a treaty with the Miami tribe of Indians concluded on the 6th ultimo. In doing so I beg to call your attention to that section which reserves from the cession made by the Miamies a tract of land supposed to contain 10 square miles, and to other reservations according to a schedule appended to the treaty. The commissioner who negotiated this treaty is of opinion that it could not have been concluded if he had not so far departed from his instructions as to admit these reservations. And it is to be feared that if the rules adopted by the Department in this particular be insisted upon on this occasion it will very much increase the difficulty, if it does not render it impracticable to acquire this land and remove these Indians—objects of so much importance to the United States and especially to the State of Indiana.

Very respectfully, your most obedient servant,

J. R. POINSETT.

WASHINGTON, *December 18, 1838.*

To the House of Representatives of the United States:

I transmit the accompanying documents, marked from 1 to 5,* in reply to a resolution of yesterday's date, calling for copies of correspondence between the Executive of the General Government and the governor of Pennsylvania in relation to "a call of the latter for an armed force of United States troops since the present session of Congress," and requiring information "whether any officer of the United States instigated or participated" in the riotous proceedings referred to in the resolution, and "what measures, if any, the President has taken to investigate and punish the said acts, and whether any such officer still remains in the service of the United States."

M. VAN BUREN.

*Relating to the "Buckshot war."

WASHINGTON, *December 20, 1838.*

To the House of Representatives:

I have the honor to transmit herewith additional letters and documents* embraced in the resolution of the House of Representatives of the 17th instant.

M. VAN BUREN.

WASHINGTON, *December 20, 1838.*

To the House of Representatives:

An important difference of opinion having arisen concerning the construction of an act of Congress making a grant of land to the State of Indiana,† and in which she feels a deep interest, I deem it proper to submit all the material facts to your consideration, with a view to procure such additional legislation as the facts of the case may appear to render proper.

The report of the Secretary of the Treasury and the documents annexed from the General Land Office will disclose all the circumstances deemed material in relation to the subject, and are herewith presented.

M. VAN BUREN.

WASHINGTON, *December 26, 1838.*

To the Senate and House of Representatives of the United States:

I transmit for your consideration the inclosed communication and accompanying documents from the Secretary of War, relative to the present state of the Pea Patch Island, in the Delaware River, and of the operations going on there for the erection of defenses for that important channel of commerce.

It will be seen from these documents that a complete stop has been put to those operations in consequence of the island having been taken possession of by the individual claimant under the decision, in his favor, of the United States district court for the district of New Jersey, and that unless early measures are taken to bring the island within the jurisdiction of the Government great loss and injury will result to the future operations for carrying on the works. The importance of the subject would seem to render it worthy of the early attention of Congress.

M. VAN BUREN.

WASHINGTON, *December, 1838.*

To the Senate:

I transmit a letter from the Secretary of War, accompanied by a communication from the Commissioner of Indian Affairs, on the subject of granting to the Chickasaw Indians subsistence for the further term of

---

* Relating to the "Buckshot war."
† In aid of the construction of the Wabash and Erie Canal.

seven months. Should it be the pleasure of the Senate to give its sanction to the measure suggested by the Commissioner for this purpose, my own will not be withheld.

M. VAN BUREN.

WASHINGTON, *January 7, 1839.*

To the Senate of the United States:

In compliance with the resolution of the Senate of the 20th December last, I communicate to the Senate reports from the several Executive Departments, containing the information * called for by said resolution.

. M. VAN BUREN.

WASHINGTON, *January 9, 1839.*

The PRESIDENT OF THE SENATE OF THE UNITED STATES.

SIR: I transmit herewith a report from the Secretary of the Navy, in answer to the resolution of the Senate of the 3d instant, calling for information in regard to the examinations of inventions designed to prevent the calamities resulting from the explosion of steam boilers, directed by the acts of Congress of the 28th of June and the 9th of July last.

M. VAN BUREN.

WASHINGTON, *January 10, 1839.*

To the House of Representatives:

I communicate to the House of Representatives, in compliance with its resolution of the 3d instant, reports† from the Secretaries of State and War, containing all the information called for by said resolution now in possession of the Executive.

M. VAN BUREN.

WASHINGTON, *January 11, 1839.*

To the Senate of the United States:

I transmit herewith a report of the Secretary of War, in reply to the resolution of the Senate of yesterday's date, calling for information respecting the agreement between him and the United States Bank of Pennsylvania on the subject of the sale or payment of certain bonds of that institution held by the United States, and respecting the disposition made of the proceeds thereof.

M. VAN BUREN.

---

*Copies of orders and instructions issued since April 14, 1836, relative to the kind of money and bank notes to be paid out on account of the United States.

†Relating to the invasion of the southwestern frontier of the United States by an armed force from the Republic of Texas.

WASHINGTON, *January 15, 1839.*

To the Senate of the United States:

In compliance with a resolution of the Senate of the 9th of July last, I transmit reports* from the several Departments of the Government to which that resolution was referred.

M. VAN BUREN.

WASHINGTON, *January 16, 1839.*

To the Senate and House of Representatives of the United States:

I lay before you a communication from the Secretary of War, which is accompanied by one from the Commissioner of Indian Affairs, suggesting the propriety of setting apart a tract of country west of the Mississippi for the Seminole Indians, so that they may be separate from the Creeks, and representing the necessity of a small appropriation for supplying the immediate wants of those who have been removed; and I respectfully recommend these subjects for the early consideration and favorable action of Congress.

M. VAN BUREN.

JANUARY 17, 1839.

To the Senate and House of Representatives:

I herewith communicate to Congress a letter from the Secretary of the Treasury, in respect to the Florida claims under the treaty of 1819 and the subsequent acts of Congress passed to enforce it.

The propriety of some additional legislation on this subject seems obvious. The period when the evidence on the claims shall be closed ought, in my opinion, to be limited, as they are already of long standing, and, as a general consequence, the proof of their justice every day becoming more and more unsatisfactory.

It seems also that the task of making the final examination into the justice of the awards might advantageously be devolved upon some other officer or tribunal than the Secretary of the Treasury, considering the other responsible, laborious, and numerous duties imposed on him at the present juncture.

M. VAN BUREN.

WASHINGTON, *January 17, 1839.*

To the Senate and House of Representatives of the United States:

I transmit herewith a communication from the Secretary of the Treasury, which presents for the consideration of Congress the propriety of so changing the second section of the act of March 2, 1837, as that the

---

*Transmitting statements of cases in which a per centum has been allowed to public officers on disbursements of public moneys.

existing humane provisions of the laws for the relief of certain insolvent debtors of the United States may be extended to such cases of insolvency as shall have occurred on or before the 1st day of January, 1839

M. VAN BUREN.

WASHINGTON, *January 17, 1839.*

The SPEAKER OF THE HOUSE OF REPRESENTATIVES:

In answer to the resolution of the House of Representatives of the 14th instant, calling for information as to the proceedings under the act of Congress of the 28th of June last, providing for examinations of inventions designed to prevent the explosion of steam boilers, I transmit herewith a copy of a report of the Secretary of the Navy, which was made to the Senate in answer to a similar call from that body, as containing the information called for.

M. VAN BUREN.

WASHINGTON, *January 18, 1839.*

To the House of Representatives:

In addition to the information contained in a report from the Secretary of State communicated with my message of the 30th April, 1838, I transmit to the House of Representatives a report* from the Secretary of War, dated the 16th instant, in answer to a resolution of the House of the 19th March last, and containing so much of the information called for by said resolution as could be furnished by his Department.

M. VAN BUREN.

WASHINGTON, *January 21, 1839.*

To the Senate of the United States:

I transmit herewith to the Senate, for their consideration in reference to its ratification, a treaty of commerce and navigation between the United States of America and His Majesty the King of the Netherlands, signed at this place on the 19th instant by the Secretary of State and the chargé d'affaires of the Netherlands in the United States.

M. VAN BUREN.

WASHINGTON, *January 21, 1839.*

To the Senate of the United States:

I transmit for the consideration of the Senate with a view to its ratification a convention for the adjustment of claims of citizens of the United States upon the Government of the Mexican Republic, concluded and

---

*Relating to the intermeddling of any foreign government, or subjects or officers thereof, with the Indian tribes in Michigan, Wisconsin, the territory beyond the Rocky Mountains, or elsewhere within the limits of the United States, etc.

signed in this city on the 10th of September last by John Forsyth, Secretary of State of the United States, and Francisco Pizarro Martinez, envoy extraordinary and minister plenipotentiary of the Mexican Republic, on the part of their respective Governments.

M. VAN BUREN.

WASHINGTON, *January 21, 1839.*

To the Senate of the United States:

I transmit a treaty negotiated with the New York Indians, which was submitted to your body in June last and amended. The amendments have, in pursuance of the requirement of the Senate, been submitted to each of the tribes, assembled in council, for their free and voluntary assent or dissent thereto. In respect to all the tribes except the Senecas the result of this application has been entirely satisfactory. It will be seen by the accompanying papers that of this tribe, the most important of those concerned, the assent of only 42 out of 81 chiefs has been obtained. I deem it advisable under these circumstances to submit the treaty in its modified form to the Senate, for its advice in regard of the sufficiency of the assent of the Senecas to the amendments proposed.

M. VAN BUREN.

WASHINGTON, *January 24, 1839.*

To the Senate of the United States:

I transmit herewith to the Senate, for their consideration in reference to its ratification, a treaty of commerce and navigation between the United States of America and His Majesty the King of Sardinia, signed at Genoa on the 26th of November last by the plenipotentiaries of the contracting parties.

M. VAN BUREN.

WASHINGTON, *January 25, 1839.*

To the Senate of the United States:

I herewith transmit to the Senate a report* from the Secretary of State, in answer to their resolution of the 22d instant.

M. VAN BUREN.

WASHINGTON, *January 26, 1839.*

To the Senate of the United States:

I lay before you, for your consideration, a treaty concluded with the Omaha, Ioway, and Otoe tribes of Indians, and sanctioned by the Yancton and Santie bands of Sioux, by which a tract of land situated on the

---

* Stating that there has been no correspondence with Great Britain in relation to the northeastern boundary since December 3, 1838.

south side of the Missouri between the Great and Little Nemahaw rivers has been ceded to the United States.

It appears that the consent of the half-breeds of the above-mentioned tribes and bands is wanting to perfect the treaty. This tract of land was ceded by the treaty of 15th July, 1830, to them by the above-mentioned tribes and bands of Indians, and can not be taken from them, even for such a valuable consideration as will relieve their wants, without their assent. In order to avoid unnecessary delay, I submit it to your consideration in order to receive an expression of your opinion as to the manner of obtaining the assent of the minors, whereby all unnecessary delay in the final action upon the treaty will be avoided.

M. VAN BUREN.

JANUARY 28, 1839.

To the Senate and House of Representatives of the United States:

I transmit herewith a communication received from the Secretary of the Treasury, on the subject of the balances reported on the books of the Treasury against collecting and disbursing agents of the Government, to which I beg leave to invite the early attention of Congress.

M. VAN BUREN.

WASHINGTON, *January 30, 1839.*

To the Senate and House of Representatives:

I herewith transmit a report from the Secretary of the Treasury, on the subject of commissions claimed by agents or officers employed by the General Government.

The propriety of new legislation regulating the whole matter by express laws seems very apparent, and is urgently recommended to the early attention of Congress.

M. VAN BUREN.

WASHINGTON, *February 2, 1839.*

To the Senate of the United States:

I transmit a report from the Secretary of State, assigning reasons which render it probable that the time limited for the exchange of the ratifications of the convention for the adjustment of claims of citizens of the United States on the Government of the Mexican Republic may expire before that exchange can be effected, and suggesting that the consent of the Senate be requested for an extension of that time. The object of this communication, accordingly, is to solicit the approval by the Senate of such an extension upon the conditions mentioned in the report of the Secretary of State.

M. VAN BUREN.

DEPARTMENT OF STATE,
Washington, February 2, 1839.

The PRESIDENT OF THE UNITED STATES:

The Secretary of State has the honor to report to the President that, according to his instructions, Mr. Martinez, the Mexican minister plenipotentiary, was invited to the Department of State in order to ascertain if he had any recent information on the subject of the convention between the United States and Mexico, transmitted by him to Mexico for ratification by his Government. Mr. Martinez called yesterday and stated that he was without definite information, but expected daily to receive it. He supposed the delay was occasioned by the troubled condition of Mexican affairs, and hoped we would make all due allowances for unavoidable delays. When asked if he had power to enlarge the time for the exchange of ratifications, he said that all his instructions had been fulfilled on the signature of the treaty. The Secretary called his attention to information just received at the Department from Mexico that the treaty was about to be submitted to the Mexican Congress, and he was requested to state what had changed the views of his Government on the question of ratifying the convention, he himself having stated, pending the negotiation, that the President, Bustamente, believed he had full power under the decree of the 20th of May, 1837, to ratify the convention without a reference of it to Congress. He replied that he did not know the causes which had produced this change of opinion. Mr. Martinez appeared to be very solicitous to have it understood that he had done everything in his power to hasten the exchange of ratifications, and to have every allowance made in consequence of the disturbed state of Mexico and her pending war with France. From this conversation and the accompanying extracts from two letters from the consul of the United States at Mexico the President will see that it is by no means improbable, if the ratification of the convention should have been decreed by the Congress of Mexico, that the ratification may not reach the city of Washington until after the 10th of February. The Secretary therefore respectfully represents to the President whether it is not advisable to ask the consent of the Senate to the exchange of the ratifications after the expiration of the time limited, if such exchange shall be offered by the Mexican Government by their agent duly authorized for that purpose. Unless this authority can be granted, a new convention will have to be negotiated and the whole subject passed over until after the next session of Congress.

All which is respectfully submitted.

JOHN FORSYTH.

[Extract of a letter from the consul of the United States at Mexico, dated November 17, 1838.]

On the 13th Mr. Basave did me the honor to call on me, and informed me that he was requested by his excellency the minister of foreign relations, Mr. Cuevas, to inform me that in consequence of his having to go to Jalapa to meet Admiral Baudin, the French minister plenipotentiary, he could not attend to the matters relating to the American question in time for Mr. Basave to go back in the *Woodbury*, and wished, therefore, that she might not be detained, as was intended, for the purpose of conveying to the United States Messrs. Basave and Murphy.

[Extract of a letter from the consul of the United States at Mexico, dated December 31, 1838.]

On a visit to the minister of foreign relations yesterday he informed me that he was writing a friendly letter to the President of the United States and another to Mr. Forsyth, and said he was about to lay the convention entered into between the two Governments before the new Congress, and if ratified should request of me to procure for it a conveyance to the United States by one of our men-of-war, the time for its ratification being nearly expired.

WASHINGTON, D. C., *February 6, 1839.*

To the House of Representatives of the United States:

I transmit to the House of Representatives a report* from the Secretary of State, with accompanying documents, in answer to a resolution of that body bearing date on the 28th ultimo.

M. VAN BUREN.

WASHINGTON, *February 6, 1839.*

To the Senate of the United States:

In compliance with a resolution of the Senate of the 19th December last, I communicate to the Senate a report† from the Secretary of State, accompanying copies of the correspondence called for by said resolution.

M. VAN BUREN.

WASHINGTON, *February 6, 1839.*

The SPEAKER OF THE HOUSE OF REPRESENTATIVES.

SIR: I transmit herewith the report of the commissioners appointed under the act of 28th of June last and the supplementary act of July following to test the usefulness of inventions to improve and render safe the boilers of steam engines against explosions.

M. VAN BUREN.

WASHINGTON, D. C., *February 9, 1839.*

To the House of Representatives of the United States:

I transmit herewith to the House of Representatives a report from the Secretary of State, together with the documents which accompanied it, in answer to the resolution of the 28th ultimo, requesting information touching certain particulars in the territorial relations of the United States and Great Britain on this continent.

M. VAN BUREN.

WASHINGTON, *February 13, 1839.*

To the Senate of the United States:

I herewith transmit to the Senate a report‡ from the Secretary of State, with accompanying documents, in answer to their resolution of the 1st instant.

M. VAN BUREN.

*Relating to the demand upon the British Government for satisfaction for the burning of the steamboat *Caroline* and murdering of unarmed citizens on board, at Schlosser, N. Y., December 29, 1837.

†Relating to the commerce and navigation carried on within the Turkish dominions and in the Pashalic of Egypt.

‡Relating to compensation by Great Britain in the cases of the brigs *Enterprise, Encomium,* and *Comet,* slaves on board which were forcibly seized and detained by local authorities of Bermuda and Bahama islands.

WASHINGTON, *February 16, 1839.*

To the Senate:

I transmit for the constitutional action of the Senate treaties recently concluded with the Creek, Osage, and Iowa tribes of Indians, with communications from the Department of War.

M. VAN BUREN.

WASHINGTON, *February 19, 1839.*

To the House of Representatives:

I transmit a report from the War Department in relation to the investigations had by the commissioners under the resolution of 1st July, 1836, on the sales of reservations of deceased Creek Indians.

M. VAN BUREN.

WASHINGTON, *February 21, 1839.*

To the Senate of the United States:

I transmit for the constitutional action of the Senate articles supplementary to the treaty with the Chippewas, for the purchase of 40 acres of land at the mouth of the Saginaw River, which are esteemed necessary in the erection and use of a light-house at that point.

M. VAN BUREN.

WASHINGTON, *February 22, 1839.*

The SPEAKER OF THE HOUSE OF REPRESENTATIVES:

I herewith transmit a report from the Secretary of State, with accompanying documents, on the subject of the blockades of the Mexican coast and of the Rio de la Plata, in answer to the resolution of the House of Representatives of the 11th instant.

M. VAN BUREN.

WASHINGTON, *February 25, 1839.*

To the Senate:

I transmit for the constitutional action of the Senate a supplemental article to the treaty with the Chippewas of Saganaw, which accompanied my communication of the 21st instant, and explanatory papers from the War Department.

M. VAN BUREN.

WASHINGTON, *February 26, 1839.*

To the Senate and House of Representatives:

I lay before Congress several dispatches from his excellency the governor of Maine, with inclosures, communicating certain proceedings of the legislature of that State, and a copy of the reply of the Secretary of State, made by my direction, together with a note from H. S. Fox, esq., envoy extraordinary and minister plenipotentiary of Great Britain, with the answer of the Secretary of State to the same.

It will appear from those documents that a numerous band of lawless and desperate men, chiefly from the adjoining British Provinces, but without the authority or sanction of the provincial government, had trespassed upon that portion of the territory in dispute between the United States and Great Britain which is watered by the river Aroostook and claimed to belong to the State of Maine, and that they had committed extensive depredations there by cutting and destroying a very large quantity of timber. It will further appear that the governor of Maine, having been officially apprised of the circumstance, had communicated it to the legislature with a recommendation of such provisions in addition to those already existing by law as would enable him to arrest the course of said depredations, disperse the trespassers, and secure the timber which they were about carrying away; that, in compliance with a resolve of the legislature passed in pursuance of his recommendation, his excellency had dispatched the land agent of the State, with a force deemed adequate to that purpose, to the scene of the alleged depredations, who, after accomplishing a part of his duty, was seized by a band of the trespassers at a house claimed to be within the jurisdiction of Maine, whither he had repaired for the purpose of meeting and consulting with the land agent of the Province of New Brunswick, and conveyed as a prisoner to Frederickton, in that Province, together with two other citizens of the State who were assisting him in the discharge of his duty.

It will also appear that the governor and legislature of Maine, satisfied that the trespassers had acted in defiance of the laws of both countries, learning that they were in possession of arms, and anticipating (correctly, as the result has proved) that persons of their reckless and desperate character would set at naught the authority of the magistrates without the aid of a strong force, had authorized the sheriff and the officer appointed in the place of the land agent to employ, at the expense of the State, an armed posse, who had proceeded to the scene of these depredations with a view to the entire dispersion or arrest of the trespassers and the protection of the public property.

In the correspondence between the governor of Maine and Sir John Harvey, lieutenant-governor of the Province of New Brunswick, which has grown out of these occurrences and is likewise herewith communicated, the former is requested to recall the armed party advanced into the disputed territory for the arrest of trespassers, and is informed that a strong body of British troops is to be held in readiness to support and protect the authority and subjects of Great Britain in said territory. In answer to that request the provincial governor is informed of the determination of the State of Maine to support the land agent and his party in the performance of their duty, and the same determination, for the execution of which provision is made by a resolve of the State legislature, is communicated by the governor to the General Government.

The lieutenant-governor of New Brunswick, in calling upon the governor of Maine for the recall of the land agent and his party from the disputed territory, and the British minister, in making a similar demand upon the Government of the United States, proceed upon the assumption that an agreement exists between the two nations conceding to Great Britain, until the final settlement of the boundary question, exclusive possession of and jurisdiction over the territory in dispute. The important bearing which such an agreement, if it existed, would have upon the condition and interests of the parties, and the influence it might have upon the adjustment of the dispute, are too obvious to allow the error upon which this assumption seems to rest to pass for a moment without correction. The answer of the Secretary of State to Mr. Fox's note will show the ground taken by the Government of the United States upon this point. It is believed that all the correspondence which has passed between the two Governments upon this subject has already been communicated to Congress and is now on their files. An abstract of it, however, hastily prepared, accompanies this communication. It is possible that in thus abridging a voluminous correspondence, commencing in 1825 and continuing to a very recent period, a portion may have been accidentally overlooked; but it is believed that nothing has taken place which would materially change the aspect of the question as therein presented. Instead of sustaining the assumption of the British functionaries, that correspondence disproves the existence of any such agreement. It shows that the two Governments have differed not only in regard to the main question of title to the territory in dispute, but with reference also to the right of jurisdiction and the fact of the actual exercise of it in different portions thereof.

Always aiming at an amicable adjustment of the dispute, both parties have entertained and repeatedly urged upon each other a desire that each should exercise its rights, whatever it considered them to be, in such a manner as to avoid collision and allay to the greatest practicable extent the excitement likely to grow out of the controversy. It was in pursuance of such an understanding that Maine and Massachusetts, upon the remonstrance of Great Britain, desisted from making sales of lands, and the General Government from the construction of a projected military road in a portion of the territory of which they claimed to have enjoyed the exclusive possession; and that Great Britain on her part, in deference to a similar remonstrance from the United States, suspended the issue of licenses to cut timber in the territory in controversy and also the survey and location of a railroad through a section of country over which she also claimed to have exercised exclusive jurisdiction.

The State of Maine had a right to arrest the depredations complained of. It belonged to her to judge of the exigency of the occasion calling for her interference, and it is presumed that had the lieutenant-governor of New Brunswick been correctly advised of the nature of the proceedings of the State of Maine he would not have regarded the transaction as requiring on his part any resort to force. Each party claiming a right to the territory, and hence to the exclusive jurisdiction over it, it is manifest that to prevent the destruction of the timber by trespassers, acting against the authority of both, and at the same time avoid forcible collision between the contiguous governments during the pendency of negotiations concerning the title, resort must be had to the mutual exercise of jurisdiction in such extreme cases or to an amicable and temporary arrangement as to the limits within which it should be exercised by each party. The understanding supposed to exist between the United States and Great Britain has been found heretofore sufficient for that purpose, and I believe will prove so hereafter if the parties on the frontier directly interested in the question are respectively governed by a just spirit of conciliation and forbearance. If it shall be found, as there is now reason to apprehend, that there is, in the modes of construing that understanding by the two Governments, a difference not to be reconciled, I shall not hesitate to propose to Her Britannic Majesty's Government a distinct arrangement for the temporary and mutual exercise of jurisdiction by means of which similar difficulties may in future be prevented.

But between an effort on the part of Maine to preserve the property in dispute from destruction by intruders and a military occupation by that State of the territory with a view to hold it by force while the settlement is a subject of negotiation between the two Governments there is an essential difference, as well in respect to the position of the State as to the duties of the General Government. In a letter addressed by the Secretary of State to the governor of Maine on the 1st of March last, giving a detailed statement of the steps which had been taken by the Federal Government to bring the controversy to a termination, and designed to apprise the governor of that State of the views of the Federal Executive in respect to the future, it was stated that while the obligations of the Federal Government to do all in its power to effect the settlement of the boundary question were fully recognized, it had, in the event of being unable to do so specifically by mutual consent, no other means to accomplish that object amicably than by another arbitration, or by a commission, with an umpire, in the nature of an arbitration; and that in the event of all other measures failing the President would feel it his duty to submit another proposition to the Government of Great Britain to refer the decision of the question to a third power. These are still my views upon the subject, and until this step shall have been taken I can not think it proper to invoke the attention of Congress to other than amicable means for the settlement of the controversy, or to cause the military power of the Federal Government to be brought in aid of the State of Maine in any attempt to effect that object by a resort to force.

On the other hand, if the authorities of New Brunswick should attempt to enforce the claim of exclusive jurisdiction set up by them by means of a military occupation on their part of the disputed territory, I shall feel myself bound to consider the contingency provided by the Constitution as having occurred, on the happening of which a State has the right to call for the aid of the Federal Government to repel invasion.

I have expressed to the British minister near this Government a confident expectation that the agents of the State of Maine, who have been arrested under an obvious misapprehension of the object of their mission, will be promptly released, and to the governor of Maine that a similar course will be pursued in regard to the agents of the Province of New Brunswick. I have also recommended that any militia that may have been brought together by the State of Maine from an apprehension of a collision with the government or people of the British Province will be voluntarily and peaceably disbanded.

I can not allow myself to doubt that the results anticipated from these representations will be seasonably realized. The parties more immediately interested can not but perceive that an appeal to arms under existing circumstances will not only prove fatal to their present interests, but would postpone, if not defeat, the attainment of the main objects which they have in view. The very incidents which have recently occurred will necessarily awaken the Governments to the importance of promptly adjusting a dispute by which it is now made manifest that the peace of the two nations is daily and imminently endangered. This expectation is further warranted by the general forbearance which has hitherto characterized the conduct of the Government and people on both sides of the line. In the uniform patriotism of Maine, her attachment to the Union, her respect for the wishes of the people of her sister States (of whose interest in her welfare she can not be unconscious), and in the solicitude felt by the country at large for the preservation of peace with our neighbors, we have a strong guaranty that she will not disregard the request that has been made of her.

As, however, the session of Congress is about to terminate and the agency of the Executive may become necessary during the recess, it is important that the attention of the Legislature should be drawn to the consideration of such measures as may be calculated to obviate the necessity of a call for an extra session. With that view I have thought it my duty to lay the whole matter before you and to invite such action thereon as you may think the occasion requires.

M. VAN BUREN.

WASHINGTON, D. C., *February 27, 1839.*

To the House of Representatives of the United States:

I herewith transmit to the House of Representatives, in answer to their resolution of the 26th instant, a report from the Secretary of State, with the document* therein referred to.

M. VAN BUREN.

WASHINGTON, *February 27, 1839.*

To the House of Representatives:

In further compliance with the resolution of the House of Representatives of the 28th of January last, I communicate a report† from the Secretary of War, which, with its inclosures, contains additional information called for by said resolution.

M. VAN BUREN.

WASHINGTON, *February 27, 1839.*

To the Senate and House of Representatives of the United States:

I transmit to Congress copies of various other documents received from the governor of Maine, relating to the dispute between that State and the Province of New Brunswick, which formed the subject of my message of the 26th instant, and also a copy of a memorandum, signed by the Secretary of State of the United States and Her Britannic Majesty's envoy extraordinary and minister plenipotentiary near the United States, of the terms upon which it is believed that all hostile collision can be avoided on the frontier consistently with and respecting the claims on either side.

As the British minister acts without specific authority from his Government, it will be observed that this memorandum has but the force of recommendation on the provincial authorities and on the government of the State.

M. VAN BUREN.

EXECUTIVE DEPARTMENT,
Augusta, February 22, 1839.

His Excellency M. VAN BUREN,
    President United States.

SIR: I have the honor to inclose herewith copies of letter from the lieutenant-governor of New Brunswick, under date of February 18, with my reply thereto; letter from the solicitor-general of the Province of New Brunswick to the Hon. Charles Jarvis, temporary land agent, under date of the 17th instant, with Mr. Jarvis's reply; parole of honor given by Messrs. McIntire, Cushman, Bartlett, and Webster, dated 18th February; my message to the legislature of the 21st instant.

---

*Letter of Mr. Stevenson, minister to England, relative to the duties and restrictions imposed by Great Britain upon the tobacco trade of the United States.

†Relating to troubles in the British Provinces of Upper and Lower Canada and to alleged violations of neutrality on the part of the United States or Great Britain, and whether the authorities of Upper Canada have undertaken to interdict or restrict the ordinary intercourse between said Province and the United States, inconsistent with subsisting treaties.

These papers will give Your Excellency all the additional information of any importance not heretofore communicated that has been received in relation to the state of affairs upon our eastern frontier. I can not but persuade myself that Your Excellency will see that an attack upon the citizens of this State by a British armed force is in all human probability inevitable, and that the interposition of the General Government at this momentous crisis should be promptly afforded.

I have the honor to be, with high respect, Your Excellency's obedient servant,

JOHN FAIRFIELD,
Governor of Maine.

GOVERNMENT HOUSE,
Frederickton, New Brunswick, February 18, 1839.

His Excellency the GOVERNOR OF MAINE.

SIR: I have the honor to acknowledge the receipt, by the hands of Hon. Mr. Rogers, of your excellency's letter of the 15th instant. Mr. McIntire and the gentlemen with him have been subjected to an examination before Her Majesty's attorney-general of this Province, who has reported to me that the offense of which they stand charged is one rather against the law of nations and of treaties than against those of this Province. They must accordingly be regarded as "state offenders." In this view, their disposal rests exclusively with Her Majesty's Government, to which I shall accordingly report the case. In the meantime I have had pleasure in directing that they shall immediately be allowed to return to the State of Maine upon pledging their parole of honor to present themselves to the Government of this Province whenever Her Majesty's decision may be received, or when required to do so. The high respectability of their characters and situations and my desire to act in all matters relating to the disputed territory in such a manner as may evince the utmost forbearance consistent with the fulfillment of my instructions have influenced me in my conduct toward these gentlemen; but it is necessary that I should upon this occasion distinctly state to your excellency—

First. That if it be the desire of the State of Maine that the friendly relations subsisting between Great Britain and the United States should not be disturbed, it is indispensable that the armed force from that State now understood to be within the territory in dispute be immediately withdrawn, as otherwise I have no alternative but to take military occupation of that territory, with a view to protect Her Majesty's subjects and to support the civil authorities in apprehending all persons claiming to exercise jurisdiction within it.

Second. That it is my duty to require that all persons subjects of Her Majesty who may have been arrested in the commission of acts of trespass within the disputed territory be given up to the tribunals of this Province, there to be proceeded against according to law.

Third. That in the event of the rumor which has just reached me relative to the arrest, detention, or interruption of James Maclauchlan, esq., the warden of the disputed territory, being correct, that that officer be enlarged and the grounds of his detention explained.

Mr. Rogers takes charge of this letter, of which a duplicate will be placed in the hands of the Hon. Mr. McIntire, with both of whom I have conversed and communicated to them my views in regard to the actual position in which I shall be placed and the measures which will be forced upon me if the several demands contained in this letter be not complied with; and I have reason to believe that Mr. McIntire leaves me fully impressed with the anxious desire which I feel to be spared the necessity of acting as the letter of my instructions would both warrant and prescribe.

With regard to trespasses upon the lands of the disputed territory, I beg to assure you that the extent to which those trespasses appear to have been carried, as brought to my knowledge by recent occurrences, will lead me to adopt without any delay the strongest and most effectual measures which may be in my power for putting a stop to and preventing the recurrence of such trespasses.

With high respect, I have the honor to be, your excellency's most obedient servant,

J. HARVEY,
Major-General, Lieutenant-Governor.

EXECUTIVE DEPARTMENT,
Augusta, February 21, 1839.

His Excellency SIR JOHN HARVEY,
Lieutenant-Governor New Brunswick.

SIR: I have the honor to acknowledge the receipt of your excellency's communication of the 18th instant, by the hand of Colonel J. P. Rogers.

To your demand for the discharge of the persons arrested by the authorities of this State for being engaged in acts of trespass upon the public lands of this State I have to say that the persons named are now in the *custody of the law.* With that custody I have neither the disposition nor the authority to interfere.

In regard to James Maclauchlan, esq., provincial land agent, and Mr. Tibbets, his assistant, I have advised that they be released upon the *same terms* upon which the Hon. Rufus McIntire and his assistants were released, to wit, upon their *parole of honor* to return to Bangor whenever they should be thereto required by the executive government of this State, to answer to any charges that may be brought against them for their acts and proceedings upon what your excellency is pleased to call "the disputed territory."

For a reply to the remainder of your excellency's communication I must refer you to my letter of the 18th instant, which you will receive by the hand of R. English, esq.

I have the honor to be, with high respect, your excellency's obedient servant,

JOHN FAIRFIELD,
Governor of Maine.

AT THE MOUTH OF THE ARESTOOK, RIVER ST. JOHN,
Province of New Brunswick, February 17, 1839.

The OFFICER COMMANDING THE ARMED FORCE ON THE DISPUTED TERRITORY.

SIR: I am directed by His Excellency Major-General Sir John Harvey, lieutenant-governor and commander in chief of this Province, to express to you his great surprise at the very extraordinary occurrence of an armed force of the description now with you having entered upon the disputed territory (so called) and attempted to exercise a jurisdiction there foreign to the British Government, seizing upon and maltreating British subjects and retaining many of them prisoners without having in the first instance given any notice or made any communication whatever to the government authorities of this Province of such your intention, or the causes which have led to these acts of aggression. If you are acting under any authority from your own government, the proceedings are still more unjustifiable, being in direct defiance and breach of the existing treaties between the Central Government of the United States and England. If you have not any such authority, you and those with you have placed yourselves in a situation to be treated by both Governments as persons rebelling against the laws of either country. But be that as it may, I am directed by his excellency to give you notice that unless you immediately remove with the force you have with you from any part of the disputed territory (so called) and discharge all British subjects whom you have taken prisoners and at once cease attempting to exercise any authority in the said territory not authorized by the British Government every person of your party that can be found or laid hold of will be taken by the

British authorities in this Province and detained as prisoners to answer for this offense, as his excellency is expressly commanded by his Sovereign to hold this territory inviolate and to defend it from any foreign aggression whatever until the two Governments have determined the question of to whom it shall belong; and to enable him to carry these commands into full effect, a large military force is now assembling at this place, part of which has already arrived, and will be shortly completed to any extent that the service may require. In doing this his excellency is very desirous to avoid any collision between Her Majesty's troops and any of the citizens of the United States that might lead to bloodshed, and if you remove from the territory peaceably and quietly without further opposition such collision will be avoided, as in that case his excellency will not think it necessary to move the British troops farther; but if you do not he will, in the execution of the commands of the British Government, find it necessary to take military possession of the territory in order to defend it from such innovation; and the consequences must be upon your own heads or upon the authority, if any, under which you act. The three gentlemen who were with you, and were taken prisoners by some of our people, have been forwarded on to Frederickton by the magistrates of the country and will be detained (as all persons heretofore have been who on former occasions were found endeavoring to set up or exercise any foreign jurisdiction or authority in the territory in question). They will, however, be well treated and every necessary attention paid to their comfort; but I have no doubt they will be detained as prisoners, to be disposed of as may hereafter be directed by the British Government. The warden of the disputed territory, Mr. Maclauchlan, went out, I understood, a few days since to explain all this to you; but he not having returned we are led to suppose you have still further violated the laws and treaties of the two nations by detaining him, who was a mere messenger of communication, together with Mr. Tibbets, the person who was employed to convey him. But as Mr. Maclauchlan was an accredited officer, acknowledged by the American Government as well as the British, and appointed for the very purpose of looking after this territory, I trust you will on reflection see the great impropriety and risk you run, even with your own government, by detaining him or his attendant, Mr. Tibbets, any longer.

I shall await at this place to receive your answer to this.

I am, sir, your most obedient, humble servant,

GEO. FRED'K STREET,
Solicitor-General of the Provinces.

CONFLUENCE OF THE ST. CROIX, STREAM ARESTOOK RIVER,
Township No. 10, State of Maine, February 19, 1839.

GEO. FRED. STREET, Esq.,
Solicitor-General of Province New Brunswick.

SIR: Your communication of the 17th instant has been this moment received. The solicitor-general of the Provinces must have been misinformed as to the place where the force under my direction is now located, or he would have been spared the impropriety of addressing such a communication to me, a citizen of the State of Maine, one of the North American Confederacy of United States.

It is also to be hoped, for the honor of the British Empire, that when Major-General Sir John Harvey, lieutenant-governor and commander in chief of the Province of New Brunswick, is made acquainted with the place where the Hon. Rufus McIntire, land agent of the State of Maine, and the two other gentlemen with him were forcibly arrested by a lawless mob, that he will direct their immediate discharge and bring the offenders to justice.

The officer to whom you allude and the person in company with him were arrested for serving a precept on a citizen of Maine. He was sent on immediately to Augusta, the seat of government, to be dealt with by the authorities of the State. Their persons are not, therefore, in my power, and application for their discharge must be made to the government of the State.

If, however, I have been in error as to your being under a mistake as to the place where I am now stationed, on land which was run out into townships by the State of Massachusetts and covered by grants from that State before Maine was separated from Massachusetts, and which has therefore been under the jurisdiction of Maine since she has taken her rank among the independent States of the North American Union, therefore, as a citizen of Maine, in official capacity, I have but one answer to return to the threat conveyed: I am here under the direction of the executive of the State, and must remain until otherwise ordered by the only authority recognized by me; and deeply as I should regret a conflict between our respective countries, I shall consider the approach to my station by an armed force as an act of hostility, which will be met by me to the best of my ability.

I am, sir, your most obedient servant,

CHARLES JARVIS, *Land Agent.*

FREDERICKTON, NEW BRUNSWICK, *February 18, 1839.*

Hon. RUFUS McINTIRE, GUSTAVUS G. CUSHMAN, THOMAS BARTLETT, and EBENEZER WEBSTER, Esqs.:

Whereas the offense wherewith you stand charged has been pronounced by the law officers of this Province as one rather against the law of nations and of treaties than against the municipal laws of this country, and as such must be referred for the decision of Her Majesty's Government, you are hereby required to pledge your parole of honor to present yourselves at Frederickton, in this Province of New Brunswick, whenever such decision shall be communicated, or you shall be otherwise required by or on the part of this government; and for this purpose you shall make known the place or places to which such requisition shall be sent.

J. HARVEY.

FEBRUARY 18, 1839.

We have no hesitation in giving, and hereby do give, the parole of honor above referred to.

Witness:

W. EARL.

COUNCIL CHAMBER, *February 21, 1839.*

To the House of Representatives:

Under the order of the House of Representatives of the 19th instant, I herewith lay before you certain correspondence since had with the lieutenant-governor of New Brunswick, and the correspondence between Geo. Frederick Street, esq., solicitor-general for the Province of New Brunswick, and Charles Jarvis, esq., provisional land agent of this State.

The reply of Mr. Jarvis to the inadmissible and preposterous claims and pretensions of Her Majesty's solicitor-general for the Province of New Brunswick must, I think, command the unqualified approbation of everyone having a just regard for the honor of his State. It is in the true spirit, and I have every reason to believe that the same spirit animates the whole body of our citizens. While it prevails, though success will be deserved, defeat can bring no disgrace.

You will see by the accompanying papers (and I take great pleasure in communicating the fact) that Mr. McIntire and his assistants have been released. It was, however, upon their parole of honor to return when thereto required by the government of that Province. Immediately upon the receipt of this information I advised the release of James Maclauchlan, esq., provincial land agent, and his assistant, *upon the same terms.*

Since my last communication the land agent's forces at the Aroostook have been reenforced by about 600 good and effective men, making the whole force now about 750.

I have a letter from Mr. Jarvis dated the 19th, before the reenforcement had arrived, and when his company consisted of only 100 men. He says he found the men in good spirits and that they had been active in making temporary but most effectual defenses of logs, etc.

After describing his defenses, he says: "By to-morrow noon a force of 100 men would make good our position against 500. *Retreating, therefore, is out of the question.* We shall make good our stand against any force that we can reasonably expect would be brought against us." He says further: "I take pleasure in saying to you that a finer looking set of men I never saw than those now with me, and that the honor of our State, so far as they are concerned, is in safe-keeping."

The draft of 1,000 men from the third division has been made with great dispatch. The troops, I understand, arrived promptly at the place of rendezvous at the time appointed in good spirits and anxious for the order to march to the frontier. The detachment from this second division will be ordered to march at the earliest convenient day—probably on Monday next. Other military movements will be made, which it is unnecessary to communicate to you at this time.

The mission of Colonel Rogers to the lieutenant-governor of New Brunswick has resulted successfully so far as relates to the release of the land agent and his assistants, and has been conducted in a manner highly satisfactory.

JOHN FAIRFIELD.

[Memorandum.]

WASHINGTON, *February 27, 1839.*

Her Majesty's authorities consider it to have been understood and agreed upon by the two Governments that the territory in dispute between Great Britain and the United States on the northeastern frontier should remain exclusively under British jurisdiction until the final settlement of the boundary question.

The United States Government have not understood the above agreement in the same sense, but consider, on the contrary, that there has been no agreement whatever for the exercise by Great Britain of exclusive jurisdiction over the disputed territory or any portion thereof, but a mutual understanding that pending the negotiation the jurisdiction then exercised by either party over small portions of the territory in dispute should not be enlarged, but be continued merely for the preservation of local tranquillity and the public property, both forbearing, as far as practicable, to exert any authority, and when any should be exercised by either placing upon the conduct of each other the most favorable construction.

A complete understanding upon the question thus placed at issue of present jurisdiction can only be arrived at by friendly discussion between the Governments of the United States and Great Britain, and as it is confidently hoped that there will be an early settlement of the general question, this subordinate point of difference can be of but little moment.

In the meantime the government of the Province of New Brunswick and the government of the State of Maine will act as follows: Her Majesty's officers will not seek to expel by military force the armed party which has been sent by Maine into the district bordering on the Restook River, but the government of Maine will voluntarily and without needless delay withdraw beyond the bounds of the disputed territory any armed force now within them; and if future necessity shall arise for dispersing notorious trespassers or protecting public property from depredation by armed force, the operation shall be conducted by concert, jointly or separately, according to agreement between the governments of Maine and New Brunswick.

The civil officers in the service, respectively, of New Brunswick and Maine who have been taken into custody by the opposite parties shall be released.

Nothing in this memorandum shall be construed to fortify or to weaken in any respect whatever the claim of either party to the ultimate possession of the disputed territory.

The minister plenipotentiary of Her Britannic Majesty having no specific authority to make any arrangement on this subject, the undersigned can only recommend, as they now earnestly do, to the governments of New Brunswick and Maine to regulate their future proceedings according to the terms hereinbefore set forth until the final settlement of the territorial dispute or until the Governments of the United States and Great Britain shall come to some definite conclusion on the subordinate point upon which they are now at issue.

JOHN FORSYTH,
Secretary of State of the United States of North America.

H. S. FOX,
Her Britannic Majesty's Envoy Extraordinary
and Minister Plenipotentiary.

WASHINGTON, *February 27, 1839.*

To the House of Representatives of the United States:

In compliance with the resolution of the House of Representatives of the 22d instant, requesting information on the subject of the existing relations between the United States and the Mexican Republic, I transmit a report from the Secretary of State, to whom the resolution was referred, and the documents by which the report was accompanied.

M. VAN BUREN.

WASHINGTON, *February 28, 1839.*

To the House of Representatives:

I transmit herewith a report from the Secretary of the Treasury, accompanied by a letter from the Commissioner of the General Land Office, and other documents therein referred to, touching certain information directed to be communicated to the House of Representatives by a resolution dated the 7th of July last.*

M. VAN BUREN.

WASHINGTON, *February 28, 1839.*

To the Senate and House of Representatives of the United States:

I transmit herewith a communication from the Secretary of War, respecting the importance of requiring the officers who may be employed to take the next general census to make a return of the names and ages of pensioners, and, for the reasons given by the Secretary of War, I recommend the subject for your favorable consideration.

M. VAN BUREN.

* Relating to attempts to keep down the price of public lands.

WASHINGTON, *March 1, 1839.*

To the Senate of the United States:

Understanding from the decision of the Senate that the regulation of the Navy Department requiring that a commander "shall serve in active employ as such one year before he can be promoted to a captain" does not under the circumstances of the case constitute an objection to the promotion of Commander Robert F. Stockton, I nominate him to be a captain in the Navy from the 8th of December, 1838, at the same time renominating Commanders Isaac McKeever and John P. Zantzingers to be captains in the Navy, the former from the 8th of December, 1838, and the latter from the 22d of December, 1838, and withdrawing the nomination of Commander William D. Salter.

M. VAN BUREN.

WASHINGTON, *March 1, 1839.*

To the Senate of the United States:

I have received the resolution of the Senate of this day, upon the subject of a communication made to you by the Postmaster-General on the 27th ultimo,* and have the satisfaction of laying before the Senate the accompanying letter from that officer, in which he fully disclaims any intended disrespect to the Senate in the communication referred to.

M. VAN BUREN.

WASHINGTON, *March 2, 1839.*

The SPEAKER OF THE HOUSE OF REPRESENTATIVES OF THE UNITED STATES.

I transmit herewith reports of the Secretaries of the State, Treasury, War, and Navy Departments, in reply to a resolution of the 28th ultimo, calling for information respecting the amounts paid to persons concerned in negotiating treaties with the Indians since the year 1829, and in regard to the disbursement of public money by clerks in the above Departments and the bureaus and offices thereof.

M. VAN BUREN.

VETO MESSAGE.†

MARCH 5, 1839.

The annexed joint resolution was presented to me by Messrs. Foster and Merrick, of the Senate, on the 4th of March at half past 3 o'clock a. m. at the President's house, after a joint committee had informed me at the Capitol that the two Houses had completed their business and

---

*Stating that the only reason he had not sent an answer to a resolution of the Senate was because it was not ready, which was considered disrespectful.

†Pocket veto.

were ready to adjourn, and had communicated my answer that I had no further communication to make to them. The committee of the Senate, on presenting the joint resolution for my signature, stated in explanation of the circumstance that they were not attended by the Committee on Enrolled Bills of the House of Representatives (as is required by the joint rules of the two Houses); that that body had adjourned about two hours before.

The joint resolution is not certified by the clerk of the House in which it originated, as is likewise required by the joint rules. Under these circumstances, and without reference to its provisions, I withheld my approval from the joint resolution.

M. VAN BUREN.

To be placed on file in the State Department.

M. V. B.

A RESOLUTION for the distribution in part of the Madison Papers.

Resolved by the Senate and House of Representatives of the United States of America in Congress assembled, That the Secretary of the Senate and Clerk of the House of Representatives be, and they are hereby, directed to distribute by mail, or otherwise, to each member of the Senate and House of Representatives and Delegates of the Twenty-fifth Congress one copy of the compilation now in progress of execution under the act entitled "An act authorizing the printing of the Madison Papers," when the same shall have been completed; and that of the said compilation there be deposited in the Library of Congress ten copies, in the Library of the House of Representatives twenty copies, and in the office of the Secretary of the Senate ten copies, and one copy in each of the committee rooms of the Senate; and that the residue of said copies shall remain under the care of the said officers subject to the future disposition of Congress.

JAMES K. POLK,
Speaker of the House of Representatives.

W. R. KING,
President of the Senate pro tempore.

I certify that this resolution did originate in the Senate.

————— —————,
Secretary.

THIRD ANNUAL MESSAGE.

WASHINGTON, *December 2, 1839.*

Fellow-Citizens of the Senate and House of Representatives:

I regret that I can not on this occasion congratulate you that the past year has been one of unalloyed prosperity. The ravages of fire and disease have painfully afflicted otherwise flourishing portions of our country, and serious embarrassments yet derange the trade of many of our cities. But notwithstanding these adverse circumstances, that general prosperity which has been heretofore so bountifully bestowed upon us by the

Author of All Good still continues to call for our warmest gratitude. Especially have we reason to rejoice in the exuberant harvests which have lavishly recompensed well-directed industry and given to it that sure reward which is vainly sought in visionary speculations. I can not, indeed, view without peculiar satisfaction the evidences afforded by the past season of the benefits that spring from the steady devotion of the husbandman to his honorable pursuit. No means of individual comfort is more certain and no source of national prosperity is so sure. Nothing can compensate a people for a dependence upon others for the bread they eat, and that cheerful abundance on which the happiness of everyone so much depends is to be looked for nowhere with such sure reliance as in the industry of the agriculturist and the bounties of the earth.

With foreign countries our relations exhibit the same favorable aspect which was presented in my last annual message, and afford continued proof of the wisdom of the pacific, just, and forbearing policy adopted by the first Administration of the Federal Government and pursued by its successors. The extraordinary powers vested in me by an act of Congress for the defense of the country in an emergency, considered so far probable as to require that the Executive should possess ample means to meet it, have not been exerted. They have therefore been attended with no other result than to increase, by the confidence thus reposed in me, my obligations to maintain with religious exactness the cardinal principles that govern our intercourse with other nations. Happily, in our pending questions with Great Britain, out of which this unusual grant of authority arose, nothing has occurred to require its exertion, and as it is about to return to the Legislature I trust that no future necessity may call for its exercise by them or its delegation to another Department of the Government.

For the settlement of our northeastern boundary the proposition promised by Great Britain for a commission of exploration and survey has been received, and a counter project, including also a provision for the certain and final adjustment of the limits in dispute, is now before the British Government for its consideration. A just regard to the delicate state of this question and a proper respect for the natural impatience of the State of Maine, not less than a conviction that the negotiation has been already protracted longer than is prudent on the part of either Government, have led me to believe that the present favorable moment should on no account be suffered to pass without putting the question forever at rest. I feel confident that the Government of Her Britannic Majesty will take the same view of this subject, as I am persuaded it is governed by desires equally strong and sincere for the amicable termination of the controversy.

To the intrinsic difficulties of questions of boundary lines, especially those described in regions unoccupied and but partially known, is to be added in our country the embarrassment necessarily arising out of our Constitution by which the General Government is made the organ of negotiating and deciding upon the particular interests of the States on whose frontiers these lines are to be traced. To avoid another controversy in which a State government might rightfully claim to have her wishes consulted previously to the conclusion of conventional arrangements concerning her rights of jurisdiction or territory, I have thought it necessary to call the attention of the Government of Great Britain to another portion of our conterminous dominion of which the division still remains to be adjusted I refer to the line from the entrance of Lake Superior to the most northwestern point of the Lake of the Woods, stipulations for the settlement of which are to be found in the seventh article of the treaty of Ghent. The commissioners appointed under that article by the two Governments having differed in their opinions, made separate reports, according to its stipulations, upon the points of disagreement, and these differences are now to be submitted to the arbitration of some friendly sovereign or state. The disputed points should be settled and the line designated before the Territorial government of which it is one of the boundaries takes its place in the Union as a State, and I rely upon the cordial cooperation of the British Government to effect that object.

There is every reason to believe that disturbances like those which lately agitated the neighboring British Provinces will not again prove the sources of border contentions or interpose obstacles to the continuance of that good understanding which it is the mutual interest of Great Britain and the United States to preserve and maintain.

Within the Provinces themselves tranquillity is restored, and on our frontier that misguided sympathy in favor of what was presumed to be a general effort in behalf of popular rights, and which in some instances misled a few of our more inexperienced citizens, has subsided into a rational conviction strongly opposed to all intermeddling with the internal affairs of our neighbors. The people of the United States feel, as it is hoped they always will, a warm solicitude for the success of all who are sincerely endeavoring to improve the political condition of mankind. This generous feeling they cherish toward the most distant nations, and it was natural, therefore, that it should be awakened with more than common warmth in behalf of their immediate neighbors; but it does not belong to their character as a community to seek the gratification of those feelings in acts which violate their duty as citizens, endanger the peace of their country, and tend to bring upon it the stain of a violated faith toward foreign nations. If, zealous to confer benefits on others, they appear for a moment to lose sight of the permanent obligations imposed upon them as citizens, they are seldom long misled. From all the information I receive, confirmed to some extent by personal observation, I am satisfied that no one can now hope to engage in such enterprises without encountering public indignation, in addition to the severest penalties of the law.

Recent information also leads me to hope that the emigrants from Her Majesty's Provinces who have sought refuge within our boundaries are disposed to become peaceable residents and to abstain from all attempts to endanger the peace of that country which has afforded them an asylum. On a review of the occurrences on both sides of the line it is satisfactory to reflect that in almost every complaint against our country the offense may be traced to emigrants from the Provinces who have sought refuge here. In the few instances in which they were aided by citizens of the United States the acts of these misguided men were not only in direct contravention of the laws and well-known wishes of their own Government, but met with the decided disapprobation of the people of the United States.

I regret to state the appearance of a different spirit among Her Majesty's subjects in the Canadas. The sentiments of hostility to our people and institutions which have been so frequently expressed there, and the disregard of our rights which has been manifested on some occasions, have, I am sorry to say, been applauded and encouraged by the people, and even by some of the subordinate local authorities, of the Provinces. The chief officers in Canada, fortunately, have not entertained the same feeling, and have probably prevented excesses that must have been fatal to the peace of the two countries.

I look forward anxiously to a period when all the transactions which have grown out of this condition of our affairs, and which have been made the subjects of complaint and remonstrance by the two Governments, respectively, shall be fully examined, and the proper satisfaction given where it is due from either side.

Nothing has occurred to disturb the harmony of our intercourse with Austria, Belgium, Denmark, France, Naples, Portugal, Prussia, Russia, or Sweden. The internal state of Spain has sensibly improved, and a well-grounded hope exists that the return of peace will restore to the people of that country their former prosperity and enable the Government to fulfill all its obligations at home and abroad. The Government of Portugal, I have the satisfaction to state, has paid in full the eleventh and last installment due to our citizens for the claims embraced in the settlement made with it on the 3d of March, 1837.

I lay before you treaties of commerce negotiated with the Kings of Sardinia and of the Netherlands, the ratifications of which have been exchanged since the adjournment of Congress. The liberal principles of these treaties will recommend them to your approbation. That with Sardinia is the first treaty of commerce formed by that Kingdom, and it will, I trust, answer the expectations of the present Sovereign by aiding the development of the resources of his country and stimulating the enterprise of his people. That with the Netherlands happily terminates a long-existing subject of dispute and removes from our future commercial intercourse all apprehension of embarrassment. The King of the Netherlands has also, in further illustration of his character for justice and of his desire to remove every cause of dissatisfaction, made compensation for an American vessel captured in 1800 by a French privateer, and carried into Curaçoa, where the proceeds were appropriated to the use of the colony, then, and for a short time after, under the dominion of Holland.

The death of the late Sultan has produced no alteration in our relations with Turkey. Our newly appointed minister resident has reached Constantinople, and I have received assurances from the present ruler that the obligations of our treaty and those of friendship will be fulfilled by himself in the same spirit that actuated his illustrious father.

I regret to be obliged to inform you that no convention for the settlement of the claims of our citizens upon Mexico has yet been ratified by the Government of that country. The first convention formed for that purpose was not presented by the President of Mexico for the approbation of its Congress, from a belief that the King of Prussia, the arbitrator in case of disagreement in the joint commission to be appointed by the United States and Mexico, would not consent to take upon himself that friendly office. Although not entirely satisfied with the course pursued by Mexico, I felt no hesitation in receiving in the most conciliatory spirit the explanation offered, and also cheerfully consented to a new convention, in order to arrange the payments proposed to be made to our citizens in a manner which, while equally just to them, was deemed less onerous and inconvenient to the Mexican Government. Relying confidently upon the intentions of that Government, Mr. Ellis was directed to repair to Mexico, and diplomatic intercourse has been resumed between the two countries. The new convention has, he informs us, been recently submitted by the President of that Republic to its Congress under circumstances which promise a speedy ratification, a result which I can not allow myself to doubt.

Instructions have been given to the commissioner of the United States under our convention with Texas for the demarcation of the line which separates us from that Republic. The commissioners of both Governments met in New Orleans in August last. The joint commission was organized, and adjourned to convene at the same place on the 12th of October. It is presumed to be now in the performance of its duties.

The new Government of Texas has shown its desire to cultivate friendly relations with us by a prompt reparation for injuries complained of in the cases of two vessels of the United States.

With Central America a convention has been concluded for the renewal of its former treaty with the United States. This was not ratified before the departure of our late chargé d'affaires from that country, and the copy of it brought by him was not received before the adjournment of the Senate at the last session. In the meanwhile, the period limited for the exchange of ratifications having expired, I deemed it expedient, in consequence of the death of the chargé d'affaires, to send a special agent to Central America to close the affairs of our mission there and to arrange with the Government an extension of the time for the exchange of ratifications.

The commission created by the States which formerly composed the Republic of Colombia for adjusting the claims against that Government has by a very unexpected construction of the treaty under which it acts decided that no provision was made for those claims of citizens of the United States which arose from captures by Colombian privateers and were adjudged against the claimants in the judicial tribunals. This decision will compel the United States to apply to the several Governments formerly united for redress. With all these—New Granada, Venezuela, and Ecuador—a perfectly good understanding exists. Our treaty with Venezuela is faithfully carried into execution, and that country, in the enjoyment of tranquillity, is gradually advancing in prosperity under the guidance of its present distinguished President, General Paez. With Ecuador a liberal commercial convention has lately been concluded, which will be transmitted to the Senate at an early day.

With the great American Empire of Brazil our relations continue unchanged, as does our friendly intercourse with the other Governments of South America—the Argentine Republic and the Republics of Uruguay, Chili, Peru, and Bolivia. The dissolution of the Peru-Bolivian Confederation may occasion some temporary inconvenience to our citizens in that quarter, but the obligations on the new Governments which have arisen out of that Confederation to observe its treaty stipulations will no doubt be soon understood, and it is presumed that no indisposition will exist to fulfill those which it contracted with the United States.

The financial operations of the Government during the present year have, I am happy to say, been very successful. The difficulties under which the Treasury Department has labored, from known defects in the existing laws relative to the safe-keeping of the public moneys, aggravated by the suspension of specie payments by several of the banks holding public deposits or indebted to public officers for notes received in payment of public dues, have been surmounted to a very gratifying extent. The large current expenditures have been punctually met, and the faith of the Government in all its pecuniary concerns has been scrupulously maintained.

The nineteen millions of Treasury notes authorized by the act of Congress of 1837, and the modifications thereof with a view to the indulgence of merchants on their duty bonds and of the deposit banks in the payment of public moneys held by them, have been so punctually redeemed as to leave less than the original ten millions outstanding at any one time, and the whole amount unredeemed now falls short of three millions. Of these the chief portion is not due till next year, and the whole would have been already extinguished could the Treasury have realized the payments due to it from the banks. If those due from them during the next year shall be punctually made, and if Congress shall keep the appropriations within the estimates, there is every reason to believe that all the outstanding Treasury notes can be redeemed and the ordinary expenses defrayed without imposing on the people any additional burden, either of loans or increased taxes.

To avoid this and to keep the expenditures within reasonable bounds is a duty second only in importance to the preservation of our national character and the protection of our citizens in their civil and political rights. The creation in time of peace of a debt likely to become permanent is an evil for which there is no equivalent. The rapidity with which many of the States are apparently approaching to this condition admonishes us of our own duties in a manner too impressive to be disregarded. One, not the least important, is to keep the Federal Government always in a condition to discharge with ease and vigor its highest functions should their exercise be required by any sudden conjuncture of public affairs—a condition to which we are always exposed and which may occur when it is least expected. To this end it is indispensable that its finances should be untrammeled and its resources as far as practicable unencumbered. No circumstance could present greater obstacles to the accomplishment of these vitally important objects than the creation of an onerous national debt. Our own experience and also that of other nations have demonstrated the unavoidable and fearful rapidity with which a public debt is increased when the Government has once surrendered itself to the ruinous practice of supplying its supposed necessities by new loans. The struggle, therefore, on our part to be successful must be made at the threshold. To make our efforts effective, severe economy is necessary. This is the surest provision for the national welfare, and it is at the same time the best preservative of the principles on which our institutions rest. Simplicity and economy in the affairs of state have never failed to chasten and invigorate republican principles, while these have been as surely subverted by national prodigality, under whatever specious pretexts it may have been introduced or fostered.

These considerations can not be lost upon a people who have never been inattentive to the effect of their policy upon the institutions they have created for themselves, but at the present moment their force is augmented by the necessity which a decreasing revenue must impose. The check lately given to importations of articles subject to duties, the derangements in the operations of internal trade, and especially the reduction gradually taking place in our tariff of duties, all tend materially to lessen our receipts; indeed, it is probable that the diminution resulting from the last cause alone will not fall short of $5,000,000 in the year 1842, as the final reduction of all duties to 20 per cent then takes effect. The whole revenue then accruing from the customs and from the sales of public lands, if not more, will undoubtedly be wanted to defray the

necessary expenses of the Government under the most prudent administration of its affairs. These are circumstances that impose the necessity
of rigid economy and require its prompt and constant exercise. With the
Legislature rest the power and duty of so adjusting the public expenditure as to promote this end. By the provisions of the Constitution it is
only in consequence of appropriations made by law that money can be
drawn from the Treasury. No instance has occurred since the establishment of the Government in which the Executive, though a component
part of the legislative power, has interposed an objection to an appropriation bill on the sole ground of its extravagance. His duty in this respect
has been considered fulfilled by requesting such appropriations only as
the public service may be reasonably expected to require. In the present
earnest direction of the public mind toward this subject both the Executive and the Legislature have evidence of the strict responsibility to which
they will be held; and while I am conscious of my own anxious efforts
to perform with fidelity this portion of my public functions, it is a satisfaction to me to be able to count on a cordial cooperation from you.

At the time I entered upon my present duties our ordinary disbursements, without including those on account of the public debt, the Post-
Office, and the trust funds in charge of the Government, had been
largely increased by appropriations for the removal of the Indians, for
repelling Indian hostilities, and for other less urgent expenses which
grew out of an overflowing Treasury. Independent of the redemption
of the public debt and trusts, the gross expenditures of seventeen and
eighteen millions in 1834 and 1835 had by these causes swelled to
twenty-nine millions in 1836, and the appropriations for 1837, made
previously to the 4th of March, caused the expenditure to rise to the
very large amount of thirty-three millions. We were enabled during
the year 1838, notwithstanding the continuance of our Indian embarrassments, somewhat to reduce this amount, and that for the present
year (1839) will not in all probability exceed twenty-six millions, or
six millions less than it was last year. With a determination, so far as
depends on me, to continue this reduction, I have directed the estimates
for 1840 to be subjected to the severest scrutiny and to be limited to the
absolute requirements of the public service. They will be found less
than the expenditures of 1839 by over $5,000,000.

The precautionary measures which will be recommended by the Secretary of the Treasury to protect faithfully the public credit under the
fluctuations and contingencies to which our receipts and expenditures
are exposed, and especially in a commercial crisis like the present, are
commended to your early attention.

On a former occasion your attention was invited to various considerations in support of a preemption law in behalf of the settlers on the public lands, and also of a law graduating the prices for such lands as had
long been in the market unsold in consequence of their inferior quality.

The execution of the act which was passed on the first subject has been attended with the happiest consequences in quieting titles and securing improvements to the industrious, and it has also to a very gratifying extent been exempt from the frauds which were practiced under previous preemption laws. It has at the same time, as was anticipated, contributed liberally during the present year to the receipts of the Treasury.

The passage of a graduation law, with the guards before recommended, would also, I am persuaded, add considerably to the revenue for several years, and prove in other respects just and beneficial.

Your early consideration of the subject is therefore once more earnestly requested.

The present condition of the defenses of our principal seaports and navy-yards, as represented by the accompanying report of the Secretary of War, calls for the early and serious attention of Congress; and, as connecting itself intimately with this subject, I can not recommend too strongly to your consideration the plan submitted by that officer for the organization of the militia of the United States.

In conformity with the expressed wishes of Congress, an attempt was made in the spring to terminate the Florida war by negotiation. It is to be regretted that these humane intentions should have been frustrated and that the effort to bring these unhappy difficulties to a satisfactory conclusion should have failed; but after entering into solemn engagements with the commanding general, the Indians, without any provocation, recommenced their acts of treachery and murder. The renewal of hostilities in that Territory renders it necessary that I should recommend to your favorable consideration the plan which will be submitted to you by the Secretary of War, in order to enable that Department to conduct them to a successful issue.

Having had an opportunity of personally inspecting a portion of the troops during the last summer, it gives me pleasure to bear testimony to the success of the effort to improve their discipline by keeping them together in as large bodies as the nature of our service will permit. I recommend, therefore, that commodious and permanent barracks be constructed at the several posts designated by the Secretary of War. Notwithstanding the high state of their discipline and excellent police, the evils resulting to the service from the deficiency of company officers were very apparent, and I recommend that the staff officers be permanently separated from the line.

The Navy has been usefully and honorably employed in protecting the rights and property of our citizens wherever the condition of affairs seemed to require its presence. With the exception of one instance, where an outrage, accompanied by murder, was committed on a vessel of the United States while engaged in a lawful commerce, nothing is known to have occurred to impede or molest the enterprise of our citizens on that element, where it is so signally displayed. On learning this daring act of piracy, Commodore Reed proceeded immediately to the spot, and receiving no satisfaction, either in the surrender of the murderers or the restoration of the plundered property, inflicted severe and merited chastisement on the barbarians.

It will be seen by the report of the Secretary of the Navy respecting the disposition of our ships of war that it has been deemed necessary to station a competent force on the coast of Africa to prevent a fraudulent use of our flag by foreigners.

Recent experience has shown that the provisions in our existing laws which relate to the sale and transfer of American vessels while abroad are extremely defective. Advantage has been taken of these defects to give to vessels wholly belonging to foreigners and navigating the ocean an apparent American ownership. This character has been so well simulated as to afford them comparative security in prosecuting the slave trade—a traffic emphatically denounced in our statutes, regarded with abhorrence by our citizens, and of which the effectual suppression is nowhere more sincerely desired than in the United States. These circumstances make it proper to recommend to your early attention a careful revision of these laws, so that without impeding the freedom and facilities of our navigation or impairing an important branch of our industry connected with it the integrity and honor of our flag may be carefully preserved. Information derived from our consul at Havana showing the necessity of this was communicated to a committee of the Senate near the close of the last session, but too late, as it appeared, to be acted upon. It will be brought to your notice by the proper Department, with additional communications from other sources.

The latest accounts from the exploring expedition represent it as proceeding successfully in its objects and promising results no less useful to trade and navigation than to science.

The extent of post-roads covered by mail service on the 1st of July last was about 133,999 miles and the rate of annual transportation upon them 34,496,878 miles. The number of post-offices on that day was 12,780 and on the 30th ultimo 13,028.

The revenue of the Post-Office Department for the year ending with the 30th of June last was $4,476,638, exhibiting an increase over the preceding year of $241,560. The engagements and liabilities of the Department for the same period are $4,624,117.

The excess of liabilities over the revenue for the last two years has been met out of the surplus which had previously accumulated. The cash on hand on the 30th ultimo was about $206,701.95, and the current income of the Department varies very little from the rate of current expenditures. Most of the service suspended last year has been restored, and most of the new routes established by the act of 7th July, 1838, have been set in operation, at an annual cost of $136,963. Notwithstanding the pecuniary difficulties of the country, the revenue of the

Department appears to be increasing, and unless it shall be seriously checked by the recent suspension of payment by so many of the banks it will be able not only to maintain the present mail service, but in a short time to extend it. It is gratifying to witness the promptitude and fidelity with which the agents of this Department in general perform their public duties.

Some difficulties have arisen in relation to contracts for the transportation of the mails by railroad and steamboat companies. It appears that the maximum of compensation provided by Congress for the transportation of the mails upon railroads is not sufficient to induce some of the companies to convey them at such hours as are required for the accommodation of the public. It is one of the most important duties of the General Government to provide and maintain for the use of the people of the States the best practicable mail establishment. To arrive at that end it is indispensable that the Post-Office Department shall be enabled to control the hours at which the mails shall be carried over railroads, as it now does over all other roads. Should serious inconveniences arise from the inadequacy of the compensation now provided by law, or from unreasonable demands by any of the railroad companies, the subject is of such general importance as to require the prompt attention of Congress.

In relation to steamboat lines, the most efficient remedy is obvious and has been suggested by the Postmaster-General. The War and Navy Departments already employ steamboats in their service; and although it is by no means desirable that the Government should undertake the transportation of passengers or freight as a business, there can be no reasonable objection to running boats, temporarily, whenever it may be necessary to put down attempts at extortion, to be discontinued as soon as reasonable contracts can be obtained.

The suggestions of the Postmaster-General relative to the inadequacy of the legal allowance to witnesses in cases of prosecutions for mail depredations merit your serious consideration. The safety of the mails requires that such prosecutions shall be efficient, and justice to the citizen whose time is required to be given to the public demands not only that his expenses shall be paid, but that he shall receive a reasonable compensation.

The reports from the War, Navy, and Post-Office Departments will accompany this communication, and one from the Treasury Department will be presented to Congress in a few days.

For various details in respect to the matters in charge of these Departments I would refer you to those important documents, satisfied that you will find in them many valuable suggestions which will be found well deserving the attention of the Legislature.

From a report made in December of last year by the Secretary of State to the Senate, showing the trial docket of each of the circuit courts and the number of miles each judge has to travel in the performance of his duties, a great inequality appears in the amount of labor assigned to each judge. The number of terms to be held in each of the courts composing the ninth circuit, the distances between the places at which they sit and from thence to the seat of Government, are represented to be such as to render it impossible for the judge of that circuit to perform in a manner corresponding with the public exigencies his term and circuit duties. A revision, therefore, of the present arrangement of the circuit seems to be called for and is recommended to your notice.

I think it proper to call your attention to the power assumed by Territorial legislatures to authorize the issue of bonds by corporate companies on the guaranty of the Territory. Congress passed a law in 1836 providing that no act of a Territorial legislature incorporating banks should have the force of law until approved by Congress, but acts of a very exceptionable character previously passed by the legislature of Florida were suffered to remain in force, by virtue of which bonds may be issued to a very large amount by those institutions upon the faith of the Territory. A resolution, intending to be a joint one, passed the Senate at the same session, expressing the sense of Congress that the laws in question ought not to be permitted to remain in force unless amended in many material respects; but it failed in the House of Representatives for want of time, and the desired amendments have not been made. The interests involved are of great importance, and the subject deserves your early and careful attention.

The continued agitation of the question relative to the best mode of keeping and disbursing the public money still injuriously affects the business of the country. The suspension of specie payments in 1837 rendered the use of deposit banks as prescribed by the act of 1836 a source rather of embarrassment than aid, and of necessity placed the custody of most of the public money afterwards collected in charge of the public officers. The new securities for its safety which this required were a principal cause of my convening an extra session of Congress, but in consequence of a disagreement between the two Houses neither then nor at any subsequent period has there been any legislation on the subject. The effort made at the last session to obtain the authority of Congress to punish the use of public money for private purposes as a crime—a measure attended under other governments with signal advantage—was also unsuccessful, from diversities of opinion in that body, notwithstanding the anxiety doubtless felt by it to afford every practicable security. The result of this is still to leave the custody of the public money without those safeguards which have been for several years earnestly desired by the Executive, and as the remedy is only to be found in the action of the Legislature it imposes on me the duty of again submitting to you the propriety of passing a law providing for the safe-keeping of the public moneys, and especially to ask that its use for private purposes by any officers intrusted with it may be declared to be a felony, punishable with penalties proportioned to the magnitude of the offense.

These circumstances, added to known defects in the existing laws and unusual derangement in the general operations of trade, have during the last three years much increased the difficulties attendant on the collection, keeping, and disbursement of the revenue, and called forth corresponding exertions from those having them in charge. Happily these have been successful beyond expectation. Vast sums have been collected and disbursed by the several Departments with unexpected cheapness and ease, transfers have been readily made to every part of the Union, however distant, and defalcations have been far less than might have been anticipated from the absence of adequate legal restraints. Since the officers of the Treasury and Post-Office Departments were charged with the custody of most of the public moneys received by them there have been collected $66,000,000, and, excluding the case of the late collector at New York, the aggregate amount of losses sustained in the collection can not, it is believed, exceed $60,000. The defalcation of the late collector at that city, of the extent and circumstances of which Congress have been fully informed, ran through all the modes of keeping the public money that have been hitherto in use, and was distinguished by an aggravated disregard of duty that broke through the restraints of every system, and can not, therefore, be usefully referred to as a test of the comparative safety of either. Additional information will also be furnished by the report of the Secretary of the Treasury, in reply to a call made upon that officer by the House of Representatives at the last session requiring detailed information on the subject of defaults by public officers or agents under each Administration from 1789 to 1837. This document will be submitted to you in a few days. The general results (independent of the Post-Office, which is kept separately and will be stated by itself), so far as they bear upon this subject, are that the losses which have been and are likely to be sustained by any class of agents have been the greatest by banks, including, as required in the resolution, their depreciated paper received for public dues; that the next largest have been by disbursing officers, and the least by collectors and receivers. If the losses on duty bonds are included, they alone will be threefold those by both collectors and receivers. Our whole experience, therefore, furnishes the strongest evidence that the desired legislation of Congress is alone wanting to insure in those operations the highest degree of security and facility. Such also appears to have been the experience of other nations. From the results of inquiries made by the Secretary of the Treasury in regard to the practice among them I am enabled to state that in twenty-two out of twenty-seven foreign governments from which undoubted information has been obtained the public moneys are kept in charge of public officers. This concurrence of opinion in favor of that system is perhaps as great as exists on any question of internal administration.

In the modes of business and official restraints on disbursing officers no legal change was produced by the suspension of specie payments.

The report last referred to will be found to contain also much useful information in relation to this subject.

I have heretofore assigned to Congress my reasons for believing that the establishment of an independent National Treasury, as contemplated by the Constitution, is necessary to the safe action of the Federal Government. The suspension of specie payments in 1837 by the banks having the custody of the public money showed in so alarming a degree our dependence on those institutions for the performance of duties required by law that I then recommended the entire dissolution of that connection. This recommendation has been subjected, as I desired it should be, to severe scrutiny and animated discussion, and I allow myself to believe that notwithstanding the natural diversities of opinion which may be anticipated on all subjects involving such important considerations, it has secured in its favor as general a concurrence of public sentiment as could be expected on one of such magnitude.

Recent events have also continued to develop new objections to such a connection. Seldom is any bank, under the existing system and practice, able to meet on demand all its liabilities for deposits and notes in circulation. It maintains specie payments and transacts a profitable business only by the confidence of the public in its solvency, and whenever this is destroyed the demands of its depositors and note holders, pressed more rapidly than it can make collections from its debtors, force it to stop payment. This loss of confidence, with its consequences, occurred in 1837, and afforded the apology of the banks for their suspension. The public then acquiesced in the validity of the excuse, and while the State legislatures did not exact from them their forfeited charters, Congress, in accordance with the recommendation of the Executive, allowed them time to pay over the public money they held, although compelled to issue Treasury notes to supply the deficiency thus created.

It now appears that there are other motives than a want of public confidence under which the banks seek to justify themselves in a refusal to meet their obligations. Scarcely were the country and Government relieved in a degree from the difficulties occasioned by the general suspension of 1837 when a partial one, occurring within thirty months of the former, produced new and serious embarrassments, though it had no palliation in such circumstances as were alleged in justification of that which had previously taken place. There was nothing in the condition of the country to endanger a well-managed banking institution; commerce was deranged by no foreign war; every branch of manufacturing industry was crowned with rich rewards, and the more than usual abundance of our harvests, after supplying our domestic wants, had left our granaries and storehouses filled with a surplus for exportation. It is in the midst of this that an irredeemable and depreciated paper currency is entailed upon the people by a large portion of the banks. They are not driven to it by the exhibition of a loss of public confidence or of a sudden pressure from their depositors or note holders, but they excuse themselves by alleging that the current of business and exchange with foreign countries, which draws the precious metals from their vaults, would require in order to meet it a larger curtailment of their loans to a comparatively small portion of the community than it will be convenient for them to bear or perhaps safe for the banks to exact. The plea has ceased to be one of necessity. Convenience and policy are now deemed sufficient to warrant these institutions in disregarding their solemn obligations. Such conduct is not merely an injury to individual creditors, but it is a wrong to the whole community, from whose liberality they hold most valuable privileges, whose rights they violate, whose business they derange, and the value of whose property they render unstable and insecure. It must be evident that this new ground for bank suspensions, in reference to which their action is not only disconnected with, but wholly independent of, that of the public, gives a character to their suspensions more alarming than any which they exhibited before, and greatly increases the impropriety of relying on the banks in the transactions of the Government.

A large and highly respectable portion of our banking institutions are, it affords me unfeigned pleasure to state, exempted from all blame on account of this second delinquency. They have, to their great credit, not only continued to meet their engagements, but have even repudiated the grounds of suspension now resorted to. It is only by such a course that the confidence and good will of the community can be preserved, and in the sequel the best interests of the institutions themselves promoted.

New dangers to the banks are also daily disclosed from the extension of that system of extravagant credit of which they are the pillars. Formerly our foreign commerce was principally founded on an exchange of commodities, including the precious metals, and leaving in its transactions but little foreign debt. Such is not now the case. Aided by the facilities afforded by the banks, mere credit has become too commonly the basis of trade. Many of the banks themselves, not content with largely stimulating this system among others, have usurped the business, while they impair the stability, of the mercantile community; they have become borrowers instead of lenders; they establish their agencies abroad; they deal largely in stocks and merchandise; they encourage the issue of State securities until the foreign market is glutted with them; and, unsatisfied with the legitimate use of their own capital and the exercise of their lawful privileges, they raise by large loans additional means for every variety of speculation. The disasters attendant on this deviation from the former course of business in this country are now shared alike by banks and individuals to an extent of which there is perhaps no previous example in the annals of our country. So long as a willingness of the foreign lender and a sufficient export of our productions to meet any necessary partial payments leave the flow of credit undisturbed all appears to be prosperous, but as soon as it is checked by any hesitation abroad or by an inability to make payment there in our productions the evils of the system are disclosed. The paper currency, which might serve for domestic purposes, is useless to pay the debt due in Europe. Gold and silver are therefore drawn in exchange for their notes from the banks. To keep up their supply of coin these institutions are obliged to call upon their own debtors, who pay them principally in their own notes, which are as unavailable to them as they are to the merchants to meet the foreign demand. The calls of the banks, therefore, in such emergencies of necessity exceed that demand, and produce a corresponding curtailment of their accommodations and of the currency at the very moment when the state of trade renders it most inconvenient to be borne. The intensity of this pressure on the community is in proportion to the previous liberality of credit and consequent expansion of the currency. Forced sales of property are made at the time when the means of purchasing are most reduced, and the worst calamities to individuals are only at last arrested by an open violation of their obligations by the banks—a refusal to pay specie for their notes and an imposition upon the community of a fluctuating and depreciated currency.

These consequences are inherent in the present system. They are not influenced by the banks being large or small, created by National or State Governments. They are the results of the irresistible laws of trade or credit. In the recent events, which have so strikingly illustrated the certain effects of these laws, we have seen the bank of the largest capital in the Union, established under a national charter, and lately strengthened, as we were authoritatively informed, by exchanging that for a State charter with new and unusual privileges—in a condition, too, as it was said, of entire soundness and great prosperity—not merely unable to resist these effects, but the first to yield to them.

Nor is it to be overlooked that there exists a chain of necessary dependence among these institutions which obliges them to a great extent to follow the course of others, notwithstanding its injustice to their own immediate creditors or injury to the particular community in which they are placed. This dependence of a bank, which is in proportion to the extent of its debts for circulation and deposits, is not merely on others in its own vicinity, but on all those which connect it with the center of trade. Distant banks may fail without seriously affecting those in our principal commercial cities, but the failure of the latter is felt at the extremities of the Union. The suspension at New York in 1837 was everywhere, with very few exceptions, followed as soon as it was known. That recently at Philadelphia immediately affected the banks of the South and West in a similar manner. This dependence of our whole banking system on the institutions in a few large cities is not found in the laws of their organization, but in those of trade and exchange. The banks at that center, to which currency flows and where it is required in payments for merchandise, hold the power of controlling those in regions whence it comes, while the latter possess no means of restraining them; so that the value of individual property and the prosperity of trade through the whole interior of the country are made to depend on the good or bad management of the banking institutions in the great seats of trade on the seaboard.

But this chain of dependence does not stop here. It does not terminate at Philadelphia or New York. It reaches across the ocean and ends in London, the center of the credit system. The same laws of trade which give to the banks in our principal cities power over the whole banking system of the United States subject the former, in their turn, to the money power in Great Britain. It is not denied that the suspension of the New York banks in 1837, which was followed in quick succession throughout the Union, was produced by an application of that power, and it is now alleged, in extenuation of the present condition of so large a portion of our banks, that their embarrassments have arisen from the same cause.

From this influence they can not now entirely escape, for it has its origin in the credit currencies of the two countries; it is strengthened by the current of trade and exchange which centers in London, and is rendered almost irresistible by the large debts contracted there by our merchants, our banks, and our States. It is thus that an introduction of a new bank into the most distant of our villages places the business of that village within the influence of the money power in England; it is thus that every new debt which we contract in that country seriously affects our own currency and extends over the pursuits of our citizens its powerful influence. We can not escape from this by making new banks, great or small, State or national. The same chains which bind those now existing to the center of this system of paper credit must equally fetter every similar institution we create. It is only by the extent to which this system has been pushed of late that we have been made fully aware of its irresistible tendency to subject our own banks and currency to a vast controlling power in a foreign land, and it adds a new argument to those which illustrate their precarious situation. Endangered in the first place by their own mismanagement and again by the conduct of every institution which connects them with the center of trade in our own country, they are yet subjected beyond all this to the effect of whatever measures policy, necessity, or caprice may induce those who control the credits of England to resort to. I mean not to comment upon these measures, present or past, and much less to discourage the prosecution of fair commercial dealing between the two countries, based on reciprocal benefits; but it having now been made manifest that the power of inflicting these and similar injuries is by the resistless law of a credit currency and credit trade equally capable of extending their consequences through all the ramifications of our banking system, and by that means indirectly obtaining, particularly when our banks are used as depositories of the public moneys, a dangerous political influence in the United States, I have deemed it my duty to bring the subject to your notice and ask for it your serious consideration.

Is an argument required beyond the exposition of these facts to show the impropriety of using our banking institutions as depositories of the public money? Can we venture not only to encounter the risk of their individual and mutual mismanagement, but at the same time to place our foreign and domestic policy entirely under the control of a foreign moneyed interest? To do so is to impair the independence of our Government, as the present credit system has already impaired the independence of our banks; it is to submit all its important operations, whether of peace or war, to be controlled or thwarted, at first by our own banks and then by a power abroad greater than themselves. I can not bring myself to depict the humiliation to which this Government and people might be sooner or later reduced if the means for defending their rights are to be made dependent upon those who may have the most powerful of motives to impair them.

Nor is it only in reference to the effect of this state of things on the independence of our Government or of our banks that the subject presents itself for consideration; it is to be viewed also in its relations to the general trade of our country. The time is not long passed when a deficiency of foreign crops was thought to afford a profitable market for the surplus of our industry, but now we await with feverish anxiety the news of the English harvest, not so much from motives of commendable sympathy, but fearful lest its anticipated failure should narrow the field of credit there. Does not this speak volumes to the patriot? Can a system be beneficent, wise, or just which creates greater anxiety for interests dependent on foreign credit than for the general prosperity of our own country and the profitable exportation of the surplus produce of our labor?

The circumstances to which I have thus adverted appear to me to afford weighty reasons, developed by late events, to be added to those which I have on former occasions offered when submitting to your better knowledge and discernment the propriety of separating the custody of the public money from banking institutions. Nor has anything occurred to lessen, in my opinion, the force of what has been heretofore urged. The only ground on which that custody can be desired by the banks is the profitable use which they may make of the money. Such use would be regarded in individuals as a breach of trust or a crime of great magnitude, and yet it may be reasonably doubted whether, first and last, it is not attended with more mischievous consequences when permitted to the former than to the latter. The practice of permitting the public money to be used by its keepers, as here, is believed to be peculiar to this country and to exist scarcely anywhere else. To procure it here improper influences are appealed to, unwise connections are established between the Government and vast numbers of powerful State institutions, other motives than the public good are brought to bear both on the executive and legislative departments, and selfish combinations leading to special legislation are formed. It is made the interest of banking institutions and their stockholders throughout the Union to use their exertions for the increase of taxation and the accumulation of a surplus revenue, and while an excuse is afforded the means are furnished for those excessive issues which lead to extravagant trading and speculation and are the forerunners of a vast debt abroad and a suspension of the banks at home.

Impressed, therefore, as I am with the propriety of the funds of the Government being withdrawn from the private use of either banks or individuals, and the public money kept by duly appointed public agents, and believing as I do that such also is the judgment which discussion, reflection, and experience have produced on the public mind, I leave the subject with you. It is, at all events, essential to the interests of the community and the business of the Government that a decision should be made.

Most of the arguments that dissuade us from employing banks in the custody and disbursement of the public money apply with equal force to the receipt of their notes for public dues. The difference is only in form. In one instance the Government is a creditor for its deposits, and in the other for the notes it holds. They afford the same opportunity for using the public moneys, and equally lead to all the evils attendant upon it, since a bank can as safely extend its discounts on a deposit of its notes in the hands of a public officer as on one made in its own vaults. On the other hand, it would give to the Government no greater security, for in case of failure the claim of the note holder would be no better than that of a depositor.

I am aware that the danger of inconvenience to the public and unreasonable pressure upon sound banks have been urged as objections to requiring the payment of the revenue in gold and silver. These objections have been greatly exaggerated. From the best estimates we may safely fix the amount of specie in the country at $85,000,000, and the portion of that which would be employed at any one time in the receipts and disbursements of the Government, even if the proposed change were made at once, would not, it is now, after fuller investigation, believed exceed four or five millions. If the change were gradual, several years would elapse before that sum would be required, with annual opportunities in the meantime to alter the law should experience prove it to be oppressive or inconvenient. The portions of the community on whose business the change would immediately operate are comparatively small, nor is it believed that its effect would be in the least unjust or injurious to them.

In the payment of duties, which constitute by far the greater portion of the revenue, a very large proportion is derived from foreign commission houses and agents of foreign manufacturers, who sell the goods consigned to them generally at auction, and after paying the duties out of the avails remit the rest abroad in specie or its equivalent. That the amount of duties should in such cases be also retained in specie can hardly be made a matter of complaint. Our own importing merchants, by whom the residue of the duties is paid, are not only peculiarly interested in maintaining a sound currency, which the measure in question will especially promote, but are from the nature of their dealings best able to know when specie will be needed and to procure it with the least difficulty or sacrifice. Residing, too, almost universally in places where the revenue is received and where the drafts used by the Government for its disbursements must concentrate, they have every opportunity to obtain and use them in place of specie should it be for their interest or convenience. Of the number of these drafts and the facilities they may afford, as well as of the rapidity with which the public funds are drawn and disbursed, an idea may be formed from the fact that of nearly $20,000,000 paid to collectors and receivers during the present year the average amount in their hands at any one time has not exceeded a million and a half, and of the fifteen millions received by the collector of New York alone during the present year the average amount held by him subject to draft during each week has been less than half a million.

The ease and safety of the operations of the Treasury in keeping the public money are promoted by the application of its own drafts to the public dues. The objection arising from having them too long outstanding might be obviated and they yet made to afford to merchants and banks holding them an equivalent for specie, and in that way greatly lessen the amount actually required. Still less inconvenience will attend the requirement of specie in purchases of public lands. Such purchases, except when made on speculation, are in general but single transactions, rarely repeated by the same person; and it is a fact that for the last year and a half, during which the notes of sound banks have been received, more than a moiety of these payments has been voluntarily made in specie, being a larger proportion than would have been required in three years under the graduation proposed.

It is, moreover, a principle than which none is better settled by experience that the supply of the precious metals will always be found adequate to the uses for which they are required. They abound in countries where no other currency is allowed. In our own States, where small notes are excluded, gold and silver supply their place. When driven to their hiding places by bank suspensions, a little firmness in the community soon restores them in a sufficient quantity for ordinary purposes. Postage and other public dues have been collected in coin without serious inconvenience even in States where a depreciated paper currency has existed for years, and this, with the aid of Treasury notes for a part of the time, was done without interruption during the suspension of 1837. At the present moment the receipts and disbursements of the Government are made in legal currency in the largest portion of the Union. No one suggests a departure from this rule, and if it can now be successfully carried out it will be surely attended with even less difficulty when bank notes are again redeemed in specie.

Indeed, I can not think that a serious objection would anywhere be raised to the receipt and payment of gold and silver in all public transactions were it not from an apprehension that a surplus in the Treasury might withdraw a large portion of it from circulation and lock it up unprofitably in the public vaults. It would not, in my opinion, be difficult to prevent such an inconvenience from occurring; but the authentic statements which I have already submitted to you in regard to the actual amount in the public Treasury at any one time during the period embraced in them and the little probability of a different state of the Treasury for at least some years to come seem to render it unnecessary to dwell upon it. Congress, moreover, as I have before observed, will in every year have an opportunity to guard against it should the occurrence of any circumstances lead us to apprehend injury from this source. Viewing the subject in all its aspects, I can not believe that any period will be more auspicious than the present for the adoption of all measures necessary to maintain the sanctity of our own engagements and to aid in securing to the community that abundant supply of the precious metals which adds so much to their prosperity and gives such increased stability to all their dealings.

In a country so commercial as ours banks in some form will probably always exist, but this serves only to render it the more incumbent on us, notwithstanding the discouragements of the past, to strive in our respective stations to mitigate the evils they produce; to take from them as rapidly as the obligations of public faith and a careful consideration of the immediate interests of the community will permit the unjust character of monopolies; to check, so far as may be practicable, by prudent legislation those temptations of interest and those opportunities for their dangerous indulgence which beset them on every side, and to confine them strictly to the performance of their paramount duty—that of aiding the operations of commerce rather than consulting their own exclusive advantage. These and other salutary reforms may, it is believed, be accomplished without the violation of any of the great principles of the social compact, the observance of which is indispensable to its existence, or interfering in any way with the useful and profitable employment of real capital.

Institutions so framed have existed and still exist elsewhere, giving to commercial intercourse all necessary facilities without inflating or depreciating the currency or stimulating speculation. Thus accomplishing

their legitimate ends, they have gained the surest guaranty for their protection and encouragement in the good will of the community.   Among
a people so just as ours the same results could not fail to attend a similar
course.   The direct supervision of the banks belongs, from the nature
of our Government, to the States who authorize them.   It is to their
legislatures that the people must mainly look for action on that subject.
But as the conduct of the Federal Government in the management of
its revenue has also a powerful, though less immediate, influence upon
them, it becomes our duty to see that a proper direction is given to it.
While the keeping of the public revenue in a separate and independent
treasury and of collecting it in gold and silver will have a salutary influence on the system of paper credit with which all banks are connected,
and thus aid those that are sound and well managed, it will at the same
time sensibly check such as are otherwise by at once withholding the
means of extravagance afforded by the public funds and restraining them
from excessive issues of notes which they would be constantly called
upon to redeem.

I am aware it has been urged that this control may be best attained
and exerted by means of a national bank.   The constitutional objections
which I am well known to entertain would prevent me in any event
from proposing or assenting to that remedy; but in addition to this, I
can not after past experience bring myself to think that it can any
longer be extensively regarded as effective for such a purpose.   The
history of the late national bank, through all its mutations, shows that it
was not so.   On the contrary, it may, after a careful consideration of the
subject, be, I think, safely stated that at every period of banking excess
it took the lead; that in 1817 and 1818, in 1823, in 1831, and in 1834 its
vast expansions, followed by distressing contractions, led to those of the
State institutions.   It swelled and maddened the tides of the banking
system, but seldom allayed or safely directed them.   At a few periods
only was a salutary control exercised, but an eager desire, on the contrary, exhibited for profit in the first place; and if afterwards its measures
were severe toward other institutions, it was because its own safety compelled it to adopt them.   It did not differ from them in principle or in
form; its measures emanated from the same spirit of gain; it felt the
same temptation to overissues; it suffered from and was totally unable
to avert those inevitable laws of trade by which it was itself affected
equally with them; and at least on one occasion, at an early day, it was
saved only by extraordinary exertions from the same fate that attended
the weakest institution it professed to supervise.   In 1837 it failed
equally with others in redeeming its notes (though the two years allowed
by its charter for that purpose had not expired), a large amount of which
remains to the present time outstanding.   It is true that, having so
vast a capital and strengthened by the use of all the revenues of the
Government, it possessed more power; but while it was itself by that

circumstance freed from the control which all banks require, its paramount object and inducement were left the same—to make the most for its stockholders, not to regulate the currency of the country. Nor has it, as far as we are advised, been found to be greatly otherwise elsewhere. The national character given to the Bank of England has not prevented excessive fluctuations in their currency, and it proved unable to keep off a suspension of specie payments, which lasted for nearly a quarter of a century. And why should we expect it to be otherwise? A national institution, though deriving its charter from a different source than the State banks, is yet constituted upon the same principles, is conducted by men equally exposed to temptation, and is liable to the same disasters, with the additional disadvantage that its magnitude occasions an extent of confusion and distress which the mismanagement of smaller institutions could not produce. It can scarcely be doubted that the recent suspension of the United States Bank of Pennsylvania, of which the effects are felt not in that State alone, but over half the Union, had its origin in a course of business commenced while it was a national institution, and there is no good reason for supposing that the same consequences would not have followed had it still derived its powers from the General Government. It is in vain, when the influences and impulses are the same, to look for a difference in conduct or results. By such creations we do, therefore, but increase the mass of paper credit and paper currency, without checking their attendant evils and fluctuations. The extent of power and the efficiency of organization which we give, so far from being beneficial, are in practice positively injurious. They strengthen the chain of dependence throughout the Union, subject all parts more certainly to common disaster, and bind every bank more effectually in the first instance to those of our commercial cities, and in the end to a foreign power. In a word, I can not but believe that, with the full understanding of the operations of our banking system which experience has produced, public sentiment is not less opposed to the creation of a national bank for purposes connected with currency and commerce than for those connected with the fiscal operations of the Government.

Yet the commerce and currency of the country are suffering evils from the operations of the State banks which can not and ought not to be overlooked. By their means we have been flooded with a depreciated paper, which it was evidently the design of the framers of the Constitution to prevent when they required Congress to "coin money and regulate the value of foreign coins," and when they forbade the States "to coin money, emit bills of credit, make anything but gold and silver a tender in payment of debts," or "pass any law impairing the obligation of contracts." If they did not guard more explicitly against the present state of things, it was because they could not have anticipated that the few banks then existing were to swell to an extent which would expel to so great a degree the gold and silver for which they had provided from the channels of circulation, and fill them with a currency that defeats the objects they had in view. The remedy for this must chiefly rest with the States from whose legislation it has sprung. No good that might accrue in a particular case from the exercise of powers not obviously conferred on the General Government would authorize its interference or justify a course that might in the slightest degree increase at the expense of the States the power of the Federal authorities; nor do I doubt that the States will apply the remedy. Within the last few years events have appealed to them too strongly to be disregarded. They have seen that the Constitution, though theoretically adhered to, is subverted in practice; that while on the statute books there is no legal tender but gold and silver, no law impairing the obligations of contracts, yet that in point of fact the privileges conferred on banking corporations have made their notes the currency of the country; that the obligations imposed by these notes are violated under the impulses of interest or convenience, and that the number and power of the persons connected with these corporations or placed under their influence give them a fearful weight when their interest is in opposition to the spirit of the Constitution and laws. To the people it is immaterial whether these results are produced by open violations of the latter or by the workings of a system of which the result is the same. An inflexible execution even of the existing statutes of most of the States would redress many evils now endured, would effectually show the banks the dangers of mismanagement which impunity encourages them to repeat, and would teach all corporations the useful lesson that they are the subjects of the law and the servants of the people. What is still wanting to effect these objects must be sought in additional legislation, or, if that be inadequate, in such further constitutional grants or restrictions as may bring us back into the path from which we have so widely wandered.

In the meantime it is the duty of the General Government to cooperate with the States by a wise exercise of its constitutional powers and the enforcement of its existing laws. The extent to which it may do so by further enactments I have already adverted to, and the wisdom of Congress may yet enlarge them. But above all, it is incumbent upon us to hold erect the principles of morality and law, constantly executing our own contracts in accordance with the provisions of the Constitution, and thus serving as a rallying point by which our whole country may be brought back to that safe and honored standard.

Our people will not long be insensible to the extent of the burdens entailed upon them by the false system that has been operating on their sanguine, energetic, and industrious character, nor to the means necessary to extricate themselves from these embarrassments. The weight which presses upon a large portion of the people and the States is an enormous debt, foreign and domestic. The foreign debt of our States, corporations, and men of business can scarcely be less than $200,000,000, requiring more than $10,000,000 a year to pay the interest. This sum has to be paid out of the exports of the country, and must of necessity cut off imports to that extent or plunge the country more deeply in debt from year to year. It is easy to see that the increase of this foreign debt must augment the annual demand on the exports to pay the interest, and to the same extent diminish the imports, and in proportion to the enlargement of the foreign debt and the consequent increase of interest must be the decrease of the import trade. In lieu of the comforts which it now brings us we might have our gigantic banking institutions and splendid, but in many instances profitless, railroads and canals absorbing to a great extent in interest upon the capital borrowed to construct them the surplus fruits of national industry for years to come, and securing to posterity no adequate return for the comforts which the labors of their hands might otherwise have secured. It is not by the increase of this debt that relief is to be sought, but in its diminution. Upon this point there is, I am happy to say, hope before us; not so much in the return of confidence abroad, which will enable the States to borrow more money, as in a change of public feeling at home, which prompts our people to pause in their career and think of the means by which debts are to be paid before they are contracted. If we would escape embarrassment, public and private, we must cease to run in debt except for objects of necessity or such as will yield a certain return. Let the faith of the States, corporations, and individuals already pledged be kept with the most punctilious regard. It is due to our national character as well as to justice that this should on the part of each be a fixed principle of conduct. But it behooves us all to be more chary in pledging it hereafter. By ceasing to run in debt and applying the surplus of our crops and incomes to the discharge of existing obligations, buying less and selling more, and managing all affairs, public and private, with strict economy and frugality, we shall see our country soon recover from a temporary depression, arising not from natural and permanent causes, but from those I have enumerated, and advance with renewed vigor in her career of prosperity.

Fortunately for us at this moment, when the balance of trade is greatly against us and the difficulty of meeting it enhanced by the disturbed state of our money affairs, the bounties of Providence have come to relieve us from the consequences of past errors. A faithful application of the immense results of the labors of the last season will afford partial relief for the present, and perseverance in the same course will in due season accomplish the rest. We have had full experience in times past of the extraordinary results which can in this respect be brought about in a short period by the united and well-directed efforts of a community like ours. Our surplus profits, the energy and industry of our population, and the wonderful advantages which Providence has bestowed upon our country in its climate, its various productions, indispensable to other nations, will in due time afford abundant means to perfect the most useful of those objects for which the States have been plunging themselves of late in embarrassment and debt, without imposing on ourselves or our children such fearful burdens.

But let it be indelibly engraved on our minds that relief is not to be found in expedients. Indebtedness can not be lessened by borrowing more money or by changing the form of the debt. The balance of trade is not to be turned in our favor by creating new demands upon us abroad. Our currency can not be improved by the creation of new banks or more issues from those which now exist. Although these devices sometimes appear to give temporary relief, they almost invariably aggravate the evil in the end. It is only by retrenchment and reform—by curtailing public and private expenditures, by paying our debts, and by reforming our banking system—that we are to expect effectual relief, security for the future, and an enduring prosperity. In shaping the institutions and policy of the General Government so as to promote as far as it can with its limited powers these important ends, you may rely on my most cordial cooperation.

That there should have been in the progress of recent events doubts in many quarters and in some a heated opposition to every change can not surprise us. Doubts are properly attendant on all reform, and it is peculiarly in the nature of such abuses as we are now encountering to seek to perpetuate their power by means of the influence they have been permitted to acquire. It is their result, if not their object, to gain for the few an ascendency over the many by securing to them a monopoly of the currency, the medium through which most of the wants of mankind are supplied; to produce throughout society a chain of dependence which leads all classes to look to privileged associations for the means of speculation and extravagance; to nourish, in preference to the manly virtues that give dignity to human nature, a craving desire for luxurious enjoyment and sudden wealth, which renders those who seek them dependent on those who supply them; to substitute for republican simplicity and economical habits a sickly appetite for effeminate indulgence and an imitation of that reckless extravagance which impoverished and enslaved the industrious people of foreign lands, and at last to fix upon us, instead of those equal political rights the acquisition of which was alike the object and supposed reward of our Revolutionary struggle, a system of exclusive privileges conferred by partial legislation. To remove the influences which had thus gradually grown up among us, to deprive them of their deceptive advantages, to test them by the light of wisdom and truth, to oppose the force which they concentrate in their support—all this was necessarily the work of time, even among a people so enlightened and pure as that of the United States. In most other countries, perhaps, it could only be accomplished through that series of revolutionary movements which are too often found necessary to effect any great and radical reform; but it is the crowning merit of our institutions that they create and nourish in the vast majority of our people a disposition and a power peaceably to remedy abuses which have elsewhere caused the effusion of rivers of blood and the sacrifice of thousands of the human race. The result thus far is most honorable to the self-denial, the intelligence, and the patriotism of our citizens; it justifies the confident hope that they will carry through the reform which has been so well begun, and that they will go still further than they have yet gone in illustrating the important truth that a people as free and enlightened as ours will, whenever it becomes necessary, show themselves to be indeed capable of self-government by voluntarily adopting appropriate remedies for every abuse, and submitting to temporary sacrifices, however great, to insure their permanent welfare.

My own exertions for the furtherance of these desirable objects have been bestowed throughout my official career with a zeal that is nourished by ardent wishes for the welfare of my country, and by an unlimited reliance on the wisdom that marks its ultimate decision on all great and controverted questions. Impressed with the solemn obligations imposed upon me by the Constitution, desirous also of laying before my fellow-citizens, with whose confidence and support I have been so highly honored, such measures as appear to me conducive to their prosperity, and anxious to submit to their fullest consideration the grounds upon which my opinions are formed, I have on this as on preceding occasions freely offered my views on those points of domestic policy that seem at the present time most prominently to require the action of the Government. I know that they will receive from Congress that full and able consideration which the importance of the subjects merits, and I can repeat the assurance heretofore made that I shall cheerfully and readily cooperate with you in every measure that will tend to promote the welfare of the Union.

M. VAN BUREN.

SPECIAL MESSAGES.

CITY OF WASHINGTON, *December 4, 1839.*

To the Senate and House of Representatives of the United States:

I transmit herewith a report from the Secretary of the Treasury, exhibiting certain transfers of appropriations that have been made in that Department in pursuance of the powers vested in the President of the United States by the act of Congress of the 3d of March, 1809, entitled "An act further to amend the several acts for the establishment and regulation of the Treasury, War, and Navy Departments."

M. VAN BUREN.

CITY OF WASHINGTON, *December 4, 1839.*

To the Senate and House of Representatives of the United States:

I transmit herewith a report from the Secretary of War, which exhibits certain transfers of appropriations made in the War Department under the authority conferred upon the President of the United States by the acts of Congress of March 3, 1809, and May 1, 1820, passed in addition to and to amend the several acts for the establishment and regulation of the Treasury, War, and Navy Departments.

M. VAN BUREN.

WASHINGTON, *December 11, 1839.*

To the Senate of the United States:

I transmit for the consideration and advice of the Senate a treaty concluded on the 3d day of September last with the Stockbridge and Munsee tribes of Indians, with a report from the Secretary of War and other documents in relation to it.

M. VAN BUREN.

WASHINGTON, *December 12, 1839.*

To the Senate of the United States:

I nominate the persons named in the accompanying list for promotion and appointment in the Army to the several grades annexed to their names, as proposed by the Secretary of War.

M. VAN BUREN.

WAR DEPARTMENT, *December 11, 1839.*

The PRESIDENT OF THE UNITED STATES.

SIR: In submitting the accompanying list* of promotions and appointments, which I respectfully recommend for your approval, I beg leave to call your attention to that part of it which relates to the Quartermaster's Department.

The seventh section of the act of 2d of March, 1821, fixing the military peace establishment, provides "that there shall be one Quartermaster-General; that there shall be two quartermasters with the rank, pay, and emoluments of majors of cavalry, and ten assistant quartermasters, who shall, in addition to their pay in the line, receive a sum not less than ten nor more than twenty dollars per month, to be regulated by the Secretary of War."

The third section of the act of the 18th May, 1826, provides for "two additional quartermasters and ten assistant quartermasters, to be taken from the line of the Army, who shall have the same rank and compensation as are provided for like grades by the act of the 2d March, 1821," above quoted; that is to say, the two additional quartermasters shall have the "rank, pay, and emoluments of majors of cavalry," and the ten additional assistant quartermasters "shall, in addition to their pay in the line, receive a sum not less than $10 nor more than $20 per month."

The ninth section of the act of the 5th July, 1838, provides "that the President of the United States be authorized, by and with the advice and consent of the Senate,

* Omitted.

to add to the Quartermaster's Department not exceeding two assistant quartermasters-general with the rank of colonel, two deputy quartermasters-general with the rank of lieutenant-colonel, and eight assistant quartermasters with the rank of captain; that the assistant quartermasters now in service shall have the same rank as is provided by this act for those hereby authorized: * * * *Provided,* That all the appointments in the Quartermaster's Department shall be made from the Army, * * * and that promotions in said Department shall take place as in regiments and corps."

These are believed to be the only laws now in force which provide for the organization of the Quartermaster's Department, and they are here cited with a view to a full and clear understanding of the question of precedence of rank between certain officers of that Department.

Prior to the act of the 5th of July, 1838, last quoted, the assistant quartermasters were selected from the several regiments of the line to perform duty in the Quartermaster's Department. They were never commissioned in the Department; they merely received letters of appointment as assistant quartermasters, and were allowed the additional pay provided by the act of the 2d March, 1821, and 16th May, 1826. They held no rank in the Department separate from their rank in the line, and were liable to be returned to their regiments according to the wants of the service or at the pleasure of the President. In completing the organization of the Department provided by the act of 5th July, 1838, several officers were selected from regiments for appointment as assistant quartermasters whose lineal rank was greater than that held by the assistant quartermasters then doing duty in the Department, and on the 7th of July, the list being nearly completed, it was submitted to the Senate for confirmation. All the assistant quartermasters thus submitted to the Senate were confirmed to take rank from the 7th of July, and in the order they were nominated, which was according to their seniority in the line and agreeably to what was conceived to be the intention of the law. Had the opposite course been pursued, the lieutenants serving in the Department must either have outranked some of the captains selected or else the selections must have been confined altogether to the subaltern officers of the Army. It will appear, therefore, that the relative rank of these officers has been properly settled, both by a fair construction of the law and the long-established regulation of the service which requires that "in cases where commissions of the same grade and date interfere a retrospect is to be had to former commissions in actual service at the time of appointment." But as several of the assistant quartermasters who were doing duty in the Department prior to the act of the 5th of July, 1838, have felt themselves aggrieved by this construction of the law, and have urged a consideration of their claims to priority of rank, I have felt it my duty to lay their communications before you, with a view to their being submitted to the Senate with the accompanying list,* should you think proper to do so.

I have the honor to be, very respectfully, your most obedient servant,

J. R. POINSETT.

WASHINGTON, *December 17, 1839.*

Hon. WM. R. KING,
   President of the Senate.

SIR: I transmit herewith a report made to me by the Secretary of the Treasury, with accompanying documents, in regard to some difficulties which have occurred concerning the kind of papers deemed necessary to be provided by law for the use and protection of American vessels

* Omitted.

engaged in the whale fisheries, and would respectfully invite the consideration of Congress to some new legislation on a subject of so much interest and difficulty.

M. VAN BUREN.

[The same message was addressed to the Speaker of the House of Representatives.]

WASHINGTON CITY, *December 23, 1839.*

To the Senate and House of Representatives of the United States:

I herewith communicate to Congress copies of a letter from the governor of Iowa to the Secretary of State and of the documents transmitted with it, on the subject of a dispute respecting the boundary line between that Territory and the State of Missouri. The disagreement as to the extent of their respective jurisdictions has produced a state of such great excitement that I think it necessary to invite your early attention to the report of the commissioner appointed to run the line in question under the act of the 18th of June, 1838, which was sent to both Houses of Congress by the Secretary of State on the 30th of January last.

M. VAN BUREN.

DECEMBER 24, 1839.

To the Senate and House of Representatives of the United States:

I transmit herewith to Congress a report from the Secretary of State, on the subject of the law providing for taking the Sixth Census of the United States, to which I invite your early attention.

M. VAN BUREN.

WASHINGTON, *December 28, 1839.*

To the Senate and House of Representatives of the United States:

I herewith transmit a report from the Secretary of the Treasury, in relation to the employment of steam vessels in the Revenue-Cutter Service, and recommend the subject to the special and favorable consideration of Congress.

M. VAN BUREN.

WASHINGTON, *December 30, 1839.*

To the Senate and House of Representatives:

I transmit to Congress copies of a communication from Governor Lucas, and of additional documents, in relation to the disputed boundary line between the Territory of Iowa and the State of Missouri.

M. VAN BUREN.

WASHINGTON, *December 31, 1839.*

To the Senate and House of Representatives of the United States:

I communicate to Congress a report from the Secretary of State, in relation to applications on the part of France for the extension to vessels coming from the colonies of French Guiana and Senegal of the benefits granted by the act of the 9th of May, 1828, to vessels of the same nation coming from the islands of Guadaloupe and Martinique, and for the repayment of duties levied in the district of Newport upon the French ship *Alexandre* and part of her cargo. The circumstances under which these duties were demanded being, as stated by the Secretary of the Treasury, of a character to entitle the parties to relief, I recommend the adoption of the necessary legislative provisions to authorize their repayment. I likewise invite your attention to the evidence contained in the accompanying documents as to the treatment of our vessels in the port of Cayenne, which will doubtless be found by Congress such as to authorize the application to French vessels coming from that colony of the liberal principles of reciprocity which have hitherto governed the action of the Legislature in analogous cases.

M. VAN BUREN.

WASHINGTON, *January 6, 1840.*

To the Senate and House of Representatives of the United States:

I herewith communicate to Congress copies of a communication received from the chief magistrate of the State of Maryland in respect to the cession to that State of the interest of the General Government in the Chesapeake and Ohio Canal. Having no authority to enter into the proposed negotiation, I can only submit the subject to the consideration of Congress. That body will, I am confident, give to it a careful and favorable consideration and adopt such measures in the premises within their competency as will be just to the State of Maryland and to all the other interests involved.

M. VAN BUREN.

WASHINGTON CITY, *January 8, 1840.*

To the Senate and House of Representatives of the United States:

I transmit herewith for your consideration and action a communication from the Secretary of War, which is accompanied by documents from the military and topographical engineer bureaus, referred to in his late annual report as relating to the system of internal improvement carried on by the General Government, and showing the operations during the past year in that branch of the public service intrusted to the topographical bureau.

M. VAN BUREN.

WASHINGTON CITY, *January 8, 1840.*

To the Senate and House of Representatives of the United States:

In addition to the papers accompanying my messages of the 23d and 30th ultimo, I communicate to Congress a copy of a letter, with its inclosure, since received at the Department of State from the governor of Iowa, in relation to the disputed boundary between that Territory and the State of Missouri.

M. VAN BUREN.

WASHINGTON CITY, *January 8, 1840.*

To the Senate of the United States:

In compliance with a resolution that passed the Senate the 30th ultimo, calling for information as to the banks which had recently suspended specie payments and those which had resumed, as well as the cases where they had refused payment of the public demands in specie, with several other particulars, I requested the different Departments to prepare reports on the whole subject so far as connected with the business with each.

Having received an answer from the Treasury Department which, with the documents annexed, will probably cover most of the inquiries, I herewith submit the same to your consideration, and will present the reports from the other Departments so soon as they are completed.

M. VAN BUREN.

WASHINGTON, *January 10, 1840.*

To the Senate of the United States:

I transmit herewith, in compliance with a resolution of the 30th ultimo, the proceedings of the court of inquiry in the case of Lieutenant-Colonel Brant,* held at St. Louis in November last, and the papers connected therewith, together with a copy of that officer's resignation.

The report of the Secretary of War which accompanies these papers contains the reasons for withholding the proceedings of the court-martial.

M. VAN BUREN.

WASHINGTON, *January 11, 1840.*

To the Senate of the United States:

I transmit to the Senate, in compliance with its resolutions of the 30th ultimo, two reports of the Secretary of State, containing the answers of the Commissioner of Patents and the disbursing agent of the Department of State to the inquiries embraced in said resolutions.†

M. VAN BUREN.

---

*Relating to his administration of the affairs of the Quartermaster's Department at St. Louis.
†Relating to the sale or exchange of Government drafts, etc.

WASHINGTON, *January 11, 1840.*

To the Senate of the United States:

I transmit herewith a report and statement of the Secretary of the Treasury, furnishing the information called for by the resolution of the 30th ultimo, in relation to the amount of money drawn from the Treasury in each of the five years preceding the commencement of the present session of Congress, except the amount drawn under the special pension laws. The statement showing the amount, it will be seen from the accompanying communication of the Secretary of War, will take some little time, but will be prepared as early as possible and transmitted.

M. VAN BUREN.

WASHINGTON, *January 13, 1840.*

To the Senate of the United States:

I again submit to you the amended treaty of June 11, 1838, with the New York Indians. It is accompanied by minutes of the proceedings of a council held with them at Cattaraugus on the 13th and 14th days of August, 1839, at which were present on the part of the United States the Secretary of War and on the part of the State of Massachusetts General H. A. S. Dearborn, its commissioner; by various documentary testimony, and by a memorial presented in behalf of the several committees on Indian concerns appointed by the four yearly meetings of Friends of Genesee, New York, Philadelphia, and Baltimore. In the latter document the memorialists not only insist upon the irregularity and illegality of the negotiation, but urge a variety of considerations which appear to them to be very conclusive against the policy of the removal itself. The motives by which they have been induced to take so deep an interest in the subject are frankly set forth, and are doubtless of the most beneficent character. They have, however, failed to remove my decided conviction that the proposed removal, if it can be accomplished by proper means, will be alike beneficial to the Indians, to the State in which the land is situated, and to the more general interest of the United States upon the subject of Indian affairs.

The removal of the New York Indians is not only important to the tribes themselves, but to an interesting portion of western New York, and especially to the growing city of Buffalo, which is surrounded by lands occupied by the Senecas. To the Indians themselves it presents the only prospect of preservation. Surrounded as they are by all the influences which work their destruction, by temptation they can not resist and artifices they can not counteract, they are rapidly declining, and, notwithstanding the philanthropic efforts of the Society of Friends, it is believed that where they are they must soon become extinct; and to this portion of our country the extraordinary spectacle is presented of densely populated and highly improved settlements inhabited by industrious, moral, and respectable citizens, divided by a wilderness on one side of which is a city of more than 20,000 souls, whose advantageous position in every other respect and great commercial prospects would insure its rapid increase in population and wealth if not retarded by the circumstance of a naturally fertile district remaining a barren waste in its immediate vicinity. Neither does it appear just to those who are entitled to the fee simple of the land, and who have paid a part of the purchase money, that they should suffer from the waste which is constantly committed upon their reversionary rights and the great deterioration of the land consequent upon such depredations without any corresponding advantage to the Indian occupants.

The treaty, too, is recommended by the liberality of its provisions. The cession contained in the first article embraces the right, title, and interest secured to "the Six Nations of the New York Indians and St. Regis tribe" in lands at Green Bay by the Menomonee treaty of 8th February, 1831, the supplement thereto of 17th of same month, and the conditions upon which they were ratified by the Senate, except a tract on which a part of the New York Indians now reside. The Menomonee treaty assigned them 500,000 acres, coupled with the original condition that they should remove to them within three years after the date of the treaty, modified by the supplement so as to empower the President to prescribe the term within which they should remove to the Green Bay lands, and that if they neglected to do so within the period limited so much of the land as should be unoccupied by them at the termination thereof should revert to the United States. To these lands the New York Indians claimed title, which was resisted, and, for quieting the controversy, by the treaty of 1831 the United States paid a large consideration; and it will be seen that by using the power given in the treaty the Executive might put an end to the Indian claim. Instead of this harsher measure, for a grant of all their interest in Wisconsin, which, deducting the land in the actual occupancy of New York Indians, amounts to about 435,000 acres, the treaty as amended by the Senate gives 1,824,000 acres of lands in the West and the sum of $400,000 for their removal and subsistence, for education and agricultural purposes, the erection of mills and the necessary houses, and the promotion of the mechanic arts. Besides, there are special money provisions for the Cayugas, the Onondagas, the Oneidas of New York, the Tuscaroras, and St. Regis Indians, and an engagement to receive from Ogden and Fellows for the Senecas $202,000; to invest $100,000 of this sum in safe stocks and to distribute $102,000 among the owners of improvements in New York according to an appraisement; to sell for the Tuscaroras 5,000 acres of land they hold in Niagara County, N. Y., and to invest the proceeds, exclusive of what may be received for improvements, "the income from which shall be paid to the nation at their new homes annually, and the money which shall be received for improvements on said lands shall be paid to the owners of the improvements when the lands are sold." These are the substantial parts of the treaty, and are so careful of Indian advantage that one might suppose they would be satisfactory to those most anxious for their welfare. The right they cede could be extinguished by a course that treaty provisions justify and authorize. So long as they persevere in their determination to remain in New York it is of no service to them, and for this naked right it is seen what the United States propose to give them besides the sum of $202,000, which will be due from the purchasers of their occupant right to the Senecas, and $9,600 to the Tuscaroras for their title to 1,920 acres of land in Ontario County, N. Y., exclusive of the 5,000 acres above mentioned.

But whilst such are my views in respect to the measure itself, and while I shall feel it to be my duty to labor for its accomplishment by the proper use of all the means that are or shall be placed at my disposal by Congress, I am at the same time equally desirous to avoid the use of any which are inconsistent with those principles of benevolence and justice which I on a former occasion endeavored to show have in the main characterized the dealings of the Federal Government with the Indian tribes from the Administration of President Washington to the present time. The obstacles to the execution of the treaty grow out of the following considerations: The amended treaty was returned to me by your body at the close of its last session, accompanied by a resolution setting forth that "whenever the President of the United States shall be satisfied that the assent of the Seneca tribe of Indians has been given to the amended treaty of June 11, 1838, with the New York Indians, according to the true intent and meaning of the resolution of the 11th of June, 1838, the Senate recommend that the President make proclamation of said treaty and carry the same into effect." The resolution of the 11th of June, 1838, provided that "the said treaty shall have no force or effect whatever as relates to any of the said tribes, nations, or bands of New York Indians, nor shall it be understood that the Senate have assented to any of the contracts connected with it until the same, with the amendments herein proposed, is submitted and fully explained by the commissioner of the United States to each of the said tribes or bands separately assembled in council, and they have given their free and voluntary consent thereto." The amended treaty was submitted to the chiefs of the several tribes and its provisions explained to them in council. A majority of the chiefs of each of the tribes of New York Indians signed the treaty in council, except the Senecas. Of them only 16 signed in council, 13 signed at the commissioner's office, and 2, who were confined by indisposition, at home. This was reported to the War Department in October, 1838, and in January, 1839, a final return of the proceedings of the commissioner was made, by which it appeared that 41 signatures of chiefs, including 6 out of the 8 sachems of the nation, had been affixed to the treaty. The number of chiefs of the Seneca Nation entitled to act for the people is variously estimated from 74 to 80, and by some at a still higher number. Thus it appears that, estimating the number of chiefs at 80—and it is believed there are at least that number— there was only a bare majority of them who signed the treaty, and only 16 gave their assent to it in council. The Secretary of War was under these circumstances directed to meet the chiefs of the New York Indians in council, in order to ascertain, if possible, the views of the several tribes, and especially of the Senecas, in relation to the amended treaty. He did so in the month of August last, and the minutes of the proceedings of that council are herewith submitted. Much opposition was manifested by a party of the Senecas, and from some cause or other some of the chiefs of the other tribes who had in former councils consented to the treaty appeared to be now opposed to it. Documents were presented showing that some of the Seneca chiefs had received assurances of remuneration from the proprietors of the land, provided they assented to the treaty and used their influence to obtain that of the nation, while testimony was offered on the other side to prove that many had been deterred from signing and taking part in favor of the treaty by threats of violence, which, from the late intelligence of the cruel murders committed upon the signers of the Cherokee treaty, produced a panic among the partisans of that now under consideration. Whatever may have been the means used by those interested in the fee simple of these lands to obtain the assent of Indians, it appears from the disinterested and important testimony of the commissioner appointed by the State of Massachusetts that the agent of the Government acted throughout with the utmost fairness, and General Dearborn declares himself to be perfectly satisfied that were it not for the unremitted and disingenuous exertions of a certain number of white men who are actuated by their private interests, to induce the chiefs not to assent to the treaty, it would immediately have been approved by an immense majority—an opinion which he reiterated at Cattaraugus. Statements were presented to the Secretary of War at Cattaraugus to show that a vast majority of the New York Indians were adverse to the treaty, but no reasonable doubt exists that the same influence which obtained this expression of opinion would, if exerted with equal zeal on the other side, have produced a directly opposite effect and shown a large majority in favor of emigration. But no advance toward obtaining the assent of the Seneca tribe to the amended treaty in council was made, nor can the assent of a majority of them in council be now obtained. In the report of the committee of the Senate, upon the subject of this treaty, of the 28th of February last it is stated as follows:

But it is in vain to contend that the signatures of the last ten, which were obtained on the second mission, or of the three who have sent on their assent lately, is such a signing as was contemplated by the resolution of the Senate. It is competent, however, for the Senate to waive the usual and customary forms in this instance and consider the signatures of these last thirteen as good as though they had been obtained in open council. But the committee can not recommend the adoption of such a practice in making treaties, for divers good reasons, which must be obvious to the Senate; and among those reasons against these secret individual negotiations is the distrust created that the chiefs so acting are doing what a majority of their people do not approve of, or else that they are improperly acted upon by bribery or threats or unfair influences. In this case we have most ample illustrations. Those opposed to the treaty accuse several of those who signed their assent to the amended treaty with having been bribed, and in at least one instance they make out the charge very clearly.

Although the committee, being four in number, were unable to agree upon any recommendation to the Senate, it does not appear that there was any diversity of opinion amongst them in regard to this part of the report. The provision of the resolution of the Senate of the 11th of June, 1838, requiring the assent of each of the said tribes of Indians to the amended treaty to be given in council, and which was also made a condition precedent to the recommendation to me of the Senate of the 2d of March, 1839, to carry the same into effect, has not, therefore, been complied with as it respects the Seneca tribe.

It is, however, insisted by the advocates for the execution of the treaty that it was the intention of the Senate by their resolution of the 2d of March, 1839, to waive so much of the requirement of that of the 11th of June, 1838, as made it necessary that the assent of the different tribes should be given in council. This assumption is understood to be founded upon the circumstances that the fact that only sixteen of the chiefs had given their assent in that form had been distinctly communicated to the Senate before the passage of the resolution of the 2d of March, and that instead of being a majority that number constituted scarcely one-fifth of the whole number of chiefs, and it is hence insisted that unless the Senate had so intended there would have been no use in sending the amended treaty to the President with the advice contained in that resolution. This has not appeared to me to be a necessary deduction from the foregoing facts, as the Senate may have contemplated that the assent of the tribe in the form first required should be thereafter obtained, and before the treaty was executed, and the phraseology of the resolution, viz, "that whenever the President shall be satisfied," etc., goes far to sustain this construction. The interpretation of the acts of the Senate set up by the advocates for the treaty is, moreover, in direct opposition to the disclaimer contained in the report of the committee which has been adverted to. It is at best an inference only, in respect to the truth of which the Senate can alone speak with certainty, and which could not with propriety be regarded as justifying the desired action in relation to the execution of the treaty.

This measure is further objected to on the ground of improper inducements held out to the assenting chiefs by the agents of the proprietors of the lands, which, it is insisted, ought to invalidate the treaty if even the requirement that the assent of the chiefs should be given in council was dispensed with. Documentary evidence upon this subject was laid before you at the last session, and is again communicated, with additional evidence upon the same point. The charge appears by the proceedings of the Senate to have been investigated by your committee, but no conclusion upon the subject formed other than that which is contained in the extract from the report of the committee I have referred to, and which asserts that at least in one instance the charge of bribery has been clearly made out. That improper means have been employed to obtain the assent of the Seneca chiefs there is every reason to believe, and I have not been able to satisfy myself that I can, consistently with the resolution of the Senate of the 2d of March, 1839, cause the treaty to be carried into effect in respect to the Seneca tribe.

You will perceive that this treaty embraces the Six Nations of New York Indians, occupying different reservations, but bound together by common ties, and it will be expedient to decide whether in the event of that part of it which concerns the Senecas being rejected it shall be considered valid in relation to the other tribes, or whether the whole confederacy shall share one fate. In the event of the Senate not advising the ratification of the amended treaty, I invite your attention to the proposal submitted by the dissentients to authorize a division of the lands, so that those who prefer it may go West and enjoy the advantages of a permanent home there, and of their proportion of the annuities now payable, as well as of the several pecuniary and other beneficiary provisions of the amended treaty.

M. VAN BUREN.

WASHINGTON CITY, *January 17, 1840.*
To the Senate of the United States:

I transmit herewith a communication and statement from the Secretary of War, containing the balance of the information, not heretofore furnished, called for by a resolution of the 30th ultimo, in relation to the amount of money drawn from the Treasury during the five years immediately preceding the commencement of the present session of Congress, in consequence of the legislation of that body upon private claims.

M. VAN BUREN.

WASHINGTON, *January 20, 1840.*
To the Senate and House of Representatives of the United States:

I transmit a report from the Secretary of State, explaining the causes which have prevented a compliance with the resolution of Congress for the distribution of the Biennial Register.

M. VAN BUREN.

WASHINGTON, *January, 1840.*

To the Senate of the United States:

I transmit to the Senate, for their consideration with a view to its ratification, a treaty of peace, friendship, navigation, and commerce between the United States of America and the Republic of Ecuador, signed at Quito on the 13th day of June last. With a view to enable the Senate to understand the motives which led to this compact, the progress of its negotiation, and the grounds upon which it was concluded, I also communicate a copy of the instructions from the Secretary of State to Mr. Pickett in relation to it, and the original official dispatches of the latter. It is requested that the dispatches may be returned when the convention shall have been disposed of by the Senate. M. VAN BUREN.

WASHINGTON, *January 21, 1840.*

To the Senate of the United States:

I transmit to the Senate, in compliance with the request of the governor of Massachusetts, a copy of a letter addressed to him by one of the chiefs of the Seneca tribe of Indians in the State of New York, written on behalf of that portion of the tribe opposed to the treaty of Buffalo.

M. VAN BUREN.

WASHINGTON, *January 22, 1840.*

To the Senate of the United States:

In compliance with the resolution of the Senate of the 17th instant, I communicate a report and documents from the Secretary of State and a report from the Secretary of War.* M. VAN BUREN.

WASHINGTON, *January 23, 1840.*

To the Senate and House of Representatives of the United States:

I herewith transmit a communication from the Secretary of the Treasury, inclosing a letter addressed to him from the Solicitor of the Treasury, and have to invite the earliest attention of Congress to the subject contained therein.† M. VAN BUREN.

WASHINGTON, *January 25, 1840.*

To the Senate of the United States:

The accompanying report ‡ from the Secretary of State is, with its inclosures, communicated to the Senate in compliance with their resolution of the 14th instant. M. VAN BUREN.

---

* Transmitting correspondence with the British Government on the subject of the northeastern boundary and the jurisdiction of the disputed territory; also with the governor of Maine and the minister of Great Britain relative to the invasion of Maine, etc.

† Relating to the discharge of liens and incumbrances upon real estate which has or may become the property of the United States.

‡ Relating to the compensation by Great Britain in the case of the brigs *Enterprise, Encomium,* and *Comet,* slaves on board which were forcibly seized and detained by local authorities of Bermuda and Bahama islands.

WASHINGTON, *January 25, 1840.*

The PRESIDENT OF THE SENATE.

SIR: I transmit a report from the Secretary of the Navy, containing information required by a resolution of the Senate of the 2d of March, 1839, in relation to the military and naval defenses of the United States.

M. VAN BUREN.

WASHINGTON CITY, *January 28, 1840.*

To the Senate and House of Representatives of the United States:

I present for your information a communication from the Secretary of War, accompanied by a report and documents from the Chief Engineer, in relation to certain works* under the superintendence of that officer during the past year. These documents were intended as a supplement to the annual report of the Chief Engineer, which was laid before Congress at the commencement of the session.

M. VAN BUREN.

WASHINGTON, *January 29, 1840.*

To the Senate of the United States:

I herewith transmit to the Senate, with reference to their resolutions of the 17th instant, copies of two official notes which have passed subsequently to the date of my message of the 22d between the Secretary of State and the British minister at Washington, containing additional information in answer to the resolutions referred to.

M. VAN BUREN.

Mr. Fox to Mr. Forsyth.

WASHINGTON, *January 26, 1840.*

Hon. JOHN FORSYTH, etc.:

The undersigned, Her Britannic Majesty's envoy extraordinary and minister plenipotentiary, has the honor to acquaint Mr. Forsyth, Secretary of State of the United States, that since the date of his last official note, of the 12th instant, he has been furnished by Her Majesty's authorities in North America with more correct information than he then possessed respecting certain reported movements of British troops within the disputed territory, which formed the subject of a part of that official note, as well as of the two official notes addressed by the Secretary of State to the undersigned on the 24th of December and on the 16th of the present month. The same reported movements of troops were referred to in a recent message from the governor of Maine to the legislature of the State, and also in a published official letter addressed by the governor of Maine to the President of the United States on the 23d of December.

It appears from accurate information now in the possession of the undersigned that the governor of Maine and through him the President and General Government of the United States have been misinformed as to the facts. In the first place, no reenforcement has been marched to the British post at the Lake Temiscouata; the

---

*Operations in the Missouri, Arkansas, Ohio, and Mississippi rivers, etc.

only change occurring there has been the relief of a detachment of Her Majesty's Twenty-fourth Regiment by a detachment of equal force of the Eleventh Regiment, this force of one company being now stationed at the Temiscouata post, as it always has been, for the necessary purpose of protecting the stores and accommodations provided for the use of Her Majesty's troops who may be required, as heretofore, to march by that route to and from the Provinces of Canada and New Brunswick. In the second place, it is not true that the British authorities either have built or are building barracks on both sides of the St. John River or at the mouth of the Madawaska River; no new barracks have in fact been built anywhere. In the third place, Her Majesty's authorities are not concentrating a military force at the Grand Falls; the same trifling force of sixteen men is now stationed at the post of the Grand Falls which has been stationed there for the last twelvemonth. It was perhaps, however, needless for the undersigned to advert to this last matter at all, as the post of the Grand Falls is beyond the bounds of the disputed territory and within the acknowledged limits of New Brunswick.

The undersigned, while conveying the above information upon a matter of fact to the Secretary of State of the United States, takes occasion to repeat distinctly his former declaration that there exists no intention on the part of Her Majesty's authorities to infringe the terms of those provisional agreements which were entered into at the beginning of last year so long as there is reason to trust that the same will be faithfully adhered to by the opposite party; but it is the duty of the undersigned at the same time clearly to state that Her Majesty's authorities in North America, taking into view the attitude assumed by the State of Maine with reference to the boundary question, will, as at present advised, be governed entirely by circumstances in adopting such measures of defense and protection (whether along the confines of the disputed territory or within that portion of it where, it has been before explained, the authority of Great Britain, according to the existing agreements, was not to be interfered with) as may seem to them necessary for guarding against or for promptly repelling the further acts of hostile aggression over the whole of the disputed territory which it appears to be the avowed design of the State of Maine sooner or later to attempt.

For the undersigned has to observe that not only is the extensive system of encroachment which was denounced and remonstrated against by the undersigned in his official note of the 2d of last November still carried on and persisted in by armed bands employed by the authorities of Maine in the districts above the Aroostook and Fish rivers, but that acts, as above stated, of a character yet more violent and obnoxious to the rights of Great Britain and more dangerous to the preservation of the general peace are with certainty meditated by the inhabitants of that State. The existence of such designs has for months past been a matter of notoriety by public report. Those designs were plainly indicated in the recent message of the governor of Maine to the legislature of the State, and they are avowed in more explicit terms in the letter addressed to the President of the United States by the governor of Maine on the 21st of November, which letter has within the last few days been communicated to Congress and published.

The undersigned, it is true, has been assured by the Secretary of State, in his note of the 16th instant, that the General Government see no reason to doubt the disposition of the governor of Maine to adhere to the existing arrangements and to avoid all acts tending to render more difficult and distant the final adjustment of the boundary question; but in face of the above clear indications of the intentions of Maine as given out by the parties themselves the Secretary of State has not given to the undersigned any adequate assurance that Maine will be constrained to desist from carrying those intentions into effect if, contrary to the expectation of the General Government, the legislature or the executive of the State should think fit to make the attempt.

The undersigned not only preserves the hope, but he entertains the firm belief, that if the duty of negotiating the boundary question be left in the hands of the two national Governments, to whom alone of right it belongs, the difficulty of conducting the negotiation to an amicable issue will not be found so great as has been by many persons apprehended. But the case will become wholly altered if the people of the State of Maine, who, though interested in the result, are not charged with the negotiation, shall attempt to interrupt it by violence.

Her Majesty's authorities in North America have on their part no desire or intention to interfere with the course of the pending negotiation by an exertion of military force, but they will, as at present advised, consult their own discretion in adopting the measures of defense that may be rendered necessary by the threats of a violent interruption to the negotiation which have been used by all parties in Maine and which the undersigned regrets to find confirmed by the language (as above referred to) employed by the highest official authority in that State.

The undersigned avails himself of this occasion to renew to the Secretary of State of the United States the assurance of his distinguished consideration.

H. S. FOX.

Mr. Forsyth to Mr. Fox.

DEPARTMENT OF STATE,
Washington, January 28, 1840.

HENRY S. FOX, Esq., etc.:

The undersigned, Secretary of State of the United States, has the honor to reply, by direction of the President, to the note addressed to him on the 26th instant by Mr. Fox, envoy extraordinary and minister plenipotentiary of Great Britain.

The President derives great satisfaction from the information conveyed by Mr. Fox's note that, with reference to the reported movements of British troops within the territory in dispute, no actual change has taken place in the attitude of Her Majesty's authorities in the territory since the arrangements entered into by the two Governments at the commencement of last year for the preservation of tranquillity within its limits, and from his assurances that there exists no intention on the part of Her Majesty's authorities to infringe the terms of those arrangements so long as they are faithfully observed on the side of the United States. The President, however, can not repress a feeling of regret that the British colonial authorities, without graver motives than the possibility of a departure from the arrangements referred to by the State of Maine, should take upon themselves the discretion, and along with it the fearful responsibility of probable consequences, of being guided by circumstances liable, as these are, to be misapprehended and misjudged in the adoption within the disputed territory of measures of defense and precaution in manifest violation of the understanding between the two countries whenever they may imagine that acts of hostile aggression over the disputed territory are meditated or threatened on the part of the State of Maine. The President can not but hope that when Her Majesty's Government at home shall be apprised of the position assumed in this regard by its colonial agents proper steps will be taken to place the performance of express and solemn agreements upon a more secure basis than colonial discretion, to be exercised on apprehended disregard of such agreements on the part of the State of Maine.

It is gratifying to the President to perceive that Mr. Fox entertains the firm belief that the difficulty of conducting to an amicable issue the pending negotiation for the adjustment of the question of boundary is not so great as has by many persons been apprehended. As, under a corresponding conviction, the United States have, with a view to the final settlement of that exciting question, submitted a proposition for the consideration of Her Majesty's Government, the President hopes that the sentiments expressed by Mr. Fox have their foundation in an expectation of his having it in his power at an early day to communicate to this Government a result of the deliberations had by that of Her Britannic Majesty upon the proposition alluded to which will present the prospect of a prompt and satisfactory settlement, and which, when known by the State of Maine, will put an end to all grounds of apprehensions of intentions or disposition on her part to adopt any measures calculated to embarrass the negotiation or to involve a departure from the provisional arrangements. In the existence of those arrangements the United States behold an earnest of the mutual desire of the two Governments to divest a question abounding in causes of deep and growing excitement of as much as possible of the asperity and hostile feeling it is calculated to engender; but unless attended with the most scrupulous observance of the spirit and letter of their provisions, it would prove but one more cause added to the many already prevailing of enmity and discord. Mr. Fox has already been made the channel of conveyance to his Government of the desire and determination of the President that the obligations of the country shall be faithfully discharged; that desire is prompted by a sense of expediency as well as of justice, and by an anxious wish to preserve the amicable relations now, so manifestly for the advantage of both, subsisting between the United States and Great Britain.

The undersigned avails himself of the occasion to renew to Mr. Fox assurances of his distinguished consideration. JOHN FORSYTH.

To the Senate of the United States:

In compliance with two resolutions of the Senate, dated the 30th ultimo, calling for information in relation to the disputed boundary between the State of Missouri and the Territory of Iowa, I transmit a report from the Secretary of State, which, with inclosures, contains all the information in the executive department on the subject not already communicated to Congress. M. VAN BUREN.

JANUARY 31, 1840.

WASHINGTON, *February 4, 1840.*

To the Honorable the House of Representatives:

I lay before you a report from the Secretary of the Treasury, with several documents annexed, by which it will be seen that judicial constructions have been given to the existing laws for the collection of imposts, affecting extensively and injuriously the accruing revenue.

They embrace, with many others, the important articles of linens, woolens, and cottons, the last two of which are often treated as silks, because that material constitutes a component part of them, and thus exempted them from duty altogether. Assessments of duties which have prevailed for years, and in some cases since the passage of the laws themselves, are in this manner altered, and uncertainty and litigation introduced in regard to the future.

The effects which these proceedings have already produced in diminishing the amount of the revenue, and which are likely to increase hereafter, deserve your early consideration.

I have therefore deemed it necessary to bring the matter to your notice, with a view to such legislative action as the exigencies of the case may in your judgment require. It is not believed that any law which can now be passed upon the subject can affect the revenue favorably for several months to come, and could not, therefore, be safely regarded as a substitute for the early provision of certain and adequate means to enable the Treasury to guard the public credit and meet promptly and faithfully any deficiencies that may occur in the revenue, from whatever cause they may arise.

The reasons in favor of the propriety of adopting at an early period proper measures for that purpose were explained by the Secretary of the Treasury in his annual report and recommended to your attention by myself. The experience of the last two months, and especially the recent decisions of the courts, with the continued suspension of specie payments by the banks over large sections of the United States, operating unfavorably upon the revenue, have greatly strengthened the views then taken of the subject.

M. VAN BUREN.

WASHINGTON CITY, *February 14, 1840.*

To the House of Representatives of the United States:

I lay before you a communication from the Secretary of War, accompanied by a report of the Commissioner of Pensions, showing the great importance of early action on the bill from the Senate providing for the continuance of the office of Commissioner of Pensions. The present law will expire by its own limitation on the 4th day of the next month, and, sensible of the suffering which would be experienced by the pensioners from its suspension, I have deemed it my duty to bring the subject to your notice and invite your early attention to it.

M. VAN BUREN.

FEBRUARY 17, 1840.

To the Senate and House of Representatives of the United States:

I submit to Congress a communication from the Secretary of the Treasury, repeating suggestions contained in his annual report in regard to the necessity of an early provision by law for the protection of the Treasury against the fluctuations and contingencies to which its receipts are exposed, with additional facts and reasons in favor of the propriety of the legislation then desired.

The application assumes that although the means of the Treasury for the whole year may be equal to the expenditures of the year, the Department may, notwithstanding, be rendered unable to meet the claims upon it at the times when they fall due.

This apprehension arises partly from the circumstance that the largest proportion of the charges upon the Treasury, including the payment of pensions and the redemption of Treasury notes, fall due in the early part of this year, viz, in the months of March and May, while the resources on which it might otherwise rely to discharge them can not be made available until the last half of the year, and partly from the fact that a portion of the means of the Treasury consists of debts due from banks, for some of which delay has already been asked, and which may not be punctually paid.

Considering the injurious consequences to the character, credit, and business of the country which would result from a failure by the Government for ever so short a period to meet its engagements; that the happening of such a contingency can only be effectually guarded against by the exercise of legislative authority; that the period when such disability must arise, if at all, and which at the commencement of the session was comparatively remote, has now approached so near as a few days; and that the provision asked for is only intended to enable the Executive to fulfill existing obligations, and chiefly by anticipating funds not yet due, without making any additions to the public burdens, I have deemed the subject of sufficient urgency and importance again to ask for it your early attention.

M. VAN BUREN.

WASHINGTON, *February 21, 1840.*

To the House of Representatives of the United States:

In compliance with a resolution of the House of Representatives of the 7th instant, I communicate a report* from the Secretary of State, containing all the information in possession of the Executive respecting the matters referred to in that resolution.

M. VAN BUREN.

WASHINGTON, *February 27, 1840.*

To the Senate of the United States:

I transmit to the Senate, for their consideration with a view to its ratification, a convention for the adjustment of claims of citizens of the United States upon the Government of the Mexican Republic, concluded and signed in the city of Washington on the 11th of April last. I also communicate, as explanatory of the motives to the adoption of a new convention and illustrative of the course of the negotiation, the correspondence between the Secretary of State and Mr. Martinez, the late minister of Mexico accredited to this Government, and also such parts of the correspondence between the former and Mr. Ellis as relate to the same subject. By the letters of Mr. Ellis it will be seen that the convention now transmitted to the Senate has been already ratified by the Government of Mexico. As some of the papers are originals, it is requested that they may be returned to the Department of State when the convention shall have been disposed of by the Senate.

M. VAN BUREN.

* Relating to the trade with China, etc.

WASHINGTON, *March 4, 1840.*

To the Senate:

I communicate a report from the Secretary of State, with documents*
accompanying it, in compliance with the resolution of the Senate of the
17th of February last.

M. VAN BUREN.

WASHINGTON, *March 9, 1840.*

To the Senate:

In addition to information already communicated in compliance with
the resolutions of the Senate of the 17th January last, I think it proper
to transmit to the Senate copies of two letters, with inclosures, since
received from the governor of Maine, and of a correspondence relative
thereto between the Secretary of State and the British minister.

M. VAN BUREN.

EXECUTIVE DEPARTMENT,
Augusta, February 15, 1840.

His Excellency M. VAN BUREN,
President United States.

SIR: A communication from Mr. Fox, the British minister, to Mr. Forsyth, Secretary of State, under date of January 26, contains the following statement:

"It appears from *accurate* information now in possession of the undersigned that
the governor of Maine and through him the President and General Government of
the United States have been misinformed as to the facts. In the first place, no *reenforcement* has been marched to the British post at the Lake Temiscouata; the *only*
change occurring there has been the relief of a detachment of Her Majesty's Twenty-
fourth Regiment by a detachment of *equal force* of the Eleventh Regiment, this force
of *one company* being now stationed at the Temiscouata post, as it *always has been,*
for the necessary purpose of protecting the stores and accommodations provided for
the use of Her Majesty's troops who may be required, as heretofore, to march by that
route to and from the Provinces of Canada and New Brunswick. In the second place,
it is not true that the British authorities either have built or are building barracks
on both sides of the St. John River or at the mouth of the Madawaska River; *no*
new barracks have in fact been built anywhere."

This statement has been read by the citizens of this State with the most profound
astonishment, and however high may be the source from which it emanates I must
be permitted to say, in the language of that high functionary, that "it is not true,"
though in justice to him I should add that he has undoubtedly been misinformed.
Though this State, in the vindication of her rights and maintenance of her interests
relative to her territorial boundary, from past experience had no reason to expect any
material admissions of the truth on the part of the British authorities, she was not
prepared to meet such a positive and unqualified denial of facts as the foregoing
exhibits, especially of facts so easily susceptible of proof. The "*accuracy*" of the
information alleged to be in the possession of the minister is only equaled by
the *justice* of the pretensions heretofore set up in regard to title.

But not to be bandying assertions where proof is abundant, I deem it my duty to
transmit to Your Excellency the depositions † of a number of gentlemen, citizens of

---

*Containing information relative to the necessity of amending the existing law regulating the
transfer of property in American vessels abroad.
† Omitted

this State, of great respectability, and whose statements are entitled to the most implicit confidence.

These depositions abundantly prove that up to May last, nearly two months subsequent to the arrangement entered into through the mediation of General Scott, *no troops* whatever were stationed at Temiscouata Lake; that in August, September, and October the number did not exceed 25, while now it has been increased to about 200; that prior to May no barracks had been erected at Temiscouata, but that since that time two have been built at the head of the lake, besides some five or six other buildings apparently adapted to the establishment of a permanent military post, and at the foot of the lake two or more buildings for barracks and other military purposes; that though no *new* barracks have been erected at Madawaska, certain buildings heretofore erected have been engaged for use as such; that a road has been constructed connecting the military post at the head and foot of the lake, a towpath made the whole length of the Madawaska River, the road from the head of the lake to the military post at the river Des Loup thoroughly repaired, transport boats built, etc.

I would further inform Your Excellency that an agent has been dispatched to Temiscouata and Madawaska for the purpose of procuring exact information of the state of things there at the present moment; but having incidentally found some evidence of the state of things prior to November last, I have thought best to forward it without delay for the purpose of disabusing the Government and the country of the errors into which they may have been led by the communication before alluded to. The report of the agent will be transmitted as soon as received, which may not be short of two weeks.

Under these circumstances, I have only to repeat my official call upon the General Government for the protection of this State from *invasion*.

I have the honor to be, with great respect, Your Excellency's most obedient servant,

JOHN FAIRFIELD,
Governor of Maine.

DEPARTMENT OF STATE,
Washington, February 27, 1840.

His Excellency JOHN FAIRFIELD,
   Governor of Maine.

SIR: I have the honor to acknowledge the receipt at this Department of your excellency's letter to the President of the 15th instant, inclosing three depositions of citizens of Maine in relation to certain movements of British troops in the disputed territory. The depositions have been informally communicated to the British minister by direction of the President, who desires me to apprise your excellency of his intention to cause an official communication to be addressed to the minister on the subject so soon as the report of the agent dispatched by your order to Temiscouata and Madawaska for the purpose of procuring exact information as to the present state of things there shall have been received.

I have the honor to be, sir, your obedient servant,

JOHN FORSYTH.

EXECUTIVE DEPARTMENT,
Augusta, February 27, 1840.

His Excellency M. VAN BUREN,
   President United States.

SIR: Having received the report of Benjamin Wiggin, esq., the agent referred to in my last communication, dispatched by me to the disputed territory to obtain exact information of British military movements in that quarter and of the existing state of things, I hasten to lay the same* before you, accompanied by his plan* of the British military post at the head of Lake Temiscouata. It will be perceived that it goes to confirm in every essential particular the evidence already forwarded in the depositions of Messrs. Varnum, Bartlett, and Little, and is directly opposed to the statement contained in the letter of Mr. Fox to Mr. Forsyth under date of 26th of January last.

The course thus clearly proved to have been pursued by the British Government upon the disputed territory is utterly inconsistent with the arrangement heretofore subsisting, and evinces anything but a disposition to submit to an *amicable* termination of the question relating to the boundary.

Permit me to add that the citizens of Maine are awaiting with deep solicitude that action on the part of the General Government which shall vindicate the national honor and be fulfilling in part a solemn obligation to a member of the Union.

I have the honor to be, with high respect, your most obedient servant,

JOHN FAIRFIELD,
Governor of Maine.

Mr. Forsyth to Mr. Fox.

DEPARTMENT OF STATE,
Washington, March 6, 1840.

HENRY S. FOX, Esq., etc.:

By the directions of the President, the undersigned, Secretary of State of the United States, communicates to Mr. Fox, envoy extraordinary and minister plenipotentiary of Great Britain, the inclosed copy of a report* made to the governor of the State of Maine by the agent commissioned on the part of the authorities of that State to ascertain the precise character and extent of the occupation of parts of the disputed territory by troops of Her Britannic Majesty and of the buildings and other public works constructed for their use and accommodation.

By that report and the three depositions which the undersigned informally communicated to Mr. Fox a few days since he will perceive that there must be some extraordinary misapprehension on his part of the facts in relation to the occupation by British troops of portions of the disputed territory. The statements contained in these documents and that given by Mr. Fox in his note of the 20th of January last exhibit a striking discrepancy as to the number of troops now in the territory as compared with those who were in it when the arrangement between Governor Fairfield and Lieutenant-Governor Harvey was agreed upon, and also as to the present and former state of the buildings there. The extensive accommodations prepared and preparing at an old and at new stations, the works finished and in the course of construction on the land and on the water, are not in harmony with the assurance that the only object is the preservation of a few unimportant buildings and storehouses for the temporary protection of the number of troops Her Majesty's ordinary service can require to pass on the road from New Brunswick to Canada.

The undersigned will abstain from any remarks upon these contradictory statements until Mr. Fox shall have had an opportunity to obtain the means of fully explaining them. How essential it is that this should be promptly done, and that the steps necessary to a faithful observance on the part of Her Majesty's colonial authorities of the existing agreements between the two Governments should be immediately taken, Mr. Fox can not fail fully to understand.

The undersigned avails himself of the occasion to renew to Mr. Fox assurances of his high consideration.

JOHN FORSYTH.

*Omitted.

Mr. Fox to Mr. Forsyth.

WASHINGTON, *March 7, 1840.*

The undersigned, Her Britannic Majesty's envoy extraordinary and minister pleni-potentiary, has the honor to acknowledge the receipt of the official note of yester-day's date addressed to him by Mr. Forsyth, Secretary of State of the United States, to which is annexed the copy of a report from Mr. Benjamin Wiggin, an agent employed by the State of Maine to visit the British military post at Lake Temiscouata, and in which reference is made to other papers upon the same subject, which were informally communicated to the undersigned by Mr. Forsyth a few days before; and the attention of the undersigned is called by Mr. Forsyth to different points upon which the information contained in the said papers is considered to be mate-rially at variance with that which was conveyed to the United States Government by the undersigned in his official note of the 26th of last January.

The undersigned had already been made acquainted by the lieutenant-governor of New Brunswick with the circumstance of Mr. Wiggin's visit to the military post at Lake Temiscouata, where the officer in command very properly furnished to Mr. Wig-gin the requisite information upon all matters connected with the British station which he appeared desirous to inquire about.

The alleged points of variance, after deducting what is fanciful and conjectural in the reports now produced and after comparing what is there stated in contradiction to other reports before produced from the same quarters, do not appear to the under-signed to be by any means so material as they seem to have been considered by the Government of the United States. The British military detachment stationed at Lake Temiscouata, which the agents employed by the State of Maine had, in the first instance with singular exaggeration represented as amounting to two regiments, is now discovered by the same parties to amount to 175 men, which instead of two regiments is something less than two companies. It is indeed true, should such a point be considered worth discussing, that the undersigned might have used a more technically correct expression in his note of the 26th of January if he had stated the detachment in question to consist of from one to two companies instead of stating it to consist of one company. But a detachment of Her Majesty's troops has been stationed at the Lake Temiscouata from time to time ever since the winter of 1837 and 1838, when the necessity arose from marching reenforcements by that route from New Brunswick to Canada; and it will be remembered that a temporary right of using that route for the same purpose was expressly reserved to Great Britain in the pro-visional agreement entered into at the beginning of last year.

It is not, therefore, true that the stationing a military force at the Lake Temis-couata is a new measure on the part of Her Majesty's authorities; neither is it true that that measure has been adopted for other purposes than to maintain the security of the customary line of communication and to protect the buildings, stores, and accommodations provided for the use of Her Majesty's troops when on march by that route; and it was with a view to correct misapprehensions which appeared to exist upon these points, and thus to do away with one needless occasion of dispute, that the undersigned conveyed to the United States Government the information contained in his note of the 26th of January.

With regard again to the construction of barracks and other buildings and the preserving them in an efficient state of repair and defense, a similar degree of error and misapprehension appears still to prevail in the minds of the American authorities.

The erection of those buildings within the portion of the disputed territory now referred to, for the shelter of Her Majesty's troops while on their march and for the safe lodgment of the stores, is no new act on the part of Her Majesty's authorities. The buildings in question have been in the course of construction from a period antecedent to the provisional agreements of last year, and they are now maintained and occupied along the line of march with a view to the same objects above specified, for which the small detachments of troops also referred to are in like manner. there stationed.

The undersigned will not refrain from here remarking upon one point of comparison exhibited in the present controversy. It is admitted by the United States authorities that the armed bands stationed by the government of Maine in the neighborhood of the Aroostook River have fortified those stations with artillery, and it is now objected as matter of complaint against the British authorities with reference to the buildings at Lake Temiscouata, not that those buildings are furnished with artillery, but only that they are defended by palisades capable of resisting artillery. It would be difficult to adduce stronger evidence of the acts on the one side being those of aggression and on the other of defense.

The fact, shortly, is (and this is the essential point of the argument) that Her Majesty's authorities have not as yet altered their state of preparation or strengthened their military means within the disputed territory with a view to settling the question of the boundary, although the attitude assumed by the State of Maine with reference to that question would be a clear justification of such measures, and it is much to be apprehended that the adoption of such measures will sooner or later become indispensable if the people of Maine be not compelled to desist from the extensive system of armed aggression which they are continuing to carry on in other parts of the same disputed territory.

The undersigned avails himself of this occasion to renew to the Secretary of State of the United States the assurance of his distinguished consideration.

H. S. FOX.

WASHINGTON, *March 9, 1840.*

To the Senate and House of Representatives of the United States:

I transmit to Congress, for their consideration, copies and translations of a correspondence between the Secretary of State and the Spanish legation, growing out of an application on the part of Spain for a reduction of tonnage duty on her vessels in certain cases.

By a royal order issued on the 29th of April, 1832, by the King of Spain, in consequence of a representation made to his Government by the minister of the United States against the discriminating tonnage duty then levied in the ports of Spain upon American vessels, said duty was reduced to 1 real de vellon, equal to 5 cents, per ton, without reference to the place from whence the vessel came, being the same rate as paid by those of all other nations, including Spain.

By the act approved on the 13th of July, 1832, a corresponding reduction of tonnage duty upon Spanish vessels in ports of the United States was authorized, but confined to vessels coming from ports in Spain; in consequence of which said reduction has been applied to such Spanish vessels only as came directly from ports in the Spanish Peninsula.

The application of the Spanish Government is for the extension of the provisions of the act to vessels coming from other places, and I submit for the consideration of Congress whether the principle of reciprocity would not justify it in regard to all vessels owned in the Peninsula and its dependencies of the Balearic and Canary islands, and coming from all places other than the islands of Cuba, Porto Rico, and the Philippine, and the repayment of such duties as may have been levied upon Spanish vessels of that class which have entered our ports since the act of 1832 went into operation.

M. VAN BUREN.

WASHINGTON, *March 10, 1840.*

To the House of Representatives of the United States:

In compliance with a resolution of the House of Representatives of the 2d of March, 1839, I communicate reports* from the several Departments, containing the information requested by the resolution.

M. VAN BUREN.

WASHINGTON, *March 11, 1840.*

To the Senate:

In compliance with the resolution of the Senate dated the 4th of February, 1840, I have the honor to transmit herewith copies of the correspondence between the Department of War and Governor Call concerning the war in Florida.

Very respectfully, your obedient servant,

M. VAN BUREN.

WASHINGTON CITY, *March, 1840.*

To the Senate and House of Representatives of the United States:

I lay before you for your consideration a communication of the Secretary of War, accompanied by a report of the Surgeon-General of the Army, in relation to sites for marine hospitals selected in conformity with the provisions of the act of March 3, 1837, from which it will be seen that some action on the subject by Congress seems to be necessary.

M. VAN BUREN.

WASHINGTON, D. C., *March 12, 1840.*

To the House of Representatives of the United States:

I transmit to the House of Representatives, in answer to resolution of that body dated on the 9th instant, the inclosed report of the Secretary of State.

M. VAN BUREN.

DEPARTMENT OF STATE,
Washington, March 12, 1840.

The PRESIDENT OF THE UNITED STATES:

The Secretary of State, to whom has been referred a resolution of the House of Representatives dated the 9th instant, requesting the President to communicate to that body "whether any, and, if any, what, measures have been taken since the rejection

---

*Transmitting lists of removals from office since March 3, 1789.

of the recommendation of the King of Holland of a new line of boundary between the United States and the Province of New Brunswick to obtain information in respect to the topography of the territory in dispute by a survey or exploration of the same on the part of the United States alone, and also whether any measures have been adopted whereby the accuracy of the survey lately made under the authority of the British Government, when communicated, may be tested or examined," has the honor to report to the President that no steps have been thought necessary by this Government since the date above referred to to obtain topographical information regarding the disputed territory, either by exploration or survey on its part alone, nor has it thought proper to adopt any measures to test the accuracy of the topographical examination recently made by a British commission, the result of which has not been made public or communicated to the United States.

Respectfully submitted.

JOHN FORSYTH.

WASHINGTON CITY, *March 19, 1840.*

To the Senate of the United States:

I submit herewith for your consideration and constitutional action the treaty accompanying the inclosed communication of the Secretary of War, made with the Shawnee Indians west of the Mississippi River, for the purchase of a portion of their lands, with the view of procuring for the Wyandot Indians of Ohio a satisfactory residence west.

M. VAN BUREN.

WAR DEPARTMENT, *March, 1840.*

The PRESIDENT OF THE UNITED STATES.

SIR: I have the honor to submit for your consideration, and, if it meets your approbation, for transmission to the Senate, a treaty concluded on the 18th December last with the Shawnee Indians by their chiefs, headmen, and counselors, and an explanatory communication of the 17th instant from the Commissioner of Indian Affairs.

Very respectfully, your obedient servant,

J. R. POINSETT.

WAR DEPARTMENT, OFFICE INDIAN AFFAIRS,
March 17, 1840.

Hon. J. R. POINSETT,
Secretary of War.

SIR: Negotiations with the Wyandots for a cession of their lands in Ohio and removal to the country west of the Mississippi have been pending for some years. During the past season two exploring parties from that tribe have visited the West and were tolerably well pleased with the district to which it was proposed to remove them, but expressed a strong preference for a tract which the Shawnees and Delawares offered to sell to the United States for them. The commissioner charged with the business of treating with the Wyandots was of opinion that if this tract could be procured there would be little difficulty in concluding a treaty. He was therefore under these circumstances instructed to make the purchase, subject to the ratification of the President and Senate and dependent on the condition that the Wyandots will accept it, and on the 18th of December last effected a treaty with the Shawnees by which they ceded a tract of about 58,000 acres on those conditions at the price of $1.50 per acre. No purchase has been made from the Delawares, as they refuse to sell at a less price than $5 per acre, and it is thought that the land ceded by the Shawnees will be amply sufficient for the present.

I have the honor herewith to submit the treaty with the Shawnees, to be laid, if you think proper, before the President and Senate for ratification.

Very respectfully, your obedient servant,

T. HARTLEY CRAWFORD.

WASHINGTON, *March 24, 1840.*

To the House of Representatives of the United States:

I transmit herewith a report from the Secretaries of State, Treasury, and Navy and the Postmaster-General, with the documents which accompanied it, in compliance with the resolution of the House of Representatives of the 5th instant, relative to the General Post-Office building and the responsibilities of the architect and Commissioner of the Public Buildings, etc.

M. VAN BUREN.

WASHINGTON, *March 26, 1840.*

To the Senate of the United States:

I transmit to the Senate herewith copies of official notes which have passed between the Secretary of State and the British minister since my last message on the subject of the resolutions of the 17th of January.

M. VAN BUREN.

Mr. Fox to Mr. Forsyth.

WASHINGTON, *March 13, 1840.*

Hon. JOHN FORSYTH, etc.:

The undersigned, Her Britannic Majesty's envoy extraordinary and minister plenipotentiary, has been instructed by his Government to make the following communication to the Secretary of State of the United States in reference to the boundary negotiation and the affairs of the disputed territory.

Her Majesty's Government have had under their consideration the official note addressed to the undersigned by the Secretary of State of the United States on the 24th of last December in reply to a note from the undersigned of the 2d of November preceding, in which the undersigned protested in the name of his Government against the extensive system of aggression pursued by the people of the State of Maine within the disputed territory, to the prejudice of the rights of Great Britain and in manifest violation of the provisional agreements entered into between the authorities of the two countries at the beginning of the last year.

Her Majesty's Government have also had their attention directed to the public message transmitted by the governor of Maine to the legislature of the State on the 3d of January of the present year.

Upon a consideration of the statements contained in these two official documents, Her Majesty's Government regret to find that the principal acts of encroachment which were denounced and complained of on the part of Great Britain, so far from being either disproved or discontinued or satisfactorily explained by the authorities of the State of Maine, are, on the contrary, persisted in and publicly avowed.

Her Majesty's Government have consequently instructed the undersigned once more formally to protest against those acts of encroachment and aggression.

Her Majesty's Government claim and expect, from the good faith of the Government of the United States, that the people of Maine shall replace themselves in the situation in which they stood before the agreements of last year were signed; that they shall, therefore, retire from the valley of the St. John and confine themselves to the valley of the Aroostook; that they shall occupy that valley in a temporary manner only, for the purpose, as agreed upon, of preventing depredations; and that they shall not construct fortifications nor make roads or permanent settlements.

Until this be done by the people of the State of Maine, and so long as that people shall persist in the present system of aggression, Her Majesty's Government will feel it their duty to make such military arrangements as may be required for the protection of Her Majesty's rights. And Her Majesty's Government deem it right to declare that if the result of the unjustifiable proceedings of the State of Maine should be collision between Her Majesty's troops and the people of that State the responsibility of all the consequences that may ensue therefrom, be they what they may, will rest with the people and Government of the United States.

The undersigned has been instructed to add to this communication that Her Majesty's Government are only waiting for the detailed report of the British commissioners recently employed to survey the disputed territory, which report it was believed would be completed and delivered to Her Majesty's Government by the end of the present month, in order to transmit to the Government of the United States a reply to their last proposal upon the subject of the boundary negotiation.

The undersigned avails himself of this occasion to renew to the Secretary of State of the United States the assurance of his distinguished consideration.

H. S. FOX.

Mr. Forsyth to Mr. Fox.

DEPARTMENT OF STATE,
Washington, March 25, 1840.

HENRY S. FOX, Esq., etc.:

The undersigned, Secretary of State of the United States, acknowledges to have received Mr. Fox's communication of the 13th instant, in reference to the boundary negotiation and the affairs of the disputed territory. The information given in the closing part of it—that a reply to the last proposition of the United States upon the subject of the boundary may be expected in a short time—is highly gratifying to the President, who has, however, given directions to the undersigned, in making this acknowledgment, to accompany it with the expression of his profound regret that Mr. Fox's note is in no other respect satisfactory.

After the arrangements which in the beginning of last year were entered into on the part of the two Governments with regard to the occupation of the disputed territory, the President had indulged the hope that the causes of irritation which had grown out of this branch of the subject could have been removed. Relying on the disposition of Maine to cooperate with the Federal Government in all that could lead to a pacific adjustment of the principal question, the President felt confident that his determination to maintain order and peace on the border would be fully carried out. He looked upon all apprehensions of designs by the people of Maine to take possession of the territory as without adequate foundation, deeming it improbable that on the eve of an amicable adjustment of the question any portion of the American people would without cause and without object jeopard the success of the negotiation and endanger the peace of the country. A troublesome, irritating, and comparatively unimportant, because subordinate, subject being thus disposed of, the President hoped that the parties would be left free at once to discuss and finally adjust the principal question. In this he has been disappointed. While the proceedings of Her Majesty's Government at home have been attended with unlooked-for delays, its attention has been diverted from the great subject in controversy by repeated complaints imputing to a portion of the people of the United States designs to violate the engagements of their Government—designs which have never been entertained, and which Mr. Fox knows would receive no countenance from this Government.

It is to be regretted that at this late hour so much misapprehension still exists on the side of the British Government as to the object and obvious meaning of the existing arrangements respecting the disputed territory. The ill success which appears to have attended the efforts made by the undersigned to convey through Mr. Fox to Her Majesty's Government more correct impressions respecting them calls for a recurrence to the subject, and a brief review of the correspondence which has grown out of it may tend to remove the erroneous views which prevail as to the manner in which the terms of the arrangements referred to have been observed.

As Mr. Fox had no authority to make any agreement respecting the exercise of jurisdiction over the disputed territory, that between him and the undersigned of the 27th of February, 1839, had for its object some provisional arrangement for the restoration and preservation of peace in the territory. To accomplish this object it provided that Her Majesty's officers should not seek to expel by military force the armed party which had been sent by Maine into the district bordering on the Restook River, and that, on the other hand, the government of Maine would voluntarily and without needless delay withdraw beyond the bounds of the disputed territory any armed force then within them. Besides this, the arrangement had other objects—the dispersion of notorious trespassers and the protection of public property from depredation. In case future necessity should arise for this, the operation was to be conducted by concert, jointly or separately, according to agreement between the governments of Maine and New Brunswick.

In this last-mentioned respect the agreement looked to some further arrangement between Maine and New Brunswick. Through the agency of General Scott one was agreed to on the 23d and 25th of March following, by which Sir John Harvey bound himself not to seek, without renewed instructions to that effect from his Government, to take military possession of the territory or to expel from it by military force the armed civil posse or the troops of Maine. On the part of Maine it was agreed by her governor that no attempt should be made, without renewed instructions from the legislature, to disturb by arms the Province of New Brunswick in the possession of the Madawaska settlements or interrupt the usual communications between that and the upper Provinces. As to possession and jurisdiction, they were to remain unchanged—each party holding, in fact, possession of part of the disputed territory, but each denying the right of the other to do so. With that understanding Maine was without unnecessary delay to withdraw her military force, leaving only, under a land agent, a small civil posse, armed or unarmed, to protect the timber recently cut and to prevent further depredations.

In the complaints of infractions of the agreements by the State of Maine addressed to the undersigned Mr. Fox has assumed two positions which are not authorized by the terms of those agreements: First. Admitting the right of Maine to maintain a civil posse in the disputed territory for the purposes stated in the agreement, he does so with the restriction that the action of the posse was to be confined within certain limits; and, second, by making the advance of the Maine posse into the valley of the Upper St. John the ground of his complaint of encroachment upon the Madawaska settlement, he assumes to extend the limits of that settlement beyond those it occupied at the date of the agreement.

The United States can not acquiesce in either of these positions.

In the first place, nothing is found in the agreement subscribed to by Governor Fairfield and Sir John Harvey defining any limits in the disputed territory within which the operations of the civil posse of Maine were to be circumscribed. The task of preserving the timber recently cut and of preventing further depredations *within the disputed territory* was assigned to the State of Maine after her military force should have been withdrawn from it, and it was to be accomplished by a civil posse, armed or unarmed, which was to continue in the territory and to operate in every part of it where its agency might be required to protect the timber already cut and prevent further depredations, without any limitation whatever or any restrictions except such as might be construed into an attempt to disturb by arms the Province of New Brunswick in her possession of the Madawaska settlement or interrupt the usual communication between the Provinces.

It is thus, in the exercise of a legitimate right and in the conscientious discharge of an obligation imposed upon her by a solemn compact, that the State of Maine has done those acts which have given rise to complaints for which no adequate cause is perceived. The undersigned feels confident that when those acts shall have been considered by Her Majesty's Government at home as explained in his note to Mr. Fox of the 24th of December last and in connection with the foregoing remarks they will no longer be viewed as calculated to excite the apprehensions of Her Majesty's Government that the faith of existing arrangements is to be broken on the part of the United States.

With regard to the second position assumed by Mr. Fox—that the advance of the Maine posse along the valley of the Restook to the mouth of Fish River and into the valley of the Upper St. John is at variance with the terms and spirit of the agreements—the undersigned must observe that if at variance with any of their provisions it could only be with those which secure Her Majesty's Province of New Brunswick against any attempt to disturb the possession of the Madawaska settlements and to interrupt the usual communications between New Brunswick and the upper Provinces. The agreement could only have reference to the Madawaska settlements as confined within their actual limits at the time it was subscribed. The undersigned in his note of the 24th of December last stated the reasons why the mouth of Fish River and the portion of the valley of the St. John through which it passes could in no proper sense be considered as embraced in the Madawaska settlements. Were the United States to admit the pretension set up on the part of Great Britain to give to the Madawaska settlements a degree of constructive extension that might at this time suit the purposes of Her Majesty's colonial authorities, those settlements might soon be made with like justice to embrace any portions of the disputed territory, and the right given to the Province of New Brunswick to occupy them temporarily and for a special purpose might by inference quite as plausible give the jurisdiction exercised by Her Majesty's authorities an extent which would render the present state of the question, so long as it could be maintained, equivalent to a decision on the merits of the whole controversy in favor of Great Britain. If the small settlement at Madawaska on the north side of the St. John means the whole valley of that river, if a boom across the Fish River and a station of a small posse on the south side of the St. John at the mouth of Fish River is a disturbance of that settlement, which is 25 miles below, within the meaning of the agreement, it is difficult to conceive that there are any limitations to the pretensions of Her Majesty's Government under it or how the State of Maine could exercise the preventive power with regard to trespassers, which was on her part the great object of the temporary arrangement. The movements of British troops lately witnessed in the disputed territory and the erection of military works for their protection and accommodation, of which authentic information recently received at the Department of State has been communicated to Mr. Fox, impart a still graver aspect to the matter immediately under consideration. The fact of those military operations, established beyond a doubt, left unexplained or unsatisfactorily accounted for by Mr. Fox's note of the 7th instant, continues an abiding cause of complaint on the part of the United States against Her Majesty's colonial agents as inconsistent with arrangements whose main object was to divest a question already sufficiently perplexed and complicated from such embarrassments as those with which the proceedings of the British authorities can not fail to surround it.

If, as Mr. Fox must admit, the objects of the late agreements were the removal of all military force and the preservation of the property from further spoliations, leaving the possession and jurisdiction as they stood before the State of Maine found itself compelled to act against the trespassers, the President can not but consider that the conduct of the American local authorities strongly and most favorably contrasts with that of the colonial authorities of Her Majesty's Government. While the one, promptly withdrawing its military force, has confined itself to the use of the small posse, armed as agreed upon, and has done no act not necessary to the accomplishment of the conventional objects, every measure taken or indicated by the other party is essentially military in its character, and can be justified only by a well-founded apprehension that hostilities must ensue.

With such feelings and convictions the President could not see without painful surprise the attempt of Mr. Fox, under instructions from his Government, to give to the existing state of things a character not warranted by the friendly disposition of the United States or the conduct of the authorities and people of Maine; much more is he surprised to find it alleged as a ground for strengthening a military force and preparing for a hostile collision with the unarmed inhabitants of a friendly State, pursuing within their own borders their peaceful occupations or exerting themselves in compliance with their agreements to protect the property in dispute from unauthorized spoliation.

The President wishes that he could dispel the fear that these dark forebodings can be realized. Unless Her Majesty's Government shall forthwith arrest all military interference in the question, unless it shall apply to the subject more determined efforts than have hitherto been made to bring the dispute to a certain and pacific adjustment, the misfortunes predicted by Mr. Fox in the name of his Government may most unfortunately happen.

But no apprehension of the consequences alluded to by Mr. Fox can be permitted to divert the Government and people of the United States from the performance of their duty to the State of Maine. That duty is as simple as it is imperative. The construction which is given by her to the treaty of 1783 has been again and again, and in the most solemn manner, asserted also by the Federal Government, and must be maintained unless Maine freely consents to a new boundary or unless that construction of the treaty is found to be erroneous by the decision of a disinterested and independent tribunal selected by the parties for its final adjustment. The President on assuming the duties of his station avowed his determination, all other means of negotiation failing, to submit a proposition to the Government of Great Britain to refer the decision of the question once more to a third party.

In all the subsequent steps which have been taken upon the subject by his direction he has been actuated by the same spirit. Neither his dispositions in the matter nor his opinion as to the propriety of that course has undergone any change. Should the fulfillment of his wishes be defeated, either by an unwillingness on the part of Her Majesty's Government to meet the offer of the United States in the spirit in which it is made or from adverse circumstances of any description, the President will in any event derive great satisfaction from the consciousness that no effort on his part has been spared to bring the question to an amicable conclusion, and that there has been nothing in the conduct either of the Governments and people of the United States or of the State of Maine to justify the employment of Her Majesty's forces as indicated by Mr. Fox's letter. The President can not under such circumstances apprehend that the responsibility for any consequences which may unhappily ensue will by the just judgment of an impartial world be imputed to the United States.

The undersigned avails himself, etc.

JOHN FORSYTH.

Mr. Fox to Mr. Forsyth.

WASHINGTON, *March 26, 1840.*

Hon. JOHN FORSYTH, etc.:

The undersigned, Her Britannic Majesty's envoy extraordinary and minister plenipotentiary, has had the honor to receive the official note of yesterday's date addressed to him by Mr. Forsyth, Secretary of State of the United States, in reply to a note dated the 13th instant, wherein the undersigned, in conformity with instructions received from his Government, had anew formally protested against the acts of encroachment and aggression which are still persisted in by armed bands in the employment of the State of Maine within certain portions of the disputed territory.

It will be the duty of the undersigned immediately to transmit Mr. Forsyth's note to Her Majesty's Government in England, and until the statements and propositions which it contains shall have received the due consideration of Her Majesty's Government the undersigned will not deem it right to add any further reply thereto excepting to refer to and repeat, as he now formally and distinctly does, the several declarations which it has from time to time been his duty to make to the Government of the United States with reference to the existing posture of affairs in the disputed territory, and to record his opinion that an inflexible adherence to the resolutions that have been announced by Her Majesty's Government for the defense of Her Majesty's rights pending the negotiation of the boundary question offers to Her Majesty's Government the only means of protecting those rights from being in a continually aggravated manner encroached upon and violated.

The undersigned avails himself of this occasion to renew to the Secretary of State of the United States the assurance of his distinguished consideration.

H. S. FOX.

WASHINGTON, *March 28, 1840.*

To the Senate:

I communicate to the Senate, in compliance with their resolution of the 12th instant, a report from the Secretary of War, containing information on the subject of that resolution.

M. VAN BUREN.

WAR DEPARTMENT, *March 27, 1840.*

The PRESIDENT OF THE UNITED STATES.

SIR: The resolution of the Senate of the 12th instant, "that the President of the United States be requested to communicate to the Senate, if in his judgment compatible with the public interest, any information which may be in the possession of the Government, or which can be conveniently obtained, of the military and naval preparations of the British authorities on the northern frontier of the United States from Lake Superior to the Atlantic Ocean, designating the permanent from the temporary and field works, and particularly by noting those which are within the claimed limits of the United States," having been referred by you to this Department, it was immediately referred to Major-General Scott and other officers who have been stationed on the frontier referred to for such information on the subjects as they possessed and could readily procure, and an examination is now in progress for such as may be contained in the files of this Department. General Scott is the only officer yet heard from, and a copy of his report is herewith submitted, together with a copy of that to which he refers, made upon the resolution of the House of Representatives of the 9th instant. As soon as the other officers who have been called upon are heard from and the examination of the files of the Department is completed, any further information which may be thus acquired will be immediately laid before you.

Very respectfully, your most obedient servant,

J. R. POINSETT.

HEADQUARTERS, EASTERN DIVISION,
Elizabethtown, N. J., March 23, 1840.

Brigadier-General R. JONES,
 Adjutant-General United States Army.

SIR: I have received from your office copies of two resolutions, passed, respectively, the 12th and 9th instant, one by the Senate and the other by the House of Representatives, and I am asked for "any information on the subject of both or either of the resolutions that may be in [my] possession."

In respect to the naval force recently maintained upon the American lakes by Great Britain, I have just had the honor to report to the Secretary of War, by whom the resolution of the House of Representatives (of the 9th instant) was directly referred to me.

I now confine myself to the Senate's resolution, respecting "military [I omit *naval*] preparations of the British authorities on the northern frontiers of the United States from Lake Superior to the Atlantic Ocean, distinguishing the permanent from the temporary and field works, and particularly noting those which are within the claimed limits of the United States."

I will here remark that however well my duties have made me acquainted with the greater part of the line in question, I have paid but slight attention to the forts and barracks erected by the British authorities near the borders of Maine *above* Frederickton, in New Brunswick, or in Upper Canada *above* Cornwall, being of the fixed opinion (which need not here be developed) that all such structures would be of little or no military value to either of the parties in the event of a new war between the United States and Great Britain.

I was last summer at the foot of Lake Superior, and neither saw nor heard of any British fort or barrack on the St. Marys River, the outlet of that lake.

Between Lakes Huron and Erie the British have three sets of barracks—one at Windsor, opposite to Detroit; one at Sandwich, a little lower down; and the third at Malden, 18 miles from the first—all built of sawed logs, strengthened by blockhouses, loopholes, etc. Malden has long been a military post, with slight defenses. These have been recently strengthened. The works at Sandwich and Windsor have also, I think, been erected within the last six or eight months.

Near the mouth of the Niagara the British have two small forts—George and Mississauga; both existed during the last war. The latter may be termed a permanent work. Slight barracks have been erected within the last two years on the same side near the Falls and at Chippewa, with breastworks at the latter place, but nothing, I believe, above the works first named on the Niagara which can be termed a fort.

Since the commencement of recent troubles in the Canadas and (consequent thereupon) within our limits Fort William Henry, at Kingston, and Fort Wellington, opposite to Ogdensburg (old works), have both been strengthened within themselves, besides the addition of dependencies. These forts may be called permanent.

On the St. Lawrence below Prescott, and confronting our territory, I know of no other military post. Twelve miles above, at Brockville, there may be temporary barracks and breastworks. I know that of late Brockville has been a military station.

In the system of defenses on the approaches to Montreal the Isle aux Noix, a few miles below our line, and in the outlet of Lake Champlain, stands at the head. This island contains within itself a system of permanent works of great strength. On them the British Government has from time to time since the peace of 1815 expended much skill and labor.

Odletown, near our line, on the western side of Lake Champlain, has been a station for a body of Canadian militia for two years, to guard the neighborhood from refugee incendiaries from our side. I think that barracks have been erected there for the accommodation of those troops, and also at a station, with the like object, near Alburgh, in Vermont.

It is believed that there are no important British forts or extensive British barracks on our borders from Vermont to Maine.

In respect to such structures on *the disputed territory*, Governor Fairfield's published letters contain fuller information than has reached me through any other channel. I have heard of no new military preparations by the British authorities on the St. Croix or Passamaquoddy Bay.

Among such preparations, perhaps I ought not to omit the fact that Great Britain. besides numerous corps of well-organized and well-instructed militia, has at this time within her North American Provinces more than 20,000 of her best regular troops. The whole of those forces might be brought to the verge of our territory in a few days. Two-thirds of that regular force has arrived out since the spring of 1838.

I remain, sir, with great respect, your most obedient servant,

WINFIELD SCOTT.

WASHINGTON, *March 28, 1840.*

To the House of Representatives of the United States:

I communicate to the House of Representatives, in compliance with their resolution of the 9th instant, reports* from the Secretaries of State and War, with documents, which contain information on the subject of that resolution.

M. VAN BUREN.

WASHINGTON, *March 31, 1840.*

To the House of Representatives of the United States:

I communicate to the House of Representatives a report† from the Secretary of State, with documents, containing the information called for by their resolution of the 23d instant.

M. VAN BUREN.

WASHINGTON CITY, *April 3, 1840.*

Hon. R. M. T. HUNTER,

    Speaker of the House of Representatives.

SIR: In compliance with a resolution of the House of Representatives of the 9th ultimo, I communicate herewith, accompanied by a report from the Secretary of War, ''copies of the arrangement entered into between the governor of Maine and Sir John Harvey, lieutenant-governor of New Brunswick, through the mediation of Major-General Scott, in the month of March last (1839), together with copies of the instructions given to

---

*Relating to the British naval armament on the American lakes, etc.

†Relating to the demand of the minister of Spain for the surrender of the schooner *Amistad*, with Africans on board, detained by the American brig of war *Washington*, etc.

General Scott and of all correspondence with him relating to the subject of controversy between the State of Maine and the Province of New Brunswick.''

M. VAN BUREN.

WASHINGTON, *April 10, 1840.*

To the House of Representatives of the United States:

In compliance with the resolution of the House of Representatives of the 23d March last, I transmit a report* from the Secretary of State, which, with the documents accompanying it, contains the information in possession of the Department in relation to the subject of the resolution.

M. VAN BUREN.

WASHINGTON, *April, 1840.*

To the House of Representatives of the United States:

I transmit herewith communications from the Secretary of War and Commissioner of Indian Affairs, giving the information ''in possession of the Government respecting the assemblage of Indians on the northwestern frontier, and especially as to the interference of the officers or agents of any foreign power with the Indians of the United States in the vicinity of the Great Lakes,'' which I was requested to communicate by the resolution of the House of Representatives of the 9th ultimo.

M. VAN BUREN.

WASHINGTON, *April 14, 1840.*

To the House of Representatives of the United States:

I transmit to the House of Representatives a report† from the Secretary of State, with documents, containing the information required by their resolution of the 9th March last.

M. VAN BUREN.

APRIL 15, 1840.

To the Senate of the United States:

In further compliance with a resolution of the Senate passed December 30, 1839, I herewith submit reports‡ from the Secretary of the Navy and the Postmaster-General, together with a supplemental statement from the Secretary of the Treasury, and the correspondence annexed.

M. VAN BUREN.

---

*Relating to the seizure and condemnation by British authorities of American vessels engaged in the fisheries.

†Relating to the tobacco trade between the United States and foreign countries.

‡Relating to the sale or exchange of Government drafts for bank notes and the payment of Government creditors in depreciated currency.

WASHINGTON, *April 15, 1840.*

To the Senate and House of Representatives of the United States:

I transmit a copy of a convention for the adjustment of claims of citizens of the United States upon the Government of the Mexican Republic, for such legislative action on the part of Congress as may be necessary to carry the engagements of the United States under the convention into full effect.

M. VAN BUREN.

WASHINGTON CITY, *Abril 18, 1840.*

To the House of Representatives of the United States:

I transmit herewith a communication from the Secretary of War, accompanied by a letter from the Commissioner of Indian Affairs, indicating the importance of an extension of the authority given by the sixteenth clause of the first section of the act entitled "An act providing for the salaries of certain officers therein named, and for other purposes," approved 9th May, 1836.

M. VAN BUREN.

WASHINGTON CITY, *April 24, 1840.*

To the Senate of the United States:

I transmit herewith a report and accompanying documents from the Secretary of War, which furnish the information in relation to that portion of the defenses* of the country intrusted to the charge and direction of the Department of War, called for by the resolution of the Senate of the 2d of March, 1839.

M. VAN BUREN.

WASHINGTON, *April 27, 1840.*

To the Senate of the United States:

I lay before the Senate a report† of the Postmaster-General, in further compliance with a resolution of the Senate of the 30th December, 1839.

M. VAN BUREN.

WASHINGTON, *May 2, 1840.*

To the Senate of the United States:

I transmit to the Senate a report‡ from the Secretary of State, which, with the papers accompanying it, contains in part the information requested by a resolution of the Senate of the 30th December last.

M. VAN BUREN.

---

* Military and naval.
† Relating to the sale or exchange of Government drafts, etc.
‡ Relating to bonds of the Territory of Florida.

WASHINGTON, *May 9, 1840.*

To the House of Representatives of the United States:

I communicate to the House of Representatives a report* from the Secretary of State, which, with the documents accompanying it, furnishes the information requested by their resolution of the 23d of March last.

M. VAN BUREN.

MAY 11, 1840.

To the Senate of the United States:

In part compliance with the resolution of the Senate of the 29th of December last, I herewith submit a report† from the Secretary of the Treasury, with the documents therein referred to.

M. VAN BUREN.

WASHINGTON, *May 12, 1840.*

To the Senate of the United States:

I communicate to the Senate a copy of a letter‡ from the secretary of the Territory of Florida, with documents accompanying it, received at the Department of State since my message of the 2d instant and containing additional information on the subject of the resolution of the Senate of the 30th of December last.

M. VAN BUREN.

WASHINGTON, *May 16, 1840.*

To the House of Representatives of the United States:

I transmit the report of the Secretary of War furnishing a statement of the amounts paid to persons concerned in negotiating Indian treaties since 1829, etc., which completes the information called for by the resolution of the House of Representatives dated the 28th January, 1839, upon that subject and the disbursing officers in the War Department.

M. VAN BUREN.

WASHINGTON, *May 18, 1840.*

To the Senate of the United States:

I communicate to the Senate a copy of a letter‡ from the governor of Florida to the Secretary of State, containing, with the documents accompanying it, further information on the subject of the resolution of the Senate of the 30th of December last.

M. VAN BUREN.

---

*Transmitting correspondence with France, Sweden, Denmark, and Prussia relating to the surrender to the United States of persons charged with piracy and murder on board the United States schooner *Plattsburg* in 1817; correspondence relating to the demand by the chargé d'affaires of Great Britain for the surrender of a mutineer in the British armed ship *Lee* in 1819; opinion of the Attorney-General with regard to the right of the President of the United States or the governor of a State to deliver up, on the demand of any foreign government, persons charged with crimes committed without the jurisdiction of the United States.

†Relating to the sale or exchange of Government drafts, etc.

‡Relating to bonds of the Territory of Florida.

WASHINGTON, *May 21, 1840.*

To the Senate and House of Representatives of the United States:

I communicate to Congress sundry papers, from which it will be perceived that the Imaum of Muscat has transmitted to this country and, through the agency of the commander of one of his vessels, offered for my acceptance a present, consisting of horses, pearls, and other articles of value. The answer of the Secretary of State to a letter from the agents of the vessel communicating the offer of the present, and my own letter to the Imaum in reply to one which he addressed to me, were intended to make known in the proper quarter the reasons which had precluded my acceptance of the proffered gift. Inasmuch, however, as the commander of the vessel, with the view, as he alleges, of carrying out the wishes of his Sovereign, now offers the presents to the Government of the United States, I deem it my duty to lay the proposition before Congress for such disposition as they may think fit to make of it; and I take the opportunity to suggest for their consideration the adoption of legislative provisions pointing out the course which they may deem proper for the Executive to pursue in any future instances where offers of presents by foreign states, either to the Government, its legislative or executive branches, or its agents abroad, may be made under circumstances precluding a refusal without the risk of giving offense.

The correspondence between the Department of State and our consul at Tangier will acquaint Congress with such an instance, in which every proper exertion on the part of the consul to refrain from taking charge of an intended present proved unavailing. The animals constituting it may consequently, under the instructions from the Secretary of State, be expected soon to arrive in the United States, when the authority of Congress as to the disposition to be made of them will be necessary.

M. VAN BUREN.

WASHINGTON, *May 23, 1840.*

To the Senate of the United States:

I transmit a communication from the Secretary of War, together with the papers therein referred to, relative to the proceedings instituted under a resolution of Congress to try the title to the Pea Patch Island, in the Delaware River, and recommend that Congress pass a special act giving to the circuit court of the district of Maryland jurisdiction to try the cause.

M. VAN BUREN.

JUNE 4, 1840.

To the House of Representatives:

I herewith submit a report from the Secretary of the Treasury, showing the progress made in complying with the requirements of a resolution passed February 6, 1839, concerning mineral lands of the United States.

The documents he communicates contain much important information on the subject of those lands, and a plan for the sale of them is in a course of preparation and will be presented as soon as completed.

M. VAN BUREN.

WASHINGTON, *June 5, 1840.*

To the Senate of the United States:

In compliance with the resolution of the Senate dated the 30th December, 1839, I transmit herewith the report* of the Secretary of War, furnishing so much of the information called for by said resolution as relates to the Executive Department under his charge.

M. VAN BUREN.

WASHINGTON, *June 5, 1840.*

To the Senate of the United States:

In compliance with the resolution of the Senate of the 30th December, 1839, I communicate the report† of the Secretary of War, containing the information called for by that resolution as far as it relates to the Department under his charge.

M. VAN BUREN.

WASHINGTON, *June 6, 1840.*

To the House of Representatives:

I herewith submit a report from the Secretary of the Treasury, in relation to certain lands falling within the Chickasaw cession which have been sold at Chocchuma and Columbus, in Mississippi, and invite the attention of Congress to the subject of further legislation in relation to them.

M. VAN BUREN.

WASHINGTON, *June 13, 1840.*

To the House of Representatives:

I communicate to the House of Representatives a report‡ from the Secretary of State, with documents, containing the information requested by their resolution of the 26th of May last.

M. VAN BUREN.

WASHINGTON, *June 19, 1840.*

The SPEAKER OF THE HOUSE OF REPRESENTATIVES OF THE UNITED STATES.

SIR: I transmit a communication from the Secretary of the Navy, suggesting that an appropriation of $50,000 be made by Congress to

---

*Relating to the refusal of banks to pay the Government demands in specie since the general resumption in 1838, and the payment of Government creditors in depreciated currency.

†Relating to the manner in which the public funds have been paid out by disbursing officers and agents during 1838 and 1839.

‡Relating to charges preferred by Dr. John Baldwin, of Louisiana, against Marmaduke Burroughs, consul at Vera Cruz.

'meet claims of navy pensioners, payable on the 1st of July next, reimbursable by a transfer of stocks belonging to the fund at their nominal value to the amount so appropriated, and respectfully recommend the measure to the consideration and action of Congress.

M. VAN BUREN.

WASHINGTON, *June 22, 1840.*

To the Senate of the United States:

I lay before you, for your consideration, a treaty of commerce and navigation between the United States of America and His Majesty the King of Hanover, signed by their ministers on the 20th day of May last.

M. VAN BUREN.

WASHINGTON, *June 27, 1840.*

To the Senate:

The importance of the subject to the tranquillity of our country makes it proper that I should communicate to the Senate, in addition to the information heretofore transmitted in reply to their resolution of the 17th of January last, the copy of a letter just received from Mr. Fox, announcing the determination of the British Government to consent to the principles of our last proposition for the settlement of the question of the northeastern boundary, with a copy of the answer made to it by the Secretary of State. I can not doubt that, with the sincere disposition which actuates both Governments to prevent any other than an amicable termination of the controversy, it will be found practicable so to arrange the details of a conventional agreement on the principles alluded to as to effect that object.

The British commissioners, in their report communicated by Mr. Fox, express an opinion that the true line of the treaty of 1783 is materially different from that so long contended for by Great Britain. The report is altogether *ex parte* in its character, and has not yet, as far as we are informed, been adopted by the British Government. It has, however, assumed a form sufficiently authentic and important to justify the belief that it is to be used hereafter by the British Government in the discussion of the question of boundary; and as it differs essentially from the line claimed by the United States, an immediate preparatory exploration and survey on our part, by commissioners appointed for that purpose, of the portions of the territory therein more particularly brought into view would, in my opinion, be proper. If Congress concur with me in this view of the subject, a provision by them to enable the Executive to carry it into effect will be necessary.

M. VAN BUREN.

Mr. Fox to Mr. Forsyth.

WASHINGTON, *June 22, 1840.*

Hon. JOHN FORSYTH, etc.:

The undersigned, Her Britannic Majesty's envoy extraordinary and minister plenipotentiary, has the honor to transmit to the Secretary of State of the United States, by order of his Government, the accompanying printed copies of a report and map which have been presented to Her Majesty's Government by Colonel Mudge and Mr. Featherstonhaugh, the commissioners employed during the last season to survey the disputed territory.

The undersigned is instructed to say that it will of course have become the duty of Her Majesty's Government to lay the said report and map before Parliament; but Her Majesty's Government have been desirous, as a mark of courtesy and consideration toward the Government of the United States, that documents bearing upon a question of so much interest and importance to the two countries should in the first instance be communicated to the President. The documents had been officially placed in the hands of Her Majesty's Government only a few days previously to the date of the instruction addressed to the undersigned.

Her Majesty's Government feel an unabated desire to bring the long-pending questions connected with the boundary between the United States and the British possessions in North America to a final and satisfactory settlement, being well aware that questions of this nature, as long as they remain open between two countries, must be the source of frequent irritation on both sides and are liable at any moment to lead to events that may endanger the existence of friendly relations.

It is obvious that the questions at issue between Great Britain and the United States must be beset with various and really existing difficulties, or else those questions would not have remained open ever since the year 1783, notwithstanding the frequent and earnest endeavors made by each Government to bring them to an adjustment; but Her Majesty's Government do not relinquish the hope that the sincere desire which is felt by both parties to arrive at an amicable settlement will at length be attended with success.

The best clew to guide the two Governments in their future proceedings may perhaps be obtained by an examination of the causes of past failure; and the most prominent amongst these causes has certainly been a want of correct information as to the topographical features and physical character of the district in dispute.

This want of adequate information may be traced as one of the difficulties which embarrassed the Netherlands Government in its endeavors to decide the points submitted to its arbitration in 1830. The same has been felt by the Government in England; it has been felt and admitted by the Government of the United States, and even by the local government of the contiguous State of Maine.

The British Government and the Government of the United States agreed, therefore, two years ago that a survey of the disputed territory by a joint commission would be the measure best calculated to elucidate and solve the questions at issue. The President proposed such a commission and Her Majesty's Government consented to it, and it was believed by Her Majesty's Government that the general principles upon which the commission was to be guided in its local operations had been settled by mutual agreement, arrived at by means of a correspondence which took place between the two Governments in 1837 and 1838. Her Majesty's Government accordingly transmitted in April of last year, for the consideration of the President, the draft of a convention to regulate the proceedings of the proposed commission. The preamble of that draft recited textually the agreement that had been come to by means of notes which had been exchanged between the two Governments, and the articles of the draft were framed, as Her Majesty's Government considered, in strict conformity with that agreement.

But the Government of the United States did not think proper to assent to the convention so proposed.

The United States Government did not, indeed, allege that the proposed convention was at variance with the result of the previous correspondence between the two Governments, but it thought that the convention would establish a commission of "mere exploration and survey," and the President was of opinion that the step next to be taken by the two Governments should be to contract stipulations bearing upon the face of them the promise of a final settlement under some form or other and within a reasonable time.

The United States Government accordingly transmitted to the undersigned, for communication to Her Majesty's Government, in the month of July last a counter draft of convention varying considerably in some parts (as the Secretary of State of the United States admitted in his letter to the undersigned of the 29th of July last) from the draft proposed by Great Britain, but the Secretary of State added that the United States Government did not deem it necessary to comment upon the alterations so made, as the text itself of the counter draft would be found sufficiently perspicuous.

Her Majesty's Government might certainly well have expected that some reasons would have been given to explain why the United States Government declined to confirm an arrangement which was founded upon propositions made by that Government itself and upon modifications to which that Government had agreed, or that if the American Government thought the draft of convention thus proposed was not in conformity with the previous agreement it would have pointed out in what respect the two were considered to differ.

Her Majesty's Government, considering the present state of the boundary question, concur with the Government of the United States in thinking that it is on every account expedient that the next measure to be adopted by the two Governments should contain arrangements which will necessarily lead to a final settlement, and they think that the convention which they proposed last year to the President, instead of being framed so as to constitute a mere commission of exploration and survey, did, on the contrary, contain stipulations calculated to lead to the final ascertainment of the boundary between the two countries.

There was, however, undoubtedly one essential difference between the British draft and the American counter draft. The British draft contained no provision embodying the principle of arbitration; the American counter draft did contain such a provision.

The British draft contained no provision for arbitration, because the principle of arbitration had not been proposed on either side during the negotiations upon which that draft was founded, and because, moreover, it was understood at that time that the principle of arbitration would be decidedly objected to by the United States.

But as the United States Government have now expressed a wish to embody the principle of arbitration in the proposed convention, Her Majesty's Government are perfectly willing to accede to that wish.

The undersigned is accordingly instructed to state officially to Mr. Forsyth that Her Majesty's Government consent to the two principles which form the main foundation of the American counter draft, namely: First, that the commission to be appointed shall be so constituted as necessarily to lead to a final settlement of the questions of boundary at issue between the two countries, and, secondly, that in order to secure such a result the convention by which the commission is to be created shall contain a provision for arbitration upon points as to which the British and American commissioners may not be able to agree.

The undersigned is, however, instructed to add that there are many matters of detail in the American counter draft which Her Majesty's Government can not adopt. The undersigned will be furnished from his Government, by an early opportunity, with an amended draft in conformity with the principles above stated, to be submitted to the consideration of the President. And the undersigned expects to be at the same time furnished with instructions to propose to the Government of the United States a fresh, local, and temporary convention for the better prevention of incidental border collisions within the disputed territory during the time that may be occupied in carrying through the operations of survey or arbitration.

The undersigned avails himself of this occasion to renew to the Secretary of State the assurance of his distinguished consideration. H. S. FOX.

Mr. Forsyth to Mr. Fox.

DEPARTMENT OF STATE,
Washington, June 26, 1840.

H. S. Fox, Esq., etc.:

The undersigned, Secretary of State of the United States, has had the honor to receive a note addressed to him on the 22d instant by Mr. Fox, envoy extraordinary and minister plenipotentiary of Great Britain, inclosing printed copies of the report and map laid before the British Government by the commissioners employed during the last season to survey the territory in dispute between the two countries, and communicating the consent of Her Britannic Majesty's Government to the two principles which form the main foundation of the counter proposition of the United States for the adjustment of the question.

The undersigned, having laid Mr. Fox's note before the President, is instructed to say in answer that the President duly appreciates the motives of courtesy which prompted the British Government to communicate to that of the United States the documents referred to, and that he derives great satisfaction from the announcement that Her Majesty's Government do not relinquish the hope that the sincere desire which is felt by both parties to arrive at an amicable settlement will at length be attended with success, and from the prospect held out by Mr. Fox of his being accordingly furnished by an early opportunity with the draft of a proposition amended in conformity with the principles to which Her Majesty's Government has acceded, to be submitted to the consideration of this Government.

Mr. Fox states that his Government might have expected that when the American counter draft was communicated to him some reasons would have been given to explain why the United States Government declined accepting the British draft of convention, or that if it thought the draft was not in conformity with previous agreement it would have pointed out in what respect the two were considered to differ.

In the note which the undersigned addressed to Mr. Fox on the 29th July of last year, transmitting the American counter draft, he stated that in consequence of the then recent events on the frontier and the danger of collision between the citizens and subjects of the two Governments a mere commission of exploration and survey would be inadequate to the exigencies of the occasion and fall behind the just expectations of the people of both countries, and referred to the importance of having the measure next adopted bear upon its face stipulations which must result in a final settlement under some form and in a reasonable time. These were the reasons which induced the President to introduce in the new project the provisions which he thought calculated for the attainment of so desirable an object, and which in his opinion rendered obviously unnecessary any allusion to the previous agreements referred to by Mr. Fox. The President is gratified to find that a concurrence in those views has brought the minds of Her Majesty's Government to a similar conclusion, and from this fresh indication of harmony in the wishes of the two cabinets he permits himself to anticipate the most satisfactory result from the measure under consideration.

The undersigned avails himself of the opportunity to offer to Mr. Fox renewed assurances of his distinguished consideration. JOHN FORSYTH.

WASHINGTON, *June 29, 1840.*

To the Senate of the United States:

I transmit, in answer to a resolution of the Senate of the 12th of March last, a communication of the Secretary of War, accompanied by such information as could be obtained in relation to the military and naval preparations of the British authorities on the northern frontier of the United States from Lake Superior to the Atlantic Ocean.

M. VAN BUREN.

WAR DEPARTMENT, *June 27, 1840.*

The PRESIDENT OF THE UNITED STATES.

SIR: I have the honor to transmit herewith a report of the Commanding General, embracing the substance of the answers of the several officers who were applied to to furnish the information required by a resolution of the Senate of the 12th March last, referred by you to this Department, requesting the President to communicate to the Senate, if in his judgment compatible with the public interests, any information which may be in the possession of the Government, or which can be conveniently obtained, of the military and naval preparations of the British authorities on the northern frontier of the United States from Lake Superior to the Atlantic Ocean, distinguishing the permanent from the temporary and field works, and particularly by noticing those which are within the claimed limits of the United States.

This report and a letter of General Scott on the subject, which was transmitted to the Senate on the 27th of March last, furnish all the information the Department is in possession of in relation to the requirements of the above resolution.

Very respectfully, your most obedient servant,

J. R. POINSETT.

HEADQUARTERS OF THE ARMY,
Washington, June 26, 1840.

The SECRETARY OF WAR.

SIR: I have the honor to report that in obedience to your instructions letters have been addressed to the various officers who it was supposed might be able to procure the information required by the resolution of the Senate of the 12th of March, to wit: "*Resolved*, That the President of the United States be requested to communicate to the Senate, if in his judgment compatible with the public interest, any information which may be in possession of the Government, or which can be conveniently obtained, of the military and naval preparations of the British authorities on the northern frontier of the United States from Lake Superior to the Atlantic Ocean, distinguishing the permanent from the temporary and field works, and particularly by noting those which are within the claimed limits of the United States." In answer to the letter addressed to him on the subject, and with regard to the Senate's resolution as far as relates to "military preparations of the British authorities on the northern frontier of the United States," General Scott communicates the following facts: That he has paid but little attention to the forts and barracks erected by the British authorities near the borders of Maine *above* Frederickton, in New Brunswick, or in Upper Canada *above* Cornwall, being of the fixed opinion that all such structures would be of little or no military value to either of the parties in the event of a new war between the United States and Great Britain; that he was last summer at the foot of Lake Superior, and neither saw nor heard of any British fort or barracks on the St. Marys River; that between Lakes Huron and Erie the British have three sets of barracks—one at Windsor, opposite to Detroit; one at Sandwich, a little lower down; and the third at Malden, 18 miles below the first—all built of sawed logs, strengthened by blockhouses, loopholes, etc.; that Malden has long been a military post, with slight defenses; these have been recently strengthened. The works at Sandwich and Windsor have also, he thinks, been erected within the last six or eight months. That near the mouth of the Niagara the British have two small forts—George and Mississauga; both existed during the last war; the latter may be termed a permanent work. Slight barracks have been erected within the last two years on the same side near the Falls and at Chippewa, with breastworks at the latter place, but nothing, he believes, above the work first named on the Niagara which can be termed a fort.

That since the commencement of recent troubles and (consequent thereon) within our own limits Fort William Henry, at Kingston, and Fort Wellington, opposite to Ogdensburg (old works), have both been strengthened within themselves, besides the addition of dependencies. These forts may be called permanent. That on the St. Lawrence below Prescott, and confronting our territory, he knows of no other military post. Twelve miles above, at Brockville, there may be temporary barracks and breastworks; that he knows that of late Brockville has been a military station.

That in the system of defenses on the approaches to Montreal the Isle aux Noix, a few miles below our line, and in the outlet of Lake Champlain, stands at the head. This island contains within itself a system of permanent works of great strength; on them the British Government has from time to time expended much skill and labor.

That Odletown, near our line, on the western side of Lake Champlain, has been a station for a body of Canadian militia for two years, to guard the neighborhood from refugee incendiaries from our side. He thinks that barracks have been erected there for the accommodation of those troops, and also at a station, with the like object, near Alburgh, Vt. He believes that there are no important British forts or extensive British barracks on our borders from Vermont to Maine. In respect to such structures on the disputed territory, that Governor Fairfield's published letters contain fuller information than has reached him through any other channel; that he has heard of no new military preparations by the British authorities on the St. Croix or Passamaquoddy Bay.

That among such preparations, perhaps he ought not to omit the fact that Great Britain, besides numerous corps of well-organized and well-instructed militia, has at this time within her North American Provinces more than 20,000 of her best regular troops. The whole of those forces might be brought to the verge of our territory in a few days. Two-thirds of that regular force has arrived out since the spring of 1838. General Scott states that he has had the honor to report directly to the Secretary of War with regard to the naval force recently maintained upon the American lakes by Great Britain. In answer to a similar letter to that addressed to General Scott, General Brady writes from Detroit that the only permanent work of which he has any knowledge is the one at Fort Malden, which has in the last year been thoroughly repaired, and good substantial barracks of wood have been erected within the works, sufficient, he thinks, to contain six if not eight hundred men; that the timber on the island of Bois Blanc has been partly taken off and three small blockhouses erected on the island. These are all the military improvements he knows of between the mouth of Detroit River and the outlet of Lake Superior. That temporary barracks of wood capable of containing perhaps 150 men have been erected opposite to Detroit; that some British militia are stationed along the St. Clair River.

Colonel Bankhead writes that of the military and naval preparations of the British on the northern frontier of the United States, he can only state that Fort Mississauga, nearly opposite our Fort Niagara, has been enlarged and strengthened; that permanent and extensive barracks were commenced last summer at Toronto and are probably completed by this time, and that a large vessel for a steamer was being constructed last fall at Niagara City by and for the service of the Government; that the British Government has on Lake Ontario a steamboat commanded and officered by officers of the navy, and is commissioned, he presumes, as a Government vessel;

that the authorities of Upper Canada had last summer in their service on Lake Erie two steamboats, which were at first hired from citizens of Buffalo, but which they subsequently purchased, as he was informed.

Lieutenant-Colonel Crane writes from Buffalo that the only military work in that vicinity undergoing repairs (within his knowledge) is Fort Mississauga, at the mouth of the Niagara River, on the Canada side, which the English have been repairing and extending for two years past, and it is believed to be now in a very efficient state; that there have been rumors of armed steamers being built or building at Chippewa, but on inquiry he could learn of none except the ordinary steamboats for the navigation of the lakes. It has been said, however, that one is building on Lake Ontario by the English, and intended for the revenue service, but he does not know what truth there is in this statement.

Lieutenant-Colonel Pierce reports from Plattsburg that he has no knowledge of any military or naval preparations of the British authorities on the line of frontier adjacent to his command, comprising what is generally called the Lake Champlain frontier, except the introduction of troops at Odletown and Napierville, near the boundary line between New York and Canada, on the west side of the lake, and also the establishment of a line of posts from Missisquoi Bay, on the east side of the lake, along and near to the Vermont frontier as far as the Connecticut River, the erection of a new barrack and fieldwork at St. John, and the repairs and armament of the Isle aux Noix, with increased force at both of these posts; that none of the positions so occupied by British troops are within the claimed limits of the United States; that these military preparations (it has been heretofore understood) have been made by the British authorities to suppress rebellion and insurrection among the Canadian population.

Captain Johnson reports from Fort Brady that he has heard nothing on the subject of the resolution but mere rumors, and that there is no appearance of any works going up anywhere on the Canada side of the St. Marys River. The files of the Adjutant-General's Office have been examined, but no further information has been elicited.

Respectfully submitted.

ALEX. MACOMB,
Major-General.

WASHINGTON, *June 29, 1840.*

To the House of Representatives of the United States:

I transmit herewith a communication of the Secretary of War, accompanied by a report of the Commanding General of the Army, embracing all the information which can be obtained in answer to a resolution of the House of Representatives of the 6th of April, 1840, requesting to be furnished with any information in possession of the executive department showing the military preparation of Great Britain by introducing troops into Canada or New Brunswick or erecting or repairing fortifications on our northern or northeastern boundary or by preparing naval armaments on any of the great northern lakes, and what preparations, if any, have been made by this Government to put the United States, and especially those frontiers, in a posture of defense against Great Britain in case of war.

M. VAN BUREN.

WASHINGTON CITY, *June 29, 1840.*

To the House of Representatives of the United States:

I transmit the inclosed report of the Secretary of War, with accompanying documents, furnishing all the information the Department has been able to obtain in relation to any violation of or desire on the part of Great Britain to annul the agreement entered into between that Government and the United States in the month of April, 1817, relative to the naval force to be maintained upon the American lakes, called for by a resolution of the House of Representatives of the 9th March last.

M. VAN BUREN.

Hon. R. M. JOHNSON,
   President of the Senate.

SIR: I transmit herewith to the Senate a statement from the Secretary of the Navy of the transfers which have been made since the commencement of the present year from different appropriations for the naval service to other appropriations for the same service, which had become necessary for the public interests.

The law under which these transfers were made conveys no authority for refunding the different amounts which may be transferred. On the contrary, so soon as the appropriations for the year shall pass and the means be furnished for refunding these sums the repayments would be prohibited by the law of 3d March, 1809, in relation to general transfers.

Some authority to refund the amounts which may be transferred under the law of 30th of June, 1834, seems so obviously indispensable to any beneficial exercise of the power which it grants that its omission may be presumed to have been accidental.

The subject is respectfully referred to the consideration of Congress for such action as they may deem proper to accomplish the restoration of these transfers, and thus confirm the original appropriations as they are established by Congress, instead of leaving their expenditure discretionary with the Executive.

M. VAN BUREN.

JULY 2, 1840.

[The same message was addressed to the Speaker of the House of Representatives.]

WASHINGTON, *July 20, 1840.*

To the Senate of the United States:

I transmit herewith, in reply to the resolution of the Senate of the 11th March last, a report* from the Secretary of War, accompanied by a communication and other documents from the Commissioner of Indian Affairs.

M. VAN BUREN.

---

*Relating to purchases of Indian lands since the establishment of the Federal Government.

JULY 25, 1840.

The President of the United States, in pursuance of a resolution of the Senate of the 20th instant, herewith transmits to the honorable Secretary of the Senate a copy of the report of Captain M. C. Perry in relation to the light-houses of England and France.

M. VAN BUREN.

EXECUTIVE ORDER.

WASHINGTON CITY, *March 31, 1840.*

The President of the United States, finding that different rules prevail at different places as well in respect to the hours of labor by persons employed on the public works under the immediate authority of himself and the Departments as also in relation to the different classes of workmen, and believing that much inconvenience and dissatisfaction would be removed by adopting a uniform course, hereby directs that all such persons, whether laborers or mechanics, be required to work only the number of hours prescribed by the ten-hour system.

M. VAN BUREN.

FOURTH ANNUAL MESSAGE.

WASHINGTON, *December 5, 1840.*

Fellow-Citizens of the Senate and House of Representatives:

Our devout gratitude is due to the Supreme Being for having graciously continued to our beloved country through the vicissitudes of another year the invaluable blessings of health, plenty, and peace. Seldom has this favored land been so generally exempted from the ravages of disease or the labor of the husbandman more amply rewarded, and never before have our relations with other countries been placed on a more favorable basis than that which they so happily occupy at this critical conjuncture in the affairs of the world. A rigid and persevering abstinence from all interference with the domestic and political relations of other States, alike due to the genius and distinctive character of our Government and to the principles by which it is directed; a faithful observance in the management of our foreign relations of the practice of speaking plainly, dealing justly, and requiring truth and justice in return as the best conservatives of the peace of nations; a strict impartiality in our manifestations of friendship in the commercial privileges we concede and those we require from others—these, accompanied by a disposition as prompt to maintain in every emergency our own rights as we are from principle averse to the invasion of those of others, have given to our country and Government a standing in the great family of nations of which we have just cause to be proud and the advantages of which are experienced by our citizens throughout every portion of the earth to which their enterprising and adventurous spirit may carry them. Few, if any, remain insensible to the value of our friendship or ignorant of the terms on which it can be acquired and by which it can alone be preserved.

A series of questions of long standing, difficult in their adjustment and important in their consequences, in which the rights of our citizens and the honor of the country were deeply involved, have in the course of a few years (the most of them during the successful Administration of my immediate predecessor) been brought to a satisfactory conclusion; and the most important of those remaining are, I am happy to believe, in a fair way of being speedily and satisfactorily adjusted.

With all the powers of the world our relations are those of honorable peace. Since your adjournment nothing serious has occurred to interrupt or threaten this desirable harmony. If clouds have lowered above the other hemisphere, they have not cast their portentous shadows upon our happy shores. Bound by no entangling alliances, yet linked by a common nature and interest with the other nations of mankind, our aspirations are for the preservation of peace, in whose solid and civilizing triumphs all may participate with a generous emulation. Yet it behooves us to be prepared for any event and to be always ready to maintain those just and enlightened principles of national intercourse for which this Government has ever contended. In the shock of contending empires it is only by assuming a resolute bearing and clothing themselves with defensive armor that neutral nations can maintain their independent rights.

The excitement which grew out of the territorial controversy between the United States and Great Britain having in a great measure subsided, it is hoped that a favorable period is approaching for its final settlement. Both Governments must now be convinced of the dangers with which the question is fraught, and it must be their desire, as it is their interest, that this perpetual cause of irritation should be removed as speedily as practicable. In my last annual message you were informed that the proposition for a commission of exploration and survey promised by Great Britain had been received, and that a counter project, including also a provision for the certain and final adjustment of the limits in dispute, was then before the British Government for its consideration. The answer of that Government, accompanied by additional propositions of its own, was received through its minister here since your separation. These were promptly considered, such as were deemed correct in principle and consistent with a due regard to the just rights of the United

States and of the State of Maine concurred in, and the reasons for dissenting from the residue, with an additional suggestion on our part, communicated by the Secretary of State to Mr. Fox. That minister, not feeling himself sufficiently instructed upon some of the points raised in the discussion, felt it to be his duty to refer the matter to his own Government for its further decision. Having now been for some time under its advisement, a speedy answer may be confidently expected. From the character of the points still in difference and the undoubted disposition of both parties to bring the matter to an early conclusion, I look with entire confidence to a prompt and satisfactory termination of the negotiation. Three commissioners were appointed shortly after the adjournment of Congress under the act of the last session providing for the exploration and survey of the line which separates the States of Maine and New Hampshire from the British Provinces. They have been actively employed until their progress was interrupted by the inclemency of the season, and will resume their labors as soon as practicable in the ensuing year.

It is understood that their respective examinations will throw new light upon the subject in controversy and serve to remove any erroneous impressions which may have been made elsewhere prejudicial to the rights of the United States. It was, among other reasons, with a view of preventing the embarrassments which in our peculiar system of government impede and complicate negotiations involving the territorial rights of a State that I thought it my duty, as you have been informed on a previous occasion, to propose to the British Government, through its minister at Washington, that early steps should be taken to adjust the points of difference on the line of boundary from the entrance of Lake Superior to the most northwestern point of the Lake of the Woods by the arbitration of a friendly power in conformity with the seventh article of the treaty of Ghent. No answer has yet been returned by the British Government to this proposition.

With Austria, France, Prussia, Russia, and the remaining powers of Europe I am happy to inform you our relations continue to be of the most friendly character. With Belgium a treaty of commerce and navigation, based upon liberal principles of reciprocity and equality, was concluded in March last, and, having been ratified by the Belgian Government, will be duly laid before the Senate. It is a subject of congratulation that it provides for the satisfactory adjustment of a long-standing question of controversy, thus removing the only obstacle which could obstruct the friendly and mutually advantageous intercourse between the two nations. A messenger has been dispatched with the Hanoverian treaty to Berlin, where, according to stipulation, the ratifications are to be exchanged. I am happy to announce to you that after many delays and difficulties a treaty of commerce and navigation between the United States and Portugal was concluded and signed at Lisbon on the 26th of

August last by the plenipotentiaries of the two Governments. Its stipulations are founded upon those principles of mutal liberality and advantage which the United States have always sought to make the basis of their intercourse with foreign powers, and it is hoped they will tend to foster and strengthen the commercial intercourse of the two countries.

Under the appropriation of the last session of Congress an agent has been sent to Germany for the purpose of promoting the interests of our tobacco trade.

The commissioners appointed under the convention for the adjustment of claims of citizens of the United States upon Mexico having met and organized at Washington in August last, the papers in the possession of the Government relating to those claims were communicated to the board. The claims not embraced by that convention are now the subject of negotiation between the two Governments through the medium of our minister at Mexico.

Nothing has occurred to disturb the harmony of our relations with the different Governments of South America. I regret, however, to be obliged to inform you that the claims of our citizens upon the late Republic of Colombia have not yet been satisfied by the separate Governments into which it has been resolved.

The chargé d'affaires of Brazil having expressed the intention of his Government not to prolong the treaty of 1828, it will cease to be obligatory upon either party on the 12th day of December, 1841, when the extensive commercial intercourse between the United States and that vast Empire will no longer be regulated by express stipulations.

It affords me pleasure to communicate to you that the Government of Chili has entered into an agreement to indemnify the claimants in the case of the *Macedonian* for American property seized in 1819, and to add that information has also been received which justifies the hope of an early adjustment of the remaining claims upon that Government.

The commissioners appointed in pursuance of the convention between the United States and Texas for marking the boundary between them have, according to the last report received from our commissioner, surveyed and established the whole extent of the boundary north along the western bank of the Sabine River from its entrance into the Gulf of Mexico to the thirty-second degree of north latitude. The commission adjourned on the 16th of June last, to reassemble on the 1st of November for the purpose of establishing accurately the intersection of the thirty-second degree of latitude with the western bank of the Sabine and the meridian line thence to Red River. It is presumed that the work will be concluded in the present season.

The present sound condition of their finances and the success with which embarrassments in regard to them, at times apparently insurmountable, have been overcome are matters upon which the people and Government of the United States may well congratulate themselves. An overflowing Treasury, however it may be regarded as an evidence of public prosperity, is seldom conducive to the permanent welfare of any people, and experience has demonstrated its incompatibility with the salutary action of political institutions like those of the United States. Our safest reliance for financial efficiency and independence has, on the contrary, been found to consist in ample resources unencumbered with debt, and in this respect the Federal Government occupies a singularly fortunate and truly enviable position.

When I entered upon the discharge of my official duties in March, 1837, the act for the distribution of the surplus revenue was in a course of rapid execution. Nearly $28,000,000 of the public moneys were, in pursuance of its provisions, deposited with the States in the months of January, April, and July of that year. In May there occurred a general suspension of specie payments by the banks, including, with very few exceptions, those in which the public moneys were deposited and upon whose fidelity the Government had unfortunately made itself dependent for the revenues which had been collected from the people and were indispensable to the public service.

This suspension and the excesses in banking and commerce out of which it arose, and which were greatly aggravated by its occurrence, made to a great extent unavailable the principal part of the public money then on hand, suspended the collection of many millions accruing on merchants' bonds, and greatly reduced the revenue arising from customs and the public lands. These effects have continued to operate in various degrees to the present period, and in addition to the decrease in the revenue thus produced two and a half millions of duties have been relinquished by two biennial reductions under the act of 1833, and probably as much more upon the importation of iron for railroads by special legislation.

Whilst such has been our condition for the last four years in relation to revenue, we have during the same period been subjected to an unavoidable continuance of large extraordinary expenses necessarily growing out of past transactions, and which could not be immediately arrested without great prejudice to the public interest. Of these, the charge upon the Treasury in consequence of the Cherokee treaty alone, without adverting to others arising out of Indian treaties, has already exceeded $5,000,000; that for the prosecution of measures for the removal of the Seminole Indians, which were found in progress, has been nearly fourteen millions, and the public buildings have required the unusual sum of nearly three millions.

It affords me, however, great pleasure to be able to say that from the commencement of this period to the present day every demand upon the Government, at home or abroad, has been promptly met. This has been done not only without creating a permanent debt or a resort to additional taxation in any form, but in the midst of a steadily progressive reduction of existing burdens upon the people, leaving still a considerable balance of available funds which will remain in the Treasury at the end of the year. The small amount of Treasury notes, not exceeding $4,500,000, still outstanding, and less by twenty-three millions than the United States have in deposit with the States, is composed of such only as are not yet due or have not been presented for payment. They may be redeemed out of the accruing revenue if the expenditures do not exceed the amount within which they may, it is thought, be kept without prejudice to the public interest, and the revenue shall prove to be as large as may justly be anticipated.

Among the reflections arising from the contemplation of these circumstances, one, not the least gratifying, is the consciousness that the Government had the resolution and the ability to adhere in every emergency to the sacred obligations of law, to execute all its contracts according to the requirements of the Constitution, and thus to present when most needed a rallying point by which the business of the whole country might be brought back to a safe and unvarying standard—a result vitally important as well to the interests as to the morals of the people. There can surely now be no difference of opinion in regard to the incalculable evils that would have arisen if the Government at that critical moment had suffered itself to be deterred from upholding the only true standard of value, either by the pressure of adverse circumstances or the violence of unmerited denunciation. The manner in which the people sustained the performance of this duty was highly honorable to their fortitude and patriotism. It can not fail to stimulate their agents to adhere under all circumstances to the line of duty and to satisfy them of the safety with which a course really right and demanded by a financial crisis may in a community like ours be pursued, however apparently severe its immediate operation.

The policy of the Federal Government in extinguishing as rapidly as possible the national debt, and subsequently in resisting every temptation to create a new one, deserves to be regarded in the same favorable light. Among the many objections to a national debt, the certain tendency of public securities to concentrate ultimately in the coffers of foreign stockholders is one which is every day gathering strength. Already have the resources of many of the States and the future industry of their citizens been indefinitely mortgaged to the subjects of European Governments to the amount of twelve millions annually to pay the constantly accruing interest on borrowed money—a sum exceeding half the ordinary revenues of the whole United States. The pretext which this relation affords to foreigners to scrutinize the management of our domestic affairs, if not actually to intermeddle with them, presents a subject for earnest attention, not to say of serious alarm. Fortunately, the Federal Government, with the exception of an obligation entered into in behalf of the District of Columbia, which must soon be discharged, is wholly exempt from any such embarrassment. It is also, as is believed, the only Government which, having fully and faithfully paid all its creditors, has also relieved itself entirely from debt. To maintain a distinction so desirable and so honorable to our national character should be an object of earnest solicitude. Never should a free people, if it be possible to avoid it, expose themselves to the necessity of having to treat of the peace, the honor, or the safety of the Republic with the governments of foreign creditors, who, however well disposed they may be to cultivate with us in general friendly relations, are nevertheless by the law of their own condition made hostile to the success and permanency of political institutions like ours. Most humiliating may be the embarrassments consequent upon such a condition. Another objection, scarcely less formidable, to the commencement of a new debt is its inevitable tendency to increase in magnitude and to foster national extravagance. He has been an unprofitable observer of events who needs at this day to be admonished of the difficulties which a government habitually dependent on loans to sustain its ordinary expenditures has to encounter in resisting the influences constantly exerted in favor of additional loans; by capitalists, who enrich themselves by government securities for amounts much exceeding the money they actually advance—a prolific source of individual aggrandizement in all borrowing countries; by stockholders, who seek their gains in the rise and fall of public stocks; and by the selfish importunities of applicants for appropriations for works avowedly for the accommodation of the public, but the real objects of which are too frequently the advancement of private interests. The known necessity which so many of the States will be under to impose taxes for the payment of the interest on their debts furnishes an additional and very cogent reason why the Federal Government should refrain from creating a national debt, by which the people would be exposed to double taxation for a similar object. We possess within ourselves ample resources for every emergency, and we may be quite sure that our citizens in no future exigency will be unwilling to supply the Government with all the means asked for the defense of the country. In time of peace there can, at all events, be no justification for the creation of a permanent debt by the Federal Government. Its limited range of constitutional duties may certainly under such circumstances be performed without such a resort. It has, it is seen, been avoided during four years of greater fiscal difficulties than have existed in a similar period since the adoption of the Constitution, and one also remarkable for the occurrence of extraordinary causes of expenditures.

But to accomplish so desirable an object two things are indispensable: First, that the action of the Federal Government be kept within the boundaries prescribed by its founders, and, secondly, that all appropriations for objects admitted to be constitutional, and the expenditure of them also, be subjected to a standard of rigid but well-considered and practical economy. The first depends chiefly on the people themselves—the opinions they form of the true construction of the Constitution and the confidence they repose in the political sentiments of those they select as their representatives in the Federal Legislature; the second rests upon the fidelity with which their more immediate representatives and other public functionaries discharge the trusts committed to them. The duty of economizing the expenses of the public service is admitted on all hands; yet there are few subjects upon which there exists a wider difference of opinion than is constantly manifested in regard to the fidelity with which that duty is discharged. Neither diversity of sentiment nor even mutual recriminations upon a point in respect to which the public mind is so justly sensitive can well be entirely avoided, and least so at periods of great political excitement. An intelligent people, however, seldom fail to arrive in the end at correct conclusions in such a matter. Practical economy in the management of public affairs can have no adverse influence to contend with more powerful than a large surplus revenue, and the unusually large appropriations for 1837 may without doubt, independently of the extraordinary requisitions for the public service growing out of the state of our Indian relations, be in no inconsiderable degree traced to this source. The sudden and rapid distribution of the large surplus then in the Treasury and the equally sudden and unprecedentedly severe revulsion in the commerce and business of the country, pointing with unerring certainty to a great and protracted reduction of the revenue, strengthened the propriety of the earliest practicable reduction of the public expenditures.

But to change a system operating upon so large a surface and applicable to such numerous and diversified interests and objects was more than the work of a day. The attention of every department of the Government was immediately and in good faith directed to that end, and has been so continued to the present moment. The estimates and appropriations for the year 1838 (the first over which I had any control) were somewhat diminished. The expenditures of 1839 were reduced $6,000,000. Those of 1840, exclusive of disbursements for public debt and trust claims, will probably not exceed twenty-two and a half millions, being between two and three millions less than those of the preceding year and nine or ten millions less than those of 1837. Nor has it been found necessary in order to produce this result to resort to the power conferred by Congress of postponing certain classes of the public works, except by deferring expenditures for a short period upon a limited portion of them, and which postponement terminated some time since—at the moment the Treasury Department by further receipts from the indebted banks became fully assured of its ability to meet them without prejudice to the public service in other respects. Causes are in operation which will, it is believed, justify a still further reduction without injury to any important national interest. The expenses of sustaining the troops employed in Florida have been gradually and greatly reduced through the persevering efforts of the War Department, and a reasonable hope may be entertained that the necessity for military operations in that quarter will soon cease. The removal of the Indians from within our settled borders is nearly completed. The pension list, one of the heaviest charges upon the Treasury, is rapidly diminishing by death. The most costly of our public buildings are either finished or nearly so, and we may, I think, safely promise ourselves a continued exemption from border difficulties.

The available balance in the Treasury on the 1st of January next is estimated at $1,500,000. This sum, with the expected receipts from all sources during the next year, will, it is believed, be sufficient to enable the Government to meet every engagement and have a suitable balance in the Treasury at the end of the year, if the remedial measures connected with the customs and the public lands heretofore recommended are adopted and the new appropriations by Congress shall not carry the expenditures beyond the official estimates.

The new system established by Congress for the safe-keeping of the public money, prescribing the kind of currency to be received for the public revenue and providing additional guards and securities against losses, has now been several months in operation. Although it might be premature upon an experience of such limited duration to form a definite opinion in regard to the extent of its influences in correcting many evils under which the Federal Government and the country have hitherto suffered, especially those that have grown out of banking expansions, a depreciated currency, and official defalcations, yet it is but right to say that nothing has occurred in the practical operation of the system to weaken in the slightest degree, but much to strengthen, the confident anticipations of its friends. The grounds of these have been heretofore so fully explained as to require no recapitulation. In respect to the facility and convenience it affords in conducting the public service, and the ability of the Government to discharge through its agency every duty attendant on the collection, transfer, and disbursement of the public money with promptitude and success, I can say with confidence that the apprehensions of those who felt it to be their duty to oppose its adoption have proved to be unfounded. On the contrary, this branch of the fiscal affairs of the Government has been, and it is believed may always be, thus carried on with every desirable facility and security. A few changes and improvements in the details of the system, without affecting any principles involved in it, will be submitted to you by the Secretary of the Treasury, and will, I am sure, receive at your hands that attention to which they may on examination be found to be entitled.

I have deemed this brief summary of our fiscal affairs necessary to the due performance of a duty specially enjoined upon me by the Constitution. It will serve also to illustrate more fully the principles by which

I have been guided in reference to two contested points in our public policy which were earliest in their development and have been more important in their consequences than any that have arisen under our complicated and difficult, yet admirable, system of government. I allude to a national debt and a national bank. It was in these that the political contests by which the country has been agitated ever since the adoption of the Constitution in a great measure originated, and there is too much reason to apprehend that the conflicting interests and opposing principles thus marshaled will continue as heretofore to produce similar if not aggravated consequences.

Coming into office the declared enemy of both, I have earnestly endeavored to prevent a resort to either.

The consideration that a large public debt affords an apology, and produces in some degree a necessity also, for resorting to a system and extent of taxation which is not only oppressive throughout, but is likewise so apt to lead in the end to the commission of that most odious of all offenses against the principles of republican government, the prostitution of political power, conferred for the general benefit, to the aggrandizement of particular classes and the gratification of individual cupidity, is alone sufficient, independently of the weighty objections which have already been urged, to render its creation and existence the sources of bitter and unappeasable discord. If we add to this its inevitable tendency to produce and foster extravagant expenditures of the public moneys, by which a necessity is created for new loans and new burdens on the people, and, finally, refer to the examples of every government which has existed for proof, how seldom it is that the system, when once adopted and implanted in the policy of a country, has failed to expand itself until public credit was exhausted and the people were no longer able to endure its increasing weight, it seems impossible to resist the conclusion that no benefits resulting from its career, no extent of conquest, no accession of wealth to particular classes, nor any nor all its combined advantages, can counterbalance its ultimate but certain results—a splendid government and an impoverished people.

If a national bank was, as is undeniable, repudiated by the framers of the Constitution as incompatible with the rights of the States and the liberties of the people; if from the beginning it has been regarded by large portions of our citizens as coming in direct collision with that great and vital amendment of the Constitution which declares that all powers not conferred by that instrument on the General Government are reserved to the States and to the people; if it has been viewed by them as the first great step in the march of latitudinous construction, which unchecked would render that sacred instrument of as little value as an unwritten constitution, dependent, as it would alone be, for its meaning on the interested interpretation of a dominant party, and affording no security to the rights of the minority—if such is undeniably the case, what rational grounds could have been conceived for anticipating aught but determined opposition to such an institution at the present day.

Could a different result have been expected when the consequences which have flowed from its creation, and particularly from its struggles to perpetuate its existence, had confirmed in so striking a manner the apprehensions of its earliest opponents; when it had been so clearly demonstrated that a concentrated money power, wielding so vast a capital and combining such incalculable means of influence, may in those peculiar conjunctures to which this Government is unavoidably exposed prove an overmatch for the political power of the people themselves; when the true character of its capacity to regulate according to its will and its interests and the interests of its favorites the value and production of the labor and property of every man in this extended country had been so fully and fearfully developed; when it was notorious that all classes of this great community had, by means of the power and influence it thus possesses, been infected to madness with a spirit of heedless speculation; when it had been seen that, secure in the support of the combination of influences by which it was surrounded, it could violate its charter and set the laws at defiance with impunity; and when, too, it had become most apparent that to believe that such an accumulation of powers can ever be granted without the certainty of being abused was to indulge in a fatal delusion?

To avoid the necessity of a permanent debt and its inevitable consequences I have advocated and endeavored to carry into effect the policy of confining the appropriations for the public service to such objects only as are clearly within the constitutional authority of the Federal Government; of excluding from its expenses those improvident and unauthorized grants of public money for works of internal improvement which were so wisely arrested by the constitutional interposition of my predecessor, and which, if they had not been so checked, would long before this time have involved the finances of the General Government in embarrassments far greater than those which are now experienced by any of the States; of limiting all our expenditures to that simple, unostentatious, and economical administration of public affairs which is alone consistent with the character of our institutions; of collecting annually from the customs, and the sales of public lands a revenue fully adequate to defray all the expenses thus incurred; but under no pretense whatsoever to impose taxes upon the people to a greater amount than was actually necessary to the public service conducted upon the principles I have stated.

In lieu of a national bank or a dependence upon banks of any description for the management of our fiscal affairs, I recommended the adoption of the system which is now in successful operation. That system affords every requisite facility for the transaction of the pecuniary concerns of the Government; will, it is confidently anticipated, produce in other respects many of the benefits which have been from time to time expected from the creation of a national bank, but which have never been realized;

avoid the manifold evils inseparable from such an institution; diminish to a greater extent than could be accomplished by any other measure of reform the patronage of the Federal Government—a wise policy in all governments, but more especially so in one like ours, which works well only in proportion as it is made to rely for its support upon the unbiased and unadulterated opinions of its constituents; do away forever all dependence on corporate bodies either in the raising, collecting, safekeeping, or disbursing the public revenues, and place the Government equally above the temptation of fostering a dangerous and unconstitutional institution at home or the necessity of adapting its policy to the views and interests of a still more formidable money power abroad.

It is by adopting and carrying out these principles under circumstances the most arduous and discouraging that the attempt has been made, thus far successfully, to demonstrate to the people of the United States that a national bank at all times, and a national debt except it be incurred at a period when the honor and safety of the nation demand the temporary sacrifice of a policy which should only be abandoned in such exigencies, are not merely unnecessary, but in direct and deadly hostility to the principles of their Government and to their own permanent welfare.

The progress made in the development of these positions appears in the preceding sketch of the past history and present state of the financial concerns of the Federal Government. The facts there stated fully authorize the assertion that all the purposes for which this Government was instituted have been accomplished during four years of greater pecuniary embarrassment than were ever before experienced in time of peace, and in the face of opposition as formidable as any that was ever before arrayed against the policy of an Administration; that this has been done when the ordinary revenues of the Government were generally decreasing as well from the operation of the laws as the condition of the country, without the creation of a permanent public debt or incurring any liability other than such as the ordinary resources of the Government will speedily discharge, and without the agency of a national bank.

If this view of the proceedings of the Government for the period it embraces be warranted by the facts as they are known to exist; if the Army and Navy have been sustained to the full extent authorized by law, and which Congress deemed sufficient for the defense of the country and the protection of its rights and its honor; if its civil and diplomatic service has been equally sustained; if ample provision has been made for the administration of justice and the execution of the laws; if the claims upon public gratitude in behalf of the soldiers of the Revolution have been promptly met and faithfully discharged; if there have been no failures in defraying the very large expenditures growing out of that long-continued and salutary policy of peacefully removing the Indians to regions of comparative safety and prosperity; if the public faith has at all times and everywhere been most scrupulously maintained by a prompt discharge of the numerous, extended, and diversified claims on the Treasury—if all these great and permanent objects, with many others that might be stated, have for a series of years, marked by peculiar obstacles and difficulties, been successfully accomplished without a resort to a permanent debt or the aid of a national bank, have we not a right to expect that a policy the object of which has been to sustain the public service independently of either of these fruitful sources of discord will receive the final sanction of a people whose unbiased and fairly elicited judgment upon public affairs is never ultimately wrong?

That embarrassments in the pecuniary concerns of individuals of unexampled extent and duration have recently existed in this as in other commercial nations is undoubtedly true. To suppose it necessary now to trace these reverses to their sources would be a reflection on the intelligence of my fellow-citizens. Whatever may have been the obscurity in which the subject was involved during the earlier stages of the revulsion, there can not now be many by whom the whole question is not fully understood.

Not deeming it within the constitutional powers of the General Government to repair private losses sustained by reverses in business having no connection with the public service, either by direct appropriations from the Treasury or by special legislation designed to secure exclusive privileges and immunities to individuals or classes in preference to or at the expense of the great majority necessarily debarred from any participation in them, no attempt to do so has been either made, recommended, or encouraged by the present Executive.

It is believed, however, that the great purposes for the attainment of which the Federal Government was instituted have not been lost sight of. Intrusted only with certain limited powers, cautiously enumerated, distinctly specified, and defined with a precision and clearness which would seem to defy misconstruction, it has been my constant aim to confine myself within the limits so clearly marked out and so carefully guarded. Having always been of opinion that the best preservative of the union of the States is to be found in a total abstinence from the exercise of all doubtful powers on the part of the Federal Government rather than in attempts to assume them by a loose construction of the Constitution or an ingenious perversion of its words, I have endeavored to avoid recommending any measure which I had reason to apprehend would, in the opinion even of a considerable minority of my fellow-citizens, be regarded as trenching on the rights of the States or the provisions of the hallowed instrument of our Union. Viewing the aggregate powers of the Federal Government as a voluntary concession of the States, it seemed to me that such only should be exercised as were at the time intended to be given.

I have been strengthened, too, in the propriety of this course by the conviction that all efforts to go beyond this tend only to produce dissatisfaction and distrust, to excite jealousies, and to provoke resistance. Instead of adding strength to the Federal Government, even when successful they must ever prove a source of incurable weakness by alienating a portion of those whose adhesion is indispensable to the great aggregate of united strength and whose voluntary attachment is in my estimation far more essential to the efficiency of a government strong in the best of all possible strength—the confidence and attachment of all those who make up its constituent elements.

Thus believing, it has been my purpose to secure to the whole people and to every member of the Confederacy, by general, salutary, and equal laws alone, the benefit of those republican institutions which it was the end and aim of the Constitution to establish, and the impartial influence of which is in my judgment indispensable to their preservation. I can not bring myself to believe that the lasting happiness of the people, the prosperity of the States, or the permanency of their Union can be maintained by giving preference or priority to any class of citizens in the distribution of benefits or privileges, or by the adoption of measures which enrich one portion of the Union at the expense of another; nor can I see in the interference of the Federal Government with the local legislation and reserved rights of the States a remedy for present or a security against future dangers.

The first, and assuredly not the least, important step toward relieving the country from the condition into which it had been plunged by excesses in trade, banking, and credits of all kinds was to place the business transactions of the Government itself on a solid basis, giving and receiving in all cases value for value, and neither countenancing nor encouraging in others that delusive system of credits from which it has been found so difficult to escape, and which has left nothing behind it but the wrecks that mark its fatal career.

That the financial affairs of the Government are now and have been during the whole period of these wide-spreading difficulties conducted with a strict and invariable regard to this great fundamental principle, and that by the assumption and maintenance of the stand thus taken on the very threshold of the approaching crisis more than by any other cause or causes whatever the community at large has been shielded from the incalculable evils of a general and indefinite suspension of specie payments, and a consequent annihilation for the whole period it might have lasted of a just and invariable standard of value, will, it is believed, at this period scarcely be questioned.

A steady adherence on the part of the Government to the policy which has produced such salutary results, aided by judicious State legislation and, what is not less important, by the industry, enterprise, perseverance, and economy of the American people, can not fail to raise the whole country at an early period to a state of solid and enduring prosperity, not subject to be again overthrown by the suspension of banks or the explosion of a bloated credit system. It is for the people and their representatives to decide whether or not the permanent welfare of the country (which all good citizens equally desire, however widely they may differ as to the means of its accomplishment) shall be in this way secured, or whether the management of the pecuniary concerns of the Government, and by consequence to a great extent those of individuals also, shall be carried back to a condition of things which fostered those contractions and expansions of the currency and those reckless abuses of credit from the baleful effects of which the country has so deeply suffered—a return that can promise in the end no better results than to reproduce the embarrassments the Government has experienced, and to remove from the shoulders of the present to those of fresh victims the bitter fruits of that spirit of speculative enterprise to which our countrymen are so liable and upon which the lessons of experience are so unavailing. The choice is an important one, and I sincerely hope that it may be wisely made.

A report from the Secretary of War, presenting a detailed view of the affairs of that Department, accompanies this communication.

The desultory duties connected with the removal of the Indians, in which the Army has been constantly engaged on the northern and western frontiers and in Florida, have rendered it impracticable to carry into full effect the plan recommended by the Secretary for improving its discipline. In every instance where the regiments have been concentrated they have made great progress, and the best results may be anticipated from a continuance of this system. During the last season a part of the troops have been employed in removing Indians from the interior to the territory assigned them in the West—a duty which they have performed efficiently and with praiseworthy humanity—and that portion of them which has been stationed in Florida continued active operations there throughout the heats of summer.

The policy of the United States in regard to the Indians, of which a succinct account is given in my message of 1838, and of the wisdom and expediency of which I am fully satisfied, has been continued in active operation throughout the whole period of my Administration. Since the spring of 1837 more than 40,000 Indians have been removed to their new homes west of the Mississippi, and I am happy to add that all accounts concur in representing the result of this measure as eminently beneficial to that people.

The emigration of the Seminoles alone has been attended with serious difficulty and occasioned bloodshed, hostilities having been commenced by the Indians in Florida under the apprehension that they would be compelled by force to comply with their treaty stipulations. The execution of the treaty of Paynes Landing, signed in 1832, but not ratified until 1834, was postponed at the solicitation of the Indians until 1836, when they again renewed their agreement to remove peaceably to their new homes in the West. In the face of this solemn and renewed compact they broke their faith and commenced hostilities by the massacre of Major Dade's command, the murder of their agent, General Thompson, and other acts of cruel treachery. When this alarming and unexpected intelligence reached the seat of Government, every effort appears to have been made to reenforce General Clinch, who commanded the troops then in Florida. General Eustis was dispatched with reenforcements from Charleston, troops were called out from Alabama, Tennessee, and Georgia, and General Scott was sent to take the command, with ample powers and ample means. At the first alarm General Gaines organized a force at New Orleans, and without waiting for orders landed in Florida, where he delivered over the troops he had brought with him to General Scott.

Governor Call was subsequently appointed to conduct a summer campaign, and at the close of it was replaced by General Jesup. These events and changes took place under the Administration of my predecessor. Notwithstanding the exertions of the experienced officers who had command there for eighteen months, on entering upon the administration of the Government I found the Territory of Florida a prey to Indian atrocities. A strenuous effort was immediately made to bring those hostilities to a close, and the army under General Jesup was reenforced until it amounted to 10,000 men, and furnished with abundant supplies of every description. In this campaign a great number of the enemy were captured and destroyed, but the character of the contest only was changed. The Indians, having been defeated in every engagement, dispersed in small bands throughout the country and became an enterprising, formidable, and ruthless banditti. General Taylor, who succeeded General Jesup, used his best exertions to subdue them, and was seconded in his efforts by the officers under his command; but he too failed to protect the Territory from their depredations. By an act of signal and cruel treachery they broke the truce made with them by General Macomb, who was sent from Washington for the purpose of carrying into effect the expressed wishes of Congress, and have continued their devastations ever since. General Armistead, who was in Florida when General Taylor left the army by permission, assumed the command, and after active summer operations was met by propositions for peace, and from the fortunate coincidence of the arrival in Florida at the same period of a delegation from the Seminoles who are happily settled west of the Mississippi and are now anxious to persuade their countrymen to join them there hopes were for some time entertained that the Indians might be induced to leave the Territory without further difficulty. These hopes have proved fallacious and hostilities have been renewed throughout the whole of the Territory. That this contest has endured so long is to be attributed to causes beyond the control of the Government. Experienced generals have had the command of the troops, officers and soldiers have alike distinguished themselves for their activity, patience, and enduring courage, the army has been constantly furnished with supplies of every description, and we must look for the causes which have so long procrastinated the issue of the contest in the vast extent of the theater of hostilities, the almost insurmountable obstacles presented by the nature of the country, the climate, and the wily character of the savages.

The sites for marine hospitals on the rivers and lakes which I was authorized to select and cause to be purchased have all been designated, but the appropriation not proving sufficient, conditional arrangements only have been made for their acquisition. It is for Congress to decide whether these conditional purchases shall be sanctioned and the humane intentions of the law carried into full effect.

The Navy, as will appear from the accompanying report of the Secretary, has been usefully and honorably employed in the protection of our commerce and citizens in the Mediterranean, the Pacific, on the coast of Brazil, and in the Gulf of Mexico. A small squadron, consisting of the frigate *Constellation* and the sloop of war *Boston*, under Commodore Kearney, is now on its way to the China and Indian seas for the purpose of attending to our interests in that quarter, and Commander Aulick, in the sloop of war *Yorktown*, has been instructed to visit the Sandwich and Society islands, the coasts of New Zealand and Japan, together with other ports and islands frequented by our whale ships, for the purpose of giving them countenance and protection should they be required. Other smaller vessels have been and still are employed in prosecuting the surveys of the coast of the United States directed by various acts of Congress, and those which have been completed will shortly be laid before you.

The exploring expedition at the latest date was preparing to leave the Bay of Islands, New Zealand, in further prosecution of objects which have thus far been successfully accomplished. The discovery of a new continent, which was first seen in latitude 66° 2' south, longitude 154° 27' east, and afterwards in latitude 66° 31' south, longitude 153° 40' east, by Lieutenants Wilkes and Hudson, for an extent of 1,800 miles, but on which they were prevented from landing by vast bodies of ice which encompassed it, is one of the honorable results of the enterprise. Lieutenant Wilkes bears testimony to the zeal and good conduct of his officers and men, and it is but justice to that officer to state that he appears to have performed the duties assigned him with an ardor, ability, and perseverance which give every assurance of an honorable issue to the undertaking.

The report of the Postmaster-General herewith transmitted will exhibit the service of that Department the past year and its present condition. The transportation has been maintained during the year to the full extent authorized by the existing laws; some improvements have been effected which the public interest seemed urgently to demand, but not involving any material additional expenditure; the contractors have generally performed their engagements with fidelity; the postmasters, with few exceptions, have rendered their accounts and paid their quarterly balances with promptitude, and the whole service of the Department has maintained the efficiency for which it has for several years been distinguished.

The acts of Congress establishing new mail routes and requiring more expensive services on others and the increasing wants of the country have for three years past carried the expenditures something beyond the accruing revenues, the excess having been met until the past year by the surplus which had previously accumulated. That surplus having been exhausted and the anticipated increase in the revenue not having been realized owing to the depression in the commercial business of the country, the finances of the Department exhibit a small deficiency at the close of the last fiscal year. Its resources, however, are ample, and the reduced rates of compensation for the transportation service which may be expected on the future lettings from the general reduction of prices, with the increase of revenue that may reasonably be anticipated from the revival of commercial activity, must soon place the finances of the Department in a prosperous condition.

Considering the unfavorable circumstances which have existed during the past year, it is a gratifying result that the revenue has not declined as compared with the preceding year, but, on the contrary, exhibits a small increase, the circumstances referred to having had no other effect than to check the expected income.

It will be seen that the Postmaster-General suggests certain improvements in the establishment designed to reduce the weight of the mails, cheapen the transportation, insure greater regularity in the service, and secure a considerable reduction in the rates of letter postage—an object highly desirable. The subject is one of general interest to the community, and is respectfully recommended to your consideration.

The suppression of the African slave trade has received the continued attention of the Government. The brig *Dolphin* and schooner *Grampus* have been employed during the last season on the coast of Africa for the purpose of preventing such portions of that trade as were said to be prosecuted under the American flag. After cruising off those parts of the coast most usually resorted to by slavers until the commencement of the rainy season, these vessels returned to the United States for supplies, and have since been dispatched on a similar service.

From the reports of the commanding officers it appears that the trade is now principally carried on under Portuguese colors, and they express the opinion that the apprehension of their presence on the slave coast has in a great degree arrested the prostitution of the American flag to this inhuman purpose. It is hoped that by continuing to maintain this force in that quarter and by the exertions of the officers in command much will be done to put a stop to whatever portion of this traffic may have been carried on under the American flag and to prevent its use in a trade which, while it violates the laws, is equally an outrage on the rights of others and the feelings of humanity. The efforts of the several Governments who are anxiously seeking to suppress this traffic must, however, be directed against the facilities afforded by what are now recognized as legitimate commercial pursuits before that object can be fully accomplished.

Supplies of provisions, water casks, merchandise, and articles connected with the prosecution of the slave trade are, it is understood, freely carried by vessels of different nations to the slave factories, and the effects of the factors are transported openly from one slave station to another without interruption or punishment by either of the nations to which they belong engaged in the commerce of that region. I submit to your judgments whether this Government, having been the first to prohibit by adequate penalties the slave trade, the first to declare it piracy, should not be the first also to forbid to its citizens all trade with the slave factories on the coast of Africa, giving an example to all nations in this respect which if fairly followed can not fail to produce the most effective results in breaking up those dens of iniquity.

M. VAN BUREN.

SPECIAL MESSAGES.

WASHINGTON, *December 7, 1840.*

Hon. R. M. T. HUNTER,
  Speaker of the House of Representatives.

SIR: I herewith transmit a letter from the Secretary of the Navy, in relation to the navy pension fund, to which the attention of Congress is invited, and recommend an immediate appropriation of $151,352.39 to meet the payment of pensions becoming due on and after the 1st of January, 1841.

M. VAN BUREN.

WASHINGTON, *December 10, 1840.*

To the Senate of the United States:

I transmit, for the action of the Senate, a communication from the Secretary of War, on the subject of the transfer of Chickasaw stock to the Choctaw tribe, which the accompanying papers explain.

M. VAN BUREN.

WAR DEPARTMENT, *December 10, 1840.*

The PRESIDENT OF THE UNITED STATES.

SIR: I have the honor to lay before you a communication from the Commissioner of Indian Affairs, relative to the transfer of $500,000 Chickasaw stock to the Choctaws in execution of the compact of 17th January, 1837, between those tribes, that if you think it advisable you may assent to the proposed transfer and lay the matter before the Senate for the sanction of that body.

Very respectfully, your most obedient servant,   J. R. POINSETT.

WAR DEPARTMENT, OFFICE INDIAN AFFAIRS,
December, 1840.

Hon. J. R. POINSETT,
        Secretary of War.

SIR: A compact was made on the 17th January, 1837, "subject to the approval of the President and Senate of the United States," which it received from the former on the 24th March, 1837, in conformity with the resolution of the Senate of 25th February, between the Choctaw and Chickasaw tribes of Indians, of which I have the honor to inclose a copy.

By this instrument the right to occupy a portion of the Choctaw country west of the Mississippi was, with certain privileges, secured to the Chickasaws, who agreed to pay therefor $530,000, of which $30,000 were paid in 1837, and the remaining $500,000 it was agreed should be invested under the direction of the Government of the United States and that the interest should be paid annually to the Choctaws.

There being no money to place in the hands of the United States, but a very large amount of Chickasaw stock under the direction of the Treasury, the reasonable desire of the Choctaws that this large fund belonging to them should be put in their own names on the books of the Government can be gratified by a transfer of so much of the stock to the Secretary of War for their use, upon which the interest will be received and paid over to them. This will be an execution of the agreement of the parties. A sale of stocks to raise the money and then a reinvestment of it according to the letter of the compact ought not to be resorted to on account of their present low price in the market.

In considering this subject in the course of the autumn the thirteenth article of the treaty of 24th May, 1834, with the Chickasaws was adverted to, by which it is provided: "If the Chickasaws shall be so fortunate as to procure a home within the limits of the United States, it is agreed that, with the consent of the President and Senate, so much of their invested stock as may be necessary to the purchase of a country for them to settle in shall be permitted to them to be sold, or the United States will advance the necessary amount upon a guaranty and pledge of an equal amount of their stocks." The compact before referred to having been ratified by the President and Senate, it was doubted whether that was not a virtual consent to the application of so much of the stock as would be required to pay for the land and privileges contracted for by the said compact, and an authority for the transfer of it. The question was referred to the Attorney-General, who was of opinion that the transfer could not be legally made without the assent of the President and Senate to the particular act.

I have therefore respectfully to request that you will lay the matter before the President, that if he concurs in the propriety of so doing he may give his own and ask the consent of the Senate to the proposed proceeding.

Very respectfully, your most obedient,   T. HARTLEY CRAWFORD.

WASHINGTON, *December 10, 1840.*

To the Senate:

I communicate a report * of the Secretary of State, with the documents accompanying it, in compliance with the resolution of the Senate of the 20th of July last.

M. VAN BUREN.

* Relating to sales and donations of public lots in Washington, D. C.

WASHINGTON, *December 21, 1840.*

To the Senate of the United States:

I transmit herewith, for the consideration of the Senate with a view to its ratification, a treaty of commerce and navigation between the United States of America and His Majesty the King of the Belgians, signed at Washington on the 29th day of March, 1840.

M. VAN BUREN.

WASHINGTON, *December 23, 1840.*

To the House of Representatives of the United States:

Herewith I transmit a communication * from the Secretary of the Treasury and also copies of certain papers accompanying it, which are believed to embrace the information contemplated by a resolution of the House of Representatives of the 17th instant.

M. VAN BUREN.

WASHINGTON, *December 28, 1840.*

To the House of Representatives of the United States:

I herewith transmit to the House of Representatives a report † from the Secretary of State, with accompanying papers, in answer to their resolution of the 21st instant.

M. VAN BUREN.

WASHINGTON, *December 28, 1840.*

To the Senate of the United States:

I transmit herewith, for the consideration of the Senate with a view to its ratification, a treaty of commerce and navigation between the United States and Portugal, signed at Lisbon on the 26th day of August, 1840, and certain letters relating thereto, of which a list is annexed.

M. VAN BUREN.

WASHINGTON, *December 29, 1840.*

To the House of Representatives of the United States:

I herewith transmit to the House of Representatives a report ‡ from the Secretary of State, with accompanying papers, in answer to their resolution of the 23d instant.

M. VAN BUREN.

---

* Relating to the suspension of appropriations made at the last session of Congress.

† Transmitting correspondence with Great Britain relative to the burning of the steamboat *Caroline* at Schlosser, N. Y., December 29, 1837.

‡ Transmitting correspondence with Great Britain relative to proceedings on the part of that Government which may have a tendency to interrupt our commerce with China.

WASHINGTON, *January 2, 1841.*

To the House of Representatives of the United States:

I think proper to communicate to the House of Representatives, in further answer to their resolution of the 21st ultimo, the correspondence which has since occurred between the Secretary of State and the British minister on the same subject.

M. VAN BUREN.

Mr. Fox to Mr. Forsyth.

WASHINGTON, *December 29, 1840.*

Hon. JOHN FORSYTH, etc.

SIR: I have the honor to acknowledge the receipt of your letter of the 26th instant, in which, in reply to a letter which I had addressed to you on the 13th, you acquaint me that the President is not prepared to comply with my demand for the liberation of Mr. Alexander McLeod, of Upper Canada, now imprisoned at Lockport, in the State of New York, on a pretended charge of murder and arson, as having been engaged in the destruction of the piratical steamboat *Caroline* on the 29th of December, 1837.

I learn with deep regret that such is the decision of the President of the United States, for I can not but foresee the very grave and serious consequences that must ensue if, besides the injury already inflicted upon Mr. McLeod of a vexatious and unjust imprisonment, any further harm should be done to him in the progress of this extraordinary proceeding.

I have lost no time in forwarding to Her Majesty's Government in England the correspondence that has taken place, and I shall await the further orders of Her Majesty's Government with respect to the important question which that correspondence involves.

But I feel it my duty not to close this communication without likewise testifying my vast regret and surprise at the expressions which I find repeated in your letter with reference to the destruction of the steamboat *Caroline*. I had confidently hoped that the first erroneous impression of the character of that event, imposed upon the mind of the United States Government by partial and exaggerated representations, would long since have been effaced by a more strict and accurate examination of the facts. Such an investigation must even yet, I am willing to believe, lead the United States Government to the same conviction with which Her Majesty's authorities on the spot were impressed—that the act was one, in the strictest sense, of self-defense, rendered absolutely necessary by the circumstances of the occasion for the safety and protection of Her Majesty's subjects, and justified by the same motives and principles which upon similar and well-known occasions have governed the conduct of illustrious officers of the United States. The steamboat *Caroline* was a hostile vessel engaged in piratical war against Her Majesty's people, hired from her owners for that express purpose, and known to be so beyond the possibility of doubt. The place where the vessel was destroyed was nominally, it is true, within the territory of a friendly power, but the friendly power had been deprived through overbearing piratical violence of the use of its proper authority over that portion of territory. The authorities of New York had not even been able to prevent the artillery of the State from being carried off publicly at midday to be used as instruments of war against Her Majesty's subjects. It was under such circumstances, which it is to be hoped will never recur, that the vessel was attacked by a party of Her Majesty's people, captured, and destroyed. A remonstrance against the act in question has been addressed by the United States to Her Majesty's Government in England. I am not authorized to pronounce the decision of Her Majesty's Government upon that remonstrance, but I have felt myself bound to record in the meantime the above opinion.

in order to protest in the most solemn manner against the spirited and loyal conduct of a party of Her Majesty's officers and people being qualified, through an unfortunate misapprehension, as I believe, of the facts, with the appellation of outrage or of murder.

I avail myself of this occasion to renew to you the assurance of my distinguished consideration.

H. S. FOX.

Mr. Forsyth to Mr. Fox.

DEPARTMENT OF STATE,
Washington, December 31, 1840.

SIR: I have the honor to acknowledge the receipt of your note of the 29th instant, in reply to mine of the 26th, on the subject of the arrest and detention of Alexander McLeod as one of the perpetrators of the outrage committed in New York when the steamboat *Caroline* was seized and burnt. Full evidence of that outrage has been presented to Her Britannic Majesty's Government with a demand for redress, and of course no discussion of the circumstances here can be either useful or proper, nor can I suppose it to be your desire to invite it. I take leave of the subject with this single remark, that the opinion so strongly expressed by you on the facts and principles involved in the demand for reparation on Her Majesty's Government by the United States would hardly have been hazarded had you been possessed of the carefully collected testimony which has been presented to your Government in support of that demand.

I avail myself of the occasion to renew to you the assurance of my distinguished consideration.

JOHN FORSYTH.

WASHINGTON, *January 4, 1841.*
To the Senate of the United States:

I submit herewith a treaty concluded with the Miami Indians for the cession of their lands in the State of Indiana. The circumstances attending this negotiation are fully set forth in the accompanying communication from the Secretary of War. Although the treaty was concluded without positive instructions and the usual official preliminaries, its terms appear to be so advantageous and the acquisition of these lands are deemed so desirable by reason of their importance to the State of Indiana and the Government, as well as on account of the Indians themselves, who will be greatly benefited by their removal west, that I have thought it advisable to submit it to the action of the Senate.

M. VAN BUREN.

WAR DEPARTMENT, *January 4, 1841.*
The PRESIDENT OF THE UNITED STATES.

SIR: I have the honor to transmit herewith a treaty concluded with the Miami Indians of the State of Indiana, to be laid before the Senate for their ratification if upon due consideration of the circumstances under which this treaty was negotiated you should think proper to do so. These circumstances are fully and correctly set forth in the accompanying communication from the Commissioner of Indian Affairs, to which I beg leave respectfully to refer you.

I have the honor to be, very respectfully, your most obedient servant,

J. R. POINSETT.

WAR DEPARTMENT, OFFICE INDIAN AFFAIRS,
December 29, 1840.

Hon. J. R. POINSETT,
    Secretary of War.

SIR: A treaty made with the Miami tribe of Indians in the State of Indiana on the 28th day of November last for the residue of their lands in that State has been unexpectedly received.

Great anxiety has been manifested by the citizens of Indiana and made known by their representatives in both Houses of Congress that a cession of the Miami land should be procured, and it seems to have been met by a correspondent disposition on the part of the leading men among the Indians. On the 25th May last a communication was received from General Samuel Milroy, subagent, etc., expressing the belief that the Miamies would treat and that their principal chief was desirous before the close of his life, now drawing near, to effect a negotiation, as in his opinion the emigration or extinction of the tribe were the alternatives before them, and suggesting that the most judicious course would be to conduct the business informally at the annuity payment. In reply he was informed on the 2d July that the Department did not open negotiations for the purchase of Indian lands unless thereto previously authorized by Congress, and that at the request of a portion of the representation of Indiana an estimate had been furnished of the sum that would be required to hold a treaty, and that if the presumed intention of obtaining the estimate should be realized an effort would be made to execute the purpose for which the appropriation would be obtained. (Extracts from these letters, so far as they relate to the subject, are herewith sent, marked A.*) On the 31st July he renewed the subject, accompanied by an extract of a letter of 22d July to himself from Allen Hamilton, esq., the confidential friend of Chief Richardville, urging the propriety of a negotiation. (B.*)

On the 12th August, no appropriation having been made by Congress, a letter was addressed to you by the Hon. O. H. Smith, of the Senate of the United States from Indiana, inclosing a letter from Mr. Hamilton, dated on the 11th, urging the vast importance of treating with the Miamies, as well to them as to the State, and giving the reasons which in the judgment of both led to the conclusion that their particular case should form an exception to the general rule that obtains in regard of Indian treaties, and recommending strongly the appointment of General Milroy as a suitable person to conduct the negotiation. A communication of similar character (except the last feature), dated 20th August, was received from Mr. Milroy. The letter of the Hon. Mr. Smith was referred by you to this office, and on the 27th August, after a conference with you on the subject, I replied that exceptions to the rule stated might under very peculiar circumstances exist, but that as the Senate certainly, and it was believed the House too, had rejected an application for an appropriation, the opening of a negotiation might be considered to be opposed to an expression of legislative opinion. In answer to the suggestion that little or perhaps no expense need be incurred, as the treaty could be made at the payment of the annuities, it was remarked that the consideration money must necessarily be large, as the Miami lands were very valuable, and an appropriation of it required, which Congress might be disinclined to grant after what had happened; that it was therefore deemed advisable to decline treating, and that perhaps a future application for legislative sanction might be more successful. Of this letter a copy was sent to General Milroy as a reply on the subject in hand to his communication of 31st July, and his letter of 20th August was further answered on 2d September. (C.*)

In consequence of the representations referred to, and probably others which did not reach me, you addressed me an unofficial note on 14th September, suggesting that Allen Hamilton, esq., might at the payment of the annuities make an arrangement with the Miamies that would be "gratifying to the people as well as beneficial to

*Omitted.

the service." With this expressed wish of the head of the Department, and after consultation with you, I wrote unofficial letters to General Samuel Milroy and to Allen Hamilton, esq., on the 18th September, setting forth the views of the Department as hereinbefore expressed in regard of precedent legislative sanction and the importance to Indiana of treating with the Miamies, whose disposition to cede their remaining lands on just and equitable terms might not continue. It was thought, however, to be in keeping with the rule adopted to ascertain informally from the Miamies what they would be willing to take for their lands when it was their pleasure to emigrate, etc. It was doubted whether it would be judicious to reduce the terms to writing, however informally, on account of the difficulty there might be in convincing the Indians that it was not a treaty, although it was desirable, if it could be safely done, that it should be so; and they were informed that a report from them would answer "all my purposes, as my object is to be able to say to each branch of Congress upon what terms the Miami lands can be had by the United States, so that if the terms are approved the necessary law may be passed." It was suggested that the annuity payment would afford a good opportunity for procuring the information desired, which it was expected could be had without any expense, for which there were no funds, and that if there were it would not be proper to expend them in the way proposed. (D.*)

I desire to state the facts as they exist so fully as to exhibit precisely what has been the action of the Department, without going into more detail than may be necessary, and therefore annex extracts and copies of the papers referred to instead of embodying them in this communication.

On the 28th day of November last a treaty was concluded by Messrs. Samuel Milroy and Allen Hamilton with "the chiefs, warriors, and headmen of the Miami tribe of Indians," which was received here on the 19th instant, accompanied by a letter explanatory of the treaty and stating it to have been made by "the undersigned, acting under instructions contained in your unofficial letter dated September 18, 1840;" that it was made at the annuity payment, when "the views and instructions of the Department" were "communicated to the Miami Indians in full council," and that "after full consideration of the subject they decided to reduce to treaty form a proposition or the terms upon which they would consent to cede their remaining lands in Indiana to the United States, subject, as they understand it, to the approval of the Department and the approval and ratification of the President and Senate of the United States before being of any binding force or efficiency as a treaty." With the original treaty I send a copy of the explanatory letter and of a communication from General Milroy giving the reasons for the money provisions made for the chief Richardville and the family of Chief Godfroy. (E.*)

It will be thus seen that the negotiation of a treaty was not authorized; but if in the opinion of the President and Senate it shall be advisable to adopt and confirm it, I do not see any legal objection to such a course. The quantity of land ceded is estimated at about 500,000 acres, for which the consideration is fixed at $550,000, or $1.10 per acre, of which $250,000 are payable presently and the balance in annual payments of $15,000, which will be discharged in twenty years. In addition, we will be bound to remove them west of the Mississippi within five years, the period stipulated for their emigration, and to subsist them for one year after their arrival. These are the chief provisions in which the United States are interested. By the second (it is called in the treaty now submitted the "22," which, if the President should decide to lay it before the Senate, can be corrected by that body) article of the treaty of 6th November, 1838, there is reserved from the cession contained in that instrument 10 miles square for the band of Ma-to-sin-ia, in regard of which the seventh article says:

"It is further stipulated that the United States convey by patent to Me-shing-go-

* Omitted.

me-zia, son of Ma-to-sin-ia, the tract of land reserved by the twenty-second article of the treaty of 6th of November, 1838, to the band of Ma-to-sin-ia.''

This is a change as to the title of a reservation heretofore sanctioned and not now ceded, and so far as the United States are concerned does not vary the aspect of the present compact. There are reserved to the chief Richardville seven sections of land, and to him and the family of the deceased chief Godfroy are to be paid, respectively, considerable sums of money, which it seems from the statement of General Milroy were debts due to them and acknowledged by the tribe.

The treaty of November, 1838, which was ratified on the 8th February, 1839, extinguished the Indian title to about 177,000 acres of land and cost the United States $335,680, or nearly $2 per acre. Measured by this price the present arrangement would seem to be very advantageous. It is stated by Messrs. Milroy and Hamilton that more favorable terms will not be assented to by the Miamies under any circumstances, and considering the great importance of the adoption of this compact, however irregularly made, to the State of Indiana, as well as the belief that any postponement will probably swallow up what remains to these Indians in debts which they most improvidently contract and the conviction that nothing can save them from moral ruin but their removal west, I think it would be judicious in all views of the matter to adopt and ratify this treaty, and respectfully recommend that it, with the accompanying papers, be laid before the President, and, if he and you concur in my views, that the sanction of it by the Senate be asked.

Respectfully submitted.

T. HARTLEY CRAWFORD.

WASHINGTON, *January 5, 1841.*

To the Senate of the United States:

I communicate to the Senate sundry papers,* in further answer to its resolution of the 30th of December, 1839, which have been received from the governor of Florida since the adjournment of the last session of Congress.

M. VAN BUREN.

WASHINGTON, *January 6, 1841.*

Hon. R. M. JOHNSON,
    President of the Senate.

SIR: The report of the Secretary of War herewith and the accompanying documents are respectfully submitted in reply to the resolution of the Senate of June 30, 1840, calling for information in relation to the number of soldiers enlisted in the late war and entitled to bounty land, etc.

M. VAN BUREN.

WASHINGTON, *January 7, 1841.*

Hon. R. M. JOHNSON,
    President of the Senate.

SIR: The communication of the Secretary of War and the accompanying report of the colonel of Topographical Engineers are respectfully submitted in reply to the resolution of the 15th of June last, calling for a

---

* Relating to bonds of the Territory of Florida.

plan and estimate for the improvement of Pennsylvania avenue west of the President's square and for the construction of a stone bridge across Rock Creek, etc.

M. VAN BUREN.

WASHINGTON, *January 18, 1841.*

To the Senate of the United States:

I herewith transmit to the Senate, in reply to their resolution of the 20th of July last, a report from the Secretary of State, with accompanying papers.*

M. VAN BUREN.

WASHINGTON, *January 19, 1841.*

To the House of Representatives of the United States:

I herewith transmit to the House of Representatives a report, with accompanying papers,† from the Secretary of State, in answer to the resolution of the House of the 16th of December last.

M. VAN BUREN.

WASHINGTON, *January 22, 1841.*

To the House of Representatives of the United States:

I transmit herewith to the House of Representatives of the United States a report from the Director of the Mint, exhibiting the operations of that institution during the year 1840, and I have to invite the special attention of Congress to that part of the Director's report in relation to the overvaluation given to the gold in foreign coins by the act of Congress of June 28, 1834, ''regulating the value of certain foreign gold coin within the United States.''

Applications have been frequently made at the Mint for copies of medals voted at different times by Congress to the officers who distinguished themselves in the War of the Revolution and in the last war (the dies for which are deposited in the Mint), and it is submitted to Congress whether authority shall be given to the Mint to strike off copies of those medals, in bronze or other metal, to supply those persons making application for them, at a cost not to exceed the actual expense of striking them off.

M. VAN BUREN.

WASHINGTON, *January 29, 1841.*

To the Senate and House of Representatives:

By the report of the Secretary of State herewith communicated and the accompanying papers it appears that an additional appropriation is

---

* Correspondence imputing malpractices to N. P. Trist, American consul at Havana, in regard to granting papers to vessels engaged in the slave trade, etc.

† Relating to the origin of any political relations between the United States and the Empire of China, etc.

necessary if it should be the pleasure of Congress that the preparatory exploration and survey of the northeastern boundary of the United States should be completed.

M. VAN BUREN.

WASHINGTON, *February 1, 1841.*

To the Senate of the United States:

I respectfully transmit herewith a report and accompanying documents from the Secretary of War, in answer to a resolution of the 22d of December, 1840, requesting the President to transmit to the Senate any information in his possession relative to the survey directed by the act of the 12th of June, 1838, entitled "An act to ascertain and designate the boundary line between the State of Michigan and Territory of Wiskonsin."

M. VAN BUREN.

WASHINGTON, *February 8, 1841.*

To the Senate and House of Representatives:

I transmit herewith the copy of a report from the commissioners for the exploration and survey of the northeastern boundary, in addition to the documents sent to Congress, with reference to a further appropriation for the completion of the duty intrusted to the commission.

M. VAN BUREN.

Report of the commissioners appointed by the President of the United States under the act of Congress of 20th July, 1840, for the purpose of exploring and surveying the boundary line between the States of Maine and New Hampshire and the British Provinces.

NEW YORK, *January 6, 1841.*

Hon. JOHN FORSYTH,
    Secretary of State.

SIR: The commissioners, having assembled in this city in conformity with your orders under date of 29th of July, beg leave respectfully to report—

That the extent of country and the great length of the boundary line included in the objects of their commission would have rendered it impossible to have completed the task assigned them within the limits of a single season. In addition to this physical impossibility, the work of the present year was entered upon under circumstances very unfavorable for making any great progress. The law under which they have acted was passed at the last period of a protracted session, when nearly half of the season during which working parties can be kept in the field had elapsed; and although no delay took place in the appointment of commissioners to carry it into effect, the organization of the board was not effected, in consequence of the refusal of one of the commissioners and the agent to accept of their nomination. The commissioners, acting under these disadvantages, have done all that lay in their power to accomplish the greatest practicable extent of work, and have obtained many results which can not but be important in the examination of the vexed and important question which has been committed to them; but after having fully and maturely considered the subject and interchanged the results of their respective operations they have come to the conclusion that it would be premature to embody the partial results which they have attained in a general report for the purpose of being laid before the political and scientific world. The meridian line of the St. Croix has not been carried to a distance of more than 50 miles from the monument at the source of that river, and the operations of the other commissioners, although they have covered a wide extent of country, have fulfilled but one part of the duty assigned them, namely, that of exploration; while even in the parts explored actual surveys will be necessary for the purpose of presenting the question in such form as can admit of no cavil. In particular, the results of the examination of the most northern part of the line appear to differ in some points from the conclusions of the late British commission. Satisfied that the latter have been reached in too hasty a manner and without a sufficient time having been expended upon comparative observations, they are cautioned by this example against committing a like error. In respect to the argumentative part of the report of the British commissioners, the duty of furnishing a prompt and immediate reply to such parts of it as rest upon the construction of treaties and the acts of diplomacy has been rendered far less important than it might at one time have appeared by the publication of the more important parts of the argument laid before the King of the Netherlands as umpire. This argument, the deliberate and studied work of men who well understood the subject, is a full exposition of the grounds on which the claim of the United States to the whole of the disputed territory rests. It has received the sanction of successive Administrations of opposite politics, and may therefore be considered, in addition to its original official character, as approved by the whole nation. To this publication your commission beg leave to refer as embodying an argument which may be styled unanswerable.

The operations of the parties under the command of the several commissioners were as follows:

The party under the direction of Professor Renwick left Portland in detachments on the 26th and 27th of August. The place of general rendezvous was fixed at Woodstock, or, failing that, at the Grand Falls of the St. John. The commissary of the party proceeded as speedily as possible to Oldtown, in order to procure boats and engage men. Professor Renwick passed by land through Brunswick, Gardiner, and Augusta. At the former place barometer No. 1 was compared with that of Professor Cleaveland, at Gardiner with that of Hallowel Gardiner, esq.; and arrangements were made with them to keep registers, to be used as corresponding observations with those of the expedition. At Augusta some additional articles of equipment were obtained from the authorities of the State, but the barometer which it had been hoped might have been procured was found to be unfit for service. At Houlton two tents and a number of knapsacks, with some gunpowder, were furnished by the politeness of General Eustis from the Government stores.

The boats and all the stores reached Woodstock on the 3d September, and all the party were collected except one engineer, who had been left behind at Bangor in the hopes of obtaining another barometer. A bateau was therefore left to bring him on. The remainder of the boats were loaded, and the party embarked on the St. John on the morning of the 4th of September. This, the main body, reached the Grand Falls at noon on the 8th of September. The remaining bateau, with the engineer, arrived the next evening, having ascended the rapids of the St. John in a time short beyond precedent. On its arrival it was found that the barometer, on whose receipt reliance had been placed, had not been completed in time, and although, as was learnt afterwards, it had been committed as soon as finished by the maker to the care of Major Graham, the other commissioners felt compelled to set out before he had joined them. The want of this barometer, in which defects observed in the others had been remedied, was of no little detriment.

A delay of eighteen days had occurred in Portland in consequence of the refusal of Messrs. Cleaveland and Jarvis to accept their appointments, and it was known from the experience of the commissioners sent out in 1838 by the State of Maine that it would require at least three weeks to reach the line claimed by the United States from Bangor. It was therefore imperative to push forward, unless the risk of having the whole of the operations of this party paralyzed by the setting in of winter was to be encountered. It was also ascertained at the Grand Falls that the streams which were to be ascended were always shallow and rapid, and that at the moment they were extremely low, so that the boats would not carry more stores than would be consumed within the time required to reach the region assigned to Professor Renwick as his share of the duty and return. It became, therefore, necessary, as it had been before feared it must, to be content with an exploration instead of a close and accurate survey. Several of the men employed had been at the northern extremity of the meridian line, but their knowledge was limited to that single object. Inquiry was carefully made for guides through the country between the sources of the Grande Fourche of Restigouche and of Tuladi, but none were to be found. One Indian only had passed from the head of Green River to the Grande Fourche, but his knowledge was limited to a single path, in a direction not likely to shed any light on the object of the commission. He was, however, engaged. The French hunters of Madawaska had never penetrated beyond the sources of Green River, and the Indians who formerly resided on the upper waters of the St. John were said to have abandoned the country for more than twelve years.

The party was now divided into four detachments, the first to proceed down the Restigouche to the tide of the Bay of Chaleurs, the second to ascend the Grande Fourche of Restigouche to its source, the third to be stationed on Green River Mountain, the fourth to convey the surplus stores and heavy baggage to Lake Temiscouata and thence to ascend the Tuladi and Abagusquash to the highest accessible point of the latter. It was resolved that the second and fourth detachments should endeavor to cross the country and meet each other, following as far as possible the height of land. A general rendezvous was again fixed at Lake Temiscouata.

In compliance with this plan, the first and second detachments ascended the Grande River together, crossed the Wagansis portage, and reached the confluence of the Grande Fourche and southwest branch of Restigouche.

The first detachment then descended the united stream, returned by the same course to the St. John, and reached the portage at Temiscouata on the 7th October. All the intended objects of the detachment were happily accomplished.

The second detachment, under the personal direction of the commissioner, reached the junction of the north and south branches of the Grande Fourche on the 22d September. Two engineers, with two men to carry provisions, were then dispatched to cross the country to the meridian line, and thence to proceed westward to join the detachment at Kedgwick Lake. This duty was performed and many valuable observations obtained, but an accident, by which the barometer was broken, prevented all the anticipated objects of the mission from being accomplished.

All the stores which could possibly be spared were now placed in a depot at the junction of the south branch, and the commissioner proceeded with the boats thus lightened toward Kedgwick Lake. The lightening of the boats was rendered necessary in consequence of the diminution of the volume of the river and the occurrence of falls, over which it would have been impossible to convey them when fully loaded. For want of a guide, a branch more western than that which issues from the lake was entered. One of the boats was therefore sent round into the lake to await the return of the engineers dispatched to the meridian line. The stores, which were all that could be brought up in the state of the waters, were now found to be wholly insufficient to allow of committing the party to the unexplored country between this stream and Tuladi. Even the four days which must intervene before the return of the engineers could be expected would do much to exhaust them. The commissioner therefore resolved to proceed across the country, with no other companion than two men, carrying ten days' provisions. It was hoped that four or five days might suffice for the purpose, but ten of great toil and difficulty were spent before Lake Tuladi was reached. The remainder of the detachment, united by the return of the engineers, descended the north branch of the Grande Fourche to the junction of the south branch, ascended the latter, and made the portage to Green River. In this the boats were completely worn out, and the last of their food exhausted just at the moment that supplies sent up the Green River to meet them arrived at their camp.

No arrangement which could have been made would have sufficed to prevent the risk of famine which was thus encountered by the second detachment. A greater number of boats would have required more men, and these would have eaten all they could have carried. No other actual suffering but great fatigue and anxiety were encountered; and it is now obvious that had the rains which were so abundant during the first week of October been snow (as they sometimes are in that climate) there would have been a risk of the detachment perishing.

The third detachment reached their station on Green River Mountain on the 13th September and continued there until the 12th October. A full set of barometric observations was made, the latitude well determined by numerous altitudes, and the longitude approximately by some lunar observations.

The fourth detachment, after depositing the stores intended for the return of the party in charge of the British commissary at Fort Ingall, who politely undertook the care of them, ascended the Tuladi, and taking its northern branch reached Lake Abagusquash. Here one of the engineers wounded himself severely and was rendered unfit for duty. The commissary then proceeded a journey of five days toward the east, blazing a path and making signals to guide the second detachment.

The difference between the country as it actually exists and as represented on any maps prevented the commissioner from meeting this party. It found the source of the central or main branch of Tuladi to the north of that of the Abagusquash, and following the height of land reached the deep and narrow valley of the Rimouski at the point where, on the British maps, that stream is represented as issuing from a ridge of mountains far north of the line offered to the King of the Netherlands as the bounds of the American claim. The commissary therefore found it impossible to ascend Rimouski to its source, and crossing its valley found himself again on a dividing ridge, where he soon struck a stream running to the southeast. This, from a comparison of courses and distances, is believed to be the source of the main branch of the Grande Fourche of Ristaymoh; and thus the second and fourth detachments had reached points within a very short distance of each other. The greater breadth of the dividing ridge has thus been explored, but it will remain to trace the limits of the valley of the Rimouski, which will form a deep indenture in the boundary line. This line having been explored, a party was formed, after the assemblage of the several divisions at Temiscouata, for the purpose of leveling it with the barometer; but the expedition was frustrated by a heavy snowstorm, which set in on the 12th October. This, the most important part of the whole northern line, therefore remains for future investigation. It can only be stated that strong grounds exist for the belief that its summits are not only higher than any point which has been measured, but that, although cut by the Rimouski, it exceeds in average elevation any part of the disputed territory.

The leveling of the Temiscouata portage appeared to be an object of great importance, not only on its own account, but as furnishing a base for future operations. As soon as a sufficient force had been assembled at Lake Temiscouata a party was therefore formed to survey the portage with a theodolite. Orders were also given by the commissioner that the first barometer which should be returned should be carried over the portage. It was believed that this double provision would have secured the examination of this point beyond the chance of failure. A snowstorm, however (the same which interrupted the last operation referred to), set in after the level had been run to the mountain of Biort, and one of the laboring men, worn out by his preceding fatigues, fell sick. The party being thus rendered insufficient, the engineer in command found himself compelled to return. The contemplated operation with the barometer was also frustrated, for on examination at Temiscouata it was found that all were unfit for further service. In order that the desired object might be accomplished, a new expedition was dispatched from New York on the 12th of November, furnished with four barometers. This party, by great exertions, reached St. André, on the St. Lawrence, on the eighth day and accomplished the object of its mission. The operation was rendered possible at this inclement season by its being confined to a beaten road and in the vicinity of human habitations.

The country which has been the object of this reconnoissance is, as may already be understood, of very difficult access from the settled parts of the State of Maine. It is also, at best, almost impenetrable except by the water courses. It furnishes no supplies except fish and small game, nor can these be obtained by a surveying party which can not be strong enough to allow for hunters and fishermen as a constituent part. The third detachment alone derived any important benefit from these sources. The best mode of supplying a party moving on the eastern section would be to draw provisions and stores from the St. Lawrence. It is, indeed, now obvious, although it is contrary to the belief of any of the persons professing to be acquainted with the subject, that had the commissioner proceeded from New York by the way of Montreal and Quebec he must have reached the district assigned to him a fortnight earlier and have accomplished twice as much work as his party was able to perform.

Although much remains to be done in this region, an extensive knowledge of a country hitherto unknown and unexplored has been obtained; and this not only sheds much light upon the boundary question in its present state, but will be of permanent service in case of a further *ex parte* examination, or of a joint commission being agreed upon by the Governments of Great Britain and the United States.

The season was too late for any efficient work, as the line to be explored was not reached before the 22d September. Not only were the rivers at their lowest ebb, but ice was met in the progress of the parties as early as the 12th September, and snow fell on the 21st and 22d September. The actual setting in of winter, which sometimes occurs in the first week of October, was therefore to be dreaded. From this time the country becomes unfit for traveling of any description until the streams are bound with solid ice and a crust formed on the snow of sufficient firmness to make it passable on snowshoes. The only road is that along the St. John River, and it would be almost impossible for a party distant more than 10 or 12 miles from that stream to extricate itself after the winter begins.

No duty could be well imagined more likely to be disagreeable than that assigned to Professor Renwick. The only feasible modes of approach lay for hundreds of miles through the acknowledged limits of the British territory, and the line he was directed to explore was included within the military post of that nation. It may be likened to the entry upon the land of a neighbor for the purpose of inquiring into his title. Under these circumstances of anticipated difficulty it becomes his duty, as well as his pleasure, to acknowledge the uniform attention and civilities he has experienced from all parties, whether in official or in private stations. All possibility of interruption by the local authorities was prevented by a proclamation of His Excellency Sir John Harvey, K. C. B., lieutenant-governor of the Province of New Brunswick, and the British warden, Colonel Maclauchlan, was personally instrumental in promoting the comforts of the commissioner and his assistants. Similar attentions were received from the officers of the garrison at Fort Ingall, and the commandant of the citadel of Quebec, and from His Excellency the Governor-General. Even the private persons whose property might be affected by the acknowledgment of the American claim exhibited a generous hospitality.

The party under the direction of Captain Talcott left the settlements on Halls Stream on the 6th of September. The main branch of this was followed to its source in a swamp, in which a branch of the St. Francis also had its origin. From this point the party followed the ridge dividing the Atlantic from the St. Lawrence waters until it was supposed that all the branches of Indian Stream had been headed. In this work the party was employed until the 14th September. It had now arrived at a point where the Magalloway River should be found to the left, according to the most authentic map of the country, especially that prepared by the New Hampshire commissioner appointed in 1836 to explore the boundary of that State, and accompanying that report.* The party accordingly bore well north to avoid being led from the true "height of land" by the dividing ridge between the Connecticut and Androscoggin rivers. After crossing several small streams, it came on the afternoon of the 15th to a rivulet about 12 feet wide running to the east, which was supposed to be the main Magalloway. The 16th was spent in exploring it to its source. The next day it was discovered that what had been taken for the Magalloway was a tributary of Salmon River, a large branch of the St. Francis, and consequently the party was considerably to the north of the boundary.

The supply of provisions did not allow the party to retrace its steps to the point where it had diverged from the true dividing ridge. The course was therefore changed until it bore a little south; but it was not until the 22d that the party found itself again on the dividing ridge, and then upon the waters of the Magalloway.

The party reached Arnold River, or Chaudiere, above Lake Megantic, on the 24th September. After having recruited and taken a fresh supply of provisions from the depot established there, the party was divided into two detachments. One returned westward to find the corner of the State of New Hampshire as marked by the commission in 1789 appointed to trace the boundary line.

It was there ascertained that the corner was on the true *dividing* ridge, and not from 8 to 10 miles south, as has been erroneously reported by the surveyor employed by the New Hampshire commissioners in 1836 and reiterated in several official papers. From the State corner the dividing ridge was followed to where it had been previously explored by the party. Thence a course was taken to the northeast so as to reach the head of Lake Megantic, and thence to Lake Magaumac, where on the 8th October the two detachments were again united. The detachment led by the assistant, Mr. Cutts, had successfully followed the dividing ridge from the camp of the 24th on Arnold River to this place.

It was now ascertained that the provisions remaining were not sufficient to subsist all of the company until the Kennebec road could be reached by following the *height of land*. It was thought advisable again to separate into two detachments—one to follow the ridge, supplied with provisions for twenty days, and the other to strike for the nearest settlement, which it was supposed could be reached in four or five days. This movement commenced on the 10th October, and the detachment, following the high land, reached the Kennebec road on the 23d, and on the following day provisions for the party for fifteen days were placed there and a like quantity at the mouth of the Metjarmette. It was intended that the two detachments should move simultaneously from these two points on the 26th to explore the boundary line as far as Lake Etchemin. A deep snow, which commenced falling on the night of the 25th, compelled the commissioner to abandon further explorations at that time; and there was not the slightest probability that they could be resumed before another year.

The result of these explorations may be stated as follows:

About 160 miles of country along or near the "*height of land*" have been traversed, the traveled distances carefully estimated, and the courses measured with a compass. Barometrical observations were made as often as necessary for giving a profile of the

---

*Also see report No. 176, House of Representatives, Twenty-fifth Congress, third session.

route from the head of Halls Stream to Arnold or the Chaudiere River, and thence to Lake Magaumac via the corner of the State of New Hampshire. Some further barometrical observations were made between the lake and the Kennebec road, but for a portion of that distance the barometer was unserviceable in consequence of air having entered the tube. Astronomical observations were made as often as there was an opportunity, but, owing to the prevalence of clouds, not as often as was desirable. They will serve for correcting the courses and estimated distances traveled. Barometrical observations for comparison were made at the intersection of the Kennebec road and height of land hourly from 7 a. m. to 5 p. m. while the parties were on the dividing ridge.

The only discovery of interest made by this party is that the Magalloway River does not head any of the branches of the Connecticut, as it was generally believed it did, and consequently our claim to Halls Stream is deprived of the support it would have had from the fact that *all* the other branches were headed by an Atlantic river, and consequently could not be reached by the line along the height of land from the northwest angle of Nova Scotia.

The other commissioner (Major Graham) did not receive his appointment until 16th August to fill the place left vacant by the nonacceptance of Professor Cleaveland, and to him was assigned the survey and examination of the due north line, commencing at the source of the river St. Croix and extending to the highlands which divide the waters that flow into the river St. Lawrence from those which flow into the Atlantic Ocean.

Immediately after receiving his appointment he took the necessary steps for organizing his party, and in addition to two officers of the Corps of Topographical Engineers, assigned to him by the commandant of the Corps for this service, he called to his aid two civil engineers possessing the requisite qualifications for the duties to be performed. So soon as the requisite instruments could be procured and put in proper order he left New York for Portland, Me., where he arrived on the 5th of September, expecting there to join his colleagues of the commission. They had, however, proceeded to the points designated for the commencement of their respective duties, the season being too far advanced to justify their incurring any further delay.

At Portland a short conference was had with Mr. Stubbs, the agent of the State Department, who furnished the necessary means for procuring an outfit for the party in provisions, camp equipage, etc.

The party then proceeded to Bangor, where it was occupied until the 12th in procuring the necessary supplies of provisions, camp equipage, transportation, etc., to enable it to take the field; and a few astronomical observations were made here for the purpose of testing the rates of the chronometers which were to be used upon this service, as well as of obtaining additional data for computing the longitude of this place, which, together with the latitude, had been determined by the commissioner by a very near approximation in the summer of 1838, while occupied upon the military reconnoissances of the northeastern frontier.

On the 12th the party left Bangor for Houlton, where it arrived on the evening of the 13th. A depot of provisions was established here for supplying the line of their future operations, and the services of the requisite number of men as axmen, chain bearers, instrument carriers, etc., were engaged.

Pending these preparations and the time necessarily occupied in cutting a roadway through the forest from a convenient point on the Calais road to the monument at the source of the river St. Croix, a series of astronomical observations was made, both by day and by night, by which the latitude and longitude of Houlton were satisfactorily determined and the rates of the chronometers further tested.

By the 24th of September the roadway was sufficiently opened to permit a camp to be established upon the experimental line traced by the United States and British surveyors in the year 1817, when an attempt was made to mark this portion of the boundary between the two countries agreeably to the provisions of the treaty of Ghent of 1815.

The provisions and camp equipage were transported upon a strong but roughly constructed sled, drawn by horses, whilst the instruments were carried by hand, the surface of the country over which this roadway was opened being too rough for any wheeled vehicle to pass.

The point decided upon as the true source of the river St. Croix by the United States and British commissioners appointed for that purpose under the fifth article of the treaty of 1794 was found and identified, both by the inscriptions upon the monument erected there to mark the spot and also by the testimony of a living witness of high respectability, who has known the locality since it was first designated by the commissioners under the treaty of 1794.

The avenue which had been cleared through a dense forest from the monument to a distance of 12 miles north of it by the surveyors in 1817 was easily recognized by the new and thick growth of young timber, which, having a width of from 40 to 50 feet, now occupied it. Axmen were at once set at work to reopen this avenue, under the supposition that the due north line would at least fall within its borders for a distance of 12 miles. In the meantime the first astronomical station and camp were established, and the transit instrument set up at a distance of 4,578 feet north of the monument, upon an eminence 45½ feet above the level of its base. This position commanded a distinct view of the monument to the south, and of the whole line to the north for a distance of 11 miles, reaching to Parks Hill. Whilst the work of clearing the line of its young growth of timber was progressing a series of astronomical observations was commenced at this first camp, and continued both day and night without intermission (except when interrupted by unfavorable weather), with the sextant, the repeating circle of reflection, and the transit instrument, until the latitude and longitude of the monument and of this first camp were satisfactorily ascertained, and also the direction of the true meridian from the said monument established. For this latter purpose several observations were in the first place made upon the polar star (α Ursæ Minoris) when at its greatest eastern diurnal elongation, and the direction thus obtained was afterwards verified and corrected by numerous transit observations upon stars passing the meridian at various altitudes both north and south of the zenith. These were multiplied with every degree of care, and with the aid of four excellent chronometers, whose rates were constantly tested, not only by the transit observations, but also by equal altitudes of the sun in the day, to correct the time at noon and midnight, and by observed altitudes of east and west stars for correcting the same at various hours of the night.

The direction of this meridian, as thus established by the commissioner, was found to vary from the experimental line traced by the surveyors of 1817 by running in the first place to the west of their line, then crossing it, and afterwards deviating considerably to the east of it.

At the second principal station erected by the party, distant 6 miles and 3,952 feet north of the first camp, or 7 miles and 3,240 feet north of the monument, it found itself 60 feet to the west of the line of 1817. This appeared to be the maximum deviation to the west of that line as near as its trace could be identified, which was only marked by permanent objects recognized by the party at the termination of each mile from the monument. Soon after passing this station the line of 1817 was crossed, and the party did not afterwards touch it, but deviated more and more to the east of it as it progressed north by an irregular proportion to the distance advanced.

In order to obtain a correct profile or vertical section along the whole extent of this meridian line, in the hopes of furnishing data for accurate comparisons of elevations so far as they might be considered relevant to the subject in dispute between the two Governments, and also to afford an accurate base of comparison for the barometers along an extended line which must traverse many ridges that will be objects of minute exploration for many miles of lateral extent, an officer was detailed to trace a line of levels from the base of the monument marking the source of the river St. Croix to tide water at Calais, in Maine, by which means the elevation of the base of the monument above the planes of mean low and mean high water, and also the elevations of several intermediate points of the river St. Croix on its expanded lake surface, have been accurately ascertained.

Another officer was at the same time charged with tracing a line of levels from the base of the same monument along the due north line as marked by the commissioner, by which it is intended that every undulation with the absolute heights above the plane of mean low water at Calais shall be shown along the whole extent of that line.

At Parks Hill, distant only 12 miles from the monument, a second station for astronomical observations was established, and a camp suitable for that purpose was formed. On the 26th day of October, whilst occupied in completing the prolongation of the meridian line to that point and in establishing a camp there, the party was visited by a snowstorm, which covered the ground to a depth of 4 inches in the course of six hours. This was succeeded by six days of dark, stormy weather, which entirely interrupted all progress, and terminated by a rain, with a change to a milder temperature, which cleared away the snow. During this untoward event the parties made themselves as comfortable as practicable in their tents, and were occupied in computing many of the astronomical and other observations previously made.

On the 2d of November the weather became clear, and the necessary astronomical observations were immediately commenced at Parks Hill. From this elevated point the first station could be distinctly seen by means of small heliotropes during the day and bright lights erected upon it at night. Its direction, with that of several intermediate stations due south of Parks Hill, was verified by a new series of transit observations upon high and low stars, both north and south of the zenith. By the same means the line was prolonged to the north.

In one week after commencing the observations at Parks Hill the weather became again unfavorable. The sky was so constantly overcast as to preclude all astronomical observations, and the atmosphere so thick as to prevent a view to the north which would permit new stations to be established with sufficient accuracy in that direction. Unwilling to quit the field while there was a prospect of the weather becoming sufficiently favorable to enable the party to reach the latitude of Mars Hill, or even proceed beyond it, it was determined that some of the party should continue in the tents, and there occupy themselves with such calculations as ought to be made before quitting the field. The officers charged with the line of levels and with the reconnoissances in advance for the selection of new positions for stations continued their labors in the field, notwithstanding they were frequently exposed to slight rain and snow storms, as these portions of the work could go on without a clear sky.

On the 13th of November a severe snowstorm occurred, which in a single night and a portion of the following morning covered the surface of the whole country and the roofs of the tents to a depth of 16 inches. The northern extremity of the avenue which had been cleared by the surveyors of 1817 was now reached, and, in addition to the young growth which had sprung up since that period upon the previous part of the line, several miles had been cleared through the dense forest of heavy timber in order to proceed with the line of levels, which had reached nearly to the Meduxna-keag. The depth of snow now upon the ground rendered it impracticable to continue the leveling with the requisite accuracy any further, and that part of the work was accordingly suspended for the season. The thermometer had long since assumed a range extending during the night and frequently during a great portion of the day to many degrees below the freezing point.

The highlands bordering on the Aroostook, distant 40 miles to the north of the party, were distinctly seen from an elevated position whenever the atmosphere was clear, and a long extent of intermediate country of inferior elevation to the position then occupied presented itself to the view, with the two peaks of Mars Hill rising abruptly above the general surface which surrounded their base. The eastern extremity of the base of the easternmost peak was nearly 2 degrees of arc, or nine-tenths of a mile in space, to the west of the line as it passed the same latitude.

To erect stations opposite to the base of Mars Hill and upon the heights of the Aroostook, in order to obtain exact comparisons with the old line at these points, were considered objects of so much importance as to determine the commissioner to continue the operations in the field to the latest practicable period in hopes of accomplishing these ends.

On the 18th day of November the party succeeded in erecting a station opposite Mars Hill and very near the meridian line. It was thus proved that the line would pass from nine-tenths of a mile to 1 mile east of the eastern extremity of the base of the northeast peak of Mars Hill.

On the 30th of November a series of signals was commenced to be interchanged at night between the position of the transit instrument on Parks Hill and the highlands of the Aroostook. These were continued at intervals whenever the weather was sufficiently clear until by successive approximations a station was on the 9th of December established on the heights 1 mile south of that river and on the meridian line. The point thus reached is more than 50 miles from the monument at the source of the St. Croix, as ascertained from the land surveys made under the authority of the States of Maine and Massachusetts. The measurements of the party could not be extended to this last point, owing to the depth of the snow which lay upon the ground since the middle of November, but the distance derived from the land surveys must be a very near approximation to the truth. A permanent station was erected at the position established on the Aroostook heights and a measurement made from it due west to the experimental or exploring line of 1817, by which the party found itself 2,400 feet to the east of that line.

Between the 1st and 15th of December the observations were carried on almost exclusively during the night, and frequently with the thermometer ranging from 0 to 10 and 12 degrees below that point by Fahrenheit's scale. Although frequently exposed to this temperature in the performance of their duties in the open air at night, and to within a few degrees of that temperature during the hours of sleep, with no other protection than the tents and camp beds commonly used in the Army, the whole party, both officers and men, enjoyed excellent health.

During the day the tents in which the astronomical computations were carried on were rendered quite comfortable by means of small stoves, but at night the fire would become extinguished and the temperature reduced to within a few degrees of that of the outward air. Within the observatory tent the comfort of a fire could not be indulged in, in consequence of the too great liability to produce serious errors of observation by the smoke passing the field of the telescope. The astronomical observations were therefore always made in the open air or in a tent open to the heavens at top during the hours of observation, and without a fire.

On the 16th of December the tents were struck and this party retired from the field for the season, there being then more than 2 feet of snow on the ground. To the unremitting zeal amidst severe exposures, and to the scientific and practical attainments of the officers, both civil and military, who served under the orders of the commissioner on this duty, he acknowledges himself in a great measure indebted for the progress that he was enabled to make, notwithstanding the many difficulties encountered.

Observations were made during portions of three lunations of the transit of the moon's bright limb and of such tabulated stars as differed but little in right ascension and declination from the moon, in order to obtain additional data to those furnished by chronometrical comparisons with the meridian of Boston for computing the longitude of this meridian line.

At the first station, 4,578 feet north of the monument, and also at the Parks Hill station, the dip of the magnetic needle was ascertained by a series of observations—in the one case upon two and in the other upon three separate needles. The horizontal declination was also ascertained at both these stations by a full set of observations upon six different needles.

The details of these and of all the astronomical observations alluded to will be prepared as soon as practicable for the use of the commission, should they be required. To His Excellency Major-General Sir John Harvey, K. C. B., lieutenant-governor of the Province of New Brunswick, Major Graham acknowledges himself greatly indebted for having in the most obliging manner extended to him every facility within his power for prosecuting the examinations. From Mr. Connell, of Woodstock, a member of the colonial parliament, and from Lieutenant-Colonel Maclauchlan, the British land agent, very kind attentions were received.

Major Graham has also great pleasure in acknowledging his obligations to General Eustis, commandant of the Eastern Department; to Colonel Pierce, commanding the garrison at Houlton, and to his officers; and also to Major Ripley, of the Ordnance Department, commanding the arsenal at Augusta, for the prompt and obliging manner in which they supplied many articles useful to the prosecution of the labors of his party.

The transit instrument with which the meridian line was traced had been loaned to the commission by the Hon. William A. Duer, president of Columbia College, New York, and the commissioners feel bound to return their acknowledgments for the liberality with which the use of this astronomical instrument was granted at a time when it would have been difficult, and perhaps impossible, to have procured one as well suited to the object.

All which is respectfully submitted.

JAS. RENWICK,
JAMES D. GRAHAM,
A. TALCOTT,
Commissioners.

WASHINGTON, *February 12, 1841.*

To the Senate of the United States:

I transmit a report of the Secretary of State, containing the information asked for by the resolution of the Senate of the 5th instant, relative to the negroes taken on board the schooner *Amistad.*

M. VAN BUREN.

WASHINGTON, *March 2, 1841.*

To the House of Representatives:

I transmit to the House of Representatives a report from the Attorney-General, with accompanying documents,* in compliance with the request contained in their resolution of the 23d of March last.

M. VAN BUREN.

*Opinions of the Attorneys-General of the United States from the commencement of the Government to March 1, 1841.

WASHINGTON, *March 2, 1841.*

To the House of Representatives:

I transmit the accompanying report from the Secretary of State, in relation to the resolution of the House of Representatives of the 12th ultimo, on the subject of claims of citizens of the United States on the Government of Hayti. The information called for thereby is in the course of preparation and will be without doubt communicated at the commencement of the next session of Congress.

M. VAN BUREN.

WASHINGTON, *March 3, 1841.*

To the House of Representatives:

I transmit to the House of Representatives, in compliance with their resolution of the 30th January last, a report* from the Secretary of State, with accompanying documents.

M. VAN BUREN.

PROCLAMATION.

[From Senate Journal, Twenty-sixth Congress, second session, p. 247.]

WASHINGTON, *January 6, 1841.*

The President of the United States to ——, Senator for the State of ——:

Certain matters touching the public good requiring that the Senate of the United States should be convened on Thursday, the 4th day of March next, you are desired to attend at the Senate Chamber, in the city of Washington, on that day, then and there to receive and deliberate on such communications as shall be made to you.

M. VAN BUREN.

*Relating to the search or seizure of United States vessels on the coast of Africa or elsewhere by British cruisers or authorities, and to the African slave trade, etc.